Explore Your World!

Focus on case studies to understand your world.

To learn about **The United States and Canada**, you will take a close look at specific countries. In each case study, the story of that country will be told through an important world theme—such as the relationship between people and their environment or a nation's quest for independence. After studying each country, you can apply what you've learned to understand other parts of the world.

Interact with exciting online activities.

Journey to different parts of the world by using dynamic online activities on geography, history and culture. Use the web codes listed in the Go Online boxes and in the chart below to tour this region.

The United States and Canada Activities

Web Code	Activity
	History Interactive
lhp-5001	Discover a Steam Engine
lhp-5003	The Sharecropping Cycle
lhp-5009	Explore the Boston Tea Party
lhp-5010	Explore the Northwest Territory
lhp-5011	The Mexican American War
lhp-5013	Find Out How Tariffs Work
lhp-5018	The Trans-Continental Railroad
lhp-5022	Explore Capitalism
lhp-5024	Explore the Magna Carta
lhp-5025	Explore the Lessons of Battle
lhp-5026	Inside Fort Sumter
	MapMaster
lhp-5000	The Western Front
lhp-5002	The American Revolution
lhp-5004	Growth of the United States to 1853
lhp-5005	States Take Sides
lhp-5006	Land Taken from Native Americans
lhp-5007	Native American Territory
lhp-5008	Exploring the Louisiana Purchase
lhp-5012	Industrial Centers, 1865-1914
lhp-5014	Slavery After the Kansas-Nebraska Act
lhp-5015	Western Land Claims
lhp-5016	North America in 1830
lhp-5017	Early Days of War
lhp-5019	Travels to the West
lhp-5020	Final Battle of the Civil War
lhp-5021	The Texas War for Independence
lhp-5023	The Seasons

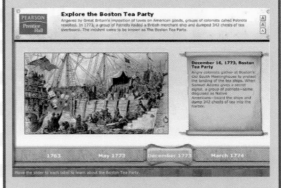

For: An activity on the Civil War
Visit:: PHSchool.com
Web Code: lhd-4202

Get hands-on with the Geographer's Apprentice Activity Pack.

Explore the geography, history and culture of the world's regions through hands-on activities. Each activity pack includes maps, data and primary sources to make learning geography fun!

Teacher's Edition

PRENTICE HALL
WORLD STUDIES
The UNITED STATES and CANADA

Geography • History • Culture

In association with
DK

DISCOVERY
CHANNEL
SCHOOL

PEARSON

Prentice
Hall

Boston, Massachusetts
Upper Saddle River, New Jersey

Program Consultants

Heidi Hayes Jacobs

Heidi Hayes Jacobs, Ed.D., has served as an education consultant to more than 1,000 schools across the nation and abroad. Dr. Jacobs serves as an adjunct professor in the Department of Curriculum on Teaching at Teachers College, Columbia University. She has written two best-selling books and numerous articles on curriculum reform. She received an M.A. from the University of Massachusetts, Amherst, and completed her doctoral work at Columbia University's Teachers College in 1981. The core of Dr. Jacobs's experience comes from her years teaching high school, middle school, and elementary school students. As an educational consultant, she works with K–12 schools and districts on curriculum reform and strategic planning.

Michal L. LeVasseur

Michal L. LeVasseur is the Executive Director of the National Council for Geographic Education. She is an instructor in the College of Education at Jacksonville State University and works with the Alabama Geographic Alliance. Her undergraduate and graduate work were in the fields of anthropology (B.A.), geography (M.A.), and science education (Ph.D.). Dr. LeVasseur's specialization has moved increasingly into the area of geography education. Since 1996 she has served as the Director of the National Geographic Society's Summer Geography Workshops. As an educational consultant, she has worked with the National Geographic Society as well as with schools and organizations to develop programs and curricula for geography.

Senior Reading Consultants

Kate Kinsella

Kate Kinsella, Ed.D., is a faculty member in the Department of Secondary Education at San Francisco State University. A specialist in second-language acquisition and content area literacy, she consults nationally on school-wide practices that support adolescent English learners and striving readers to make academic gains. Dr. Kinsella earned her M.A. in TESOL from San Francisco State University, and her Ed.D. in Second Language Acquisition from the University of San Francisco.

Kevin Feldman

Kevin Feldman, Ed.D., is the Director of Reading and Early Intervention with the Sonoma County Office of Education (SCOE) and an independent educational consultant. At the SCOE, he develops, organizes, and monitors programs related to K–12 literacy. Dr. Feldman has an M.A. from the University of California, Riverside, in Special Education, Learning Disabilities and Instructional Design. He earned his Ed.D. in Curriculum and Instruction from the University of San Francisco.

Acknowledgments appear on pages 225–226, which constitutes an extension of this copyright page.

Copyright © 2008 by Pearson Education, Inc., publishing as Pearson Prentice Hall, Boston, Massachusetts 02116.

MapMaster™ is a trademark of Pearson Education, Inc.
Pearson Prentice Hall™ is a trademark of Pearson Education, Inc.
Pearson® is a registered trademark of Pearson plc.
Prentice Hall® is a registered trademark of Pearson Education, Inc.
Discovery Channel School® is a registered trademark of Discovery Communications, Inc.
ExamView® is a registered trademark of FSCreations, Inc.

 is a registered trademark of Dorling Kindersley Limited. Prentice Hall World Studies is published in collaboration with DK Designs, Dorling Kindersley Limited, 80 Strand, London WC2R 0RL. A Penguin Company.

Cartography Consultant

 Andrew Heritage

Andrew Heritage has been publishing atlases and maps for more than 25 years. In 1991, he joined the leading illustrated nonfiction publisher Dorling Kindersley (DK) with the task of building an international atlas list from scratch. The DK atlas list now includes some 10 titles, which are constantly updated and appear in new editions either annually or every other year.

ISBN 0-13-204159-6
2345678910   11 10 09 08 07

Academic Reviewers

Africa
Barbara B. Brown, Ph.D.
African Studies Center
Boston University
Boston, Massachusetts

Ancient World
Evelyn DeLong Mangie, Ph.D.
Department of History
University of South Florida
Tampa, Florida

Central Asia and the Middle East
Pamela G. Sayre
History Department,
    Social Sciences Division
Henry Ford Community College
Dearborn, Michigan

East Asia
Huping Ling, Ph.D.
History Department
Truman State University
Kirksville, Missouri

Eastern Europe
Robert M. Jenkins, Ph.D.
Center for Slavic, Eurasian and
    East European Studies
University of North Carolina
Chapel Hill, North Carolina

Latin America
Dan La Botz
Professor, History Department
Miami University
Oxford, Ohio

Medieval Times
James M. Murray
History Department
University of Cincinnati
Cincinnati, Ohio

North Africa
Barbara E. Petzen
Center for Middle Eastern Studies
Harvard University
Cambridge, Massachusetts

Religion
Charles H. Lippy, Ph.D.
Department of Philosophy
    and Religion
University of Tennessee
    at Chattanooga
Chattanooga, Tennessee

Russia
Janet Vaillant
Davis Center for Russian
    and Eurasian Studies
Harvard University
Cambridge, Massachusetts

United States and Canada
Victoria Randlett
Geography Department
University of Nevada, Reno
Reno, Nevada

Western Europe
Ruth Mitchell-Pitts
Center for European Studies
University of North Carolina
    at Chapel Hill
Chapel Hill, North Carolina

Reviewers

Sean Brennan
Brecksville-Broadview Heights
    City School District
Broadview Heights, Ohio

Stephen Bullick
Mt. Lebanon School District
Pittsburgh, Pennsylvania

Louis P. De Angelo, Ed.D.
Archdiocese of Philadelphia
Philadelphia, Pennsylvania

Paul Francis Durietz
Social Studies
    Curriculum Coordinator
Woodland District #50
Gurnee, Illinois

Gail Dwyer
Dickerson Middle School,
    Cobb County
Marietta, Georgia

Michal Howden
Social Studies Consultant
Zionsville, Indiana

Rosemary Kalloch
Springfield Public Schools
Springfield, Massachusetts

Deborah J. Miller
Office of Social Studies,
    Detroit Public Schools
Detroit, Michigan

Steven P. Missal
Plainfield Public Schools
Plainfield, New Jersey

Catherine Fish Petersen
Social Studies Consultant
Saint James, Long Island,
    New York

Joe Wieczorek
Social Studies Consultant
Baltimore, Maryland

The UNITED STATES and CANADA

Develop Skills

Use these pages to develop students' reading, writing, and geography skills.

Build a Regional Background

Introduce students to the geography, history, and culture of the region.

Focus on Countries

Create an understanding of the United States and Canada
by focusing on specific regions.

MAP MASTER

- Learn map skills with the MapMaster Skills Handbook.
- Practice your skills with every map in this book.
- Interact with every map online and on CD-ROM.

DK

Maps and illustrations created by DK help build your understanding of the world. The DK World Desk Reference Online keeps you up to date.

Discovery CHANNEL SCHOOL Video/DVD

The World Studies Video Program takes you on field trips to study countries around the world.

Interactive Textbook

The *World Studies* Interactive Textbook online and on CD-ROM uses interactive maps and other activities to help you learn.

COUNTRY DATABANK

Read about the states that make up the United States.

Read about the provinces and the territories that make up Canada.

REGIONAL PROFILES

Theme-based maps and charts provide a closer look at regions, provinces, and territories.

Links

See the fascinating links between social studies and other disciplines.

Literature

A selection by an American author brings social studies to life.

Skills for Life

Teach skills that students will use all of their lives.

Citizen Heroes

Introduce people who have made a difference in their country.

Target Reading Skills

Chapter-by-chapter reading skills help students read and understand social studies concepts.

DK Eyewitness Technology

Detailed drawings show how technology shapes places and societies.

Discovery Channel School — Video/DVD

Explore the geography, history, and cultures of the United States and Canada.

MAP✦MASTER™ Interactive

Go online to find an interactive version of every MapMaster map in this book. Use the Web Code provided to gain direct access to these maps.

How to Use Web Codes:

1. Go to **www.PHSchool.com**.
2. Enter the Web Code.
3. Click Go!

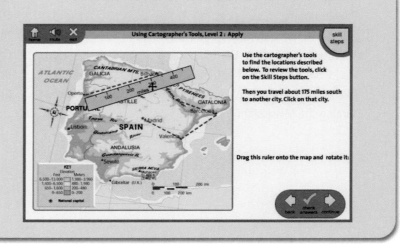

NCLB Implications for Social Studies

The No Child Left Behind (NCLB) legislation was a landmark in educational reform designed to improve student achievement and create a fundamental shift in American education. In the essay that follows, we will explore the implications of NCLB on social studies curriculum, instruction, assessment, and instructional programs.

Facts about NCLB

The No Child Left Behind Act of 2001 (NCLB) calls for sweeping educational reform, requiring all students to perform proficiently on standardized tests in reading, mathematics, and (soon to be added) science by the year 2014. Under NCLB, schools will be held accountable for students' academic progress. In exchange for this accountability, the law offers more flexibility to individual states and school districts to decide how best to use federal education funds. NCLB places an emphasis on implementing scientifically proven methods in teaching reading and mathematics, and promotes teacher quality. It also offers parental choice for students in failing schools.

Effects on Curriculum, Instruction, and Assessment

Since the primary focus of NCLB is on raising the achievement of students in reading and mathematics, some educators have wondered how it relates to social studies. Some teachers have expressed concerns that since NCLB does not require yearly testing of social studies, state and school districts may decide to shift resources and class time away from teaching social studies. However, NCLB considers the social studies areas of history, geography, economics, and government and civics to be core academic subjects. Many states are requiring middle grades social studies teachers to be highly qualified in history and geography in order to comply with the principle of improving teacher quality in NCLB.

NCLB sets the goal of having every child meet state-defined education standards. Since social studies educators have been leaders in the development of standards-based education and accountability through student testing over the past decade, many state and local districts have their own standards and assessments for social studies already in place. Assessment, including screening, diagnostic, progress-monitoring—including end-of-year, end-of-schooling, grade level, district, and state testing—and large-scale assessments, will continue to play a significant role in shaping social studies curriculum and instruction in the near future.

Integrating Reading into Social Studies Instruction

Due to the increased emphasis on reading and mathematics required by NCLB, social studies teachers may be called on to help improve their students' reading and math skills. For example, a teacher might use a graph about exports and imports to reinforce math skills, or a primary source about a historical event to improve reading skills. The connection between reading and social studies is especially important. Since many state and local assessments of reading require students to read and interpret informational texts, social studies passages are often used in the exams. Therefore, social studies teachers may assist in raising reading scores by integrating reading instruction into their teaching of social studies content.

Implications for Instructional Programs

The environment created by the NCLB legislation has implications for instructional programs. In keeping with the spirit of NCLB, social studies programs should clearly tie their content to state and local standards. Programs should also provide support so that all students can master these standards, ensuring that no child is left behind. An ideal instructional program is rooted in research, embeds reading instruction into the instructional design, and provides assessment tools that inform instruction—helping teachers focus on improving student performance.

Prentice Hall Response

We realize that raising the achievement level of all students is the number one challenge facing teachers today. To assist you in meeting this challenge, Prentice Hall enlisted a team of respected consultants who specialize in middle grades issues, reading in the content areas, and geographic education. This team created a middle grades world studies program that breaks new ground and meets the changing needs of you and your students.

With Prentice Hall, you can be confident that your students will not only be motivated, inspired, and excited to learn world studies, but they will also achieve the success needed in today's environment of the No Child Left Behind (NCLB) legislation and testing reform.

In the following pages, you will find the key elements woven throughout this World Studies program that truly set it apart and assure success for you and your students.

Teacher's Edition Contents in Brief

Research on Effective Reading Instruction

Why do many students have difficulty reading textbooks? How can we help students read to learn social studies? In the pages that follow, we examine the research on the challenge of reading textbooks; explain the direct, systematic, and explicit instruction needed to help students; and then show how Prentice Hall has responded to this research.

What is skilled reading?

Recent research (Snow et al., 2002) suggests that skillful and strategic reading is a long-term developmental process in which "readers learn how to simultaneously extract and construct meaning through interaction with written language." In other words, successful readers know how to decode all kinds of words, read with fluency and expression, have well-developed vocabularies, and possess various comprehension strategies such as note-taking and summarizing to employ as the academic reading task demands.

Many students lack reading skills

Sadly, many secondary students do not have solid reading skills. In the early years, students read mainly engaging and accessible narratives, such as stories, poems, and junior biographies. But in the upper elementary years, they shift toward conceptually dense and challenging nonfiction, or expository texts. It is no accident that the infamous "Fourth-Grade Slump" (Chall and Jacobs, 2003; Hirsch 2003)—a well-documented national trend of declining literacy after grade four—occurs during this time. The recent National Assessment of Educational Progress (NAEP, 2002) found that only 33 percent of eighth-grade students scored at or above the proficient level in reading.

Even students quite skilled in reading novels, short stories, and adolescent magazines typically come to middle school ill-equipped for the rigors of informational texts or reading to learn. They tend to dive right into a social studies chapter as if reading a recreational story. They don't first preview the material to create a mental outline and establish a reading purpose. They have not yet learned other basic strategies, including reading a section more than once, taking notes as they read, and reading to answer specific questions.

Dr. Kate Kinsella
Reading Consultant for *World Studies*
Department of Secondary Education
San Francisco State University, CA

Dr. Kevin Feldman
Reading Consultant for *World Studies*
Director of Reading and Early Intervention
Sonoma County, CA

"Even students quite skilled in reading novels, short stories, and adolescent magazines typically come to middle school ill-equipped for the rigors of informational texts or reading to learn."

The unique demands of textbooks

The differences between textbooks and the narratives students are used to reading are dramatic. The most distinctive challenges include dense conceptual content, heavy vocabulary load, unfamiliar paragraph and organizational patterns, and complex sentence structures. Academic texts present such a significant challenge to most students that linguists and language researchers liken them to learning a foreign language (Schleppegrell, 2002). In other words, most secondary students are second language learners: they are learning the academic language of informational texts!

Effective reading instruction

Research illustrates that virtually all students benefit from direct, systematic, and explicit instruction in reading informational texts (Baker & Gersten, 2000). There are three stages to the instructional process for content-area reading:

(1) **before reading:** instructional frontloading;

(2) **during reading:** guided instruction;

(3) **after reading:** reflection and study.

Before reading

Placing a major emphasis on preteaching, or "front-loading" your instruction—building vocabulary, setting a purpose for reading, and explicitly teaching students strategies for actively engaging with the text—helps you structure learning to ensure student success (see Strategies 1 and 2 on pages T32-T33). Frontloading strategies are especially critical in mixed-ability classrooms with English language learners, students with special needs, and other students performing below grade level in terms of literacy.

During reading

In guided instruction, the teacher models approaches for actively engaging with text to gain meaning. The teacher guides students through the first reading of the text using passage reading strategies (see Strategies 3-7 on pages T33-35), and then guides discussion about the content using participation strategies (see Strategies 8-11 on pages T35-T37). Finally, students record key information in a graphic organizer.

After reading

During the reflection and study phase, the teacher formally checks for student understanding, offers remediation if necessary, and provides activities that challenge students to apply content in a new way. To review the chapter, students recall content, analyze the reading as a whole, and study key vocabulary and information likely to be tested.

References

Baker, Scott and Russell Gersten. "What We Know About Effective Instructional Practices for English Language Learners." *Exceptional Children*, 66 (2000):454–470.

Chall, Jeanne S. and Vicki A. Jacobs. "Poor Children's Fourth-Grade Slump." *American Educator* (Spring 2003):14.

Donahue, P.L., et al. *The 1998 NAEP Reading Report Card for the Nation and the States* (NCES 1999-500). Washington, D.C.: U.S. Department of Education, Office of Education Research and Improvement, National Center for Education Statistics, 1999.

Grigg, W.S. et al. *The Nation's Report Card: Reading 2002* (NCES 2003-521). Washington, D.C.: U.S. Department of Education, Institute of Education Sciences, National Center for Education Statistics, 2003.

Hirsch, E.D., Jr. "Reading Comprehension Requires Knowledge—of Words and the World." *American Educator* (Spring 2003):10-29.

Kinsella, Kate, et al. *Teaching Guidebook for Universal Access*. Upper Saddle River, NJ: Prentice Hall, 2002.

Schleppegrell, M. "Linguistic Features of the Language of Schooling." *Linguistics and Education*, 12, no. 4 (2002): 431–459.

Snow, C., et al. *Reading for Understanding: Toward an R&D Program in Reading Comprehension*. Santa Monica, California: The Rand Corporation, 2002.

Putting Research Into Practice

Prentice Hall enlisted the assistance of Dr. Kate Kinsella and Dr. Kevin Feldman to ensure that the new middle grades world studies program would provide the direct, systematic, and explicit instruction needed to foster student success in reading informational texts. To help students rise to the challenge of reading an informational text, *World Studies* embedded reading support right into the student text.

Embedded Reading Support in the Student Text

Before students read

- **Objectives** set the purpose for what students will read.
- **Target Reading Skill** for the section is explained.
- **Key Terms** are defined up front with pronunciation and part of speech.

During the section

- **Target Reading Skill** is applied to help students read and understand the narrative.
- **Key Terms** are defined in context, with terms and definitions called out in blue type.
- **Reading Checks** reinforce students' understanding by slowing them down to review after every concept is discussed.
- **Caption Questions** draw students into the art and photos, helping them to connect the content to the images.

After students read

- **Section Assessment** revisits the **Key Terms**, provides an opportunity to master the **Target Reading Skill**, allows student to rehearse their understanding of the text through the **Writing Activity**.

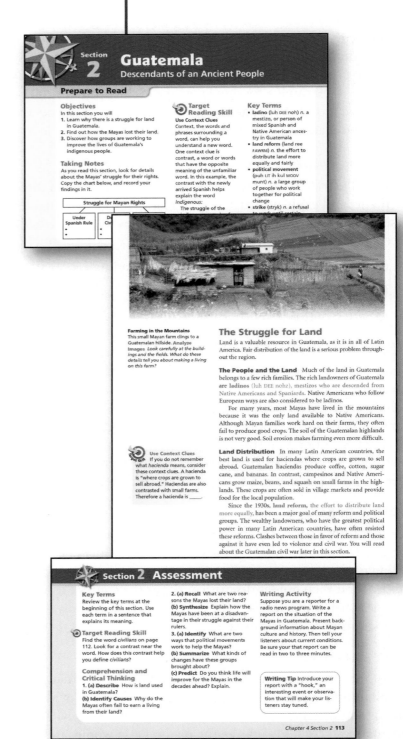

Putting Research Into Practice

World Studies offers teachers guidance in direct, systematic, and explicit reading instruction. The instructional sequence in the Teacher's Edition explicitly guides you in the use of effective strategies at each stage of the instructional process.

Reading Instruction in *World Studies* Teacher's Edition

Before Reading

Every lesson plan begins with suggestions that help you integrate frontloading strategies into your teaching. Build Background Knowledge activates and builds prior knowledge. Set a Purpose for Reading prompts students to predict and anticipate content and motivates students to engage with the text. Preview Key Terms helps students learn Key Terms to understand the text. Target Reading Skill models a reading strategy to help students gain meaning from the text. Vocabulary Builder gives teachers definitions and sample sentences to help teach high-use words.

During Reading

In the Instruct part of the lesson plan, you can use suggestions for getting students actively engaged in the text. Guided Instruction clarifies high-use words, applies a passage-reading strategy to promote text comprehension, and guides discussion to construct meaning. Independent Practice prompts students to reread and take notes in the graphic organizer provided to rehearse understanding.

After Reading

The lesson plan closes with specific strategies for the reflection and study phase after reading is completed. Monitor Progress checks students' note taking, and verifies students' prereading predictions. Assess and Reteach measures students' recall of content and provides additional instruction if needed. Review Chapter Content promotes retention of key concepts and vocabulary.

Integrated Reading Resources

The *World Studies* program provides instructional materials to support the reading instruction in the Teacher's Edition.

The **All-in-One Teaching Resources** provides reading instruction support worksheets, such as a Reading Readiness Guide, Word Knowledge, and Vocabulary Development.

Students can use the **Reading and Vocabulary Study Guide** (English and Spanish) to reinforce reading instruction and vocabulary development, and to review section summaries of every section of the student text.

Research on Differentiated Instruction

It's basic, but it's true—not all our students learn in the same manner and not all our students have the same academic background or abilities. As educators, we need to respond to this challenge through the development and utilization of instructional strategies that address the needs of diverse learners, or the number of children who "fall through the cracks" will continue to rise (Kame'enui & Carnine, 1998).

Providing universal access

Universal access happens when curriculum and instruction are provided in ways that allow all learners to participate and to achieve (Kinsella, et al., 2002). Teachers who teach in heterogeneous, inclusive classrooms can provide universal access by modifying their teaching to respond to the needs of typical learners, gifted learners, less proficient readers, English language learners, and special needs students. Many of these learner populations benefit from extensive reading support (see pages T14-T17).

It is also critical to properly match the difficulty level of tasks with the ability level of students. Giving students tasks that they perceive as too hard lowers their expectations of success. However, giving students assignments that they think are too easy, undermines their feelings of competence (Stipek, 1996). Therefore, it is important for a program to give teachers leveled activities that allow them to match tasks with the abilities of their individual students.

When students connect to and are engaged with the content, comprehension and understanding increase. Technology, such as online activities, can provide an ideal opportunity for such engagement. It also can be used to provide additional opportunities to access content. For example, a less proficient reader may reinforce understanding of a key concept through watching a video. A complete social studies program makes content available in a variety of formats, including text, audio, visuals, and interactivities.

> "Universal access happens when curriculum and instruction are provided in ways that allow all learners to participate and to achieve (Kinsella, et al., 2002)."

Kame'enui, Edward and Douglas Carnine. *Effective Teaching Strategies that Accommodate Diverse Learners.* Upper Saddle River, NJ: Prentice Hall, 1998.

Kinsella, Kate, et al. *Teaching Guidebook for Universal Access.* Upper Saddle River, NJ: Prentice Hall, 2002.

Stipek, D.J. "Motivation and Instruction," in R.C. Clafee and D.C. Berlinger (Eds.), *Handbook of Educational Psychology.* New York: Macmillan, 1996.

Putting Research Into Practice

Prentice Hall recognizes that today's classrooms include students with diverse backgrounds and ability levels. Accordingly, the *World Studies* program was designed to provide access to the content for all students. The program provides both the instructional materials to meet the learning needs of all students and the guidance you need to accommodate these needs.

Differentiated Instruction in the Teacher's Edition

The Teacher's Edition was designed to make it easy for teachers to modify instruction for diverse learners. Teaching strategies, provided by Dr. Kate Kinsella and Dr. Kevin Feldman, to help you modify your teaching are incorporated into every lesson plan. Specific activities help you differentiate instruction for individual students in five categories—less proficient readers, advanced readers, special needs students, gifted and talented, and English language learners. Resources are identified as being appropriate for use by each of these categories. All resources are also assigned a level—basic, average, and above average—so you know exactly how to assign tasks of appropriate difficulty level.

All-in-One Teaching Resources

Everything you need to provide differentiated instruction for each lesson, including reading support, activities and projects, enrichment, and assessment—in one convenient location.

World Studies Video Program

Students will benefit from our custom-built video program—the result of an exclusive partnership with Discovery Channel School—making content accessible through dynamic footage and high-impact stories.

Student Edition on Audio CD

The complete narrative is read aloud, section by section, providing extra support for auditory learners, English language learners, and reluctant readers. Also available is the Guided Reading Audio CD (English/Spanish), containing section summaries read aloud.

Interactive Textbook—The Student Edition Online and on CD-ROM

The Interactive Textbook allows students to interact with the content, including reading aids, visual and interactive learning tools, and instant feedback assessments.

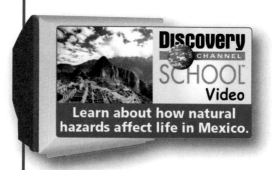

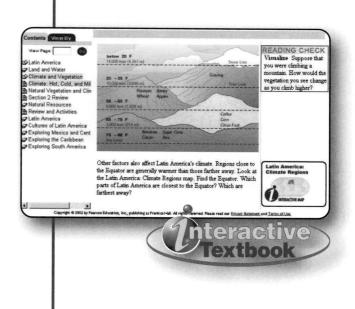

Research on Geographic Literacy

As the *Geography for Life: National Geography Standards* (1994) state, "There is now a widespread acceptance among the people of the United States that being literate in geography is essential if students are to leave school equipped to earn a decent living, enjoy the richness of life, and participate responsibly in local, national, and international affairs." A middle grades social studies program needs to help teachers produce students who are literate in geography.

Geographic literacy defined

Results for the 2001 National Assessment of Educational Progress (NAEP) Geography assessment show that the average scores of fourth- and eighth-grade students have improved since 1994. The average score of twelfth-grade students, however, has not changed significantly. In order to make the critical leap from basic geography skills to the kind of geographic literacy needed by the twelfth grade and beyond, a program must teach both geography content and geography skills, and then help students think critically. Geography content is made up of the essential knowledge that students need to know about the world. Geography skills are the ability to ask geographic questions, acquire and analyze geographic information, and answer these questions. To be truly literate in geography, students must be able to apply their knowledge and skills to understand the world.

Elements for success in middle grades

Students in the elementary grades don't always get enough training in geography. In order to help all students gain a base upon which to build middle grades geographic literacy, a program should introduce basic geography skills at the beginning of the school year.

The quality of maps is also vital to the success of a middle grades world studies program. Maps must be developmentally appropriate for middle grades students. They should be clean, clear, and accurate. Maps should be attractive and present subject matter in appealing ways, so that students *want* to use them to learn.

Another element that can lead to success is the incorporation of technology into the teaching and learning of geography, specifically the Internet. Research has shown that 8th grade students with high Internet usage scored higher in geography (NAEP, 2001).

U.S. Department of Education, Office of Educational Research and Improvement, National Center for Education Statistics, National Assessment of Educational Progress (NAEP), 2001 Geography Assessment.

Andrew Heritage
Head of Cartography
Dorling Kindersley (DK)

"Maps should be attractive and present subject matter in appealing ways, so that students *want* to use them to learn."

Putting Research Into Practice

Prentice Hall partnered with DK—internationally known for their dynamic atlases—to develop the *World Studies* program. DK's Andrew Heritage and his world-renowned cartography team designed all maps, resulting in stunning, high quality maps that are middle grades appropriate.

The MapMaster™ System

World Studies offers the first interactive geography instruction system available with a world studies textbook.

Introduce Basic Map Skills

The MapMaster™ Skills Handbook, a DK-designed introduction to the basics, brings students up to speed with a complete overview at the beginning of every book.

Build Geographic Literacy with Every Map

Scaffolded questions start with questions that require basic geography content and skills, and then ask students to demonstrate geographic literacy by thinking critically about the map.

Activate Learning Online

MapMaster™ Interactive—online and on CD-ROM—allows students to put their knowledge of geography skills and content into practice through interactivities.

Extend Learning with DK

- **DK World Desk Reference Online** is filled with up-to-date data, maps, and visuals that connect students to a wealth of information about the world's countries.

- **DK Compact Atlas of the World** with Map Master™ Teacher's Companion provides activities to introduce, develop, and master geography and map skills.

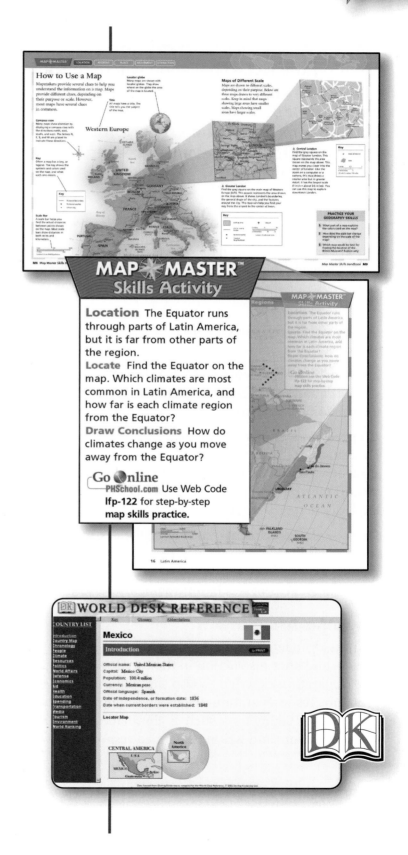

Research on Assessment

Meeting the NCLB challenge will necessitate an integrated approach to assessment with a variety of assessment tools. With the spotlight now on *improving* student performance, it is essential to use assessment results to inform instruction.

Assessments Tools for Informing Instruction

The key to success is using a variety of assessment tools coupled with data analysis and decision making. Teachers work with information coming from four kinds of assessment.

Screening assessments are brief procedures used to identify at-risk students who are not ready to work at grade level.

Diagnostic assessments provide a more in-depth analysis of strengths and weaknesses that can help teachers make instructional decisions and plan intervention strategies.

Progress-monitoring assessments (sometimes referred to as benchmark tests) provide an ongoing, longitudinal record of student achievement detailing individual student progress toward meeting end-of-year and end-of-schooling, grade level, district, or state standards.

Large-scale assessments, such as state tests and standardized tests, are used to determine whether individual students have met the expected standards and whether a school system has made adequate progress in improving its performance.

Ongoing Assessment

Daily assessment should be embedded in the program before, during, and after instruction in the core lessons. Legitimate test preparation experiences also should be embedded in the program. Test preparation involves teaching students strategies for taking tests, such as eliminating answers, reading comprehension, and writing extended response answers.

Eileen Depka
Supervisor of Standards and Assessment
Waukesha, WI

"Meeting the NCLB challenge will necessitate an integrated approach to assessment with a variety of assessment tools."

Putting Research Into Practice

Prentice Hall developed the *World Studies* program with a variety of assessment tools, including ongoing assessment in the student text.

Assessments for Informing Instruction

World Studies was designed to provide you with all four kinds of assessment.

- **Screening test** identifies students who are reading 2-3 years below grade level.

- **Diagnostic tests** focus on skills needed for success in social studies, including subtests in geographic literacy, visual analysis, critical thinking and reading, and communications skills, as well as vocabulary and writing.

- **Benchmark tests**, to be given six times throughout the year, monitor student progress in the course.

- **Outcome test**, to be administered at the end of the year, evaluates student mastery of social studies content standards.

Ongoing Assessment

- **Student Edition** offers section and chapter assessments with questions building from basic comprehension to critical thinking and writing.

- **Test Prep Workbook** and **Test-taking Strategies with Transparencies** develop students' test-taking skills and improve their scores on standardized tests.

- *ExamView® Test Bank CD-ROM* allows you to quickly and easily develop customized tests from a bank of thousands of questions.

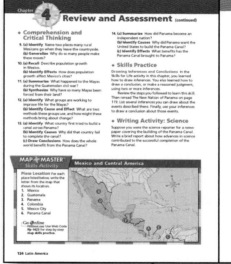

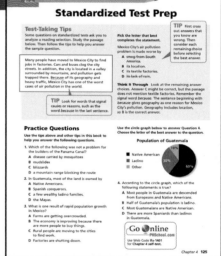

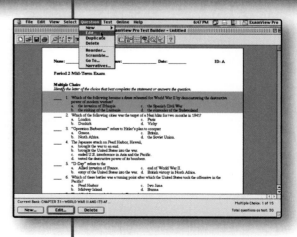

The United States and Canada Skills
Scope and Sequence

Prentice Hall *World Studies* contains a comprehensive program of core skills. Each skill is taught in every book of the series. A Target Reading Skill is located at the beginning of each chapter and expanded upon in each section within the chapter. Core skills are also taught either in the "Skills for Life Activity" in the Student Edition, or in a "Skills Mini Lesson" in the Teacher's Edition. In addition, worksheets for the students' use in completing each skill are located in the All-in-One Teaching Resources. The chart below lists the skills covered in *Prentice Hall World Studies: The United States and Canada* and the page where each skill is taught.

The United States and Canada Analysis Skills	SE	TE
Analyzing Graphic Data	pp. 62–63, 82–83, 124–125	pp. 62–63, 82–83, 124–125
Analyzing Images		p. 22
Analyzing Primary Sources		p. 51
Clarifying Meaning	pp. 34, 36, 40, 41, 42, 46, 48, 49, 50, 54, 55, 58, 61, 64, 68, 70	pp. 34B, 36, 42, 49, 55, 64
Comparing and Contrasting	pp. 96, 110, 113, 116, 117, 121, 123, 126, 129, 132, 133, 137, 138	pp. 96B, 110, 117, 126, 133
Decision Making		p. 79
Distinguishing Fact and Opinion		p. 136
Drawing Inferences and Conclusions		p. 78
Identifying Cause and Effect/Making Predictions		p. 40
Identifying Frame of Reference and Point of View	pp. 16–17	pp. 16–17
Identifying Main Ideas/Summarizing	pp. 74, 76, 79, 82–83, 84, 86, 91, 178–179	pp. 74B, 76, 79, 81, 82–83, 84, 86, 89, 91, 178–179
Making Valid Generalizations		p. 27
Problem Solving		p. 57
Recognizing Bias and Propaganda		p. 156
Sequencing		p. 183
Supporting a Position		p. 157
Synthesizing Information		p. 112
Transferring Information From One Medium to Another		p. 45
Using the Cartographer's Tools	pp. M8–M9	pp. M8–M9, 131
Using Context	pp. 146, 152, 157, 160, 164, 166, 169, 172, 173, 174, 177, 180, 181, 184	pp. 146B, 152, 160, 166, 173, 180
Using the Reading Process	pp. 8, 10, 13, 15, 18, 21, 24, 25, 28, 30	pp. 8B, 10, 18, 25
Using Reliable Information		p. 87
Using Special-Purpose Maps	pp. M12–M17	pp. 119

Pacing Options

World Studies offers many aids to help you plan your instruction time, whether regular class periods or block scheduling. Section-by-section lesson plans for each chapter include suggested times, based on the 9-week course configuration below. Teacher Express CD-ROM will help you manage your time electronically.

The United States and Canada Pacing Options			9-week unit	12-week unit
Chapter 1	Section 1	Land and Water	4.5	7
	Section 2	Climate and Vegetation	1.5	2
	Section 3	Resources and Land Use	3	3.5
Chapter 2	Section 1	The Arrival of the Europeans	1.5	2
	Section 2	Growth and Conflict in the United States	1.5	2
	Section 3	The United States on the Brink of Change	1.5	2
	Section 4	The History of Canada	2.5	3.5
	Section 5	The United States and Canada Today	3	4
Chapter 3	Section 1	A Heritage of Diversity and Exchange	3	3.5
	Section 2	The United States: A Nation of Immigrants	1.5	2
	Section 3	The Canadian Mosaic	3	4
Chapter 4	Section 1	The Northeast: An Urban Center	2.5	3
	Section 2	The South: The Growth of Industry	3	3.5
	Section 3	The Midwest: Leaving the Farm	1.5	2
	Section 4	The West: Using and Preserving Resources	3	4
Chapter 5	Section 1	Ontario and Quebec: Bridging Two Cultures	2	2.5
	Section 2	The Prairie Provinces: Canada's Breadbasket	1	1.5
	Section 3	British Columbia: Economic and Cultural Changes	1	1.5
	Section 4	The Atlantic Provinces: Relying on the Sea	2	3
	Section 5	The Northern Territories: New Frontiers	2.5	3.5
		Total Number of Days	**45**	**60**

Correlation to *Geography for Life*, the National Geography Standards

On the following pages, *Prentice Hall World Studies The United States and Canada* is correlated with *Geography for Life*, the National Geography Standards. These standards were prepared in response to the Goals 2000, Educate America Act, by the Geography Education Standards Project. Participating in the project were the American Geographical Society, the Association of American Geographers, the National Council for Geographic Education, and the National Geographic Society. Concepts and skills contained in the Geography Standards are incorporated throughout the program. This correlation displays places where the standards are directly addressed.

Standard	The United States and Canada
The World in Spatial Terms	
Standard 1 Use maps and other geographic representations, tools, and technologies to acquire, process, and report information from a spatial perspective.	MapMaster Skills Handbook, Regional Overview, 1:1–3, 2:1, 2:2, 2:4, 2:5, 3:1, 4:1–4, 5:1–5, Review and Assessment: Chs. 1–5
Standard 2 Use mental maps to organize information about people, places, and environments in a spatial context.	MapMaster Skills Handbook, 1:1, 1:3
Standard 3 Analyze the spatial organization of people, places, and environments on Earth's surface.	MapMaster Skills Handbook, Regional Overview, 1:1–3, 2:1–5, 3:1, 4:1–4, 5:1–5, Review and Assessment: Chs. 1–5
Places and Regions	
Standard 4 Understand the physical and human characteristics of places.	MapMaster Skills Handbook, Regional Overview, 1:1–3, 2:1–5, 3:1–3, 4:1–4, 5:1–5, Country Databanks: Chs. 4, 5, Review and Assessment: Chs. 1–5
Standard 5 Understand that people create regions to interpret Earth's complexity.	MapMaster Skills Handbook, Regional Overview, 1:1, 1:2, 4:1–4, 5:1–5, Review and Assessment: Chs. 1–5
Standard 6 Understand how culture and experience influence people's perception of places and regions.	MapMaster Skills Handbook, Regional Overview, 2:1–5, 3:1–3, 4:1–4, 5:1–5, Review and Assessment: Chs. 2, 3, 5
Physical Systems	
Standard 7 Understand the physical processes that shape the patterns of Earth's surface.	1:1–3, 2:1, 3:2, 4:3, 4:4, 5:1–5, Review and Assessment: Ch. 4
Standard 8 Understand the characteristics and spatial distribution of ecosystems on Earth's surface.	MapMaster Skills Handbook, 1:1–3, 2:5, 4:2, 5:1–5, Review and Assessment: Ch. 1

Correlation to *Geography for Life*, the National Geography Standards *(continued)*

Standard	The United States and Canada
Human Systems	
Standard 9 Understand the characteristics, distribution, and migration of human populations on Earth's surface.	MapMaster Skills Handbook, Regional Overview, 2:1, 2:2, 2:3, 2:4, 3:1–3, 4:1, 4:2, 4:4, 5:1–5, Review and Assessment: Chs. 3, 4, 5
Standard 10 Understand the characteristics, distribution, and complexity of Earth's cultural mosaics.	MapMaster Skills Handbook, Regional Overview, 2:1, 2:4, 3:1–3, 4:1, 5:1–5, Review and Assessment: Chs. 3, 5
Standard 11 Understand the patterns and networks of economic interdependence on Earth's surface.	MapMaster Skills Handbook, 1:3, 2:3, 2:4, 2:5, 3:1, 4:1–4, 5:2, 5:3, 5:4, Review and Assessment: Chs. 2, 3, 4, 5
Standard 12 Understand the processes, patterns, and functions of human settlement.	MapMaster Skills Handbook, 2:1, 2:2, 2:3, 2:4, 3:1–3, 4:1–4, 5:1–5, Review and Assessment: Chs. 2, 3, 4, 5
Standard 13 Understand how the forces of cooperation and conflict among people influence division and control of Earth's surface.	1:1, 2:1, 2:2, 2:3, 2:4, 3:1–3, 4:4, 5:1, 5:2, 5:3, 5:4, Review and Assessment: Chs. 2, 3, 4, 5
Environment and Society	
Standard 14 Understand how human actions modify the physical environment.	1:1, 2:5, 4:3, 4:4, 5:2, 5:3, 5:4 Review and Assessment: Ch. 2
Standard 15 Understand how physical systems affect human systems.	1:1–3, 2:1, 2:5, 3:1, 4:2, 4:4, 5:2, 5:3, 5:4, 5:5, Review and Assessment: Chs. 1, 2, 4, 5
Standard 16 Understand the changes that occur in the meaning, use, distribution, and importance of resources.	1:1–3. 2:2, 2:4, 2:5, 3:1, 3:2, 4:1–4, 5:1–5, Review and Assessment: Chs. 1, 2, 4
The Uses of Geography	
Standard 17 Understand how to apply geography to interpret the past.	MapMaster Skills Handbook, Regional Overview, 1:1, 2:1, 2:2, 2:3, 3:1, 4:1, 4:3, 4:4, 5:1, 5:2, 5:3, 5:4, Review and Assessment: Chs. 2, 4
Standard 18 Understand how to apply geography to interpret the present and plan for the future.	MapMaster Skills Handbook, Regional Overview, 1:2, 1:3, 2:5, 4:1–4, 5:1–5, Review and Assessment: Chs. 1, 4, 5

Correlation to the NCSS Curriculum Standards

On the following pages *Prentice Hall World Studies The United States and Canada* is correlated with *Expectations of Excellence*, the Curriculum Standards for Social Studies. These standards were developed by the National Council for the Social Studies to address overall curriculum design and comprehensive student performance expectations.

Standard	The United States and Canada
Performance Expectations 1: Culture	
• compare similarities and differences in the ways groups, societies, and cultures meet human needs and concerns • explain how information and experiences may be interpreted by people from diverse cultural perspectives and frames of reference • explain and give examples of how language, literature, the arts, architecture, other artifacts, traditions, beliefs, values, and behaviors contribute to the development and transmission of culture • explain why individuals and groups respond differently to their physical and social environments and/or changes to them on the basis of shared assumptions, values, and beliefs • articulate the implications of cultural diversity, as well as cohesion, within and across groups	MapMaster Skills Handbook, Regional Overview, 2:1–5, 3:1–3, 4:1–4, 5:1–5, Review and Assessment: Chs. 2, 3, 5
Performance Expectations 2: Time, Continuity, and Change	
• demonstrate an understanding that different scholars may describe the same event or situation in different ways but must provide reasons or evidence for their view • identify and use key concepts such as chronology, causality, change, conflict, and complexity to explain, analyze, and show connections among patterns of historical change and continuity • identify and describe selected historical periods and patterns of change within and across cultures • identify and use processes important to reconstructing and reinterpreting the past • develop critical sensitivities regarding attitudes, values, and behaviors of people in different historical contexts • use knowledge of facts and concepts drawn from history, along with methods of historical inquiry, to inform decision-making about and action-taking on public issues	Regional Overview, 2:1–5, 3:1–3, 4:2, 4:3, 4:4, 5:1–5, Review and Assessment: Chs. 2, 3, 4, 5
Performance Expectations 3: People, Places, and Environment	
• elaborate mental maps of locales, regions, and the world that demonstrate understanding of relative location, direction, size, and shape • create, interpret, use, and distinguish various representations of the earth • use appropriate resources, data sources, and geographic tools to generate, manipulate, and interpret information • estimate distance, calculate scale, and distinguish geographic relationships • locate and describe varying landforms and geographic features and explain their relationship with the ecosystem • describe physical system changes and identify geographic patterns associated with them • describe how people create places that reflect cultural values and ideals • examine, interpret, and analyze physical and cultural patterns and their interactions • describe ways that historical events have been influenced by, and have influenced, physical and human geographic factors in local, regional, national, and global settings • observe and speculate about social and economic effects of environmental changes and crises resulting from natural phenomena • propose, compare, and evaluate alternative uses of land and resources in communities, regions, nations, and the world	MapMaster Skills Handbook, Regional Overview, 1:1–3, 2:1, 2:2, 2:4, 2:5, 3:1–3, 4:1–4, 5:1–5, Skills for Life: Ch. 1, Review and Assessment: Chs. 1– 5

Correlation to the NCSS Curriculum Standards *(continued)*

Standard	The United States and Canada
Performance Expectations 4: Individual Development and Identity	
• relate personal changes to social, cultural, and historical contexts • describe personal connections to place—as associated with community, nation, and world • describe the ways family, gender, ethnicity, nationality, and institutional affiliations contribute to personal identity • relate such factors as physical endowment and capabilities, learning, motivation, personality, perception, and behavior to individual development • identify and describe ways regional, ethnic, and national cultures influence individuals' daily lives • identify and describe the influence of perception, attitudes, values, and beliefs on personal identity • identify and interpret examples of stereotyping, conformity, and altruism • work independently and cooperatively to accomplish goals	2:1, 2:2, 2:4, 3:1–3, 4:1–4, 5:1, Skills for Life: Ch. 1, Review and Assessment: Chs. 1, 2, 3, 4
Performance Expectations 5: Individuals, Groups, & Institutions	
• demonstrate an understanding of concepts such as role, status, and social class in describing interactions of individuals and social groups • analyze group and institutional influences on people, events, and elements of culture • describe the various forms institutions take and the interactions of people with institutions • identify and analyze examples of tensions between expressions of individuality and group or institutional efforts to promote social conformity • identify and describe examples of tensions between belief systems and government policies and laws • describe the role of institutions in furthering both continuity and change • apply knowledge of how groups and institutions work to meet individual needs and promote the common good	2:1–5, 3:1–3, 5:1–5, Review and Assessment: Chs. 2, 3, 5
Performance Expectations 6: Power, Authority, and Governance	
• examine persistent issues involving the rights, roles, and status of the individual in relation to general welfare • describe the purpose of government and how its powers are acquired, used, and justified • analyze and explain ideas and governmental mechanisms to meet needs and wants of citizens, regulate territory, manage conflict, and establish order and security • describe the ways nations and organizations respond to forces of unity and diversity affecting order and security • identify and describe the basic features of the political system in the United States, and identify representative leaders from various levels and branches of government • explain conditions, actions, and motivations that contribute to conflict and cooperation within and among nations • describe and analyze the role of technology as it contributes to or helps resolve conflicts • explain how power, role, status, and justice influence the examination of persistent issues and social problems • give examples and explain how governments attempt to achieve their stated ideals at home and abroad	2:1–5, 3:1–3, 4:1, 4:2, 4:4, 5:1–5, Review and Assessment: Chs. 2, 3, 5

Correlation to the NCSS Curriculum Standards *(continued)*

Standard	The United States and Canada
Performance Expectation 7: Production, Distribution, and Consumption	
• give examples of ways that economic systems structure choices about how goods and services are to be produced and distributed • describe the role that supply and demand, prices, incentives, and profits play in determining what is produced and distributed in a competitive market system • explain differences between private and public goods and services • describe a range of examples of the various institutions that make up economic systems • describe the role of specialization and exchange in the economic process • explain and illustrate how values and beliefs influence different economic decisions • differentiate among various forms of exchange and money • compare basic economic systems according to who determines what is produced, distributed, and consumed • use economic concepts to help explain historical and current events in local, national, or global concepts • use economic reasoning to compare different proposals for dealing with contemporary social issues	1:3, 2:1–5, 3:1, 4:1–4, 5:2, 5:3, 5:4, Review and Assessment: Chs. 2, 3, 4, 5
Performance Expectation 8: Science, Technology, and Society	
• examine and describe the influence of culture on scientific and technological choices and advancement • show through specific examples how science and technology have changed peoples' perceptions of their social and natural world • describe examples in which values, beliefs, and attitudes have been influenced by new scientific and technological knowledge • explain the need for laws and policies to govern scientific and technological applications • seek reasonable and ethical solutions to problems that arise when scientific advancements and social norms or values come into conflict	1:1, 1:3, 2:2, 2:3, 2:4, 2:5, 4:2, 4:3, 4:4, 5:2, 5:3, 5:4, Review and Assessment: Chs. 4, 5
Performance Expectation 9: Global Connections	
• describe instances in which language, art, music, and belief systems, and other cultural elements can facilitate global understanding or cause misunderstanding • analyze examples of conflict, cooperation, and interdependence among groups, societies, and nations • describe and analyze the effects of changing technologies on the global community • explore the causes, consequences, and possible solutions to persistent contemporary and emerging global interests • describe and explain the relationships and tensions between national sovereignty and global interests • demonstrate understanding of concerns, standards, issues, and conflicts related to universal human rights • identify and describe the roles of international and multinational organizations	1: 3, 2:1–5, 3:1–3, 5:1–5, Review and Assessment: Chs. 2, 3, 5

Correlation to the NCSS Curriculum Standards *(continued)*

Standard	The United States and Canada
Performance Expectation 10: Civic Ideals and Practices	
• examine the origins and continuing influence of key ideals of the democratic republican form of government, such as individual human dignity, liberty, justice, equality, and rule of law • identify and interpret sources and examples of the rights and responsibilities of citizens • locate, access, analyze, organize, and apply information about selected public issues—recognizing and explaining multiple points of view • practice forms of civic discussion and participation consistent with the ideals of citizens in a democratic republic • explain and analyze various forms of citizen action that influence public policy decisions • identify and explain the roles of formal and informal political actors in influencing and shaping public policy and decision-making • analyze the influence of diverse forms of public opinion on the development of public policy and decision-making • analyze the effectiveness of selected public policies and citizen behaviors in realizing the stated ideals of a democratic republican form of government • explain the relationship between policy statements and action plans used to address issues of public concern • examine strategies designed to strengthen the "common good," which consider a range of options for citizen action	2:1–5, 4:4, 5:1, 5:5, Review and Assessment: Ch. 2

Instructional Strategies for Improving Student Comprehension

In response to today's environment of the NCLB legislation and testing reform, Prentice Hall asked Dr. Kate Kinsella and Dr. Kevin Feldman to provide specific instructional strategies you can use to improve student comprehension. Their guidance informed the development of the *World Studies* Teacher's Edition. The lesson plans in this Teacher's Edition incorporate the following instructional strategies to enhance students' comprehension.

There is no single magical strategy that will solve all of the difficulties students encounter in reading challenging content area texts. Secondary students in mixed-ability classrooms depend on teachers to use a consistent set of research-informed and classroom-tested strategies in a patient and recursive manner—not the occasional or random use of different strategies. Students will not become skillful readers of content area texts in a week or two of instruction. However, when teachers engage students in the consistent use of a well-chosen set of content reading strategies appropriately matched to the demands of the text and the students' level of knowledge, their ability to comprehend difficult grade level texts will be dramatically enhanced.

Strategy 1: Set a Purpose for Reading

This program has two types of activities designed to help students set a purpose for reading: an Anticipation Guide and a KWL chart. The two types rotate by section.

A. Anticipation Guide

Purpose: To focus students' attention on key concepts, and guide them to interact with ideas in the text

1. Distribute the *Reading Readiness Guide*. Read each statement aloud, and then ask students to react to the statements individually and in groups, marking their responses in the Before Reading column.

2. Use the worksheet as a springboard for discussing the section's key concepts as a unified class. Refrain from revealing the correct responses at this time, to avoid taking away the need for them to read the text.

3. Have students read the section with the purpose of finding evidence that confirms, disproves, or elaborates each statement in the *Reading Readiness Guide*.

4. After students finish reading, have them return to the statements and mark the After Reading column on their worksheets. Have them locate information from the text that supports or disproves each statement.

5. Discuss what the class has learned and probe for any lingering confusion about key concepts.

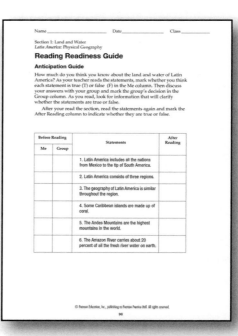

B. KWL

Purpose: To engage students before, during, and after reading

The KWL worksheet guides students to recall what they **K**now, determine what they **W**ant to learn, and identify what they **L**earn as they read.

1. Distribute the *Reading Readiness Guide*. Brainstorm with the group about what they already know about the topic. List students' ideas on the board. Encourage students to generate questions at points of ambiguity.

2. Students then list pieces of information they already know and questions they want to answer in the first two columns of their worksheets.

3. As students read the section, ask them to note information that answers their questions or adds to what they know.

4. After reading, facilitate a class discussion about what the students have learned. Clarify any lingering confusion about key concepts.

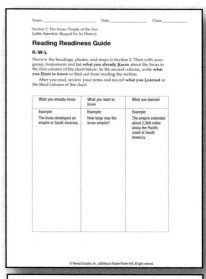

Strategy 2: Teach High-Use Academic Words

Purpose: To teach students words used often in academic texts, beyond the content-specific Key Terms

How to Do It

1. Have students rate how well they know each word on their *Word Knowledge* worksheets. Tell them there is no penalty for a low rating.

2. Survey students' ratings to decide which words need the most instruction.

3. Provide a brief definition or sample sentence for each word. (See Vocabulary Builder at the beginning of each section for definitions and sample sentences.) Rephrase your explanation, leaving out the word and asking students to substitute it aloud.

4. Work with students as they fill in the "Definition or Example" column of their *Word Knowledge* worksheets.

5. Point out each word in context as you read the chapters. Consider allowing students to earn extra credit if they use a word correctly in class discussion or assignments.

Strategy 3: Oral Cloze

Purpose: To help students read actively while the teacher reads aloud

How to Do It

1. Choose a passage and direct students to "read aloud silently using their inner voices." Be sure students understand reading is an active process, not simply a listening activity, and their job is to follow along—eyes riveted to each word, saying the words to themselves as you read aloud.

2. Tell students to be on their "reading toes," for you will be leaving out an occasional word and their task is to chorally supply the word.

3. The first few times you use the Oral Cloze, demonstrate by telling the students in advance what word you will be leaving out, directing them to read the word at the right time. Practice this a few times until they have the feel for the procedure. Leave out fewer words as students become more familiar with the Oral Cloze and require less direction to remain focused during teacher read alouds.

Strategies for Improving Student Comprehension (continued)

Strategy 4: Choral Reading

Purpose: To have students attend to the text in a non-threatening atmosphere

How to Do It

1. Choose a relatively short passage.

2. Tell students that you will all read the text aloud at once. Direct students to "keep your voice with mine" as they read.

3. Read the passage slowly and clearly.

4. Have students read the text again silently.

Strategy 5: Structured Silent Reading

Purpose: To give students a task as they read silently to increase their attentiveness and accountability

How to Do It

1. Assign a section to read silently. Pose a question for the whole class to answer from their silent reading, such as the Reading Check question at the end of each subsection. Model how one thinks while reading to find answers to a question.

2. When students get used to reading to answer the Reading Check question, pose more in-depth questions, progressing from factual recall to questions that stimulate interpretive or applied thinking.

3. Teach students to ask and answer their own questions as they read. Model this process by reading a section aloud and asking and answering your own questions as you read.

4. After the students have finished reading, engage the class in a brief discussion to clarify questions, vocabulary, and key concepts.

Strategy 6: Paragraph Shrinking

Purpose: To increase comprehension during reading

How to Do It

1. Partner struggling students with more proficient students and assign a manageable portion of the text.

2. Ask one member of each pair to identify the "who or what" the paragraph is about and tell the other.

3. Have the other member of the pair identify important details about the "who or what" and tell the other.

4. Ask the first member to summarize the paragraph in fifteen to twenty words or less using the most important details. The second member of the pair monitors the number of words and says "Shrink it!" if the summary goes over twenty words.

5. Have the partners reverse roles and continue reading.

6. Discuss the reading as a class to make sure students' paragraphs have correctly hit upon the main ideas of the passage.

Strategy 7: ReQuest (Reciprocal Questioning)

Purpose: To ask and answer questions during reading to establish a purpose for reading and monitor one's own comprehension

How to Do It

1. Prepare students to read by doing the section's Build Background Knowledge, Set a Purpose for Reading, and Preview Key Terms activities.

2. Begin reading a brief portion of the text aloud. Ask and answer your own questions about the text, progressing from recall to critical thinking questions.

3. After modeling this question and response pattern with a brief passage, ask students to read the next section of the text. Tell students that they will be taking turns asking you questions about what they read, and you will answer their questions, just like you modeled for them.

4. Ask students to read the next section. Inform them that you will be asking them questions about the section and they will be answering your questions.

5. Continue to alternate between student-generated questions and teacher-generated questions until the entire designated passage has been read. As students become used to the strategy, they gradually assume more responsibility in the process.

6. When the students have read enough information to make predictions about the remainder of the assignment, stop the exchange of comprehension questions. Instead, ask prediction questions, such as, "What do you think will be discussed in the next section? Why do you think so?"

7. Assign the remaining portion for students to read silently. Then lead a wrap-up discussion of the material.

Strategy 8: Idea Wave

Purpose: To engage students in active class discussions

How to Do It

1. Pose a question or task.

2. Give students quiet time to consider what they know about the topic and record a number of responses.

3. Whip around the class in a fast-paced and structured manner (e.g. down rows, around tables), allowing as many students as possible to share an idea in 15 seconds or less.

4. After several contributions, if there tends to be repetition, ask students to point out similarities in responses rather than simply stating that their idea has already been mentioned.

Strategies for Improving Student Comprehension *(continued)*

Strategy 9: Numbered Heads

Purpose: To engage students in active class discussions

How to Do It

1. Seat students in groups of four and number off one through four (if possible, combine established partners to form groups of four).

2. After giving the discussion prompt, allow students to discuss possible responses for an established amount of time.

3. Remind students to pay close attention to the comments of each group member because you will be randomly selecting one student to represent the best thinking of the entire group.

4. Call a number (one through four), and ask all students with that number to raise their hands, ready to respond to the topic at hand in a teacher-directed, whole-class discussion.

5. Add comments, extend key ideas, ask follow-up questions, and make connections between individual student's comments to create a lively whole-class discussion.

6. Provide any summary comments required to ensure that all students understand critical points.

Strategy 10: Think–Write–Pair–Share

Purpose: To engage students in responding to instruction

How to Do It

1. **Think**—Students listen while the teacher poses a question or a task related to the reading or classroom discussion. The level of questions should vary from lower level literal to higher order inferential or analytical.

2. **Write**—Provide quiet thinking or writing time for students to deal with the question, and go back to the text or review notes. Have students record their ideas in their notebooks.

3. **Pair/Share**—Cue students to find a partner and discuss their responses, noting similarities and differences. Teach students to encourage one another to clarify and justify responses.

4. Randomly call on students to share during a unified class discussion after they have all rehearsed answers with their partners.

5. Invite any volunteers to contribute additional ideas and points of view to the discussion after calling on a reasonable number of students randomly.

6. Direct students to go back to notes and add any important information garnered during the partner and class discussions.

Strategy 11: Give One, Get One

Purpose: To foster independent reflection and peer interaction prior to a unified class discussion

How to Do It

1. Pose a thought-provoking question or a concrete task to the class.

2. Allow three to five minutes of quiet time for students to consider what they may already know about the topic and jot down a number of potential responses.

3. Ask students to place a check mark next to the two or three ideas that they perceive as their strongest and then draw a line after their final idea to separate their ideas from those that they will gather from classmates.

4. Give students a set amount of time (about eight to ten minutes) to get up from their seats and share ideas with classmates. After finding a partner, the two students exchange papers and first quietly read each other's ideas. They discuss the ideas briefly, then select one idea from their partner's list and add it to their own, making sure to accurately copy the idea alongside the partner's name.

5. When one exchange is completed, students move on to interact with a new partner.

6. At the end of the exchange period, facilitate a unified class discussion. Call on a volunteer to share one new idea acquired from a conversation partner. The student whose idea has just been reported then shares the next idea, gleaned from a different conversation partner.

Professional Development

For more information about these strategies, see the end of each chapter's Interleaf.

Objectives

- Learn how to read nonfiction critically by analyzing an author's purpose, distinguishing between facts and opinions, identifying evidence, and evaluating credibility.

Prepare to Read

Build Background Knowledge   L2

Write the phrase "Don't believe everything you read" on the board. Ask students to brainstorm examples that illustrate the saying. Provide a few simple examples to get them started (*tall tales, advertisements.*)

Instruct

Reading Informational Texts   L2

Guided Instruction

- Tell students that they must actively evaluate the information in most of the nonfiction they read.

- Read the sample editorial on this page aloud. Tell students that an editorial usually expresses a person's opinion. Ask students to consider why the author wrote this editorial. (*The author expresses the opinion that the proposal to build the new shopping center should have been approved.*) Ask **How might this purpose affect what the editorial says?** (*The author may present information in the best possible light to prove his or her belief.*)

- Another important step in evaluating nonfiction is distinguishing between facts and opinions. Ask each student to write one fact and one opinion, on any subject, in their notebooks. Use the Idea Wave strategy (TE, p. T35) to get students to share their facts and opinions. If students have incorrectly categorized examples, help them to see why.

Reading Informational Texts

Reading a magazine, an Internet page, or a textbook is not the same as reading a novel. The purpose of reading nonfiction texts is to acquire new information. On page M18 you'll read about some ⟲ Target Reading Skills that you'll have a chance to practice as you read this textbook. Here we'll focus on a few skills that will help you read nonfiction with a more critical eye.

Analyze the Author's Purpose

Different types of materials are written with different purposes in mind. For example, a textbook is written to teach students information about a subject. The purpose of a technical manual is to teach someone how to use something, such as a computer. A newspaper editorial might be written to persuade the reader to accept a particular point of view. A writer's purpose influences how the material is presented. Sometimes an author states his or her purpose directly. More often, the purpose is only suggested, and you must use clues to identify the author's purpose.

Distinguish Between Facts and Opinions

It's important when reading informational texts to read actively and to distinguish between fact and opinion. A fact can be proven or disproven. An opinion cannot—it is someone's personal viewpoint or evaluation.

For example, the editorial pages in a newspaper offer opinions on topics that are currently in the news. You need to read newspaper editorials with an eye for bias and faulty logic. For example, the newspaper editorial at the right shows factual statements in blue and opinion statements in red. The underlined words are examples of highly charged words. They reveal bias on the part of the writer.

> More than 5,000 people voted last week in favor of building a new shopping center, but the opposition won out. The margin of victory is irrelevant. Those radical voters who opposed the center are obviously self-serving elitists who do not care about anyone but themselves.
>
> This month's unemployment figure for our area is 10 percent, which represents an increase of about 5 percent over the figure for this time last year. These figures mean unemployment is getting worse. But the people who voted against the mall probably do not care about creating new jobs.

- Tell students that identifying evidence is another way to read nonfiction critically. Ask students to look again at the facts highlighted in the sample editorial. **Does the evidence presented in these facts convince you that building a new shopping center is a good idea?** (*The evidence is incomplete—the author has not shown that the new shopping center would solve the unemployment problem.*)

- Tell students that analyzing an author's purpose, distinguishing between facts and opinions, and identifying evidence are all ways to evaluate the credibility of the author. Tell students to look at the checklist for evaluating Web sites. Ask students to think about Web sites they have visited. Do those Web sites pass the checklist's test? Why or why not?

Identify Evidence

Before you accept an author's conclusion, you need to make sure that the author has based the conclusion on enough evidence and on the right kind of evidence. An author may present a series of facts to support a claim, but the facts may not tell the whole story. For example, what evidence does the author of the newspaper editorial on the previous page provide to support his claim that the new shopping center would create more jobs? Is it possible that the shopping center might have put many small local businesses out of business, thus increasing unemployment rather than decreasing it?

Evaluate Credibility

Whenever you read informational texts, you need to assess the credibility of the author. This is especially true of sites you may visit on the Internet. All Internet sources are not equally reliable. Here are some questions to ask yourself when evaluating the credibility of a Web site.

- ❑ Is the Web site created by a respected organization, a discussion group, or an individual?
- ❑ Does the Web site creator include his or her name as well as credentials and the sources he or she used to write the material?
- ❑ Is the information on the site balanced or biased?
- ❑ Can you verify the information using two other sources?
- ❑ Is there a date telling when the Web site was created or last updated?

Reading and Writing Handbook **RW1**

Independent Practice

Ask students to bring in an editorial from the local newspaper, or distribute copies of an appropriate editorial. Ask students to critically assess their editorial by analyzing the author's purpose; underlining facts and circling opinions in the text of the editorial; summarizing the evidence presented in the editorial; and finally drawing a conclusion about the credibility of the editorial.

Monitor Progress

Pair students and have them share their editorial assessments. Ask them to explain the reasoning behind the conclusions they drew about the editorial's credibility. Circulate and offer assistance as needed.

Assess and Reteach

Assess Progress   L2
Collect students' papers and review their assessments.

Reteach   L1
If students are struggling, tell them to approach the task by asking themselves the following questions as they read a piece of nonfiction: **Why** did the author write this? **How** has the author made his or her points, using facts or opinions? **What** evidence has the author used to support the main idea? **Who** is the author, and what sources has he or she used?

Extend   L3
To extend this lesson, tell students to turn to the Table of Contents in the Student Edition and pick a chapter name that intrigues them. Then, ask them to search the Internet and find two Web sites about the chapter's topic. Finally, ask them to use the checklist on this page to evaluate each web site and compare the two in terms of credibility.

Differentiated Instruction

For Advanced Readers   L3
Draw students' attention to the checklist under the heading "Evaluate Credibility." Ask students to create a similar checklist for analyzing an author's purpose, distinguishing between fact and opinion, and identifying evidence.

For Special Needs Students   L1
If special needs students are having trouble making the distinction between facts and opinions, partner them with more proficient students to do the *Distinguishing Fact and Opinion* lesson on the Social Studies Skill Tutor CD-ROM.

◉ *Distinguishing Fact and Opinion,* **Social Studies Skill Tutor CD-ROM**

Objectives

- Use a systematic approach to write narrative, persuasive, expository, and research essays.

Prepare to Read

Build Background Knowledge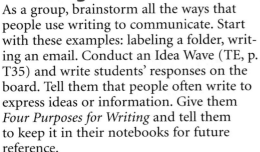

As a group, brainstorm all the ways that people use writing to communicate. Start with these examples: labeling a folder, writing an email. Conduct an Idea Wave (TE, p. T35) and write students' responses on the board. Tell them that people often write to express ideas or information. Give them *Four Purposes for Writing* and tell them to keep it in their notebooks for future reference.

All in One United States and Canada Teaching Resources, *Four Purposes for Writing,* p. 5

Instruct

Narrative Essays

Guided Instruction

- Tell students that narrative essays tell a story about their own experiences. Discuss the steps listed in the Student Edition.

- Choose an event in your own life (or invent one) such as visiting friends in another city. Write your topic on the board and model how to list details. *(what the trip was like, what you did while you were there, what your friends are like)* Cross out the least interesting details.

- Think aloud as you form your topic into a sentence that conveys the main idea of your essay.

- Tell students that you will go on to flesh out the details into a colorful story.

Independent Practice

- Tell students to write a narrative essay about a recent positive experience. Have student pairs brainstorm topics.

Writing for Social Studies

Writing is one of the most powerful communication tools you will ever use. You will use it to share your thoughts and ideas with others. Research shows that writing about what you read actually helps you learn new information and ideas. A systematic approach to writing—including prewriting, drafting, revising, and proofing—can help you write better, whether you're writing an essay or a research report.

Narrative Essays

Writing that tells a story about a personal experience

1 Select and Narrow Your Topic

A narrative is a story. In social studies, it might be a narrative essay about how an event affected you or your family.

2 Gather Details

Brainstorm a list of details you'd like to include in your narrative.

3 Write a First Draft

Start by writing a simple opening sentence that conveys the main idea of your essay. Continue by writing a colorful story that has interesting details. Write a conclusion that sums up the significance of the event or situation described in your essay.

4 Revise and Proofread

Check to make sure you have not begun too many sentences with the word *I*. Replace general words with more colorful ones.

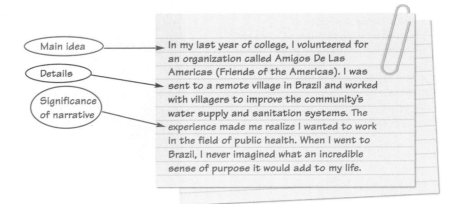

Main idea
Details
Significance of narrative

In my last year of college, I volunteered for an organization called Amigos De Las Americas (Friends of the Americas). I was sent to a remote village in Brazil and worked with villagers to improve the community's water supply and sanitation systems. The experience made me realize I wanted to work in the field of public health. When I went to Brazil, I never imagined what an incredible sense of purpose it would add to my life.

RW2 Reading and Writing Handbook

- Give students *Writing to Describe* to help them write their essays. After they have written the body of their essay, give them *Writing the Conclusion* to help them complete it.

All in One United States and Canada Teaching Resources, *Writing to Describe,* p. 6; *Writing the Conclusion,* p. 7

Monitor Progress

Have students share their drafts with their partners. Give them *Using the Revision Checklist* and ask them to review their partners' papers. Urge them to provide constructive criticism and suggestions for improvement.

All in One United States and Canada Teaching Resources, *Using the Revision Checklist,* p. 8

Persuasive Essays

Writing that supports an opinion or position

① Select and Narrow Your Topic
Choose a topic that provokes an argument and has at least two sides. Choose a side. Decide which argument will appeal most to your audience and persuade them to understand your point of view.

② Gather Evidence
Create a chart that states your position at the top and then lists the pros and cons for your position below, in two columns. Predict and address the strongest arguments against your stand.

③ Write a First Draft
Write a strong thesis statement that clearly states your position. Continue by presenting the strongest arguments in favor of your position and acknowledging and refuting opposing arguments.

④ Revise and Proofread
Check to make sure you have made a logical argument and that you have not oversimplified the argument.

Main Idea → It is vital to vote in elections. When people vote, they tell public officials how to run the government. Not every proposal is carried out; however, politicians do their best to listen to what the majority of people want. Therefore, every vote is important.

Supporting (pro) argument

Opposing (con) argument

Transition words

Reading and Writing Handbook **RW3**

Guided Instruction
- Tell students that the purpose of writing a persuasive essay is to convince other people to believe your point of view. However, you must use solid, reliable evidence and arguments to make your points.
- Model the thought process by pointing out how the writer presents his or her argument in the paragraph on this page.

Independent Practice
- Tell students to write a persuasive essay about a topic that is important to them. Have students form pairs. One student in each pair should state his or her position. The other student then shares opposing arguments, which the first student should refute in his or her essay. Then the pairs switch roles.
- Give students *Writing to Persuade* to help them write their essays.

  All in One **United States and Canada Teaching Resources,** *Writing to Persuade,* p. 9

Monitor Progress
If students are having trouble structuring their paragraphs, give them *Structuring Paragraphs* and *Creating Paragraph Outlines* to provide a framework.

  All in One **United States and Canada Teaching Resources,** *Structuring Paragraphs,* p. 10; *Creating Paragraph Outlines,* p. 11

Differentiated Instruction

For Less Proficient Readers L1
Tell students to use looping to help them focus on a topic. Have them follow these steps: Write freely on your topic for about five minutes. Read what you have written and circle the most important idea. Write for five minutes on the circled idea. Repeat the process until you isolate a topic narrow enough to cover well in a short essay.

Expository Essays L2

Guided Instruction

- Read the steps for writing expository essays with students.

- Tell students that the graphic organizer example given on the Student Edition page is for a cause-and-effect expository essay. They might use a Venn diagram for a compare-and-contrast essay and a flow-chart for a problem-and-solution essay.

- Model how to create a topic sentence from the information in the cause-and-effect graphic organizer. (*Sample topic sentence: In Mexico, several factors are causing rural families to move from the countryside to the city.*)

- Create a brief outline showing how you will organize the paragraphs in your essay.

Independent Practice

Tell students to write an expository essay based on a recent current event. Have them brainstorm ideas with a partner, then choose which type of essay best suits their topic (cause and effect, compare and contrast, or problem and solution.) Give them *Writing to Inform and Explain* and *Gathering Details* to help them start drafting their essays.

All in One United States and Canada Teaching Resources, *Writing to Inform and Explain*, p. 12; *Gathering Details*, p. 13

Monitor Progress

If students are struggling with their essays, give them *Writing a Cause-and-Effect Essay* or *Writing a Problem-and-Solution Essay.*

All in One United States and Canada Teaching Resources, *Writing a Cause-and-Effect Essay,* p. 14; *Writing a Problem-and-Solution Essay,* p. 15

Research Papers L2

Guided Instruction

Go over the steps for writing a research paper carefully. Ask students to share questions about the process, using the Idea Wave strategy (TE, p. T35). Answer any questions they might have.

Expository Essays

Writing that explains a process, compares and contrasts, explains causes and effects, or explores solutions to a problem

1 Identify and Narrow Your Topic

Expository writing is writing that explains something in detail. It might explain the similarities and differences between two or more subjects (compare and contrast). It might explain how one event causes another (cause and effect). Or it might explain a problem and describe a solution.

2 Gather Evidence

Create a graphic organizer that identifies details to include in your essay.

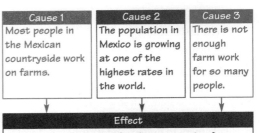

Cause 1	Cause 2	Cause 3
Most people in the Mexican countryside work on farms.	The population in Mexico is growing at one of the highest rates in the world.	There is not enough farm work for so many people.

Effect

As a result, many rural families are moving from the countryside to live in Mexico City.

3 Write Your First Draft

Write a topic sentence and then organize the essay around your similarities and differences, causes and effects, or problem and solutions. Be sure to include convincing details, facts, and examples.

4 Revise and Proofread

Research Papers

Writing that presents research about a topic

1 Narrow Your Topic

Choose a topic you're interested in and make sure that it is not too broad. For example, instead of writing a report on Panama, write about the construction of the Panama Canal.

2 Acquire Information

Locate several sources of information about the topic from the library or the Internet. For each resource, create a source index card like the one at the right. Then take notes using an index card for each detail or subtopic. On the card, note which source the information was taken from. Use quotation marks when you copy the exact words from a source.

> Source #1
> McCullough, David. *The Path Between the Seas: The Creation of the Panama Canal, 1870-1914.* N.Y., Simon and Schuster, 1977.

3 Make an Outline

Use an outline to decide how to organize your report. Sort your index cards into the same order.

> Outline
> I. Introduction
> II. Why the canal was built
> III. How the canal was built
>   A. Physical challenges
>   B. Medical challenges
> IV. Conclusion

RW4 Reading and Writing Handbook

Differentiated Instruction

For Gifted and Talented L3

Tell students that a verb is in active voice when the subject performs the action named by the verb. A verb is in passive voice when the subject undergoes the action named by the verb.

Give these examples:

Passive voice: The house is being painted by my sister and me.

Active voice: My sister and I are painting the house.

Tell students that using the active voice whenever possible will make their writing more dynamic and concise.

Introduction

Building the Panama Canal

Ever since Christopher Columbus first explored the Isthmus of Panama, the Spanish had been looking for a water route through it. They wanted to be able to sail west from Spain to Asia without sailing around South America. However, it was not until 1914 that the dream became a reality.

Conclusion

It took eight years and more than 70,000 workers to build the Panama Canal. It remains one of the greatest engineering feats of modern times.

④ Write a First Draft

Write an introduction, a body, and a conclusion. Leave plenty of space between lines so you can go back and add details that you may have left out.

⑤ Revise and Proofread

Be sure to include transition words between sentences and paragraphs. Here are some examples:

To show a contrast—*however, although, despite.*

To point out a reason—*since, because, if.*

To signal a conclusion—*therefore, consequently, so, then.*

Evaluating Your Writing

Use this table to help you evaluate your writing.

	Excellent	Good	Acceptable	Unacceptable
Purpose	Achieves purpose—to inform, persuade, or provide historical interpretation—very well	Informs, persuades, or provides historical interpretation reasonably well	Reader cannot easily tell if the purpose is to inform, persuade, or provide historical interpretation	Purpose is not clear
Organization	Develops ideas in a very clear and logical way	Presents ideas in a reasonably well-organized way	Reader has difficulty following the organization	Lacks organization
Elaboration	Explains all ideas with facts and details	Explains most ideas with facts and details	Includes some supporting facts and details	Lacks supporting details
Use of Language	Uses excellent vocabulary and sentence structure with no errors in spelling, grammar, or punctuation	Uses good vocabulary and sentence structure with very few errors in spelling, grammar, or punctuation	Includes some errors in grammar, punctuation, and spelling	Includes many errors in grammar, punctuation, and spelling

Reading and Writing Handbook **RW5**

Differentiated Instruction

For English Language Learners L2

To help students understand the tasks you have given them, provide them with an example of a well-executed essay from a different class or a previous year. The example essay should be well written and organized but not above grade level. You could look for and save good examples each year you teach.

Independent Practice

- Have students consider topics for a research paper. Give them *Choosing a Topic* to help them learn how to evaluate potential topics.

  All in One **United States and Canada Teaching Resources,** *Choosing a Topic,* p. 16

- Once students have selected a topic, tell them they will need facts to support their ideas. Give them *Using the Library, Summarizing and Taking Notes,* and *Preparing Note Cards* to help them start their research.

  All in One **United States and Canada Teaching Resources,** *Using the Library,* p. 17; *Summarizing and Taking Notes,* p. 18; *Preparing Note Cards,* p. 19

Monitor Progress

Give students *Writing an Introduction* and *Writing the Body of an Essay* to help them write their essays.

All in One **United States and Canada Teaching Resources,** *Writing an Introduction,* p. 20; *Writing the Body of an Essay,* p. 21

Assess and Reteach

Assess Progress L2

Ask students to pick the best essay they have written so far and evaluate it using the rubric on this page.

Reteach L1

Collect students' essays and self-evaluations. Meet with students to go over good points and areas for improvement. Revisit each type of essay as needed with the whole class.

Extend L3

To extend this lesson, tell students there are many other different types of writing. Have them complete *Writing for Assessment* and *Writing a Letter* to learn about two more types of writing.

All in One **United States and Canada Teaching Resources,** *Writing for Assessment,* p. 22; *Writing a Letter,* p. 23

MapMaster Skills Handbook
Step-by-Step Instruction

Objective
- Identify and define the five themes of geography.

Prepare to Read

Build Background Knowledge `L2`
Assign students to small groups and give them five minutes to write a definition of geography. Then write the five themes of geography on the board. Remind students that a theme is an important underlying idea. As a class, decide which parts of their definitions go under each of the geography themes. For example, "landforms" would fall under the theme of place.

Instruct

Five Themes of Geography `L2`

Guided Instruction
- Divide the text using the headings and ask students to read the pages using the Structured Silent Reading technique (TE, p. T34). Clarify the meanings of any unfamiliar words.

- Ask students to give the relative locations of their homes.

- Mention the popularity of different kinds of ethnic foods in the United States. Ask **What theme of geography are these foods a good example of?** *(movement)* Encourage students to name other examples of the movement of cultural traditions from one region to another.

- Discuss the climate in your area. Ask **How does the environment affect how we live?** *(affects dress, travel, sports and other recreational activities, the way homes are built)*

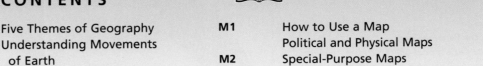

MAP★MASTER™ SKILLS HANDBOOK

CONTENTS

Go Online PHSchool.com Use Web Code **lap-0000** for all of the maps in this handbook.

Five Themes of Geography

Studying the geography of the entire world is a huge task. You can make that task easier by using the five themes of geography: location, regions, place, movement, and human-environment interaction. The themes are tools you can use to organize information and to answer the where, why, and how of geography.

▲ **Location**
This museum in England has a line running through it. The line marks its location at 0° longitude.

LOCATION

1 Location answers the question, "Where is it?" You can think of the location of a continent or a country as its address. You might give an absolute location such as 22 South Lake Street or 40° N and 80° W. You might also use a relative address, telling where one place is by referring to another place. *Between school and the mall* and *eight miles east of Pleasant City* are examples of relative locations.

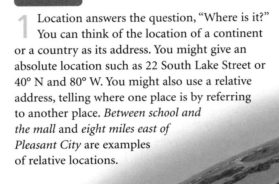

MapMaster Skills Handbook

Differentiated Instruction

For English Language Learners `L1`
Students may find it difficult to pronounce some of the multisyllable words in this section such as *relative, environment, interaction, government, signature,* and *communicate.* Show students how to break down these words into smaller parts to help them sound out the pronunciation.

For Advanced Readers `L3`
Have students find articles in newspapers or magazines that illustrate the five themes of geography. Have students underline the relevant sections and identify the theme or themes they illustrate. Suggest that students create a bulletin board to share their examples with the class.

REGIONS

2 Regions are areas that share at least one common feature. Geographers divide the world into many types of regions. For example, countries, states, and cities are political regions. The people in any one of these places live under the same government. Other features, such as climate and culture, can be used to define regions. Therefore the same place can be found in more than one region. For example, the state of Hawaii is in the political region of the United States. Because it has a tropical climate, Hawaii is also part of a tropical climate region.

MOVEMENT

4 Movement answers the question, "How do people, goods, and ideas move from place to place?" Remember that what happens in one place often affects what happens in another. Use the theme of movement to help you trace the spread of goods, people, and ideas from one location to another.

PLACE

3 Place identifies the natural and human features that make one place different from every other place. You can identify a specific place by its landforms, climate, plants, animals, people, language, or culture. You might even think of place as a geographic signature. Use the signature to help you understand the natural and human features that make one place different from every other place.

INTERACTION

5 Human-environment interaction focuses on the relationship between people and the environment. As people live in an area, they often begin to make changes to it, usually to make their lives easier. For example, they might build a dam to control flooding during rainy seasons. Also, the environment can affect how people live, work, dress, travel, and communicate.

◄ **Interaction**
These Congolese women interact with their environment by gathering wood for cooking.

PRACTICE YOUR GEOGRAPHY SKILLS

1 Describe your town or city, using each of the five themes of geography.

2 Name at least one thing that comes into your town or city and one that goes out. How is each moved? Where does it come from? Where does it go?

MapMaster Skills Handbook **M1**

Independent Practice

Partner students and have them complete *The Five Themes of Geography.*

All in One **United States and Canada Teaching Resources,** *The Five Themes of Geography,* p. 27

Monitor Progress

As students complete the worksheet, circulate to make sure that individuals comprehend the material. Provide assistance as needed.

Assess and Reteach

Assess Progress   L2

Have students complete the questions under Practice Your Geography Skills.

Reteach   L1

Help students create a concept web that identifies the five themes of geography. Start filling in blank *Transparency B17: Concept Web* to model how to identify information to clarify each theme. For example, under Regions students might write "share common features such as government, climate, and culture." Encourage students to refer to their webs to review the themes.

📖 **United States and Canada Transparencies,** *Transparency B17: Concept Web*

Extend   L3

To extend the lesson, ask students to find out about any plans for new buildings, highways, or other types of construction in your area. Ask students to predict how these changes will affect the community's environment.

Answers

PRACTICE YOUR GEOGRAPHY SKILLS

1. Answers should include an example of how each of the five themes relates to your community.

2. Students' answers should provide examples of goods, ideas, or things that move into and out of your community.

MapMaster Skills Handbook **M1**

Objective

- Explain how the movements of the Earth cause night and day, as well as the seasons.

Prepare to Read

Build Background Knowledge L2

Remind students that while the Earth revolves around the sun, it also rotates on its own axis. Review the meanings of "revolve" and "rotate" in this context. Ask students to brainstorm ways that the Earth's revolving and rotating might affect their lives. Conduct an Idea Wave (TE, p. T35) to generate a list of ideas.

Instruct

Understanding Movements of Earth L2

Guided Instruction

- Read the text as a class using the Oral Cloze technique (TE, p. T33). Explain that the illustrations on pages M2 and M3 show the information in the text visually. Clarify the meanings of any unfamiliar words.

- Ask students **How does Earth rotating on its axis cause day and night?** (*It is daytime on the side of Earth facing the sun, while the side facing away from the sun is dark.*)

- Ask **How does the tilt of Earth affect the seasons?** (*The farther away a part of Earth is from the sun's rays, the colder it is.*)

Independent Practice

Partner students and have them complete *Understanding the Movements of the Earth.*

 United States and Canada Teaching Resources, *Understanding Movements of the Earth,* p. 28

Understanding Movements of Earth

The planet Earth is part of our solar system. Earth revolves around the sun in a nearly circular path called an orbit. A revolution, or one complete orbit around the sun, takes 365 ¼ days, or one year. As Earth orbits the sun, it also spins on its axis, an invisible line through the center of Earth from the North Pole to the South Pole. This movement is called a rotation.

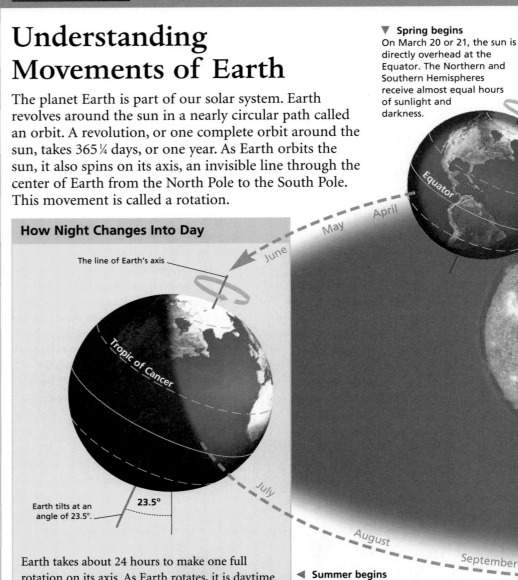

How Night Changes Into Day

The line of Earth's axis

Tropic of Cancer

Earth tilts at an angle of 23.5°.   **23.5°**

Earth takes about 24 hours to make one full rotation on its axis. As Earth rotates, it is daytime on the side facing the sun. It is night on the side away from the sun.

▼ **Spring begins**
On March 20 or 21, the sun is directly overhead at the Equator. The Northern and Southern Hemispheres receive almost equal hours of sunlight and darkness.

◄ **Summer begins**
On June 21 or 22, the sun is directly overhead at the Tropic of Cancer. The Northern Hemisphere receives the greatest number of sunlight hours.

M2 MapMaster Skills Handbook

Background: Links Across Place

Sunrise and Sunset Most people have heard the saying "The sun rises in the east and sets in the west." However, the sun does not ever actually change position. Every day, Earth rotates on its axis so that as each region faces the sun, it experiences day. The rotation continues so that as a region turns away from the sun, it experiences night. The sun stays in the same place. A person viewing sunrise or sunset is really seeing Earth's slow turn on its axis, not the sun rising or setting.

The Seasons

Earth's axis is tilted at an angle. Because of this tilt, sunlight strikes different parts of Earth at different times in the year, creating seasons. The illustration below shows how the seasons are created in the Northern Hemisphere. In the Southern Hemisphere, the seasons are reversed.

Earth orbits the sun at 66,600 miles per hour (107,244 kilometers per hour).

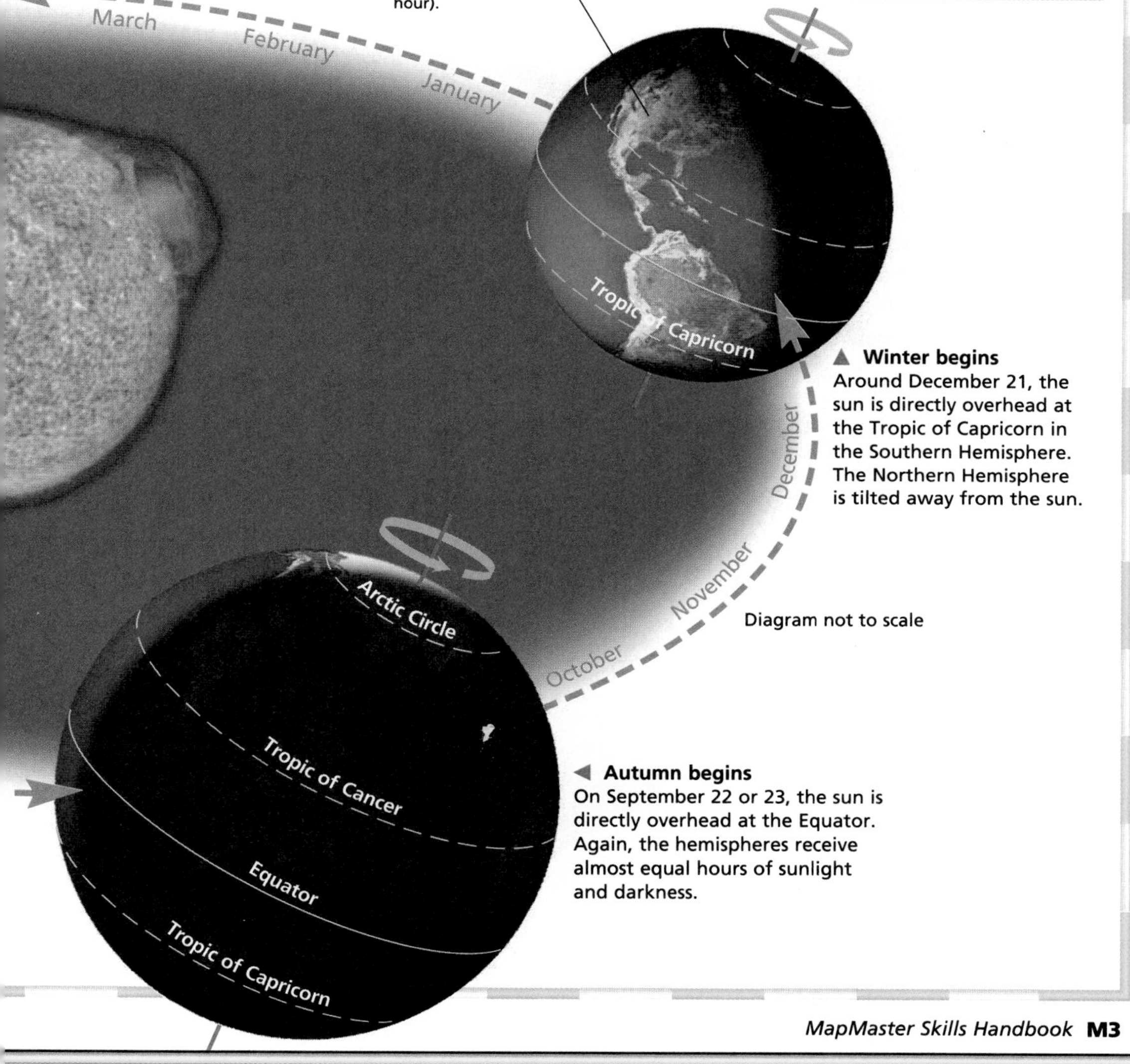

PRACTICE YOUR GEOGRAPHY SKILLS

1 What causes the seasons in the Northern Hemisphere to be the opposite of those in the Southern Hemisphere?

2 During which two days of the year do the Northern Hemisphere and Southern Hemisphere have equal hours of daylight and darkness?

March February January

Tropic of Capricorn

December

November

October

Arctic Circle

Tropic of Cancer

Equator

Tropic of Capricorn

▲ **Winter begins**
Around December 21, the sun is directly overhead at the Tropic of Capricorn in the Southern Hemisphere. The Northern Hemisphere is tilted away from the sun.

Diagram not to scale

◄ **Autumn begins**
On September 22 or 23, the sun is directly overhead at the Equator. Again, the hemispheres receive almost equal hours of sunlight and darkness.

MapMaster Skills Handbook **M3**

Differentiated Instruction

For Special Needs Students L1

Have students act out the revolution of Earth around the sun. Assign one student the role of "the sun," and other students the roles of Earth at four different times of the year. Have them walk through a year's cycle. Show *Color Transparency USC 1: The Earth's Revolution and the Seasons* to guide them. Ask them to simulate the tilt of the Earth's axis as shown in the illustrations on pp. M2–M3.

📖 **United States and Canada Transparencies,** *Color Transparency USC 1: The Earth's Revolution and the Seasons*

Monitor Progress

As students do the worksheet, circulate to make sure individuals comprehend the key concepts. Provide assistance as needed.

Assess and Reteach

Assess Progress L2

Have students complete the Practice Your Geography Skills questions.

Reteach L1

If students are having trouble understanding these concepts, create a model to demonstrate Earth's revolution. Use a foam ball to represent Earth. Insert a pencil through the ball to represent Earth's axis, labeling the ends "North Pole" and "South Pole." Draw the Equator perpendicular to the axis. Place a light source in the center of a table to represent the sun. Then tilt the ball at a slight angle and move it around the light to mimic Earth's revolution. Have students notice the point at which each pole is nearest the sun and identify what season it would be in each hemisphere.

Extend L3

To extend the lesson, ask students to consider Earth's relationship to its satellite, the Moon. Ask them to research on the Internet to answer these questions: "Does the Moon rotate like Earth? Does the Moon revolve around Earth as Earth revolves around the sun?" To help students start their research, give them *Doing Searches on the Internet*.

All in One United States and Canada Teaching Resources, *Doing Searches on the Internet*, p. 29

Answers

PRACTICE YOUR GEOGRAPHY SKILLS

1. The seasons are reversed in the Northern Hemisphere and Southern Hemisphere because the Earth is tilted. When one hemisphere is tilted towards the sun, the other hemisphere is tilted away from the sun.

2. September 22–23 and March 20–21

Objectives

- Understand how a globe is marked with a grid to measure features on Earth.

- Learn how to use longitude and latitude to locate a place.

Prepare to Read

Build Background Knowledge   L2

Tell students that in this lesson, they will learn how to use globes. Ask students what it would be like to see Earth from a spacecraft. Discuss the shape that students would see. Then discuss why a globe is a more accurate rendering of Earth than a flat map. Point out that a globe is like a model car in that it is a small version of something larger. If a globe is available, have students examine it.

Instruct

Understanding Globes   L2

Guided Instruction

- Read the text as a class using the Oral Cloze technique (TE, p. T33). Have students study the illustrations carefully.

- Ask **What line of latitude divides the Northern and Southern Hemispheres?** *(the Equator)* **At what degrees latitude is this line?** *(0°)*

- Ask **Where do the lines of longitude come together?** *(at the North and South Poles)* **What is the name of the meridian at 0 degrees?** *(Prime Meridian)*

- Have students look at the global grid on *Color Transparency USC 3: The Global Grid.* Ask **What is the global grid?** *(a pattern of lines formed where the parallels of latitude and meridians of longitude cross)* **What continent in the Eastern Hemisphere does the 100° E meridian pass through?** *(Asia)*

  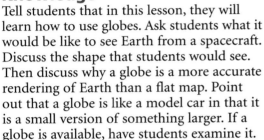 **United States and Canada Transparencies,** *Color Transparency USC 3: The Global Grid*

Understanding Globes

A globe is a scale model of Earth. It shows the actual shapes, sizes, and locations of all Earth's landmasses and bodies of water. Features on the surface of Earth are drawn to scale on a globe. This means that a small unit of measure on the globe stands for a large unit of measure on Earth.

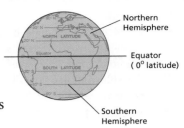

Northern Hemisphere

Equator (0° latitude)

Southern Hemisphere

Parallels of Latitude

Geographers divide the globe along imaginary horizontal lines called parallels of latitude. One of these latitude lines is the Equator, located halfway between the North and South poles. Parallels of latitude are measured in degrees (°). One degree of latitude represents a distance of about 69 miles (111 kilometers).

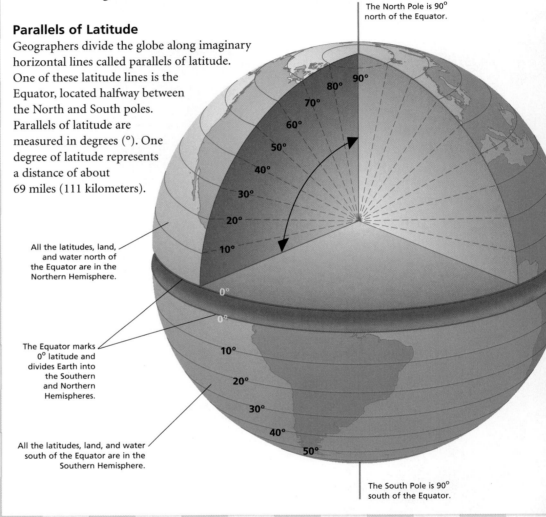

The North Pole is 90° north of the Equator.

All the latitudes, land, and water north of the Equator are in the Northern Hemisphere.

The Equator marks 0° latitude and divides Earth into the Southern and Northern Hemispheres.

All the latitudes, land, and water south of the Equator are in the Southern Hemisphere.

The South Pole is 90° south of the Equator.

Background: Links Across Time

The First Globes Historians believe that the first globe may have been made in the second century B.C. by a Greek geographer known as Crates of Mallus. The mathematician Ptolemy represented Earth as a globe in his written works in the second century A.D. In late 1492 Martin Behaim made a terrestrial globe that, although inaccurate by today's knowledge, reflected the best geographical knowledge of the time. This globe still exists and is on display in Behaim's hometown of Nuremberg, Germany.

Meridians of Longitude

Geographers also divide the globe along imaginary vertical lines called meridians of longitude, which are measured in degrees (°). The longitude line called the Prime Meridian runs from pole to pole through Greenwich, England. All meridians of longitude come together at the North and South Poles.

PRACTICE YOUR GEOGRAPHY SKILLS

1 Which continents lie completely in the Northern Hemisphere? In the Western Hemisphere?

2 Is there land or water at 20° S latitude and the Prime Meridian? At the Equator and 60° W longitude?

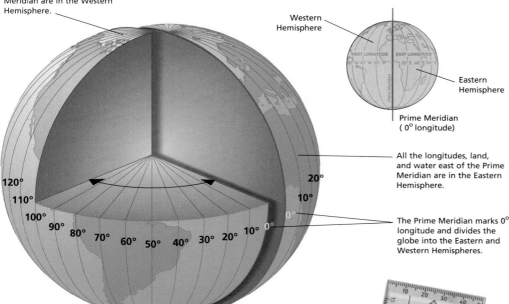

All the longitudes, land, and water west of the Prime Meridian are in the Western Hemisphere.

Western Hemisphere

Eastern Hemisphere

Prime Meridian (0° longitude)

All the longitudes, land, and water east of the Prime Meridian are in the Eastern Hemisphere.

The Prime Meridian marks 0° longitude and divides the globe into the Eastern and Western Hemispheres.

120° 110° 100° 90° 80° 70° 60° 50° 40° 30° 20° 10° 0°

20° 10° 0°

The Global Grid

Together, the pattern of parallels of latitude and meridians of longitude is called the global grid. Using the lines of latitude and longitude, you can locate any place on Earth. For example, the location of 30° north latitude and 90° west longitude is usually written as 30° N, 90° W. Only one place on Earth has these coordinates—the city of New Orleans, in the state of Louisiana.

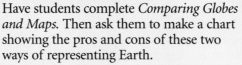

▲ **Compass**
Wherever you are on Earth, a compass can be used to show direction.

Differentiated Instruction

For Less Proficient Readers [L1]

For students having difficulty understanding the concept of a global grid, give them *Understanding Grids* and help them complete it. Then follow up with *Using a Grid*.

All in One United States and Canada Teaching Resources, *Understanding Grids*, p. 34; *Using a Grid*, p. 35

For Advanced Readers [L3]

Have students complete *Comparing Globes and Maps*. Then ask them to make a chart showing the pros and cons of these two ways of representing Earth.

All in One United States and Canada Teaching Resources, *Comparing Globes and Maps*, p. 36

Independent Practice

Have students work in pairs to complete *Understanding Hemispheres* and *Understanding Latitude and Longitude*.

All in One United States and Canada Teaching Resources, *Understanding Hemispheres*, p. 30; *Understanding Latitude and Longitude*, p. 31

Monitor Progress

As students do the worksheets, circulate to make sure pairs understand the key concepts. Show *Color Transparency USC 2: The Hemispheres* to help students.

United States and Canada Transparencies, *Color Transparency USC 2: The Hemispheres*

Assess and Reteach

Assess Progress [L2]

Have students answer the questions under Practice Your Geography Map Skills.

Reteach [L1]

Use the DK Atlas activity *Understanding Latitude and Longitude* to review these skills with students. Have students complete the activity in pairs.

All in One United States and Canada Teaching Resources, *DK Compact Atlas of the World Activity: Understanding Latitude and Longitude*, p. 32

Extend [L3]

To extend the lesson, have students complete *Using Latitude and Longitude*. Then have students use the map and with a partner, play a game of Can You Find …? Each partner takes a turn giving the coordinates for a place on the map and the other partner must name the place.

All in One United States and Canada Teaching Resources, *Using Latitude and Longitude*, p. 33

Answers

PRACTICE YOUR GEOGRAPHY SKILLS

1. Northern Hemisphere: North America; Europe; Western Hemisphere: North America; South America

2. water; land

Objectives

- Compare maps of different projections.
- Describe distortions in map projections.

Prepare to Read

Build Background Knowledge   **L1**

In this lesson, students will learn how cartographers depict Earth on a two-dimensional map. Remind students that if they were traveling in a spaceship, they would see Earth as a globe. Ask if they could ever see the entire Earth at one time from space. Help students recognize that a flat map is the only way to see all of Earth at once.

Instruct

Map Projections   **L2**

Guided Instruction

- Read the text as a class using the Choral Reading technique (TE, p. T34). Direct students to look at the relevant maps after you read each section together. Follow up by having students do a second silent reading.

- Help students locate Greenland on the Mercator and Robinson maps. Ask **What difference do you notice in the way Greenland is shown?** *(It appears much larger on the Mercator Map.)* **How would you explain this?** *(The Mercator is a same-shape map and the shapes toward the poles are enlarged.)*

- Ask **Where does the distortion usually occur on an equal-area map?** *(at the edges of the map)*

- Have students compare Antarctica on the three projections. *(It is largest and most distorted on the Mercator map; smallest on the equal-area map; covers the entire bottom edge of the Robinson map.)*

Map Projections

Maps are drawings that show regions on flat surfaces. Maps are easier to use and carry than globes, but they cannot show the correct size and shape of every feature on Earth's curved surface. They must shrink some places and stretch others. To make up for this distortion, mapmakers use different map projections. No one projection can accurately show the correct area, shape, distance, and direction for all of Earth's surface. Mapmakers use the projection that has the least distortion for the information they are presenting.

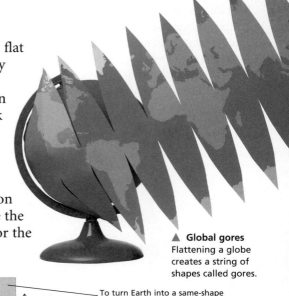

▲ **Global gores**
Flattening a globe creates a string of shapes called gores.

Same-Shape Maps

Map projections that accurately show the shapes of landmasses are called same-shape maps. However, these projections often greatly distort, or make less accurate, the size of landmasses as well as the distance between them. In the projection below, the northern and southern areas of the globe appear more stretched than the areas near the Equator.

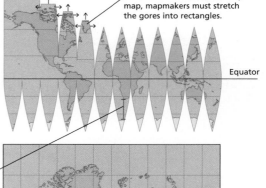

To turn Earth into a same-shape map, mapmakers must stretch the gores into rectangles.

Equator

Stretching the gores makes parts of Earth larger. This enlargement becomes greater toward the North and South Poles.

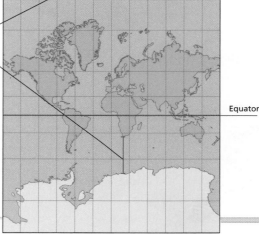

Mercator projection ▶
One of the most common same-shape maps is the Mercator projection, named for the mapmaker who invented it. The Mercator projection accurately shows shape and direction, but it distorts distance and size. Because the projection shows true directions, ships' navigators use it to chart a straight-line course between two ports.

Equator

Differentiated Instruction

For Special Needs Students   **L1**

If students have difficulty understanding why distortion occurs, draw a simple picture on an orange. Then have students try to peel the orange in one piece. Challenge students to place the peel flat on a piece of paper without any tears and spaces. Talk about what happens to the drawing. Explain that mapmakers face this same challenge when drawing Earth on a flat paper.

For Gifted and Talented   **L3**

Have students complete *Great Circles and Straight Lines.* Then ask them to use their completed page and a globe to explain the concept of great circles to the class.

All in One **United States and Canada Teaching Resources,** *Great Circles and Straight Lines,* p. 38

Equal-Area Maps

Map projections that show the correct size of landmasses are called equal-area maps. In order to show the correct size of landmasses, these maps usually distort shapes. The distortion is usually greater at the edges of the map and less at the center.

PRACTICE YOUR GEOGRAPHY SKILLS

1 What feature is distorted on an equal-area map?

2 Would you use a Mercator projection to find the exact distance between two locations? Tell why or why not.

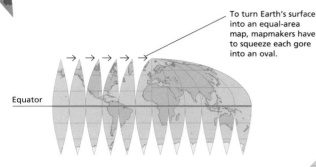

To turn Earth's surface into an equal-area map, mapmakers have to squeeze each gore into an oval.

Equator

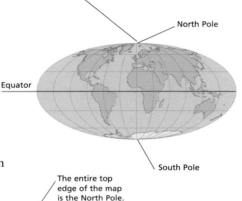

The tips of all the gores are then joined together. The points at which they join form the North and South Poles. The line of the Equator stays the same.

North Pole

Equator

South Pole

Robinson Maps

Many of the maps in this book use the Robinson projection, which is a compromise between the Mercator and equal-area projections. The Robinson projection gives a useful overall picture of the world. It keeps the size and shape relationships of most continents and oceans, but distorts the size of the polar regions.

The entire top edge of the map is the North Pole.

The map is least distorted at the Equator.

Equator

The entire bottom edge of the map is the South Pole.

MapMaster Skills Handbook **M7**

Independent Practice

Have students work with partners to complete *Understanding Projection.*

All in One United States and Canada Teaching Resources, *Understanding Projection,* p. 37

Monitor Progress

As students do the worksheet, circulate to make sure individuals comprehend the key concepts. Provide assistance as needed.

Assess and Reteach

Assess Progress   L2

Have students complete the Practice Your Geography Skills questions.

Reteach   L1

Use *Maps with Accurate Shapes: Conformal Maps* and *Maps with Accurate Areas: Equal-Area Maps* to help students go over the information in the lesson. Model thinking for each question and partner students to complete each page together. Circulate to provide explanations and help as students work.

All in One United States and Canada Teaching Resources, *Maps with Accurate Shapes: Conformal Maps,* p. 39; *Maps with Accurate Areas: Equal-Area Maps,* p. 40

Extend   L3

To extend the lesson, ask students to complete *Maps with Accurate Direction: Azimuthal Maps.* Then have students write a sentence or two describing the different projections they have learned about.

All in One United States and Canada Teaching Resources, *Maps with Accurate Directions: Azimuthal Maps,* p. 41

Background: Biography

Gerardus Mercator (1512–1594) The Mercator projection takes its name from a Flemish geographer, Gerhard Kremer. Kremer, who used the Latin form of his name, Gerardus Mercator, wrote books on ancient geography and cartography. He made his first world map in 1538. In 1554 he made a map of Europe. In 1568, the first map using the Mercator projection bearing his name appeared. Mercator also began an atlas of his maps which was finished by his son and published in 1594.

Answers

PRACTICE YOUR GEOGRAPHY SKILLS

1. shapes

2. No; the Mercator projection distorts distances.

Objective

- Identify and use the parts of a map.

Prepare to Read

Build Background Knowledge　L1

In this lesson, students will learn about the practical aspects of maps. Ask students to name reasons that they might use a map; for example, to find directions, boundaries, distances. Conduct an Idea Wave (TE, p. T35) to generate a list of ideas. List the ideas on the board.

Instruct

How to Use a Map　L2

Guided Instruction

- Divide the text and captions in the lesson using the headings and ask students to read the pages using the Structured Silent Reading strategy (TE, p. T34). Remind students to use the illustrations to acquire additional understanding. Refer to the list on the board, then ask students which map part (key, compass rose, scale, symbol, title) would be helpful in using a map for a specific purpose.

- Ask **What is the purpose of a compass rose?** *(to show directions)*

- Talk about how the three maps show different amounts of Earth's surface. Ask **Which map shows the largest area?** *(Western Europe)* **Which map shows the smallest area?** *(Central London)*

- Ask **What are some symbols that you might find on a map key?** *(border, national capital, city, airport, park, point of interest)*

Independent Practice

Partner students and have them complete *Using the Map Key* and *Using the Compass Rose.*

> **All in One United States and Canada Teaching Resources,** *Using the Map Key,* p. 42; *Using the Compass Rose,* p. 43

MAP★MASTER™　　LOCATION　REGIONS　PLACE　MOVEMENT　INTERACTION

How to Use a Map

Mapmakers provide several clues to help you understand the information on a map. Maps provide different clues, depending on their purpose or scale. However, most maps have several clues in common.

Locator globe
Many maps are shown with locator globes. They show where on the globe the area of the map is located.

Title
All maps have a title. The title tells you the subject of the map.

Compass rose
Many maps show direction by displaying a compass rose with the directions north, east, south, and west. The letters N, E, S, and W are placed to indicate these directions.

Key
Often a map has a key, or legend. The key shows the symbols and colors used on the map, and what each one means.

Western Europe

Key

——	National border
⊛	National capital
•	Other city

Scale bar
A scale bar helps you find the actual distances between points shown on the map. Most scale bars show distances in both miles and kilometers.

0 miles　　　　300
0 kilometers　　300
Lambert Azimuthal Equal Area

M8 MapMaster Skills Handbook

SHETLAND ISLANDS (U.K.)
Glasgow
North Sea
Copenhagen
DENMARK
Dublin
IRELAND
UNITED KINGDOM
London
The Hague
NETHERLANDS
Amsterdam
Hamburg
Berlin
GERMANY
Brussels
Frankfurt
Prague
CZECH REPUBLIC
BELGIUM
LUXEMBOURG
Luxembourg
Munich
Vienna
AUSTRIA
Paris
Bern LIECHTENSTEIN
FRANCE
SWITZERLAND
English Channel
Bay of Biscay
Lyon
Milan
SAN MARINO
Toulouse
Marseille
MONACO
ITALY
Adriatic Sea
ANDORRA
CORSICA (France)
VATICAN CITY
Rome
PORTUGAL
Madrid
Barcelona
SARDINIA (Italy)
Lisbon
SPAIN
BALEARIC ISLANDS (Spain)
Tyrrhenian Sea
Seville
Mediterranean Sea
SICILY (Italy)

Differentiated Instruction

For Less Proficient Readers　L2

If students have difficulty recalling the purposes of different parts of a map, have them make a table using each map part as a heading. Under each heading, help students list the important function or functions of that map part. Suggest that students refer to their table when they are working with maps.

For English Language Learners　L1

Some of the words in the lesson, such as *symbol* and *scale,* may be unfamiliar to students acquiring English. Have students identify difficult words, look them up in the dictionary, and write sentences explaining what the terms mean.

Maps of Different Scales

Maps are drawn to different scales, depending on their purpose. Here are three maps drawn to very different scales. Keep in mind that maps showing large areas have smaller scales. Maps showing small areas have larger scales.

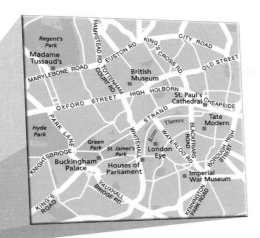

▲ **Greater London**
Find the gray square on the main map of Western Europe (left). This square represents the area shown on the map above. It shows London's boundaries, the general shape of the city, and the features around the city. This map can help you find your way from the airport to the center of town.

▲ **Central London**
Find the gray square on the map of Greater London. This square represents the area shown on the map above. This map moves you closer into the center of London. Like the zoom on a computer or a camera, this map shows a smaller area but in greater detail. It has the largest scale (1 inch represents about 0.9 mile). You can use this map to explore downtown London.

Key

■ Point of interest

◤ Park

0 miles   0.5   1
0 kilometers   1

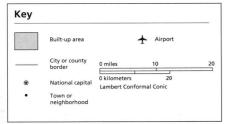

Key

▭ Built-up area   ✈ Airport

── City or county border

0 miles   10   20
0 kilometers   20
Lambert Conformal Conic

⊛ National capital

• Town or neighborhood

PRACTICE YOUR GEOGRAPHY SKILLS

1 What part of a map explains the colors used on the map?

2 How does the scale bar change depending on the scale of the map?

3 Which map would be best for finding the location of the British Museum? Explain why.

Monitor Progress

Circulate around the room as students complete the worksheets. Make sure that individuals comprehend the material. Provide assistance as needed.

Assess and Reteach

Assess Progress   L2
Have students complete the questions under Practice Your Geography Skills.

Reteach   L1
Some DK Atlas Activities will be helpful in reteaching the lesson. Give students more practice using these concepts by doing the activities for *Using the Map Key; Using the Compass Rose;* and *Using the Map Scale.*

All in One United States and Canada Teaching Resources, *DK Compact Atlas of the World Activity: Using the Map Key,* p. 44; *DK Compact Atlas of the World Activity: Using the Compass Rose,* p. 45; *DK Compact Atlas of the World Activity: Using the Map Scale,* p. 46

Extend   L3
To extend the lesson, have students complete *Comparing Maps of Different Scale* and *Maps with Accurate Distances: Equidistant Maps.*

All in One United States and Canada Teaching Resources, *Comparing Maps of Different Scale,* p. 47; *Maps with Accurate Distances: Equidistant Maps,* p. 48

Answers

PRACTICE YOUR GEOGRAPHY SKILLS

1. key

2. The larger the scale of the map, the smaller the distance shown on the scale bar.

3. the map of Central London; it shows the streets in more detail and includes the British Museum as a point of interest

Objectives

- Understand and use political maps.
- Understand and use physical maps.

Prepare to Read

Build Background Knowledge L1

Tell students that they will learn about political maps and physical maps in this lesson. Explain that a political map is one that shows the boundaries and cities of an area as established by its people. Physical maps show information about the physical features of the area. These physical features would exist whether people lived in a place or not.

Instruct

Political Maps L2
Physical Maps L2

Guided Instruction

- Read the text as a class using the Choral Reading technique (TE, p. T34) and ask students to study the map.

- Ask students to identify what river forms the boundary between Zimbabwe and South Africa. *(Limpopo River)* Then ask them to name at least two capitals on the Mediterranean Sea. *(Tripoli, Algiers, Tunis)*

- Read the text with the class and draw students' attention to the map and its key.

- Explain that sea level is the average height of the ocean's surface; sea level is at zero elevation. Ask students what color represents sea level on the map key. *(dark green)*

- Have students find the Qattara Depression. Ask **What is its elevation?** *(from 0 to 650 feet)*

- Ask **What is the difference between elevation and relief?** *(Elevation is the height of land above sea level while relief shows how quickly the land rises or falls.)*

Answers

PRACTICE YOUR GEOGRAPHY SKILLS

1. solid line, star in a circle, dot

2. Luanda

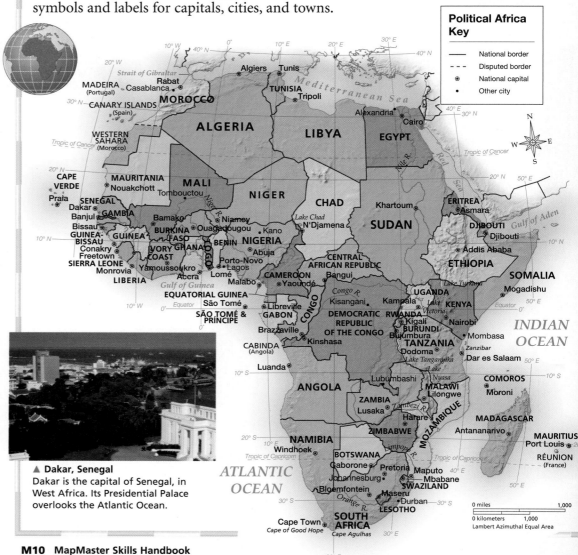

Political Maps

Political maps show political borders: continents, countries, and divisions within countries, such as states or provinces. The colors on political maps do not have any special meaning, but they make the map easier to read. Political maps also include symbols and labels for capitals, cities, and towns.

PRACTICE YOUR GEOGRAPHY SKILLS

1 What symbols show a national border, a national capital, and a city?

2 What is Angola's capital city?

Political Africa Key

——— National border
- - - - Disputed border
⊛ National capital
• Other city

▲ **Dakar, Senegal**
Dakar is the capital of Senegal, in West Africa. Its Presidential Palace overlooks the Atlantic Ocean.

M10 **MapMaster Skills Handbook**

Background: Global Perspectives

Africa's Highest Peaks Africa's two highest mountains are both extinct volcanoes that rise near the equator on the eastern part of the continent. The tallest mountain, Kilimanjaro in Tanzania, reaches 19,340 feet (5,895 meters) at its highest point. Although snow covers its peaks, farmers raise coffee and plantains on the lower southern slopes of Kilimanjaro. Africa's second highest mountain is Mt. Kenya at 17,058 feet (5,199 meters) located in central Kenya. Like Kilimanjaro, it is snowcapped in its highest regions. Both Kilimanjaro and Mt. Kenya are attractions for mountain climbers from all over the world.

Physical Maps

Physical maps represent what a region looks like by showing its major physical features, such as hills and plains. Physical maps also often show elevation and relief. Elevation, indicated by colors, is the height of the land above sea level. Relief, indicated by shading, shows how sharply the land rises or falls.

PRACTICE YOUR GEOGRAPHY SKILLS

1 Which areas of Africa have the highest elevation?

2 How can you use relief to plan a hiking trip?

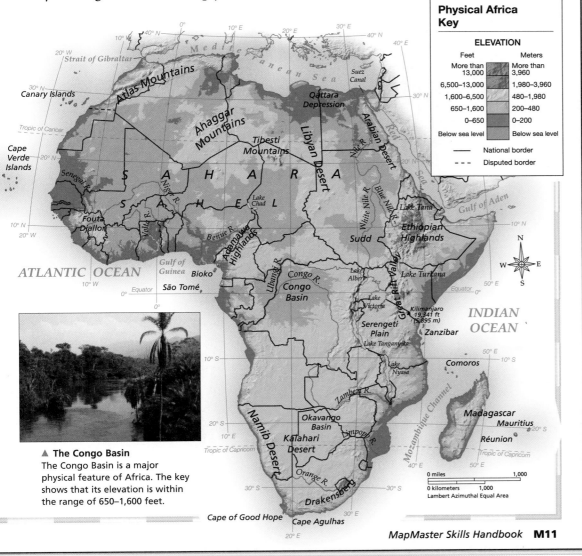

Physical Africa Key

ELEVATION

Feet		Meters
More than 13,000		More than 3,960
6,500–13,000		1,980–3,960
1,600–6,500		480–1,980
650–1,600		200–480
0–650		0–200
Below sea level		Below sea level

——— National border

- - - Disputed border

▲ **The Congo Basin**
The Congo Basin is a major physical feature of Africa. The key shows that its elevation is within the range of 650–1,600 feet.

MapMaster Skills Handbook **M11**

Independent Practice

Have students complete *Reading a Political Map*, *Reading a Physical Map* and *Elevation on a Map* working with partners.

All in One **United States and Canada Teaching Resources,** *Reading a Political Map,* p. 49; *Reading a Physical Map,* p. 54; *Elevation on a Map,* p. 55

Monitor Progress

As students complete the worksheets, circulate around the room to make sure individuals understand the key concepts. Provide assistance as needed.

Assess and Reteach

Assess Progress   L2

Have students answer the questions under Practice Your Geography Skills on pages M10 and M11.

Reteach   L1

Use the DK Atlas Activities *Reading a Political Map* and *Reading a Physical Map* to review the concepts in this lesson.

All in One **United States and Canada Teaching Resources,** *DK Compact Atlas of the World Activity: Reading a Political Map,* p. 50; *DK Compact Atlas of the World Activity: Reading a Physical Map,* p. 56

Extend   L3

To extend the lesson, have students fill in the name of each country and its capital on the outline maps *North Africa*, *West and Central Africa*, and *East and Southern Africa*. Also, ask them to use colors and shading to indicate the Atlas Mountains, the Ethiopian Highlands, the Congo Basin, and the Namib Desert.

All in One **United States and Canada Teaching Resources,** *Outline Map 22: North Africa,* p. 51; *Outline Map 23: West and Central Africa,* p. 52; *Outline Map 24: East and Southern Africa,* p. 53

Differentiated Instruction

For Special Needs Students   L1
Reuse *Reading a Political Map* to help students understand political maps. Point to the symbol for a national border in the key, then trace the borders of several countries. Invite students to trace others.

All in One **United States and Canada Teaching Resources,** *Reading a Political Map,* p. 49

For Advanced Readers   L3
Challenge students to explore the concepts of relief and elevation further by completing *Relief on a Map* and *Maps of the Ocean Floor*.

All in One **United States and Canada Teaching Resources,** *Relief on a Map,* p. 57; *Maps of the Ocean Floor,* p. 58

Answers

PRACTICE YOUR GEOGRAPHY SKILLS

1. Ethiopian Highlands and Great Rift Valley

2. It can help you find out where the land rises and falls.

Objectives

- Understand and use climate maps.
- Understand and use language maps.

Prepare to Read

Build Background Knowledge **L1**

Ask students to think of as many meanings for the word *special* as they can. Tell them that maps can be special too. Ask **What do you think a special-purpose map might show?** List suggestions on the board.

Instruct

Special-Purpose Maps: Climate **L1**

Guided Instruction

- Ask students to read the text using the Structured Silent Reading strategy (TE, p. T34). Point out that the map shows Bangladesh, Bhutan, Nepal, and parts of Myanmar and Pakistan as well as India.

- Point out the map and key. Ask **What areas have a tropical wet climate?** (*area along the southern western coast; eastern part of Bangladesh*)

- Ask **What color represents an arid climate?** (*brown*)

Independent Practice

Partner students and have them complete *Reading a Climate Map.*

All in One United States and Canada Teaching Resources, *Reading a Climate Map*, p. 59

Monitor Progress

As students complete the worksheet, circulate around the room to make sure individuals comprehend the key concepts. Provide assistance as needed.

Answers

PRACTICE YOUR GEOGRAPHY SKILLS

1. the key

2. the northwestern part; No major cities are in the arid region.

Special-Purpose Maps: Climate

Unlike the boundary lines on a political map, the boundary lines on climate maps do not separate the land into exact divisions. For example, in this climate map of India, a tropical wet climate gradually changes to a tropical wet and dry climate.

PRACTICE YOUR GEOGRAPHY SKILLS

1 What part of a special-purpose map tells you what the colors on the map mean?

2 Where are arid regions located in India? Are there major cities in those regions?

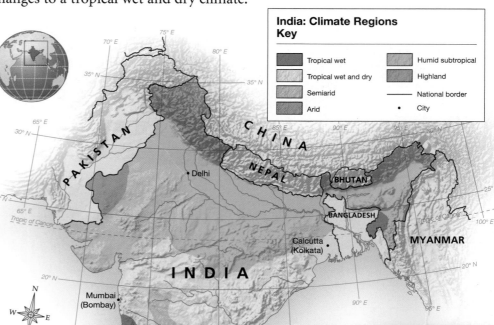

India: Climate Regions Key

- Tropical wet
- Tropical wet and dry
- Semiarid
- Arid
- Humid subtropical
- Highland
- — National border
- • City

▲ Rain in Delhi
One of Delhi's features as a place is its humid subtropical climate. During its rainy season, Delhi receives heavy rainfall.

M12 MapMaster Skills Handbook

Differentiated Instruction

For English Language Learners **L1**

If students are unfamiliar with words in the lesson, help them identify and look up those words in the dictionary. For example: *arid*—adj. having little or no rainfall; dry *humid*—adj. having a lot of water; damp *semi*—adj. part or partially

Follow up by having students determine the meaning of *semiarid*.

For Gifted and Talented **L3**

Give students *Reading a Climate Graph*. Ask students to compare the information in the graph with the information on the map above. Ask them to write a sentence synthesizing about the climate of Mumbai.

All in One United States and Canada Teaching Resources, *Reading A Climate Graph*, p. 60

Special-Purpose Maps: Language

This map shows the official languages of India. An official language is the language used by the government. Even though a region has an official language, the people there may speak other languages as well. As in other special-purpose maps, the key explains how the different languages appear on the map.

PRACTICE YOUR GEOGRAPHY SKILLS

1 What color represents the Malayalam language on this map?

2 Where in India is Tamil the official language?

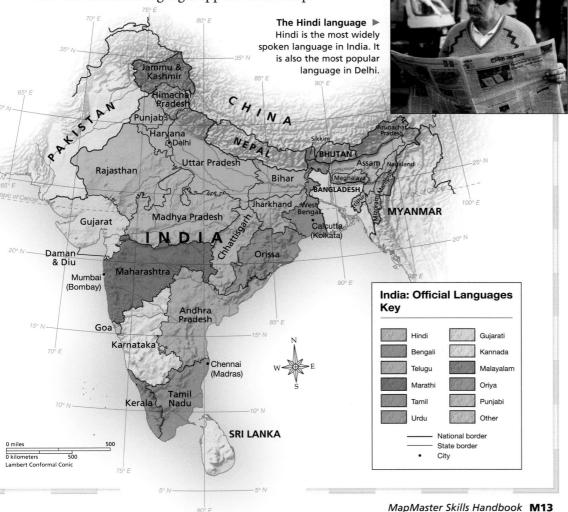

The Hindi language ▶
Hindi is the most widely spoken language in India. It is also the most popular language in Delhi.

India: Official Languages Key

Hindi	Gujarati
Bengali	Kannada
Telugu	Malayalam
Marathi	Oriya
Tamil	Punjabi
Urdu	Other

— National border
— State border
• City

MapMaster Skills Handbook **M13**

Background: Daily Life

The Hindi Language Hindi is the official language of India and is the primary language for about 300 million people. English is also spoken by many Indians and is considered the language of politics and commerce. However, the diversity of the country is reflected in the enormous number of languages spoken there, more than 1,500 in all. Ten of India's major states are organized along linguistic lines, and the Indian constitution recognizes 15 regional languages.

Special-Purpose Maps: Language L2

Guided Instruction
- Read the text as a class. Draw students' attention to the map and its key.

- Have students consider the diversity of official languages. Ask **Why might it be important for a state to have a common language in addition to local ones?** *(Communication is easier with a common language.)*

Independent Practice
Have students work with partners to read another special purpose map, *Reading a Natural Vegetation Map.*

> **All in One United States and Canada Teaching Resources,** *Reading a Natural Vegetation Map,* p. 61

Monitor Progress
As students complete the worksheet, circulate around the room and make sure individuals understand key concepts. Provide assistance as needed.

Assess and Reteach

Assess Progress L2
Have students answer the questions under Practice Your Geography Skills on pages M12 and M13.

Reteach L1
Have students practice using a special purpose map by completing *Analyzing and Interpreting Special Purpose Maps.*

> ⊙ *Analyzing and Interpreting Special-Purpose Maps,* **Social Studies Skills Tutor CD-ROM**

Extend L3
Have students learn about another type of special-purpose map by completing *Reading a Time Zone Map.* Then ask students to find out the time zones in India and create their own time zone map, using *Outline Map 26: South Asia.*

> **All in One United States and Canada Teaching Resources,** *Reading a Time Zone Map.* p. 63; *Outline Map 26: South Asia,* p. 62

Answers
PRACTICE YOUR GEOGRAPHY SKILLS
1. dark purple
2. southeast India

Objectives
- Learn why people migrate.
- Understand how migration affects environments.

Prepare to Read

Build Background Knowledge L1
Remind students that they studied the theme of movement earlier in this unit. Brainstorm with students why people move from place to place, particularly those who move from one country to another. Use the Numbered Heads participation strategy (TE, p. T36) to generate ideas.

Instruct

Human Migration L2

Guided Instruction
- Divide the text using the headings and ask students to read the pages using the Paragraph Shrinking strategy (TE, p. T34). Clarify the meanings of any unfamiliar words.
- Have students look at the map. Ask **From what European countries did people migrate to the Americas in the years between 1500 and 1800?** *(Portugal, Spain, France, Netherlands, England)*
- Ask **Where did the French settle in the Americas?** *(French Guiana and Haiti)* **Which European country had the most possessions in the Americas?** *(Spain)*
- Ask **Why were some Africans forced to migrate?** *(They were imported as slaves from their homeland. Europeans wanted them to work on the land they claimed in the Americas.)*

MAP MASTER | LOCATION | REGIONS | PLACE | MOVEMENT | INTERACTION

Human Migration

Migration is an important part of the study of geography. Since the beginning of history, people have been on the move. As people move, they both shape and are shaped by their environments. Wherever people go, the culture they bring with them mixes with the cultures of the place in which they have settled.

Explorers arrive ▼
In 1492, Christopher Columbus set sail from Spain for the Americas with three ships. The ships shown here are replicas of those ships.

▲ **Native American pyramid**
When Europeans arrived in the Americas, the lands they found were not empty. Diverse groups of people with distinct cultures already lived there. The temple-topped pyramid shown above was built by Mayan Indians in Mexico, long before Columbus sailed.

Migration to the Americas, 1500–1800
A huge wave of migration from the Eastern Hemisphere began in the 1500s. European explorers in the Americas paved the way for hundreds of years of European settlement there. Forced migration from Africa started soon afterward, as Europeans began to import African slaves to work in the Americas. The map to the right shows these migrations.

M14 MapMaster Skills Handbook

Differentiated Instruction

For Less Proficient Readers L1
Review with students the meaning of "push" and "pull" factors in terms of human migration. Model for students how to make a table with the headings Push and Pull. Then work with students to list as many factors as they can under each heading.

For Advanced Readers L3
Have students complete *Analyzing Statistics*. When they have finished, have them write a paragraph explaining how economic and social statistics are related to "push" and "pull" factors.

All in One United States and Canada Teaching Resources, *Analyzing Statistics,* p. 65

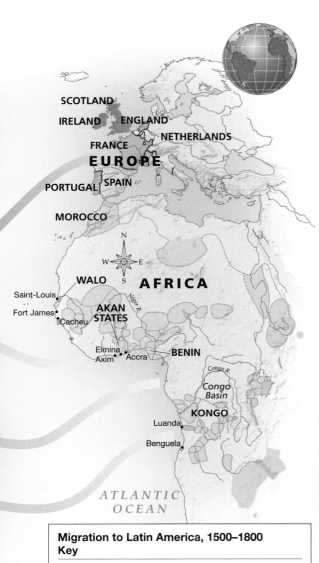

SCOTLAND
IRELAND   ENGLAND
          NETHERLANDS
FRANCE
E U R O P E
PORTUGAL SPAIN
MOROCCO

WALO   A F R I C A
Saint-Louis
Fort James
  Cacheu   AKAN
            STATES
  Elmina   BENIN
  Axim   Accra
          Congo R.
          Congo
          Basin
          KONGO
  Luanda
  Benguela

A T L A N T I C
O C E A N

Migration to Latin America, 1500–1800
Key

⬅ European migration	▨ Spain and possessions
⬅ African migration	▨ Portugal and possessions
— National or colonial border	▨ Netherlands and possessions
⋯ Traditional African border	▨ France and possessions
▨ African State	▨ England and possessions

PRACTICE YOUR GEOGRAPHY SKILLS

1 Where did the Portuguese settle in the Americas?

2 Would you describe African migration at this time as a result of both push factors and pull factors? Explain why or why not.

"Push" and "Pull" Factors

Geographers describe a people's choice to migrate in terms of "push" factors and "pull" factors. Push factors are things in people's lives that push them to leave, such as poverty and political unrest. Pull factors are things in another country that pull people to move there, including better living conditions and hopes of better jobs.

▲ **Elmina, Ghana**
Elmina, in Ghana, is one of the many ports from which slaves were transported from Africa. Because slaves and gold were traded here, stretches of the western African coast were known as the Slave Coast and the Gold Coast.

Independent Practice

Have students work with partners to complete *Reading a Historical Map.* Have students be ready to explain how the movement of European groups changed the map of Africa. (*Much of Africa was colonized by Europeans.*)

All in One **United States and Canada Teaching Resources,** *Reading a Historical Map,* p. 64

Monitor Progress

As students complete the worksheet, circulate around the room to make sure individuals comprehend the key concepts. Provide assistance as needed.

Assess and Reteach

Assess Progress   L2

Have students complete the questions under Practice Your Geography Skills.

Reteach   L1

Help students make an outline of the lesson. Show *Transparency B15: Outline* as a model. Then work with students to identify the main points. Encourage students to refer to their outlines to review the material.

📖 **United States and Canada Transparencies,** *Transparency B15: Outline*

Extend   L3

To extend the lesson, have students complete *The Global Refugee Crisis.* Then ask them to choose a specific region on the graph and find out more about refugees from one country in that region.

Go Online
PHSchool.com **For:** Environmental and Global Issues: *The Global Refugee Crisis*
Visit: PHSchool.com
Web Code: lhd-4001

Answers

PRACTICE YOUR GEOGRAPHY SKILLS

1. Brazil

2. most likely push factors because people were forced to leave; the need for workers in the Americas was a pull factor although it was the Europeans who responded to it by importing Africans as slaves

Objectives
- Understand and use a land use map.
- Learn how land use and economic structures are linked.

Prepare to Read

Build Background Knowledge **L1**

Discuss with the class the ways that people in your community are using land. For example, is all the land used for homes? How much is used for commercial purposes? What kinds? Are there farms or manufacturing facilities? Point out that communities in all parts of the world use land in different ways.

Instruct

World Land Use **L2**

Guided Instruction
- Read the text as a class using the Oral Cloze strategy (TE, p. T33). Follow up by having students do a second silent reading. Encourage students to study the map and photographs.
- Talk about the difference between commercial and subsistence farming. Have them look closely at the photographs on pages M16 and M17. Ask **How do the tools and equipment people use differ in these types of farming?** (*Large power machines are used in commercial farming; hand tools are used in subsistence farming.*) **Why might people use more land in commercial farming?** (*Machines make it possible to cultivate more land. The more land cultivated, the more sales possible.*)
- Ask **What color represents nomadic herding on this map?** (*light purple*) **In what parts of the world is this an economic activity?** (*Africa, Asia, Europe*)
- Ask **Why might some parts of the world have little or no land use activity?** (*Land and/or climate might not be suitable for farming or other activity.*)

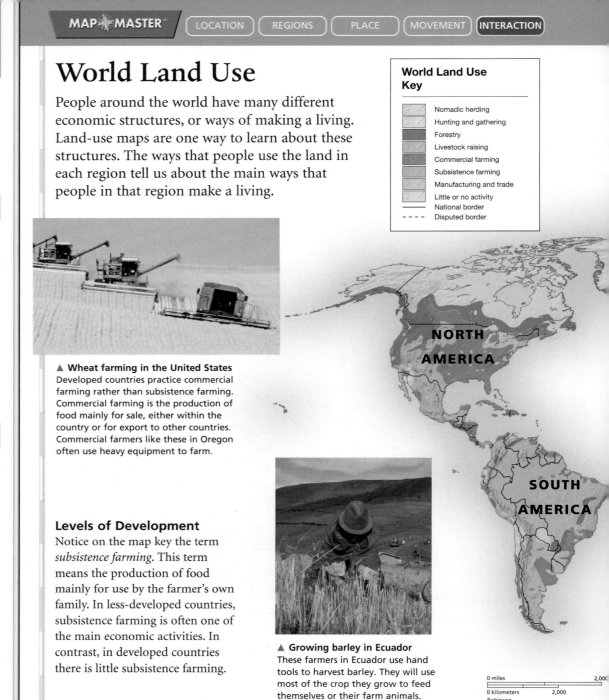

World Land Use

People around the world have many different economic structures, or ways of making a living. Land-use maps are one way to learn about these structures. The ways that people use the land in each region tell us about the main ways that people in that region make a living.

World Land Use Key

- Nomadic herding
- Hunting and gathering
- Forestry
- Livestock raising
- Commercial farming
- Subsistence farming
- Manufacturing and trade
- Little or no activity
- —— National border
- - - - Disputed border

▲ **Wheat farming in the United States**
Developed countries practice commercial farming rather than subsistence farming. Commercial farming is the production of food mainly for sale, either within the country or for export to other countries. Commercial farmers like these in Oregon often use heavy equipment to farm.

Levels of Development
Notice on the map key the term *subsistence farming*. This term means the production of food mainly for use by the farmer's own family. In less-developed countries, subsistence farming is often one of the main economic activities. In contrast, in developed countries there is little subsistence farming.

▲ **Growing barley in Ecuador**
These farmers in Ecuador use hand tools to harvest barley. They will use most of the crop they grow to feed themselves or their farm animals.

NORTH AMERICA

SOUTH AMERICA

0 miles 2,000
0 kilometers 2,000
Robinson

M16   MapMaster Skills Handbook

Background: Global Perspectives

Agriculture Almost 50 percent of the world's population is occupied in agriculture. A much higher proportion of this is in developing countries where dense populations, small land holdings, and traditional techniques predominate. In areas where there is intense cultivation using people and animals but few machines, the yield is low in relation to the output of energy. In leading food producing countries such as the United States, industrial farms make use of new technology and crop specialization to increase output.

▲ **Growing rice in Vietnam**
Women in Vietnam plant rice in wet rice paddies, using the same planting methods their ancestors did.

PRACTICE YOUR GEOGRAPHY SKILLS

1 In what parts of the world is subsistence farming the main land use?

2 Locate where manufacturing and trade are the main land use. Are they found more often near areas of subsistence farming or areas of commercial farming? Why might this be so?

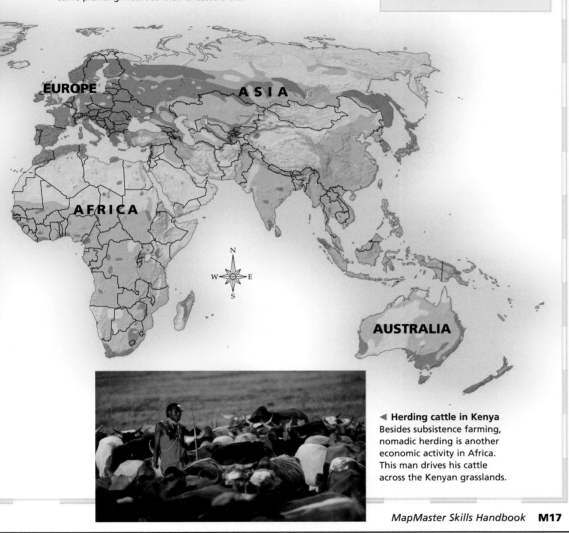

EUROPE

ASIA

AFRICA

AUSTRALIA

◄ **Herding cattle in Kenya**
Besides subsistence farming, nomadic herding is another economic activity in Africa. This man drives his cattle across the Kenyan grasslands.

MapMaster Skills Handbook **M17**

Independent Practice

Partner students and have them complete *Reading an Economic Activity Map*. Have students be ready to offer explanations for how the economic activity in Somalia might affect the lives of people there.

All in One United States and Canada Teaching Resources, *Reading an Economic Activity Map*, p. 66

Monitor Progress

Circulate around the room as students complete the worksheet to make sure individuals comprehend the key concepts. Provide assistance as needed.

Assess and Reteach

Assess Progress   L2

Have students complete the questions under Practice Your Geography Skills.

Reteach   L1

Help students make a table to identify the main kinds of land use. Draw a model on the board for students to follow. Use these headings: Nomadic Herding, Forestry, Livestock Raising, Commercial Farming, Subsistence Farming, Manufacturing and Trade. Under each heading, help students write a short explanation. Then have students find one or two places on the map in their books where that activity takes place.

Extend   L3

To extend the lesson, have students complete *Reading a Natural Resources Map*. Point out that this map shows mineral resources. Then ask students to write a paragraph relating mineral resources to land use.

All in One United States and Canada Teaching Resources, *Reading a Natural Resources Map*, p. 67

Differentiated Instruction

For English Language Learners   L3
Students may find it difficult to pronounce some of the multisyllable words in this section, such as *nomadic, subsistence, commercial,* and *forestry.* Model how to break down these words into smaller parts to help students sound out the pronunciation.

Answers

PRACTICE YOUR GEOGRAPHY SKILLS

1. Africa, Asia, South America, North America

2. areas of commercial farming; both manufacturing and trade and commercial farming require technology that subsistence farmers do not have

MapMaster Skills Handbook **M17**

Teaching the Target Reading Skills

The Prentice Hall *World Studies* program has interwoven essential reading skills instruction throughout the Student Edition, Teacher's Edition, and ancillary resources. In United States and Canada, students will learn five reading skills.

Student Edition The *World Studies* Student Edition provides students with reading skills instruction, practice, and application opportunities in each chapter within the program.

Teacher's Edition The *World Studies* Teacher Edition supports your teaching of each skill by providing full modeling in each chapter's interleaf and modeling of the specific sub-skills in each section lesson.

All in One Teaching Resources The *World Studies* All-in-One Teaching Resources provides a worksheet explaining and supporting the elements of each Target Reading Skill. Use these to help struggling students master skills, or as more practice for every student.

Target Reading Skills

The Target Reading Skills introduced on this page will help you understand the words and ideas in this book and in other social studies reading you do. Each chapter focuses on one of these reading skills. Good readers develop a bank of reading strategies, or skills. Then they draw on the particular strategies that will help them understand the text they are reading.

Chapter 1 Target Reading Skills

Reading Process Previewing can help you understand and remember what you read. In this chapter you will practice using these previewing skills: setting a purpose for reading, predicting what the text will be about, and asking questions before you read.

Chapter 2 Target Reading Skills

Clarifying Meaning If you do not understand something you are reading right away, you can use several skills to clarify the meaning of the word or idea. In this chapter you will practice these strategies for clarifying meaning: rereading, reading ahead, paraphrasing, and summarizing.

Chapter 3 Target Reading Skills

Main Idea Since you cannot remember every detail of what you read, it is important to identify the main ideas. The main idea of a section or paragraph is the most important point and the one you want to remember. In this chapter you will practice these skills: identifying both stated and implied main ideas and identifying supporting details.

Chapter 4 Target Reading Skills

Comparison and Contrast You can use comparison and contrast to sort out and analyze information you are reading. Comparing means examining the similarities between things. Contrasting is looking at differences. In this chapter you will practice these skills: comparing and contrasting, using signal words, identifying contrasts, and making comparisons.

Chapter 5 Target Reading Skills

Using Context Using the context of an unfamiliar word can help you understand its meaning. Context includes the words, phrases, and sentences surrounding a word. In this chapter you will practice using these context clues: definitions, interpreting nonliteral meanings, your own general knowledge, and cause and effect.

M18 United States and Canada

Assessment Resources

Use the diagnosing readiness tests from **AYP Monitoring Assessments** to help you identify problems before students begin to study the United States and Canada.

Determine students' reading level and identify challenges:

📄 *Screening Tests,* pp. 1–10

Evaluate students' verbal skills:

📄 *Critical Thinking and Reading Tests,* pp. 25–34

📄 *Vocabulary Tests,* pp. 45–52

📄 *Writing Tests,* pp. 53–60

The UNITED STATES and CANADA

Spreading "from sea to shining sea," the United States and Canada take up nearly seven eighths of North America. In this book, you'll see how the United States and Canada are working to create a good life for every citizen in these vast countries.

Guiding Questions
The text, photographs, maps, and charts in this book will help you discover answers to these Guiding Questions.

1 **Geography** How has physical geography affected the cultures of the United States and Canada?

2 **History** How have historical events affected the cultures of the United States and Canada?

3 **Culture** How has the variety of people in the United States and Canada benefited and challenged the two nations?

4 **Government** How do the governments of the United States and Canada differ? How are they alike?

5 **Economics** How did the United States and Canada become two of the wealthiest nations in the world?

Project Preview
You can also discover answers to the Guiding Questions by working on projects. Several project possibilities are listed on page 188 of this book.

Assess students' social studies skills:
- 📄 *Geographic Literacy Tests*, pp. 13–20
- 📄 *Visual Analysis Tests*, pp. 21–24
- 📄 *Communications Tests*, pp. 35–44

The World Studies program provides instruction and practice for all of these skills. Use students' test results to pinpoint the skills your students have mastered and the skills they need to practice. Then use *Correlation to Program Resources* to prescribe skills practice and reinforcement.
- 📄 *Correlation to Program Resources*, pp. 64–77

The UNITED STATES and CANADA

Guiding Questions
- This book was developed around five Guiding Questions about the United States and Canada. They appear on the reduced Student Edition page to the left. The Guiding Questions are intended as an organizational focus for the book. The Guiding Questions act as a kind of umbrella under which all of the material falls.

- You may wish to add your own Guiding Questions to the list in order to tailor them to your particular course.

- Draw students' attention to the Guiding Questions. Ask them to write the questions in their notebooks for future reference.

- In the Teacher's Edition, each section's themes are linked to a specific Guiding Question at the beginning of each chapter. Then, an activity at the end of the chapter returns to the Guiding Questions to review key concepts.

Project Preview
- The projects for this book are designed to provide students with hands-on involvement in the content area. Students are introduced to some projects on page 188.

- *Book Projects* give students directions on how to complete these projects, and more.

  All in One **United States and Canada Teaching Resources**, *Book Project: Set Up a Weather Station*, pp. 73–75; *Book Project: Write a Children's Book*, pp. 76–78; *Book Project: Make a Timeline of Local History*, pp. 79–81; *Book Project: Create a Diorama*, pp. 82–84

- Assign projects as small group activities, whole-class projects, or individual projects. Consider assigning a project at the beginning of the course.

Objectives

- Describe the size and relative location of the United States and Canada.

- Locate and name the major bodies of water surrounding the United States and Canada.

- Analyze the range of climates in the United States and Canada.

- Examine the different regions of the United States and Canada.

Prepare to Read

Build Background Knowledge L2

Have students describe the location of their community. Tell students that they will compare their home to other parts of the United States and Canada as they study this region.

Instruct

Investigate the United States and Canada L2

Guided Instruction

- Read the introductory, Location, and Regions paragraphs as a class. Divide the class into small groups of three or four.

- Hand out the *Regional Overview* worksheet. Direct students to fill in the worksheet as they study the Regional Overview.

  All in One United States and Canada Teaching Resources, *Regional Overview*, pp. 89–91

Independent Practice

Ask groups to write a statement comparing the location and size of the United States and Canada.

Monitor Progress

Circulate and make sure the groups are communicating effectively.

Answers

LOCATION Canada; the U.S.; Canada; Canada must have a colder climate.
REGIONS Canada is longer and wider.

Investigate the United States and Canada

Stretching from the Pacific Ocean to the Atlantic Ocean, the United States is the world's fourth largest country. Canada is slightly larger and stretches across five time zones. Though roughly the same size, the United States has far more people—nearly 10 times the population of Canada.

▲ **The Northern Territories, Canada**
Snowmobiles and dogsleds make travel possible in the far north.

CANADA

UNITED STATES

LOCATION
1 Locate the United States and Canada

How would you describe Canada's location? One way would be to compare its location to that of the United States. Which country extends farther north? Which country is closer to Russia? Which country has more of its land touching the Arctic Ocean? Based on the relative locations of these two countries, estimate which has a colder climate.

REGIONS
2 Estimate the Length of the United States and Canada

How does Canada's length from north to south compare to the length of the continental United States? With a ruler, measure the United States from its southernmost border to its border with Canada. Now measure the length of Canada. Which is longer? Now measure both countries from east to west. Which is wider?

Mental Mapping

Everything in Its Place Distribute *Outline Map 11: The United States: Political.* Ask students to locate and label as many of the states as they can from memory, without looking in their textbooks. Tell them to name some of the states they cannot locate and write these state names on the board. Ask students to keep this outline map so they can update it as they study the region.

All in One United States and Canada Teaching Resources, *Outline Map 11: The United States: Political*, p. 92

Political United States and Canada

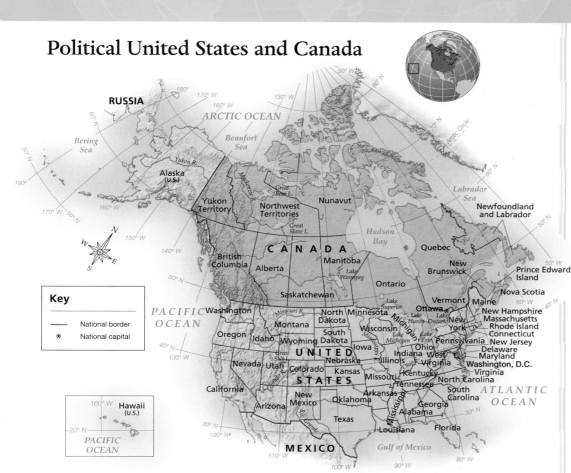

RUSSIA

ARCTIC OCEAN

Bering Sea

Beaufort Sea

Yukon R.

Alaska (U.S.)

Yukon Territory

Northwest Territories

Great Bear L.

Great Slave L.

Nunavut

Hudson Bay

Labrador Sea

Newfoundland and Labrador

Key

—— National border

⊛ National capital

PACIFIC OCEAN

CANADA

British Columbia

Alberta

Saskatchewan

Manitoba

Lake Winnipeg

Ontario

Quebec

New Brunswick

Prince Edward Island

Nova Scotia

Washington

Oregon

Idaho

Montana

Wyoming

Missouri R.

North Dakota

South Dakota

Nebraska

Minnesota

Lake Superior

Wisconsin

Iowa

Lake Michigan

Lake Huron

Lake Ontario

Lake Erie

Michigan

Illinois

Indiana

Ohio

Ottawa

Vermont

Maine

New Hampshire

Massachusetts

Rhode Island

Connecticut

New York

Pennsylvania

New Jersey

Delaware

Maryland

Washington, D.C.

Virginia

West Virginia

Kentucky

North Carolina

South Carolina

Tennessee

ATLANTIC OCEAN

Nevada

Utah

California

Colorado

UNITED STATES

Kansas

Missouri

Arkansas

Oklahoma

New Mexico

Arizona

Texas

Mississippi

Alabama

Georgia

Louisiana

Florida

Gulf of Mexico

MEXICO

Rio Grande

Hawaii (U.S.)

PACIFIC OCEAN

0 miles 1,000
0 kilometers 1,000
Lambert Azimuthal Equal Area

PLACE

3 Find States, Provinces, and Territories

Which two of the 50 United States do not share a border with any other state? Which Canadian territory reaches the farthest north? Which states border Canada? Which provinces border the United States? Name the cities that are the national capitals of the United States and Canada. Notice that the United States and Canada together make up most of the continent of North America. What other country is on the same continent?

▲ Niagara Falls
The Niagara Falls lie on the border between Canada and the United States.

Background: Global Perspectives

The Longest Borders The United States and Canada share 5,526 miles (8,893 kilometers) of border. This is often called "the world's longest undefended border," since most of the long border is not fenced or guarded by armies. Some of the other long international borders are: Russia and Kazakhstan, 4,254 miles (6,846 kilometers); Argentina and Chile, 3,200 miles (5,150 kilometers); Mongolia and China, 2,906 miles (4,677 kilometers); Brazil and Bolivia, 2,113 miles (3,400 kilometers); United States and Mexico, 1,951 miles (3,141 kilometers); India and Pakistan, 1,809 miles (2,912 kilometers).

Political United States and Canada [L2]

Guided Instruction

- Read the Place paragraph. Direct students' attention to the political map of the United States and Canada. Ask students to try to locate the three biggest states in the United States and write their answers on the board. Direct students to the Country Databank on pages 98–109 to check their answers. (*Alaska, Texas, California*)

- Ask students **Which Canadian province borders the Pacific Ocean?** (*British Columbia*) **Which states in the United States border Mexico?** (*Texas, New Mexico, Arizona, California*)

- Ask students to continue completing the *Regional Overview* worksheet.

  All in One **United States and Canada Teaching Resources,** *Regional Overview,* pp. 89–91

Independent Practice

Provide students with *Outline Map 10: The United States and Canada: Political.* Have students label the United States and Canada, and the oceans surrounding these countries. Ask them to label Alaska and Hawaii, indicating which country each is a part of. Have students label the capital of each country. Encourage students to include other details on their maps.

  All in One **United States and Canada Teaching Resources,** *Outline Map 10: The United States and Canada: Political,* p. 93

Monitor Progress

Circulate while students complete their maps and provide assistance where needed.

Answers

PLACE Alaska and Hawaii do not border any other states; Nunavut is the farthest north; Alaska, Washington, Idaho, Montana, North Dakota, Minnesota, Michigan, New York, Vermont, New Hampshire, and Maine border Canada; British Columbia, Alberta, Saskatchewan, Manitoba, Ontario, Quebec, and New Brunswick border the United States; Washington, D.C., is the capital of the United States, Ottawa is the capital of Canada; Mexico is also in North America.

Physical United States and Canada L2

Guided Instruction

- Read the Interaction paragraph. Have students study the physical map of the United States and Canada, noting the location of major bodies of water.

- Ask students to identify the major mountain chains in the United States and Canada. *(Rocky Mountains, Appalachian Mountains.)* Ask students **Which of these ranges has higher mountains?** *(the Rocky Mountains)*

- Tell students that the highest peak in the United States and Canada is located in Alaska. Ask them to name this peak and give its height *(Mt. McKinley, 20,320 feet [6,194 meters]).*

- Ask **Where is most of the land in the 0–650 feet elevation range located?** *(along the coasts)*

- Ask students to continue completing the Regional Overview worksheet.

  All in One United States and Canada Teaching Resources, *Regional Overview,* pp. 89–91

Independent Practice

To give students practice working with physical maps, provide them with the *Elevation on a Map* worksheet. Ask students to study the map and map key, and then answer the questions at the bottom of the worksheet.

All in One United States and Canada Teaching Resources, *Elevation on a Map,* p. 94

Monitor Progress

Circulate while students complete their worksheets. Make sure individuals understand how to use the map key.

Answers

INTERACTION The Atlantic, Pacific, and Arctic oceans surround the United States and Canada; lakes Superior, Michigan, Huron, Erie, and Ontario, which are known as the Great Lakes, lie between the countries; Hudson Bay; the Atlantic Ocean.

Physical United States and Canada

INTERACTION
4 Find Important Bodies of Water

What three oceans surround the United States and Canada? What bodies of water lie on the border between the United States and Canada? The largest bay in the world is located in Canada. What is its name? Would you enter the bay from the Pacific Ocean or from the Atlantic Ocean?

▲ **Lake Superior**
One of the five Great Lakes, Superior is the farthest north. It lies along the border of the United States and Canada.

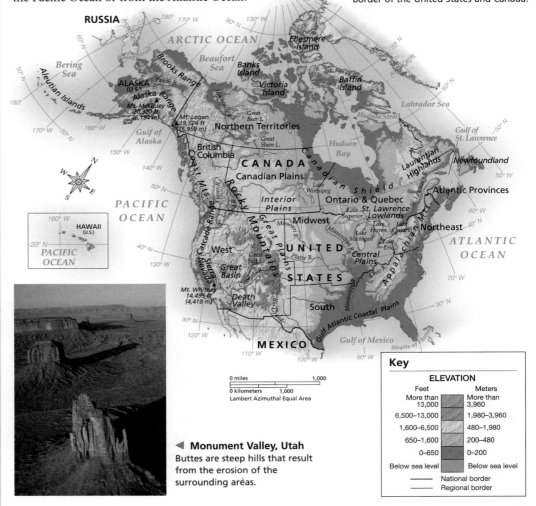

◄ **Monument Valley, Utah**
Buttes are steep hills that result from the erosion of the surrounding areas.

Key

ELEVATION		
Feet		Meters
More than 13,000		More than 3,960
6,500–13,000		1,980–3,960
1,600–6,500		480–1,980
650–1,600		200–480
0–650		0–200
Below sea level		Below sea level
—— National border		
—— Regional border		

0 miles 1,000
0 kilometers 1,000
Lambert Azimuthal Equal Area

Differentiated Instruction

For Special Needs Students L1
If possible, show students the United States and Canada flyover segment on the Passport to the World CD-ROM. Ask students to list several of the region's major landforms on the board after viewing the segment.

⊙ *Flyover segment,* **Passport to the World CD-ROM**

Climates of the United States and Canada

The climates of the United States and Canada range widely. Average annual temperatures vary from 71° F in Florida to 27° F in Alaska. Because of its greater distance from the Equator, Canada has much cooler temperatures than the United States. In both countries it is hotter in the interior in the summer and colder and windier in the winter.

Key

——	National border
■	Tropical wet
■	Tropical wet and dry
■	Semiarid
■	Arid
■	Mediterranean
■	Humid continental
■	Marine west coast
■	Humid subtropical
■	Subarctic
■	Tundra
■	Highland

REGIONS
5 Explore Influences on Climate
Compare the physical map of the United States and Canada on the previous page with the climate map above. How might landforms affect weather and rainfall? Notice that from Miami, Florida to Yellowknife, Canada the climate changes from tropical wet and dry to subarctic. Give reasons for this great shift in climates.

▲ **Mount Rainier National Park, Washington**

PRACTICE YOUR GEOGRAPHY SKILLS

1. On your hike in the western mountains you camped at the foot of Mount Rainier. Then you crossed an international border. What country are you in now?

2. You just flew over the mouth of the Mackenzie River and are headed for Victoria Island in Canada. Are you north or south of the Arctic Circle?

3. You are traveling through the Gulf of St. Lawrence toward the Great Lakes. What river will you take?

Regional Overview **5**

Differentiated Instruction

For Gifted and Talented   L3
Have students use an almanac or the Internet to locate average monthly temperatures and precipitation figures for four of the cities shown on the climate map in their textbooks. Have students collect data for the months of January and July. Then have students find the same data for your community. Students may display the data in a chart or a graph. Have students use their charts or graphs to identify which cities experience climatic conditions most similar to your community.

Climates of the United States and Canada   L2

Guided Instruction
- Read the introductory paragraph and the Regions paragraph. Have students study the climate map, referring to the map key to locate the warmest and coldest regions of these two countries.

- Ask students **In what climate region is the city of Toronto?** (*humid continental*) **In what climate region is Seattle located?** (*marine west coast*)

- Ask students **Where are the coldest climates shown on this map located?** (*northern Canada*) **Does Hawaii get a lot of rain? How can you tell?** (*Yes; the state is located in a tropical wet region.*)

- Direct students to finish the Regional Overview worksheet.

  All in One United States and Canada Teaching Resources, *Regional Overview,* pp. 89–91

Independent Practice
Ask students to write a brief statement describing the climate of their own community. Then ask them to find the location of their community on the climate map. Have them compare their descriptions to the information on the map.

Monitor Progress
If students are having trouble with their statements, have them focus on typical summer and winter weather in their area. You may want to help students find the location of their community on the climate map.

Answers
REGIONS The Rocky Mountains are shaped like the highlands climate region; mountains effect weather in that temperatures are usually lower at higher elevations and there is usually less rainfall on one side of a mountain range; Reasons for the shift in climate from Florida to Nunavut are: their respective distances from the Equator; the bodies of water each area borders.

PRACTICE YOUR GEOGRAPHY SKILLS
1. Canada
2. north of the Arctic Circle
3. St. Lawrence River

Regional Overview **5**

Focus on Regions of the United States and Canada

L2

Guided Instruction

- Read the introduction and photo captions as a class. Students will notice that not every region of the United States and Canada is discussed in a photo caption.

- Point out that Alaska and Hawaii are part of the West. Ask **Which region of the United States is the largest?** *(the West)* Ask students to identify the smallest region. *(the Northeast)*

- Ask students to name Canada's two most populous provinces. *(Ontario and Quebec)* Ask them to give two reasons why Vancouver is a busy trading center. *(Its harbor never freezes and it handles almost all Canadian trade with Pacific Rim countries.)*

Independent Practice

Ask students to take out their copy of *Outline Map 11: The United States: Political.* Have students draw in the borders of the four regions of the United States. Ask them to label each region and put a star in the region that they live in.

All in One **United States and Canada Teaching Resources,** *Outline Map 11: The United States: Political,* p. 92

Monitor Progress

Circulate while students complete their maps and provide assistance where needed.

Focus on Regions of the United States and Canada

Now that you've investigated the geography of the United States and Canada, take a closer look at some of the regions that make up these two countries.

Go Online PHSchool.com **Use Web Code lhp-4000 for the interactive maps on these pages.**

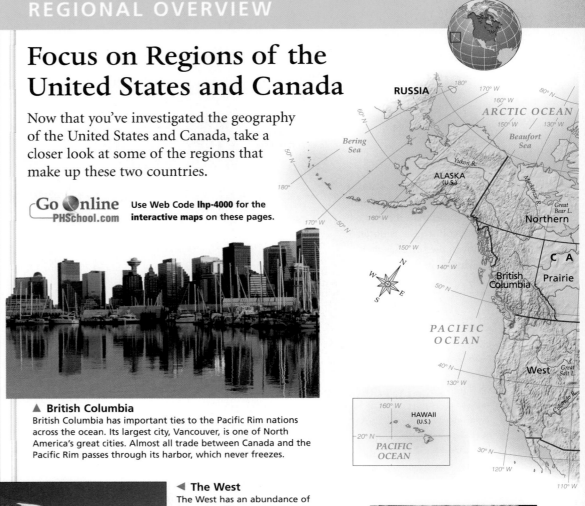

▲ **British Columbia**
British Columbia has important ties to the Pacific Rim nations across the ocean. Its largest city, Vancouver, is one of North America's great cities. Almost all trade between Canada and the Pacific Rim passes through its harbor, which never freezes.

◄ **The West**
The West has an abundance of natural and human resources. Although the West produces 85 percent of America's gold, water is one of the most precious natural resources in the region.

The South ►
The South is a warm region with a climate perfect for growing crops. Its booming industries have drawn many people from within the country and overseas. The Mardi Gras festival is one example of the region's cultural diversity.

6 United States and Canada

Background: Links Across Place

Pollution Crosses Borders Activities in one region can contribute to environmental problems in another region. For example, air pollution generated by power plants in the Midwestern United States rises into the atmosphere and is blown east by the wind. These pollutants combine with moisture in the air and fall as acid rain in the Northeastern United States and eastern Canada. The governments of the United States and Canada have recognized that they need to work together to solve problems that affect both countries.

Atlantic Provinces ▶
The four Canadian provinces that make up the Atlantic Provinces all border the Atlantic Ocean. Fishing and other maritime industries have always supported the economy and way of life of this region.

▲ **Ontario and Quebec**
These two provinces are Canada's most populous provinces. Ontario contains Ottawa, the national capital, shown above. French speakers make up a majority of the population of Quebec.

0 miles 1,000
0 kilometers 1,000
Lambert Azimuthal Equal Area

Key

——— National border
——— Regional border
⊛ Capital city

◀ **The Midwest**
Though the Midwest is still "America's Breadbasket," most family farms there have given way to larger corporate farms. The region is also an important transportation center.

Assess and Reteach

Assess Progress
- Have students revisit the ideas they brainstormed in Build Background Knowledge. Using the information they have learned so far, ask them to expand on their description of their region of the United States. How does it differ from other regions of the United States and Canada?

- Ask students to complete Practice Your Geography Skills on page 5.

Reteach
For more exploration of the region, have students view the United States and Canada portion of the Passport to the World CD-ROM and complete the Customs Quiz.

⊙ *The United States and Canada,* **Passport to the World CD-ROM**

Extend

Portfolio Activity One way of assessing student accomplishments is by having them build a portfolio of their best work. To begin their portfolios for the United States and Canada, have students choose a region of the United States or a Canadian province from the map on pages 6–7. Then have them complete a project on this region or province. Students can choose what type of project they would like to do. Options include physical maps, resource maps, travel brochures, brief history reports, and more.

- Give students *Choosing a Topic* to help them get started on their project.

All in One **United States and Canada Teaching Resources,** *Choosing a Topic,* p. 95

Differentiated Instruction

For English Language Learners L2
Pair English learners with native speakers and have each pair write three questions based on the information on pages 6–7.

Have pairs discuss any words or ideas in the text that are unfamiliar. Ask each pair to share its questions with the class.

The United States and Canada: Physical Geography

Chapter Overview

Overview

1 Land and Water
Section 1
1. Learn where the United States and Canada are located.
2. Find out about the major landforms of the United States and Canada.
3. Explore major bodies of water that are important to the United States and Canada.

2 Climate and Vegetation
Section 2
1. Learn what climate zones the United States and Canada have.
2. Identify the natural vegetation zones of the United States and Canada.

3 Resources and Land Use
Section 3
1. Learn about the major resources of the United States.
2. Find out about the major resources of Canada.

DISCOVERY
CHANNEL
SCHOOL Video

The Geography of the United States and Canada
Length: 5 minutes, 40 seconds
Use with Section 1
This segment provides an overview of the geography of the United States and Canada. It also describes the different climates and major resources in the countries.

Technology Resources

Go Online
PHSchool.com

Interactive Textbook

PRENTICE HALL
TeacherEXPRESS
Plan · Teach · Assess

Students use embedded Web codes to access Internet activities, chapter self-tests, and additional map practice. They may also access Dorling Kindersley's Online Desk Reference to learn more about each country they study.

Use the Interactive Textbook to make content and concepts come alive through animations, videos, and activities that accompany the complete basal text—online and on CD-ROM.

Use this complete suite of powerful teaching tools to make planning lessons and administering tests quicker and easier.

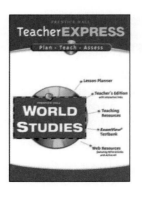

Reading and Assessment

Reading and Vocabulary Instruction

⟳ Model the Target Reading Skill

Reading Process Ask students to consider the difference between passive and active reading. Passive readers simply look at the words. Active readers think about what they are reading, how it relates to previous knowledge, and what might come next. Setting a purpose before reading is one way to remain active and engaged with the text. As students read, they can continually return to their stated purpose to make sure it is being fulfilled. Model setting a purpose for reading by thinking aloud about the chapter:

I want to set a purpose for reading this chapter to help me focus. The chapter's title is *The U.S. and Canada: Physical Geography,* and the titles of the three sections are *Land and Water, Climate and Vegetation,* and *Resources and Land Use.* For the chapter as a whole, my purpose for reading will be to learn about the major landforms and bodies of water, the major climate and vegetation zones, and different kinds of natural resources in the United States and Canada. If I take notes as I read, it will be easier for me to keep track of the information I have learned and how it relates to my purpose.

Use the following worksheets from All-in-One United States and Canada Teaching Resources (pp. 110–112) to support this chapter's Target Reading Skill.

Vocabulary Builder
High-Use Academic Words

Use these steps to teach this chapter's high-use words:

1. Have students rate how well they know each word on their Word Knowledge worksheets (All-in-One United States and Canada Teaching Resources, p. 113).

2. Pronounce each word and ask students to repeat it.

3. Give students a brief definition and sample sentence (provided on TE pp. 11, 19, and 26).

4. Work with students as they fill in the "Definition or Example" column of their Word Knowledge worksheets.

Assessment

Formal Assessment

Test students' understanding of core knowledge and skills.

> **Chapter Tests A and B,** All-in-One United States and Canada Teaching Resources, pp. 129–134

Customize the Chapter Tests to suit your needs.
ExamView® Test Bank CD-ROM

Skills Assessment

Assess geographic literacy.
> MapMaster Skills, Student Edition, pp. 9, 20, 22, 26, 32

Assess reading and comprehension.
> **Target Reading Skills,** Student Edition, pp. 13, 21, 28, and in Section Assessments

> **Chapter 1 Assessment,** United States and Canada Reading and Vocabulary Study Guide, p. 15

Performance Assessment

Assess students' performance on this chapter's Writing Activities using the following rubrics from All-in-One United States and Canada Teaching Resources.

> **Rubric for Assessing a Writing Assignment,** p. 127

> **Rubric for Assessing a Map Produced by a Student,** p. 128

Assess students' work through performance tasks.

> **Small Group Activity: Creating Travel Posters for National Parks,** United States and Canada Teaching Resources, pp. 116–119

Online Assessment

Have students check their own understanding.
> **Chapter Self-Test**

Test Preparation

Assess students' skills and diagnose problems as students begin their study of this region.

> **Screening Tests and Diagnosing Readiness Tests,** AYP Monitoring Assessments, pp. 1–11, 13–63

Section 1 Land and Water

 2 periods, 1 block (includes Skills for Life)

Social Studies Objectives

1. Learn where the United States and Canada are located.
2. Find out about the major landforms of the United States and Canada.
3. Explore major bodies of water that are important to the United States and Canada.

Reading/Language Arts Objective

Learn how to set a purpose for reading.

Prepare to Read	Instructional Resources	Differentiated Instruction
Build Background Knowledge Use a video to prompt discussion about the physical geography of the United States and Canada. **Set a Purpose for Reading** Have students evaluate statements on the *Reading Readiness Guide*. **Preview Key Terms** Teach the section's Key Terms. **Target Reading Skill** Introduce the section's Target Reading Skill of **setting a purpose for reading.**	**All in One United States and Canada Teaching Resources** **L2** Reading Readiness Guide, p. 99 **L2** Preview and Set a Purpose, p. 110 **World Studies Video Program** **L2** The Geography of the United States and Canada	**Spanish Reading and Vocabulary Study Guide** **L1** Chapter 1, Section 1, pp. 7–8 ELL

Instruct	Instructional Resources	Differentiated Instruction
A Global Perspective Discuss the locations of the United States and Canada. **Landforms** Discuss physical features of the United States and Canada. **Target Reading Skill** Review **setting a purpose for reading.** **Major Bodies of Water** Discuss the key bodies of water in the United States and Canada.	**All in One United States and Canada Teaching Resources** **L2** Guided Reading and Review, p. 100 **L2** Reading Readiness Guide, p. 99 **United States and Canada Transparencies** **L2** Section Reading Support Transparency USC 43	**All in One United States and Canada Teaching Resources** **L1** Outline Map 9: The United States and Canada: Physical, p. 120 ELL, LPR, SN **L2** Skills for Life, p. 115 AR, GT, LPR, SN **Teacher's Edition** **L1** For English Language Learners, TE p. 12 **L1** For Less Proficient Readers, TE p. 12 **L3** For Gifted and Talented, TE p. 14 **United States and Canada Transparencies** **L1** Color Transparency USC 22: United States and Canada: Physical and Political ELL, LPR, SN

Assess and Reteach	Instructional Resources	Differentiated Instruction
Assess Progress Evaluate student comprehension with the section assessment and section quiz. **Reteach** Assign the Reading and Vocabulary Study Guide to help struggling students. **Extend** Extend the lesson by assigning a Book Project.	**All in One United States and Canada Teaching Resources** **L2** Section Quiz, p. 101 Rubric for Assessing a Writing Assignment, p. 127 **L3** Book Project: Create a Diorama, pp. 82–84 **Reading and Vocabulary Study Guide** **L1** Chapter 1, Section 1, pp. 6–8	**Teacher's Edition** **L1** For Special Needs Students, TE p. 17 **Spanish Support** **L2** Section Quiz (Spanish), p. 5 ELL **Social Studies Skills Tutor CD-ROM** **L1** Identifying Frame of Reference and Point of View ELL, LPR, SN

Key

L1 Basic to Average   **L3** Average to Advanced

L2 For All Students

LPR Less Proficient Readers

AR Advanced Readers

SN Special Needs Students

GT Gifted and Talented

ELL English Language Learners

Section 2 Climate and Vegetation

 1.5 periods, .75 block

Social Studies Objectives
1. Learn what climate zones the United States and Canada have.
2. Identify the natural vegetation zones of the United States and Canada.

Reading/Language Arts Objective
Learn how to make predictions about what you read.

Prepare to Read	Instructional Resources	Differentiated Instruction
Build Background Knowledge Discuss the local climate with students. **Set a Purpose for Reading** Have students evaluate statements on the *Reading Readiness Guide*. **Preview Key Terms** Teach the section's Key Terms. **Target Reading Skill** Introduce the section's Target Reading Skill of **predicting**.	**All in One United States and Canada Teaching Resources** **L2** Reading Readiness Guide, p. 103 **L2** Preview and Predict, p. 111	**Spanish Reading and Vocabulary Study Guide** **L1** Chapter 1, Section 2, pp. 9–10 ELL

Instruct	Instructional Resources	Differentiated Instruction
Climate Zones Describe how Canada's climate differs by region. **Target Reading Skill** Review **predicting**. **Natural Vegetation Zones** Study a map and review vegetation zones.	**All in One United States and Canada Teaching Resources** **L2** Guided Reading and Review, p. 104 **L2** Reading Readiness Guide, p. 103 **United States and Canada Transparencies** **L2** Transparency B3: Tree Map/Flow Chart **L2** Section Reading Support Transparency USC 44	**All in One United States and Canada Teaching Resources** **L3** Enrichment, p. 114 AR, GT **L3** Hatchet, pp. 122–125 AR, ELL, GT **Teacher's Edition** **L1** For Special Needs Students, TE p. 21 **L3** For Gifted and Talented, TE pp. 20, 21 **L3** For Advanced Readers, TE p. 23 **L2** For English Language Learners, TE p. 23 **United States and Canada Transparencies** **L3** Color Transparency USC 22: The United States and Canada: Physical-Political (Base) AR, GT **L3** Color Transparency USC 24: The United States and Canada: Population Distribution (Overlay) AR, GT

Assess and Reteach	Instructional Resources	Differentiated Instruction
Assess Progress Evaluate student comprehension with the section assessment and section quiz. **Reteach** Assign the Reading and Vocabulary Study Guide to help struggling students. **Extend** Extend the lesson by assigning a Book Project.	**All in One United States and Canada Teaching Resources** **L2** Section Quiz, p. 105 **L3** Book Project: Set Up a Weather Station, pp. 73–75 Rubric for Assessing a Writing Assignment, p. 127 **Reading and Vocabulary Study Guide** **L1** Chapter 1, Section 2, pp. 9–11	**Spanish Support** **L2** Section Quiz (Spanish), p. 7 ELL

Key
L1 Basic to Average
L2 For All Students
L3 Average to Advanced

LPR Less Proficient Readers
AR Advanced Readers
SN Special Needs Students

GT Gifted and Talented
ELL English Language Learners

Section 3 Resources and Land Use

 3 periods, 1.5 blocks (includes Chapter Review and Assessment)

Social Studies Objectives
1. Learn about the major resources of the United States.
2. Find out about the major resources of Canada.

Reading/Language Arts Objective
Learn how to preview and ask questions to see what a reading selection is about.

Prepare to Read	**Instructional Resources**	**Differentiated Instruction**
Build Background Knowledge Brainstorm about resources in the United States and Canada. **Set a Purpose for Reading** Have students evaluate statements on the *Reading Readiness Guide*. **Preview Key Terms** Teach the section's Key Terms. **Target Reading Skill** Introduce the section's Target Reading Skill of **previewing and asking questions**.	**All in One United States and Canada Teaching Resources** **L2** Reading Readiness Guide, p. 107 **L2** Preview and Ask Questions, p. 112	**Spanish Reading and Vocabulary Study Guide** **L1** Chapter 1, Section 3, pp. 11–12 ELL

Instruct	**Instructional Resources**	**Differentiated Instruction**
Resources of the United States Derive information from a map and discuss the United States' natural resources. **Target Reading Skill** Review **previewing and asking questions**. **Resources of Canada** Ask questions about and discuss the resources of Canada.	**All in One United States and Canada Teaching Resources** **L2** Guided Reading and Review, p. 108 **L2** Reading Readiness Guide, p. 107 **United States and Canada Transparencies** **L2** Section Reading Support Transparency USC 45	**All in One United States and Canada Teaching Resources** **L1** Reading a Natural Resources Map, p. 121 ELL, LPR, SN **Teacher's Edition** **L3** For Gifted and Talented, TE p. 28 **L1** For Less Proficient Readers, TE p. 28 **Spanish Support** **L2** Guided Reading and Review (Spanish), p. 8 ELL

Assess and Reteach	**Instructional Resources**	**Differentiated Instruction**
Assess Progress Evaluate student comprehension with the section assessment and section quiz. **Reteach** Assign the Reading and Vocabulary Study Guide to help struggling students. **Extend** Extend the lesson by assigning a Small Group Activity.	**All in One United States and Canada Teaching Resources** **L2** Section Quiz, p. 109 **L3** Small Group Activity: Creating Travel Posters for National Parks, pp. 116–119 Rubric for Assessing a Writing Assignment, p. 127 **L2** Vocabulary Development, p. 126 **L2** Word Knowledge, p. 113 Rubric for Assessing a Map Produced by a Student, p. 128 **L2** Chapter Tests A and B, pp. 129–134 **Reading and Vocabulary Study Guide** **L1** Chapter 1, Section 3, pp. 12–14	**Spanish Support** **L2** Section Quiz (Spanish), p. 9 ELL **L2** Chapter Summary (Spanish), p. 10 ELL **L2** Vocabulary Development (Spanish), p. 11 ELL

Key
L1 Basic to Average	**L3** Average to Advanced	**LPR** Less Proficient Readers	**GT** Gifted and Talented
L2 For All Students		**AR** Advanced Readers	**ELL** English Language Learners
		SN Special Needs Students	

Professional Development

Reading Background

Previewing and Prereading

This chapter's Target Reading Skill asks students to preview each section and set a purpose for reading. Students who do a brief, preliminary reading of complex material are in a strategic position to take control of their learning and comprehension. Previewing helps students consider what they already know about a topic they will be studying and gives some idea of what a text selection is about before they read it. Previewing also helps students identify the text structure and develop a mental framework for ideas to be encountered in the text. This can help them in formulating a more realistic reading and study plan.

Follow the steps below to teach students how to preview and preread.

1. Tell students that previewing will help them identify the text structure and develop a mental outline of ideas they will encounter in the text.
2. List the various text features you will be previewing in the order in which you would like students to examine them: section title, text headings, introduction, list of key terms, questions or tasks in the reading selection, photographs, drawings, maps, charts and other visuals in the text. Focus students' attention on some of these items, or ask them to look at all of them.
3. Prompt students to reflect after examining various text features. They may ask themselves questions such as: What is this reading selection about? What are some key words I will learn? How should I tackle this reading and divide up the task?

Using Paragraph Shrinking Effectively

In this chapter, students will use the Paragraph Shrinking technique to help them learn the important ideas in the text. Students will first read the paragraph independently. Because everyone reads at a different pace, minimize anxiety by telling students that you will not have them move on to the next step until everyone has finished reading. If they finish the paragraph before the time is up, they can read it again more slowly. Then monitor the class for signs that all students have finished reading silently before asking students to continue.

When the partner work begins, remind students of polite ways to express disagreement, such as, "I have a different idea. Can I share it with you?" or, "I hadn't thought of that. I was going to say …."

World Studies Background

Mississippi River

The Mississippi, the largest river in the United States, provides a home to more than 240 kinds of fish, about 50 kinds of mammals, and 40 percent of the migratory birds in the United States—not to mention the 12 million people who live along its banks. The Mississippi River rises in Lake Itasca in Minnesota and flows south to empty into the Gulf of Mexico. With its tributaries, the Mississippi drains all or part of 31 states and two Canadian provinces.

The Canadian Shield

The Canadian Shield is a layer of ancient rock that covers more than half of Canada, most of Greenland, and stretches into the northern United States. This makes it one of the largest continental shields. More than 540 million years old, the rock that makes up the shield is constantly being eroded by atmospheric factors, making it relatively flat. During the ice age, glaciers scraped across the shield, carving out lakes and creating smooth hills. Although the area is mostly undeveloped, it is a good source of natural resources.

Infoplease® provides a wealth of useful information for the classroom. You can use this resource to strengthen your background on the subjects covered in this chapter. Have students visit this advertising-free site as a starting point for projects requiring research.

 Use Web Code **lhd-4100** for **Infoplease®**.

Chapter 1

Guiding Questions

Remind students about the Guiding Questions introduced at the beginning of the book.

Section 1 relates to **Guiding Question** ⑤
How has physical geography affected the cultures of the United States and Canada? *(The physical geography of the United States and Canada varies greatly, ranging from tall mountain ranges to rolling plains. People work different types of jobs and engage in different types of recreational activities based on the physical geography in their region.)*

Section 2 relates to **Guiding Question** ②
How has physical geography affected the cultures of the United States and Canada? *(The various climates and vegetation zones across the two countries affect the way people live and work.)*

Section 3 relates to **Guiding Question** ⑤
How did the United States and Canada become two of the wealthiest nations in the world? *(The abundant natural resources found in these countries helped them to build two of the world's leading economies.)*

⟳ Target Reading Skill

In this chapter, students will learn and apply the reading skill of reading process. Use the following worksheets to help students practice this skill:

> **All in One** **United States and Canada Teaching Resources,** *Preview and Set a Purpose,* p. 110; *Preview and Predict,* p. 111; *Preview and Ask Questions,* p. 112

> ### Differentiated Instruction

The following Teacher's Edition strategies are suitable for students of varying abilities.

Advanced Readers, p. 23
English Language Learners, pp. 12, 23
Gifted and Talented, pp. 14, 20, 21, 28
Less Proficient Readers, pp. 12, 28
Special Needs Students, pp. 17, 21

Chapter

1 The U.S. and Canada: Physical Geography

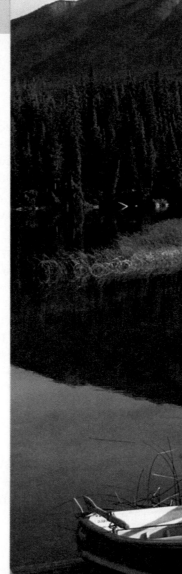

Chapter Preview

This chapter will introduce you to the geography of the United States and Canada and show how geography affects the people who live in the region.

Section 1
Land and Water

Section 2
Climate and Vegetation

Section 3
Resources and Land Use

⟳ Target Reading Skill

Reading Process In this chapter you will use previewing to help you understand and remember what you read.

 Talbot Lake, Canada

Bibliography

For the Teacher
Dennis, Jerry. *The Living Great Lakes: Searching for the Heart of the Inland Seas.* St. Martin's Press, 2003.
Hudson, John C. *Across This Land: A Regional Geography of the United States and Canada.* Johns Hopkins University Press, 2002.

For the Student
L1 Ylvisaker, Anne and Rosanne W. Fortner. *Lake Erie.* Capstone Press, 2003.
L1 Rau, Dana Meachen. *North America.* The Child's World Incorporated, 2003.
L2 Beckett, Harry. *Manitoba.* Weigl Educational Associates, 2003.
L3 Currie, Stephen. *Mississippi.* Lucent Books, 2003.

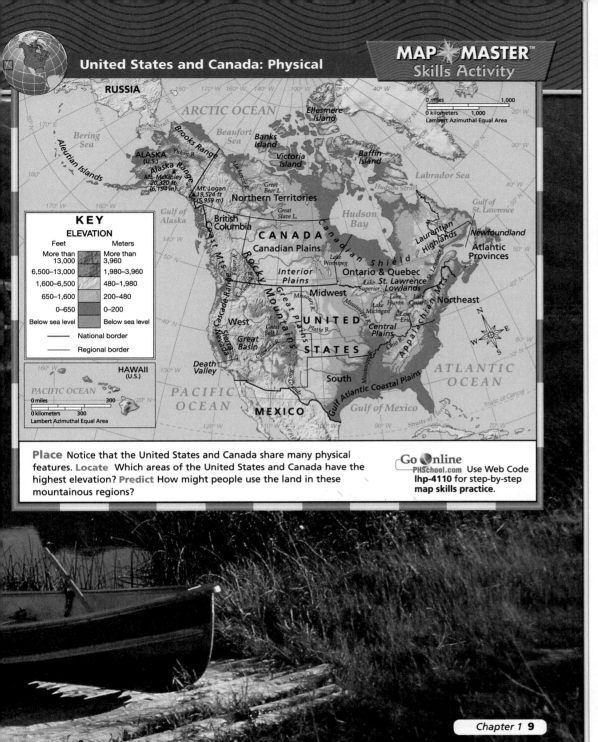

United States and Canada: Physical

MAP MASTER™ Skills Activity

KEY

ELEVATION

Feet	Meters
More than 13,000	More than 3,960
6,500–13,000	1,980–3,960
1,600–6,500	480–1,980
650–1,600	200–480
0–650	0–200
Below sea level	Below sea level

— National border
— Regional border

Place Notice that the United States and Canada share many physical features. **Locate** Which areas of the United States and Canada have the highest elevation? **Predict** How might people use the land in these mountainous regions?

Go Online PHSchool.com Use Web Code lhp-4110 for step-by-step map skills practice.

Chapter 1 **9**

MAP MASTER™ Skills Activity

- Have students create a table listing the regions of the United States and the physical features and elevations found in each region, as shown on the map. Remind them to label the columns and rows and give the table a title. Then have them create a similar table for Canada.

Go Online PHSchool.com Students may practice their map skills using the interactive online version of this map.

Using the Visual L2

Reach Into Your Background Draw students' attention to the photograph on this spread. Ask them if a photograph containing similar physical features could be taken in their town. Tell them to explain what would be the same and what would be different about the photograph. What physical features might a scenic photograph taken in their town or city include?

Answers

MAP MASTER™ Skills Activity **Locate** areas in the Rocky Mountains, Sierra Nevada, and Alaska Range **Predict** Possible answer: for ski resorts and other recreational businesses.

Chapter Resources

Teaching Resources
Letter Home, p. 97
- L2 Vocabulary Development, p. 126
- L2 Skills for Life, p. 115
- L2 Chapter Tests A and B, pp. 129–134

Spanish Support
Spanish Letter Home, p. 3
- L2 Spanish Chapter Summary, p. 10
- L2 Spanish Vocabulary Development, p. 11

Media and Technology
- L1 Student Edition on Audio CD
- L1 Guided Reading Audiotapes, English and Spanish
- L2 Social Studies Skills Tutor CD-ROM
  ExamView® Test Bank CD-ROM

PRENTICE HALL Presentation EXPRESS™
Teach · Connect · Inspire

Teach this chapter's content using the PresentationExpress™ CD-ROM including:
- slide shows
- transparencies
- interactive maps and media
- *ExamView®* QuickTake Presenter

Objectives

Social Studies

1. Learn where the United States and Canada are located.
2. Find out about the major landforms of the United States and Canada.
3. Explore major bodies of water that are important in the United States and Canada.

Reading/Language Arts

Learn how to set a purpose for reading.

Prepare to Read

Build Background Knowledge L2

Tell students that they will start their study of the United States and Canada by learning about their land and water. Show the video *The Geography of the United States and Canada.* Ask students to note three to five facts about the land and water of United States and Canada as they watch. Have students engage in a Give One, Get One activity (TE, p. T37) to share the information they gathered.

📼 *The Geography of the United States and Canada,* **World Studies Video Program**

Set a Purpose for Reading L2

- Preview the Objectives.

- Read each statement in the *Reading Readiness Guide* aloud. Ask students to mark the statements true or false.

- Have students discuss the statements in pairs or groups of four, then mark their worksheets again. Use the Numbered Heads participation strategy (TE, p. T36) to call on students to share their group's perspectives.

All in One United States and Canada Teaching Resources, *Reading Readiness Guide,* p. 99

Vocabulary Builder
Preview Key Terms L2

Create a three-column "See It—Remember It" chart of the Key Terms on the board. Write a term in the first column, a short definition in the second column, and a sketch in the third column. Guide students as they copy and complete the chart.

Land and Water

Prepare to Read

Objectives

In this section you will

1. Learn where the United States and Canada are located.
2. Find out about the major landforms of the United States and Canada.
3. Explore major bodies of water that are important to the United States and Canada.

Taking Notes

As you read the section, look for the main ideas about land and water. Copy the table below and record your findings in it.

Country	Landforms	Bodies of Water
United States		
Canada		

🎯 Target Reading Skill

Set a Purpose for Reading
Before you read this section, look at the headings, maps, and photographs to see what the section is about. Then set a purpose for reading this section. For example, your purpose might be to find out about the geography of the United States and Canada. Use the Taking Notes table to help you meet your purpose.

Key Terms

- **Rocky Mountains** (RAHK ee MOWN tunz) *n.* the major mountain range in western North America
- **glacier** (GLAY shur) *n.* a huge, slow-moving mass of snow and ice
- **Great Lakes** (grayt layks) *n.* the world's largest group of freshwater lakes
- **tributary** (TRIB yoo tehr ee) *n.* a river or stream that flows into a larger river

Alaska's Mount McKinley is the highest mountain in North America. In 1992, Ruth Kocour joined a team of climbers to scale the 20,320-foot (6,194-meter) peak. After the team had set up camp at 9,500 feet (2,896 meters), the first storm arrived. The team quickly built walls of packed snow to shield their tents from the wind. They dug a snow cave to house their kitchen and waited for the storm to end. Kocour recalls, "Someone on another team went outside for a few minutes, came back, and had a hot drink. His teeth cracked."

Maybe camping in the mountains is not for you. Perhaps you would prefer the sunny beaches of Florida, the giant forests of the Northwest, or the rugged coastline of Nova Scotia. Maybe you would like to see the Arizona desert or the plains of central Canada. The landscape of the United States and Canada varies greatly.

Climbers on Mount McKinley

10 United States and Canada

🎯 Target Reading Skill L2

Set a Purpose for Reading Draw students' attention to the Target Reading Skill. Tell students that setting a purpose for reading means choosing a focus for reading before they begin. Encourage students to preview photographs, maps, diagrams, captions, and headings before they begin reading. Explain that these items can be clues to what their purpose for reading might be.

Model the skill using the photographs on pages 10 and 11 of the Student Edition. Tell students that because the photographs show mountains, a river, a field and trees, a reasonable purpose for reading these pages would be to learn about the geographic features of the United States and Canada.

Give students *Preview and Set a Purpose.* Have them complete the activity in groups.

All in One United States and Canada Teaching Resources, *Preview and Set a Purpose,* p. 110

A Global Perspective

The United States and Canada are located in North America. To the east is the Atlantic Ocean, and to the west is the Pacific Ocean. To the north, Canada borders the Arctic Ocean, while to the south, the United States borders Mexico and the Gulf of Mexico. The United States also includes Alaska, a huge state bordering northwest Canada, and Hawaii, a group of Pacific islands more than 2,000 miles (3,220 kilometers) west of California.

✓ **Reading Check** **Which bodies of water border the United States and Canada?**

Landforms

From outer space, the United States and Canada appear as one landmass, with mountain ranges or systems, and vast plains running from north to south. Locate these mountains and plains on the United States and Canada: Physical map on page 9.

Extending about 3,000 miles (4,830 kilometers) along the western section of the continent, the **Rocky Mountains** are the largest mountain system in North America. In the east, the Appalachian (ap uh LAY chun) Mountains are the United States' second-largest mountain system. They stretch about 1,500 miles (2,415 kilometers). In Canada, the Appalachian Mountains meet the Laurentian (law REN shun) Highlands.

Between the Rockies and the Appalachians lies a huge plains area. In Canada, these lowlands are called the Interior Plains. In the United States, they are called the Great Plains and the Central Plains. Much of this region has rich soil. In the wetter, eastern area, farmers grow crops like corn and soybeans. In the drier, western area, farmers grow wheat and ranchers raise livestock.

A Scenic Landscape
This view of the Pioneer Valley along the Connecticut River in Massachusetts was taken from Mount Sugarloaf. **Draw Conclusions** *What can you conclude about the northeastern region of the United States from this photo?*

DISCOVERY CHANNEL SCHOOL Video
Explore the geography of the U.S. and Canada.

Chapter 1 Section 1 **11**

Landforms

L2

Guided Instruction

- **Vocabulary Builder** Clarify the high-use words **unique** and **notable** before reading.

- Ask students to read Landforms of the United States and Canada. Circulate to make sure that students can answer the Reading Check question.

- Have students contrast the Gulf-Atlantic Coastal Plain with the Great Basin. *(Students should note that the Gulf-Atlantic Coastal Plain is flat, fertile, and close to water, while the Great Basin is bowl-shaped, very hot, and dry.)*

- Ask students to discuss ways in which the physical geography of the United States and Canada affects the people who live there. Ask students to provide specific examples of the geography's effects. *(Answers will vary, but may include that areas with rich soil, such as the Great Plains, encourage farming; places with access to the sea, such as the Gulf-Atlantic Coastal Plain, promote shipping and fishing; people cannot easily live in areas with glaciers, such as the valleys of Alaska, or very rugged areas, such as the Canadian Shield; more than half of Canada's population lives in the small St. Lawrence Lowlands because of good conditions for manufacturing and farming.)*

Independent Practice

Ask students to create the Taking Notes graphic organizer on a blank piece of paper. Then have them fill in the "Landforms" column with the information they have just learned. Model one example of choosing a detail to record in the Landforms column.

Monitor Progress

Circulate among the students as they work on the first column of the organizer, and offer help to individuals as needed.

Links

Read the **Links to Science** on this page. Ask students **How do scientists know that Loihi erupts?** *(Scientists know that the volcano is erupting because it is growing in height as layers of lava from the eruptions pile on top of one another.)*

Links to Science

The Next Hawaiian Island Volcanic eruptions in the Pacific Ocean, like the one shown above in Volcano National Park, created the islands of Hawaii. Loihi (loh EE hee), off the southern tip of Hawaii, is the world's most active volcano. But no one has seen it erupt. Its peak is 3,000 feet (914 meters) below the ocean's surface. Years of continuous eruption have produced layer after layer of molten lava. Scientists predict that in 100,000 years or less, Loihi will rise above the surface of the ocean and become the next Hawaiian island.

Special Features of the United States The United States has several unique features. The Gulf-Atlantic Coastal Plain runs along its eastern and southern coasts. In the Northeast, this plain is narrow; it broadens as it spreads south and west. Flat, fertile land and access to the sea attracted many settlers to this area.

A region of plateaus and basins lies west of the Rockies. Perhaps the most notable feature of this area is the Great Basin. In the northeast section of this bowl-shaped region is the Great Salt Lake. Death Valley is in the southwest section. Much of Death Valley lies below sea level. It is also the hottest place in North America. Summer temperatures there exceed 125°F (52°C).

Volcanoes To the west of this region lie three more mountain ranges. They are the Coast Ranges along the Pacific, the Sierra Nevada in California, and the Cascades in Washington and Oregon. Volcanoes produced the Cascades. Volcanoes form when magma, or molten rock, breaks through Earth's crust. Once it comes up to the surface, the molten rock is called lava. One of the volcanoes in the Cascades—Mount St. Helens—erupted in 1980. The eruption was so powerful that people as far away as Montana had to sweep volcanic ash off of their cars.

Glaciers Far to the north, snow and ice cover Alaska's many mountains. **Glaciers,** huge, slow-moving sheets of ice, fill many of the valleys among these mountains. Glaciers form over many years when layers of snow press together, thaw a little, and then turn to ice. Valley glaciers are found in high mountain valleys where the climate is too cold for the ice to melt. In North America, these valley glaciers move through the Rocky and Cascade mountains, the Sierra Nevada, and the Alaskan ranges.

12 United States and Canada

Differentiated Instruction

For English Language Learners L1
Show *Color Transparency USC 22: United States and Canada: Physical and Political.* Ask individual students to take turns coming up to trace the geographical features mentioned in the text on the transparency's map.

📖 **United States and Canada Transparencies,** *Color Transparency USC 22: United States and Canada: Physical and Political*

For Less Proficient Readers L1
Distribute *Outline Map 9: The United States and Canada: Physical.* As students read A Global Perspective, have them label The United States, Canada, and Mexico and fill in the names of the bodies of water described in the text. Provide assistance as needed.

All in One United States and Canada Teaching Resources, *Outline Map 9: The United States and Canada: Physical,* p. 120

Special Features of Canada Canada, too, has a number of unique features. East of Alaska lies the Yukon (YOO kahn) Territory. Mount Logan, Canada's highest peak, is located there in a range called the Coast Mountains. The Coast Mountains, which stretch south along the Pacific Ocean, are located only in Canada. They are not part of the United States Coast Ranges.

Farther east, beyond the Interior Plains, lies the Canadian Shield. This huge region of ancient rock covers about half of Canada. The land on the shield is rugged, so few people live there.

Southeast of the shield along the St. Lawrence River are the St. Lawrence Lowlands. These lowlands are Canada's smallest land region. However, they are home to more than half of the country's population. The region is also Canada's manufacturing center. And because the lowlands have fertile soil, farmers in this region produce about one third of the country's crops.

✓ **Reading Check** Describe two physical features of the United States and Canada.

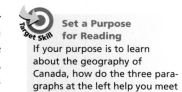

Set a Purpose for Reading If your purpose is to learn about the geography of Canada, how do the three paragraphs at the left help you meet your goal?

Major Bodies of Water

Both the United States and Canada have important lakes and rivers. People use these bodies of water for transportation, recreation, and industry. Many American and Canadian cities developed near these bodies of water. Find these waterways on the United States and Canada: Physical map on page 9.

The Great Lakes Lakes Superior, Michigan, Huron, Erie, and Ontario make up the **Great Lakes,** the world's largest group of freshwater lakes. Lake Superior is the deepest lake, with a mean depth of 487 feet (148 meters). Lake Erie is the shallowest lake at only 62 feet (19 meters) deep. Only Lake Michigan lies entirely in the United States. The other four lie on the border between the United States and Canada.

Glaciers formed the Great Lakes during an ice age long ago. As the glaciers moved, they dug deep trenches in the land. Water from the melting glaciers filled these trenches to produce the Great Lakes. Today, the Great Lakes are important waterways in both the United States and Canada. Shipping on the Great Lakes has helped to develop the industries of both countries.

A satellite image of the Great Lakes, which create a natural border between the United States and Canada

Background: Links Across Place

The Mother of Rivers Canada's Columbia Icefield, which overlaps part of the British Columbia–Alberta border, is the largest accumulation of permanent ice and snow in the Rocky Mountains. Because the icefield's main accumulation of ice lies on the Continental Divide, its glacial melt waters feed major rivers on either side of the divide—hence its nickname, "the mother of rivers." Meltwater from one glacier follows a river-and-lake network eastward through Alberta, Saskatchewan, and Manitoba and finally drains into Hudson Bay. Water from the northwestern part of the icefield flows into the Fraser and Columbia rivers, eventually emptying into the Pacific Ocean.

Independent Practice
Have students complete the Taking Notes graphic organizer by filling in the "Bodies of Water" column.

Monitor Progress
- Show *Section Reading Support Transparency USC 43* and ask students to check their graphic organizers individually. Go over key concepts and clarify key vocabulary as needed.

    📖 **United States and Canada Transparencies,** *Section Reading Support Transparency USC 43*

- Tell students to fill in the last column of the *Reading Readiness Guide.* Probe for what they learned that confirms or invalidates each statement.

    All in One **United States and Canada Teaching Resources,** *Reading Readiness Guide,* p. 99

Assess and Reteach

Assess Progress   **L2**
Have students complete the Section Assessment. Administer the *Section Quiz.*

   All in One **United States and Canada Teaching Resources,** *Section Quiz,* p. 101

Reteach   **L1**
If students need more instruction, have them read this section in the Reading and Vocabulary Study Guide.

   📖 Chapter 1, Section 1, **United States and Canada Reading and Vocabulary Study Guide,** pp. 6–8

Extend   **L3**
To learn more about the geographic features of the United States and Canada, have students complete the *Book Project: Create a Diorama.*

   All in One **United States and Canada Teaching Resources,** *Book Project: Create a Diorama,* pp. 82–84

Answer

Explain The Flathead River flows west because it is west of the Continental Divide.

The Continental Divide
The Rocky Mountains form the continental divide and are the site of several national parks, including Grand Teton National Park in Wyoming (large photo). White-water rafters paddle along Flathead River in Montana, west of the Rockies (small photo).
Explain *In what direction does the Flathead River flow?*

Major Rivers of the United States   The largest river in the United States is the Mississippi River. Its source, or starting point, is in Minnesota. From there, the river flows through the Central Plains to the Gulf of Mexico. Two other major rivers, the Ohio and the Missouri, are tributaries of the Mississippi. A **tributary** (TRIB yoo tehr ee) is a stream or river that flows into a larger river. The Mississippi River system includes hundreds of tributaries and branches. Together they form about 12,000 miles (19,000 kilometers) of navigable water.

The Mighty Mississippi   Water levels tend to rise in the spring when heavy rain combines with melting snow from the mountains. If the soil cannot soak up the excess water, flooding can occur. In 1993, the Upper Mississippi Valley experienced a disastrous flood. It caused nearly 50 deaths and damages totaling more than 15 billion dollars.

People have used the Mississippi River as an important transportation route for hundreds of years. Today, it is one of the busiest waterways in the world. Cargo ships transport many products, including iron, steel, chemicals, and even space rockets.

Look at the United States and Canada: Physical map on page 9 and find the Rocky Mountains. Notice that the Fraser, Columbia, and Colorado rivers form in the Rockies and flow west. Now find the Platte and Missouri rivers. They flow east from the Rockies. This is because the Rockies form the Continental Divide, the boundary that separates rivers flowing to the Pacific Ocean from those flowing to the Atlantic Ocean.

Major Rivers of Canada   The Mackenzie River, Canada's longest, forms in the Rocky Mountains and flows north to the Arctic Ocean. It runs for more than 2,600 miles (4,197 kilometers). Although for most of its course the Mackenzie winds through sparsely populated, dense forest area, it is an important transportation route.

14 United States and Canada

Differentiated Instruction

For Gifted and Talented   **L3**
Have students conduct research on locks and canals, individually or in groups. Ask them to find out why locks and canals are needed to help larger ships navigate the St. Lawrence River. If possible, ask students to find or create a visual representation of a lock system. Have students share their findings with the class.

In the 1880s, steamboats on the Mackenzie took supplies to local trading posts. Today, ships carry energy and mineral resources from the oil and natural gas fields in the region.

Canada's second major river is the St. Lawrence River. It is one of North America's most important transportation routes, flowing from the Great Lakes to the Atlantic Ocean. A system of locks and canals enables large ships to navigate it. From the St. Lawrence, ships can reach the Great Lakes ports that serve the farmland and industries of the region. Thus, the St. Lawrence is an important trade route between the United States and Canada. Millions of tons of cargo move along the St. Lawrence River each year.

✓ Reading Check **Name the five Great Lakes.**

Section 1 Assessment

Key Terms
Review the key terms at the beginning of this section. Use each term in a sentence that explains its meaning.

Target Reading Skill
How did having a purpose for reading help you to understand important ideas in this section?

Comprehension and Critical Thinking
1. (a) Recall Describe the borders of the United States and Canada.
(b) Predict How do you think the climates of Hawaii and Alaska differ?

2. (a) Describe What is the largest mountain system in North America?
(b) Identify Effects How have the physical features of the United States and Canada affected the lives of the people there?
3. (a) Locate Which bodies of water lie on the border between the United States and Canada?
(b) Explain Why are these bodies of water important?
(c) Draw Conclusions Why did many people coming to the United States and Canada hundreds of years ago settle along coastal plains and rivers?

Writing Activity
Suppose that you are on vacation in the United States or Canada. Write a postcard to a friend describing the physical features that you have seen. Before you begin, review the information you recorded in your Taking Notes table.

For: An activity on Mt. McKinley
Visit: PHSchool.com
Web Code: lhd-4101

Objective

Learn how to identify and understand frame of reference.

Prepare to Read

Build Background Knowledge `L2`

Ask students what it might be like if they had to attend school in another country for one week. Have students brainstorm what kinds of things they might experience that they would find unusual or surprising such as the language the classes are taught in, the food served in the cafeteria, and what time school starts and ends. Then explain that these judgments would be based on their frame of reference, or background.

Instruct

Identifying Frame of Reference `L2`

Guided Instruction

■ Read the steps to identify frame of reference as a class and write them on the board.

■ Practice the skill by following the steps on p. 17 as a class. First choose an appropriate title for the boxed text. *(Possible answer: "An Inuit Homeland")* Then identify descriptive parts of the text *(the first two paragraphs)*, and opinions *(the last paragraph)*. Next, list facts about the authors. *(They are tenth-grade students at a high school in Nunavut.)* Finally, suggest how your own frame of reference might make you have a different opinion about Nunavut. *(Possible answer: Because you are not Canadian or Inuit, the creation of Nunavut might not seem as important to you as it does to the authors.)*

■ Ask students to return to the Build Background Knowledge activity, to identify their own frame of reference, and to explain how that frame of reference would affect their opinions about attending school overseas.

Identifying Frame of Reference

"It's a freak storm," Ian e-mailed excitedly to his friends. "Four inches of snow already, and we might get six inches total. It's awful!"

"Awful?" Janet replied. "It's just a few inches. What's the big deal?"

"JUST a few inches?" Ian typed. "This city is paralyzed. Cars are stuck everywhere. Our camping trip this weekend is cancelled. It's a disaster."

Luann responded to both of her friends. "Of course it's a disaster to Ian. He lives in Georgia. No way is the South prepared to deal with a snowstorm in April."

"Well, up here in Quebec, we're not afraid of a little snow!" Janet wrote back.

"Okay, calm down," wrote Luann. "Your opinion depends on what you're used to."

In other words, your opinion depends on your frame of reference.

16 United States and Canada

Learn the Skill

Follow the steps below to understand frame of reference.

1 **Identify the topic being discussed.** Look for evidence that an opinion is being expressed. When people state their opinions, they often reveal information about their frame of reference.

2 **Identify the author's opinion on the issue.** An opinion is what someone believes. It is not a fact, which is something that can be proved.

3 **Identify what you know about the author's background.** Some background factors are age, personality, family, culture, nationality, concerns, and historical era.

4 **Ask how the author's background might have influenced his or her beliefs.** Think about whether the person's opinions would be different if he or she came from a different place, culture, family, or time in history.

Independent Practice

Assign *Skills for Life* and have students complete it individually.

All in One **United States and Canada Teaching Resources,** *Skills for Life,* p. 115

Monitor Progress

Monitor the students doing the *Skills for Life* worksheet, checking to make sure they understand the skills steps.

Practice the Skill

The text in the box on the right comes from Inuit students in Nunavut. The Inuit, a Native American culture group, persuaded the Canadian government to create the territory of Nunavut in 1999. Read what the students wrote just before the creation of their new homeland.

1. This text has no title, but you can give it a title that reflects the main topic. What title would you give it?

2. The students give both description and opinion. Which parts of the text are description, and which are opinion?

3. You already know some facts about the students' background: They are Canadian, and they are Inuit. What else can you discover about the students' background?

4. The students' opinions are shaped by their frame of reference. Explain how your own frame of reference might make you feel differently about Nunavut.

"There are not very many people, but all of us are friends. We share the same culture and language, Inuktitut. You can learn from elders. We help each other. . . .

"[W]e go to school, church, cadets, the hall, and the gym. We play [games], watch T.V., listen to music, play and watch sports (especially hockey), . . . dance, and sleep. We also stay home, visit with our parents, clean, look after children, and try to finish our homework. . . . We eat seal meat, caribou, arctic char, walrus, . . . and also we eat various types of birds. . . .

"Nunavut is independence. The creation of Nunavut means that we, the Inuit, are going to have our own land. . . . It means a lot to us, the Inuit youth. It means making choices for ourselves. We are proud of Nunavut."
—*Grade 10 students at Ataguttaaluk High in Igloolik, a town in central Nunavut, above the Arctic Circle*

Inuit sculptor

Apply the Skill

Think of an issue that you feel strongly about. Describe your own frame of reference, and show how it has influenced your opinion.

Differentiated Instruction

For Special Needs Students L1
Partner special needs students with more proficient students to do Level 1 of the *Identifying Frame of Reference and Point of View* lesson on the Social Studies Skills Tutor CD-ROM together.

When the students feel more confident, they can move onto Level 2 alone.

◉ *Identifying Frame of Reference and Point of View,* **Social Studies Skills Tutor CD-ROM**

Assess and Reteach

Assess Progress L2
Ask students to do the Apply the Skill activity.

Reteach L1
If students are having trouble applying the skill steps, have them review the skill using the interactive Social Studies Skills Tutor CD-ROM.

◉ *Identifying Frame of Reference and Point of View,* **Social Studies Skills Tutor CD-ROM**

Extend L3
Ask students to bring in an editorial or a letter to the editor from a recent newspaper. Working individually or in pairs, have students follow the four steps they have learned in the skills lesson in order to identify the possible frame of reference of the editorial or letter.

Answers
Apply the Skill

Answers will vary, but should reflect an accurate frame of reference (age, nationality, culture, etc.) and show a reasonable influence on the stated opinion.

Section 2
Climate and Vegetation

Objectives

Social Studies

1. Learn what climate zones the United States and Canada have.
2. Identify the natural vegetation zones of the United States and Canada.

Reading/Language Arts

Learn how to make predictions about what you read.

Prepare to Read

Build Background Knowledge [L2]

In this section students will learn about the climate and vegetation of the United States and Canada. Have students preview the headings and visuals of this section with the following question in mind: **What would best describe the climate and vegetation of the region I live in?** Use the Think-Write-Pair-Share participation strategy (TE, p. T36) to share students responses.

Set a Purpose for Reading [L2]

- Preview the Objectives.

- Read each statement in the *Reading Readiness Guide* aloud. Ask students to mark the statements true or false.

- Have students discuss the statements in pairs or groups of four, then mark their worksheets again. Use the Numbered Heads participation strategy (TE, p. T36) to call on students to share their group's perspectives.

  All in One **United States and Canada Teaching Resources,** *Reading Readiness Guide,* p. 103

Vocabulary Builder

Preview Key Terms [L2]

Pronounce each Key Term, then ask the students to say the word with you. Provide a simple explanation such as, "Just as Montana is a state in the United States, Alberta is a province in Canada."

Prepare to Read

Objectives

In this section you will
1. Learn what climate zones the United States and Canada have.
2. Identify the natural vegetation zones of the United States and Canada.

Taking Notes

As you read the section, look for details about climate and vegetation. Copy the chart below and write each detail under the correct heading.

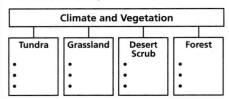

```
                  Climate and Vegetation
        ┌──────────┬──────────┬──────────┬──────────┐
     Tundra    Grassland    Desert     Forest
                             Scrub
      •           •           •           •
      •           •           •           •
      •           •           •           •
```

Target Reading Skill

Predict Making predictions about your text helps you set a purpose for reading and remember what you read. Before you begin, preview the section by looking at the headings, photographs, and maps. Then predict what the text might discuss about climate and vegetation. As you read the section, connect what you read to your prediction. If what you learn doesn't support your prediction, change it.

Key Terms

- **tundra** (TUN druh) *n.* a cold, dry region covered with snow for more than half the year
- **permafrost** (PUR muh frawst) *n.* a permanently frozen layer of ground below the top layer of soil
- **prairie** (PREHR ee) *n.* a region of flat or rolling land covered with grasses
- **province** (PRAH vins) *n.* a political division of land in Canada

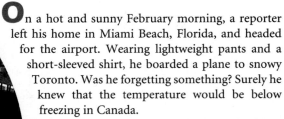

On a hot and sunny February morning, a reporter left his home in Miami Beach, Florida, and headed for the airport. Wearing lightweight pants and a short-sleeved shirt, he boarded a plane to snowy Toronto. Was he forgetting something? Surely he knew that the temperature would be below freezing in Canada.

He did, indeed, know all about the bitter cold that would greet him when he got off the plane. But he was going to research an article on Toronto's tunnels and underground malls. He wanted to find out whether people could really visit hotels, restaurants, and shops without having to go outside and brave the harsh Canadian winter.

A climate-controlled shopping center in Toronto, Ontario

18 United States and Canada

Target Reading Skill [L2]

Predict Point out the Target Reading Skill. Tell students that predicting is making an educated guess. Remind students that a prediction can be revised at any time if they discover it is not accurate.

Model the skill by pointing out the title of the map on page 20 of the Student Edition. Make a prediction about what students will learn from the map. (*I predict that students will learn about the patterns of tornadoes in the United States.*)

Give students *Preview and Predict.* Have them complete the activity in groups.

All in One **United States and Canada Teaching Resources,** *Preview and Predict,* p. 111

Climate Zones

Climate is weather patterns that an area experiences over a long period of time. Climate zones in the United States and Canada range from a desert climate to a polar climate. Factors such as latitude, or a location's distance north or south of the Equator, mountains, and oceans all affect the climates found in different regions.

Climates of Canada   Generally, the farther a location is from the Equator, the colder its climate. Look at the climate regions map on page 5 of the Regional Overview. Notice that much of Canada lies well north of the 40° N line of latitude, a long way from the Equator. Therefore, much of Canada is very cold!

Ocean Effects   The ocean affects Canada's climates, too. Water heats up and cools down more slowly than land. Winds blowing across water on to land tend to warm the land in winter and cool the land in summer. Therefore, areas that are near an ocean generally have milder climates. Also, winds blowing across the ocean pick up moisture. When these winds blow over land, they drop the moisture in the form of rain or snow.

Being a great distance from the ocean also affects climate. Inland areas often have climate extremes. Find Winnipeg, in Canada's Interior Plains, on the climate map. Winter temperatures here are very cold, averaging around 0°F (−18°C). Yet summer temperatures run between 70°F and 90°F (20°C and 32°C).

Mountain Effects   Mountains are another factor that influence climate. Winds blowing from the Pacific Ocean rise as they meet mountain ranges in the west. As they rise, the winds cool and drop their moisture. The air is dry by the time it reaches the other side of the mountains, and it warms up as it returns to lower altitudes. This is called the Chinook effect. The area on the side of the mountains away from the wind is in a rain shadow. A rain shadow is an area on the dry, sheltered side of a mountain, which receives little rainfall.

■ Graph Skills

Located in different climate regions, Miami, Florida, and Toronto, Canada, experience very different average temperatures. **Identify**   In which month does Miami experience the coolest temperatures? Which month is the coolest in Toronto?
Compare   Which month has the least difference between the average temperature in Miami and Toronto?

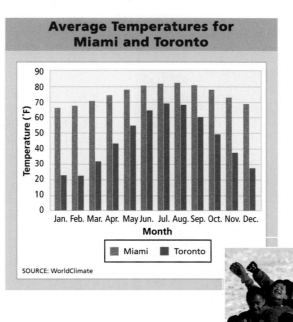

Average Temperatures for Miami and Toronto

SOURCE: WorldClimate

Legend: Miami, Toronto

Chapter 1 Section 2 **19**

Vocabulary Builder

Use the information below to teach students this section's high-use words.

High-Use Word	Definition and Sample Sentence
ideal, p. 22	*adj.* perfect The amount of snow on the hill made it **ideal** for skiing.
support, p. 23	*v.* to promote or provide for The income from the bake sale helped **support** the chess club.

Guided Instruction (continued)

■ Have students describe the climate of the United States east of the Great Plains. *(This part of the country has a continental climate with cold winters and warm summers in the north, and mild winters and long, hot summers in the south.)*

■ Ask students to use the map on this page to determine the line of latitude closest to your area. Then ask students to think about the words they used to describe the area's climate in the Build Background Knowledge activity at the beginning of this section. How might those climate characteristics be related to the distance of the area from the Equator? *(Answers will vary according to region, but students should be able to make the correlation that areas closer to the Equator are generally hotter than those farther away from it).*

Independent Practice

Assign *Guided Reading and Review*.

All in One **United States and Canada Teaching Resources,** *Guided Reading and Review,* p. 104

Monitor Progress

As students work on the *Guided Reading and Review*, circulate to check their answers and comprehension of the section.

Answers

✓ Reading Check oceans, mountains, and proximity to the Equator

MAP MASTER Skills Activity **Explain** The area has more tornadoes each year than other parts of the United States. **Draw Conclusions** The Plains areas do not have many hills or mountains to stall or impede the tornadoes.

Go Online PHSchool.com Students may practice their map skills by using the interactive online version of this map.

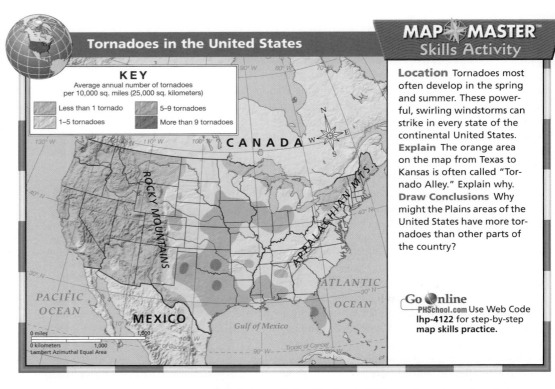

Tornadoes in the United States

MAP MASTER Skills Activity

KEY
Average annual number of tornadoes per 10,000 sq. miles (25,000 sq. kilometers)

- Less than 1 tornado
- 1–5 tornadoes
- 5–9 tornadoes
- More than 9 tornadoes

Location Tornadoes most often develop in the spring and summer. These powerful, swirling windstorms can strike in every state of the continental United States. **Explain** The orange area on the map from Texas to Kansas is often called "Tornado Alley." Explain why. **Draw Conclusions** Why might the Plains areas of the United States have more tornadoes than other parts of the country?

Go Online PHSchool.com Use Web Code lhp-4122 for step-by-step map skills practice.

A tornado produces high winds and flying debris that can cause heavy damage to structures in its path.

Climates of the United States Location also influences climate. On the climate map on page 5, notice that Alaska lies north of the 60° N line of latitude. Far from the Equator, Alaska is cold for much of the year. Now find Hawaii and the southern tip of Florida. They lie near or within the tropics, the area between the 23 1/2° N and 23 1/2° S lines of latitude. There, it is almost always warm.

The Pacific Ocean and mountains affect climate in the western United States. Wet winds from the ocean drop their moisture before they cross the mountains. As a result, the eastern sections of California and Arizona are semiarid or desert. Death Valley, which is located there, has the lowest average rainfall in the country—about 2 inches (5 centimeters) a year.

East of the Great Plains, the country has continental climates. In the north, summers are warm and winters are cold and snowy. In the south, summers tend to be long and hot, while winters are mild. The coastal regions of these areas sometimes experience violent weather. In summer and fall, hurricanes and tropical storms develop in the Atlantic Ocean.

✓ Reading Check What factors affect climate?

20 United States and Canada

Differentiated Instruction

For Gifted and Talented Students **L3**
Display *Color Transparency USC 24: United States and Canada: Population Distribution.* Briefly review how to read the map. Then have students compare it with the climate map on p. 20 and identify

what climate zones are the most densely populated.

📖 **United States and Canada Transparencies,** *Color Transparency USC 22: United States and Canada: Physical and Political (Base); Color Transparency USC 24: Population Distribution (Overlay)*

Natural Vegetation Zones

Climate in the United States and Canada helps produce four major kinds of natural vegetation, or plant life. As you can see on the United States and Canada: Vegetation map on page 22, these are tundra, grassland, desert scrub, and forest.

Northern Tundras   The **tundra,** found in the far north, is a cold, dry region that is covered with snow for more than half the year. The Arctic tundra contains **permafrost,** a layer of permanently frozen soil. During the short, cool summer, the soil above the permafrost thaws. Mosses, grasses, and bright wildflowers grow there. Life is hard in the tundra. However, some Inuits (IN oo its), a native people of Canada and Alaska, once called Eskimos, live there. They make a living by fishing and hunting.

Grasslands   Grasslands are regions of flat or rolling land covered with grasses. They are located in areas where there is enough rain to support grasses but not enough to support forests. In North America, grasslands are called **prairies.** The world's largest prairie lies in the Central and Great Plains of North America. It stretches from the American central states into the Canadian provinces of Alberta, Saskatchewan (sas KACH uh wahn), and Manitoba. These three provinces are sometimes called the Prairie Provinces. **A province** is a political division of Canada, much like one of our states. Look at the temperate grasslands region of the United States and Canada: Vegetation map on page 22 to locate the prairies, or plains areas, of the United States and Canada.

Predict
Based on what you've read so far, is your prediction on target? If not, revise or change your prediction now.

Two Vegetation Zones
The natural vegetation of the northern tundra (large photo) differs greatly from the natural vegetation of the grasslands (smaller photo).
Draw Conclusions *How does climate affect the vegetation that grows in the tundra and grasslands?*

Predict As a follow up, ask students to answer the Target Reading skill question in the Student Edition. *(Answers will vary. Students should be able to recognize whether their original prediction is accurate or needs to be revised.)*

Natural Vegetation Zones   L2

Guided Instruction

- **Vocabulary Builder** Clarify the high-use words **ideal** and **support** before reading.

- Read about tundras, grasslands, desert scrub, and forests in Natural Vegetation Zones. Circulate to make sure that students can answer the Reading Check question.

- Have students study the map. Then ask them to list all of the vegetation zones of the United States and Canada. *(tropical rain forest, mixed forest, deciduous forest, coniferous forest, Mediterranean forest, tropical savanna, temperate grassland, desert scrub, desert, tundra, ice cap)*

- Ask students **Why do you think few plants grow in the tundra?** *(Possible answer: Snow covers the ground for more than half the year, and permafrost, or permanently frozen soil, does not support growth.)*

- Ask students **Why do you think few people live in the tundra?** *(Possible answer: The region is very cold and crops cannot be grown in the frozen soil.)*

Differentiated Instruction

For Special Needs Students   L1
Have students listen to the recorded version of the section on the Student Edition on Audio CD. Pause the CD several times to discuss correlations between the audio text and the photos and maps on these pages.

⊙ Chapter 1, Section 2, **United States and Canada Student Edition on Audio CD**

For Gifted and Talented   L3
Have students learn more about Canada's national parks by completing the *Enrichment* activity. Students should read the passage and then select a project to complete from the list provided. Students should present their projects to the class.

All in One **United States and Canada Teaching Resources,** *Enrichment,* p.114

Answers

Draw Conclusions Few types of vegetation grow in the harsh climate of the tundra, and the climate of the grasslands can support grasses but not forests.

Guided Instruction (continued)

- Have students describe the location of the Great Basin, and identify one kind of animal that can thrive in the Great Basin. (*The Great Basin is located between the Rocky Mountains and the Sierras. Sheep graze on the area's vegetation.*)

- Ask students to name Canada's Prairie Provinces. (*Alberta, Manitoba, and Saskatchewan*) Then have them explain why they are called the Prairie Provinces. (*The world's largest prairie stretches into the provinces.*)

- Tell students that forests are an important type of vegetation. Ask students whether coniferous or deciduous forests are more prevalent in your area. Have the class brainstorm names of different kinds of deciduous trees. (*Answers will vary. Students may know the names of some deciduous trees, such as oak, birch, ash, willow, or others.*)

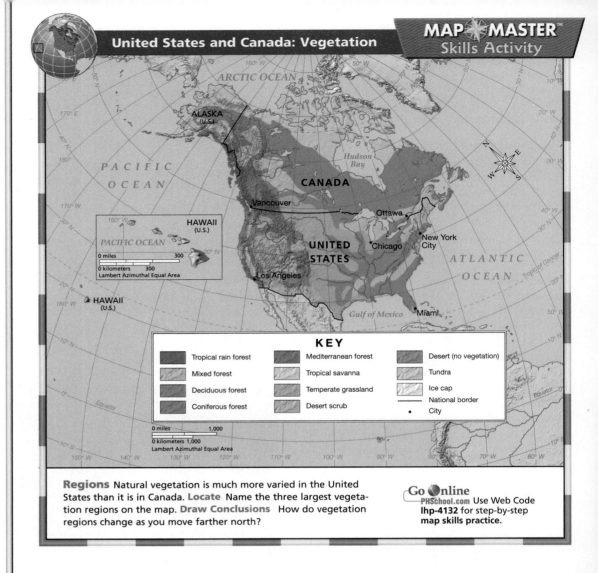

MAP MASTER Skills Activity

United States and Canada: Vegetation

KEY

- Tropical rain forest
- Mixed forest
- Deciduous forest
- Coniferous forest
- Mediterranean forest
- Tropical savanna
- Temperate grassland
- Desert scrub
- Desert (no vegetation)
- Tundra
- Ice cap
- — National border
- • City

Regions Natural vegetation is much more varied in the United States than it is in Canada. **Locate** Name the three largest vegetation regions on the map. **Draw Conclusions** How do vegetation regions change as you move farther north?

Go Online PHSchool.com Use Web Code lhp-4132 for step-by-step map skills practice.

When pioneers first encountered the prairies in what is now the Midwest, they described it as "a sea of grass." Today, farmers grow fields of corn and soybeans there. Farther west, the Great Plains receive less rainfall. Therefore, only short grasses will grow. These grasses are ideal for grazing cattle. The land is also suitable for growing wheat. The Prairie Provinces, too, have many wheat farms and cattle ranches.

22 United States and Canada

Answers

MAP MASTER Skills Activity Locate coniferous forest, temperate grassland, and tundra **Draw Conclusions** There are primarily tundra, mixed forest, and coniferous forest regions as you move farther north.

Go Online PHSchool.com Students may practice their map skills by using the interactive online version of this map.

Skills for Life — Skills Mini Lesson

Analyzing Images ▢ L2

1. Teach the skill by telling students that images supply important information. Tell them to study images carefully and read their captions. While studying images students should ask themselves the following questions: Who or what is the image showing? Where and when does the scene take place? What feeling do I get from it? Why do I think this image was created?

2. Help students practice the skill by helping them answer these questions as they look at the larger photo on page 21. (*The image shows a polar bear in the northern tundra; student answers will vary as to how the image makes them feel and why they think it was created.*)

3. Have students apply the skill by answering the questions as they study the smaller image on page 21.

Desert Scrub With little rainfall, desert and semiarid regions have limited vegetation. What plants there are have adapted to drought conditions or survive through their deep root systems. The Great Basin, a large, dry region between the Rocky Mountains and the Sierra Nevada in the United States, is one example of a desert region. It covers about 190,000 square miles (492,000 square kilometers) of the West and includes Death Valley. The majority of Nevada and western Utah lie within the Great Basin.

The Sierras block the Great Basin from moisture-bearing winds that come off the Pacific Ocean. Thus, the entire region is in a rain shadow. With annual rainfall of only six to twelve inches (15 to 30 centimeters), the basin cannot support large numbers of people. But, many sheep graze on the area's shrubs.

For many years, the Great Basin was an obstacle that delayed the development of the West, because conditions made it difficult for explorers to cross it. Many people sought alternate routes around the Great Basin as they headed west during the California Gold Rush in 1849.

Life in the Desert
Despite little rain and scorching heat, hundreds of plants and animals, such as the scorpion below, live in the desert. **Draw Conclusions** *How might these plants and animals have adapted to the harsh desert environment?*

Independent Practice

Have students create the Taking Notes graphic organizer on a blank piece of paper. Ask them to fill in the climate and vegetation information for "Tundra" and "Grassland." Display the *Tree Map/Flow Chart* transparency and model how to fill in a few details to get them started. Then have students complete the graphic organizer by filling in the "Desert Scrub" and "Forest" sections.

📖 **United States and Canada Transparencies,** *Transparency B3: Tree Map/Flow Chart*

Monitor Progress

■ Show *Section Reading Support Transparency USC 44* and ask students to check their graphic organizers individually. Go over key concepts and clarify key vocabulary as needed.

📖 **United States and Canada Transparencies,** *Section Reading Support Transparency USC 44*

■ Tell students to fill in the last column of the *Reading Readiness Guide*. Probe for what they learned that confirms or invalidates each statement.

All in One United States and Canada Teaching Resources, *Reading Readiness Guide,* p. 103

Differentiated Instruction

For Advanced Readers ⬛3

To get a sense of what it might be like to experience a forest in Canada, have students read *Hatchet* and discuss what resources the forest offered to Brian when he was stranded there.

All in One United States and Canada Teaching Resources, *Hatchet,* pp. 122–125

For English Language Learners ⬛2

Pair native English-speaking students with English learners and have them read *Hatchet* together. Encourage students to answer each other's questions about the material. Circulate and ask students questions about the material to be sure they understand what they have read.

All in One United States and Canada Teaching Resources, *Hatchet,* pp. 122–125

Answer

Draw Conclusions Possible answer: They might have adapted by finding ways to store water and protect themselves from the heat of the sun.

Assess and Reteach

Assess Progress L2
Have students complete the Section Assessment Administer the *Section Quiz.*

 United States and Canada Teaching Resources, *Section Quiz,* p. 105

Reteach L1
If students need more instruction, have them read this section in the Reading and Vocabulary Study Guide.

Chapter **1**, Section 2, **United States and Canada Reading and Vocabulary Study Guide,** pp. 9–11

Extend L3
Students can extend their knowledge of climate and its effects on your local environment by working in teams to complete the *Book Project: Set Up a Weather Station.*

 United States and Canada Teaching Resources, *Book Project: Set Up a Weather Station,* pp. 73–75

Answers

✓ **Reading Check** tundra, grassland, desert scrub, forest

Section 2 Assessment

Key Terms
Students' sentences should reflect knowledge of each Key Term.

⟳ **Target Reading Skill**
Answers will vary, but students' predictions should involve learning about the climate and vegetation of the United States and Canada.

Comprehension and Critical Thinking
1. (a) The climate on the Pacific coast is generally mild and rainy. The climate just east of the Rocky Mountains is dryer and warmer. Much of the east coast has a continental climate with warm summers and cold winters. Northern Canada has a colder climate than much of the United States.
(b) Water heats up and cools down more slowly than land, making coastal climates more moderate. Winds pick up moisture as they move across the water, bringing more rain to some coastal areas. **(c)** Vancouver, close to the Pacific coast, has mild temperatures all year long. Winnipeg, which is

inland, has more extreme temperatures and winters get very cold.

2. (a) It stretches from the American central states into the Canadian provinces of Alberta, Saskatchewan, and Manitoba. **(b)** The tundra is extremely cold, so very little can grow there. The prairies have a much warmer climate, more rainfall, and a great deal of natural vegetation. **(c)** The prairies support numerous crops, so many people there make their living as farmers. The natural grasses of the prairies are ideal for cattle ranching.

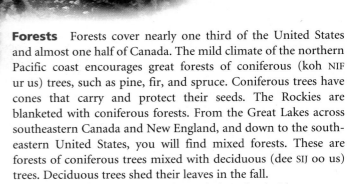

Forests Forests cover nearly one third of the United States and almost one half of Canada. The mild climate of the northern Pacific coast encourages great forests of coniferous (koh NIF ur us) trees, such as pine, fir, and spruce. Coniferous trees have cones that carry and protect their seeds. The Rockies are blanketed with coniferous forests. From the Great Lakes across southeastern Canada and New England, and down to the southeastern United States, you will find mixed forests. These are forests of coniferous trees mixed with deciduous (dee SIJ oo us) trees. Deciduous trees shed their leaves in the fall.

One of Canada's best-known symbols is the deciduous sugar maple tree. The sugar maple leaf appears on Canada's flag. In addition, sugar maples produce a sweet sap that can be made into maple syrup and maple sugar—two Canadian specialties.

An autumn landscape in the Charlevoix region of Quebec, Canada

✓ **Reading Check** **Name the four major kinds of natural vegetation in the United States and Canada.**

 ## Section 2 Assessment

Key Terms
Review the key terms at the beginning of this section. Use each term in a sentence that explains its meaning.

⟳ **Target Reading Skill**
What did you predict about this section? How did your prediction guide your reading?

Comprehension and Critical Thinking
1. (a) Recall Describe the major climate zones of the United States and Canada.

(b) Summarize How do oceans influence climate?
(c) Generalize What geographic features might lead someone to settle in Vancouver rather than in Winnipeg?
2. (a) Locate Where is the largest prairie in the world?
(b) Infer Why do more people live in the prairies than in the tundra?
(c) Identify Effects How does the vegetation of the prairies affect economic activity there?

Writing Activity
Describe the climate zones you would pass through if you traveled from northwestern Canada to the southeastern United States.

For: An activity on Florida's Everglades
Visit: PHSchool.com
Web Code: lhd-4102

Writing Activity
Use the *Rubric for Assessing a Writing Assignment* to evaluate students' descriptions.

United States and Canada Teaching Resources, *Rubric for Assessing a Writing Assignment,* p. 127

Go Online Typing in the Web code when prompted will bring students directly to detailed instructions for this activity.

Section 3 — Resources and Land Use

Prepare to Read

Objectives
In this section you will
1. Learn about the major resources of the United States.
2. Find out about the major resources of Canada.

Taking Notes
As you read the section, look for details about the resources of the United States and Canada. Copy the table below and write each detail under the correct subject heading.

Resource	United States	Canada
Farmland		
Water		
Energy and minerals		
Forests		

Target Reading Skill

Preview and Ask Questions Before you read this section, preview the headings and photographs to see what the section is about. Write one or two questions that will help you understand or remember something important in the section. Then read to answer your questions.

Key Terms
- **alluvial soil** (uh LOO vee ul soyl) *n.* fertile topsoil left by a river, especially after a flood
- **agribusiness** (AG ruh biz niz) *n.* a large company that runs huge farms
- **hydroelectricity** (hy droh ee lek TRIH suh tee) *n.* electric power produced by moving water
- **fossil fuel** (FAHS ul FYOO ul) *n.* a fuel formed over millions of years from animal and plant remains

Surrounded by majestic redwood forests, Carlotta, California, has little more than a gas station and a general store. Yet on one day in September 1996, police arrested more than 1,000 people there. Was Carlotta filled with outlaws like some old Wild West town? No, but it was the scene of a showdown. A logging company wanted to cut down some of the oldest redwood trees in the world. Protesters wanted to preserve the forest and the animals that live there. Both sides believed in the importance of natural resources. But they disagreed strongly about how to use them. As in Carlotta, people all over North America use their natural resources for recreation, industry, and energy.

Redwood National Park, California

Chapter 1 Section 3 **25**

Target Reading Skill

Preview and Ask Questions Ask students to focus on the Target Reading Skill. Tell them that they can preview a section to see what they will learn about and create questions that will help them remember important information.

Model previewing and asking questions using page 26. Have students read the page heading and identify what the map shows to preview the page. Tell them they can use this information to write a question such as, "What are the major resources of the United States?" Have students read the subsection, and then reinforce the skill by modeling the answer to the questions.

Give students *Preview and Ask Questions.* Have them complete the activity in groups.

All in One **United States and Canada Teaching Resources,** *Preview and Ask Questions,* p. 112

Section 3
Step-by-Step Instruction

Objectives
Social Studies
1. Learn about the major resources of the United States.
2. Find out about the major resources of Canada.

Reading/Language Arts
Learn how to preview and ask questions to see what a reading selection is about.

Prepare to Read

Build Background Knowledge `L2`
Tell students that in this section they will learn about the natural resources that are available in the United States and Canada. Have students preview the headings and visuals in the section with the following question in mind: **How are the resources of the United States and Canada similar?** Use the Idea Wave participation strategy (TE, p. T35) to solicit answers.

Set a Purpose for Reading `L2`
- Preview the Objectives.
- Read each statement in the *Reading Readiness Guide* aloud. Ask students to mark the statements true or false.
- Have students discuss the statements in pairs or groups of four, then mark their worksheets again. Use the Numbered Heads participation strategy (TE, p. T36) to call on students to share their group's perspectives.

All in One **United States and Canada Teaching Resources,** *Reading Readiness Guide,* p. 107

Vocabulary Builder
Preview Key Terms `L2`
Pronounce each Key Term, then ask the students to say the word with you. Provide a simple explanation such as, "Hydroelectricity comes from dams built on rivers. Hoover Dam in the Colorado River supplies much of the electric power for portions of the United States and Canada."

Instruct

Resources of the United States L2

Guided Instruction

- **Vocabulary Builder** Clarify the high-use words **abundant** and **generate** before reading.

- Read Resources of the United States using the Paragraph Shrinking strategy (TE, p. T34).

- Ask students to explain why they think soil is considered an important natural resource of the United States. *(Possible answer: Without fertile soil, Americans would not be able to grow the crops needed to feed the people of the United States and to sell to other countries to help our economy.)*

- Lead a discussion about what life would be like if the United States did not have access to so much water. *(An absence of water would affect how much Americans were able to drink, make it difficult for farmers to raise crops, make it hard for factories to operate, decrease routes of transportation, and eliminate hydroelectricity as an available energy source.)*

Answers

MAP MASTER Skills Activity **List** The two countries share all of the resources mentioned in the key except for bauxite and phosphates, which only the United States has.

Draw Conclusions Canada's location between the Pacific and Atlantic oceans allows the country to export goods by sea, and its long border with the United States allows for easy trade between the two countries.

Resources of the United States

Native Americans, pioneers, and explorers in North America knew centuries ago that it was a land of plenty. Abundant resources helped to build two of the world's leading economies.

Farmland Both the Midwest and the South have rich, dark soils that are suitable for farming. Along the Mississippi and other river valleys are **alluvial** (uh LOO vee ul) **soils**, the fertile topsoil left by a river after a flood. Until the 1900s, most American farms were owned by families. Since then, large companies have bought many family farms. Southern California's Imperial Valley has vast vegetable fields operated by agribusinesses. An **agribusiness** is a large company that runs huge farms.

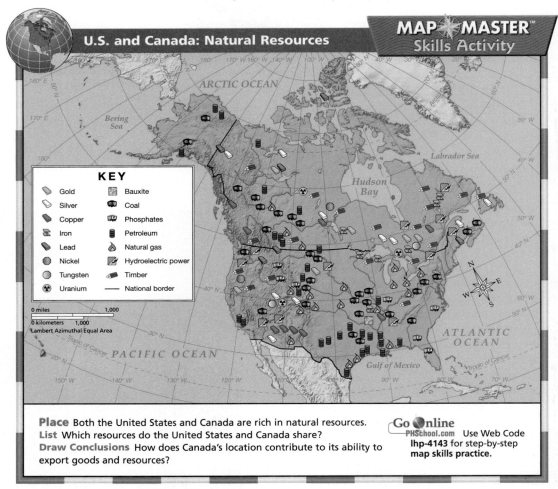

MAP MASTER Skills Activity

U.S. and Canada: Natural Resources

KEY
- Gold
- Silver
- Copper
- Iron
- Lead
- Nickel
- Tungsten
- Uranium
- Bauxite
- Coal
- Phosphates
- Petroleum
- Natural gas
- Hydroelectric power
- Timber
- National border

0 miles 1,000
0 kilometers 1,000
Lambert Azimuthal Equal Area

Place Both the United States and Canada are rich in natural resources.
List Which resources do the United States and Canada share?
Draw Conclusions How does Canada's location contribute to its ability to export goods and resources?

Go Online PHSchool.com Use Web Code lhp-4143 for step-by-step map skills practice.

26 United States and Canada

Vocabulary Builder

Use the information below to teach students this section's high-use words.

High-Use Word	Definition and Sample Sentence
abundant, p. 26	*adj.* plentiful The perfect weather allowed the farmer to grow an **abundant** crop of corn.
generate, p. 27	*v.* produce The energy **generated** by the battery powered the flashlight.
suitable, p. 29	*adj.* appropriate, fitting The gym was a **suitable** place to hold the dance.
harness, p. 29	*v.* to use or control The dam **harnessed** the power of the waterfall.

Water Water is a vital resource. People need water to drink and to grow crops. Factories rely on water for many industrial processes, including cooling machinery. Both industry and farmers use rivers to transport goods. The Mississippi, Ohio, and Missouri rivers are important shipping routes.

Water is used for other purposes, too. Dams along many rivers produce **hydroelectricity** (hy droh ee lek TRIH suh tee), or electric power generated by moving water. The Grand Coulee (KOO lee) Dam on the Columbia River in the state of Washington produces more hydroelectricity than any other dam in the United States.

An irrigation system watering several fields on a California farm

Forests People have claimed that before Europeans arrived, a squirrel could leap from one tree to another all the way from the Atlantic Coast to the Mississippi River. That is no longer true, but America's forests are still an important resource. Large forests extend across the Pacific Northwest, the South, the Appalachians, and areas around the Great Lakes. They produce lumber, wood pulp for paper, and fine wood for furniture.

Energy and Mineral Resources The United States produces and consumes more fossil fuels than any other country. **Fossil fuels** are sources of energy that formed from animal and plant remains. Petroleum, natural gas, and coal are all fossil fuels. Although the United States imports most of its oil from other countries, the biggest oil reserves in North America are along the northern coast of Alaska. A pipeline carries oil from the wells in Prudhoe Bay to the port of Valdez in the south. From here, giant tankers carry the oil away to be refined.

The Trans-Alaska Pipeline Workers prepare a section of the 800-mile (1,280-kilometer) pipeline for welding. **Identify Effects** *How did the construction of the Trans-Alaska Pipeline produce growth for both the population and the economy of Alaska?*

■ Direct students' attention to the map on page 26, and ask them to identify the major products and resources of Alaska. *(petroleum and coal)*

■ Ask students to list the United States' energy and mineral resources. *(Energy resources—petroleum, natural gas, coal, oil; mineral resources—copper, gold, iron ore, lead)*

Skills Mini Lesson

Making Generalizations L2

1. Teach the skill by explaining to students that a generalization is a conclusion drawn from specific facts and applied to a broader situation.

2. Have students practice the skill by reading the text under the heading Water on this page. Point out that the first sentence is a generalization. Then point out that the facts in the rest of the paragraph and in the next paragraph support this generalization.

3. Have students apply the skill by reading the text under the heading Energy and Mineral Resources. Have them make a generalization based on what they read. Then have them write down the sentences from the reading that support their generalizations.

Answer

Identify Effects Workers needed to build and maintain the pipeline may have increased the population of Alaska. The pipeline brings both income and jobs to Alaska, which aids the economy.

Independent Practice

Have students create the Taking Notes graphic organizer on a blank piece of paper and ask them to record details about the resources of the United States. Model how to choose details by selecting one detail and recording it in the correct column.

Monitor Progress

As students fill in the graphic organizer, circulate and make sure students are choosing the correct details. Help students as needed.

↺ Target Reading Skill   L2

Preview and Ask Questions As a follow up, ask students to perform the Target Reading Skill activity in the student edition. *(Students should ask a question that reflects important information from the paragraph, such as "Why is coal a useful natural resource?")*

Preview and Ask Questions
Ask yourself a question about the paragraph at the right.

Natural Gas Natural gas is a mixture of gases found beneath Earth's surface. To be usable, natural gas must be processed after it is removed from the ground. Its major use is as a fuel. Natural gas heats many homes in the United States. Large gas fields can be found in the Texas Panhandle, Louisiana, and Alaska. Natural gas can be transported by pipeline or in specially designed tanker ships.

Coal Coal is another important fossil fuel. Many power plants burn coal to produce electricity. It is also used to produce steel, as well as to heat and power industrial facilities. The United States has about 2,500 coal mines, totaling nearly 25 percent of the world's coal reserves. Over the past 30 years, modern mining equipment has nearly tripled the productivity of these mines. Wyoming, Kentucky, West Virginia, and Pennsylvania are the main coal-producing states in the country.

Mining In addition, the United States has valuable deposits of copper, gold, iron ore, and lead. Mining accounts for a small percentage of the country's economy and employs less than one percent of its workers. But these minerals are very important to other industries and have fueled industrial expansion.

✓ **Reading Check** **Why is water an important natural resource?**

Mining Machinery
A coal miner uses a mining machine to dig into the face of a coal deposit. **Analyze** *Why is coal such an important resource in the United States?*

28 United States and Canada

Differentiated Instruction

For Gifted and Talented   L3

Have students conduct Internet or library research to find out the major exports of the United States. Then have them look at the map on page 26 to find out which states produce these products or resources related to the products. Have them create a table showing their findings.

For Less Proficient Readers   L1

Have students complete the *Reading a Natural Resources Map* activity to help them read the map on page 26.

All in One **United States and Canada Teaching Resources,** *Reading a Natural Resources Map,* p. 121

Answers

✓ **Reading Check** Water is an important natural resource because it is needed to drink, grow crops, cool moving parts in industrial processes, and transport goods by ship.

Analyze Energy gained from coal supports industry in the United States.

Resources of Canada

Canada's first European settlers earned their living as fur trappers, loggers, fishers, and farmers. Today, the economic picture has changed. Less than five percent of Canada's workers earn their living in these ways.

Farmland Less than 10 percent of Canada's land is suitable for farming. Most is located in the Prairie Provinces. This region produces most of Canada's wheat and beef. The St. Lawrence Lowlands are another major agricultural region. This area produces grains, milk, vegetables, and fruits.

Water Canada has more lakes than any other country in the world. About nine percent of the world's fresh water is in Canada. Before the first railroads were built in the 1800s, the only way to reach some parts of the country was by water. Today, the St. Lawrence and Mackenzie rivers serve as important shipping routes.

Minerals and Energy Resources The Canadian Shield contains much of Canada's mineral wealth. Most of the nation's iron ore comes from mines near the Quebec-Newfoundland border. The region also has large deposits of gold, silver, zinc, copper, and uranium. The Prairie Provinces, particularly Alberta, have large oil and natural gas deposits.

Canada harnesses the rivers of Quebec Province to make hydroelectricity. These rivers generate enough hydroelectric power that some of it can be sold to the northeastern United States.

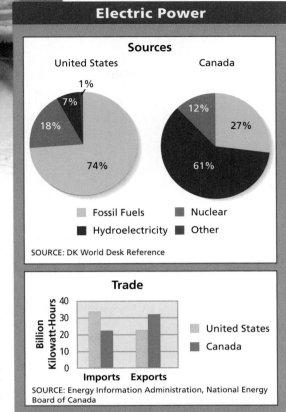

Electric Power

Sources

United States

- 1%
- 7%
- 18%
- 74%

Canada

- 12%
- 27%
- 61%

Fossil Fuels ■ Nuclear
Hydroelectricity ■ Other

SOURCE: DK World Desk Reference

Trade

Billion Kilowatt-Hours: 0, 10, 20, 30, 40

Imports Exports

United States ■ Canada

SOURCE: Energy Information Administration, National Energy Board of Canada

■ Chart Skills

Both the United States and Canada use fossil fuels to produce electricity. Fossil fuels are nonrenewable resources, meaning that once used they are not easily replaced. The United States and Canada also make use of renewable resources such as the hydroelectricity produced by the dam above. **Name** What energy source produces the largest percentage of Canada's electricity? **Analyze** Which nation is more dependent on the other for its energy? Explain.

Chapter 1 Section 3 **29**

Background: Global Perspectives

Canadian Inventions If necessity is the mother of invention, the world can thank Canada's northerly climate and abundant natural resources for many practical and familiar innovations. For example, kerosene, snowmobiles, and snow blowers all appeared first in Canada. Canada also lays claim to the McIntosh variety of apple.

Assess and Reteach

Assess Progress L2
Have students complete the Section Assessment. Administer the *Section Quiz*.

All in One **United States and Canada Teaching Resources,** *Section Quiz,* p. 109

Reteach L1
If students need more instruction, have them read this section in the Reading and Vocabulary Study Guide.

📖 Chapter 1, Section 3, **United States and Canada Reading and Vocabulary Study Guide,** pp. 12–14

Extend L3
Have students work in groups to complete the *Small Group Activity: Creating Travel Posters for National Parks.*

All in One **United States and Canada Teaching Resources,** *Small Group Activity: Creating Travel Posters for National Parks,* pp. 116–119

Answers

✓ **Reading Check** The Canadian Shield contains many mineral resources, including iron ore, gold, silver, zinc, copper, and uranium.

Section 3 Assessment

Key Terms
Students' sentences should reflect knowledge of each Key Term.

🔲 **Target Reading Skill**
Students' questions should reflect that they previewed the section and identified important information.

Comprehension and Critical Thinking
1. (a) The major natural resources of the United States include fertile soil, water, energy and mineral resources, and forests. **(b)** Because the United States is rich in many energy resources, the country is able to both provide them to its residents and sell them to other countries at a profit. **(c)** Possible answer: A country with few natural resources would have to find a way to buy the resources it needed from other countries.

2. (a) Less than 10 percent of Canada's land can be used for farming. **(b)** Canada uses its water resources as major shipping routes and to generate hydroelectricity. **(c)** The United States and Canada are located on the same continent, and share many physical features,

Tugboats tow huge booms, or lines of connected floating logs, harvested from Canada's forests.

Forests With almost half its land covered in forests, Canada is a leading producer and exporter of timber products. These products include lumber, paper, plywood, and wood pulp. The climate in British Columbia produces Canada's densest tall-timber forests. Large amounts of rain and a long growing season contribute to the growth of large evergreens with hard wood ideal for construction lumber. The provinces of Ontario and Quebec also produce large amounts of timber.

✓ **Reading Check** What resources are found in the Canadian Shield?

 Section 3 Assessment

Key Terms
Review the key terms at the beginning of this section. Use each term in a sentence that explains its meaning.

🔲 **Target Reading Skill**
What questions did you ask that helped you to learn and remember something from this section?

Comprehension and Critical Thinking
1. (a) List Describe the major natural resources of the United States.

(b) Explain How have energy resources shaped the economy and the standard of living of the United States?
(c) Infer What economic challenges might a country with few natural resources face?
2. (a) Note How much of Canada's land can be used for farming?
(b) Summarize How is water used as a resource in Canada?
(c) Compare Based on what you know about the physical geography of the two countries, in what ways do you think the resources are similar?

Writing Activity
What do you think is the most important resource in the United States and Canada? Write a paragraph explaining your choice.

Writing Tip Be sure to include examples, details, facts, and reasons that support the main idea of your paragraph.

30 United States and Canada

including the Great Lakes, the Interior and Great Plains, and the Rocky Mountains. Thus, the two countries have many similar resources.

Writing Activity
Use *Rubric for Assessing a Writing Assignment* to evaluate students' paragraphs.

All in One **United States and Canada Teaching Resources,** *Rubric for Assessing a Writing Assignment,* p. 127

Review and Assessment

◆ Chapter Summary

Section 1: Land and Water
- Both the United States and Canada are located in North America.
- The United States and Canada have many mountain ranges and plains areas.
- Bodies of water such as the Great Lakes provide transportation and support industry.

Section 2: Climate and Vegetation
- Climate zones in the United States and Canada range from a desert climate to a polar climate.
- Varied climates in the United States and Canada help to produce varied vegetation.

Section 3: Resources and Land Use
- Farmland, forests, water, and minerals are all important resources for the United States and Canada.
- Natural resources affect the economies of the United States and Canada.

Montana

Scorpion in a desert in California

◆ Key Terms

Use each key term below in a sentence that shows the meaning of the term.

1. agribusiness
2. alluvial soil
3. glacier
4. Great Lakes
5. hydroelectricity
6. Rocky Mountains

7. tributary
8. tundra
9. permafrost
10. prairie
11. province
12. fossil fuel

Chapter 1 **31**

┌ Vocabulary Builder

Revisit this chapter's high-use words:

border	ideal	generate
unique	support	suitable
notable	abundant	harness
navigate		

Ask students to review the definitions they recorded on their *Word Knowledge* worksheets.

All in One United States and Canada Teaching Resources, *Word Knowledge,* p. 113

Consider allowing students to earn extra credit if they use the words in their answers to the questions in the Chapter Review and Assessment. The words must be used correctly and in a natural context to win the extra points.

Review and Assessment

Review Chapter Content

- Review the major themes of this chapter by asking students to match the correct Guiding Question to each bulleted statement in the Chapter Summary. Have students determine the number of the Guiding Question that relates to each statement individually, then pair students and have them discuss their classifications with their partner. Refer to page 1 in the Student Edition for text of Guiding Questions.

- Assign *Vocabulary Development* for students to review Key Terms.

  All in One United States and Canada Teaching Resources, *Vocabulary Development,* p. 126

Answers

Key Terms

1–12. Students' sentences should reflect knowledge of each Key Term.

Review and Assessment

Comprehension and Critical Thinking

13. (a) a huge plains area, called the Interior Plains in Canada and the Great Plains and the Central Plains in the United States **(b)** In the wetter eastern part of the plains, farmers grow corn and soybeans, while in the drier west, farmers grow wheat.

14. (a) The Canadian Shield is a huge rugged region of ancient rock. **(b)** More people live in the St. Lawrence Lowlands because the Shield has rugged terrain on which nothing can grow, while the Lowlands has fertile soil.

15. (a) The Pacific Ocean heats up and cools down more slowly than land, and winds blowing across the water warm Canada's west coast in the winter and cool it in the summer. **(b)** The weather there is much more extreme, with very cold winters and very hot summers, because the winds that blow across the ocean affect the coast but never reach the country's interior.

16. (a) Regions close to the Equator are much warmer than regions far from the Equator. **(b)** Nunavut is far from the Equator, making its climate very cold. Permafrost prevents a lot of vegetation growth. People who live there must rely on hunting and fishing for food, and adapt their lifestyles to the cold temperatures.

17. (a) natural vegetation **(b)** The climate and vegetation of the tundra affects Inuit life in that they must hunt and fish for food, rather than grow crops, and their clothing, methods of transportation, and homes have been created to withstand snow and cold.

18. (a) families **(b)** Today, agribusinesses run most American farms. **(c)** This change has made it difficult for individual and family farmers to compete in the marketplace, as they cannot grow as many crops or keep their costs as low as agribusinesses can.

Skills Practice

Topic: whether or not to cut down old redwood trees in Carlotta, California
Possible reasons for differing opinions: The people who work for the logging company might feel that they need the forest to make a profit and make a living. The protesters might feel that it is more important to preserve the forest because redwood trees of that age cannot be easily replaced.

Review and Assessment (continued)

◆ Comprehension and Critical Thinking

13. (a) Identify What landform lies between the Rocky and Appalachian mountains?
(b) Draw Conclusions How does climate affect the crops grown there?

14. (a) Define What is the Canadian Shield?
(b) Compare and Contrast Why do more people live in the St. Lawrence Lowlands than on the Canadian Shield?

15. (a) Explain How does the Pacific Ocean help to keep Canada's west coast climate mild?
(b) Contrast How does the west coast climate differ from the climate that Canada's Interior Plains experiences? Explain.

16. (a) Explain How does latitude affect climate?
(b) Apply Information How might geography and climate affect the way people live in the Canadian territory of Nunavut?

17. (a) Recall Tundra, grassland, desert scrub, and forests are major types of what?
(b) Identify Cause and Effect How do the climate and vegetation of the tundra affect how Inuits live?

18. (a) Identify Until the 1900s, who owned and ran most American farms?
(b) Explore the Main Idea How are most American farms run today?
(c) Draw Conclusions How has this change in ownership affected American farmers?

◆ Skills Practice

Identifying Frame of Reference Review the steps you followed in the Skills for Life activity in this chapter. Then reread the first two paragraphs of Section 3. First, identify the topic being discussed. Then, list some reasons why the logging company and the protesters might have different opinions on how to use natural resources. Finally, identify the frames of reference for people on both sides of the issue.

◆ Writing Activity: Science

Suppose that you are a meteorologist, or a scientist who studies Earth's weather patterns. Create two possible weather maps for the United States and Canada. One map should show a typical winter day and the other a typical summer day. The weather maps should show changes in the weather across the two countries.

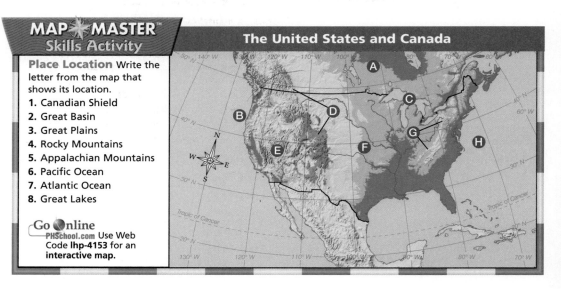

MAP MASTER™
Skills Activity

The United States and Canada

Place Location Write the letter from the map that shows its location.
1. Canadian Shield
2. Great Basin
3. Great Plains
4. Rocky Mountains
5. Appalachian Mountains
6. Pacific Ocean
7. Atlantic Ocean
8. Great Lakes

Go Online
PHSchool.com Use Web Code lhp-4153 for an **interactive map.**

32 United States and Canada

Possible frames of reference: The frame of reference for the logging company would be that of a company who wants to expand their business, provide jobs for many people, and make a profit. The frame of reference for the protesters would be that of environmentalists who want to preserve unique natural resources.

Writing Activity: Science
Students' weather maps should reflect an understanding in the general summer and winter climates for the United States and Canada. Use *Rubric for Assessing a Map Produced by a Student* to evaluate students' weather maps.

All in One **United States and Canada Teaching Resources,** *Rubric for Assessing a Map Produced by a Student,* p. 128

Standardized Test Prep

Test-Taking Tips

Some questions on standardized tests ask you to make mental maps. Read the paragraph below. Then follow the tips to answer the sample question about Canada.

Jessie is working on a crossword puzzle. She studies the following clue and knows the correct answer: Which large Canadian city is located on one of the Great Lakes?

What is her answer?

TIP Try to picture a map of the United States and Canada. Then try to place each of the cities on this mental map—from east to west.

Make a mental map of the United States and Canada. Then pick the letter that best answers the question.

A Ottawa
B Toronto
C Chicago
D Vancouver

TIP Rule out choices that do not make sense. Then choose the best answer from the remaining choices.

Think It Through You can rule out Vancouver because it is on the west coast of Canada. Chicago is on Lake Michigan, but it is in the United States. That leaves Ottawa and Toronto. Ottawa is farther north than Toronto. It is on a waterway, the Ottawa River, but not on one of the Great Lakes. The answer is B, Toronto, which is on Lake Ontario.

Practice Questions

Use the tips above and other tips in this book to help you answer the following questions.

1. Because of its location near the Pacific Ocean and the Coast Mountains, Canada's northwestern coast is
   A hot and dry.
   B bitterly cold.
   C wet and snowy.
   D wet and mild.

2. Which vegetation region shared by the United States and Canada is the largest in the world of its kind?
   A prairie
   B tundra
   C desert
   D savanna

3. The United States is the world's second-largest producer of
   A coal, petroleum, and natural gas.
   B iron ore.
   C hydroelectricity.
   D wood and wood products.

Make a mental map of Canada. Then answer the question below.

4. This region of Canada lies east of the Interior Plains. It covers about half of Canada. Few people live in this region.
   A the St. Lawrence Lowlands
   B the Canadian Shield
   C the Laurentian Highlands
   D the St. Lawrence Seaway

Use Web Code lha-4103
for a **Chapter 1 self-test.**

---

1. A   **2.** E
3. F   **4.** D
5. G   **6.** B
7. H   **8.** C

Go Online PHSchool.com Students may practice their map skills by using the interactive online version of this map.

Standardized Test Prep

Answers

1. D
2. A
3. A
4. B

Go Online PHSchool.com Students may use the Chapter 1 self-test on PHSchool.com to prepare for the Chapter Test.

Assessment Resources

Use *Chapter Tests A and B* to assess students' mastery of chapter content.

All in One **United States and Canada Teaching Resources,** *Chapter Tests A and B,* pp. 129–134

Tests are also available on the **ExamView®** **Test Bank CD-ROM.**

ExamView® Test Bank CD-ROM

The United States and Canada: Shaped by History

Overview

1 The Arrival of the Europeans
Section

1. Learn who the first Americans were.
2. Discover the effects the arrival of Europeans had on Native Americans.
3. Find out how the United States won its independence from Great Britain.

2 Growth and Conflict in the United States
Section

1. Explore the effects of westward expansion in the United States.
2. Discover the causes and effects of the Civil War.

3 The United States on the Brink of Change
Section

1. Explore what happened in the United States from 1865 to 1914.
2. Find out what happened during the World Wars.
3. Explore the challenges the United States faces at home and abroad.

4 The History of Canada
Section

1. Learn about why France and Britain were rivals in Canada.
2. Discover how Canada became an independent nation.
3. Explore how Canada became a world power in the 1900s.

5 The United States and Canada Today
Section

1. Identify the environmental concerns the United States and Canada share today.
2. Find out about the economic ties the United States and Canada have to each other and to the world.

DISCOVERY CHANNEL
SCHOOL Video

Pueblo Bonito
Length: 5 minutes, 4 seconds
Use with Section 1
This video segment provides a description of the housing complexes built by the Anasazi people in the western United States. The segment also explains how the Anasazi built structures that helped them plan when to plant and harvest corn.

Technology Resources

Go Online
PHSchool.com

Students use embedded Web codes to access Internet activities, chapter self-tests, and additional map practice. They may also access Dorling Kindersley's Online Desk Reference to learn more about each country they study.

Interactive Textbook

Use the Interactive Textbook to make content and concepts come alive through animations, videos, and activities that accompany the complete basal text—online and on CD-ROM.

PRENTICE HALL
TeacherEXPRESS
Plan • Teach • Assess

Use this complete suite of powerful teaching tools to make planning lessons and administering tests quicker and easier.

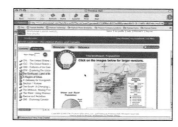

Reading and Assessment

Reading and Vocabulary Instruction

⟳ Model the Target Reading Skill

Clarifying Meaning There are several strategies readers can use to help clarify the meanings of words in passages. First, they can reread or read ahead, looking for connections among words. Next, they can paraphrase, or restate what they have read in their own words. Finally, readers can summarize, or state the main points. Write this selection from Chapter 2 on the board:

> *Many Americans believed that the United States had a right to own all the land from the Atlantic to the Pacific. This belief, called Manifest Destiny, was used to justify further westward expansion. In the 1840s, American wagon trains began to cross the continent heading for the West.*

Ask students to read the passage, stopping at the words *Manifest Destiny*. Have them reread the sentence to find words to clarify the meaning of this term. Have a volunteer come to the board and draw a line under the words that help to explain *Manifest Destiny (the United States had a right to own all the land from the Atlantic to the Pacific)*. Ask students to read ahead. Draw a double line under the words and phrases that help students further clarify the meaning *(justify further westward expansion)*. Challenge students to restate the passage in their own words and state the most important points of the passage in a sentence or two.

Use the following worksheets from All-in-One United States and Canada Teaching Resources (pp. 159–161) to support this chapter's Target Reading Skill.

Vocabulary Builder
High-Use Academic Words
Use these steps to teach this chapter's high-use words:

1. Have students rate how well they know each word on their Word Knowledge worksheets (All-in-One United States and Canada Teaching Resources, p. 162).

2. Pronounce each word and ask students to repeat it.

3. Give students a brief definition and sample sentence (provided on TE pp. 37, 43, 50, 56 and 65).

4. Work with students as they fill in the "Definition or Example" column of their Word Knowledge worksheets.

Assessment

Formal Assessment

Test students' understanding of core knowledge and skills.

Chapter Tests A and B, All-in-One United States and Canada Teaching Resources, pp. 185–190

Customize the Chapter Tests to suit your needs.
ExamView Test Bank CD-ROM

Skills Assessment

Assess geographic literacy.
MapMaster Skills, Student Edition, pp. 35, 39, 43, 44, 46, 58, 66, 72

Assess reading and comprehension.
Target Reading Skills, Student Edition, pp. 40, 46, 50, 58, 68, and in Section Assessments

Chapter Assessment, United States and Canada Reading and Vocabulary Study Guide, p. 31

Performance Assessment

Assess students' performance on this chapter's Writing Activities using the following rubrics from All-in-One United States and Canada Teaching Resources.

Rubric for Assessing a Writing Assignment, p. 183

Rubric for Assessing a Journal Entry, p. 184

Assess students' work through performance tasks.

Small Group Activity: Presenting an Oral Biography, United States and Canada Teaching Resources, pp. 165–168

Online Assessment

Have students check their own understanding.
Chapter Self-Test

Section 1 The Arrival of the Europeans

 1.5 periods, .75 block

Social Studies Objectives
1. Learn who the first Americans were.
2. Discover the effects the arrival of Europeans had on Native Americans.
3. Find out how the United States won its independence from Great Britain.

Reading/Language Arts Objective
Learn how to clarify and understand new words and ideas in a text by rereading.

Prepare to Read	Instructional Resources	Differentiated Instruction
Build Background Knowledge Preview the section and discuss settlement in North America. **Set a Purpose for Reading** Have students begin to fill out the *Reading Readiness Guide*. **Preview Key Terms** Teach the section's Key Terms. **Target Reading Skill** Introduce the section's Target Reading Skill of **rereading**.	**All in One United States and Canada Teaching Resources** **L2** Reading Readiness Guide, p. 140 **L2** Reread or Read Ahead, p. 159	**Spanish Reading and Vocabulary Study Guide** **L1** Chapter 2, Section 1, pp. 14–15 ELL

Instruct	Instructional Resources	Differentiated Instruction
The First Americans **The Europeans Arrive** Discuss the first people who came to America, and colonization of the Americas and its effects. **Eyewitness Technology** Have students read about and discuss life in a Pueblo village. **The Break With Britain** Discuss how the Revolutionary War began. **Target Reading Skill** Review **rereading**.	**All in One United States and Canada Teaching Resources** **L2** Guided Reading and Review, p. 141 **L2** Reading Readiness Guide, p. 140 Rubric for Assessing a Writing Assignment, p. 183 **United States and Canada Transparencies** **L2** Section Reading Support Transparency USC 46 **World Studies Video Program** **L2** Pueblo Bonito	**Spanish Support** **L2** Guided Reading and Review (Spanish), p. 12 ELL

Assess and Reteach	Instructional Resources	Differentiated Instruction
Assess Progress Evaluate student comprehension with the section assessment and section quiz. **Reteach** Assign the Reading and Vocabulary Study Guide to help struggling students. **Extend** Extend the lesson by assigning a primary source reading.	**All in One United States and Canada Teaching Resources** **L2** Section Quiz, p. 142 **L3** Closing Speech to the Constitutional Convention, September 17, 1787, pp. 172–173 Rubric for Assessing a Writing Assignment, p. 183 **Reading and Vocabulary Study Guide** **L1** Chapter 2, Section 1, pp. 16–18	**Spanish Support** **L2** Section Quiz (Spanish), p. 13 ELL

Key
L1 Basic to Average   **L3** Average to Advanced   **LPR** Less Proficient Readers   **GT** Gifted and Talented

L2 For All Students   **AR** Advanced Readers   **ELL** English Language Learners

SN Special Needs Students

Section 2 Growth and Conflict in the United States

 *1.5 periods, .75 block*

Social Studies Objectives
1. Explore the effects of westward expansion in the United States.
2. Discover the causes and effects of the Civil War.

Reading/Language Arts Objective
Learn how to clarify words or ideas in a text by reading ahead.

Prepare to Read	Instructional Resources	Differentiated Instruction
Build Background Knowledge Discuss what students already know about American history. **Set a Purpose for Reading** Have students begin to fill out the *Reading Readiness Guide.* **Preview Key Terms** Teach the section's Key Terms. **Target Reading Skill** Introduce the section's Target Reading Skill of **reading ahead**.	**All in One United States and Canada Teaching Resources** **L2** Reading Readiness Guide, p. 144 **L2** Reread or Read Ahead, p. 159	**Spanish Reading and Vocabulary Study Guide** **L1** Chapter 2, Section 2, pp. 16–17 ELL

Instruct	Instructional Resources	Differentiated Instruction
A Nation Grows Discuss the major events that occurred in the United States during the early to middle 1800s. **The Civil War and Reconstruction** Ask questions about abolition and the Civil War. **Target Reading Skill** Review **reading ahead**.	**All in One United States and Canada Teaching Resources** **L2** Guided Reading and Review, p. 145 **L2** Reading Readiness Guide, p. 144 **United States and Canada Transparencies** **L2** Section Reading Support Transparency USC 47	**All in One United States and Canada Teaching Resources** **L3** Morning Girl, pp. 174–176 AR, GT **L3** Journal Entry, p. 177 AR, GT **L3** Chief Joseph Surrenders, p. 178 AR, GT **Teacher's Edition** **L3** For Advanced Readers, TE p. 44 **Spanish Support** **L2** Guided Reading and Review (Spanish), p. 14 ELL

Assess and Reteach	Instructional Resources	Differentiated Instruction
Assess Progress Evaluate student comprehension with the section assessment and section quiz. **Reteach** Assign the Reading and Vocabulary Study Guide to help struggling students. **Extend** Extend the lesson by assigning a Small Group Activity.	**All in One United States and Canada Teaching Resources** **L2** Section Quiz, p. 146 **L3** Small Group Activity: Presenting an Oral Biography, pp. 165–168 Rubric for Assessing a Journal Entry, p. 184 **Reading and Vocabulary Study Guide** **L1** Chapter 2, Section 2, pp. 19–21	**Spanish Support** **L2** Section Quiz (Spanish), p. 15 ELL

Key
L1 Basic to Average   **L3** Average to Advanced
L2 For All Students

LPR Less Proficient Readers
AR Advanced Readers
SN Special Needs Students

GT Gifted and Talented
ELL English Language Learners

Section 3 The United States on the Brink of Change

 1.5 periods, .75 block

Social Studies Objectives
1. Explore what happened in the United States from 1865 to 1914.
2. Find out what happened during the World Wars.
3. Explore the challenges the United States faces at home and abroad.

Reading/Language Arts Objective
Use paraphrasing to help you understand what you read.

Prepare to Read	Instructional Resources	Differentiated Instruction
Build Background Knowledge Ask students to complete an idea web with details about the United States as a world power. **Set a Purpose for Reading** Have students evaluate statements on the *Reading Readiness Guide.* **Preview Key Terms** Teach the section's Key Terms. **Target Reading Skill** Introduce the section's Target Reading Skill of **paraphrasing**.	**All in One United States and Canada Teaching Resources** L2 Reading Readiness Guide, p. 148 L2 Paraphrase, p. 160	**Spanish Reading and Vocabulary Study Guide** L1 Chapter 2, Section 3, pp. 18–19 ELL

Instruct	Instructional Resources	Differentiated Instruction
From 1865 to 1914 Discuss different attempts to fight poverty. **Target Reading Skill** Review **paraphrasing**. **The World at War** Discuss the Great Depression and World War II. **The U.S. at Home and Abroad** Discuss the tension between the United States and the Soviet Union, and ask about the civil rights movement in the United States.	**All in One United States and Canada Teaching Resources** L2 Guided Reading and Review, p. 149 L2 Reading Readiness Guide, p. 148 **United States and Canada Transparencies** L2 Section Reading Support Transparency USC 48	**All in One United States and Canada Teaching Resources** L1 Book Project: Make a Timeline of Local History, pp. 79–81 ELL, LPR, SN **Teacher's Edition** L1 For English Language Learners, TE p. 52 L3 For Gifted and Talented, TE p. 52 L3 For Advanced Readers, TE p. 53 L1 For Special Needs Students, TE p. 53 **Spanish Support** L1 Guided Reading and Review (Spanish), p. 16 ELL

Assess and Reteach	Instructional Resources	Differentiated Instruction
Assess Progress Evaluate student comprehension with the section assessment and section quiz. **Reteach** Assign the Reading and Vocabulary Study Guide to help struggling students. **Extend** Extend the lesson by assigning a primary source reading.	**All in One United States and Canada Teaching Resources** L2 Section Quiz, p. 150 L3 A Child in Prison Camp, pp. 179–181 Rubric for Assessing a Writing Assignment, p. 183 **Reading and Vocabulary Study Guide** L1 Chapter 2, Section 3, pp. 22–24	**Spanish Support** L2 Section Quiz (Spanish), p. 17 ELL

Key

L1 Basic to Average   L3 Average to Advanced   LPR Less Proficient Readers   GT Gifted and Talented

L2 For All Students   AR Advanced Readers   ELL English Language Learners

SN Special Needs Students

Section 4 The History of Canada

 2.5 periods, 1.75 blocks (includes Skills for Life)

Social Studies Objectives
1. Learn about why France and Britain were rivals in Canada.
2. Discover how Canada became an independent nation.
3. Explore how Canada became a world power in the 1900s.

Reading/Language Arts Objective
Use summarizing to help comprehend the main points you have read.

Prepare to Read	Instructional Resources	Differentiated Instruction
Build Background Knowledge As a class, compare the histories of Canada and the United States. **Set a Purpose for Reading** Have students evaluate statements on the *Reading Readiness Guide.* **Preview Key Terms** Teach the section's Key Terms. **Target Reading Skill** Introduce the section's Target Reading Skill of **summarizing**.	**All in One United States and Canada Teaching Resources** L2 Reading Readiness Guide, p. 152 L2 Summarize, p. 161	**Spanish Reading and Vocabulary Study Guide** L1 Chapter 2, Section 4, pp. 20–21 ELL

Instruct	Instructional Resources	Differentiated Instruction
The French and the British Discuss the conflicts between the French and the British in Canada. **Canada Seeks Independence** Ask questions about and discuss Canada's independence. **Target Reading Skill** Review **summarizing**. **Canada: Postwar to the Present** Discuss how Canada changed after World War II.	**All in One United States and Canada Teaching Resources** L2 Guided Reading and Review, p. 153 L2 Reading Readiness Guide, p. 152 **United States and Canada Transparencies** L2 Section Reading Support Transparency USC 49	**All in One United States and Canada Teaching Resources** L2 Activity Shop Interdisciplinary: Transportation, pp. 169–170 ELL, LPR, SN L2 Skills for Life, p. 164 AR, GT, LPR, SN **Teacher's Edition** L1 For English Language Learners, TE p. 58 L1 For Special Needs Students, TE p. 58 L1 For Less Proficient Readers, TE p. 60 L3 For Gifted and Talented, TE p. 60 **Student Edition on Audio CD** L1 Chapter 2, Section 4 ELL, LPR, SN

Assess and Reteach	Instructional Resources	Differentiated Instruction
Assess Progress Evaluate student comprehension with the section assessment and section quiz. **Reteach** Assign the Reading and Vocabulary Study Guide to help struggling students. **Extend** Extend the lesson by assigning an Enrichment activity.	**All in One United States and Canada Teaching Resources** L2 Section Quiz, p. 154 L3 Enrichment, p. 163 Rubric for Assessing a Writing Assignment, p. 183 **Reading and Vocabulary Study Guide** L1 Chapter 2, Section 4, pp. 25–27	**All in One United States and Canada Teaching Resources** L3 Reading a Diagram, p. 171 AR, GT **Teacher's Edition** L1 For Special Needs Students, TE p. 63 L3 For Gifted and Talented, TE p. 63 **Spanish Support** L2 Section Quiz (Spanish), p. 19 ELL

Key

L1 Basic to Average	L3 Average to Advanced	LPR Less Proficient Readers	GT Gifted and Talented
L2 For All Students		AR Advanced Readers	ELL English Language Learners
		SN Special Needs Students	

Section 5 The United States and Canada Today

 3 periods, 1.5 blocks (includes Chapter Review and Assessment)

Social Studies Objectives

1. Identify the environmental concerns the United States and Canada share today.
2. Find out about the economic ties the United States and Canada have to each other and to the world.

Reading/Language Arts Objective

Use the rereading or reading ahead strategies to better understand the words and ideas in a text.

Prepare to Read	Instructional Resources	Differentiated Instruction
Build Background Knowledge Have students brainstorm different ways to protect the environment. **Set a Purpose for Reading** Have students evaluate statements on the *Reading Readiness Guide*. **Preview Key Terms** Teach the section's Key Terms. **Target Reading Skill** Introduce the section's Target Reading Skill of **rereading or reading ahead**.	**All in One United States and Canada Teaching Resources** L2 Reading Readiness Guide, p. 156 L2 Reread or Read Ahead, p. 159	**Spanish Reading and Vocabulary Study Guide** L1 Chapter 2, Section 5, pp. 22–23 ELL

Instruct	Instructional Resources	Differentiated Instruction
Environmental Issues Ask about the effects of pollution and discuss ways to combat it. **Target Reading Skill** Review **rereading**. **"Economics Has Made Us Partners"** Ask questions about and discuss the economic partnership between the United States and Canada.	**All in One United States and Canada Teaching Resources** L2 Guided Reading and Review, p. 157 L2 Reading Readiness Guide, p. 156 **United States and Canada Transparencies** L2 Section Reading Support Transparency USC 50	**All in One United States and Canada Teaching Resources** L3 Book Project: Write A Children's Book, pp. 76–78 AR, GT **Teacher's Edition** L1 For Special Needs Students, TE p. 66 L3 For Advanced Readers, TE p. 68 L1 For English Language Learners, TE p. 69 L3 For Gifted and Talented, TE p. 69 **United States and Canada Transparencies** L1 Transparency B10: Effects Chart ELL, LPR, SN **PHSchool.com** L3 For: Long-Term Integrated Projects: Mapping World Trade **Web Code:** lhd-4206 AR, GT

Assess and Reteach	Instructional Resources	Differentiated Instruction
Assess Progress Evaluate student comprehension with the section assessment and section quiz. **Reteach** Assign the Reading and Vocabulary Study Guide to help struggling students. **Extend** Extend the lesson by assigning an online activity.	**All in One United States and Canada Teaching Resources** L2 Section Quiz, p. 158 Rubric for Assessing a Writing Assignment, p. 183 L2 Vocabulary Development, p. 182 L2 Word Knowledge, p. 162 L2 Chapter Tests A and B, pp. 185–190 **Reading and Vocabulary Study Guide** L1 Chapter 2, Section 5, pp. 28–30	**Spanish Support** L2 Section Quiz (Spanish), p. 21 ELL L2 Chapter Summary (Spanish), p. 22 ELL L2 Vocabulary Development (Spanish), p. 23 ELL **PHSchool.com** L3 For: Environmental and Global Issues: The Imbalance of Energy Consumption **Web code:** lhd-4207

Key

L1 Basic to Average   L3 Average to Advanced   LPR Less Proficient Readers   GT Gifted and Talented
L2 For All Students   AR Advanced Readers   ELL English Language Learners
                                                     SN Special Needs Students

Reading Background

Pre-Teaching Vocabulary

Research literature on academic vocabulary instruction indicates that effective strategies require students to go beyond simply looking up dictionary definitions or examining the context. Vocabulary learning must be based on the learner's dynamic engagement in constructing understanding.

If students are not retaining the meaning of the Key Terms or high-use words, use this extended vocabulary sequence to engage them in learning new words.

1. Present the word in writing and point out the part of speech.
2. Pronounce the word and have students pronounce the word.
3. Provide a range of familiar synonyms (or "it's like" words) before offering definitions.
4. Provide an accessible definition and concrete examples, or "showing sentences."
5. Rephrase the simple definition or example sentence, asking students to complete the statement by substituting the word aloud.
6. Check for understanding by providing an application task/question requiring critical thinking.

Sample instructional sequence:

1. Our first word is *abolitionist.* It is a noun, a word that names a person, place, or thing. In this case, it is a person.
2. Say the word *abolitionist* after me. (Students repeat.)
3. An *abolitionist* is like a *reformer* or an *activist.*
4. The word *abolitionist* means *a person who believed that enslaving people was wrong, and wanted to end the practice.* The *abolitionist* hid runaway slaves in her home.
5. An _____ would not return a runaway slave to his or her master. (Students substitute missing word.)
6. Was Harriet Beecher Stowe an abolitionist? Yes-No-Why? (Refer students to page 47 to help them answer the question.)

Word Wizard: Going Beyond the Classroom

Challenge students to take their word knowledge beyond the classroom to find or use Key Terms in their everyday lives. Work with students to set up a system in which students earn points for bringing in evidence of having heard, seen, or used the Key Terms outside the classroom. *Boycott, free trade,* and *civil rights* are terms that are likely to appear in newspapers, or on radio or television news shows. *Bilingual* is a term that students might hear at school. And *abolitionist,* a more obscure term for everyday use, is likely to appear in books or movies about the Civil War.

World Studies Background

The Great Compromise

Written in 1787, the United States Constitution was an exercise in political compromise. Delegates argued whether the number of representatives in the legislature should be the same for each state, or different depending upon a state's population. The framers eventually adopted a proposal for a legislature that included both a *Senate,* in which all states were equally represented, and a *House of Representatives,* in which representation would be based on the state's free population, plus three fifths of its slave population. This came to be called "The Great Compromise."

Canada's Role in World War II

In 1939, Canada's Parliament voted in a virtually unanimous decision to declare war on Germany, assuming that Canadians would primarily contribute supplies to the war effort. In the summer of 1940, as Canada's allies in Europe began falling to the Germans, Canada realized it would have to take a more active part in the war.

The first step was to sign an agreement with the United States for the defense of North America. More than one million Canadians served in the armed forces. Canadian troops fought in Italy and were part of the Normandy Invasion in June 1944. In addition to soldiers, Canada provided food, money, and weapons to the war effort.

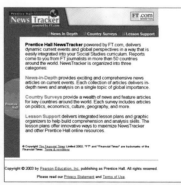

Get in-depth information on topics of global importance with **Prentice Hall Newstracker,** powered by FT.com.

Use Web code **lhd-4200** for **Prentice Hall Newstracker.**

Chapter 2

Guiding Questions

Remind students about the Guiding Questions introduced at the beginning of the book.

Section 1 relates to **Guiding Question** ❷ **How have historical events affected the cultures of the United States and Canada?** *(The United States became independent from Britain.)*

Section 2 relates to **Guiding Question** ❷ **How have historical events affected the cultures of the United States and Canada?** *(The Industrial Revolution brought new technology, and the Civil War ended slavery.)*

Section 3 relates to **Guiding Question** ❷ **How have historical events affected the cultures of the United States and Canada?** *(Reformers fought for civil rights and the United States took on greater responsibility in world affairs.)*

Section 4 relates to **Guiding Question** ❷ **How have historical events affected the cultures of the United States and Canada?** *(Canada gained its independence, grew industrially, and adopted a constitution.)*

Section 5 relates to **Guiding Question** ❺ **How did the United States and Canada become two of the wealthiest nations in the world?** *(The St. Lawrence Seaway and trade agreements have helped them become economic powers.)*

🎯 Target Reading Skill

In this chapter, students will learn and apply the reading skill of clarifying meaning. Use the following worksheets to help students practice this skill:

All in One United States and Canada Teaching Resources, *Reread or Read Ahead,* p. 159; *Paraphrase,* p. 160; *Summarize,* p. 161

Differentiated Instruction

The following Teacher Edition strategies are suitable for students of varying abilities.

Advanced Readers pp. 44, 53
English Language Learners pp. 52, 58, 69
Gifted and Talented pp. 52, 60, 63, 69
Less Proficient Readers p. 60
Special Needs Students pp. 53, 58, 63, 66

Chapter 2

The U.S. and Canada: Shaped by History

Chapter Preview

This chapter presents the history of the United States and Canada and shows how that history affects the region to this day.

Section 1
The Arrival of the Europeans

Section 2
Growth and Conflict in the United States

Section 3
The United States on the Brink of Change

Section 4
The History of Canada

Section 5
The United States and Canada Today

 Target Reading Skill

Clarifying Meaning In this chapter you will focus on skills you can use to clarify meaning as you read.

▶ The Washington Monument as seen from the Lincoln Memorial in Washington, D.C.

Bibliography

For the Teacher

Berkin, Carol. *Making America: A History of the United States.* Houghton Mifflin Co., 2002.

Brown, Craig. *The Illustrated History of Canada.* Key Porter Books, 2003.

Josephy, Alvin M. *500 Nations: An Illustrated History of North American Indians.* Knopf, 1998.

Zinn, Howard. *A People's History of the United States, Abridged and Updated Teaching Edition.* New Press, 2003.

For the Student

L1 Bowers, Vivian. *Only in Canada: From the Colossal to the Kooky (Wow Canada).* Owl Books, 2002.

L2 Hakim, Joy. *A History of Us: From Colonies to Country (A History of Us, Vol. 4.)* Oxford Univ Pr Children's Books, 2002.

L3 McPherson, James M. *Fields of Fury: The American Civil War.* Atheneum, 2002.

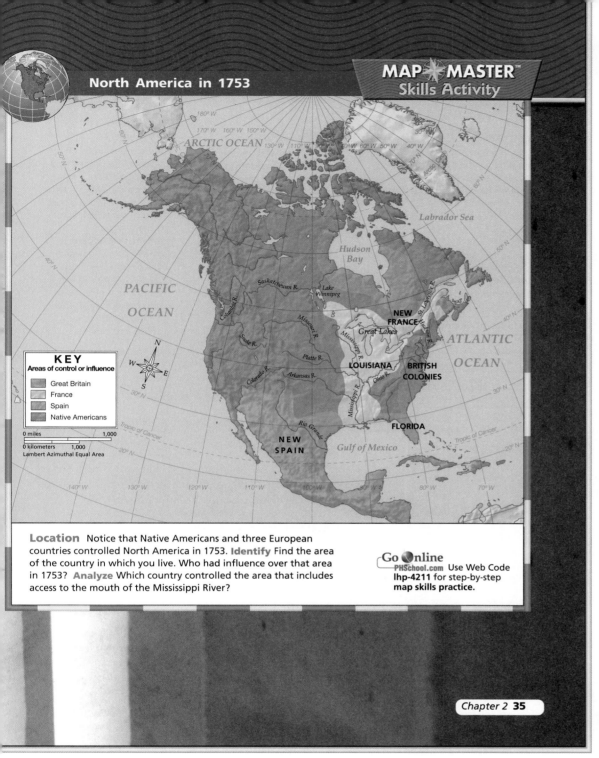

North America in 1753

ARCTIC OCEAN

Labrador Sea

Hudson Bay

PACIFIC OCEAN

Saskatchewan R.

Lake Winnipeg

Columbia R.

Missouri R.

Snake R.

NEW FRANCE

Great Lakes

St. Lawrence R.

Hudson R.

ATLANTIC OCEAN

Platte R.

LOUISIANA

BRITISH COLONIES

Colorado R.

Ohio R.

Arkansas R.

Mississippi R.

Rio Grande

FLORIDA

NEW SPAIN

Gulf of Mexico

Tropic of Cancer

KEY
Areas of control or influence

- Great Britain
- France
- Spain
- Native Americans

0 miles 1,000
0 kilometers 1,000
Lambert Azimuthal Equal Area

Location Notice that Native Americans and three European countries controlled North America in 1753. **Identify** Find the area of the country in which you live. Who had influence over that area in 1753? **Analyze** Which country controlled the area that includes access to the mouth of the Mississippi River?

Go Online
PHSchool.com Use Web Code **lhp-4211** for step-by-step **map skills practice.**

- Have students study the map of North America in 1753, directing their attention to the title and the key. Then have them write a short paragraph describing what region of North America each group controlled.

- Pair students and ask them to compare the map from the text with a current map of North America. Assign each pair a few states, provinces, territories, or cities from the current map, and ask them to identify which group or groups controlled that region in 1753.

Go Online
PHSchool.com Students may practice their map skills using the interactive online version of this map.

Using the Visual   L2

Reach Into Your Background Draw students' attention to the photograph and its caption. Ask students to name any monuments or memorials they know of or have visited. Ask them to think about how monuments keep history alive, and conduct an Idea Wave (TE, p. T35) to help them share their answers.

Answers

MAP★MASTER™ Skills Activity **Identify** Answers will vary according to where students live. **Analyze** France

---

Chapter Resources

Teaching Resources
- L2 Vocabulary Development, p. 182
- L2 Skills for Life, p. 164
- L2 Chapter Tests A and B, pp. 185–190

Spanish Support
- L2 Spanish Chapter Summary, p. 22
- L2 Spanish Vocabulary Development, p. 23

Media and Technology
- L1 Student Edition on Audio CD
- L1 Guided Reading Audiotapes, English and Spanish
- L2 Social Studies Skills Tutor CD-ROM
- *ExamView Test Bank CD-ROM*

PRENTICE HALL
Presentation EXPRESS™
Teach · Connect · Inspire

Teach this chapter's content using the PresentationExpress™ CD-ROM including:
- slide shows
- transparencies
- interactive maps and media
- *ExamView®* QuickTake Presenter

Section 1
Step-by-Step Instruction

Objectives

Social Studies

1. Learn who the first Americans were.
2. Discover the effects the arrival of Europeans had on Native Americans.
3. Find out how the United States won its independence from Great Britain.

Reading/Language Arts

Learn how to clarify and understand new words and ideas in a text by rereading.

Prepare to Read

Build Background Knowledge `L2`

Tell students that in this section they will learn about the history of settlement in North America. Have students preview the headings and visuals in this section with the following question in mind: **From where did the people who settled North America come?** Use the Idea Wave participation strategy (TE, p. T35) to solicit answers.

Set a Purpose for Reading `L2`

- Preview the Objectives.

- Form students into pairs or groups of four. Distribute the *Reading Readiness Guide.* Ask students to fill in the first two columns of the chart. Use the Numbered Heads participation strategy (TE, p. T36) to call on students to share one piece of information they already know and one piece of information they want to know.

    All in One **United States and Canada Teaching Resources,** *Reading Readiness Guide,* p. 140

Vocabulary Builder
Preview Key Terms `L2`

Pronounce each Key Term, then ask the students to say the word with you. Provide a simple explanation such as, "Indentured servants were permitted to work for their freedom, while slaves were forced to work for life."

Section 1
The Arrival of the Europeans

Prepare to Read

Objectives

In this section you will

1. Learn who the first Americans were.
2. Discover the effects the arrival of Europeans had on Native Americans.
3. Find out how the United States won its independence from Great Britain.

Taking Notes

As you read the section, look for important events that have taken place in North America. Copy the table below and write each event in the correct time period.

Events in North American History	
1400s	
1500s	
1600s	
1700s	

Target Reading Skill

Reread Rereading is a strategy that can help you understand words and ideas in the text. If you do not understand a certain passage, reread it to look for connections among the words and sentences.

Key Terms

- **indigenous** (in DIJ uh nus) *adj.* belonging to a certain place
- **missionary** (MISH un ehr ee) *n.* a person who tries to convert others to his or her religion
- **indentured servant** (in DEN churd SUR vunt) *n.* a person who must work for a period of years to gain freedom
- **boycott** (BOY kaht) *n.* a refusal to buy or use goods and services

Native American artifacts

36 United States and Canada

Louise Erdrich is an American writer. She is also part Native American. In one of her novels, she describes the variety of Native American cultures before the Europeans arrived:

❝[They] had hundreds of societies . . . whose experience had told them that the world was a pretty diverse place. Walk for a day in any direction and what do you find: A tribe with a whole new set of gods, a language as distinct from your own as Tibetan is from Dutch. . . .❞

—*Louise Erdrich,* The Crown of Columbus

The First Americans

Many scientists think that Native Americans migrated from Asia. Perhaps as early as 30,000 years ago, they theorize, small groups of hunters and gatherers reached North America from Asia.

Target Reading Skill `L2`

Reread Point out the Target Reading Skill. Tell students that going back into the text will allow them to make connections among words and sentences. In this way, rereading can help clarify or explain a new word or an idea in a passage.

Model the strategy by using rereading to determine what theory is being referenced in this sentence from The First Americans: "Many Native Americans disagree with this

theory, believing they have always lived in the Americas." *(the theory that people migrated to North America from Asia during the last ice age using an exposed land bridge)*

Give students *Reread or Read Ahead.* Have them complete the activity in their groups.

All in One **United States and Canada Teaching Resources,** *Reread or Read Ahead,* p. 159

This migration from Asia to North America took place during the last ice age. At that time, so much water froze into thick ice sheets that the sea level dropped. As a result, a land bridge was exposed between Siberia and Alaska. Hunters followed herds of bison and mammoths across this land bridge. Other migrating people may have paddled small boats and fished along the coasts.

Over time, the first Americans spread throughout North and South America. They developed different ways of life to suit the environment of the places where they settled.

Many Native Americans disagree with this theory, believing they have always lived in the Americas. In any case, all people consider Native Americans **indigenous** (in DIJ uh nus) people, meaning they belong to and are native to this place.

✓ Reading Check How did migrating people reach North America?

The Europeans Arrive

Life for the millions of indigenous people in the Americas began to change after 1492. That year, Christopher Columbus, a sea captain sailing from Spain, explored islands in the Caribbean Sea. His voyage opened the way for European colonization.

Spanish Claims to the Americas   The Spanish settlers who followed Columbus spread out across the Americas. Some went to the present-day southwestern United States and Mexico. Others went to Florida, the Caribbean islands, and South America. Spain gained great wealth from its American colonies.

Learn about early Native American houses.

Taos, New Mexico
Although Native Americans had inhabited the area for centuries, Spanish explorers arrived in present-day Taos (TAH ohs), New Mexico in 1540. They built the church below in 1617. **Predict** How might life have changed for Native Americans after Spanish explorers arrived?

Chapter 2 Section 1 **37**

Show students *Pueblo Bonito.* Ask **Why was the position of the sun important to the Anasazi when building structures?** *(It helped the Anasazi determine when to plant and harvest corn.)*

Pueblo Village [L2]

Guided Instruction
Have students read the introductory paragraph on this page. Then read the captions aloud as students study the diagram and photos. Pair students and have them discuss the Analyzing Images question.

Independent Practice
Using the information on this page, have students write a paragraph about what life might have been like in a Pueblo village. Use the *Rubric for Assessing a Writing Assignment* to evaluate students' paragraphs.

All in One **United States and Canada Teaching Resources,** *Rubric for Assessing a Writing Assignment,* p. 183

Pueblo Village

When the Pueblo Indians of the Southwest learned how to grow corn and other crops, they no longer had to move about to hunt and gather food. As they became more settled and grew larger harvests, they built stone corn cribs. Over time, these storerooms became larger, and the Pueblos began to build their houses and villages around them.

Acoma Pueblo, New Mexico
The Acoma Pueblo sits high on a 357-foot (109-meter) sandstone rock. It is also known as "Sky City."

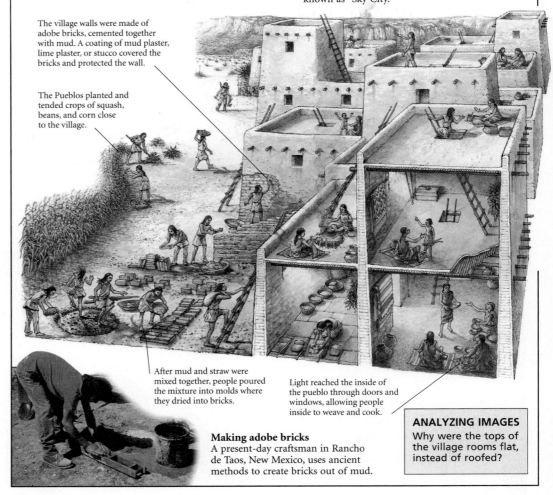

The village walls were made of adobe bricks, cemented together with mud. A coating of mud plaster, lime plaster, or stucco covered the bricks and protected the wall.

The Pueblos planted and tended crops of squash, beans, and corn close to the village.

After mud and straw were mixed together, people poured the mixture into molds where they dried into bricks.

Light reached the inside of the pueblo through doors and windows, allowing people inside to weave and cook.

Making adobe bricks
A present-day craftsman in Rancho de Taos, New Mexico, uses ancient methods to create bricks out of mud.

ANALYZING IMAGES
Why were the tops of the village rooms flat, instead of roofed?

38 United States and Canada

Answers
ANALYZING IMAGES Possible answer: The flat roofs were probably used as a safe place to work and to watch for and escape from enemies.

The colonists often enslaved Native Americans. They forced Native Americans to work in mines or on farms. Working conditions were so harsh that thousands died. Spanish missionaries tried to make Native Americans more like Europeans, often by force. **Missionaries** (MISH un ehr ees) are religious people who want to convert others to their religion.

French Claims to the Americas   Seeing Spain's success, other countries also wanted colonies in the Americas. French explorers claimed land along the St. Lawrence and Mississippi rivers. Unlike the Spanish, who were interested in gold, the French were interested in fur. French traders and missionaries often lived among the Native Americans and learned their ways. However, both the French and the Spanish brought disease along with them. Millions of Native Americans died from diseases that they had never been exposed to before, such as smallpox and measles.

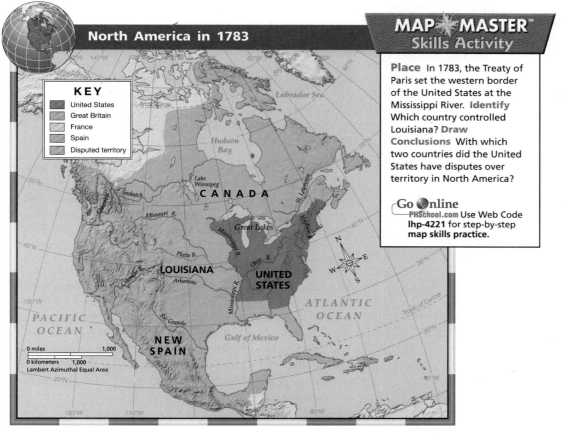

North America in 1783

MAP MASTER™ Skills Activity

KEY
- United States
- Great Britain
- France
- Spain
- Disputed territory

Place In 1783, the Treaty of Paris set the western border of the United States at the Mississippi River. **Identify** Which country controlled Louisiana? **Draw Conclusions** With which two countries did the United States have disputes over territory in North America?

Go Online PHSchool.com Use Web Code **lhp-4221** for step-by-step **map skills practice**.

Chapter 2 Section 1 **39**

Background: Biography

Pocahontas (c. 1595–1617) According to a story told by John Smith, a leading Jamestown settler, a young Native American woman named Pocahontas interceded to stop her people from executing him. She later married Englishman John Rolfe, and their marriage helped smooth uneasy relations between the English settlers and the native peoples of Virginia.

Independent Practice
Have students create the Taking Notes graphic organizer on a blank piece of paper. Then have them fill in the first three lines with what the have learned from the text. Briefly model how to identify which details to record.

Monitor Progress
As students fill in the graphic organizer, circulate and make sure individuals are choosing the correct details. Provide assistance as needed.

Answers

MAP MASTER Skills Activity **Identify** Spain **Draw Conclusions** Great Britain and Spain

Go Online PHSchool.com Students may practice their map skills using the interactive online version of this map.

The Break with Britain L2

Guided Instruction

■ **Vocabulary Builder** Clarify the high-use word **inspire** before reading.

■ Read The Break With Britain. As students read, circulate and make sure individuals can answer the Reading Check question.

■ Discuss the chain of events between Britain and the colonies that led to the Revolutionary War. *(The British taxed the colonies to help pay for the French and Indian War. Colonists thought this was unfair since they had no representation in the British government. The colonists boycotted British goods in order to avoid paying taxes. A war began and colonists delivered the Declaration of Independence to Great Britain.)*

Independent Practice

Ask students to complete their graphic organizer with the information they have just learned about the 1700s.

Monitor Progress

■ Show *Section Reading Support Transparency USC 46* and ask students to check their graphic organizers individually. Go over key concepts and clarify key vocabulary as needed.

   📖 **United States and Canada Transparencies,** *Section Reading Support Transparency USC 46*

■ Tell students to fill in the last column of the *Reading Readiness Guide.* Ask them to evaluate if what they learned was what they had expected to learn.

   All in One United States and Canada Teaching Resources, *Reading Readiness Guide,* p. 140

🔄 Target Reading Skill

Reread As a follow up, ask students to answer the Target Reading Skill question in the Student Edition. *(Britain and France went to war over land in North America. The British and their colonists fought against the French and their Native American allies.)*

Answer

✓ **Reading Check** The English settled the colonies in order to establish a new way of life. Some wanted to own land or practice their religion freely. Others wanted to escape debt.

THE LANDING OF THE PILGRIMS.
ON PLYMOUTH ROCK, DEC. 1ST 1620.

In 1620, a group of about 100 Pilgrims sailed to New England on the *Mayflower* (right). In 1682, William Penn (left) arrived in the colony of Pennsylvania, which means "Penn's woods."

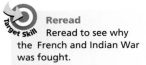
Reread
Reread to see why the French and Indian War was fought.

The English Colonists English settlers also arrived, establishing a strip of colonies along the Atlantic Coast. These settlers came to start a new life. Some wanted to be free from debt. Others wanted to own land or practice their religions freely. Some came as **indentured servants,** or people who had to work for a period of years to gain freedom.

The first permanent English settlement was Jamestown, Virginia, founded in 1607. By 1619, it had the beginnings of self-government. In the same year, the first Africans arrived there as indentured servants. Later, about 1640, Africans were brought to the colonies as slaves. Many were forced to work on plantations, or the large farms in the South where cash crops were grown.

In 1620, the Pilgrims arrived in Plymouth, Massachusetts from England. They wanted to worship God in their own way and to govern themselves. About 60 years later, William Penn founded the Pennsylvania Colony. He wanted a place where all people, regardless of race or religion, were treated fairly. Penn paid Native Americans for their land. Later, settlers took over the land, and then fought Native Americans to control it.

The French and Indian War In the 1700s, Britain and France fought several wars. When they fought, their colonists often fought, too. In 1754, Britain and France went to war over land in North America. The British fought against the French and their Native American allies. An ally is a country or person that joins with another for a special purpose. Americans call this war the French and Indian War. With the colonists' help, the British were victorious in 1763.

✓ **Reading Check** Why did English settlers establish the colonies?

40 United States and Canada

🎯 **Skills for Life** ## Skills Mini Lesson

Recognizing Cause and Effect

1. Teach the skill by surrounding a marble with an outer circle of marbles. Have a volunteer roll the center marble at the outer circle. Point out that the *cause* is the moving marble, the *effect* is the disruption of the circle. The *cause* is what makes something happen; the *effect* is what happens.

2. Help students practice the skill by rereading the first paragraph under The Break With Britain and determine what caused Britain to start taxing the colonists. *(the expense of an army to protect the colonies)*

3. Have students apply the skill by answering this question: What was the effect of the taxation? *(The colonists became angry and boycotted British goods.)*

The Break With Britain

Despite their victory, the British wanted an army in North America to protect the colonists. The British thought the colonists should help pay for the war and for their defense. They put taxes on many British goods the colonists bought. Because no one represented the colonists in the British Parliament, they could not protest these taxes. Many of them began to demand "no taxation without representation." They also **boycotted**, or refused to buy, British goods.

Resentment grew against British rule, causing the Revolutionary War to break out in 1775. Thomas Jefferson summarized the colonists' views in the Declaration of Independence. His words inspired many colonists to fight. In 1781, George Washington led the American forces to victory. The Treaty of Paris, signed in 1783, made American independence official.

Before they won independence, the 13 colonies worked on a plan of government called the Articles of Confederation. But Congress was not given the power to tax. After the war, the 13 new states agreed to form a stronger central government. They wrote the Constitution, which set up the framework for our federal government. Approved in 1788, it is still the highest law of the United States.

✓ **Reading Check** What was the problem with the Articles of Confederation?

This statue commemorates the Minutemen of the American Revolution who stood their ground against British troops on April 19, 1775.

Section 1 Assessment

Key Terms
Review the key terms at the beginning of this section. Use each term in a sentence that explains its meaning.

Target Reading Skill
What word or idea were you able to clarify by rereading?

Comprehension and Critical Thinking
1. (a) Recall Where do many scientists think the first Americans came from?

(b) Identify Point of View Why might Native Americans today disagree with the theory of migration?

2. (a) Explain Describe how different European groups settled in the Americas.

(b) Summarize How did Europeans affect Native American life?

3. (a) Name What document is the framework for the United States government?

(b) Identify Cause and Effect Why did the colonists object to the taxes placed on them by the British?

Writing Activity
Write a paragraph discussing how life in the Americas might have been different if Columbus's voyage had not taken place.

> **Writing Tip** Begin your paragraph with a topic sentence that states your main idea. Give at least two examples of how life might have been different.

Assess Progress L2
Have students complete the Section Assessment. Administer the *Section Quiz*.

 United States and Canada Teaching Resources, *Section Quiz*, p. 142

Reteach L1
If students need more instruction, have them read this section in the Reading and Vocabulary Study Guide.

📖 Chapter 2, Section 1, **United States and Canada Reading and Vocabulary Study Guide**, pp. 16–18

Extend L3
Have students read *Closing Speech to the Constitutional Convention, September 17, 1787*. Assign students to work in groups to answer the questions provided.

 United States and Canada Teaching Resources, *Closing Speech to the Constitutional Convention, September 17, 1787*, pp. 172–173

Answers

✓ **Reading Check** The Articles of Confederation did not provide for a strong central government that had the power to tax.

Writing Activity
Use the *Rubric for Assessing a Writing Assignment* to evaluate students' paragraphs.

 United States and Canada Teaching Resources, *Rubric for Assessing a Writing Assignment*, p. 183

Section 1 Assessment

Key Terms
Students' sentences should reflect knowledge of each Key Term.

Target Reading Skill
Answers will vary, but student responses should show an understanding of the reading strategy.

Comprehension and Critical Thinking
1. (a) from Asia **(b)** Some Native Americans claim they are indigenous and that they have always lived on this land.

2. (a) Spanish settlers spread out across the Americas after the arrival of Columbus. The French, who were interested in fur trade, settled along the St. Lawrence and Mississippi Rivers. The English, who came for a new way of life, settled along the Atlantic coast.

(b) Most Europeans took the land from the Native Americans then fought them to control it. Also, many Europeans tried to convert the Native Americans to their religion.

3. (a) the Constitution **(b)** They felt that they should not be forced to pay taxes to a government in which they had no representatives.

Objectives

Social Studies
1. Explore the effects of westward expansion in the United States.
2. Discover the causes and effects of the Civil War.

Reading/Language Arts
Learn how to clarify words or ideas in a text by reading ahead.

Prepare to Read

Build Background Knowledge   L2

In this section students will learn more about the growth of the United States and the challenges the country faced during the 1800s. Have students preview the headings and visuals in the section. Each student should select a heading and write two or three facts that they already know about the event they selected. Have students engage in the Think-Write-Pair-Share activity (TE, p. T36) to share their answers.

Set a Purpose for Reading   L2
- Preview the Objectives.

- Form students into pairs or groups of four. Distribute the *Reading Readiness Guide.* Ask the students to fill in the first two columns of the chart. Use the Numbered Heads participation strategy (TE, p. T36) to call on students to share one piece of information they already know and one piece of information they want to know.

All in One **United States and Canada Teaching Resources,** *Reading Readiness Guide,* p. 144

Vocabulary Builder
Preview Key Terms   L2

Pronounce each Key Term, then ask the students to say the word with you. Provide a simple explanation such as, "Immigrants have come to the United States from all parts of the world."

Prepare to Read

Objectives
In this section you will
1. Explore the effects of westward expansion in the United States.
2. Discover the causes and effects of the Civil War.

Taking Notes
As you read the section, look for details about the causes and effects of westward expansion and the Civil War. Copy the flow-chart below and write each detail under the correct heading.

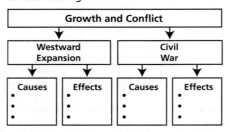

Target Reading Skill

Read Ahead Reading ahead is a strategy that can help you understand words and ideas in the text. If you do not understand a certain passage, it might help to read ahead. A word or an idea may be clarified further on.

Key Terms
- **Louisiana Purchase** (loo ee zee AN uh PUR chus) *n.* the sale of land in North America in 1803 by France to the United States
- **immigrant** (IM uh grunt) *n.* a person who moves to a new country in order to settle there
- **Industrial Revolution** (in DUS tree ul rev uh LOO shun) *n.* the change from making goods by hand to making them by machine
- **abolitionist** (ab uh LISH un ist) *n.* a person who believed that enslaving people was wrong and who wanted to end the practice
- **segregate** (SEG ruh gayt) *v.* to set apart, typically because of race or religion

Meriwether Lewis and William Clark with their Native American translator Sacajawea

In 1804, President Thomas Jefferson sent Meriwether Lewis and William Clark with a company of men to explore the land west of the Mississippi River. They would eventually travel all the way to the Pacific Coast and back—about 8,000 miles (13,000 kilometers).

As they journeyed up the Missouri River, Lewis and Clark found plants and animals completely new to them. They also created accurate, highly valuable maps of the region. As they traveled with their Native American translator, a Shoshone (shoh SHOH nee) woman named Sacajawea, Lewis and Clark met many Native American groups. Sacajawea helped Lewis and Clark communicate with the various groups. During these meetings, the two men tried to learn about the region and set up trading alliances. Few of the Native Americans they met had any idea how the visit would change their way of life.

Target Reading Skill   L2

Read Ahead Point out the Target Reading Skill. Tell students that reading ahead can help to clarify words and ideas if the words are further explained, or concepts are further developed.

Model the strategy using these sentences from p. 43: "First France, and then Spain, owned the Louisiana Territory. In 1800, war in Europe forced Spain to give it back to France." To understand exactly what land is referenced by the term "Louisiana Territory," students can read ahead to the next sentence to learn it is "all the land between the Mississippi River and the eastern slopes of the Rocky Mountains."

Give students *Reread or Read Ahead.* Have them complete the activity in their groups.

All in One **United States and Canada Teaching Resources,** *Reread or Read Ahead,* p. 159

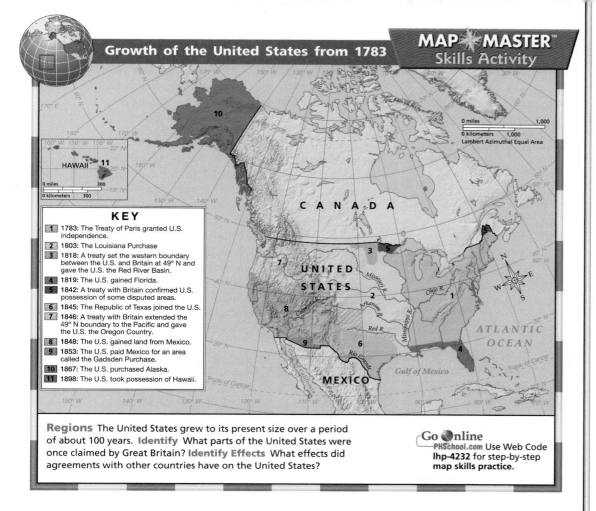

Growth of the United States from 1783

KEY

1. **1783:** The Treaty of Paris granted U.S. independence.
2. **1803:** The Louisiana Purchase
3. **1818:** A treaty set the western boundary between the U.S. and Britain at 49° N and gave the U.S. the Red River Basin.
4. **1819:** The U.S. gained Florida.
5. **1842:** A treaty with Britain confirmed U.S. possession of some disputed areas.
6. **1845:** The Republic of Texas joined the U.S.
7. **1846:** A treaty with Britain extended the 49° N boundary to the Pacific and gave the U.S. the Oregon Country.
8. **1848:** The U.S. gained land from Mexico.
9. **1853:** The U.S. paid Mexico for an area called the Gadsden Purchase.
10. **1867:** The U.S. purchased Alaska.
11. **1898:** The U.S. took possession of Hawaii.

Regions The United States grew to its present size over a period of about 100 years. **Identify** What parts of the United States were once claimed by Great Britain? **Identify Effects** What effects did agreements with other countries have on the United States?

Go Online PHSchool.com Use Web Code **lhp-4232** for step-by-step map skills practice.

A Nation Grows

The United States had not always owned the land that Lewis and Clark explored, called the Louisiana Territory. But, the purchase of this land set the country on a new course of westward expansion.

The Louisiana Purchase First France, and then Spain, owned the Louisiana Territory. In 1800, war in Europe forced Spain to give it back to France. In 1803, France offered to sell all the land between the Mississippi River and the eastern slopes of the Rocky Mountains to the United States—for only $15 million. This sale of land, called the **Louisiana Purchase**, doubled the size of the United States. The land would later be split into more than a dozen states.

Chapter 2 Section 2 **43**

Vocabulary Builder

Use the information below to teach students this section's high-use words.

High-Use Word	Definition and Sample Sentence
spur, p. 45	*v.* to encourage or motivate Losing the game **spurred** the team to practice harder.
conflict, p. 46	*n.* a disagreement A **conflict** arose between the two friends when they couldn't agree on which film to see.

Instruct

A Nation Grows [L2]

Guided Instruction

- **Vocabulary Builder** Clarify the high-use word **spur** before reading.

- Read A Growing Nation using the ReQuest Procedure (TE, p. T35).

- Ask **How much did the Louisiana Purchase cost?** *($15 million)* Tell students that the Louisiana Purchase was the sale of 828,000 square miles of land, and ask them to calculate the price per square mile. *($18.11 per square mile)* Explain that this works out to less than 3 cents per acre.

Answers

 Identify The Red River Basin, the area between the Red River Basin and the Great Lakes, the northern tip of Maine, and the Oregon Country were all disputed between the United States and Great Britain. **Identify Effects** Agreements with other countries caused the land claimed by the United States to grow.

Go Online PHSchool.com Students may practice their map skills using the interactive online version of this map.

Guided Instruction (continued)

■ Ask students to identify three major events that occurred between 1830 and 1860. *(In 1830, Congress passed the Indian Removal Act, requiring Native Americans in the Southeast to leave their homelands to make way for poor farmers, laborers, and settlers. In 1836, settlers in the territory of Texas rebelled against Mexican rule. In 1845, Texas became part of the United States.)*

■ Ask **What were the positive and negative effects of the westward expansion?** *(Positive effects: Increased land for settlers gave them an opportunity to make better lives for themselves; new states broadened voting privileges to include white men who did not own property. Negative effects: the relocation of Native Americans, and the death of many Native Americans in their forced migrations)*

Answers

Name The Seminole
Make Generalizations Native Americans probably had to face exhaustion and disease during their journeys westward, especially during winter or bad weather. It was also probably difficult for them to leave their homelands.

Go Online PHSchool.com Students may practice their map skills using the interactive online version of this map.

As the country grew, so did the meaning of democracy. In the 13 original states, only white males who owned property could vote. New states passed laws giving the vote to all white men 21 years old or older, whether they owned property or not. Eventually, all states gave every adult white male the right to vote. Women, African Americans, Native Americans, and other minorities, however, could not vote.

The Indian Removal Act Native Americans had struggled to keep their land since colonial times. Their struggle grew more difficult in 1828, when voters elected Andrew Jackson President. President Jackson looked after the interests of poor farmers, laborers, and settlers who wanted Native American lands in the Southeast. In 1830, he persuaded Congress to pass the Indian Removal Act. It required the Cherokees and other Native Americans in the area to leave their homelands. They were sent to live on new land in present-day Oklahoma. So many Cherokees died on the journey that the route they followed is known as the Trail of Tears.

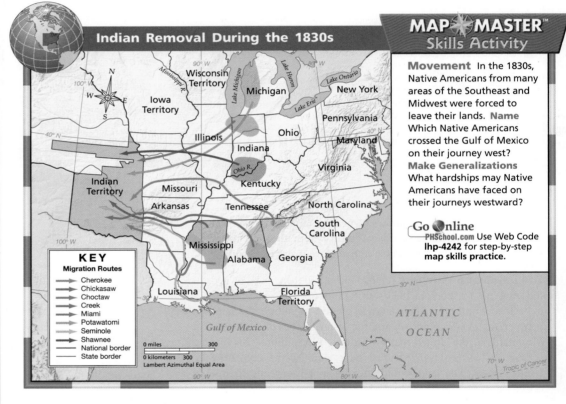

44 United States and Canada

Differentiated Instruction

For Advanced Readers L3
Have students read *Morning Girl, Journal Entry* and *Chief Joseph Surrenders.* In pairs, have students discuss how the relationship between Native Americans and Europeans changed over time.

All in One United States and Canada Teaching Resources, *Morning Girl,* pp. 174–176; *Journal Entry,* p. 177; *Chief Joseph Surrenders,* p. 178

Manifest Destiny Many Americans believed that the United States had a right to own all the land from the Atlantic to the Pacific. This belief, called Manifest Destiny, was used to justify further westward expansion. In the 1840s, American wagon trains began to cross the continent heading for the West.

The United States also looked to the Southwest. In 1836, American settlers in the Mexican territory of Texas had rebelled against Mexican rule. The Texans had then set up the Lone Star Republic. In 1845, Texas became part of the United States. Only a year later, the United States went to war with Mexico. The United States won the war and gained from Mexico much of what is now the Southwest region.

The Industrial Revolution At the same time, thousands of people were pouring into cities in the Northeast. Some had left farms to work in factories. Others were **immigrants,** or people who move to one country from another. These people came from Europe in search of jobs in the United States. They were spurred by the **Industrial Revolution,** or the change from making goods by hand to making them by machine.

The first industry to change was textiles, or cloth-making. New spinning machines and power looms enabled people to make cloth more quickly than they could by hand. Other inventions, such as the steam engine, made travel easier and faster. Steamboats and steam locomotives moved people and goods rapidly. By 1860, railroads linked most major northeastern and southeastern cities.

✓ **Reading Check** What did the Indian Removal Act do?

The Clermont, 1807
Robert Fulton demonstrates his steam-powered paddle-wheel boat, the *Clermont,* which used a steam engine improved by James Watt.
Draw Conclusions *How did the inventions of the Industrial Revolution change people's lives?*

Ask students to create the Taking Notes graphic organizer on a blank piece of paper. Then have them fill it in with information about westward expansion. Briefly model how to identify which details to record.

Monitor Progress
As students fill in the graphic organizer, circulate and make sure individuals are choosing the correct details. Provide assistance as needed.

Skills Mini Lesson

Transferring Information from One Medium to Another

1. Teach the skill by explaining to students that information from the written text on a page is often transferred to maps, charts, and photos. By looking closely at the visuals, students can learn more about the text.

2. Help students practice the skill by rereading A Nation Grows and studying the map on page 44 in the Student Edition for additional information.

3. Have students apply the skill by transferring the additional information from the map into a brief paragraph.

Answers

✓ **Reading Check** The Indian Removal Act forced Native American nations, such as the present-day Cherokee, to relocate from their homes to the Indian Territory in present-day Oklahoma. Their journey was harsh and many people died along the way.

Draw Conclusions Inventions of the Industrial Revolution allowed people to make products more quickly than they could by hand, and made travel easier and faster. Many people left farms or immigrated from other countries to work in factories.

The Civil War and Reconstruction

Guided Instruction

- **Vocabulary Builder** Clarify the high-use word **conflict** before reading.

- Read about The Civil War and Reconstruction with students. As students read, circulate and make sure individuals can answer the Reading Check question.

- Ask students to identify at least one important event that led to the Civil War. *(Possible answers: publication of* Uncle Tom's Cabin *led more Northerners to become abolitionists; California entered the nation as a free state; the Fugitive Slave Act was passed; Lincoln was elected President, causing the South to secede from the Union.)*

- Ask students to debate the following question: **Do you think the Civil War and Reconstruction achieved all of the abolitionists' goals?** *(Some students may argue that they did, because slavery was abolished. Others may say that they did not, because the Southern states passed segregation laws.)*

➲ Target Reading Skill

Read Ahead As a follow up, ask students to perform the Target Reading Skill activity in the Student Edition. *(When Eli Whitney invented the cotton gin, cotton farming boomed. To keep up production, farmers expanded into western lands and wanted to bring slavery with them.)*

Answers

MAP MASTER Skills Activity **List** Florida, Alabama, Georgia, Mississippi, Texas, Louisiana, Arkansas, Tennessee, South Carolina, North Carolina, and Virginia **Draw Conclusions** States that grew cotton depended on the labor of enslaved people; the cotton belt states joined the Confederacy.

Go Online PHSchool.com Students may practice their map skills using the interactive online version of this map.

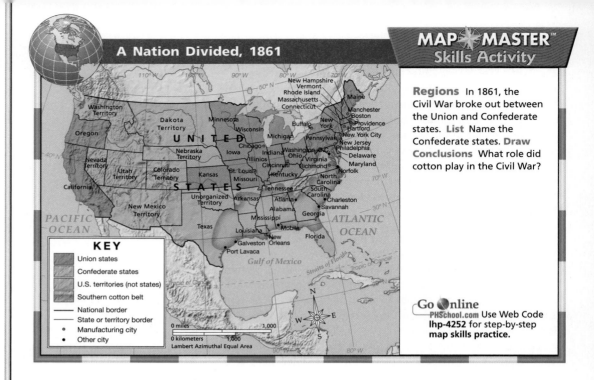

A Nation Divided, 1861

MAP MASTER™ Skills Activity

KEY
- Union states
- Confederate states
- U.S. territories (not states)
- Southern cotton belt
- National border
- State or territory border
- Manufacturing city
- Other city

0 miles 1,000
0 kilometers 1,000
Lambert Azimuthal Equal Area

Regions In 1861, the Civil War broke out between the Union and Confederate states. **List** Name the Confederate states. **Draw Conclusions** What role did cotton play in the Civil War?

Go Online PHSchool.com Use Web Code lhp-4252 for step-by-step map skills practice.

Read Ahead
Keep reading to see how harvesting cotton affected the nation's history.

The Civil War and Reconstruction

With the textile industry growing as a result of the Industrial Revolution, the demand for cotton grew as well. Cotton required many laborers for planting and harvesting. This is one reason why slaves were an important part of plantation life.

In 1793, Eli Whitney invented the cotton gin, which quickly removed seeds from cotton. The cotton gin made cotton easier to process after it was picked. Cotton farming boomed. However, growing cotton quickly wore out the soil. To keep up production, farmers wanted to expand into western lands. But that meant that slavery would spread into the new territories. Some people did not want this. The debate began. Should the states or the federal government decide about the issue of slavery in the new territories?

Causes of Conflict Before California asked to be admitted to the union as a free state in 1850, there were equal numbers of slave and free states. After a heated debate, Congress granted California's request. The Southern states were not pleased. To gain their support, Congress also passed the Fugitive Slave Act. It required that runaway slaves must be returned to their owners. This action only intensified the argument over slavery.

46 United States and Canada

Background: Biography

Harriet Tubman (c. 1820–1913) Harriet Tubman spent the first 29 years of her life in slavery. In 1849 she escaped to the North but returned to guide other slaves to freedom. Tubman soon became one of the most tireless "conductors" on the Underground Railroad. The secret flights were very dangerous for all involved, and Tubman did not tolerate any risky behavior. She kept people in line by making sure they knew she carried a gun. Such no-nonsense behavior led abolitionist John Brown to admiringly dub her "General Tubman."

The South Breaks Away   In 1852, Harriet Beecher Stowe published *Uncle Tom's Cabin,* a novel about the evils of slavery. After reading this book, thousands of Northerners became abolitionists (ab uh LISH un ists). **Abolitionists** were people who believed that slavery was wrong and wanted to end, or abolish, its practice. Many helped enslaved people escape to Canada. There, slavery was illegal. Most Southerners, however, felt that abolitionists were robbing them of their property.

The debate over slavery raged. When Abraham Lincoln, a Northerner, was elected President in 1860, many Southerners feared they would have little say in the government. As a result, some Southern states seceded, or withdrew, from the United States. They founded a new country—the Confederate States of America, or the Confederacy.

The Civil War   In 1861, the Civil War between the Northern states and the Confederacy erupted. It lasted four years. The North, known as the Union, had more industry, wealth, and soldiers. The Confederacy had experienced military officers. It also had cotton. Many foreign countries bought southern cotton. Southerners hoped that these countries would help support the Confederacy in its struggle.

Despite the North's advantages, the war dragged on. In 1863, Lincoln issued the Emancipation Proclamation. This declared that enslaved people in areas loyal to the Confederacy were free, and it gave the North a new battle cry—freedom! Thousands of African Americans joined the fight against the South.

Fighting for Their Cause
These African American soldiers are outside of their barracks at Fort Lincoln, Washington, D.C. Twenty-three African Americans received the Congressional Medal of Honor (below right), the country's highest military honor. **Draw Conclusions** *Why do you think African Americans were willing to fight for the Union?*

Chapter 2 Section 2 **47**

Independent Practice
Have students complete the graphic organizer by filling in details about the causes and effects of the Civil War.

Monitor Progress
■ Show *Section Reading Support Transparency USC 47* and ask students to check their graphic organizers individually. Go over key concepts and clarify key vocabulary as needed.

   📖 **United States and Canada Transparencies,** *Section Reading Support Transparency USC 47*

■ Tell students to fill in the last column of the *Reading Readiness Guide.* Ask them to evaluate if what they learned was what they had expected to learn.

   All in One **United States and Canada Teaching Resources,** *Reading Readiness Guide,* p. 144

Assess and Reteach

Assess Progress   L2
Have students complete the Section Assessment. Administer the *Section Quiz.*

   All in One **United States and Canada Teaching Resources,** *Section Quiz,* p. 146

Reteach   L1
If students need more instruction, have them read this section in the Reading and Vocabulary Study Guide.

   📖 Chapter 2, Section 2, **United States and Canada Reading and Vocabulary Study Guide,** pp. 19–21

Extend   L3
Assign the *Small Group Activity: Presenting an Oral Biography.* Have students work in groups to create an oral presentation about a historical figure of the Civil War.

   All in One **United States and Canada Teaching Resources,** *Small Group Activity: Presenting an Oral Biography,* pp. 165–168

Answer

Draw Conclusions Possible answer: African Americans wanted to fight to support the end of slavery in the United States.

┌─ **Background: Daily Life** ────────

Segregation Laws   The South's segregation laws were known as Jim Crow laws. These laws attempted to prevent any meeting of blacks and whites on an equal footing. For example, blacks and whites could not attend the same schools, eat in the same restaurants, or even be buried in the same cemeteries. The laws began to be outlawed in 1954, when the Supreme Court ruled that segregation in public schools was unconstitutional.

Read the **Citizens Heroes** on this page. Ask students **What sort of dangers do you think Barton and other nurses faced during the Civil War?** *(Civil War nurses may have faced dangers such as battlefield injury and disease spread in makeshift hospitals.)*

Answers

✓ **Reading Check** Some Southern states seceded after a Northerner, Abraham Lincoln, was elected President because they believed they would no longer have a voice in the government.

Section 2 Assessment

Key Terms
Students' sentences should reflect knowledge of each Key Term.

Target Reading Skill
Answers will vary, but should indicate that students understand the concept of clarifying a word or an idea by reading ahead.

Comprehension and Critical Thinking
1. (a) The United States increased its size by purchasing the Louisiana Territory, moving Native Americans off their land, and winning land in wars. **(b)** Settlers took the land of Native Americans, often fighting them to control it. Also, government actions, such as the Indian Removal Act, forced Native Americans to give up their land and relocate to Indian Territory in Oklahoma. **(c)** The Industrial Revolution spurred farmers to come to the cities to work in factories. It also encouraged immigrants to come to the United States in search of jobs. The invention of the railroad and steam engines also made transportation to big cities more efficient.

2. (a) The Southern states, which supported slavery, seceded after a Northerner, Abraham Lincoln, was elected President. They believed they would no longer have a voice in the government. **(b)** Many Northerners opposed slavery, while white Southerners felt slavery was necessary to the South's econo-

---

Clara Barton

When the Civil War began, Clara Barton learned that many soldiers were suffering because of the lack of supplies on the front lines. She decided to help by setting up an organization to deliver supplies to men wounded in battle. She also worked as a nurse in hospitals located near battlefields. Because of her gentle and helpful ways, Barton earned the name Angel of the Battlefield. Years later, she founded the American branch of the Red Cross.

Reconstruction The Civil War ended in 1865 when the Confederates surrendered. Lincoln wanted the Southern states to return willingly to the Union. This was the first step in his plan for the Reconstruction, or rebuilding, of the nation. Less than a week after the end of the war, Lincoln was assassinated, or murdered. Vice President Andrew Johnson tried to carry out Lincoln's plan. But Congress resisted his efforts. Finally, Congress took complete control of Reconstruction. The Union Army governed the South until new state officials were elected.

In 1877, the Union Army withdrew. But Southern lawmakers soon voted to **segregate,** or separate, black people from white people. Segregation affected all aspects of life. Southern states passed laws, called Jim Crow laws, that separated blacks and whites in schools, restaurants, theaters, trains, streetcars, playgrounds, hospitals, and even cemeteries. Some African Americans brought lawsuits to challenge segregation. The laws passed during Reconstruction would become the basis of the civil rights movement in later years. The difficult struggle to preserve the United States had succeeded. But the long struggle to guarantee equality to all Americans still lay ahead.

✓ **Reading Check** **Why did some Southern states secede from the United States?**

Section 2 Assessment

Key Terms
Review the key terms at the beginning of this section. Use each term in a sentence that explains its meaning.

Target Reading Skill
What word or idea were you able to clarify by reading ahead?

Comprehension and Critical Thinking
1. (a) List In what ways did the United States increase the area of its land?

(b) Identify Effects How did the growing nation affect Native Americans?
(c) Identify Causes What factors led to a population boom in northeastern cities?
2. (a) Identify Why did the Southern states withdraw from the Union?
(b) Explore the Main Idea How did the issue of slavery become a cause of the Civil War?
(c) Analyze How did segregation affect African Americans?

Writing Activity
Write an entry on a plan for Reconstruction that President Lincoln might have made in his diary.

For: An activity on the Civil War
Visit: PHSchool.com
Web Code: lhd-4202

48 United States and Canada

---

my. The debate raged on until the Southern states, seeing the balance of power tipping toward the North, finally seceded. **(c)** African Americans were separated from whites in most public places, including schools, restaurants, and trains.

Writing Activity
Use the *Rubric for Assessing a Journal Entry* to evaluate students' diary entries.

All in One **United States and Canada Teaching Resources,** *Rubric for Assessing a Journal Entry,* p. 184

Go Online PHSchool.com Typing in the Web code when prompted will bring students directly to detailed instructions for this activity.

Prepare to Read

Objectives

In this section you will
1. Explore what happened in the United States from 1865 to 1914.
2. Find out what happened during the World Wars.
3. Explore the challenges the United States faces at home and abroad.

Taking Notes

As you read the section, look for details about the United States becoming a world power. Copy the outline below and fill in each main idea and detail.

```
I. The United States from 1865 to 1914
    A. Moving to the Midwest
        1.
        2.
    B.
II.
```

Target Reading Skill

Paraphrase Paraphrasing can help you understand what you read. When you paraphrase, you restate in your own words what you have read. As you read this section, paraphrase, or "say back," the information following each red or blue heading.

Key Terms

- **labor force** (LAY bur fawrs) *n.* the supply of workers
- **Holocaust** (HAHL uh kawst) *n.* the murder of six million Jews during World War II
- **Cold War** (kohld wawr) *n.* a period of great tension between the United States and the Soviet Union
- **civil rights** (SIV ul ryts) *n.* the basic rights due to all citizens
- **terrorist** (TEHR ur ist) *n.* a person who uses violence and fear to achieve goals

---

Jacob Riis was an angry man. In one of his books, he introduced his readers to slum life in the late 1800s. He wanted other people to be angry, too—angry enough to change things.

> **Come over here. Step carefully over this baby—it is a baby, in spite of its rags and dirt—under these iron bridges called fire escapes, but loaded down . . . with broken household goods, with washtubs and barrels, over which no man could climb from a fire. . . . That baby's parents live in the rear tenement [apartment] here. . . . There are plenty of houses with half a hundred such in [them].**
>
> —*Jacob Riis*, How the Other Half Lives

An 1886 photo of a slum by Jacob Riis

Target Reading Skill L2

Paraphrase Point out the Target Reading Skill. Explain to students that paraphrasing, or restating the information you have just read in your own words, helps you understand what you read.

Model paraphrasing by reading aloud the first paragraph on page 50 and working with the class to paraphrase the information (*The Industrial Revolution improved life for the rich and middle class, but did little for the poor. Many of these people were workers who could barely speak English. They earned so little that even children had to work to help their families survive.*)

Give students *Paraphrase.* Have them complete the activity in their groups.

All in One United States and Canada Teaching Resources, *Paraphrase* p. 160

Objectives

Social Studies
1. Explore what happened in the United States from 1865 to 1914.
2. Find out what happened during the World Wars.
3. Explore the challenges the United States faces at home and abroad.

Reading/Language Arts
Use paraphrasing to help you understand what you read.

Prepare to Read

Build Background Knowledge L2

Draw the beginning of an idea web, placing the words "The United State Becomes a World Power" in the center. Ask students to glance through the section's headings, photographs, and captions. They can also recall any prior knowledge about the Industrial Revolution, World War I, World War II, or the civil rights movement. Ask students what kinds of events they think led to the United States becoming a world power, using an Idea Wave (TE, p. T35) to add students' ideas to the web.

Set a Purpose for Reading L2

- Preview the Objectives.

- Read each statement in the *Reading Readiness Guide* aloud. Ask students to mark the statements true or false.

  All in One United States and Canada Teaching Resources, *Reading Readiness Guide,* p. 148

- Have students discuss the statements in pairs or groups of four, then mark their worksheets again. Use the Numbered Heads participation strategy (TE, p. T36) to call on students to share their group's perspectives.

Vocabulary Builder

Preview Key Terms L2

Pronounce each Key Term, then ask the students to say the word with you. Provide a simple explanation such as, "The Cold War refers to the political tension and military rivalry between the United States and the Soviet Union following World War II."

Instruct

From 1865 to 1914 `L2`

Guided Instruction

- **Vocabulary Builder** Clarify the high-use word **slum** before reading.

- Read From 1865 to 1914, using the Paragraph Shrinking technique, (TE, p. T34).

- Discuss what reformers did to help fight poverty. (*Jacob Riis wrote a book exposing the hardships of the poor, Jane Addams set up a community center in Chicago, and Mary Harris Jones helped miners fight for better wages, earning the nickname Mother Jones.*)

- Ask **How did the Homestead Act help people living in cities?** (*The Homestead Act gave poor people in the cities the opportunity to own land that they could not otherwise afford.*)

Independent Practice
Ask students to create the Taking Notes graphic organizer on a blank piece of paper. Then have them fill in the outline with the information they have just learned. Briefly model how to identify which details to record.

Monitor Progress
As students fill in the graphic organizer, circulate and make sure individuals are choosing the correct details. Provide assistance as needed.

Target Reading Skill `L2`

Paraphrase As a follow up, ask students to perform the Target Reading Skill activity in the Student Edition. (*By the 1900s, the United States expanded and grew stronger by taking control of Alaska, Hawaii, Puerto Rico, Guam, and the Philippines.*)

Answers

Draw Conclusions The Homestead Act gave people incentive to settle in the Midwest, and the railroad got them there faster and easier than previous methods.

✓ **Reading Check** The United States bought Alaska from Russia.

Settling the Plains
A wagon train travels in the Oklahoma Territory around 1900 (above). Railroads such as the Hannibal and St. Joseph recruited farmers to buy and settle land, as advertised in the poster above. **Draw Conclusions** *How did the Homestead Act and the railroads help to speed up settlement of the Midwest?*

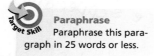

Paraphrase
Paraphrase this paragraph in 25 words or less.

From 1865 to 1914

By the late 1800s, a handful of rich people had made millions of dollars in industry. The Industrial Revolution had also made life easier for the middle class—the group of people that included skilled workers and successful farmers. But life did not improve for the poor. City slums were crowded with immigrants. These newcomers were a huge **labor force,** or supply of workers. Many couldn't speak English. Employers paid them little. Even small children worked so that families could make ends meet.

Reformers like Jacob Riis began to protest such poverty. In Chicago, Jane Addams set up a settlement house, or community center, for poor immigrants. Mary Harris Jones helped miners organize for better wages. Because of her work to end child labor, people called her Mother Jones.

Moving to the Midwest To leave poverty behind, many people moved to the open plains and prairies of the Midwest. The United States government attracted settlers to this region with the Homestead Act of 1862. This act gave free land to settlers. Settlers faced a difficult life on the plains. Still, thousands came west, helped by the development of railroads that connected the East Coast with the West.

New Territories The United States also expanded beyond its continental borders. In 1867, the United States bought the territory of Alaska from Russia. In 1898, the United States took control of Hawaii. In that same year, the United States fought and won the Spanish-American War. The victory gave the United States control of the Spanish lands of Puerto Rico, Guam, and the Philippines. By the 1900s, America had a strong economy, military might, and overseas territory.

✓ **Reading Check** How did the United States get Alaska?

┌ Vocabulary Builder

Use the information below to teach students this section's high-use words.

High-Use Word	Definition and Sample Sentence
slum, p. 49	*n.* overcrowded and poor area of housing in a city or town Many city governments are improving living conditions so there are no more **slums**.
restore, p. 51	*v.* to bring back or establish again The damaged car was **restored** and looked brand new.

The World at War

Now the United States had a major role in world affairs. As a result, the country was drawn into international conflicts. In 1914, World War I broke out in Europe. President Woodrow Wilson did not want America to take part, but when Germany began sinking American ships, Wilson had no choice. He declared war. The United States joined the Allied Powers of Great Britain and France. In 1917, thousands of American soldiers sailed to Europe. They fought against the Central Powers, which included Germany, Austria-Hungary, and Turkey. With this added strength, the Allies won the war in 1918. The terms of peace in the Treaty of Versailles punished Germany severely. Its harshness led to another worldwide conflict 20 years later.

The Economy Collapses Following World War I, the United States' economy boomed. Women enjoyed new freedoms and the hard-won right to vote. More and more people bought cars, refrigerators, radios, and other modern conveniences.

In 1929, however, the world was overcome by an economic disaster called the Great Depression. In America, factories closed, people lost their jobs, and farmers lost their farms. Many banks closed, and people lost their life's savings. In 1933, President Franklin D. Roosevelt took office. He created a plan called the New Deal. This was a series of government programs to help people get jobs and to restore the economy. Some of these programs, like Social Security, are still in place today. Social Security provides income to people who are retired or disabled.

Americans at War
Nurses place a wounded soldier on a stretcher during World War I (below). Recruitment posters such as the one below called on Americans to join the military. **Draw Inferences** *Why do you think this poster was effective in getting Americans to volunteer for military duty?*

Guided Instruction
- **Vocabulary Builder** Clarify the high-use word **restore** before reading.

- Read about The World at War with students. As students read, circulate and make sure individuals can answer the Reading Check question.

- Discuss with students how Roosevelt tried to lift America out of the Great Depression. *(Roosevelt created a plan called the New Deal, a series of government programs to help people get jobs and restore the economy.)*

- Ask students **What role did the United States play in World War II?** *(After the Japanese attacked Pearl Harbor, the United States declared war and helped the Allies win important battles in Europe and the Pacific.)*

Independent Practice
Tell students to continue to fill in their outlines with the information they have just learned.

Monitor Progress
Circulate and make sure students are choosing the correct details as they fill in their graphic organizers. Provide assistance as needed.

Skills for Life · Skills Mini Lesson

Analyze Primary Sources
1. Tell students that a *primary source* is written by someone who actually experienced what is being described. To analyze a primary source, identify who created the source and when, look for bias, then evaluate the source.
2. Help students practice by reading the primary source on page 49.

3. Have students apply the skill by answering the following questions: Who created the primary source? Does the writer have any bias? *(Jacob Riis, a writer angry about slums)* How reliable is the source? *(His statements are facts and provide a first-hand account of the conditions.)*

Answer

Draw Inferences This poster was probably very effective because the slogan and image directly address the viewer.

The U.S. At Home and Abroad

Guided Instruction

- Read about the United States after World War II in The U.S. At Home and Abroad.

- Discuss with students the postwar events that created tension between the United States and the Soviet Union. *(As the Soviet Union began to take control of many eastern European nations, the U.S. feared that it planned to spread communism throughout the world. Two wars stemmed from this tension: in Korea and Vietnam.)*

- Point out that Martin Luther King, Jr., was much admired for his nonviolent approach to social change. Ask students to think of other examples of nonviolent approaches to social change. *(Possible answers: writing to legislators; striking; demonstrating; writing letters to editors; helping candidates for public office; running for office. If not mentioned, suggest that one of the most important methods is voting.)*

- Ask students **What challenges does the United States face today?** *(the fight against terrorism; having a stable economy)*

This Rosie the Riveter poster from World War II encouraged women to join the workforce.

A Second World War The Great Depression affected people around the world. In Germany, Adolf Hitler rose to power, promising to restore Germany's wealth and power. He began World War II. In 1941, Germany's ally, Japan, attacked the United States naval base at Pearl Harbor, Hawaii. The United States declared war on Japan. Germany then declared war on the United States. The United States sent armed forces to fight in Europe and in the Pacific. President Roosevelt, who led the nation in war, did not live to see peace. He died in April 1945, and Vice President Harry S Truman became President.

In May of 1945, the Allies defeated the Germans. During the summer of 1945, President Truman decided to drop two atomic bombs on Japan. That convinced Japan to surrender. Finally, World War II was over.

By the end of the war in 1945, Europe was in ruins. People around the world learned that Hitler had forced Jews, Gypsies, Slavs, and others into brutal prison camps. Millions of people, including some six million Jews, were murdered. This horrible mass murder is called the **Holocaust** (HAHL uh kawst).

■ Timeline Skills

The United States has been involved in both domestic and international conflicts since the Civil War ended. **Identify** Which of the wars shown did not involve open warfare? **Compare** How long was this war, compared to the others shown on the timeline?

✓ **Reading Check** What led the United States to take part in World War II?

Post–Civil War to the Present

| | 1869 Transcontinental railroad completed | 1870–1900 Growth of industry | | | | | | 1929–1939 Great Depression |

1865 — 1875 — 1885 — 1895 — 1905 — 1915 — 1925 — 1935

1865–1877 Reconstruction

1898 Spanish-American War

1917–1918 World War I*

*Years of United States involvement

Differentiated Instruction

For English Language Learners
If appropriate assign *Guided Reading and Review (Spanish)* to help facilitate understanding of how the United States became a world power.

 Guided Reading and Review (Spanish), **Spanish Support,** p. 16

For Gifted and Talented
Ask students to research the art, music, literature, or drama that emerged from the Great Depression. Ask students to present their research to the class.

Answers

✓ **Reading Check** When Japan attacked the U.S. naval base at Pearl Harbor, the United States declared war on Japan. Germany then declared war on the United States.

Timeline Skills Identify the Cold War **Compare** It was the longest war, lasting 46 years. The next-longest war, the Vietnam War, lasted 20 years.

The U.S. at Home and Abroad

Following World War II, the United States was a world superpower. It faced new challenges and responsibilities both at home and abroad.

Tension with the Soviets In 1922, the Soviet Union had been created. It adopted a form of government called communism. Under this system, the state owns all property, such as farms and factories, on behalf of its citizens.

After World War II, the Soviet Union took control of many Eastern European countries. The United States feared the Soviets were trying to spread communism throughout the world. As a result, the United States and the Soviet Union entered the **Cold War**, a period of great tension. The Cold War lasted about four decades. Although the two countries never faced each other in an actual war, two wars grew out of this tension—the Korean War and the Vietnam War.

The Fight for Civil Rights The economy boomed in the post-war years, but not all citizens shared in the benefits. In the South, racial segregation was a way of life. Many African Americans began to unite to win their **civil rights**, or the rights belonging to all citizens. The movement had many leaders, including Martin Luther King, Jr. He led peaceful marches and organized boycotts against companies that practiced discrimination, or unfair treatment of a group or person. The movement's success inspired others who felt they were treated unfairly, including women and Mexican Americans.

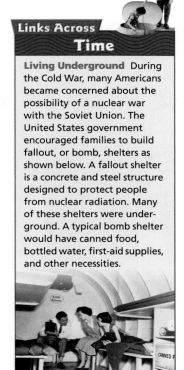

Links Across Time

Living Underground During the Cold War, many Americans became concerned about the possibility of a nuclear war with the Soviet Union. The United States government encouraged families to build fallout, or bomb, shelters as shown below. A fallout shelter is a concrete and steel structure designed to protect people from nuclear radiation. Many of these shelters were underground. A typical bomb shelter would have canned food, bottled water, first-aid supplies, and other necessities.

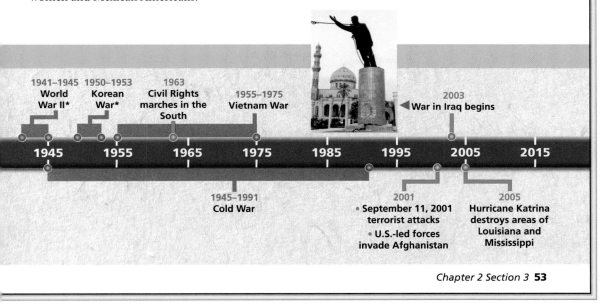

1941–1945 World War II*	1950–1953 Korean War*	1963 Civil Rights marches in the South	1955–1975 Vietnam War			2003 ◄ War in Iraq begins		

1945 **1955** **1965** **1975** **1985** **1995** **2005** **2015**

1945–1991 Cold War

2001 • September 11, 2001 terrorist attacks • U.S.-led forces invade Afghanistan

2005 Hurricane Katrina destroys areas of Louisiana and Mississippi

---

Assess and Reteach

Assess Progress `L2`

Have students complete the Section Assessment. Administer the *Section Quiz*.

All in One **United States and Canada Teaching Resources,** *Section Quiz,* p. 150

Reteach `L1`

If students need more instruction, have them read this section in the Reading and Vocabulary Study Guide.

📖 Chapter 2, Section 3, **United States and Canada Reading and Vocabulary Study Guide**, pp. 22–24

Extend `L3`

Have students learn more about the lives of the people in the United States and Canada during World War II by reading *A Child in Prison Camp.* Assign students to work in groups to discuss the questions at the end of the selection.

All in One **United States and Canada Teaching Resources,** *A Child in Prison Camp,* pp. 179–181

Answers

✓ **Reading Check** The two principal countries in the Cold War were the United States and the Soviet Union.

Section 3 Assessment

Key Terms
Students' sentences should reflect knowledge of each Key Term.

🔖 **Target Reading Skill**
Answers will vary, but should include important information such as the United States' involvement in international affairs, the United States entering the war, and the peace agreement that later caused conflict.

Comprehension and Critical Thinking
1. (a) Because poor immigrants worked for low wages, they lived in poverty in tenement slums. Even children had to work to help their families. **(b)** The United States acquired Alaska from the Russians, took control of Hawaii, won the Spanish-American War, and acquired Puerto Rico, Guam, and the Philippines.

2. (a) Germany, Austria-Hungary, and Turkey **(b)** The war began when Germany invaded Poland in 1939. The United States entered in 1941 when Japan attacked Pearl Harbor.

Firefighters walk away from the rubble of the World Trade Center towers in New York City.

America in the World Today At the beginning of the twenty-first century, Americans continued to look for solutions to long-term problems, such as homelessness, low wages, and pollution.

The economy reached new heights in the 1990s, powered by the Internet business revolution. The Internet is a network of interconnected computers that allows users to access computerized information. After a downturn in the early 2000s, the economy continued to grow. At the same time, it faced challenges such as high oil prices and rising federal debt.

The United States also faced a new challenge at home and abroad—on September 11, 2001, terrorists attacked the World Trade Center in New York City and the Pentagon in Washington, D.C. **Terrorists** use violence to frighten people or governments or to express their views. In response to these and possible future attacks, the United States took military action in both Afghanistan and Iraq. Saddam Hussein (sah DAHM hoo SAYN), Iraq's brutal dictator, was captured by coalition troops in December 2003. However, the United States continues to maintain a military presence in Iraq. The United States works with its allies around the world, especially Great Britain, to fight terrorism.

✓ **Reading Check** **What countries were involved in the Cold War?**

✦ Section 3 Assessment

Key Terms
Review the key terms at the beginning of this section. Use each term in a sentence that explains its meaning.

🔖 **Target Reading Skill**
Paraphrase the paragraph on page 51 under the red heading The World at War.

Comprehension and Critical Thinking
1. (a) Recall How did the Industrial Revolution affect poor immigrants in the late 1800s?

(b) Identify Causes What three events helped make the United States a world power?
2. (a) List What countries made up the Central Powers in World War I?
(b) Sequence Describe the events that led to World War II.
3. (a) Explain What gains in equality did African Americans make after World War II?
(b) Identify Cause and Effect How might African American gains in civil rights affect other groups?

Writing Activity
Write a paragraph about what it means for a country to be a world power. What challenges would a world power face? What special responsibilities might it have?

For: An activity on the Homestead Act
Visit: PHSchool.com
Web Code: lhp-4203

54 United States and Canada

3. (a) African Americans began winning civil rights. **4. (b)** By winning their civil rights, African Americans inspired other groups, such as women, the disabled, and Mexican Americans, to fight for their rights.

Writing Activity
Use the *Rubric for Assessing a Writing Assignment* to evaluate students' paragraphs.

All in One **United States and Canada Teaching Resources,** *Rubric for Assessing a Writing Assignment,* p. 183

Go Online PHSchool.com Typing in the Web code when prompted will bring students directly to detailed instructions for this activity.

The History of Canada

Prepare to Read

Objectives

In this section you will
1. Learn about why France and Britain were rivals in Canada.
2. Discover how Canada became an independent nation.
3. Explore how Canada became a world power in the 1900s.

Taking Notes

As you read the section, look for events that happened before and after the British North America Act in 1867. Copy the table below and write each event in the correct column.

British North America Act (1867)	
Before	After
•	•
•	•
•	•

Target Reading Skill

Summarize When you summarize, you review and state, in the correct order, the main points you have read. Summarizing what you read is a good technique to help you comprehend and study. As you read, pause occasionally to summarize what you have read.

Key Terms

• **dominion** (duh MIN yun) *n.* a self-governing area subject to Great Britain
• **bilingual** (by LIN gwul) *adj.* able to speak two languages

Haida portrait mask

The Haida people of British Columbia tell this tale. As in many Native American tales, nature plays an important role.

> **While he was crying and singing his dirge [sad song], a figure emerged from the lake. It was a strange animal, in its mouth a stick that it was gnawing. On each side of the animal were two smaller ones also gnawing sticks. Then the largest figure . . . spoke, 'Don't be so sad! It is I, your wife, and your two children. We have returned to our home in the water. . . . Call me the Beaver woman.'**
>
> —*Haida tale*

To the Haida and other native peoples in Canada, beavers were especially important. Imagine how they felt when European trappers killed almost all of the beavers to make fur hats.

Objectives

Social Studies

1. Learn about why France and Britain were rivals in Canada.
2. Discover how Canada became an independent nation.
3. Explore how Canada became a world power in the 1900s.

Reading/Language Arts

Use summarizing to help comprehend the main points you have read.

Prepare to Read

Build Background Knowledge L2

Tell students that in this section they will learn about the history of Canada. Have students preview the headers and visuals in the section with the following question in mind: **How are the histories of Canada and the United States similar and how are they different?** Conduct an Idea Wave (TE, p. T35) to generate a class list of similarities and differences on the board.

Set a Purpose for Reading L2

■ Preview the Objectives.

■ Read each statement in the *Reading Readiness Guide* aloud. Ask students to mark the statements true or false.

　All in One United States and Canada Teaching Resources, *Reading Readiness Guide,* p. 152

■ Have students discuss the statements in pairs or groups of four, then mark their worksheets again. Use the Numbered Heads participation strategy (TE, p. T36) to get students to share their group's perspective.

Target Reading Skill L2

Summarize Point out the Target Reading Skill. Tell students that a summary reviews and states what the paragraph or passage is about. To summarize, you must determine what the most important idea is and leave out the less important details.

Model the strategy by working with students to summarize the first paragraph on page 56. (*Fur trade in Canada was a source of conflict between France and Great Britain. A peace treaty in 1713 gave Great Britain what is now the southeastern corner of Canada.*)

Give students *Summarize.* Have them complete the activity in their groups.

　All in One United States and Canada Teaching Resources, *Summarize,* p. 161

Vocabulary Builder

Preview Key Terms L2

Pronounce each Key Term, then ask the students to say the word with you. Provide a simple explanation such as, "A person who is bilingual speaks more than one language fluently."

Instruct

The French and the British

Guided Instruction

■ **Vocabulary Builder** Clarify the high-use word **decisive** before reading.

■ Read The French and the British, using the Oral Cloze strategy (TE, p. T33).

■ Discuss how the first two British governors of Canada tried to keep peace with the French settlers. (*They passed the Quebec Act, giving the French people in Quebec the right to speak their own language, practice their own religion, and follow their own customs.*)

■ Ask students **What do you think was the greatest source of conflict between the French and British—control of land or cultural differences? Explain.**(*In the late 1700s, the French wanted land for trading and the British wanted land for settlements. By the 1800s, cultural differences became the greater problem and Great Britain had to divide the land into two colonies: one for the British and the other for the French.*)

Independent Practice

Ask students to create the Taking Notes graphic organizer on a blank piece of paper. Tell students that the British North America Act was accepted in 1867. Then have them fill in the table with the information they have just learned.

Monitor Progress

As students fill in the graphic organizer, circulate and make sure individuals are choosing the correct details. Provide assistance as needed.

Answers

Analyze Images Probably not, because the British would not have been able to attack Quebec.

✓ Reading Check After the American Revolution, many Loyalists moved to Canada. Most did not want to live in a French culture, so Great Britain divided the land into two colonies: Upper and Lower Canada.

The Battle of Quebec, 1759
The Battle of Quebec was a turning point in the Seven Years' War. This painting illustrates how British troops found a passage through the cliffs that protected Quebec. **Analyze Images** *Do you think that Quebec would have fallen to the British if troops had not found a passage in? Explain why or why not.*

The French and the British

The profitable fur trade in Canada was a source of conflict for France and Great Britain. They had fought wars all over the world, but had signed a peace treaty in 1713. The treaty gave Great Britain the Hudson Bay region, Newfoundland, and part of Acadia, which later became the southeastern corner of Canada.

The peace was uneasy. Against their will, French Catholics in Acadia came under the rule of British Protestants. The French controlled the lowlands south of Hudson Bay and lands around the St. Lawrence River. Both countries wanted to control the Ohio River valley, farther to the south. The French wanted the beavers for furs. The British wanted the land for settlement.

Great Britain Gains Control The contest for this region erupted into the Seven Years' War in 1756. The British won the decisive Battle of Quebec in 1759. The Treaty of Paris, signed in 1763, gave Great Britain complete control over Canada. Some French settlers returned to France. Those who stayed resisted English culture. The first two British governors of Canada were sympathetic to the French and passed the Quebec Act. It gave the French people in Quebec the right to speak their own language, practice their own religion, and follow their own customs.

Two Colonies Emerge During the American Revolution, some Americans did not want independence from Britain. They were called Loyalists. After the war, many Loyalists moved to Canada. But most did not want to live in a French culture. To avoid problems, Great Britain divided the land into two colonies, Upper Canada and Lower Canada. Most Loyalists moved into Upper Canada, which is now called Ontario. French Canadians remained in Lower Canada, which is now Quebec.

✓ Reading Check **Why was Canada divided into two colonies?**

Vocabulary Builder

Use the information below to teach students this section's high-use words.

High-Use Word	Definition and Sample Sentence
decisive, p. 56	*adj.* affecting what comes next, most important That championship match was a **decisive** moment in her career.
cooperate, p. 57	*v.* to work together for a common purpose For the team to be successful, it is important that they **cooperate.**
adopt, p. 60	*v.* to accept an idea or way of doing things The employees **adopted** the work ethic of their new supervisor.

Canada Seeks Independence

The people of Upper and Lower Canada worked together during the War of 1812. They fought to protect Canada from invasion by the United States. Once the War of 1812 ended, however, Canadians with different backgrounds stopped cooperating with one another. Both French Canadians and British Canadians hated British rule. Many felt Britain was too far away to understand their needs. But the two groups did not join in rebellion. In 1837, a French Canadian named Louis Papineau (LOO ee pah pea NOH) organized a revolt in Lower Canada. His goal was to establish the region as a separate country. The British easily defeated the rebels. The same thing happened in Upper Canada. William Mackenzie led the people against British rule. Again, the British put down the separatist rebellion.

A Peaceful Revolution   Still, British leaders were afraid more trouble was coming. They sent the Earl of Durham to learn what was wrong. When Durham returned, he had many suggestions. First, he suggested that the Canadians be given more control of their government. He also thought all of the colonies should be united. But the British government united only Upper and Lower Canada to form the Province of Canada. Nova Scotia, Newfoundland, Prince Edward Island, and New Brunswick were not included in this union. If Canada were completely united, the British feared the Canadians might make a successful rebellion.

Citizen Heroes

Louis Riel

A Voice of Protest
In 1869, the Canadian government wanted to finish the cross-country railroad across the flat plains region. Louis Riel, leader of the Métis (may TEEZ)—mixed European and Native American people—objected to the plan. The Métis said that the railroad would bring new settlers, who would take away their land. The government refused to stop, so Riel led an armed revolt. It failed, and Riel was later executed for treason, but the government did set aside land for the Métis. Today, the Métis consider Riel a hero.

The Canadian Pacific Railway
On November 7, 1885, Canada's far-flung provinces were tied together as the last spike was driven in, completing the Canadian Pacific Railway. **Draw Conclusions** *Why was a railroad connecting all of Canada important to Canadians?*

Read the **Citizens Heroes** on this page. Ask students **Why do the Métis think Riel was heroic?** *(The efforts of Riel led to land being set aside for the Métis.)*

Canada Seeks Independence L2

Guided Instruction

- **Vocabulary Builder** Clarify the high-use word **cooperate** before reading.

- Read Canada Seeks Independence. As students read, circulate and make sure individuals can answer the Reading Check question.

- Discuss the role the Earl of Durham played in helping to move Canadians toward self-rule. *(The Earl of Durham suggested that Canadians be given more control over their government and that all the colonies be united.)*

- Ask students to compare and contrast the United States and Canada's break from Great Britain. *(The United States fought a war to break from Great Britain, while Canada's break was peaceful. After the Revolutionary War, the United States became completely separate from Great Britain. Under the British North American Act, Canada was not completely independent, but had a central government to run the country.)*

Skills Mini Lesson

Problem-Solving

1. Tell students that identifying problems and their solutions in a passage can help them understand what they read.

2. Have students practice the skill by determining the problem that existed between the British and their Canadian subjects. *(Both French and British Canadians hated British rule.)*

3. Have students list attempts to solve the problem and the successful solution. *(Attempts: rebellions by French and British Canadians; uniting Upper and Lower Canada. Solution: uniting all the provinces under the British North America Act.)*

Answer

Draw Conclusions The railroad made traveling across the vast spaces of Canada much easier.

Guided Instruction (continued)

- Discuss the effects of the British North America Act. *(It made Canada more independent, but not completely self-governing. Canada could now elect their own leaders and control their own government.)*

- Ask students **Why did Canada enter World War I?** *(Because Britain entered the war, and Canada was a British subject at the time.)*

Independent Practice

Ask students to continue to fill in their graphic organizer with the information the have just learned.

Monitor Progress

Circulate and make sure students are choosing the correct details as they fill in the graphic organizer. Provide assistance as needed.

Target Reading Skill

Summarize As a follow up, ask students to answer the Target Reading Skill question in the Student Edition. *(Canada became a dominion of Great Britain in 1867. After this "peaceful revolution," Canada saw years of growth and change. When World War I broke out, Canada sent soldiers and resources overseas and contributed greatly to the Allied victory.)*

Answers

MAP MASTER Skills Activity **Name** Alberta, Saskatchewan, Newfoundland and Labrador, and Nunavut **Analyze** eastern Canada, because Britain gained control of this area in the 1700s

Go Online PHSchool.com Students may practice their map skills using the interactive online version of this map.

✓ **Reading Check** The British feared that if Canada was completely united, it might have the strength for a successful rebellion.

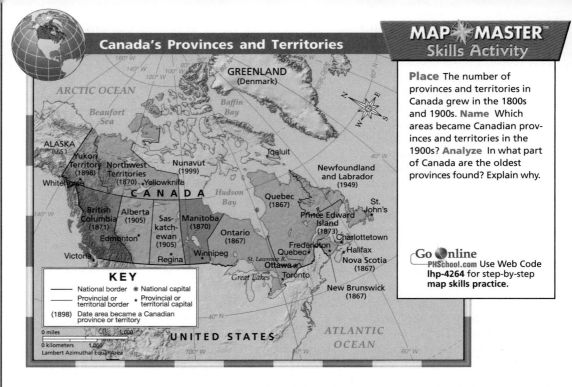

Canada's Provinces and Territories

MAP MASTER™ Skills Activity

Place The number of provinces and territories in Canada grew in the 1800s and 1900s. **Name** Which areas became Canadian provinces and territories in the 1900s? **Analyze** In what part of Canada are the oldest provinces found? Explain why.

Go Online PHSchool.com Use Web Code lhp-4264 for step-by-step map skills practice.

KEY
- National border ⊛ National capital
- Provincial or territorial border ★ Provincial or territorial capital
- (1898) Date area became a Canadian province or territory

Canadians believed that all provinces should be represented in their government. In 1864, leaders met to work out a plan to form a union. On July 1, 1867, the British Parliament accepted the British North America Act. This made Canada "one Dominion under the name of Canada." A **dominion** is a self-governing area. Canada was not completely independent from Great Britain, but now a central government would run the country. Canadians would elect their own leaders. Without a war, Canadians had won the right to control their own government.

After its "peaceful revolution," Canada saw years of growth and change. Skilled European farmers settled in Canada's western plains. Gold and other valuable minerals were discovered in the Yukon Territory in the 1890s. That brought miners to the far northwest. Canada was becoming rich and important.

Canada Becomes a World Power When Britain entered World War I, Canadians were still British subjects. Canada, therefore, entered the war, too. Canada willingly sent soldiers and resources overseas. Canada contributed so much to the Allied victory that the young country became a world power.

✓ **Reading Check** Why didn't the British want Canada to be united?

Target Skill **Summarize** Summarize this page. Be sure to include two factors that led Canada to become a world power.

58 United States and Canada

Differentiated Instruction

For English Language Learners [L1]
Have students listen to the recorded version of the section on the Student Edition on Audio CD. Check for understanding by pausing the CD and asking students to share their answers to the Reading Checks.

⊙ Chapter 2, Section 4, **Student Edition on Audio CD**

For Special Needs Students [L1]
Pair students with more proficient partners to complete the *Activity Shop Interdisciplinary: Transportation* activity.

All in One **United States and Canada Teaching Resources,** *Activity Shop Interdisciplinary: Transportation,* pp. 169–170

Canada: Postwar to the Present

During World War II, Canadians built factories. They made war supplies and goods such as clothes and shoes. Because of the war, people could not get such products from Europe. After the war, Canadian goods found a ready market in the United States and Europe.

Also, during the postwar years, immigrants poured into Canada. They came from Asia, Europe, Africa, and the Caribbean. The newcomers filled jobs in factories and businesses. Soon, Canada became one of the world's most important industrial nations.

The Growth of Industry Industrialization strengthened the economy but brought back old arguments. British Canadians built new factories in Quebec. That alarmed French Canadians. In 1969, the government passed new laws that made Canada a **bilingual** country. That is, Canada had two official languages—English and French. However, by 1976 some French Canadians did not want to be part of Canada. Quebec, they argued, should be independent. Many people in Quebec still feel that way today.

Canadian Industry
Canadians, such as this factory worker tending to spools of nylon (above), made important supplies during World War II. One year after the war, plans for the first Canadian-designed and built jet fighter (left) began. Nearly 700 planes were built to defend North America in case of a future attack and to participate in overseas operations. **Draw Conclusions** *What were the effects of WWII on Canadian industries?*

Canada: Postwar to the Present L2

Guided Instruction

- **Vocabulary Builder** Clarify the high-use word **adopt** before reading.

- Read Canada: Postwar to the Present with students.

- Discuss with students the good and bad aspects of postwar industrialization in Canada. *(Good: Canadians found ready markets in the United States and Europe for their goods. This strengthened the Canadian economy and created jobs. Bad: Industrialization brought back old arguments between French and British Canadians as British Canadians built factories in French Canadian Quebec.)*

- Ask students **How did adopting a new constitution change the relationship between Canada and Great Britain?** *(The new constitution gave Canadians the power to change their constitution without British permission. This meant that Canada was now completely independent.)*

Answer

Draw Conclusions Canadian industries grew stronger as a result of World War II. Canada became an important industrial nation.

Independent Practice

Ask students to complete the table with the information they have just learned.

Monitor Progress

- Show *Section Reading Support Transparency USC 49* and ask students to check their graphic organizers individually. Go over key concepts and clarify key vocabulary as needed.

  📖 **United States and Canada Transparencies,** *Section Reading Support Transparency USC 49*

- Tell students to fill in the last column of the *Reading Readiness Guide.* Probe for what they learned that confirms or invalidates each statement.

  All in One **United States and Canada Teaching Resources,** *Reading Readiness Guide,* p. 152

Assess and Reteach

Assess Progress   L2

Have students complete the Section Assessment. Administer the *Section Quiz.*

  All in One **United States and Canada Teaching Resources,** *Section Quiz,* p. 154

Reteach   L1

If students need more instruction, have them read this section in the Reading and Vocabulary Study Guide.

  📖 Chapter 2, Section 4, **United States and Canada Reading and Vocabulary Study Guide,** pp. 25–27

Extend   L3

Have students learn more about French traders by completing the *Enrichment* worksheet. Assign students to work in pairs to check each other's responses.

  All in One **United States and Canada Teaching Resources,** *Enrichment,* p. 163

Answer

Draw Conclusions The Parliament Buildings are in a style of architecture that developed in Western Europe between the 1100s and 1500s.

A New Constitution Although the British North America Act in 1867 gave Canadians the right to control their own government, it was still necessary for Great Britain to approve amendments to the Canadian constitution. That changed in 1982 when the Canadians adopted a new constitution. It gave Canadians the power to change their constitution without Great Britain's permission. Canada was now completely independent.

A Parliamentary System Canada's government is modeled on the British parliamentary system. Canada has a constitutional monarchy. A set of laws states what the monarch—the king or queen—can or cannot do. Because the monarch lives in Great Britain, he or she must appoint someone in Canada to act as a representative. This position is called the governor-general. Since World War II, the governor-general has been a Canadian citizen. Although the monarch is the head of state, he or she does not make any political decisions. That is the job of the prime minister, who is the head of government.

Canada is also called a parliamentary democracy. The group of representatives that makes its laws is modeled on the British parliament. Canada's Parliament, like Great Britain's, has two chambers: the House of Commons and the Senate. The House of Commons is made up of elected representatives. The governor-general appoints the members of the Senate. Senators are allowed to hold office until they are 75 years old.

Canada's Parliament Buildings
The Parliament Buildings are an example of the Gothic style of architecture, which is from medieval times. This type of architecture developed in Western Europe between the 1100s and 1500s.
Draw Conclusions *How do the Parliament Buildings reflect Canada's heritage?*

60 United States and Canada

Differentiated Instruction

For Less Proficient Readers   L1

Have students work with more advanced readers to make a diagram that shows how the Canadian government works. Encourage students to use the steps for interpreting diagrams laid out in the Skills for Life lesson, on pages 62 and 63 of the Student Edition.

For Gifted and Talented   L3

Have students research the Commonwealth of Nations in the twenty-first century, and report to the class on the following: Who are the member nations? Where and when do they meet? What has Great Britain provided to the member nations? Do you think it is important for these nations to maintain this alliance? Why or why not?

The Commonwealth of Nations Another tie between Canada and Great Britain is its membership in the Commonwealth of Nations. It is a voluntary organization, whose member countries are former British colonies. The purpose of the Commonwealth of Nations is to consult and cooperate with one another, particularly in matters of trade and economics. In addition, Great Britain gives members financial aid and advice. At one time, the Commonwealth of Nations was the only worldwide political organization besides the United Nations.

Although Great Britain's Queen Elizabeth II is the head of the Commonwealth of Nations, her role is symbolic. In 2002, for the celebration of her fiftieth year as monarch, she traveled from one end of the Commonwealth to the other, from Nunavut to Australia.

Canada in the World Today Today, Canada works both on its own and closely with international agencies to carry out foreign policy. It provides humanitarian aid to nations struck by natural disasters, such as Indonesia after a 2006 earthquake. Canada is involved in diplomatic and humanitarian missions to troubled countries from Haiti to Sudan. It has contributed to rebuilding both Afghanistan and Iraq. In addition, Canada maintains close trade and diplomatic ties with the United States.

Supporters greet Queen Elizabeth in Iqaluit, Nunavut, at the start of her twelve-day tour of Canada.

✓ **Reading Check** Why did Canadians write a new constitution?

Section 4 Assessment

Key Terms
Review the key terms at the beginning of this section. Use each term in a sentence that explains its meaning.

Target Reading Skill
Write a summary of the paragraph on page 58 called Canada Becomes a World Power.

Comprehension and Critical Thinking
1. (a) List What two countries came into conflict in Canada in the 1700s?

(b) Sequence How did the fur trade lead to war in Canada?
2. (a) Explain Why did Canadians object to British rule?
(b) Summarize How did Canadians win control of their government without going to war?
3. (a) Recall How did Canada become an industrial power after World War II?
(b) Link Past and Present How is Canada still tied to Britain today?

Writing Activity
Compare and contrast the ways in which Canada and the United States became independent nations.

> **Writing Tip** One way to organize your comparison is subject by subject, or by first explaining how the United States became independent and then how Canada did.

Chapter 2 Section 4 **61**

Answers

✓ **Reading Check** to give Canadians the power to change their constitution without Great Britain's permission and, therefore, make them independent

Section 4 Assessment

Key Terms
Students' sentences should reflect knowledge of each Key Term.

Target Reading Skill
Answers will vary, but should include that Canada entered World War I when Britain did, and was granted more independence from Britain for its contributions.

Comprehension and Critical Thinking
1. (a) France and Great Britain **(b)** The French wanted land for its beaver furs; the British wanted land for settlements.

2. (a) Canadians believed the British were too far away to understand their needs.
(b) Although Britain united a portion of Canada, Canadians believed that all the provinces should be represented in their government. Leaders met and worked out a plan to form a union. The British Parliament accepted the plan and passed the British North America Act.

3. (a) Canada built factories during the war to supply goods that European nations desperately needed. This fueled their economy and encouraged immigrants to come to Canada for jobs. With a strong economy, a strong work force, and factories in place to make goods, Canada became a world leader in industry. **(b)** Canada's government is modeled after the British Parliament; Canada is a constitutional monarchy, meaning the British monarch is head of state; Canada is part of the Commonwealth of Nations.

Writing Activity
Use the *Rubric for Assessing a Writing Assignment* to evaluate students' comparisons.

All in One United States and Canada Teaching Resources, *Rubric for Assessing a Writing Assignment,* p. 183

Objective
Interpret information in a diagram.

Prepare to Read

Build Background Knowledge `L2`
Ask students if they can think of examples of things that use both text and pictures to present information. *(Examples: catalogs, cookbooks, encyclopedia articles, instruction manuals, Web sites, newspapers)* Ask students why they think these use both pictures and words.

Instruct

Interpreting Diagrams `L2`

Guided Practice
■ Read the steps to interpreting diagrams as a class and write them on the board.

■ Practice the skill by following the steps on p. 62 as a class. Model each step in the activity by choosing a well-known item, such as a pocket calculator, and using it to draw a simple diagram. Be sure to think aloud as you create the diagram so students can follow your thought process.

■ Ask students to then write a summary describing what the diagram shows.

Independent Practice
Assign *Skills for Life* and have students complete it individually.

All in One **United States and Canada Teaching Resources,** *Skills for Life,* p. 164

Monitor Progress
As students are completing *Skills for Life,* circulate to make sure individuals are applying the skill steps effectively. Provide assistance as needed.

Interpreting Diagrams

Suppose that your pen pal in Canada wants to know what your school looks like. Which should you do: write her a letter describing your school or send her a photograph?

A photo would show her in an instant what your school looks like. But a letter could describe details a photograph might not show. Perhaps you would send both.

There is another way to show what something looks like *and* describe it in words: You could draw a diagram. A diagram is a picture that shows how something works or is made. It usually includes labels that tell about certain parts of the picture. It is a combination of the letter and the photograph you would send to your pen pal.

A diagram is like a game of show-and-tell—the picture shows and the labels tell.

Learn the Skill
To understand how to interpret information in a diagram, follow the steps below.

1. **Study the picture.** Notice the various parts of the picture. Get visual information from it.

2. **Read the labels.** Sometimes the labels will be numbered or will appear in a certain order to explain a step-by-step process.

3. **Summarize the information in the diagram.** From the information you gather by studying the picture and the labels, write a summary describing what the diagram shows you.

62 United States and Canada

Practice the Skill

Look at How a Locomotive Works, below, as you practice interpreting a diagram.

1 From the title, you can tell what the diagram shows. As you look at the picture, what information can you learn—even before you read the labels?

2 The labels in this diagram are meant to be read in a particular order. Do you know why? Notice that this diagram has both labels and arrows. What do the arrows show?

3 Write a paragraph describing how a locomotive works. Write as if the reader did not have the picture to look at. Don't simply repeat the text in the labels, but summarize the information in the labels and picture.

How a Locomotive Works

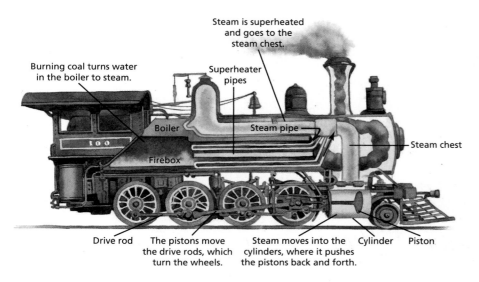

Steam is superheated and goes to the steam chest.

Burning coal turns water in the boiler to steam.

Superheater pipes

Boiler

Steam pipe

Firebox

Steam chest

Drive rod

The pistons move the drive rods, which turn the wheels.

Steam moves into the cylinders, where it pushes the pistons back and forth.

Cylinder

Piston

Apply the Skill

Find a photograph of a bicycle in a catalog or a magazine. Then, write a paragraph describing what the bicycle looks like, what parts it has, and how the parts work.

Now draw a diagram of a bicycle. Make labels showing how it works.

Compare the picture, the paragraph, and the diagram. Which one does the best job of showing and explaining how a bicycle works?

Section 5
The United States and Canada Today

Objectives

Social Studies
1. Identify the environmental concerns the United States and Canada share today.
2. Find out about the economic ties the United States and Canada have to each other and to the world.

Reading/Language Arts
Use the rereading or reading ahead strategies to better understand the words and ideas in a text.

Prepare to Read

Build Background Knowledge L2
In this section students will learn about environmental and economic issues in the United States and Canada today. Have students preview the headings and visuals in this section. Then have students make a list of two or three ways that their communities help protect their environment. Provide a few examples (*recycling, conserving water, collecting litter*) to get them started. Use the Give One, Get One strategy (TE, p. T37) to generate ideas.

Set a Purpose for Reading L2
■ Preview the Objectives.

■ Read each statement in the *Reading Readiness Guide*. Ask students to mark the statements true or false.

> **All in One** **United States and Canada Teaching Resources,** *Reading Readiness Guide,* p. 156

■ Have students discuss the statements in pairs or groups of four, then mark their guides again. Use the Numbered Heads participation strategy (TE, p. T36) to call on students to share their group's perspectives.

Vocabulary Builder
Preview Key Terms L2
Pronounce each Key Term, then ask the students to say the word with you. Provide a simple explanation such as, "Imported cars often cost more than cars made in the United States because of the tariff placed on them."

Prepare to Read

Objectives
In this section you will
1. Identify the environmental concerns the United States and Canada share today.
2. Find out about the economic ties the United States and Canada have to each other and to the world.

Taking Notes
As you read the section, look for details about the environmental concerns and economic ties that the United States and Canada share. Copy the concept web below and fill in the details.

Target Reading Skill

Reread or Read Ahead Rereading and reading ahead are strategies that can help you understand words and ideas in the text. If you do not understand a certain passage, reread it to look for connections among the words and sentences. It might also help to read ahead, because a word or an idea may be clarified further on.

Key Terms
- **acid rain** (as id rayn) n. rain containing acids that are harmful to plants and trees
- **tariff** (tar if) n. a fee charged on imported goods
- **free trade** (free trayd) n. trade without taxes on imported goods

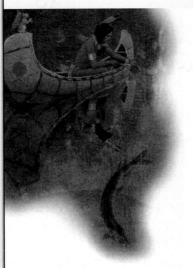

A painting of an Iroquois fishing from a canoe

64 United States and Canada

The birch-bark canoes paddled into the village of Sault Sainte Marie, on the border of the present-day United States and Canada. The canoes carried fishing nets made from strands of willow bark and baskets full of lake trout. The Native American fishermen unloaded their baskets at the shore. Any fish they did not eat that day would be dried on racks and saved for later or ground up and used as fertilizer for crops.

For centuries, the lake trout of the Great Lakes provided food for both Native Americans and European settlers. By the mid-1950s, lake trout were the most valuable fish in the Upper Great Lakes. Lake trout were soon overharvested. In some of the Great Lakes, the lake trout almost disappeared.

In 1955, Canada and the United States joined to create the Great Lakes Fishery Commission. Members of the commission worked together to find ways of protecting lake trout and many other species of fish in the Great Lakes. This is just one of the ways the United States and Canada have become cooperative neighbors.

Target Reading Skill

Reread or Read Ahead Point out the Target Reading Skill. Tell students that rereading and reading ahead often clarify words or ideas that are unfamiliar or hard to understand.

Model using these strategies using the term "cooperative neighbors" at the end of the last paragraph on page 64. By rereading the preceding sentence students learn that "members of the commission *work together.*"

By reading ahead they learn that environmental issues "concern *both* the United States and Canada." "Cooperative neighbors" work together to benefit all.

Give students *Reread or Read Ahead.* Have them complete the activity in their groups.

> **All in One** **United States and Canada Teaching Resources,** *Reread or Read Ahead,* p. 159

Environmental Issues

The United States and Canada share many geographic features—the coasts of the Atlantic and Pacific oceans, the Great Lakes, and the Rocky Mountains, for example. Both countries use natural resources in similar ways. And both have used technology to meet their needs. But technology has left its mark on their water, air, forests, and futures.

Solving Water Problems Can you picture a river on fire? Impossible, you say? In 1969, a fire started on the Cuyahoga River (ky uh HOH guh RIV er). That river flows past Cleveland, Ohio, and then empties into Lake Erie. For many years, Cleveland had poured waste, garbage, and oil into the river. The layer of pollutants was so thick that it caught on fire.

The Cuyahoga was typical of the rivers that empty into Lake Erie. So much pollution had been dumped into the lake that most of the fish had died. Swimming in the river was unthinkable. The fire on the Cuyahoga was a wake-up call. The United States and Canada signed an agreement promising to cooperate in cleaning up the lake. Agreements such as this have greatly reduced freshwater pollution in the United States. Today, people again enjoy fishing and boating on the Cuyahoga.

The Cuyahoga River
In June 1969, firefighters hosed down flames from the Cuyahoga River fire (below). **Analyze Images** *Looking at the river today (inset), what positive effects came out of the cleanup effort?*

Vocabulary Builder

Use the information below to teach students this section's high-use words.

High-Use Word	Definition and Sample Sentence
maintain, p. 67	*v.* to keep in good repair; protect To keep the fountain in working order, the plumber has to **maintain** the pipes.
expand, p. 70	*v.* to grow in size Adding water to the sponge caused it to **expand** to twice its normal size.

Instruct

Environmental Issues L2

Guided Instruction

- **Vocabulary Builder** Clarify the high-use word **maintain** before reading.

- Read Environmental Issues, using the Paragraph Shrinking strategy (TE, p. T34)

- Write the following causes of pollution on the board, and discuss with students the long-term effects of each: dumping garbage and waste in rivers; burning fossil fuels; excessive logging of trees. (*Garbage and waste pollute water and kill fish. Burning fossil fuels pollutes the air and creates acid rain. Without trees, soil washes away so that plants die and animals lose their homes.*)

Answer

Analyze Images The river is no longer dangerous and can even be used for pleasure cruising.

- Ask **What is being done to solve water problems?** *(The United States and Canada have signed agreements to clean up polluted areas.)* **How has air quality been improved?** *(by reducing pollutants released into the air)* **What steps have been taken to preserve forests?** *(Laws were passed to protect forests and create new regulations for loggers.)*

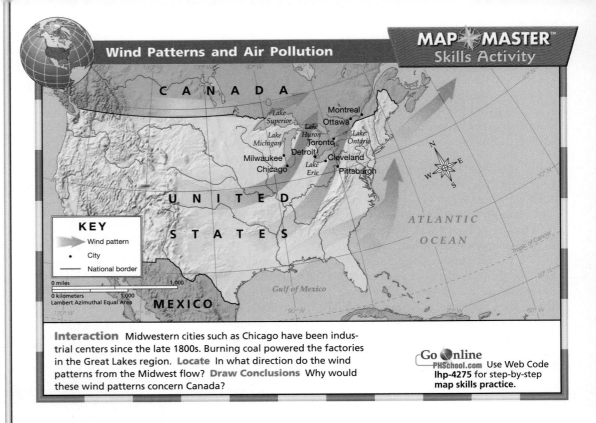

Wind Patterns and Air Pollution

MAP MASTER
Skills Activity

KEY
- → Wind pattern
- • City
- — National border

0 miles   1,000
0 kilometers   1,000
Lambert Azimuthal Equal Area

Interaction Midwestern cities such as Chicago have been industrial centers since the late 1800s. Burning coal powered the factories in the Great Lakes region. **Locate** In what direction do the wind patterns from the Midwest flow? **Draw Conclusions** Why would these wind patterns concern Canada?

Go Online
PHSchool.com Use Web Code lhp-4275 for step-by-step map skills practice.

Improving Air Quality On many days, you can look around most big cities and see that the air is filled with a brown haze. This pollution is caused by cars and factories burning fossil fuels. Not only is this air unhealthy to breathe, but it can also create other serious problems hundreds of miles away. Pollutants in the air combine with moisture to form acid. **Acid rain** is rain that dissolves these acids and carries them to Earth. This acid kills plants, trees, and fish. Coal-burning power plants in the West and Midwest United States create acid rain problems in the Northeast and in the Great Lakes area. Winds carry these acids long distances.

Acid rain caused by United States power plants has affected forests and lakes in Canada. The two countries signed agreements to control air quality in the 1980s. A 2002 government progress report showed that rain acidity was reduced in Canada by 45 percent and in the United States by 35 percent.

Aerial view of Toronto's hazy skyline and harbor, Ontario, Canada

66 United States and Canada

Answers

MAP MASTER
Skills Activity **Locate** The wind patterns from the Midwest flow in a northeastern direction. **Draw Conclusions** Wind patterns bring air pollution from the United States to Canada, where it falls in acid rain.

Go Online
PHSchool.com Students may practice their map skills using the interactive online version of this map.

Differentiated Instruction

For Special Needs Students   L1
Pair students with more proficient partners to create a cause-and-effect chart that shows the causes and effects of the following environmental problems: water pollution, acid rain, and soil erosion in forests. Have students then create a third column to show a possible solution for each one. Use the *Effects Chart* graphic organizer

transparency to help students get started. Label the four columns "Environmental Problems," "Causes," "Effects," and "Possible Solutions."

📖 **United States and Canada Transparencies,** *Transparency B10: Effects Chart*

Renewing Forests "I'm like a tree—you'll have to cut me down," cried Kim McElroy in 1993. The other demonstrators with her agreed. They were blocking the path of logging trucks trying to enter the forest of Clayoquot Sound on Vancouver Island, British Columbia. The protesters believed that cutting down the trees would damage the environment. In similar forests throughout the United States and Canada, logging companies practiced clear-cutting, or cutting down all the trees in an area. Without trees, soil washes away, other plants die, and animals lose their homes.

On the other hand, people need lumber for building. Paper companies need wood pulp to make their products. People who work for logging companies need their jobs.

The Canadian and American governments want to maintain both the forests and the timber industry. They are working to develop ways of doing that. For example, British Columbia passed a law that sets aside parts of the Clayoquot Sound's forests for logging. The law also imposes new rules on loggers to prevent damage in the areas where cutting is allowed.

√ Reading Check **Why is there disagreement about logging in some forests?**

The Old and the New
A hill in the Queen Charlotte Islands of British Columbia, Canada (below), shows clear-cut forest growth. The man in the inset photo plants new trees. **Draw Conclusions** *How does planting new trees help to keep soil from washing away? Why is that important?*

Monitor Progress
As students fill in the graphic organizer, circulate and make sure individuals are choosing the correct details. Provide assistance as needed.

Background: Links Across Place

Acid Rain in Europe Emissions from cars, trucks, power plants, and industrial facilities in Great Britain, Germany, and Poland and other countries have been causing severe acid rain problems on the continent. In fact, so many forests in Europe contain trees that have been stunted or killed by acid rain that a new word, *waldsterben* ("forest death"), has come into use. But the damage does not stop with trees. Contaminated winds blow northward from industrial facilities in nearby countries and reach Scandinavia. Rain that falls over parts of Scandinavia is, as a result, considerably more acidic than normal. Currently, about one-fifth of Swedish lakes have been damaged by acidification.

Answers

Draw Conclusions Trees keep soil from washing away. Soil erosion can cause plants to die and animals to lose their food and homes.

√ Reading Check People want to preserve the trees in order to maintain the forests that are home to plants and animals. However, people also want timber for building. Loggers also want the industry to survive in order for them to maintain their jobs.

Target Reading Skill

Reread As a follow up, ask students to perform the Target Reading Skill activity in the Student Edition. *(Reread: The U.S. and Canada maintain economic ties through lumber and fishing industries. Read ahead: The U.S. and Canada maintain economic ties through trade.)*

"Economics Has Made Us Partners" L2

Guided Instruction

- **Vocabulary Builder** Clarify the high-use word **expand** before reading.

- Read "Economics Has Made Us Partners" with students. As students read, circulate and make sure individuals can answer the Reading Check question.

- Have students provide examples of the economic partnership between the the United States and Canada. *(Possible answers: the United States and Canada built the St. Lawrence Seaway; each country is the other's largest trading partner; both have signed trade agreements.)*

- Ask students **What might be two benefits to the United States of importing goods from Canada rather than Europe?** *(cheaper transportation costs; no tariff on imported products from Canada)*

- Ask students **What is the St. Lawrence Seaway?** *(a system of locks, canals, and dams that allows ships to move from one water level to another)*

- Have students discuss how the Seaway benefits both the United States and Canada. *(It makes trade between the two countries and with Europe easier.)*

- Ask students **Where can ships leaving from Duluth, Minnesota, travel as a result of the St. Lawrence Seaway?** *(the Atlantic Ocean)*

Answers

Diagram Skills Describe The St. Lawrence Seaway's locks allow ships to be raised and lowered from one water level to another. **Identify Effects** The Seaway makes it easier for the United States and Canada to trade with each other and with Europe.

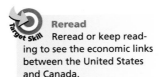

Reread
Reread or keep reading to see the economic links between the United States and Canada.

"Economics Has Made Us Partners"

Not all next-door neighbors get along as well as the United States and Canada. President John F. Kennedy once described the relationship this way: "Geography has made us neighbors. History has made us friends. Economics has made us partners." With 5,527 miles (8,895 kilometers) of border between the two countries, economic cooperation has benefited both. Part of this cooperation has been in transportation between the countries, particularly around the Great Lakes.

The St. Lawrence Seaway Have you ever heard of someone going over Niagara Falls in a barrel? The barrel would drop about 190 feet (58 meters)—a crazy stunt! Suppose you have a cargo of manufactured goods in Cleveland to send to Montreal. You would like to ship by water, because it is the cheapest and most direct means of transportation. But Niagara Falls lies between Cleveland and Montreal. And after passing the falls, your cargo would have to travel down another 250 feet (76 meters) in the St. Lawrence River before it reached Montreal. What do you do?

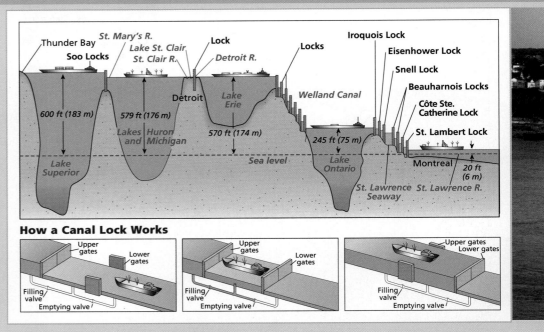

The Great Lakes and the St. Lawrence Seaway

How a Canal Lock Works

Differentiated Instruction

For Advanced Readers L3
Assign students the long-term project *Mapping World Trade*. Ask students to work in pairs or small groups to find out where imported items come from, where goods produced in their community are exported to, and how worldwide trade shapes our lives and the lives of people everywhere.

For: Long-term Integrated Projects: *Mapping World Trade*
Visit: PHSchool.com
Web Code: lhd-4206

To solve this problem, the United States and Canada built the St. Lawrence Seaway. Completed in 1959, it is a system of locks, canals, and dams that allows ships to move from one water level to another. A lock is an enclosed area on a canal that raises or lowers ships from one water level to another. Now, ships can travel from Duluth, Minnesota, on Lake Superior, all the way to the Atlantic Ocean. The St. Lawrence Seaway makes it much easier for the United States and Canada to trade with each other and with Europe. The St. Lawrence Seaway has been called Canada's highway to the sea because of the volume of goods that travels its length.

Trade What country is the biggest trading partner of the United States? It is Canada. And, the United States is Canada's largest trading partner, too. About three fourths of all of Canada's foreign trade—both exports and imports—is with the United States. Our economies are interdependent. That means that in order to be successful, each country needs to do business with the other.

■ Diagram Skills

Ships traveling from the Atlantic Ocean to Lake Superior must go through a series of locks along the St. Lawrence Seaway. **Describe** How do the locks allow ships to make the great change in elevation between the Atlantic and the Great Lakes? **Identify Effects** How did building the St. Lawrence Seaway affect the economies of the United States and Canada?

Independent Practice
Ask students to complete the concept web with the information they have just learned.

Monitor Progress
■ Show *Section Reading Support Transparency USC 50* and ask students to check their graphic organizers individually. Go over key concepts and clarify key vocabulary as needed.

📖 **United States and Canada Transparencies,** *Section Reading Support Transparency USC 50*

■ Tell students to fill in the last column of the *Reading Readiness Guide.* Probe for what they learned that confirms or invalidates each statement.

All in One **United States and Canada Teaching Resources,** *Reading Readiness Guide,* p. 156

Differentiated Instruction

For English Language Learners L1
Encourage students to examine the prefixes *im- (in), ex- (outside),* and *inter- (between),* as well as the base words *port* and *dependence,* to help understand the concepts *im*porting, *ex*porting, and *inter*dependence. Ask students to apply these concepts to their countries of origin, describing what the countries import and export, and identifying trade partners.

For Gifted and Talented L3
Assign students the *Book Project: Write a Children's Book,* encouraging them to use any person, place, event, or idea from Chapter 2 as the topic.

All in One **United States and Canada Teaching Resources,** *Book Project: Write A Children's Book,* pp. 76–78

Assess and Reteach

Assess Progress `L2`

Have students complete the Section Assessment. Administer the *Section Quiz*.

 United States and Canada Teaching Resources, *Section Quiz,* p. 158

Reteach `L1`

If students need more instruction, have them read this section in the Reading and Vocabulary Study Guide.

📖 Chapter 2, Section 5, **United States and Canada Reading and Vocabulary Study Guide,** pp. 28–30

Extend `L3`

Have students learn more about environmental issues by completing the activity *Energy and Resources: The Imbalance of Energy Consumption.* Assign students to work in groups to answer the questions.

Go Online
PHSchool.com

For: Environmental and Global Issues: *Energy and Resources: The Imbalance of Energy Consumption*
Visit: PHSchool.com
Web Code: lhd-4207

Answers

✓ Reading Check The main goals of the Organization of American States are to maintain peace in the Western Hemisphere and to prevent other countries from interfering in the region.

Section 5 Assessment

Key Terms
Students' sentences should reflect knowledge of each Key Term.

🎯 **Target Reading Skill**
Answers will vary, but should reflect that students understand the skill.

Comprehension and Critical Thinking
1. (a) water pollution, air pollution, and endangered forests **(b)** by creating treaties to clean up lakes, agreements to control air quality, and laws that set aside only specific parts of forests for the logging industry **(c)** Pollution in one country can cause acid rain in another country.

The emblem of the Organization of American States shows the furled flags of its member nations.

Since 1988, the United States and Canada have signed two important trade agreements. The Free Trade Agreement (FTA) put an end to **tariffs**, or fees charged on imported goods. Tariffs raise the cost of goods, so the amount of trade can be limited. By eliminating tariffs, Canada and the United States agreed to have **free trade**, trade without taxes on imported goods. In 1994, this agreement was expanded to include Mexico. The goal of the North American Free Trade Agreement (NAFTA) is to encourage trade and economic growth in all three countries. The agreement affects many major industries, including agriculture, trucking, and manufacturing. Since these agreements were made, trade among the three countries has increased. Although some jobs in the United States have been created because of increased imports, other jobs have been lost because American companies have moved to Mexico.

Interdependent Countries   The United States and Canada are interdependent politically as well as economically. Both Canada and the United States belong to the Organization of American States, or OAS. This international organization was formed to promote cooperation among countries in the Western Hemisphere. The member countries work with one another to promote political, economic, military, and cultural cooperation. The main goals of OAS are to maintain peace in the Western Hemisphere and to prevent other countries from interfering within the region.

✓ Reading Check **What are the main goals of the member countries in the Organization of American States?**

 ## Section 5 Assessment

Key Terms
Review the key terms at the beginning of this section. Use each term in a sentence that explains its meaning.

🎯 **Target Reading Skill**
What word or idea were you able to clarify by rereading or reading ahead?

Comprehension and Critical Thinking
1. (a) Explain What are some environmental problems the United States and Canada share?

(b) Summarize How have these two countries worked together to solve these problems?
(c) Identify Effects How can one nation's problems affect another?
2. (a) Note What country is the largest trading partner of the United States?
(b) Make Generalizations How has the St. Lawrence Seaway made trade easier for the United States and Canada?
(c) Identify the Main Idea What is the goal of NAFTA?

Writing Activity
Write a paragraph that explains the main reasons that Canada and the United States are important to each other.

Writing Tip Begin your paragraph with a topic sentence that states your main idea. Be sure to include examples, details, and facts that support your main idea.

---

70 United States and Canada

---

2. (a) Canada **(b)** The St. Lawrence Seaway allows ships to move from one water level to another through a system of locks, canals, and dams. It allows goods to be shipped easily between the United States and Canada. **(c)** to encourage trade and economic growth among Canada, the United States, and Mexico by ending tariffs on imported goods

Writing Activity
Use the *Rubric for Assessing a Writing Assignment* to evaluate students' paragraphs.

 United States and Canada Teaching Resources, *Rubric for Assessing a Writing Assignment,* p. 183

Review and Assessment

◆ Chapter Summary

Native American artifact

Section 1: The Arrival of the Europeans
- The first Americans are called Native Americans.
- The lives of Native Americans changed after Europeans arrived.
- The 13 colonies won independence after the Revolutionary War.

Section 2: Growth and Conflict in the United States
- The United States doubled its size in 1803 with the Louisiana Purchase.
- The Industrial Revolution changed the way people in America lived.
- The Civil War pitted the North against the South.

Section 3: The United States on the Brink of Change
- The Industrial Revolution helped the rich but not the poor.
- The United States fought two world wars and became a superpower.
- After years of fighting various wars, Americans faced new terrorist threats.

Section 4: The History of Canada
- Britain fought France to gain control of Canada.
- Canadians won the right to control their own government.
- Today, Canada is completely independent of Great Britain.

Section 5: The United States and Canada Today
- The United States and Canada work together to solve environmental issues.
- The United States and Canada are each other's largest trading partners.

Civil War soldiers

◆ Key Terms

Each of the statements below contains a key term from the chapter. If the statement is true, write *true*. If it is false, rewrite the statement to make it correct.

1. A **missionary** is a person who must work for a period of years to gain freedom.

2. A **tariff** is a fee charged on imported goods.

3. **Acid rain** forms over millions of years from plant and animal remains.

4. The **Industrial Revolution** was a period of great tension between the United States and the Soviet Union.

5. A **dominion** is a self-governing area that is subject to the United States.

6. Canada is a **bilingual** country, meaning that it has two official languages.

7. A **boycott** is a refusal to buy or use goods and services.

8. An **abolitionist** is a person who moves to a new country in order to settle there.

Chapter 2 **71**

┌ Vocabulary Builder ─

Revisit this chapter's high-use words:

theorize	conflict	cooperate
establish	slum	adopt
inspire	restore	maintain
spur	decisive	expand

Ask students to review the definitions they recorded on their *Word Knowledge* worksheets.

All in One United States and Canada Teaching Resources, *Word Knowledge,* p. 162

Consider allowing students to earn extra credit if they use the words in their answers to the questions in the Chapter Review and Assessment. The words must be used correctly and in a natural context to win the extra points.

Review and Assessment

Review Chapter Content

■ Review and revisit the major themes of this chapter by asking students to classify what Guiding Question each bulleted statement in the Chapter Summary answers. Have students write the Chapter Summary on a separate piece of paper and complete the activity in pairs. Each pair should write the number of the Guiding Question next to each statement on their paper. Refer to p. 1 of the Student Edition for the text of Guiding Questions.

■ Assign *Vocabulary Development* for students to review Key Terms.

All in One United States and Canada, *Vocabulary Development,* p. 182

Answers

Key Terms

1. False. A missionary is a person who wants to convert others to his or her religion.

2. True

3. False. Wind picks up pollutants in the air where they combine with moisture to form acid rain.

4. False. The Industrial Revolution was a time when handmade items began to be produced by machines.

5. False. A dominion is a self-governing area.

6. True

7. True

8. False. An abolitionist is someone who wants to end slavery.

Review and Assessment

Comprehension and Critical Thinking

9. (a) The Spanish were interested in settling the land and gaining wealth by working the farms and the mines. The French were interested in fur trade along the St. Lawrence and Mississippi Rivers. **(b)** The Spanish enslaved the Native Americans, forcing them into harsh labor on farms and in the mines. The French wanted the help of Native Americans in order to build their fur trade and so they treated them with respect.

10. (a) It helped to increase the production of textiles by converting from handmade to machine-made goods. **(b)** The Industrial Revolution provided workers with more job opportunities in factories, but diminished the need for custom-made items.

11. (a) The act gave free land to settlers. **(b)** The railroads provided faster and cheaper access from the east to the west.

12. (a) Canada **(b)** Loyalists were people who opposed the colonies separating from Great Britain, so they would be likely to oppose Canadian independence as well.

13. (a) Parliamentary government; the monarch of Great Britain is head of state, the prime minister makes the laws. **(b)** Great Britain's **(c)** Answers will vary, students answers should show an understanding that the monarch's duties would be ceremonial.

14. (a) Because the United States and Canada have a long, open border, goods can travel easily between the two countries; Canada is the United States' largest trade partner and vice versa. **(b)** The United States and Canada share the English language and similar natural resources, which contribute to a strong trade partnership.

Skills Practice

Diagrams will vary, but should be labeled clearly and include accurate information.

Writing Activity: Language and Arts

Student answers will vary, but should include the different reasons why European settlers came to each land, the different strategies by which each country gained its independence from Great Britain, the similarities in the growth of each country, and each country's contribution to the major international events of the 20th century.

Review and Assessment (continued)

◆ Comprehension and Critical Thinking

9. (a) Compare Why were Spanish and French explorers interested in the Americas?
(b) Identify Cause and Effect How did the treatment of Native Americans reflect the different interests of the Spanish and the French explorers?

10. (a) Explain How did the Industrial Revolution change the textile industry?
(b) Draw Conclusions How might this change have affected workers?

11. (a) Identify What was the Homestead Act?
(b) Draw Inferences How did railroads help settle the American West more quickly?

12. (a) Name Where did some Loyalists move after the American Revolution?
(b) Identify Frame of Reference Why would Loyalists have opposed independence from Britain?

13. (a) Define What kind of government does Canada have?
(b) Name What system is the Canadian government modeled on?
(c) Draw Conclusions What duties might a monarch have, since he or she is not the head of the government?

14. (a) Describe How has geography contributed to the trade partnership between Canada and the United States?
(b) Draw Inferences What other factors might explain this strong trade relationship?

◆ Skills Practice

Interpreting Diagrams In the Skills for Life activity in this chapter, you learned how to interpret information in a diagram. You also learned that labels on a diagram often should be read in a certain order.

Review the steps you followed to learn this skill. Then reread the part of Section 5 called Improving Air Quality. Create a diagram showing the cycle of acid rain. Remember to label your diagram clearly.

◆ Writing Activity: Language Arts

Compare and contrast the histories of the United States and of Canada. Write a paragraph describing the ways in which the growth, settlement, and independence of the United States and Canada were similar and ways in which they were different.

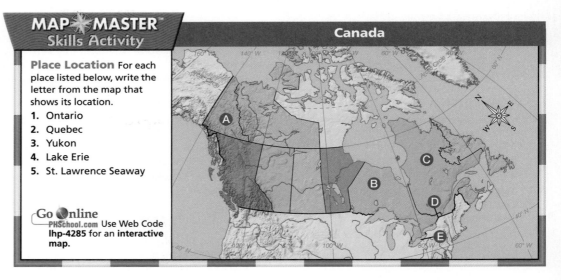

MAP MASTER™ Skills Activity

Place Location For each place listed below, write the letter from the map that shows its location.
1. Ontario
2. Quebec
3. Yukon
4. Lake Erie
5. St. Lawrence Seaway

Go Online
PHSchool.com Use Web Code lhp-4285 for an interactive map.

Canada

Use *Rubric for Assessing a Writing Assignment* to evaluate students' comparisons of the history of the United States and Canada.

All in One **United States and Canada Teaching Resources,** *Rubric for Assessing a Writing Assignment,* p. 183

Standardized Test Prep

Test-Taking Tips

Some questions on standardized tests ask you to analyze primary sources. Read the excerpt below from a famous United States document. Then follow the tips to answer the sample question.

> "All legislative Powers herein granted shall be vested in a Congress of the United States, which shall consist of a Senate and House of Representatives. . . . The House of Representatives shall be composed of Members chosen every second Year by the People of the several states. . . . The Senate of the United States shall be composed of two Senators from each State for six Years; and each Senator shall have one Vote."

TIP Try to identify the main idea, or most important point, of the passage.

Pick the letter that best answers the question.

Which document does this extract come from?

A ~~Declaration of Independence~~
B United States Constitution
C Federalist Papers
D ~~Pledge of Allegiance~~

TIP Use what you already know about United States history and government to help you find the *best* answer.

Think It Through Start with the main idea of the extract: *The Congress is supposed to make laws.* Which document explains the powers of each branch of government? You can rule out A and D. The Pledge is a statement of loyalty. The Declaration of Independence explains why colonists cut their ties to England. That leaves B and C. Maybe you aren't sure about the Federalist Papers, but you probably know that the Constitution is the plan for our government—including Congress. The correct answer is B.

Practice Questions

Use the tips above and other tips in this book to help you answer the following questions.

1. Which event encouraged immigrants and farm-workers to look for jobs in cities?
   A the Civil War
   B the Industrial Revolution
   C the Louisiana Purchase
   D the Indian Removal Act

2. What was the result of the Seven Years' War?
   A Canada became independent.
   B France lost, but kept control over Quebec.
   C Great Britain gained control over all of Canada.
   D Canada became a dominion of Great Britain.

Read the excerpt on Article 102, and then answer the question that follows.

Article 102: Objectives
a) eliminate barriers to trade in, and facilitate the cross-border movement of, goods and services between the territories of the Parties;
b) promote conditions of fair competition in the free-trade area.

3. Which document does this excerpt most likely come from?
   A the British North America Act
   B the Treaty of Paris
   C NAFTA
   D the Quebec Act

Go Online
PHSchool.com
Use Web Code lha-4205 for a Chapter 2 self-test.

Chapter 2 **73**

Cultures of the United States and Canada

Chapter Overview

Overview

Section 1 — A Heritage of Diversity and Exchange
1. Explain how cultural patterns developed in the United States and Canada.
2. Discuss the cultural patterns that exist today in the United States and Canada.

Section 2 — The United States: A Nation of Immigrants
1. Learn about the people of the United States.
2. Find out about the culture of the United States.

Section 3 — The Canadian Mosaic
1. Find out about the people of Canada.
2. Learn about Canadian culture.

DISCOVERY
CHANNEL
SCHOOL Video

Quebec's French Culture
Length: 4 minutes, 2 seconds
Use with Section 3
This video segment describes how French culture was established in Quebec and how it has been preserved. The segment also examines the political friction caused by Quebec's French identity.

Technology Resources

Go Online
PHSchool.com

Students use embedded Web codes to access Internet activities, chapter self-tests, and additional map practice. They may also access Dorling Kindersley's Online Desk Reference to learn more about each country they study.

Interactive Textbook

Use the Interactive Textbook to make content and concepts come alive through animations, videos, and activities that accompany the complete basal text—online and on CD-ROM.

PRENTICE HALL
TeacherEXPRESS
Plan • Teach • Assess

Use this complete suite of powerful teaching tools to make planning lessons and administering tests quicker and easier.

Reading and Assessment

Reading and Vocabulary Instruction

⟳ Model the Target Reading Skill

Main Idea Tell students that the main idea is the most important idea in a section. All of the details in a well-written paragraph should support the main idea. Write the paragraph below on the board. Point out that the main idea is that both the United States and Canada have diverse populations because of immigration. With students, identify and underline each supporting detail.

Because of immigration, both the United States and Canada have diverse populations. The first immigrants came mainly from West European countries, such as <u>Great Britain, France, Spain, and Germany</u>. <u>Many Africans were forced to come as slaves</u>. Later waves of immigrants included <u>Asians, Eastern Europeans, and Latin Americans</u>.

Ask yourself aloud: What do these details have in common? *(They all support the main idea that the populations of the United States and Canada are diverse because of immigration.)*

Use the following worksheets from All-in-One United States and Canada Teaching Resources (pp. 207–209) to support this chapter's Target Reading Skill.

Vocabulary Builder
High-Use Academic Words

Use these steps to teach this chapter's high-use words:

1. Have students rate how well they know each word on their Word Knowledge worksheets (All-in-One United States and Canada Teaching Resources, p. 210).

2. Pronounce each word and ask students to repeat it.

3. Give students a brief definition and sample sentence (provided on TE pp. 77, 85, and 90).

4. Work with students as they fill in the "Definition or Example" column of their Word Knowledge worksheets.

Assessment

Formal Assessment

Test students' understanding of core knowledge and skills.

Chapter Tests A and B, All-in-One United States and Canada Teaching Resources, pp. 226–231

Customize the Chapter Tests to suit your needs.
ExamView Test Bank CD-ROM

Skills Assessment

Assess geographic literacy.
MapMaster Skills, Student Edition 75, 77, 94

Assess reading and comprehension.
Target Reading Skills, Student Edition, 79, 86, 91, and in Section Assessments

Chapter 3 Assessment, United States and Canada Reading and Vocabulary Study Guide, 41

Performance Assessment

Assess students' performance on this chapter's Writing Activities using the following rubrics from All-in-One United States and Canada Teaching Resources.

Rubric for Assessing a Student Poem, p. 222

Rubric for Assessing a Journal Entry, p. 223

Rubric for Assessing a Writing Assignment, p. 224

Rubric for Assessing a Circle Graph, p. 225

Assess students' work through performance tasks.

Small Group Activity: Producing a Concert, All-in-One United States and Canada Teaching Resources, pp. 213–216

Online Assessment

Have students check their own understanding.
Chapter Self-Test

Test Preparation

United States and Canada Benchmark Test 1, AYP Monitoring Assessments, pp. 89–92

Section 1 A Heritage of Diversity and Exchange

 3 periods, 1.5 blocks (includes Skills for Life)

Social Studies Objectives

1. Explain how cultural patterns developed in the United States and Canada.
2. Discuss the cultural patterns that exist today in the United States and Canada.

Reading/Language Arts Objective

Learn to identify the main idea of a paragraph or section.

Prepare to Read	Instructional Resources	Differentiated Instruction
Build Background Knowledge Discuss diversity in the United States and Canada. **Set a Purpose for Reading** Have students evaluate statements on the *Reading Readiness Guide*. **Preview Key Terms** Teach the section's Key Terms. **Target Reading Skill** Introduce the section's Target Reading Skill of **identifying main ideas**.	**All in One United States and Canada Teaching Resources** L2 Reading Readiness Guide, p. 196 L2 Identify Main Ideas, p. 207	**Spanish Reading and Vocabulary Study Guide** L1 Chapter 3, Section 1, pp. 25–26 ELL

Instruct	Instructional Resources	Differentiated Instruction
Patterns of Culture Develop Ask questions about trading and interaction between the Native Americans and European settlers. **Cultural Patterns Today** Discuss immigration to a new country. **Target Reading Skill** Review **identifying main ideas**.	**All in One United States and Canada Teaching Resources** L2 Guided Reading and Review, p. 197 L2 Reading Readiness Guide, p. 196 **United States and Canada Transparencies** L2 Transparency B15: Outline L2 Section Reading Support Transparency USC 51	**All in One United States and Canada Teaching Resources** L1 Outline Map 12: Canada: Political, p. 217 ELL, LPR, SN L2 Skills for Life, p. 212 AR, GT, LPR, SN **Teacher's Edition** L1 For Less Proficient Readers, TE p. 80 L3 For Gifted and Talented, TE p. 80 **Spanish Support** L2 Guided Reading and Review (Spanish), p. 24 ELL

Assess and Reteach	Instructional Resources	Differentiated Instruction
Assess Progress Evaluate student comprehension with the section assessment and section quiz. **Reteach** Assign the Reading and Vocabulary Study Guide to help struggling students. **Extend** Extend the lesson by assigning an Enrichment activity.	**All in One United States and Canada Teaching Resources** L2 Section Quiz, p. 198 L3 Enrichment, p. 211 Rubric for Assessing a Student Poem, p. 222 **Reading and Vocabulary Study Guide** L1 Chapter 3, Section 1, pp. 32–34	**Teacher's Edition** L3 For Advanced Readers, TE p. 83 **United States and Canada Transparencies** L1 Transparency B17: Concept Web ELL, LPR, SN L3 Transparency B16: Venn Diagram AR, GT **Spanish Support** L2 Section Quiz (Spanish), p. 25 ELL

Key

L1 Basic to Average	L3 Average to Advanced	
L2 For All Students		
	LPR Less Proficient Readers	**GT** Gifted and Talented
	AR Advanced Readers	**ELL** English Language Learners
	SN Special Needs Students	

Section 2 The United States: A Nation of Immigrants

 1.5 periods, .75 block

Social Studies Objectives
1. Learn about the people of the United States.
2. Find out about the culture of the United States.

Reading/Language Arts Objective
Identify the supporting details of a main idea.

Prepare to Read	Instructional Resources	Differentiated Instruction
Build Background Knowledge Ask students to think about reasons immigrants come to the United States. **Set a Purpose for Reading** Have students begin to fill out the *Reading Readiness Guide*. **Preview Key Terms** Teach the section's Key Terms. **Target Reading Skill** Introduce the section's Target Reading Skill of **identifying supporting details.**	**All in One United States and Canada Teaching Resources** L2 Reading Readiness Guide, p. 200 L2 Identify Supporting Details, p. 208	**Spanish Reading and Vocabulary Study Guide** L1 Chapter 3, Section 2, pp. 27–28 ELL

Instruct	Instructional Resources	Differentiated Instruction
The People of the United States Ask questions that compare and contrast the first and second groups of immigrants that came to the United States. **Target Reading Skill** Review **identifying supporting details.** **United States Culture** Ask questions about and discuss reflections of diversity in the United States.	**All in One United States and Canada Teaching Resources** L2 Guided Reading and Review, p. 201 L2 Reading Readiness Guide, p. 200 **United States and Canada Transparencies** L2 Section Reading Support Transparency USC 52	**All in One United States and Canada Teaching Resources** L3 Small Group Activity: Producing a Concert, pp. 213–216 AR, GT L2 Doing Searches on the Internet, p. 220 AR, GT, LPR, SN **Teacher's Edition** L3 For Advanced Readers, TE p. 86 **Spanish Support** L2 Guided Reading and Review (Spanish), p. 26 ELL

Assess and Reteach	Instructional Resources	Differentiated Instruction
Assess Progress Evaluate student comprehension with the section assessment and section quiz. **Reteach** Assign the Reading and Vocabulary Study Guide to help struggling students. **Extend** Extend the lesson by having students read two poems by an American poet.	**All in One United States and Canada Teaching Resources** L2 Section Quiz, p. 202 L3 Mother to Son, p. 218 L3 Daybreak in Alabama, p. 219 Rubric for Assessing a Journal Entry, p. 223 **Reading and Vocabulary Study Guide** L1 Chapter 3, Section 2, pp. 35–37	**Spanish Support** L2 Section Quiz (Spanish), p. 27 ELL

Key
L1 Basic to Average   L3 Average to Advanced
L2 For All Students

LPR Less Proficient Readers
AR Advanced Readers
SN Special Needs Students

GT Gifted and Talented
ELL English Language Learners

Section 3 The Canadian Mosaic

 3 periods, 1.5 blocks (includes Chapter Review and Assessment)

Social Studies Objectives
1. Find out about the people of Canada.
2. Learn about Canadian culture.

Reading/Language Arts Objective
Learn to identify the implied main idea.

Prepare to Read	**Instructional Resources**	**Differentiated Instruction**
Build Background Knowledge Have students think about things they already know about Canada. **Set a Purpose for Reading** Have students evaluate statements on the *Reading Readiness Guide*. **Preview Key Terms** Teach the section's Key Terms. **Target Reading Skill** Introduce the section's Target Reading Skill of **identifying main ideas**.	**All in One United States and Canada Teaching Resources** **L2** Reading Readiness Guide, p. 204 **L2** Identifying Implied Main Ideas, p. 209	**Spanish Reading and Vocabulary Study Guide** **L1** Chapter 3, Section 3, pp. 29–30 ELL

Instruct	**Instructional Resources**	**Differentiated Instruction**
The People of Canada Discuss Canada's indigenous people. **Canadian Culture** Ask questions about and discuss Canadian culture. **Target Reading Skill** Review **identifying main ideas**.	**All in One United States and Canada Teaching Resources** **L2** Guided Reading and Review, p. 205 **L2** Reading Readiness Guide, p. 204 **United States and Canada Transparencies** **L2** Section Reading Support Transparency USC 53 **World Studies Video Program** **L2** Quebec's French Culture	**Teacher's Edition** **L3** For English Language Learners, TE p. 91 **L1** For Special Needs Students, TE p. 91 **Student Edition on Audio CD** **L1** Chapter 3, Section 3 ELL, LPR, SN **Spanish Support** **L2** Guided Reading and Review (Spanish), p. 28 ELL

Assess and Reteach	**Instructional Resources**	**Differentiated Instruction**
Assess Progress Evaluate student comprehension with the section assessment and section quiz. **Reteach** Assign the Reading and Vocabulary Study Guide to help struggling students. **Extend** Extend the lesson by assigning a CD-ROM activity.	**All in One United States and Canada Teaching Resources** **L2** Section Quiz, p. 206 Rubric for Assessing a Writing Assignment, p. 224 Rubric for Assessing a Circle Graph, p. 225 **L2** Vocabulary Development, p. 221 **L2** Word Knowledge, p. 210 **L2** Chapter Tests A and B, pp. 226–231 **Reading and Vocabulary Study Guide** **L1** Chapter 3, Section 3, pp. 38–40 **Passport to the World CD-ROM** **L3** Canada: Photo Tour	**Spanish Support** **L2** Section Quiz (Spanish), p. 29 ELL **L2** Chapter Summary (Spanish), p. 30 ELL **L2** Vocabulary Development (Spanish), p. 31 ELL

Key

L1 Basic to Average   **L3** Average to Advanced
L2 For All Students

LPR Less Proficient Readers
AR Advanced Readers
SN Special Needs Students

GT Gifted and Talented
ELL English Language Learners

Reading Background

Summarizing

Research shows that students who know how to summarize are better at comprehending and recalling text. The key to being able to summarize is the ability to recognize main ideas and their supporting details. This allows readers to state important ideas briefly and in a way that is easy to remember.

Use the following steps to model how to write a summary:

1. Preview the selection, gathering information from such features as titles, bold-faced headings, and discussion questions. Take notes on the board.
2. Invite students to use these notes to make predictions about what they will learn from the selection.
3. Read the selection, modeling aloud how to decide on main ideas and supporting details. Record these on the board.
4. Group similar ideas, taking out any extra words to make the sentences as short as possible.
5. Write your summary. Delete more unnecessary words, modeling your thinking process as you do.

Encourage Active Participation

Help students become aware of their own learning strategies by comparing them with those of others in the classroom. Below are some sentence starters with which students can express their thoughts by measuring them against the ideas of others:

One way my method is similar to _____'s is that we both _____.
I agree with this point that _____ made: _____.
I would like to add this detail to _____'s description: _____.
I disagree with _____'s description in this way: _____.
I agree with _____ that _____.
From _____'s description of the way he or she summarizes, I conclude that _____.

World Studies Background

Canadian English

Though American English and Canadian English are much alike, there are some slight differences. For example, an English-speaking Canadian might say, "Please get me a serviette, I spilled my pop on the chesterfield!" Under the same circumstances, an American might say, "Please get me a napkin, I spilled my soda on the couch!"

Cooperative Organizations

Both Canada and the United States are members of the Organization of American States, which promotes friendship and cooperation among nations of the Western Hemisphere. According to the charter of the OAS, an act of aggression against one nation is considered an act against all American nations.

The Battle of Quebec

France's defeat at the battle of Quebec in 1759, during the French and Indian War, marked the end of the French Empire in North America and began Great Britain's dominance. Among the combatants in the war were British colonists who would one day employ the military skills they gained in this conflict against Great Britain itself. One of these was George Washington, future general of the American army during the Revolutionary War.

Infoplease® provides a wealth of useful information for the classroom. You can use this resource to strengthen your background on the subjects covered in this chapter. Have students visit this advertising-free site as a starting point for projects requiring research.

Use Web Code **lhd-4300** for **Infoplease®**.

Chapter 3

Guiding Questions

Remind students about the Guiding Questions introduced at the beginning of the book.

Section 1 relates to **Guiding Question 2**
How have historical events affected the cultures of the United States and Canada? *(The United States and Canada have a long history of diversity and cultural exchange beginning with the arrival of the Europeans. Immigrants from around the world continue to come to the two countries.)*

Section 2 relates to **Guiding Question 3**
How has the variety of people in the United States and Canada benefited and challenged the two nations? *(The United States' mixture of ethnic groups produces a diversity of ideas and traditions.)*

Section 3 relates to **Guiding Question 3**
How has the variety of people in the United States and Canada benefited and challenged the two nations? *(Because immigrants to Canada preserve many of their traditions and beliefs, there are many distinct ethnic groups with their own unique identities.)*

Target Reading Skill

In this chapter, students will learn and apply the reading skill of identifying the main idea. Use the following worksheets to help students practice this skill:

All in One United States and Canada Teaching Resources, *Identify Main Ideas,* p. 207; *Identify Supporting Details,* p. 208; *Identify Implied Main Ideas,* p. 209

Differentiated Instruction

The following Teacher's Edition strategies are suitable for students of varying abilities.

Advanced Readers pp. 83, 86
English Language Learners p. 91
Gifted and Talented p. 80
Less Proficient Readers p. 80
Special Needs Students p. 91

Chapter

3 Cultures of the United States and Canada

Chapter Preview

This chapter will introduce you to the cultures of the United States and Canada.

Section 1
A Heritage of Diversity and Exchange

Section 2
The United States: A Nation of Immigrants

Section 3
The Canadian Mosaic

Target Reading Skill

Main Idea In this chapter you will focus on skills you can use to identify the main ideas as you read.

▶ Young people enjoy an amusement park ride in Orlando, Florida.

74 United States and Canada

Bibliography

For the Teacher
Mitic, Trudy Duivenvoorden. *People in Transition: Reflection on Becoming Canadian.* BPR Publishers, 2001.
Pang, Guek-Cheng. *Canada.* Cavendish, 1996.
Utter, Jack. *American Indians: Answers to Today's Questions, 2ⁿᵈ edition.* University of Oklahoma Press, 2002.

For the Student
L1 Herold, Maggie Rugg. *A Very Important Day.* Morrow, 1995.
L2 Kalman, Bobbie. *Canada: The People.* Crabtree Publishing, 2001.
L3 Bode, Janet. *The Colors of Freedom: Immigrant Stories.* Franklin Watts, Inc, 2000.

Migration to North America

ASIA
60° N
ARCTIC OCEAN
120° E   160° E   160° W   120° W   80° W   40° W   0°

NORTH
AMERICA

EUROPE

ASIA
60° N

Caribbean
Islands

PACIFIC OCEAN

AFRICA

Equator

SOUTH
AMERICA

ATLANTIC
OCEAN

INDIAN
OCEAN

Equator
0°

AUSTRALIA
40° S

20° S

N

W   E

S

20° S

40° S

0 miles   5,000
0 kilometers   5,000
Robinson

60° S

120° E   160° E   160° W   120° W   80° W   40° W   0°   40° E

KEY

United States
and Canada

Route of
Migration

Movement Both the United States and Canada have long histories of welcoming immigrants from around the world. **Locate** Where are most of the arrows pointing to on the map? **Predict** What factors in people's lives might cause them to immigrate to the United States or Canada?

Go Online
PHSchool.com Use Web Code
lhp-4311 for step-by-step map skills practice.

Chapter 3 **75**

- Draw students' attention to the origins of the arrows. Ask them to identify a continent from which many arrows originate, such as Asia. Then ask them to identify which regions these arrows point to. (*Hawaii; the western, central, and eastern United States; western Canada*)

Go Online
PHSchool.com Students may practice their map skills using the interactive online version of this map.

Using the Visual   L2

Reach Into Your Background Point out the photograph at left and its caption. Then tell students to read the section titles on p. 74. Discuss how the photograph illustrates what they will learn about in this chapter. (*The photograph shows the diversity of the United States' population.*)

Answers

MAP MASTER™
Skills Activity
Locate Most of the arrows are pointing to the United States, particularly the northeastern region. **Predict** Possible answers: strife or poverty in their home countries, desire for a better standard of living or new opportunities

---

Chapter Resources

Teaching Resources
L2 Vocabulary Development, p. 221
L2 Skills for Life, p. 212
L2 Chapter Tests A and B, pp. 226–231

Spanish Support
L2 Spanish Chapter Summary, p. 30
L2 Spanish Vocabulary Development, p. 31

Media and Technology
L1 Student Edition on Audio CD
L1 Guided Reading Audiotapes, English and Spanish
L2 Social Studies Skills Tutor CD-ROM
ExamView Test Bank CD-ROM

PRENTICE HALL
Presentation EXPRESS™
Teach · Connect · Inspire

Teach this chapter's content using the PresentationExpress™ CD-ROM including:
- slide shows
- transparencies
- interactive maps and media
- *ExamView®* QuickTake Presenter

Objectives

Social Studies

1. Explain how cultural patterns developed in the United States and Canada.
2. Discuss the cultural patterns that exist today in the United States and Canada.

Reading/Language Arts

Learn to identify the main idea of a paragraph or section.

Prepare to Read

Build Background Knowledge `L2`

In this section students will learn more about the cultural diversity of the United States and Canada. Have students preview the headings and visuals in this section with the following question in mind: **Why can the cultures of the United States and Canada be described as a "heritage of diversity and exchange?"** Conduct an Idea Wave (TE, p. T35) to create a list.

Set a Purpose for Reading `L2`

■ Preview the Objectives.

■ Read each statement in the *Reading Readiness Guide* aloud. Ask students to mark the statements true or false.

> **All in One United States and Canada Teaching Resources,** *Reading Readiness Guide,* p. 196

■ Have students discuss the statements in pairs or groups of four, then mark their worksheets again. Use the Numbered Heads participation strategy (TE, p. T36) to call on students to share their group's perspective.

Vocabulary Builder

Preview Key Terms `L2`

Pronounce each Key Term, then ask the students to say the term with you. Provide a simple explanation, such as, "A place with cultural diversity includes people who practice different traditions."

A Heritage of Diversity and Exchange

Prepare to Read

Objectives

In this section you will
1. Explain how cultural patterns developed in the United States and Canada.
2. Discuss the cultural patterns that exist today in the United States and Canada.

Taking Notes

As you read this section, add facts and details to the outline. Use Roman numerals to indicate the major headings of the section, capital letters for the subheadings, and numbers for the supporting details.

> **A Heritage of Diversity and Exchange**
> I. Patterns of culture develop
>   A.
>   B.
> II.

Target Reading Skill

Identify Main Ideas It is not possible to remember every detail that you read. Good readers therefore identify the main idea in every paragraph or section. The main idea is the most important or the biggest point—the one that includes all the other points in the section. As you read, write the main idea that is stated in each section.

Key Terms

• **cultural diversity** (KUL chur ul duh VUR suh tee) *n.* a variety of cultures
• **cultural exchange** (KUL chur ul eks CHAYNJ) *n.* the process by which different cultures share ideas and ways of doing things
• **ethnic group** (ETH nik groop) *n.* a group of people who share a common language, history, and culture

---

Fur traders at Fort Garry, present-day Winnipeg, in Manitoba, Canada

76 United States and Canada

By 1763, Canada and the eastern half of the present-day United States were one land, governed by Great Britain. When the Revolutionary War ended in 1783, new political boundaries were created. A new country, the United States, was born.

New political borders, however, did not divide cultural regions that already existed. The same patterns of **cultural diversity,** or a wide variety of cultures, continued.

> **"By 1810, many . . . merchants were . . . immigrants, as were almost all the millers, mechanics, store-keepers, . . . and the majority of the farmers. . . . [They] had been lured by economic opportunities. . . . "**
>
> —D. W. Meinig, The Shaping of America

This passage describes American immigrants to Canada. At that time, Americans in the northeastern United States were more comfortable with the culture of southern Canada than with some of the cultures within their own country.

Target Reading Skill `L2`

Identify Main Ideas Point out the Target Reading Skill. Tell students that being able to identify the main idea of a paragraph or section can help them remember what they have read.

Model reading the second paragraph on p. 76 to identify a main idea that is stated directly in the paragraph. Read the paragraph out loud and ask yourself "Which sentence speaks for the whole paragraph?"

(The first sentence: New political borders, however, did not divide cultural regions that already existed.)

Give students *Identify Main Ideas.* Have them complete the activity in their groups.

> **All in One United States and Canada Teaching Resources,** *Identify Main Ideas,* p. 207

Patterns of Culture Develop

The United States and Canada have always been culturally diverse. Both countries are geographically diverse, too—that is, they have a variety of landforms, climates, and vegetation. The cultures of the first Americans reflected their environments. Native Americans near the ocean ate a great deal of fish and told stories about the sea. Native Americans in forests learned how to trap and hunt forest animals. They also traded with each other. When groups trade, they receive more than just goods. They also get involved in **cultural exchange**, or the process by which different cultures share ideas and ways of doing things.

Cultural Exchange When Europeans arrived in North America, they changed Native American life. Some changes came from things that Europeans brought with them. For example, there were no horses in the Americas before the Spanish explorers arrived. Once horses were introduced, they became an important part of Native American culture.

Native American in the Badlands of South Dakota

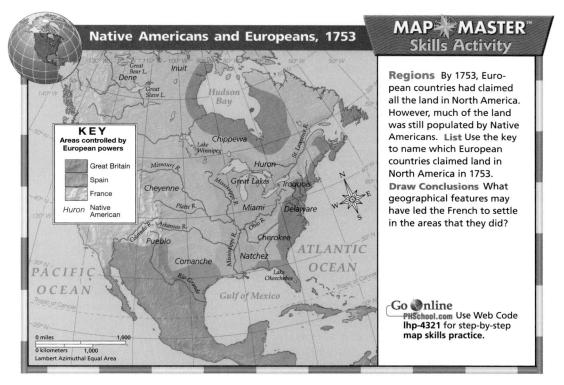

Native Americans and Europeans, 1753

MAP MASTER™ Skills Activity

KEY
Areas controlled by European powers

- Great Britain
- Spain
- France
- *Huron* Native American

Regions By 1753, European countries had claimed all the land in North America. However, much of the land was still populated by Native Americans. **List** Use the key to name which European countries claimed land in North America in 1753.
Draw Conclusions What geographical features may have led the French to settle in the areas that they did?

Go Online
PHSchool.com Use Web Code lhp-4321 for step-by-step map skills practice.

Chapter 3 Section 1 **77**

Patterns of Culture Develop L2

Guided Instruction

- **Vocabulary Builder** Clarify the high-use words **diverse** and **contribution** before reading.

- Read Patterns of Culture Develop, using the Oral Cloze technique (TE, p. T33).

- Ask students **What happens when groups trade with each other?** *(They get goods and become involved in cultural exchange.)*

- Ask students **Why do you think both Native Americans and European settlers were willing to change some of their customs after they interacted?** *(They learned something useful to add to or replace customs they already had.)*

- Ask students to give one example of a cultural exchange between Europeans and Africans. *(Africans learned English and used European tools, while Europeans absorbed African music and food into their daily lives.)*

Independent Practice
Ask students to copy the Taking Notes graphic organizer onto a piece of paper. Using the *Outline Transparency*, briefly model how to distinguish between major headings and supporting details.

📖 **United States and Canada Transparencies,** *Transparency B15: Outline*

Monitor Progress
As students fill in the graphic organizer, make sure individuals are correctly identifying major headings and supporting details. Provide assistance as needed.

Answers

MAP MASTER Skills Activity **List** Great Britain, Spain, and France **Draw Conclusions** The French were interested in trading furs, so they settled near rivers that were good trade routes.

Go Online
PHSchool.com Students may practice their map skills using the interactive online version of this map.

Vocabulary Builder

Use the information below to teach students this section's high-use words.

High-Use Word	Definition and Sample Sentence
diverse, p. 77	*adj.* different, varied He liked all styles of music, which illustrated his **diverse** taste.
contribution, p. 78	*n.* something given or shared Their research was a major **contribution** to the field of science.
tradition, p. 80	*n.* a way of doing things that is passed down over time Watching a football game is one of our Thanksgiving **traditions**.

Cultural Patterns Today

Guided Instruction

- **Vocabulary Builder** Clarify the high-use word **tradition** before reading.

- Read Cultural Patterns Today. As students read, circulate and make sure individuals can answer the Reading Check question.

- Ask students **Why do the United States and Canada share similar cultural patterns and histories?** *(They both were once British colonies.)*

- Discuss with students how immigration changes cultural patterns. Ask students **What are some reasons people immigrate to the United States and Canada?** *(Many come seeking political or religious freedom; others come to escape disease, famine, or overpopulation in their homeland. They come to improve their lives.)*

Links

Read the **Links to Math** on this page. Ask students **Why was it important for Native Americans to have a number system?** *(Having a number system is important in conducting trade and communicating.)*

Harvesting Wheat
These farmers in Manitoba, Canada, are harvesting wheat with a horse-drawn reaper, which cuts grain.
Identify Causes *Why did farming attract many immigrants to the United States and Canada?*

Native Americans also contributed to European culture. The French learned how to trap and to survive in the forest. English families learned to grow local foods such as corn. Cultural exchange also took place between enslaved Africans and their owners. The Africans learned English and used European tools. African music and foods entered the daily lives of slave owners.

Immigrant Contributions This give-and-take happens every time immigrants come to a country. When Russian and Ukrainian settlers came to Canada's Prairie Provinces, they brought a kind of hardy wheat from their home country. Farmers soon learned that it grew well in Canada's climate. These immigrants helped the region become the leading wheat-growing area in Canada today. Members of other ethnic groups have made important contributions to American and Canadian cultures, too. An **ethnic group** is a group of people who share a common language, history, and culture.

✓ **Reading Check** **What are two examples of cultural exchange?**

Cultural Patterns Today

The United States and Canada share similar cultural patterns and histories because both of them were once British colonies. Both of their cultures have also been shaped by immigration. With huge amounts of land to be cultivated, or worked on in order to raise crops, the governments of the United States and Canada first encouraged immigration to increase the work force. With the Industrial Revolution, the end of slavery, and the rise of cities, the demand for workers was great.

Links to Math

Using Your Fingers and Toes Native American groups developed number systems to help when conducting trade with others. The Chukchee, who hunted reindeer along the Bering Strait, used their fingers to count. The question *How many?* is translated "How many fingers?" Their word for *five* is "hand," for *ten*, "both hands," and for *twenty,* "man"—meaning both hands and both feet.

78 United States and Canada

Answers

Identify Causes The climate and fertile soil in the plains regions of the United States and Canada are good for farming.

✓ **Reading Check** Possible answers: Europeans brought horses to North America; Native Americans taught Europeans how to trap, survive in the forest, and grow local foods; Africans learned English and used European tools while African music and foods entered the lives of European Americans; Russian and Ukrainian settlers brought hardy wheat to Canada.

Skills for Life Skills Mini Lesson

Drawing Inferences and Conclusions L2

1. Teach how to draw conclusions based on two or more inferences by discussing the following steps with students:
1) identify what you know to be true;
2) make an educated guess based on what you assume to be true; 3) use two or more inferences to draw a conclusion; 4) check the logic of the conclusion.

2. Help students practice the skill by drawing a conclusion about what life was like before horses arrived in the Americas. *(Possible answer: Native Americans probably traveled by foot.)*

3. Have students apply the skill by drawing a conclusion based on two inferences in the text.

Today, the United States and Canada continue to attract immigrants because they are wealthy nations with stable governments. Many immigrants come seeking political asylum, religious freedom, or economic opportunities. Others come to escape famine, disease, or overcrowding in their homelands. They all come looking to improve their lives.

Fitting In   When immigrants move from their homeland to another country, they often have to make difficult decisions. As immigrants build a life in a new country, they must learn different laws and customs. Often they need to learn a new language, too. Some immigrants work hard to keep up the customs of their home culture as they settle in. Many feel torn between their cultural heritage and their new life.

For instance, when he was 14 years old, Herman immigrated to the United States from Guyana, a country in South America. Five years later, someone asked him if he felt Guyanese or American. He said, "I'm in between. Deep down inside, where I was born, that's what I am. You can't change a tiger['s] stripe."

Others, however, try to put as much of their old life behind them as they can. When Louisa and her husband immigrated to Saskatchewan, Canada, from Hong Kong, they were eager to start their new lives:

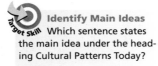
Identify Main Ideas
Which sentence states the main idea under the heading Cultural Patterns Today?

> ❝It takes time to adapt to a new environment. It is sometimes difficult for one to change one's life abruptly. However, it is the reality that we must fit in. We are determined to succeed in overcoming the difficulties and to live a Canadian way of life. ❞
>
> —Louisa, a Chinese immigrant

Celebrating Cultures
The dancers below march in a parade during Carnival Miami in Florida. The photo on the left is a busy street in Chinatown in Vancouver, British Columbia. **Analyze Images** In what ways do the photographs below show how immigrants have blended their traditional cultures with their new cultures?

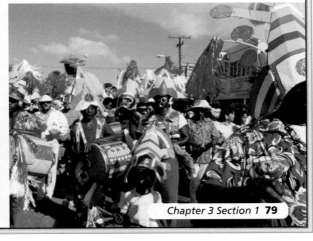

- Ask students **Do you think it would be difficult to immigrate to a new country? Why or why not?** *(Possible answers: Yes—it would be hard to leave behind friends, family, and culture and go to a new place; No—it would be an exciting adventure to learn new things and to meet new people.)*

- Discuss how customs give people a sense of identity. Ask students **Why do you think people get a sense of identity from practicing customs from their countries of origin?** *(Possible answer: It gives people a feeling that they belong and that there are others who have had shared experiences.)*

Independent Practice
Have students complete the graphic organizer by filling in the rest of the outline.

Monitor Progress
- Show *Section Reading Support Transparency USC 51*, and ask students to check their graphic organizers individually. Go over key concepts and clarify key vocabulary as needed.

    📖 **United States and Canada Transparencies,** *Section Reading Support Transparency USC 51*

- Tell students to fill in the last column of the *Reading Readiness Guide*. Probe for what they learned that confirms or invalidates each statement.

    All in One **United States and Canada Teaching Resources,** *Reading Readiness Guide*, p. 196

🎯 Target Reading Skill   L2

Identify Main Ideas As a follow-up, ask students to answer the Target Reading Skill question in the Student Edition. *(The United States and Canada share similar cultural patterns and history because both of them were once British colonies.)*

Skills Mini Lesson ——————

Decision Making   L2
1. To teach the skill, discuss with students that in order to make a decision, you must identify the problem or decision to be made, list the options, evaluate each option, and choose the option that seems best.

2. Help students practice the skill by identifying the problem that new immigrants face. *(how to adapt to their new country)*

3. Have students apply the skill by making a decision about how they might adapt to the new language used in their new country.

Answer

Analyze Images In Vancouver, Chinese immigrants have created signs in Chinese and English. The dancers in the photograph on the right continue to celebrate Carnival in Miami, Florida.

Assess and Reteach

Assess Progress L2
Have students complete the Section Assessment. Administer the *Section Quiz*.

All in One **United States and Canada Teaching Resources,** *Section Quiz,* p. 198

Reteach L1
If students need more instruction, have them read this section in the Reading and Vocabulary Study Guide.

📖 Chapter 3, Section 1, **United States and Canada Reading and Vocabulary Study Guide,** pp. 32–34

Extend L3
Point out that the United States shares a common border with Mexico as well as Canada. The culture along this border blends those of Mexico and the United States. Have students complete *Enrichment* to learn more about this border culture.

All in One **United States and Canada Teaching Resources,** *Enrichment,* p. 211

Answers
Conclusions Canadians and Americans both enjoy professional baseball, which is a money-making business.

Play Ball!
Baseball is widely considered to be the "national pastime" of the United States. It is also a popular sport in Canada. One professional baseball team in Canada competes against American teams in the major leagues. **Conclusions** *How does professional baseball link the United States and Canada both culturally and economically?*

Maintaining Traditions Almost all immigrants cling to some of the things that remind them of their former homes. Many large cities in the United States and Canada have areas where certain ethnic groups live or conduct business, such as Chinatown in Vancouver and Little Havana in Miami.

Of course, people maintain traditions in their own homes as well. Think about your family or your friends' families. Do they use special phrases from the language they learned from their parents or grandparents? Do they eat special foods? Customs give people a sense of identity. They also enrich life in both the United States and Canada.

Cultural Ties The United States and Canada are historically and economically linked. They share a border, a continent, and have felt Britain's influence on their history and language. Although the population of the United States is nearly ten times larger than that of Canada, the people are very much alike.

At least three fourths of people in both countries live in urban areas. Most Canadians live within 200 miles (320 kilometers) of the United States' border. Canadians and Americans dress alike and eat similar foods. The majority of both Canadians and Americans are either Roman Catholic or Protestant. Both nations have long life expectancies and high rates of literacy, or the ability to read and write. Canadians and Americans often read the same books and magazines, listen to the same music, and watch many of the same movies and television shows.

80 United States and Canada

Differentiated Instruction

For Less Proficient Readers L1
Students may have difficulty understanding the concept that most Canadians live within 200 miles (320 kilometers) of the United States. Have them work with a partner to show the distance on the outline map of Canada.

All in One **United States and Canada Teaching Resources,** *Outline Map 12: Canada: Political,* p. 217

For Gifted and Talented L3
Invite students to interview a community member who immigrated to the United States. Have them query the interviewee on decisions he or she had to make once in the country. Students can share their interview by playing an audiotape or writing a feature article.

Economic Ties With vast resources and strong economies, both the United States and Canada have a high standard of living. A standard of living is a measure of the amount of goods, services, and leisure time people have. Their economies are linked, too. The total amount of trade that takes place each year between the United States and Canada is larger than it is between any other two countries. Changes in business trends in the United States are quickly reflected in the Canadian business sector. The two nations trade in manufactured goods, forestry products, and food items. They also trade heavily in energy, such as oil, coal, and electricity.

In addition, millions of Canadians travel to the United States each year. Nearly two million Canadians visit Florida alone, spending more than a billion dollars there. Most of these tourists, known as Snowbirds, come to escape Canada's long, cold winters. Likewise, most of Canada's tourists are American. Americans can travel to Canada almost as easily as they would to a different state.

✓ **Reading Check** What cultural characteristics do the United States and Canada have in common?

Tourists visit the Grand Canyon (upper photo) and Quebec City (lower photo).

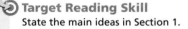

Section 1 Assessment

Key Terms
Review the key terms at the beginning of this section. Use each term in a sentence that explains its meaning.

Target Reading Skill
State the main ideas in Section 1.

Comprehension and Critical Thinking
1. (a) Recall Describe how Native American cultures reflected their environments.

(b) Analyze How did the arrival of Europeans affect Native American cultures?
2. (a) List Note the similarities between the United States and Canada.
(b) Explore the Main Idea How are the economies of the United States and Canada linked?
(c) Draw Conclusions The economy of which country—the United States or Canada—is more dependent on the other's?

Writing Activity
Write a poem about a custom that is important to your family or the family of a friend. Start by listing words or phrases that describe the details of the family custom.

Writing Tip After you write a first draft of the poem, read it aloud. Circle words that do not offer a clear picture of the custom. Replace them with more lively words.

Answers

✓ **Reading Check** Possible answers: a common British history; cultures shaped by immigration; a common language; similar dress, foods, transportation, religions, books, magazines, music, entertainment, and sports; and a high standard of living

Section 1 Assessment

Key Terms
Students' sentences should reflect knowledge of each Key Term.

Target Reading Skill
Possible answer: New patterns of culture developed in the United States and Canada because the two countries are culturally diverse. Immigrants contribute to cultural exchange in both countries. The United States and Canada share many cultural characteristics and have many economic links.

Comprehension and Critical Thinking
1. (a) The Native Americans who lived near the sea ate fish and told stories about the sea. Those who lived in the forest trapped and hunted forest animals. **(b)** The cultural exchange between Europeans and Native Americans changed Native American culture by introducing new things, such as horses.

2. (a) Possible answers: a common British history; cultures shaped by immigration; similar dress, language, foods, religions, books, magazines, music, entertainment, and sports; a high standard of living; linked economies **(b)** Many of the tourists who visit the United States are Canadian, and many of the tourists who visit Canada are from the United States. The economies are also linked by the large shared border, which leads to an exchange of goods. **(c)** Possible answer: The population of the United States is ten times larger than that of Canada. A larger population produces more goods and spends more money, so Canada's economy is probably more dependent on the United States than the United States' economy is on Canada.

Writing Activity
Use the *Rubric for Assessing a Student Poem* to evaluate students' poems.

All in One **United States and Canada Teaching Resources,** *Rubric for Assessing a Student Poem,* p. 222

Objectives

Learn how to use a concept web to organize information and how to transfer information from text to a graphic.

Prepare to Read

Build Background Knowledge **L2**

Remind students that in Section 1, they took notes about the main ideas and details in the text by using an outline. Invite students to brainstorm other helpful ways to remember information they have read. Using an Idea Wave (TE, p. T35), ask students to share their thoughts on how being able to identify main ideas and supporting details helps them to remember information.

Instruct

Using Graphic Organizers **L2**

Guided Instruction

- Read the introduction with the class, then have students study the illustration.
- Have students learn the skill by reading the numbered list on p. 82.
- Model the skill by walking students through the steps under Practice the Skill on p. 83. Model each step in the activity by referring to the concept map. Using Think-Write-Pair-Share (TE, p. T36), invite students to add supporting details relating to family history and other topics.

Independent Practice

- Assign *Skills for Life* and have students complete it individually.
  All in One **United States and Canada Teaching Resources,** *Skills for Life*, p. 212

Monitor Progress

As students are completing the *Skills for Life* worksheet, circulate to be sure individuals are applying the skill steps correctly. Provide assistance as needed.

"Today we're going to brainstorm," Ms. King told her social studies class. She drew a large circle at the center of the chalkboard, and inside it she wrote *Cultures of the United States.* "This is our topic. Now, give me the names of some important culture groups in our country."

The ideas flew fast. "European settlers!" "Before them, Native Americans." "Hispanics!" "African Americans!" "Asians!" Ms. King put each group in its own circle and connected it with a line to the center circle.

"Great start! Now give me details about each of these groups," she urged her students. "What ideas did Europeans bring here?"

She made several small circles and connected them to the large circle, saying, *"European settlers."* She filled in the circles as the students brainstormed the topic: *democracy . . . architecture . . . English language . . . banking . . . measurements . . . medicine. . . .*

By the time she finished, the chalkboard looked like a spider web. In fact, the connected circles made what is sometimes called a *web diagram.* It is also known as a *concept web.*

A concept web is a type of *graphic organizer,* a diagram that puts information into a graphic, or visual, form to make it easier to understand.

Learn the Skill

Like an outline, a concept web begins with a main topic and adds subtopics and details. Follow the steps below to learn about concept webs.

1 **Identify a main topic.** A main topic generally has at least two subtopics. Identify the subtopics.

2 **Draw a circle at the center of the concept map.** Label it with the main topic.

3 **For each subtopic, draw a circle.** Label the circles. Attach them to the main circle with lines to show that the subtopics are related to the main topic.

4 **If necessary, divide the subtopics even further.** Some subtopics have subtopics of their own. To show this, draw more circles, label them, and attach them to the circle with the subtopics.

82 United States and Canada

Background: Links Across Place

Coming to America The United States is home to many different cultures because of immigration. In the past, large numbers of people have immigrated to the United States from countries such as Ireland, Germany, and Russia. But where do immigrants come from today? In 2002, the largest number of immigrants—219,380— arrived from Mexico. The next largest group is from India, at 71,105. China is a major source of immigrants, with 61,282 people. In contrast to Mexico, people from our northern neighbor, Canada, immigrate to the United States in much smaller numbers—19,519 Canadians came to live in the United States in 2002.

Practice the Skill

Suppose you want to write a paper about your culture. Refer to the steps on the previous page and the concept web below to see how you might organize your thoughts.

1. Your topic is My Culture. You know that many factors affect a person's culture. Those factors will be your subtopics.

2. The concept web below shows My Culture in an oval at the center.

3. The ovals connected to the center show that religion, family history, languages, and the celebration of special occasions are parts of a person's culture.

4. Add supporting details that relate to family history and the other subtopics. These details go in the empty ovals shown below.

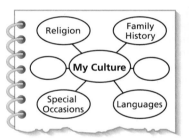

Today, many people can trace their family's history through photographs. This family has photographs of their grandfather (from top to bottom) as a baby, as a young man, with his wife and children, and with his grandson.

Apply the Skill

Choose a part of the text in Section 1. Using the steps for this skill, make a concept web that shows the main idea, subtopics, and details.

Differentiated Instruction

For Advanced Readers L3
Have students read more about the cultural similarities and differences of the United States and Canada. Ask them to create a different kind of graphic organizer, a Venn diagram, to show their findings. Show the *Venn Diagram Transparency* to help them create their own diagrams.

📖 **United States and Canada Transparencies,** *Transparency B16: Venn Diagram*

Assess and Reteach

Assess Progress L2
Ask students to do the Apply the Skill activity.

Reteach L1
If students are having trouble applying the skill steps, help them to review the skill by showing the *Concept Web Transparency*. Choose a topic of interest to the class, and write it in the central oval of the blank concept web. Then elicit details to flesh out the concept web.

 📖 **United States and Canada Transparencies,** *Transparency B17: Concept Web*

Extend L3
To extend the lesson, have pairs of students discuss some of the ways Canada and the United States are different and similar. Then have students use a concept web to organize their main idea, subtopics, and details.

Answers
Apply the Skill
Answers will vary, but student concept webs should begin with the main idea, then work outward to subtopics, and from there to details.

Objectives

Social Studies

1. Learn about the people of the United States.
2. Find out about the culture of the United States.

Reading/Language Arts

Identify the supporting details of a main idea.

Prepare to Read

Build Background Knowledge L2

Tell students that in this section they will learn about the diversity of the American people. Have students revisit the reasons early settlers originally came to North America, such as escaping religious persecution or starting new lives. Then have students discuss if these are still reasons that immigrants move to the United States today and have them brainstorm other reasons that would cause people to immigrate. Ask students to share their ideas using the Think-Write-Pair-Share strategy (TE, p. T36).

Set a Purpose for Reading L2

■ Preview the Objectives.

■ Form students into pairs or groups of four. Distribute the *Reading Readiness Guide*. Ask students to fill in the first two columns of the chart. Use the Numbered Heads participation strategy (TE, p. T36) to call on students to share one piece of information they already know and one piece of information they want to know.

All in One **United States and Canada Teaching Resources,** *Reading Readiness Guide,* p. 200

Vocabulary Builder
Preview Key Terms L2

Pronounce each Key Term, then ask the students to say the word with you. Provide a simple explanation, such as, "Some Native Americans live on reservations, or land set aside by the United States government for Native American use only."

Prepare to Read

Objectives

In this section you will

1. Learn about the people of the United States.
2. Find out about the culture of the United States.

Taking Notes

As you read this section, look for details about the cultural diversity of the United States. Copy the chart below and record your findings in it.

Target Reading Skill

Identify Supporting Details The main idea of a paragraph or section is supported by details that give further information about it. These details may explain the main idea or give examples or reasons. As you read, note the details that explain the main idea in this section: "The United States is a diverse nation."

Key Terms

- **reservation** (rez ur VAY shun) *n.* an area of land set aside for a special purpose
- **treaty** (TREE tee) *n.* a formal agreement, usually between two or more nations

The Statue of Liberty

84 United States and Canada

This view of life in the United States comes from an immigrant arriving in Ellis Island in 1920:

> **"I feel like I had two lives. You plant something in the ground, it has its roots, and then you transplant it where it stays permanently. That's what happened to me. . . . All of a sudden, I started life new, amongst people whose language I didn't understand. . . . [E]verything was different . . . but I never despaired, I was optimistic. . . . [T]his is the only country where you're not a stranger, because we are all strangers. It's only a matter of time who got here first. "**
>
> —*Lazarus Salamon, a Hungarian immigrant*

The People of the United States

The population of the United States has been growing steadily since the first national census was taken in 1790. About 4 million people lived in the nation then. Today, more than 280 million people live in the United States.

Target Reading Skill L2

Identify Supporting Details Call attention to the Target Reading Skill. Point out that supporting details give more information about the main idea.

Model reading the first paragraph under The People of the United States to identify the main idea and its supporting details: "The first sentence gives the main idea, that the population of the United States has been growing steadily." Then read each of the following sentences and ask students if the sentences supply supporting details. *(yes)*

Give students *Identify Supporting Details*. Have them complete the activity in their groups.

All in One **United States and Canada Teaching Resources,** *Identify Supporting Details,* p. 208

Despite the vast size of the United States, its people share many common attitudes and traditions. These experiences help bring Americans together. At the same time, Americans are a diverse mix of races, ethnicities, and religions.

The First People   Today's Native Americans are descendents of the first people to live in the Americas. Most experts believe that the first Americans migrated from Asia across the Bering Strait thousands of years ago. Gradually, the human population spread south across North America.

When European settlers arrived in North America, they often came into conflict with the Native Americans who were living there. As Europeans moved west, they forced the local Indians to move to land already occupied by other Native American groups.

The United States government pursued a general policy of supporting white settlement. They established **reservations,** or federal lands set aside for Native Americans, and forced Native Americans to relocate.

Conflict With Settlers   From 1778 to 1871, the United States government wrote and signed hundreds of **treaties,** or formal agreements, with American Indian groups. In these treaties, Native Americans agreed to interact peacefully with settlers. They also agreed to give up much of their land. In return, the federal government promised to pay for that land and to protect them.

Most of these treaties were broken, often because settlers wanted to expand onto reservation lands. When settlers violated these treaties, Native Americans fought back. They were fighting not only for their land but for their resources and way of life. Native Americans fought more than 1,000 battles throughout the West between 1861 and 1891.

Native Americans Today   In the 1960s, Native Americans began to seek economic and political equality. Several groups, including the American Indian Movement (AIM), formed to work for better living conditions and equal rights. They called on the government to address their concerns. The United States has since passed a series of reforms, giving money and land to Native American groups. Today, about 2.5 million people in the United States are Native American.

Fighting For Civil Rights
Dennis Banks, a leader in the American Indian Movement (AIM), leads a protest in South Dakota. **Draw Inferences** *Why do you think Banks chose Mount Rushmore as the site for the protest?*

The People of the United States   L2

Guided Instruction

- **Vocabulary Builder** Clarify the high-use words **attitude, violate,** and **reform** before reading.

- Read The People of the United States, using the Structured Silent Reading technique (TE, p. T34).

- Ask students to identify the first people who lived on the land that would become the United States. *(Native Americans)* Then ask **What conflicts arose between the Native Americans and the settlers?** *(Conflicts arose between the Native Americans and the settlers who broke federal government treaties and took Native American lands.)*

- Compare and contrast the first and second group of immigrants by asking students these questions. **From what part of Europe did the first wave of immigrants come?** *(mostly northern Europe)* **From what part of Europe did the second group of immigrants come?** *(southern and eastern Europe)* **What religion dominated the first group of immigrants?** *(Protestantism)* **What religions dominated the second group of immigrants?** *(Judaism, Catholicism, Greek Orthodox)*

Vocabulary Builder

Use the information below to teach students this section's high-use words.

High-Use Word	Definition and Sample Sentence
attitude, p. 85	*n.* opinion or feeling about something Ian studied, so he has a positive **attitude** about today's exam.
violate, p. 85	*v.* to break a promise or law They **violated** curfew by staying out after dark.
reform, p. 85	*n.* improvement or correction The mayor's **reforms** helped make the city a safer place.
enrich, p. 87	*n.* to improve the quality of something Viewing many artists' work has **enriched** my skill as an artist.

Answers

Draw Inferences Possible answers: Banks may have chosen the monument as the site for the protest to underline how Native Americans have not always shared in the freedom that the people depicted in the monument stand for.

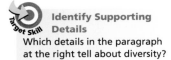
Target Reading Skill L2

Identify Supporting Details As a follow-up, ask students to answer the Target Reading Skill question in the Student Edition. (*The first major wave of immigration took place from 1830 to 1890. Immigrants were from England, Scotland, Scandinavia, and Germany. These groups continued to immigrate to the United States until World War II.*)

Independent Practice

Ask students to copy the Taking Notes graphic organizer onto a piece of paper. Briefly model how to identify which details to record.

Monitor Progress

As students fill in the graphic organizer, circulate and make sure individuals are choosing the correct details. Provide assistance as needed.

Immigrants The United States has always been a nation of immigrants. However, the first major wave of immigration took place from 1830 to 1890. These immigrants were mainly Protestants from England, Scotland, Scandinavia, and Germany who came to farm the land. They adapted fairly easily to the American ways of life because of their similar backgrounds. These ethnic groups would continue to come to the United States in large numbers until World War I.

The first large influx of Chinese immigrants came in 1849, during the California Gold Rush. More Chinese arrived in the 1860s to lay track for the transcontinental railroad. They had a more difficult time than Europeans adjusting to life in the United States. Widespread unemployment and fierce competition for gold led to violence and discrimination against many Asian immigrants.

A Second Wave of Immigrants The second major wave of immigration took place from 1880 to 1920. Unlike the first wave, these immigrants went to work in factories, mills, and mines. Immigrants from southern and eastern Europe dominated the second wave: Jews from Russia and Poland, Roman Catholics from Poland and Italy, and some of the Greek Orthodox faith. Like the Asian immigrants before them, they dressed differently, ate different foods, and spoke different languages. They often worked in poor conditions for low wages.

■ Graph Skills

Thousands of people attend the annual Ninth Avenue International Food Festival in New York City. The festival features food from nearly 30 countries along the mile-long celebration. **Identify** Where do most immigrants to the United States come from? **Draw Conclusions** What languages might the immigrants from those regions speak?

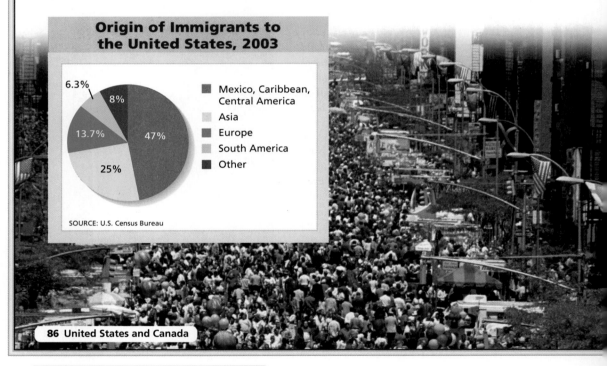

Origin of Immigrants to the United States, 2003

- 6.3%
- 8%
- 13.7%
- 47%
- 25%

- Mexico, Caribbean, Central America
- Asia
- Europe
- South America
- Other

SOURCE: U.S. Census Bureau

Differentiated Instruction

For Advanced Readers L3
Have groups of students research the music of different groups of people in the United States or Canada by completing *Small Group Activity: Producing a Concert*. Ask students to create a poster to accompany their musical presentation. Display the posters around the classroom.

All in One **United States and Canada Teaching Resources,** *Small Group Activity: Producing a Concert,* pp. 213–216

Answers

Graph Skills **Identify** The largest group is from Mexico, the Caribbean, and Central America; the second largest, from Asia.
Draw Conclusions Possible answers: Spanish, Chinese, Korean, and many other languages

The writings of Zora Neale Hurston, Ralph Waldo Emerson, and Sandra Cisneros (from far left) reflect the diversity of the books that Americans read.

Immigrants Today   Non-Europeans form the largest immigrant groups coming to the United States today. Most immigrants arrive from Asia and Latin America. The hard work of these immigrants, and of those before them, have helped develop the United States agriculturally, industrially, and economically. They also helped create a culturally diverse nation.

✓ Reading Check   **Where do most immigrants arrive from today?**

United States Culture

Have you ever eaten bagels, tacos, dim sum, or spaghetti? Have you listened to music at a Caribbean carnival or watched a dragon parade on Chinese New Year? Diverse foods, books, music, and pastimes all enrich the lives of Americans.

Literature   A distinctly American literature emerged in the nineteenth century, as Ralph Waldo Emerson and others wrote about politics and nature. By the twentieth century, America's diversity had begun to influence its literature. Playwright Eugene O'Neill had an Irish background, while Zora Neale Hurston wrote novels about what it was like to be African American. Traditions such as Native American folk tales and slave narratives also gained importance. American literature is now more varied than ever before, reflecting the diversity in today's culture.

Musical Traditions   In addition to diverse literature, Americans listen to and create many different kinds of music, from classical to popular. Popular music includes country, rap, rock, reggae, and jazz. Although it has its roots in African rhythms, jazz developed in the South, in places like New Orleans, Louisiana. African American singers and musicians, such as Louis Armstrong and Duke Ellington, made jazz popular around the world.

Pianist and composer Duke Ellington and trumpeter Louis Armstrong rehearse their first recording together in a New York City recording studio in 1946.

Chapter 3 Section 2 **87**

United States Culture   L2

Guided Instruction

- **Vocabulary Builder**   Clarify the high-use word **enrich** before reading.

- Read United States Culture with students. As students read, circulate and make sure individuals can answer the Reading Check question.

- Ask students to name some foods that came from other countries that are now part of American culture. *(bagels, tacos, dim sum, spaghetti)*

- Ask students **What does the list of writers reveal about the culture of the United States today?** *(They reflect a society in which there is diversity.)*

- Have students discuss other elements not mentioned in the section that illustrate the diversity that makes up American culture. *(Possible answers: art, holidays, religion, language)*

Independent Practice
Have students complete the graphic organizer by filling in the details on the chart.

Monitor Progress

- Show *Section Reading Support Transparency USC 52* and ask students to check their graphic organizers individually. Go over key concepts and clarify key vocabulary as needed.

    📖 **United States and Canada Transparencies,** *Section Reading Support Transparency USC 52*

- Tell students to fill in the last column of the *Reading Readiness Guide*. Probe for what they learned that confirms or invalidates each statement.

    All in One **United States and Canada Teaching Resources,** *Reading Readiness Guide*, p. 200

Answer

✓ Reading Check   Today, most immigrants arrive from Latin America and Asia.

Assess and Reteach

Assess Progress `L2`

Have students complete the Section Assessment. Administer the *Section Quiz*.

All in One **United States and Canada Teaching Resources,** *Section Quiz,* p. 202

Reteach `L1`

If students need more instruction, have them read this section in the Reading and Vocabulary Study Guide.

📖 Chapter 3, Section 2, **United States and Canada Reading and Vocabulary Study Guide,** pp. 35–37

Extend `L3`

Have students learn more about American literature by reading *Mother to Son* and *Daybreak in Alabama,* by Langston Hughes. Ask students to create illustrations for each poem.

All in One **United States and Canada Teaching Resources,** *Mother to Son,* p. 218, *Daybreak in Alabama,* p. 219

Answers

✓ **Reading Check** baseball, basketball, and football

Section 2 Assessment

Key Terms
Students' sentences should reflect knowledge of each Key Term.

🎯 **Target Reading Skill**
Answers will vary. Students may note details on p. 87 that encompass foods, traditions, literature, and music.

Comprehension and Critical Thinking
1. (a) by establishing reservations and forcing Native Americans to relocate **(b)** Possible answer: because white settlers wanted valuable land **(c)** Possible answer: The U.S. government signed and broke treaties with Native Americans, and used its powerful army to fight Native Americans, finally placing them on reservations.
2. (a) in the nineteenth century **(b)** by the twentieth century; writers from different backgrounds **(c)** Possible answer: Immigrants helped to create a culturally diverse nation in areas such as literature, music, and sports.

Basketball was invented in 1891 and quickly gained popularity in schools and colleges throughout the country.

Probably the most popular style of music to originate in the United States is rock-and-roll. A combination of rhythm and blues, gospel, and country music, rock music first became popular in the 1950s. It created a sensation all over the country and quickly spread from the United States to Europe and Asia. It remains one of the most popular musical styles throughout the world today.

Sports Many Americans watch and participate in sports activities. Sports in North America go all the way back to Native American groups who played a form of lacrosse. In the late 1800s, sports such as tennis, hiking, and golf grew in popularity. Organized team sports also began to develop a following near the end of the 1800s.

Three major sports were invented in the United States: baseball, basketball, and football. Baseball soon became the national pastime, producing sports heroes like Babe Ruth in the early 1900s. Today, baseball's popularity has spread to Japan, the Caribbean, Russia, Mexico, and Central America.

✓ **Reading Check** Which major sports were invented in the United States?

 ## Section 2 Assessment

Key Terms
Review the key terms at the beginning of this section. Use each term in a sentence that explains its meaning.

🎯 **Target Reading Skill**
State the details that support the main idea on page 87 that the United States is diverse.

Comprehension and Critical Thinking
1. (a) Explain How did the United States government support white settlement in the West?

(b) Draw Inferences Why did the government send Native Americans to live on land that was not considered valuable?
(c) Analyze Information How were Native Americans at a disadvantage in their conflict with white settlers?
2. (a) Note When did American literature begin to have a distinct voice?
(b) Identify Causes When and how did American literature become more diverse?
(c) Synthesize Information How has the immigrant experience influenced American culture?

Writing Activity
Write an entry in your journal explaining how the literature and music of the United States reflect diverse cultures. When you write a journal entry, you can let your ideas flow without stopping to edit what you write.

For: An activity on Ellis Island
Visit: PHSchool.com
Web Code: lhd-4302

Writing Activity
Use the *Rubric for Assessing a Journal Entry* to evaluate students' journals.

All in One **United States and Canada Teaching Resources,** *Rubric for Assessing a Journal Entry,* p. 223

Go Online PHSchool.com Typing in the Web code when prompted will bring students directly to detailed instructions for this activity.

Section 3
The Canadian Mosaic

Prepare to Read

Objectives
In this section you will
1. Find out about the people of Canada.
2. Learn about Canadian culture.

Taking Notes
As you read this section, look for details that show why Canadians consider their society to be a mosaic. Copy the concept web below and record your findings in it.

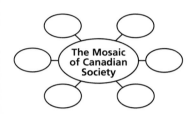

The Mosaic of Canadian Society

Target Reading Skill

Identify Main Ideas
Identifying main ideas can help you remember the most important ideas that you read. Sometimes, the main ideas are not stated directly. All the details in a section add up to a main idea, but you must state the main idea yourself. Carefully read the details in the two paragraphs below. Then, state the main idea of these paragraphs.

Key Terms
- **melting pot** (MELT ing paht) *n.* a country in which many cultures blend together to form a single culture
- **reserve** (rih ZURV) *n.* an area of land set aside by the government

A crowd celebrates Canada Day.

Over the years, Canada has been as welcoming to immigrants as the United States. However, one important difference between the countries is the way in which they view immigration. The United States considers itself to be a **melting pot,** or a country in which all cultures blend together to form a single culture. In this view, immigrants are encouraged to adopt American ways. Canadians view immigration in a slightly different way, as one Canadian journalist explains:

> **❝Canadians believe . . . in a mosaic of separate pieces, with each chunk becoming part of the whole physically but retaining its own separate identity, color, and tastes. This certainly makes for an interesting mix. Importantly, it provides Canadians with an identity peg, one major way to see themselves as different from Americans, as they must. And as they are. ❞**
>
> —*Andrew H. Malcolm*

Chapter 3 Section 3 **89**

Target Reading Skill　L2

Identify Main Ideas Point out the Target Reading Skill. Tell students that when a main idea is not specifically expressed, readers can combine important details to express the main idea.

Model identifying the implied main idea in the first paragraph on p. 91 under the heading Immigrants. Point out that the first three sentences provide background to help set up the main idea. The information in the last two sentences can be used to identify the main idea. *(Many immigrants settled in Canada until the government restricted immigration during the Great Depression.)*

Give students *Identify Implied Main Ideas.* Have them complete the activity in their groups.

All in One **United States and Canada Teaching Resources,** *Identify Implied Main Ideas,* p. 209

Section 3
Step-by-Step Instruction

Objectives
Social Studies
1. Find out about the people of Canada.
2. Learn about Canadian culture.

Reading/Language Arts
Learn to identify the implied main idea.

Prepare to Read

Build Background Knowledge　L2
Ask students to list two pieces of information they know about Canada. Model the thought process by suggesting that they recall what they have read about the similarities and differences between Canada and the United States. Use the Give One, Get One strategy (TE, p. T37) to generate a list.

Set a Purpose for Reading　L2
- Preview the Objectives.
- Read each statement in the *Reading Readiness Guide* aloud. Ask students to mark the statements true or false.

  All in One **United States and Canada Teaching Resources,** *Reading Readiness Guide,* p. 204

- Have students discuss the statements in pairs or groups of four, then mark their worksheets again. Use the Numbered Heads participation strategy (TE, p. T36) to call on students to share their group's perspective.

Vocabulary Builder
Preview Key Terms　L2
Pronounce each Key Term, then ask the students to say the word with you. Provide a simple explanation, such as, "Many of Canada's native peoples live on reserves, while many Native Americans in the United states live on reservations."

Show students *Quebec's French Culture*. Ask **How did Jacques Cartier establish France's claims to the land now known as Quebec in Canada?** *(He planted a cross on the Gaspé Peninsula in the Gulf of St. Lawrence in 1534.)*

Instruct

The People of Canada   L2

Guided Instruction

- **Vocabulary Builder** Clarify the high-use words **promote** and **restrict**.

- Read The People of Canada, using the Paragraph Shrinking technique (TE, p. T34).

- Ask students **What are Canada's indigenous peoples called?** *(First Nations)*

- Discuss how the way the Canadian government treated First Nations was similar to the way the United States first treated Native Americans. *(European settlers took over the indigenous peoples' lands. Many indigenous peoples were sent to reserves in Canada while they were sent to reservations in the United States. Others were denied equal rights.)*

- Ask students **Why has Canada's population doubled since World War II?** *(More workers were needed when the economy began to grow again after World War II. Millions of immigrants came to Canada to fill this need.)*

Independent Practice

Ask students to copy the Taking Notes graphic organizer onto a piece of paper. Briefly model how to use the concept web to record supporting details that show why Canadians consider their society to be a mosaic.

Monitor Progress

As students fill in the graphic organizer, circulate and make sure individuals are choosing the correct details. Provide assistance as needed.

Answers

Graph Skills Identify Asia and Oceania **Compare and Contrast** Similar—the areas of origin are similar; Different—the United States has a higher percentage of immigrants from Mexico, the Caribbean, and Central America than Canada, and Canada has a higher percentage of Asian immigrants.

The People of Canada

Find out more about Quebec's French culture.

Today, Canada has a population of more than 31 million people. Many of them are immigrants. At first, Canada's leaders preferred Christian European settlers. At times, laws set limits on immigrants who were Jews, Asians, or Africans. But that has changed. Today, people of all ethnic groups move to Canada.

French Canadians Sometimes, the ties among Canadians are not as strong as those among Americans. People in the United States rarely talk about forming independent states or countries. Some Canadian groups do. French Canadians in Quebec are concerned about preserving their heritage. Special laws promote French culture and language. Street and advertising signs are written in both French and English. But many French Canadians want Quebec to become a separate country. To show their determination, they have license plates that read *Je me souviens,* or "I remember." This phrase refers to remembering their French heritage.

First Nations Canada's indigenous peoples, called First Nations, also want to preserve their culture. They are trying to fix past problems by working with existing governments.

In Canada, as in the United States, early European settlers took over the native peoples' lands. Many indigenous peoples were sent to reserves, or areas that the government set aside for them, similar to reservations in the United States. Others were denied equal rights. Recently, laws have been passed allowing First Nations to use their own languages in their schools.

Graph Skills

Canada is an ethnically diverse country. **Identify** Where do most immigrants to Canada come from? **Compare and Contrast** Compare the Origin of Immigrants to Canada chart here with the similar chart on page 86. How are they similar? How do they differ?

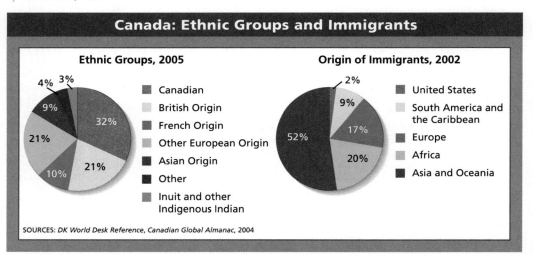

Canada: Ethnic Groups and Immigrants

Ethnic Groups, 2005

- 3%
- 4%
- 9%
- 21%
- 10%
- 21%
- 32%

- Canadian
- British Origin
- French Origin
- Other European Origin
- Asian Origin
- Other
- Inuit and other Indigenous Indian

Origin of Immigrants, 2002

- 2%
- 9%
- 17%
- 20%
- 52%

- United States
- South America and the Caribbean
- Europe
- Africa
- Asia and Oceania

SOURCES: *DK World Desk Reference, Canadian Global Almanac, 2004*

Vocabulary Builder

Use the information below to teach students this section's high-use words.

High-Use Word	Definition and Sample Sentence
promote, p. 90	*v.* to help with the growth of something Watering plants regularly helps to **promote** their growth.
restrict, p. 91	*v.* to keep within a certain amount Ann **restricts** the amount of food her dog eats so that he stays fit and healthy.

Inuits Canada's Inuits (IN oo its) lived in the Arctic for centuries as nomadic hunters and gatherers. They had excellent survival skills and were fine craftworkers. They made everything they needed using available materials, such as snow, stone, animal bones, and driftwood. Modern technology, however, allows them to buy the clothes and tools they used to make. Many Inuits have lost their traditional skills. As a result, some feel they are losing their identity.

Immigrants Because Britain and France were the first countries to colonize Canada, most Canadians were of British or French descent by the late 1800s. By the 1920s, many immigrants came from central and eastern Europe to farm the prairies in the west. But when the Depression hit in 1929, there was no longer a need for as many workers. The government restricted immigration.

After World War II, the economy began to grow again. With the need for more workers, millions of immigrants came to Canada. Many of them were from Africa, Asia, and Latin America and settled mainly in large urban areas. For example, many Asian immigrants settled in Vancouver and Toronto. Since World War II, Canada's population has more than doubled. Much of that growth is because of immigrants and their children.

✓ **Reading Check** How has technology changed the way that Inuits live?

Remembering Canada's History
The community of Chemainus, British Columbia, is famous for its collection of 35 larger-than-life historical murals. **Analyze Images** *How does this mural honor the role that the country's indigenous peoples have played in Canada's history?*

 Identify Main Ideas In one sentence, state the topic that all the details in the paragraph at the left are about.

Chapter 3 Section 3 **91**

Guided Instruction

■ Read Canadian Culture with students.

■ Ask students **What is one cultural issue that unites most Canadians?** *(They feel the United States has too much influence on their culture.)*

■ Discuss Canadian literature and music. Ask students to name Canadian writers and musicians. Encourage them to include people not mentioned in the text. *(writers: Lucy Maud Montgomery, Margaret Atwood, Robertson Davies, Alice Munro, Michael Ondaatje; musicians: Bryan Adams, Sarah McLachlan, Shania Twain, Céline Dion)*

Independent Practice
Have students complete the graphic organizer by filling in the rest of the details on the concept web.

Monitor Progress

■ Show *Section Reading Support Transparency USC 53* and ask students to check their graphic organizers individually. Go over key concepts and clarify key vocabulary as needed.

📖 **United States and Canada Transparencies,** *Section Reading Support Transparency USC 53*

■ Tell students to fill in the last column of the *Reading Readiness Guide.* Probe for what they learned that confirms or invalidates each statement.

All in One United States and Canada Teaching Resources, *Reading Readiness Guide,* p. 204

↻ Target Reading Skill

Identify Main Ideas As a follow-up, ask students to perform the Target Reading Skill activity in the Student Edition. *(Since World War II, the population of Canada has grown significantly, which has occurred in part by an increase in immigration.)*

Answers

Analyze Images The presence of the mural in the collection acknowledges the importance of indigenous peoples in history.

✓ **Reading Check** They now can buy many of the things they used to make and many Inuits have lost their traditional skills.

Differentiated Instruction

For English Language Learners [L3]
Some of the verbs used in this section may be confusing to students acquiring English as a second language. Point out irregular verbs in the section such as *made, sent,* and *came.* Help students to make a list of the section's past-tense verbs and their corresponding infinitives.

For Special Needs Students [L1]
Have students read the section as they listen to the recorded version on the Student Edition on Audio CD. Check for comprehension by pausing the CD and asking students to share their answers to the Reading Checks.

🔘 Chapter 3, Section 3, **United States and Canada Student Edition on Audio CD**

Assess and Reteach

Assess Progress L2
Have students complete the Section Assessment. Administer the *Section Quiz.*

All in One **United States and Canada Teaching Resources,** *Section Quiz,* p. 206

Reteach L1
If students need more instruction, have them read this section in the Reading and Vocabulary Study Guide.

📖 Chapter 3, Section 3, **United States and Canada Reading and Vocabulary Study Guide,** pp. 38–40

Extend L3
Have students view the Photo Tour of Canada on the Passport to the World CD, then write a letter home describing their trip.

💿 *Canada: Photo Tour,* **Passport to the World CD-ROM**

Answers

✓ Reading Check the recording and sports industries

Section 3 Assessment

Key Terms
Students' sentences should reflect knowledge of each Key Term.

 Target Reading Skill
Possible answer: The population of Canada is made up of immigrants from all over the world and Canada's indigenous peoples. Canadians share a common culture and also express their own ethnic heritages. Literature, music, and sports are all important to Canadian culture.

Comprehension and Critical Thinking
1. (a) English and French **(b)** Special laws promote French culture and language, and street and advertising signs are in French and English. **(c)** Possible answer: They feel it is the best way to protect Quebec's French culture.

2. (a) through writing, music, and sports **(b)** Possible answer: They worry that the United States has too much influence on their culture.

Playing hockey on an outdoor ice rink

Canadian Culture

Canada has made a special effort to encourage people to be Canadian and to express their ethnic heritage at the same time. One cultural issue does unite most Canadians: They feel that the United States has too much influence on their culture. Even today, Canadians search for ways to express their unique culture.

Canadian writers have long been famous for their work. From Lucy Maud Montgomery's *Anne of Green Gables* to writers of today, such as Margaret Atwood and Alice Munro, Canadian literature is popular throughout the world.

Canadian singers have made contributions to cultural life as well. Popular Canadian singers include Shania Twain and Céline Dion. Many singers maintain their ties to Canada even though their jobs often require them to be elsewhere. Since the 1960s, the Canadian recording industry has become a billion-dollar business.

Another billion-dollar industry in Canada is sports. Ice hockey is Canada's national sport. Every year, hockey teams from the United States and Canada compete for the Stanley Cup, a Canadian prize. Hockey serves not only as a national pastime but also as an important symbol of national identity.

✓ Reading Check **Which industries bring billions of dollars into the Canadian economy?**

✦ Section 3 Assessment

Key Terms
Review the key terms at the beginning of this section. Use each term in a sentence that explains its meaning.

🔄 **Target Reading Skill**
State the main ideas in Section 3.

Comprehension and Critical Thinking
1. (a) List What are two languages spoken in Canada?

(b) Identify the Main Idea In what ways do French Canadians try to preserve their culture and language?
(c) Draw Conclusions Why do many French Canadians want Quebec to be an independent country?
2. (a) Explain How do Canadians try to express their culture?
(b) Make Generalizations Why do Canadians worry about the influence of the United States on their culture?

Writing Activity
Write a brief paragraph explaining why you think ice hockey developed in Canada.

For: An activity on immigrants
Visit: PHSchool.com
Web Code: lhd-4303

Writing Activity
Use the *Rubric for Assessing a Writing Assignment* to evaluate students' paragraphs.

All in One **United States and Canada Teaching Resources,** *Rubric for Assessing a Writing Assignment,* p. 224

Go Online PHSchool.com Typing in the Web code when prompted will bring students directly to detailed instructions for this activity.

Review and Assessment

◆ Chapter Summary

Section 1: A Heritage of Diversity and Exchange

- Both the United States and Canada contain a wide variety of cultures.
- Immigrants have shaped the histories and cultures of the United States and Canada.
- The United States and Canada are important to each other for many reasons, including the cultural and economic ties that they share.

Section 2: The United States: A Nation of Immigrants

- The United States government fought many battles with Native Americans, pushing them westward.
- Millions of immigrants came to the United States to work on farms and railroads and in factories, mills, and mines.
- Diverse foods, literature, music, and sports help enrich life in the United States.

Section 3: The Canadian Mosaic

- Many immigrants come to Canada in search of a better life.
- First Nations, Inuits, and immigrants all add to the diversity of Canadian life.
- Canadians have made many contributions to the worlds of literature, music, and sports.

Quebec City

◆ Key Terms

Copy the lists of vocabulary words and definitions side by side on a sheet of paper. Then, draw a line from each term to its correct definition.

1. cultural diversity
2. cultural exchange
3. reservation
4. melting pot
5. ethnic group
6. treaty
7. reserve

A   an area of land set aside for a special purpose

B   an area of land set aside by the Canadian government

C   a variety of cultures

D   people who share a language, history, and culture

E   a formal agreement

F   the process in which different cultures share ideas and ways of doing things

G   a country in which all cultures blend together to form a single culture

Chapter 3 **93**

Review and Assessment

Review Chapter Content

- Review and revisit the major themes of this chapter by asking students to classify what Guiding Question each bulleted statement in the Chapter Summary answers. Have students work in groups to classify the statements. Use the Numbered Heads strategy (TE, p. T36) to have the groups share their answers in a class discussion. Refer to p. 1 in the Student Edition for text of Guiding Questions.

- Assign *Vocabulary Development* for students to review Key Terms.

   All in One United States and Canada Teaching Resources, *Vocabulary Development*, p. 221

◆ Vocabulary Builder

Revisit this chapter's high-use words:

diverse	attitude	enrich
contribution	violate	promote
tradition	reform	restrict

Ask students to review the definitions they recorded on their *Word Knowledge* worksheets.

All in One United States and Canada Teaching Resources, *Word Knowledge*, p. 210

Consider allowing students to earn extra credit if they use the words in their answers to the questions in the Chapter Review and Assessment. They must use the words correctly and in a natural context to win the extra points.

Answers

Key Terms

1. C
2. F
3. A
4. G
5. D
6. E
7. B

Comprehension and Critical Thinking

8. (a) to increase the work force, to have people to cultivate land, raise crops, and work in cities **(b)** They attract immigrants because they are wealthy countries with stable governments. **(c)** Possible answer: They find it hard to keep customs of their original culture when they need to learn a new language, laws, and customs in their new country. They feel torn between their cultural heritage and their new life.

9. (a) Nearly two million Canadians visit Florida each year as tourists, supporting many tourism-related industries. **(b)** Possible answer: It would harm such businesses as hotels, restaurants, and amusement centers, resulting in many job losses.

10. (a) They had similar backgrounds and languages. **(b)** Their culture and traditions were different from those of the first wave of immigrants.

11. (a) Possible answer: Because American society is diverse, Americans listen to many kinds of music and new styles of music develop, such as jazz and rock-and-roll. **(b)** Possible answer: Both originated in the United States, growing out of traditional music styles. Jazz has roots in African rhythms and rock-and-roll is a combination of rhythm and blues, gospel, and country music.

12. (a) They are working with the government to fix past problems; they are using native languages in schools. **(b)** Possible answer: Canadian culture encourages people to retain their traditional identity rather than trying to blend into one single culture. **(c)** Possible answer: Canadians wish to express their own culture rather than be influenced by the culture of the United States.

Skills Practice
Concept webs will vary, but should be labeled clearly and include accurate information.

◆ Comprehension and Critical Thinking

8. (a) Explain Why did the United States and Canada first encourage immigration?
(b) Identify Causes Why do the United States and Canada continue to attract immigrants today?
(c) Identify Frame of Reference Why do some immigrants find it challenging to balance their cultural heritage with their new environment?

9. (a) Recall How do Canadians contribute to Florida's economy?
(b) Predict In what ways would Florida's economy be affected if these tourists vacationed somewhere else?

10. (a) Recall Why did most of the first wave of immigrants adapt fairly easily to life in the United States?
(b) Draw Conclusions Why was the second wave of immigrants discriminated against when the first wave of immigrants largely was not?

11. (a) Explain How does American society influence American music?
(b) Analyze What is it about jazz or rock-and-roll music that makes them uniquely American?

12. (a) Explain How are First Nations preserving their culture?
(b) Compare and Contrast Why is Canada characterized as a mosaic rather than as a melting pot?
(c) Identify Point of View Why is it important for Canadians to see themselves as different from Americans?

◆ Skills Practice

Using Graphic Organizers In the Skills for Life activity in this chapter, you learned how to use graphic organizers. You also learned that graphic organizers put information into a visual form.

Review the steps you followed to learn this skill. Then reread Cultural Patterns Today, beginning on page 78. Create a concept web about peoples' reasons for choosing to immigrate to the United States and Canada.

◆ Writing Activity: Math

In pairs or teams, research the different ethnic or cultural groups that are represented in your state. Calculate the results in percentage form. Then display the information as a circle graph. Write a brief summary of your findings.

MAP MASTER™ Skills Activity

Native American Groups

Place Location For each Native American group listed below, write the letter from the map that shows its location.

1. Miami
2. Chippewa
3. Cherokee
4. Iroquois
5. Pueblo
6. Cheyenne
7. Comanche
8. Huron

Go Online
PHSchool.com Use Web Code lhp-4333 for an **interactive map.**

Writing Activity: Math
Student answers should include a circle graph and an informative summary. Use *Rubric for Assessing a Circle Graph* to evaluate students' graphs.

All in One **United States and Canada Teaching Resources,** *Rubric for Assessing a Circle Graph*, p. 225

Standardized Test Prep

Test-Taking Tips

Some questions on standardized tests ask you to analyze a passage to find a main idea. Read the passage below. Then follow the tips to answer the sample question.

> One Toronto radio station broadcasts in thirty languages. . . . In many Vancouver neighborhoods the street signs are in . . . English and Chinese. Toronto's city government routinely prepares its annual property tax notices in six languages: English, French, Chinese, Italian, Greek, and Portuguese.

TIP Before reading the answer choices, think of a main idea that would cover each sentence in the passage. Then match your idea to one of the answer choices.

Pick the letter that best answers the question.

What is the main idea of this passage?

A Toronto's city government prepares tax notices in many languages.

B The Chinese are an important ethnic group in Toronto.

C Many people in Toronto are bilingual, or speak two languages.

D Toronto has a diverse mix of people and ethnic groups.

TIP Read all of the answer choices before making a final choice. You can't be sure you have the right answer until you have read each one.

Think It Through You can rule out answer A, because it applies only to one of the sentences in the passage. You can rule out answer B because though it may be true, the Chinese are only one of the ethnic groups mentioned in the passage. Both answers C and D sound like they might be correct. Read answer C carefully. It isn't right because though the passage describes many languages, it does not say that most people in Toronto are bilingual. The correct answer is D.

Practice Questions

Use the tips above and other tips in this book to help you answer the following questions.

1. When two groups of people share ideas and ways of doing things, they are practicing
   A trade.   **B** cultural exchange.
   C cultural diversity.   **D** immigration.

2. What kind of standard of living do the United States and Canada have?
   A Both countries have low standards of living.
   B Both countries have high standards of living.
   C The United States has a high standard of living, while Canada's is low.
   D Canada has a high standard of living, while that of the United States is low.

3. Which group in Canada often talks about forming an independent country?
   A the Chippewa   **B** the British
   C the French Canadians   **D** the Inuit

Read the passage below, and then answer the question that follows.

> Culture here has been shaped by a history of British colonization. It has also been shaped by immigrants who have come here from all over the world, bringing their cultures with them. Music, literature, and sports are important parts of the culture.

4. Based on what you have read, which country could this passage be describing?
   A either the United States or Canada
   B the United States
   C Canada
   D neither the United States nor Canada

Use Web Code lha-4303 for a **Chapter 3** self-test.

Assessment Resources

Use *Chapter Tests A and B* to assess students' mastery of chapter content.

All in One **United States and Canada Teaching Resources,** *Chapter Tests A and B,* pp. 226–231

Tests are also available on the *ExamView®* *Test Bank CD-ROM.*

⊙ *ExamView Test Bank CD-ROM*

Use a benchmark test to evaluate students' cumulative understanding of what they have learned in Chapters 1 through 3.

📄 *United States and Canada Benchmark Test 1,* **AYP Monitoring Assessments,** pp. 89–92

Overview

Introducing the United States
1. Look at a map and study the data to learn about the states of the United States.
2. Analyze data to compare the states.
3. Identify characteristics that most states share.
4. Find some of the key differences among the states.

The Geography of the United States
Length: 3 minutes, 50 seconds
Provides an overview of the geography, natural resources, and cultures of the four regions of the United States.

The Northeast: An Urban Center
Section 1
1. Learn how the large cities of the Northeast contribute to the economy of the United States.
2. Find out how the Northeast has been a port of entry for many immigrants.

Paul Revere and the Minutemen
Length: 7 minutes, 31 seconds
Portrays the battle between the British and the American minutemen in 1775.

The South: The Growth of Industry
Section 2
1. Learn how the South's land is important to its economy.
2. Read about how the growth of industry is changing the South.

Miami's Little Havana
Length: 3 minutes, 37 seconds
Describes the Cuban community in Miami as an example of a Hispanic culture in the U.S.

The Midwest: Leaving the Farm
Section 3
1. Read about how technology is changing life on farms.
2. Learn how changes in farming are affecting the development of cities.

Taming the Mississippi
Length: 4 minutes, 26 seconds
Explains the advantages and dangers of the Mississippi River.

The West: Using and Preserving Resources
Section 4
1. Learn about the natural resources of the West.
2. Read about the challenges facing the urban West.

The Gold Rush
Length: 4 minutes, 53 seconds
Explores how the gold rushes in California in 1849 and Alaska in 1899 represent the American spirit of adventure.

Technology Resources

Go Online
PHSchool.com

Students use embedded Web codes to access Internet activities, chapter self-tests, and additional map practice. They may also access Dorling Kindersley's Online Desk Reference to learn more about each country they study.

Interactive Textbook

Use the Interactive Textbook to make content and concepts come alive through animations, videos, and activities that accompany the complete basal text—online and on CD-ROM.

PRENTICE HALL
TeacherEXPRESS
Plan • Teach • Assess

Use this complete suite of powerful teaching tools to make planning lessons and administering tests quicker and easier.

Reading and Assessment

Reading and Vocabulary Instruction

🎯 Model the Target Reading Skill

Comparison and Contrast Explain that when you compare things, you observe how they are similar. When you contrast things, you observe how they are different. By comparing and contrasting, students can sort out and analyze information. Write the following on the board. Draw attention to the phrases marked with 1 for comparisons and those marked with 2 for contrasts.

❶
Both St. Louis and New York City are important urban centers
❶
in the United States. St. Louis, Missouri, is located on the
❶
Mississippi River. New York City is also on a river, the Hudson.
❷
While St. Louis is a banking and commercial center, New York—
❷
the country's largest, wealthiest, and most influential city—is the
❷
"money capital" of the United States.

Circle the words "both," "also," and "while" because they are signifiers of comparisons and contrasts.

Use the following worksheets from All-in-One United States and Canada Teaching Resources (pp. 251–253) to support this chapter's Target Reading Skill.

Vocabulary Builder
High-Use Academic Words

Use these steps to teach this chapter's high-use words:

1. Have students rate how well they know each word on their Word Knowledge worksheets (All-in-One United States and Canada Teaching Resources, p. 254).
2. Pronounce each word and ask students to repeat it.
3. Give students a brief definition and sample sentence (provided on TE pp. 111, 118, 127, and 134).
4. Work with students as they fill in the "Definition or Example" column of their Word Knowledge worksheets.

Assessment

Formal Assessment

Test students' understanding of core knowledge and skills.

Chapter Tests A and B, All-in-One United States and Canada Teaching Resources, pp. 275–280

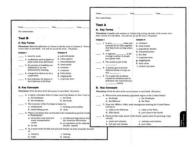

Customize the Chapter Tests to suit your needs.
ExamView Test Bank CD-ROM

Skills Assessment

Assess geographic literacy.
MapMaster Skills, Student Edition pp. 97, 111, 122, 131, 140
Regional Profile Map and Chart Skills, Student Edition pp. 112, 118, 127, 134

Assess reading and comprehension.
Target Reading Skills, Student Edition, pp. 113, 121, 129, 137, and in Section Assessments
Chapter 4 Assessment, Reading and Vocabulary Study Guide, p. 54

Performance Assessment

Assess students' performance on this chapter's Writing Activities using the following rubrics from All-in-One United States and Canada Teaching Resources.
Rubric for Assessing a Timeline, p. 272
Rubric for Assessing a Writing Assignment, p. 273
Rubric for Assessing a Newspaper Article, p. 274

Assess students' work through performance tasks.
Small Group Activity: Simulation: Town Meeting on Water Use, All-in-One United States and Canada Teaching Resources, pp. 257–260
Portfolio Suggestions, Teacher's Edition, p. 109

Online Assessment

Have students check their own understanding.
Chapter Self-Test

Section 1 The Northeast: An Urban Center

 2.5 periods, 1.25 blocks (includes Country Databank)

Social Studies Objectives
1. Learn how the large cities of the Northeast contribute to the economy of the United States.
2. Find out how the Northeast has been a port of entry for many immigrants.

Reading/Language Arts Objective
Compare and contrast to help sort out and analyze information.

Prepare to Read	**Instructional Resources**	**Differentiated Instruction**
Build Background Knowledge Have students list characteristics of some major northeastern cities. **Set a Purpose for Reading** Have students begin to fill out the *Reading Readiness Guide*. **Preview Key Terms** Teach the section's Key Terms. **Target Reading Skill** Introduce the section's Target Reading Skill of **comparing and contrasting**.	**All in One United States and Canada Teaching Resources** L2 Reading Readiness Guide, p. 236 L2 Compare and Contrast, p. 251	**Spanish Reading and Vocabulary Study Guide** L1 Chapter 4, Section 1, pp. 32–33 ELL **World Studies Video Program** L2 The Geography of the United States AR, GT, LPR, SN

Instruct	**Instructional Resources**	**Differentiated Instruction**
A Region of Cities Discuss the major cities of the Northeast. **Regional Profile** Ask students to derive information from maps, charts, and graphs. **Target Reading Skill** Review **comparing and contrasting**. **Eyewitness Technology** Have students read about and discuss skyscrapers. **Ports of Entry** Discuss the cities to which immigrants to the United States came.	**All in One United States and Canada Teaching Resources** L2 Guided Reading and Review, p. 237 L2 Reading Readiness Guide, p. 236 L2 Reading a Population Density Map, p. 263 L2 Writing a Letter, p. 270 **United States and Canada Transparencies** L2 Section Reading Support Transparency USC 54 L1 Transparency B16: Venn Diagram L2 Color Transparency USC 27: United States: Agricultural Regions **World Studies Video Program** L2 Paul Revere and the Minutemen	**All in One United States and Canada Teaching Resources** L2 Outline Map 11: The United States: Political, p. 267 AR, GT, LPR, SN **Teacher's Edition** L1 For Less Proficient Readers, TE p. 99 L3 For Advanced Readers, TE pp. 102, 115 L3 For Gifted and Talented, TE p. 106 L1 For English Language Learners, TE pp. 108, 114 L1 For Special Needs Students, TE p. 114 **PHSchool.com** L3 For: Environmental and Global Issues: Nickel-and-Diming Web Code: lhd-4405 AR, GT

Assess and Reteach	**Instructional Resources**	**Differentiated Instruction**
Assess Progress Evaluate student comprehension with the section assessment and section quiz. **Reteach** Assign the Reading and Vocabulary Study Guide to help struggling students. **Extend** Extend the lesson by having students create a television commercial about a city in the Northeast.	**All in One United States and Canada Teaching Resources** L2 Section Quiz, p. 238 Rubric for Assessing a Writing Assignment, p. 273 **Reading and Vocabulary Study Guide** L1 Chapter 4, Section 1, pp. 42–44	**All in One United States and Canada Teaching Resources** Rubric for Assessing a Timeline, p. 272 AR, GT, LPR, SN **Spanish Support** L2 Section Quiz (Spanish), p. 33 ELL

Key

L1 Basic to Average
L3 Average to Advanced
L2 For All Students

LPR Less Proficient Readers
AR Advanced Readers
SN Special Needs Students

GT Gifted and Talented
ELL English Language Learners

Section 2 The South: The Growth of Industry

 3 periods, 1.5 blocks (includes Skills for Life)

Social Studies Objectives
1. Learn how the South's land is important to its economy.
2. Read about how the growth of industry is changing the South.

Reading/Language Arts Objective
Use signal words to find relationships among ideas or events.

Prepare to Read	Instructional Resources	Differentiated Instruction
Build Background Knowledge Discuss the industries and products associated with the South's diverse economy. **Set a Purpose for Reading** Have students evaluate statements on the *Reading Readiness Guide.* **Preview Key Terms** Teach the section's Key Terms. **Target Reading Skill** Introduce the section's Target Reading Skill of **using signal words.**	**All in One United States and Canada Teaching Resources** L2 Reading Readiness Guide, p. 240 L2 Compare and Contrast, p. 251	**Spanish Reading and Vocabulary Study Guide** L1 Chapter 4, Section 2, pp. 34–35 ELL

Instruct	Instructional Resources	Differentiated Instruction
Regional Profile Ask students to derive information from maps, charts, and graphs. **The Land of the South** Ask questions about the South's land and resources. **Target Reading Skill** Review **using signal words.** **Southern Cities and Industries** Ask questions about Southern cities and industries.	**All in One United States and Canada Teaching Resources** L2 Guided Reading and Review, p. 241 L2 Reading Readiness Guide, p. 240 **United States and Canada Transparencies** L2 Section Reading Support Transparency USC 55 **World Studies Video Program** L2 Miami's Little Havana **Social Studies Skills Tutor CD-ROM** L2 Transferring Information from One Medium to Another	**All in One United States and Canada Teaching Resources** L3 Reading an Economic Activity Map, p. 264 AR, GT L2 Skills for Life, p. 256 AR, GT, LPR, SN **Teacher's Edition** L1 For English Language Learners, TE p. 121 L3 For Gifted and Talented, TE p. 122 **Spanish Support** L2 Guided Reading and Review (Spanish), p. 34 ELL

Assess and Reteach	Instructional Resources	Differentiated Instruction
Assess Progress Evaluate student comprehension with the section assessment and section quiz. **Reteach** Assign the Reading and Vocabulary Study Guide to help struggling students. **Extend** Extend the lesson by assigning a research project.	**All in One United States and Canada Teaching Resources** L2 Section Quiz, p. 242 Rubric for Assessing a Writing Assignment, p. 273 **Reading and Vocabulary Study Guide** L1 Chapter 4, Section 2, pp. 45–47	**All in One United States and Canada Teaching Resources** L1 Reading a Circle Graph, p. 265 ELL, LPR, SN **Teacher's Edition** L3 For Advanced Readers, TE p. 125 L1 For Special Needs Students, TE p. 125 **Spanish Support** L2 Section Quiz (Spanish), p. 35 ELL **Social Studies Skills Tutor CD-ROM** L1 Analyzing Graphic Data ELL, LPR, SN

Key
L1 Basic to Average   L3 Average to Advanced   LPR Less Proficient Readers   GT Gifted and Talented
L2 For All Students   AR Advanced Readers   ELL English Language Learners
     SN Special Needs Students

Section 3 The Midwest: Leaving the Farm

 1.5 periods, .75 block

Social Studies Objectives
1. Read about how technology is changing life on farms.
2. Learn how changes in farming are affecting the development of cities.

Reading/Language Arts Objective
Contrast two situations to find out how they are different.

Prepare to Read	Instructional Resources	Differentiated Instruction
Build Background Knowledge Have students brainstorm words they associate with a farm and refer to the list as they read the section. **Set a Purpose for Reading** Have students evaluate statements on the *Reading Readiness Guide.* **Preview Key Terms** Teach the section's Key Terms. **Target Reading Skill** Introduce the section's Target Reading Skill of **identifying contrasts.**	**All in One United States and Canada Teaching Resources** **L2** Reading Readiness Guide, p. 244 **L2** Identify Contrasts, p. 252	**Spanish Reading and Vocabulary Study Guide** **L1** Chapter 4, Section 3, pp. 36–37 ELL

Instruct	Instructional Resources	Differentiated Instruction
Regional Profile Ask students to derive information from maps, charts, and graphs. **Technology Changes Farm Life** Discuss how advances in technology affected farms. **Target Reading Skill** Review **identifying contrasts.** **Cities Develop in the Midwest** Discuss some of the major cities of the Midwest.	**All in One United States and Canada Teaching Resources** **L2** Guided Reading and Review, p. 245 **L2** Reading Readiness Guide, p. 244 **United States and Canada Transparencies** **L2** Transparency B7: Cause and Effect Chart **L2** Section Reading Support Transparency USC 56 **World Studies Video Program** **L2** Taming the Mississippi	**All in One United States and Canada Teaching Resources** **L1** Reading a Table, p. 266 ELL, LPR, SN **L3** Enrichment, p. 255 AR, GT **Teacher's Edition** **L2** For English Language Learners, TE p. 128 **L1** For Special Needs Students, TE p. 128 **L3** For Advanced Readers, TE p. 129 **L1** For Less Proficient Readers, TE pp. 129, 130 **L3** For Gifted and Talented, TE p. 130 **United States and Canada Transparencies** **L3** Transparency B20: Timeline AR, GT

Assess and Reteach	Instructional Resources	Differentiated Instruction
Assess Progress Evaluate student comprehension with the section assessment and section quiz. **Reteach** Assign the Reading and Vocabulary Study Guide to help struggling students. **Extend** Extend the lesson by showing a video.	**All in One United States and Canada Teaching Resources** **L2** Section Quiz, p. 246 Rubric for Assessing a Writing Assignment, p. 273 **Reading and Vocabulary Study Guide** **L1** Chapter 4, Section 3, pp. 48–50	**Spanish Support** **L2** Section Quiz (Spanish), p. 37 ELL

Key
L1 Basic to Average   **L3** Average to Advanced
L2 For All Students

LPR Less Proficient Readers
AR Advanced Readers
SN Special Needs Students

GT Gifted and Talented
ELL English Language Learners

Section 4 The West: Using and Preserving Resources

 3.5 periods, 1.75 blocks (includes Chapter Review and Assessment and Literature)

Social Studies Objectives
1. Learn about the natural resources of the West.
2. Read about the challenges facing the urban West.

Reading/Language Arts Objective
Make comparisons to see how two situations are the same.

Prepare to Read

Build Background Knowledge
Discuss recycling and conservation of natural resources.

Set a Purpose for Reading
Have students begin to fill out the *Reading Readiness Guide*.

Preview Key Terms
Teach the section's Key Terms.

Target Reading Skill
Introduce the section's Target Reading Skill of **making comparisons**.

Instructional Resources

All in One United States and Canada Teaching Resources
- L2 Reading Readiness Guide, p. 248
- L2 Make Comparisons, p. 253

Differentiated Instruction

Spanish Reading and Vocabulary Study Guide
- L1 Chapter 4, Section 4, pp. 38–39 ELL

Instruct

Regional Profile
Ask students to derive information from maps, charts, and graphs.

Natural Resources of the West
Discuss the use and management of resources in the West.

The Urban West
Discuss the issues of cities in the West.

Target Reading Skill
Review **making comparisons**.

Instructional Resources

All in One United States and Canada Teaching Resources
- L2 Guided Reading and Review, p. 249
- L2 Reading Readiness Guide, p. 248

United States and Canada Transparencies
- L2 Color Transparency USC 29: The United States: Annual Precipitation and Prevailing Winds
- L2 Section Reading Support Transparency USC 57

World Studies Video Program
- L2 The Gold Rush

Differentiated Instruction

All in One United States and Canada Teaching Resources
- L1 Reading a Table, p. 266 ELL, LPR, SN
- L3 Activity Shop Lab: Making a Model River, pp. 261–262 AR, GT

Teacher's Edition
- L1 For Less Proficient Readers, TE p. 135
- L3 For Gifted and Talented, TE pp. 135, 137
- L1 For Special Needs Students, TE p. 137
- L3 For Advanced Readers, TE p. 144

Student Edition on Audio CD
- L1 Chapter 4, Section 4 ELL, LPR, SN

Assess and Reteach

Assess Progress
Evaluate student comprehension with the section assessment and section quiz.

Reteach
Assign the Reading and Vocabulary Study Guide to help struggling students.

Extend
Extend the lesson by assigning a Small Group Activity.

Instructional Resources

All in One United States and Canada Teaching Resources
- L2 Section Quiz, p. 250
- L3 Small Group Activity, pp. 257–260 Rubric for Assessing a Writing Assignment, p. 273
- L2 Vocabulary Development, p. 271
- L2 Word Knowledge, p. 254 Rubric for Assessing a Newspaper Article, p. 274
- L2 Chapter Tests A and B, pp. 275–280

Reading and Vocabulary Study Guide
- L1 Chapter 4, Section 4, pp. 51–53

Differentiated Instruction

All in One United States and Canada Teaching Resources
- L3 Personal Experience of Maria Antonia Pico, pp. 268–269 AR, GT

Spanish Support
- L2 Section Quiz (Spanish), p. 39 ELL
- L2 Chapter Summary (Spanish), p. 40 ELL
- L2 Vocabulary Development (Spanish), p. 41 ELL

Key

- L1 Basic to Average
- L3 Average to Advanced
- L2 For All Students
- LPR Less Proficient Readers
- AR Advanced Readers
- SN Special Needs Students
- GT Gifted and Talented
- ELL English Language Learners

Reading Background

Using the Choral Reading Technique Effectively

The Choral Reading technique ensures participation by all students, including English language learners, because it provides a non-threatening reading environment. To ensure success with this technique, choose shorter passages (less than 500 words), and encourage students to stay with your voice, so that everyone reads at the same rate. When students have finished reading in unison, allow time for students to reread the passage silently, focusing on new or unfamiliar words.

Reading Passage Strategies

In this chapter, students will use the ReQuest technique to read passages. It is important to help students ask their own questions while reading. This gives them a purpose for reading and helps them monitor their comprehension.

Model this technique using the following passage from page 122 of the Student Edition. After reading the passage aloud, begin by asking questions that have students recall information and progress to more interpretive questions.

A big part of the South's economy depends on moving goods and people into and out of the region. Most of the South's largest cities play important roles in this transportation industry. Miami, Florida, and New Orleans, Louisiana, are major ports. Miami is a center for goods and people going to and from Central and South America. New Orleans is a gateway between the Gulf of Mexico and the Mississippi River system. It is also an important port for oil tankers.

Let me make sure I understand the selection: What does much of the South's economy depend on? (*moving goods and people into and out of the region*) What exactly does that mean? (*importing and exporting of goods, and tourism*) What cities therefore play a big part in the South's economy? (*Miami and New Orleans*) Why is this so? (*Miami is far south and close to the Caribbean and South America. It is a major port, allowing easy access for ships. New Orleans is at the mouth of the Mississippi River and a major port on the Gulf of Mexico.*)

Continue in this manner, alternating between teacher- and student-proposed questions. As students become more proficient, you might partner them and have them write down their questions. Ask pairs to read their questions to the group so that others can answer them.

World Studies Background

Skyscrapers

The skyscraper owes its development to various mechanical advances in the last part of the nineteenth century. An important one was the perfection of the high-speed elevator. The invention of a system in which a metal framework supported both walls and floors was another. The first skyscraper, the Home Insurance Building in Chicago, was designed in 1883 by William Le Baron Jenney. It was followed by similar buildings in Chicago and in New York City.

Mining Town Revisited

Virginia City, Nevada, was one of the many towns that were quickly built during the gold and silver mining boom years. This town, in the Sierra Nevada Mountains, grew near the rich deposit of silver called the Comstock Lode, which was discovered in 1859. As miners poured in, Virginia City went from a temporary mining camp to a town with more permanent structures including homes and more than 100 saloons! The town's population grew to about 30,000. However, within 25 years the silver ran out, and the population declined. Today, Virginia City is a well-preserved town that attracts thousands of tourists during the summer months.

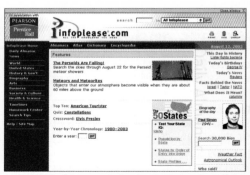

Infoplease® provides a wealth of useful information for the classroom. You can use this resource to strengthen your background on the subjects covered in this chapter. Have students visit this advertising-free site as a starting point for projects requiring research.

Use Web Code **lhd-4400** for **Infoplease®**.

Mapping Words

Research shows that the use of word maps can help students internalize word meanings and develop more comprehensive definitions of words (as opposed to simple one- or two-word definitions). Use the following steps to map word definitions:

1. Have students look at the Key Term *commute*. Ask them to answer the following questions:
   - What is it? *(traveling to get to work)*
   - What is it like? *(it can be long or short; travel can be by car, bus, subway, or train)*
   - What are some examples? *(taking the subway to work, driving from the suburbs to the city)*
2. Record responses to the questions on a word web.
3. Have students develop the answers in the word web into a definition: *(commuting is traveling to get to work, usually by car, bus, subway, or train. Driving from the suburbs to the city is one example of a commute.)*

Writing Paragraphs

It is important for students to be able to demonstrate what they have learned with strong writing skills. Help students practice writing an informative paragraph using the following steps. Model each step using the paragraph under the heading *The Land of the South*, on page 117 of the Student Edition.

1. Begin with a topic sentence.
   There are many different ways that people in the South can make a living.
2. Add three to five sentences to elaborate on the topic.
   The South's particular geography and climate make many of these jobs possible. The region has a warm climate, and most parts of it receive plenty of rain. The wide coastal plains along the Atlantic Ocean and the Gulf of Mexico have rich soil.
3. Include a summary sentence.
   Together, these features make much of the South an excellent place for growing crops and raising animals.

   Point out to students that the length of the sentences varies. Draw attention to the variety of sentence structure and transition words as well. Explain how the last sentence both summarizes the topic and adds new information.

George Washington Bridge

The George Washington Bridge, one of the longest suspension bridges in the world, spans the Hudson River. At 4,760 feet long (1,451 meters), it is one of several links between New York City and New Jersey. Other crossings include the Lincoln and Holland tunnels and railway tubes. The bridge was begun in 1927, and opened to vehicular traffic in 1931. A second level was opened in 1962.

The Sun Belt

The term "Sun Belt" gained popularity in the 1970s when there was a significant population shift to the southern part of the United States. After World War II, people of retirement age were attracted to this region by the warm climate. The relative lack of labor unions and a cheaper labor force encouraged manufacturers from the North to relocate to the region as well. The oil boom of the 1970s added to the region's wealth, as did an enormous tourism business. By the 1990s, cities in the Sun Belt, including Los Angeles, San Diego, Phoenix, and San Antonio, were among the ten largest cities in the country.

Get in-depth information on topics of global importance with **Prentice Hall Newstracker**, powered by FT.com.

 Use Web Code **lhd-4405** for **Prentice Hall Newstracker.**

Guiding Questions

Remind students about the Guiding Questions introduced at the beginning of the book.

Section 1 relates to **Guiding Question** ⑤
How did the United States and Canada become two of the wealthiest nations in the world? *(The major cities of the Northeast are centers of trade, finance, manufacturing, and communications.)*

Section 2 relates to **Guiding Question** ①
How has physical geography affected the cultures of the United States and Canada? *(The warm climate of the South provides good conditions for farming.)*

Section 3 relates to **Guiding Question** ⑤
How did the United States and Canada become two of the wealthiest nations in the world? *(The Midwest is the agricultural center of the United States. Its major cities contribute to the country's economy.)*

Section 4 relates to **Guiding Question** ①
How has physical geography affected the cultures of the United States and Canada? *(The West is rich in natural resources, attracting people to the region for hundreds of years.)*

⟲ Target Reading Skill

In this chapter, students will learn and apply the reading skill of compare and contrast. Use the following worksheets to help students practice this skill:

All in One United States and Canada Teaching Resources, *Compare and Contrast,* p. 251; *Identify Contrasts,* p. 252; *Make Comparisons,* p. 253

Differentiated Instruction

The following Teacher's Edition strategies are suitable for students of varying abilities.

Advanced Readers pp. 102, 115, 125, 129, 144

English Language Learners pp. 108, 114, 121, 128

Gifted and Talented pp. 106, 122, 130, 135, 137

Less Proficient Readers pp. 99, 129, 130, 135

Special Needs Students pp. 114, 125, 128, 137

Chapter Preview

This chapter will introduce you to the four regions of the United States.

Country Databank
The Country Databank provides data on each of the fifty states.

Section 1
The Northeast
An Urban Center

Section 2
The South
The Growth of Industry

Section 3
The Midwest
Leaving the Farm

Section 4
The West
Using and Preserving Resources

 Target Reading Skill

Comparison and Contrast In this chapter you will focus on using comparison and contrast to help you sort out and analyze information.

▶ Members of the California National Guard display an American flag.

96 United States and Canada

Bibliography

For the Teacher
Brands, H.W. *The Age of Gold: The California Gold Rush and the New American Dream.* Doubleday, 2002.
Bluestone, Barry and Mary Huff Stevenson. *The Boston Renaissance: Race, Space, and Economic Change in an American Metropolis.* Russell Sage Foundation, 2000.
Gannon, Michael. *Florida: A Short History.* University of Florida, 2003.

For the Student
L1 Ashabranner, Brent K. and Jennifer Ashabranner. *On the Mall in Washington, D.C.: A Visit to America's Front Yard.* 21st Century Books, 2002.
L2 Knowlton, Marylee and Dale Anderson. *Arriving at Ellis Island.* Gareth Stevens, 2002.
L3 Stein, R. Conrad. *Los Angeles (Cities of the World).* Children's Press, 2001.

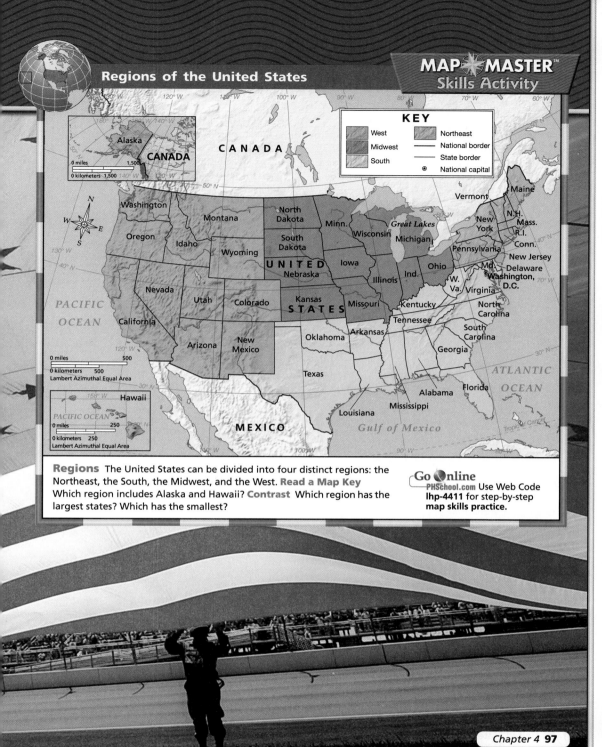

MAP MASTER™ Skills Activity

Regions of the United States

KEY

- West
- Midwest
- South
- Northeast
- — National border
- — State border
- ⊛ National capital

Regions The United States can be divided into four distinct regions: the Northeast, the South, the Midwest, and the West. **Read a Map Key** Which region includes Alaska and Hawaii? **Contrast** Which region has the largest states? Which has the smallest?

Go Online PHSchool.com Use Web Code **lhp-4411** for step-by-step **map skills practice.**

Ask students to locate their state on the map and identify the name of the region in which they live. Then ask them to identify bordering states. Are they in the same region? If not, what regions are they in?

Go Online PHSchool.com Students may practice their map skills using the interactive online version of this map.

Using the Visual L2

Reach Into Your Background Draw students' attention to the photograph on pp. 96–97. Ask students to recall and discuss what they know about the meaning of the stars and stripes in the flag.

Answers

MAP MASTER™ Skills Activity **Read a Map Key** the West **Contrast** the West; the Northeast

---

Chapter Resources

Teaching Resources
- L2 Vocabulary Development, p. 271
- L2 Skills for Life, p. 256
- L2 Chapter Tests A and B, pp. 275–280

Spanish Support
- L2 Spanish Chapter Summary, p. 40
- L2 Spanish Vocabulary Development, p. 41

Media and Technology
- L1 Student Edition on Audio CD
- L1 Guided Reading Audiotapes, English and Spanish
- L2 Social Studies Skills Tutor CD-ROM
  ExamView Test Bank CD-ROM

PRENTICE HALL Presentation EXPRESS™
Teach · Connect · Inspire

Teach this chapter's content using the PresentationExpress™ CD-ROM including:
- slide shows
- transparencies
- interactive maps and media
- *ExamView*® QuickTake Presenter

Objectives

- Look at a map and study the data to learn about the states of the United States.

- Analyze data to compare the states.

- Identify characteristics that most states share.

- Find some of the key differences among the states.

Show *The Geography of the United States.* Ask **What are the four major regions of the United States and what natural resources does each region contribute to the economy of the country?** *(Possible answers: Northeast—seafood, cities are centers for trade, business, education, and culture; South—seafood, timber, and various crops; Midwest—grains and lake fish; and the West—minerals and timber.)*

Prepare to Read

Build Background Knowledge L2

Invite students to describe what they know about the 50 states of the United States, and about their own state in particular. Ask students to share what new information they learned from the watching the World Studies Video. Conduct an Idea Wave (TE, p. T35) to generate a list of states and capitals. Keep a running list of responses on the board. See how many states and capitals students can name and tell them they will have a chance to complete the list after reading the United States Databank.

The Geography of the United States,
World Studies Video Program

Introducing
The United States

Guide for Reading

This section provides an introduction to the fifty states that make up the United States.

- Look at the map on the previous page, and then read the information below to learn about each state.
- Analyze the data to compare the states.
- What are the characteristics that most of the states share?
- What are some of the key differences among the states?

Viewing the Video Overview

View the World Studies Video Overview to learn more about each of the states. As you watch, answer this question:

- What are the four major regions of the United States, and what natural resources does each region contribute to the economy of the country?

Explore the geography of the United States.

Alabama

Year of Statehood	1819
Capital	Montgomery
Land Area	50,744 sq mi; 131,427 sq km
Population	4,447,100
Ethnic Group(s)	71.1% white; 26.0% African American; 1.7% Hispanic; 0.7% Asian; 0.5% Native American; 0.7% other
Agriculture	cotton, greenhouse products, peanuts
Industry	pulp, paper, chemicals, electronics

Alaska

Year of Statehood	1959
Capital	Juneau
Land Area	571,951 sq mi; 1,481,353 sq km
Population	626,932
Ethnic Group(s)	69.3% white; 15.6% Native American; 4.1% Hispanic; 4.0% Asian; 3.5% African American; 2.1% other
Agriculture	greenhouse products, barley, oats
Industry	petroleum, tourism, fishing

Geological formations of limestone, called tufa, in Mono Lake, California

98 United States and Canada

Arizona

Year of Statehood	1912
Capital	Phoenix
Land Area	113,635 sq mi; 294,315 sq km
Population	5,130,632
Ethnic Group(s)	75.5% white; 25.3% Hispanic; 5.0% Native American; 3.1% African American; 1.8% Asian; 11.7% other
Agriculture	cotton, lettuce, cauliflower
Industry	manufacturing, construction, tourism

Arkansas

Year of Statehood	1836
Capital	Little Rock
Land Area	52,068 sq mi; 134,856 sq km
Population	2,673,400
Ethnic Group(s)	80.0% white; 15.7% African American; 3.2% Hispanic; 0.8% Asian; 0.8% Native American; 1.6% other
Agriculture	poultry, cattle, rice, soybeans
Industry	manufacturing, agriculture, tourism, forestry

California

Year of Statehood	1850
Capital	Sacramento
Land Area	155,959 sq mi; 403,934 sq km
Population	33,871,648
Ethnic Group(s)	59.5% white; 32.4% Hispanic; 10.9% Asian; 6.7% African American; 1.0% Native American; 17.1% other
Agriculture	poultry, cattle, milk
Industry	agriculture, tourism, apparel

Colorado

Year of Statehood	1876
Capital	Denver
Land Area	103,718 sq mi; 268,630 sq km
Population	4,301,261
Ethnic Group(s)	82.8% white; 17.1% Hispanic; 3.8% African American; 2.2% Asian; 1.0% Native American; 7.3% other
Agriculture	poultry, cattle, corn, wheat
Industry	manufacturing, construction

Introducing the United States   L2

Guided Instruction

- Have students read the first two pages of data tables in the Country Databank using the Structured Silent Reading strategy (TE, p. T34).

- Ask students to identify several differences between Alabama and Alaska. Ask them to start with differences in the years of statehood and the size of each state. (*Alabama became a state in 1819; Alaska in 1959. Alaska is more than 10 times bigger than Alabama.*)

- Ask **What industries are important in both Arkansas and California?** (*agriculture, tourism*)

- Ask **Which state is more densely populated, Alabama or Alaska? How can you tell?** (*Alabama; it has far more people and a much smaller land area.*)

- Ask **In which state would you be more likely to find a cattle ranch, Colorado or Alaska? How can you tell?** (*Colorado, because cattle ranching is listed as an important agricultural activity.*)

Differentiated Instruction

For Less Proficient Readers   L1
Have students create a Venn Diagram showing the similarities and differences between California and Colorado. Ask them to focus on the agriculture and industry of these states. Display the *Venn Diagram* transparency to show students how to sketch the organizer. Circulate to make sure students are filling in the organizers correctly.

📖 **United States and Canada Transparencies,** *Transparency B16: Venn Diagram*

Guided Instruction (continued)

- Point out the Ethnic Groups data on pp. 100–101. Ask students **Which state on these pages has the highest percentage of Asian residents?** *(Hawaii)* **Which has the highest percentage of African Americans?** *(Georgia)*

- Ask **In which of these states is tourism an important industry?** *(Florida, Hawaii, Idaho)*

- Have students look at the map on p. 97. Ask them to locate both Hawaii and Florida. Discuss why warm-weather crops such as citrus fruits and sugar might be important in these states. *(These states are located farther south than most of the other states, giving them warmer climates and a longer growing season, which allows warm-weather crops to be a major source of income for their economies.)*

Introducing The United States

Connecticut

Year of Statehood	1788
Capital	Hartford
Land Area	4,845 sq mi; 12,549 sq km
Population	3,405,565
Ethnic Group(s)	81.6% white; 9.1% African American; 9.4% Hispanic; 2.4% Asian; 0.3% Native American; 4.3% other
Agriculture	nursery stock, mushrooms, vegetables, sweet corn
Industry	manufacturing, retail trade, government

Delaware

Year of Statehood	1787
Capital	Dover
Land Area	1,954 sq mi; 5,061 sq km
Population	783,600
Ethnic Group(s)	74.6% white; 19.2% African American; 4.8% Hispanic; 2.1% Asian; 0.3% Native American
Agriculture	poultry, soybeans, potatoes, corn
Industry	chemicals, agriculture, finance

An alligator at Everglades National Park, Florida

Florida

Year of Statehood	1845
Capital	Tallahassee
Land Area	53,927 sq mi; 139,671 sq km
Population	15,982,378
Ethnic Group(s)	78.0% white; 16.8% Hispanic; 14.6% African American; 1.7% Asian; 0.3% Native American; 3.1% other
Agriculture	poultry, cattle, citrus fruits
Industry	tourism, agriculture, manufacturing

Georgia

Year of Statehood	1788
Capital	Atlanta
Land Area	57,906 sq mi; 149,977 sq km
Population	8,186,453
Ethnic Group(s)	65.1% white; 28.7% African American; 5.3% Hispanic; 2.1% Asian; 0.3% Native American; 2.5% other
Agriculture	poultry, cattle, peanuts, cotton
Industry	services, manufacturing, retail trade

Hawaii

Year of Statehood	1959
Capital	Honolulu
Land Area	6,423 sq mi; 16,636 sq km
Population	1,211,537
Ethnic Group(s)	41.6% Asian; 24.3% white; 9.4% Native Hawaiian or Pacific Islander; 7.2% Hispanic; 1.8% African American; 0.3% Native American; 1.3% other
Agriculture	sugar, pineapples
Industry	tourism, defense, sugar

Idaho

Year of Statehood	1890
Capital	Boise
Land Area	82,747 sq mi; 214,315 sq km
Population	1,293,953
Ethnic Group(s)	91.0% white; 7.9% Hispanic; 1.4% Native American; 0.9% Asian; 0.4% African American; 4.3% other
Agriculture	poultry, cattle, potatoes
Industry	manufacturing, agriculture, tourism

Illinois

Year of Statehood	1818
Capital	Springfield
Land Area	55,584 sq mi; 143,963 sq km
Population	12,419,293
Ethnic Group(s)	73.5% white; 15.1% African American; 12.3% Hispanic; 3.4% Asian; 0.2% Native American; 5.8% other
Agriculture	livestock, corn, soybeans, wheat
Industry	services, manufacturing, travel

Indiana

Year of Statehood	1816
Capital	Indianapolis
Land Area	35,867 sq mi; 92,896 sq km
Population	6,080,485
Ethnic Group(s)	87.5% white; 8.4% African American; 3.5% Hispanic; 1.0% Asian; 0.3% Native American; 1.6% other
Agriculture	livestock, corn, soybeans, wheat
Industry	manufacturing, services, agriculture

Iowa

Year of Statehood	1846
Capital	Des Moines
Land Area	55,869 sq mi; 144,701 sq km
Population	2,926,324
Ethnic Group(s)	93.9% white; 2.8% Hispanic; 2.1% African American; 1.3% Asian; 0.3% Native American; 1.3% other
Agriculture	livestock, poultry, grain, corn
Industry	agriculture, communications, construction

Winner of the Indianapolis 500 race in Indiana

- Tell students that pages 100–101 include facts about some of the most important agricultural states in the country. Iowa leads the country in corn production, with Illinois and Indiana close behind. Ask students **In how many of these states is corn an important crop?** (*five: Connecticut, Delaware, Illinois, Indiana, Iowa*)

- Ask **Which industry is important to the economy of six of these states?** (*manufacturing*)

Background: Global Perspectives

Exporting Food The vast fertile plains of the Midwest have helped the United States become a major exporter of food. In fact, the United States is by far the world's leading exporter of wheat and corn, which grow very well in the Midwest. Overall, the United States has a trade deficit, meaning the country imports more than it exports.

But in the area of agriculture, the United States has a trade surplus—the country exports more food than it imports. In 2001, the United States exported $53.7 billion worth of food, while food imports were valued at $39 billion. That amounts to a surplus of nearly $15 billion.

Guided Instruction (continued)

- Ask **What is the capital of Maine?** *(Augusta)* **Of what state is Lansing the capital?** *(Michigan)*

- Tell students that two of the states on this page were among the original 13 colonies. Ask them to use the information provided to determine which two they are. *(Maryland, Massachusetts)*

- Have students turn back to the map on p. 97. Ask **In terms of location, what do the states of Maine and Massachusetts have in common?** *(Both states border the Atlantic Ocean.)* Ask students to think about how the industries of these states might be affected by their location. *(Their location on the coast has helped promote industries such as fishing and trade.)*

Introducing The United States

Kansas

Year of Statehood	1861
Capital	Topeka
Land Area	81,815 sq mi; 211,901 sq km
Population	2,688,418
Ethnic Group(s)	86.1% white; 7.0% Hispanic; 5.7% African American; 1.7% Asian; 0.9% Native American; 3.4% other
Agriculture	livestock, poultry, wheat, sorghum
Industry	manufacturing, finance, insurance

Kentucky

Year of Statehood	1792
Capital	Frankfort
Land Area	39,728 sq mi; 10,896 sq km
Population	4,041,769
Ethnic Group(s)	90.1% white; 7.3% African American; 1.5% Hispanic; 0.7% Asian; 0.2% Native American; 0.6% other
Agriculture	poultry, cattle, tobacco, corn
Industry	manufacturing, services, finance

Louisiana

Year of Statehood	1812
Capital	Baton Rouge
Land Area	43,562 sq mi; 112,826 sq km
Population	4,468,976
Ethnic Group(s)	63.9% white; 32.5% African American; 2.4% Hispanic; 1.2% Asian; 0.6% Native American; 0.7% other
Agriculture	poultry, soybeans, sugar cane
Industry	wholesale and retail trade, tourism

Maine

Year of Statehood	1820
Capital	Augusta
Land Area	30,862 sq mi; 76,933 sq km
Population	1,274,923
Ethnic Group(s)	96.9% white; 0.7% Asian; 0.7% Hispanic; 0.6% Native American; 0.5% African American; 0.2% other
Agriculture	poultry, potatoes, aquaculture
Industry	manufacturing, agriculture, fishing

Maryland

Year of Statehood	1788
Capital	Annapolis
Land Area	9,774 sq mi; 25,315 sq km
Population	5,296,486
Ethnic Group(s)	64.0% white; 27.9% African American; 4.3% Hispanic; 4.0% Asian; 0.3% Native American; 1.8% other
Agriculture	poultry, greenhouse and nursery products
Industry	manufacturing, biotechnology

Massachusetts

Year of Statehood	1788
Capital	Boston
Land Area	7,840 sq mi; 20,306 sq km
Population	6,349,097
Ethnic Group(s)	84.5% white; 6.8% Hispanic; 5.4% African American; 3.8% Asian; 0.2% Native American; 3.7% other
Agriculture	cranberries, greenhouse products, vegetables
Industry	services, trade, manufacturing

102 United States and Canada

Differentiated Instruction

For Advanced Readers   L3

Have students do Internet or library research to find out more about the states listed on this page. Ask them to find the nickname of each state. Then have them chose one state nickname and ask them to find the story behind the nickname. Have students write a short essay describing why this nickname fits this state.

Michigan

Year of Statehood	1837
Capital	Lansing
Land Area	56,804 sq mi; 147,122 sq km
Population	9,938,444
Ethnic Group(s)	80.2% white; 14.2% African American; 3.3% Hispanic; 1.8% Asian; 0.6% Native American; 1.3% other
Agriculture	poultry, corn, wheat, soybeans
Industry	manufacturing, services, tourism, agriculture

Minnesota

Year of Statehood	1858
Capital	St. Paul
Land Area	79,610 sq mi; 206,190 sq km
Population	4,919,479
Ethnic Group(s)	89.4% white; 3.5% African American; 2.9% Asian; 2.9% Hispanic; 1.1% Native American; 1.3% other
Agriculture	livestock, poultry, corn, soybeans
Industry	agribusiness, forest products, mining

Mississippi

Year of Statehood	1817
Capital	Jackson
Land Area	46,907 sq mi; 121,489 sq km
Population	2,844,658
Ethnic Group(s)	61.4% white; 36.3% African American; 1.4% Hispanic; 0.7% Asian; 0.4% Native American; 0.5% other
Agriculture	cattle, poultry, cotton, rice
Industry	warehousing/distribution, services

Missouri

Year of Statehood	1821
Capital	Jefferson City
Land Area	68,886 sq mi; 178,415 sq km
Population	5,595,211
Ethnic Group(s)	84.9% white; 11.2% African American; 2.1% Hispanic; 1.1% Asian; 0.4% Native American; 0.9% other
Agriculture	livestock, poultry, soybeans, corn
Industry	agriculture, manufacturing, aerospace

Detroit, Michigan

Chapter 4 **103**

Guided Instruction (continued)

- Have students identify the largest state on pages 102–103. *(Kansas)* Have them identify the smallest. *(Massachusetts)*

- Ask students to compare and contrast the industries of Maryland and Michigan. *(Similarities: manufacturing is important in both states. Differences: biotechnology is a major industry in Maryland, while services, tourism, and agriculture are important in Missouri.)*

- Ask **How can you tell that natural resources play an important part in Minnesota's economy?** *(Minnesota's industries—agribusiness, forest products, and mining—are all based on the use of natural resources.)*

Background: Links Across Place

Motown During the late 1950s, the city of Detroit in Michigan became an important center for rock music and African American musicians. It was here that Motown Records, named for Detroit's nickname, developed. Popular singing groups, such as the Temptations and Diana Ross and the Supremes, rose to stardom from Detroit neighborhoods. The "Motown Sound" developed into an energetic urban brand of rhythm and blues that remains popular today.

Guided Instruction (continued)

■ Have students review the states on both of these pages. Ask **In which of these states is more than 40 percent of the population Hispanic?** *(New Mexico)*

■ Tell students that the most densely populated state in the country is listed on one of these two pages. Ask them to use the data given to try to figure out which one it is. *(New Jersey, which students can see has a relatively small land area and a large population compared to other states.)*

Introducing The United States

Horses grazing in Montana

Montana

Year of Statehood	1889
Capital	Helena
Land Area	145,552 sq mi; 376,980 sq km
Population	902,195
Ethnic Group(s)	90.6% white; 6.2% Native American; 2.0% Hispanic; 0.5% Asian; 0.3% African American; 0.7% other
Agriculture	cattle, wheat, barley, sugar beets
Industry	agriculture, timber, mining, tourism

Nebraska

Year of Statehood	1867
Capital	Lincoln
Land Area	76,872 sq mi; 199,098 sq km
Population	1,711,263
Ethnic Group(s)	89.6% white; 5.5% Hispanic; 4.0% African American; 1.3% Asian; 0.9% Native American; 2.8% other
Agriculture	livestock, poultry, corn, sorghum
Industry	agriculture, manufacturing

Nevada

Year of Statehood	1864
Capital	Carson City
Land Area	109,826 sq mi; 284,449 sq km
Population	1,998,257
Ethnic Group(s)	75.2% white; 19.7% Hispanic; 6.8% African American; 4.5% Asian; 1.3% Native American; 8.4% other
Agriculture	hay, alfalfa seed, potatoes
Industry	tourism, mining, manufacturing

New Hampshire

Year of Statehood	1788
Capital	Concord
Land Area	8,968 sq mi; 23,227 sq km
Population	1,235,786
Ethnic Group(s)	96.0% white; 1.7% Hispanic; 1.3% Asian; 0.7% African American; 0.2% Native American; 0.6% other
Agriculture	dairy products, nursery and greenhouse products
Industry	tourism, manufacturing

104 United States and Canada

Background: Links Across Time

Santa Fe Santa Fe, New Mexico, is not only the highest state capital at 6,996 feet (2,132 meters) above sea level, it is also the oldest city to be a state capital. Santa Fe was founded by Spanish settlers in 1610. This region was home to the Pueblo Native Americans, who temporarily drove the Spanish out of New Mexico in the Pueblo Rebellion of 1680. Santa Fe became part of Mexico when Mexico gained independence from Spain in 1821. The city became part of the United States in 1848, as a result of the Mexican War. Santa Fe's art, food, and architecture reflect the diverse mix of cultures that have been part of this city for almost 400 years. The state's population also reflects this history, as can be seen in the large percentage of Hispanic and Native American residents.

New Jersey

Year of Statehood	1787
Capital	Trenton
Land Area	7,417 sq mi; 19,210 sq km
Population	8,414,350
Ethnic Group(s)	72.6% white; 13.6% African American; 13.3% Hispanic; 5.7% Asian; 0.2% Native American; 5.4% other
Agriculture	poultry, nursery and greenhouse products, tomatoes
Industry	pharmaceuticals, telecommunications

New Mexico

Year of Statehood	1912
Capital	Santa Fe
Land Area	121,356 sq mi; 314,312 sq km
Population	1,819,046
Ethnic Group(s)	66.8% white; 42.1% Hispanic; 9.5% Native American; 1.9% African American; 1.1% Asian; 17.1% other
Agriculture	cattle, hay, onions, chilies
Industry	government, services, trade

New York

Year of Statehood	1788
Capital	Albany
Land Area	47,214 sq mi; 122,284 sq km
Population	18,976,457
Ethnic Group(s)	67.9% white; 15.9% African American; 15.1% Hispanic; 5.5% Asian; 0.4% Native American; 7.1% other
Agriculture	cattle, poultry, apples, grapes
Industry	manufacturing, finance, communications

North Carolina

Year of Statehood	1789
Capital	Raleigh
Land Area	48,711 sq mi; 126,161 sq km
Population	8,049,313
Ethnic Group(s)	72.1% white; 21.6% African American; 4.7% Hispanic; 1.2% Native American; 2.3% other
Agriculture	livestock, poultry, tobacco, cotton
Industry	manufacturing, agriculture, tourism

The Exploris museum in Raleigh, North Carolina

Chapter 4 **105**

Guided Instruction (continued)

- Ask students to rank the four states on this page in terms of size, from largest to smallest. *(New Mexico, North Carolina, New York, New Jersey)*

- Now ask students to rank these same states in terms of populations, from largest to smallest. *(New York, New Jersey, North Carolina, New Mexico)* Ask **What can be determined by comparing the size ranking and the population ranking?** *(The two largest states in size have significantly lower population densities.)*

Guided Instruction (continued)

- Tell students that the smallest state in the country is listed on one these two pages. Ask them to figure out which one it is. *(Rhode Island)*

- Ask **Do you think there are any very large cities in North Dakota? How can you tell?** *(No; the population of the entire state is just 642,200, so there cannot be any very large cities in the state.)*

- Ask **What is one thing that the economies of Ohio, Oklahoma, Oregon, Pennsylvania, and Rhode Island have in common?** *(Manufacturing is an important industry in all five states.)*

Introducing The United States

North Dakota

Year of Statehood	1889
Capital	Bismarck
Land Area	68,976 sq mi; 178,648 sq km
Population	642,200
Ethnic Group(s)	92.5% white; 4.9% Native American; 1.2% Hispanic; 0.6% African American; 0.6% Asian; 0.4% other
Agriculture	cattle, spring wheat, durum, barley
Industry	agriculture, mining, tourism

Ohio

Year of Statehood	1803
Capital	Columbus
Land Area	40,948 sq mi; 106,055 sq km
Population	11,353,140
Ethnic Group(s)	85.0% white; 11.5% African American; 1.9% Hispanic; 1.2% Asian; 0.2% Native American; 0.8% other
Agriculture	livestock, poultry, corn, hay
Industry	manufacturing, trade, services

Oklahoma

Year of Statehood	1907
Capital	Oklahoma City
Land Area	68,667 sq mi; 177,848 sq km
Population	3,450,654
Ethnic Group(s)	76.2% white; 7.9% Native American; 7.6% African American; 5.2% Hispanic; 1.4% Asian; 4.6% other
Agriculture	livestock, poultry, wheat, cotton
Industry	manufacturing, mineral and energy exploration

Oregon

Year of Statehood	1859
Capital	Salem
Land Area	95,997 sq mi; 248,632 sq km
Population	3,421,399
Ethnic Group(s)	86.6% white; 8.0% Hispanic; 1.6% African American; 3.0% Asian; 1.3% Native American; 4.4% other
Agriculture	cattle, poultry, greenhouse products
Industry	manufacturing, services, trade, finance

Pennsylvania

Year of Statehood	1787
Capital	Harrisburg
Land Area	44,817 sq mi; 116,076 sq km
Population	12,281,054
Ethnic Group(s)	85.4% white; 10.0% African American; 3.2% Hispanic; 1.8% Asian; 0.1% Native American; 1.5% other
Agriculture	livestock, poultry, corn, hay
Industry	agribusiness, manufacturing, health care

Rhode Island

Year of Statehood	1790
Capital	Providence
Land Area	1,045 sq mi; 2,707 sq km
Population	1,048,319
Ethnic Group(s)	85.0% white; 8.7% Hispanic; 4.5% African American; 2.3% Asian; 0.5% Native American; 5.1% other
Agriculture	nursery products, turf, vegetables
Industry	services, manufacturing

106 United States and Canada

Differentiated Instruction

For Gifted and Talented   L3

Have students make a resource map of one region of the United States. They should start by drawing a large map of that region on a poster-sized piece of paper. Then they can fill in the industries shown in the Country Databank, using a small symbol to represent each industry. The map should include a key, giving the meaning of each symbol. Encourage students to do additional research to add more industries to their map.

South Carolina

Year of Statehood	1788
Capital	Columbia
Land Area	30,109 sq mi; 77,982 sq km
Population	4,012,012
Ethnic Group(s)	67.2% white; 29.5% African American; 2.4% Hispanic; 0.9% Asian; 0.3% Native American; 1.0% other
Agriculture	poultry, tobacco, cotton, soybeans
Industry	tourism, agriculture, manufacturing

South Dakota

Year of Statehood	1889
Capital	Pierre
Land Area	75,885 sq mi; 196,542 sq km
Population	754,844
Ethnic Group(s)	88.7% white; 8.3% Native American; 1.4% Hispanic; 0.6% African American; 0.6% Asian; 0.5% other
Agriculture	livestock, poultry, corn, soybeans
Industry	agriculture, services, manufacturing

Congaree Swamp National Monument, South Carolina

Tennessee

Year of Statehood	1796
Capital	Nashville
Land Area	41,217 sq mi; 106,752 sq km
Population	5,689,283
Ethnic Group(s)	80.2% white; 16.4% African American; 2.2% Hispanic; 1.0% Asian; 0.3% Native American; 1.0% other
Agriculture	cattle, poultry, tobacco, cotton
Industry	manufacturing, trade, services

Texas

Year of Statehood	1845
Capital	Austin
Land Area	261,797 sq mi; 678,054 sq km
Population	20,851,820
Ethnic Group(s)	71.0% white; 32.0% Hispanic; 11.5% African American; 2.7% Asian; 0.6% Native American; 11.8% other
Agriculture	livestock, poultry, cotton
Industry	manufacturing, trade, oil and gas extraction

Chapter 4 **107**

Guided Instruction (continued)

- Have students determine from the information provided which state is the youngest and which is the oldest on these two pages. (*Oklahoma is the youngest and Pennsylvania is the oldest.*)

- Ask students to describe the locations of South Carolina and South Dakota (*South Dakota is in the Midwest, not far from Canada. South Carolina is in the South, on the Atlantic coast.*) Ask **What are these two states south of?** (*their northern counterparts, North Dakota and North Carolina*)

Guided Instruction (continued)

- Ask **The economies of what states listed on these two pages rely on their mineral resources?** (*West Virginia, Wyoming*)

- Ask **What agricultural products do Vermont, West Virginia, and Washington have in common?** (*apples*)

- Ask **Which of Virginia's industries might be related to its location bordering Washington, D.C.?** (*government*)

Independent Practice

- Using the map of the United States on p. 97 as a model, have students fill in the names of each state on an outline map. Then ask them to use the Country Databank to help them create a map that shows whether each state joined the United States in the 1700s, 1800s, or 1900s. Tell students to choose different colors to represent each century. They should explain what each color represents in the map key.

  All in One United States and Canada Teaching Resources, *Outline Map 11: The United States: Political,* p. 267

Monitor Progress

Circulate to make sure students are filling in their maps correctly. Provide assistance as needed.

Assess and Reteach

Assess Progress   L2

Direct students' attention back to the lists of states and capitals on the board. Encourage them to use the Country Databank to complete these lists as a class. Then have students complete the Assessment questions.

Introducing **The United States**

Utah

Year of Statehood	1896
Capital	Salt Lake City
Land Area	82,144 sq mi; 212,753 sq km
Population	2,233,169
Ethnic Group(s)	89.2% white; 9.0% Hispanic; 1.7% Asian; 1.3% Native American; 0.8% African American; 4.9% other
Agriculture	poultry, hay, corn, wheat, barley
Industry	services, trade, manufacturing

Vermont

Year of Statehood	1791
Capital	Montpelier
Land Area	9,250 sq mi; 23,958 sq km
Population	608,827
Ethnic Group(s)	96.8% white; 0.9% Asian; 0.5% African American; 0.4% Native American; 1.2% other
Agriculture	dairy products, apples, maple syrup
Industry	manufacturing, tourism, agriculture

Rower in Seattle, Washington

Virginia

Year of Statehood	1788
Capital	Richmond
Land Area	39,594 sq mi; 102,548 sq km
Population	7,078,515
Ethnic Group(s)	72.3% white; 19.6% African American; 0.7% Hispanic; 3.7% Asian; 0.3% Native American; 0.1% Native Hawaiian or Pacific Islander; 2.0% other
Agriculture	cattle, poultry, tobacco
Industry	services, trade, government

Washington

Year of Statehood	1889
Capital	Olympia
Land Area	66,544 sq mi; 172,349 sq km
Population	5,894,121
Ethnic Group(s)	81.8% white; 7.5% Hispanic; 5.5% Asian; 3.2% African American; 1.6% Native American; 4.3% other
Agriculture	cattle, poultry, apples, potatoes
Industry	technology, aerospace, biotechnology

108 United States and Canada

Differentiated Instruction

For English Language Learners   L2

Tell students that each state also has a two-letter abbreviated name. List the abbreviated state names on one side of the board, and the full state names on the other. Help students identify the states and their corresponding abbreviations. If you wish, you can divide students into pairs and have each pair create a set of flash cards, with the full state name on one side of the card, and the abbreviation on the other. Then have students take turns quizzing each other.

West Virginia

Year of Statehood	1863
Capital	Charleston
Land Area	24,078 sq mi; 62,362 sq km
Population	1,808,344
Ethnic Group(s)	95.0% white; 3.2% African American; 0.7% Hispanic; 0.5% Asian; 0.2% Native American; 0.2% other
Agriculture	apples, peaches, hay, tobacco
Industry	manufacturing, services, mining

Wisconsin

Year of Statehood	1848
Capital	Madison
Land Area	54,310 sq mi; 140,663 sq km
Population	5,363,675
Ethnic Group(s)	88.9% white; 5.7% African American; 3.6% Hispanic; 1.7% Asian; 0.9% Native American; 1.6% other
Agriculture	cattle, poultry, corn, hay
Industry	services, manufacturing, trade

Wyoming

Year of Statehood	1890
Capital	Cheyenne
Land Area	97,100 sq mi; 251,489 sq km
Population	493,782
Ethnic Group(s)	92.1% white; 6.4% Hispanic; 2.3% Native American; 0.8% African American; 0.6% Asian; 2.6% other
Agriculture	cattle, wheat, beans, barley
Industry	mineral extraction, oil, natural gas, tourism and recreation

SOURCE: U.S. Census; *World Almanac*, 2003
Note: Percentages may not total 100% due to rounding. The Hispanic population may be any race and is dispersed among racial categories.

Wisconsin dairy farm

Assessment

Comprehension and Critical Thinking

1. Compare and Contrast Compare the physical sizes and the population sizes of California and Rhode Island.

2. Draw Conclusions Are there characteristics that most of the states share? Explain.

3. Compare and Contrast What are some key differences among the states?

4. Categorize What are the major products of the South and the Midwest?

5. Make Generalizations Based on the data, make a generalization about industry in the United States.

6. Make a Timeline Create a timeline showing the year of statehood for 15 states.

Keeping Current

Access the **DK World Desk Reference Online** at **PHSchool.com** for up-to-date information about the United States.

Go Online
PHSchool.com

Web Code: lhe-4401

Reteach L1

Ask students to use the Country Databank to create a table listing the agricultural products of the following states: Georgia, Hawaii, Indiana, New Mexico, and Vermont. Then show students the transparency map of United States Agricultural Regions. Have them compare this map to the information in their tables. Help them see that each state on their table is in a different agricultural region. They will notice that products on the transparency match products in their tables.

📖 **United States and Canada Transparencies,** *Color Transparency USC 27: United States Agricultural Regions*

Extend L3

Portfolio Activity Have students pick two states from the Country Databank. Ask them to do library or Internet research to learn more about the natural resources of both states. Then have them write a short essay comparing and contrasting the natural resources of the two states. Ask them to explain how the resources of each state affect that state's economy. Have students add their work to their portfolios.

Answers

Assessment

1. California is about 150 times larger than Rhode Island; its population is almost 33 times bigger than Rhode Island's.

2. Yes. In most of the states, the majority of the population is white. Many states also have large percentages of African American and Hispanic residents. Most states have several important agricultural products.

3. Possible answer: States differ in terms of size, population, ethnic groups, and their types of agriculture and major industries.

4. South: cotton, poultry, peanuts, rice, tobacco. Midwest: corn, wheat, cattle, soybeans, poultry

5. Possible answer: Industry is important in the United States. Major industries in the United States vary, but the most common industries include manufacturing, finance, services, agriculture, and tourism.

6. Students' timelines will vary. Use *Rubric for Assessing a Timeline* to assess their work.

All in One **United States and Canada Teaching Resources,** *Rubric for Assessing a Timeline*, p. 272

Objectives

Social Studies

1. Learn how the large cities of the Northeast contribute to the economy of the United States.

2. Find out how the Northeast has been a port of entry for many immigrants.

Reading/Language Arts

Compare and contrast to help sort out and analyze information.

Prepare to Read

Build Background Knowledge L2

Tell students that in this section they will learn more about the Northeast. Point out which part of the United States is the Northeast on the map on page 97. Write New York City, Philadelphia, and Boston on the board. Ask students to preview the photos in the section, reading each caption. Then have students brainstorm some characteristics of each city. Provide a few suggestions to get started. Conduct an Idea Wave (TE, p. T35) to generate a list.

Set a Purpose for Reading L2

- Preview the Objectives.

- Form students into pairs or groups of four. Distribute the *Reading Readiness Guide*. Ask students to fill in the first two columns of the chart. Use the Numbered Heads participation strategy (TE, p. T36) to call on students to share one piece of information they already know and one piece of information they want to know.

All in One United States and Canada Teaching Resources, *Reading Readiness Guide,* p. 236

Vocabulary Builder
Preview Key Terms L2

Pronounce each Key Term, then ask students to say the word with you. Provide a simple explanation such as, "Many people commute to work on a train."

Prepare to Read

Objectives

In this section, you will

1. Learn how the large cities of the Northeast contribute to the economy of the United States.

2. Find out how the Northeast has been a port of entry for many immigrants.

Taking Notes

As you read this section, look for details about Boston, Philadelphia, and New York City. Copy the chart below, and record your findings in it.

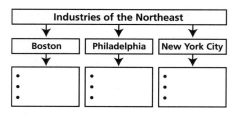

Industries of the Northeast
→ Boston
→ Philadelphia
→ New York City

Target Reading Skill

Compare and Contrast Comparing and contrasting can help you sort out and analyze information. When you compare, you examine the similarities between things. When you contrast, you look at the differences between things. As you read this section, compare and contrast the large cities of the Northeast.

Key Terms

- **commute** (kuh MYOOT) *v.* to travel to work
- **megalopolis** (meg uh LAHP uh lis) *n.* a number of cities and suburbs that blend into one very large urban area
- **population density** (pahp yuh LAY shun DEN suh tee) *n.* the average number of people per square mile or square kilometer

Rush hour in a New York City subway station

110 United States and Canada

For more than a century, life in New York City has been crowded. One hundred years ago, horse-drawn carriages caused traffic jams. Today, more than 3 million riders squeeze into New York's subway cars every day. Others travel the many miles of bus lines or catch one of the city's 12,000 taxis. And many people drive their own cars through the city's busy streets.

New York City is not unique. Washington, D.C., Boston, Massachusetts, and Philadelphia, Pennsylvania, are also crowded. In these big cities, thousands of people **commute,** or travel to work, each day. Many drive to work from suburbs that are far from the city's center. Even people who live in the city must travel from one area to another to work.

Target Reading Skill L2

Compare and Contrast Point out the Target Reading Skill. Explain that students can compare, or find similarities, and contrast, or find differences, to help them analyze information.

Model the skill by reading the Philadelphia and New York City sections on pages 113 and 115 with students, and identifying the similarities and differences between the two cities. (*Both are large cities in the Northeast located near rivers. Philadelphia is an industrial powerhouse while New York City is more of a financial powerhouse.*)

Give students *Compare and Contrast.* Have them complete the activity in groups.

All in One United States and Canada Teaching Resources, *Compare and Contrast,* p. 251

A Region of Cities

A nearly unbroken chain of cities runs from Boston to New York to Washington, D.C. This coastal region of the Northeast is a megalopolis (meg uh LAHP uh lis). A **megalopolis** is a region where the cities and suburbs have grown so close together that they form one big urban area. Find this area on the map below.

The Northeast is the most densely populated region of the United States. **Population density** is the average number of people per square mile (or square kilometer). The population density of New Jersey is 10 times greater than the density of Kentucky.

The Northeast's economy is based on its cities. Many were founded in colonial times, along rivers or near the Atlantic Ocean. These cities began as transportation and trade centers. Today, manufacturing, finance, communications, and government employ millions of urban northeasterners.

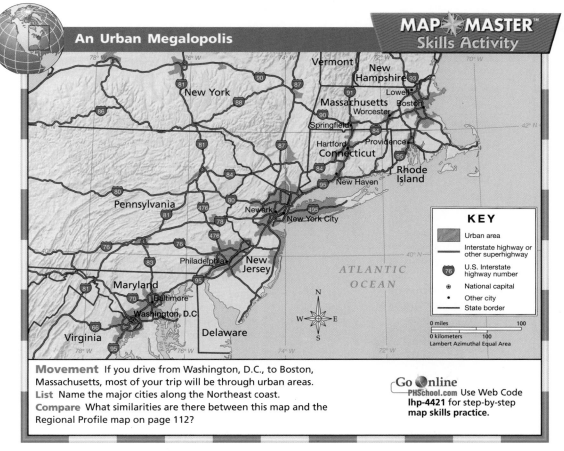

An Urban Megalopolis

MAP MASTER™ Skills Activity

KEY

- Urban area
- Interstate highway or other superhighway
- (76) U.S. Interstate highway number
- ⊛ National capital
- • Other city
- State border

0 miles 100
0 kilometers 100
Lambert Azimuthal Equal Area

Movement If you drive from Washington, D.C., to Boston, Massachusetts, most of your trip will be through urban areas.
List Name the major cities along the Northeast coast.
Compare What similarities are there between this map and the Regional Profile map on page 112?

Go Online
PHSchool.com Use Web Code
lhp-4421 for step-by-step
map skills practice.

Vocabulary Builder

Use the information below to teach students this section's high-use words.

High-Use Word	Definition and Sample Sentence
hub, p. 113	*n.* a center of activity The house's activity focuses on its **hub,** the kitchen.
institution, p. 115	*n.* an established organization They founded the **institution** fifty years ago.
innumerable, p. 116	*adj.* too many to be counted There were **innumerable** stars in the sky.

Instruct

A Region of Cities L2

Guided Instruction

- **Vocabulary Builder** Clarify the high-use words **hub** and **institution** before reading.

- Read a Region of Cities with the class using the Oral Cloze strategy (TE, p. T33). As students read, circulate around the room to make sure that students can answer the Reading Check question.

- Have students identify some places they might see if they visited Boston. (*Paul Revere's home, Harvard, MIT, hospitals*)

Answers

MAP MASTER Skills Activity **List** Boston, Providence, New Haven, New York City, Newark, Philadelphia, Baltimore, Washington, D.C.
Compare Possible answers: Both maps show the Northeast region; the areas shaded as "urban" on the map on page 111 seem to be those shaded as the most populated on page 112.

Go Online
PHSchool.com Students may practice their map skills using the interactive online version of this map.

Guided Instruction L2

- Ask students to read the text and study the map and charts on this page. As a class, answer the Map and Chart Skills questions.

- Discuss the concept of *services*. Ask students to give examples of a business or personal service. (*business—Web site developer; personal—hairdresser*)

Independent Practice

- Distribute *Reading a Population Density Map*. Have students work in pairs to complete the worksheet.

  All in One **United States and Canada Teaching Resources,** *Reading a Population Density Map,* p. 263

- Then have students return to the map on this page. Ask them to write a short paragraph explaining how they think the Northeast's population density affects its economy.

The Northeast

Although it is the nation's smallest region, the Northeast is the most heavily populated region in the United States. It has many large and old cities. New York is the center of international trade and finance, while Philadelphia was the birthplace of the Declaration of Independence and the United States Constitution. With so many people living in such a small area, services are an important part of the Northeast's economy. As you study the graphs and map, think about how population density affects an area's economy.

The Northeast: Population Density

KEY

Persons per sq. mile	Persons per sq. kilometer
More than 519	More than 199
260–519	100–199
130–259	50–99
25–129	10–49
1–24	1–9

Urban Areas
- ■ More than 9,999,999
- □ 5,000,000–9,999,999
- ◉ 1,000,000–4,999,999
- • 500,000–999,999
- · Less than 500,000
- — National border
- — State border

Types of Services

Community, business, personal
Financial, insurance, real estate
Government
Transportation, utilities, communication

Northeast Population Density, 2000

State	People per Square Mile
Connecticut	702.9
Massachusetts	809.8
New Jersey	1,134.4
New York	401.9
Pennsylvania	274.0
Rhode Island	1,003.2

SOURCE: *New York Times Almanac,* 2006

Economy of the Northeast

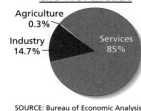

- Agriculture 0.3%
- Industry 14.7%
- Services 85%

SOURCE: Bureau of Economic Analysis

Map and Chart Skills

1. **Note** Which state has the highest population density overall?
2. **Infer** Why did most major northeastern cities develop along the coast?
3. **Explore the Main Idea** Why do you think services are the most important economic activity in this region?

 Use Web Code lhe-4411 to access the **DK World Desk Reference Online.**

Answers

Map and Chart Skills

1. New Jersey
2. They had good harbors for trade with Europe and other cities along the coast.
3. The area is heavily populated; people need services.

Go Online PHSchool.com Students can find more information about this topic on the DK World Desk Reference Online.

Skills for Life **Skills Mini Lesson**

Synthesizing Information L2

1. Explain that when you synthesize something, you put together pieces of information to draw conclusions. For each piece of information, identify the main idea and supporting details. Next, look for links between the pieces of information. Finally, draw a conclusion.

2. Help students practice the skill by synthesizing the information given in the Types of Services table and the Economy of the Northeast circle graph.

3. Have students synthesize the information from the map and the bar graph to draw a conclusion about where people live in the Northeast.

Boston In colonial times, the city of Boston was called the "hub of the universe." Boston remains an important city in the Northeast. It is a city filled with history. The American Revolution began when British troops marched from Boston to Concord in 1775. You can still visit buildings that date from before the American Revolution, including Paul Revere's house, which is the oldest building in the downtown area. Yet you will find that Boston is a very modern city, too.

The Boston area is known worldwide for its leading research centers, including dozens of colleges and universities. Cambridge (KAYM brij) is the home of Harvard, which was founded in 1636 and is the oldest university in the United States. Cambridge is also home to the Massachusetts Institute of Technology (MIT).

Boston is noted for its medical, science, and technology centers as well. Some of the best medical schools and hospitals in the country are located in Boston. Many medical firsts took place here, including the use of anesthesia (an es THEE zhuh) during surgery. Boston's universities and scientific companies often work together to carry out research and to design new products.

Philadelphia Many people consider Philadelphia to be the "cradle of the nation" because, like Boston, it was an important city in our nation's early history. It was once the capital of the country. It was in Philadelphia that America's founders wrote the Declaration of Independence and the Constitution. By the late 1700s, Philadelphia had become the political, financial, and commercial center of the nation. Home to the country's leading seaport until it was surpassed by New York's in the 1820s, Philadelphia quickly became a major shipbuilding center as well.

Today, Philadelphia is an industrial center. It is located on the Delaware River. Important land and water transportation routes pass through there. Ships, trucks, and trains bring in raw materials from other parts of Pennsylvania and from all over the world. Many factories process food, produce medical supplies, and manufacture chemicals. Hundreds of products are then shipped out for sale. In addition, Philadelphia has become a center of the health care industry, due to its several medical, dental, and pharmacology schools.

Boston's outdoor market, Haymarket, is one of the city's most famous attractions.

Learn about the Minutemen in the American Revolution.

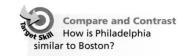

Compare and Contrast
How is Philadelphia similar to Boston?

Chapter 4 Section 1 **113**

- Ask **Why is Philadelphia called the "cradle of the nation?"** *(It is where the Declaration of Independence and Constitution were written.)* **What kinds of factories would you find in Philadelphia today?** *(food processing, medical supply production, chemical manufacturing)*

- Ask students **How do you think the location of cities in the Northeast helped them become centers of trade?** *(Their location on the coast made them accessible to ships from other countries and to cities along the Atlantic coast.)*

- Ask students **How does New York City contribute to the United States economy?** *(New York City is the center of fashion, publishing, advertising, and the arts in the United States, and contains the headquarters of many of the country's wealthiest corporations.)*

 Show students *Paul Revere and the Minutemen* and ask **Who were the Minutemen fighting against?** *(the Redcoats)*

Independent Practice
Ask students to create the Taking Notes graphic organizer on a blank piece of paper. Have students complete the graphic organizer by filling in industries for each city. Briefly model which details to record by filling in the Boston industries with them.

Monitor Progress
Show *Section Reading Support Transparency USC 54*, and ask students to check their graphic organizers individually. Go over key concepts and clarify key vocabulary as needed.

United States and Canada Transparencies, *Section Reading Support Transparency USC 54*

Target Reading Skill L2

Compare and Contrast As a follow up, ask students to answer the Target Reading Skill question in the Student Edition. *(Both were important cities in our country's history, both are home to medical schools.)*

Skills Mini Lesson

Using Cartographer's Tools

1. Teach the skill by pointing out that a map key explains symbols and special colors used on a map. Explain that it helps students interpret the information being shown on the map.

2. Help students practice the skill by looking at the map on p. 112. Read the key with students and have them identify what each color and symbol represents on the map.

3. Have students apply the skill by choosing a state and describing its population density.

The Skyscraper   L2

Guided Instruction

Ask students to study The Skyscraper by reading the text and captions, and examining the photos and diagram. As a class, answer the Analyzing Images question. Allow students to briefly discuss their responses with a partner before sharing answers.

Independent Practice

Have students use cardboard or another medium of their choice to construct their own skyscraper. Provide them with a specific size for the base, such as one foot wide and one foot long. Tell them to try to make as many floors as they can without making the structure unstable.

The Skyscraper

After the Civil War, the United States grew rapidly. People streamed into the cities to fill jobs in new factories and offices. To create more office and living space, architects used new technology to build taller and taller structures. By the 1930s, the skylines of all major American cities were dominated by tall skyscrapers. The Empire State Building, shown at right, was built in 1931. At 1,252 feet (382 meters), it is the tallest skyscraper in New York City.

Rockefeller Center, New York City
Most modern skyscrapers wear a glass skin of windows.

High-speed elevators travel as fast as 1,400 feet (426 meters) a minute.

60,000 tons of steel were used to make the skeleton that supports the building.

The outside of the building is covered with ten million bricks.

About ten minutes is all it takes for the fittest runners to race up the 1,576 steps from the lobby to the 86th floor, in the Fleet Empire State Run-Up.

Construction workers
Workers rest during the construction of New York City's Chrysler Building. Built in 1930, the building's owner hoped it would be the tallest in the world—but even taller buildings were soon built.

More than 200 steel and concrete piles support the 365,000-ton building.

ANALYZING IMAGES
How does the structure of this building allow more offices in less space?

Differentiated Instruction

For English Language Learners   L1

Students may find it difficult to pronounce some of the words in this section, such as *populated, finance, economy, density,* and *utilities.* Show students how to break down these words into smaller parts to help them sound out the pronunciation. Check to make sure students understand the meanings of the words as well.

For Special Needs Students   L1

Preteach key concepts to students by showing *Section Reading Support Transparency USC 54* before reading. Go over the key points on the transparency.

📖 **United States and Canada Transparencies,** *Section Reading Support Transparency USC 54*

Answer

ANALYZING IMAGES The building is very tall which allows more offices to fit in a smaller space.

New York City The largest, wealthiest, and most influential city in the United States is New York City. More than 8 million people live there, making it one of the 10 largest cities in the world. The city covers an area of about 300 square miles (800 square kilometers) on islands and the mainland around the mouth of the Hudson River. Tunnels and bridges connect the various parts of the city.

New York is the center of fashion, publishing, advertising, and the arts in the United States. New York's Broadway is known for its plays and musicals, Fifth Avenue for its shopping, and Wall Street for its finance.

New York City is our nation's "money capital." About 350,000 New Yorkers work for banks and other financial institutions. The headquarters of many of the country's wealthiest corporations are in New York. The New York Stock Exchange is on Wall Street. Noted for its skyscrapers, New York City's skyline is recognized by people around the world.

On September 11, 2001, the city became a target of terrorists, who crashed two planes into the towers of the World Trade Center. The World Trade Center held government agencies and businesses that were involved in international trade. Nearly 3,000 people were killed as a result of the attack.

✓ Reading Check **Which city is considered the financial capital of the United States?**

View From the Top
More than 30 million tourists visit New York City each year. Among the city's biggest tourist attractions are the theaters on 42nd Street (lower photo) and Central Park, which lies in the midst of a maze of skyscrapers (upper photo).
Identify Effects *What effect does tourism have on New York's economy?*

Ports of Entry L2

Guided Instruction
- **Vocabulary Builder** Clarify the high-use word **innumerable** before reading.

- Read about immigration to the Northeast in Ports of Entry.

- Discuss with students the meaning of a port of entry. *(the port where immigrants arrive in a country)* Ask **Which Northeast cities were ports of entry for immigrants?** *(New York, Boston, and Philadelphia)*

- Ask **How do you think this flow of immigrants helped the cities of the Northeast grow in importance?** *(They provided a workforce for factories and industry. They also brought diversity, new ideas, and skills.)*

Independent Practice
Partner students and have them write a letter that an immigrant arriving in a Northeast city might send to someone back home about his or her first impressions. Give students *Writing a Letter* to help them get started.

All in One **United States and Canada Teaching Resources,** *Writing a Letter,* p. 270

Monitor Progress
Tell students to fill in the last column of their *Reading Readiness Guides.* Ask them to evaluate if what they learned was what they had expected to learn.

All in One **United States and Canada Teaching Resources,** *Reading Readiness Guide,* p. 236

Differentiated Instruction

For Advanced Readers L3
Have students complete the *Nickel-and-Diming* Internet activity to learn about a city's infrastructure and how increased population can affect it. Ask students to find out whether the populations of Boston, Philadelphia, and New York City have increased, stayed the same, or decreased in recent years and what effect these changes have had on the infrastructure of each city.

Go Online
PHSchool.com

For: Environmental and Global Issues: *Nickel-and-Diming*
Visit: PHSchool.com
Web Code: lhd-4405

Answers
Identify Effects Tourism forms an important part of New York's economy.

✓ Reading Check New York City

Assess and Reteach

Assess Progress L2
Have students complete the Section Assessment. Administer the *Section Quiz.*

All in One United States and Canada Teaching Resources, *Section Quiz,* p. 238

Reteach L1
If students need more instruction, have them read this section in the Reading and Vocabulary Study Guide.

Chapter 4, Section 1, **United States and Canada Reading and Vocabulary Study Guide,** pp. 42–44

Extend L3
Organize students into groups of four to design a television commercial urging people to visit one of the three major cities in the Northeast. Students should supplement information in the text with more research. Encourage groups to include cultural, economic, and recreational features of the city in their presentation.

Answer

✓ Reading Check New York harbor

Section 1 Assessment

Key Terms
Students' sentences should reflect knowledge of each Key Term.

Target Reading Skill
Possible answer: Similarities—Most cities were founded in colonial times and began as transportation and trade centers. Differences—Northeastern cities vary in population size and in the businesses that fuel their economies.

Comprehension and Critical Thinking
1. (a) more than 8 million people **(b)** Although the Northeast is the smallest region in the nation, it is the most densely populated region. **(c)** Answers will vary, but may include that population density affects the types of homes people live in, the method they use to get to and from work, and the type of jobs available.

2. (a) New York City **(b)** Answers may vary, but may include that more jobs may have been available to incoming immigrants in the Northeast. **(c)** The cultures of immigrants have blended into that of the Northeast and enriched its diversity.

Ports of Entry

Louis Waldman came to the United States in 1909, when he was seventeen years old. He landed at the Ellis Island immigration station in New York harbor:

> **Behind me was the bustling harbor with its innumerable boats, the sight of which made me seasick all over again. Facing me were the tall buildings of lower Manhattan, buildings which were more magnificent and higher than any I had ever imagined, even in my wildest dreams. . . .**
>
> —*Russian immigrant Louis Waldman*

Immigrants arrive at Ellis Island in 1920.

From 1892 to 1954, millions of immigrants came to the United States through Ellis Island. Today, Ellis Island is a national monument.

Although New York was the main port of entry, Boston and Philadelphia were also important gateways for immigrants. In the 1700s, more German immigrants entered the country through Philadelphia than through any other port. In the 1800s, many Irish immigrants entered through both Philadelphia and Boston.

After arriving in these port cities, many immigrants stayed and built new lives. Today, all three cities are rich in ethnic diversity. To get a real sense of this ethnic diversity, just look at the names in the phonebooks of these big cities.

✓ Reading Check **Where is Ellis Island located?**

Section 1 Assessment

Key Terms
Review the key terms at the beginning of this section. Use each term in a sentence that explains its meaning.

Target Reading Skill
What are two ways that the cities of the Northeast are similar? What are two ways that they are different?

Comprehension and Critical Thinking
1. (a) Recall How many people live in New York City?

(b) Compare How does the population density of the Northeast compare with densities of other regions of the country?
(c) Cause and Effect How does population density affect the ways people live and work?
2. (a) Recall What city was the main port of entry for European immigrants in the 1800s?
(b) Identify the Main Idea Why might immigrants have chosen to live in the Northeast?
(c) Cause and Effect How have immigrants affected the culture of the Northeast?

Writing Activity
Which city described in this section are you most interested in learning more about? Make a list of things you would like to learn about this city. Then write a brief paragraph explaining why you want to learn these things.

For: An activity on mass transit systems
Visit: PHSchool.com
Web Code: lhd-4401

116 United States and Canada

Writing Activity
Use the *Rubric for Assessing a Writing Assignment* to evaluate students' paragraphs.

All in One United States and Canada Teaching Resources, *Rubric for Assessing a Writing Assignment,* p. 273

Go Online PHSchool.com Typing in the Web code when prompted will bring students directly to detailed instructions for this activity.

Section 2 — The South
The Growth of Industry

Prepare to Read

Objectives
In this section, you will
1. Learn how the South's land is important to its economy.
2. Read about how the growth of industry is changing the South.

Taking Notes
As you read this section, look for details about the growth of industry and how it has affected the economy. Copy the table below, and record your findings in it.

Industry	Products	Effects on Economy

Target Reading Skill
Use Signal Words Signal words point out relationships among ideas or events. Certain words, such as *however* or *like,* can signal a comparison or contrast. As you read this section, notice the contrast between what the South's economy was based on 50 years ago and what it is based on today. What signal words indicate the contrast?

Key Terms
• **petrochemical** (pet roh KEM ih kul) *n.* a substance such as plastic or paint that is made from petroleum
• **industrialization** (in dus tree ul ih ZAY shun) *n.* the process of building new industries in an area dominated by farming
• **Sun Belt** (sun belt) *n.* an area of the United States stretching from the southern Atlantic coast to the California coast

In 1895, at the age of fifteen, Catherine Evans Whitener had no idea that she was about to make history. Her friends and family liked the cotton bedspreads she made so much that she began to display them on her front porch in Dalton, Georgia. Her first sale earned her $2.50. After a large store placed an order for 24 bedspreads, an industry was born.

As interest in her work grew, Whitener began to train other girls to help produce the bedspreads. In 1917, she and her brother formed the Evans Manufacturing Company. Their company and others like it employed some 10,000 workers during the Great Depression. So many bedspreads were sold to travelers in the Dalton area that the highway through the town became known as "Bedspread Alley."

The Land of the South

There are many different ways that people in the South can make a living. The South's particular geography and climate make many of these jobs possible.

Catherine Evans Whitener

Chapter 4 Section 2 **117**

Target Reading Skill ⎗ L2

Use Signal Words Draw students' attention to the Target Reading Skill. Tell them that signal words such as *however* and *like* can help them notice a comparison or contrast.

Model using signal words by writing the following sentence on the board and identifying the signal word: "Unlike the Northeast, the South has a warm, wet climate in which oranges grow well." (*The word* unlike *signals a contrast.*)

Give students *Compare and Contrast.* Have them complete the activity in groups.

All in One **United States and Canada Teaching Resources,** *Compare and Contrast,* p. 251

Section 2
Step-by-Step Instruction

Objectives
Social Studies
1. Learn how the South's land is important to its economy.
2. Read about how the growth of industry is changing the South.

Reading/Language Arts
Use signal words to find relationships among ideas or events.

Prepare to Read

Build Background Knowledge ⬛ L2
In this section, students will learn about the southern part of the United States. Tell students to preview the visuals and headings in the section with these questions in mind: **What kinds of products are made in the South? What kinds of industries take place there?** Provide a few examples (*cotton, textiles, shipping*). Make a list on the board. Then tell the class that all of the above are part of the South's diverse economy.

Set a Purpose for Reading ⬛ L2
■ Preview the Objectives.

■ Read each statement in the *Reading Readiness Guide* aloud. Ask students to mark the statements true or false.

■ Have students discuss the statements in pairs or groups of four, then mark their worksheets again. Use the Numbered Heads participation strategy (TE, p. T36) to call on students to share their group's perspectives.

All in One **United States and Canada Teaching Resources,** *Reading Readiness Guide,* p. 240

Vocabulary Builder
Preview Key Terms ⬛ L2
Pronounce each Key Term, then ask students to say the word with you. Provide a simple explanation such as, "Many people move to the Sun Belt, located in the southern United States, because of its warm climate."

Chapter 4 Section 2 **117**

Instruct

Guided Instruction L2

- Ask students to read and study the Regional Profile on this page. Work with the class to answer the Map and Chart Skills questions. Have students briefly discuss their responses with a partner before sharing answers.

- If you have not already done so, show the video *Miami's Little Havana* for Section 2 of this chapter. The video will provide an example of how Hispanic culture is thriving in the South. Ask students to write down at least three things that they learned from it.

  📼 *Miami's Little Havana,* **World Studies Video Program**

Independent Practice

Ask students to summarize the information on one of the bar graphs in a short paragraph. If necessary, have students refer to *Transferring Information from One Medium to Another* on the Social Studies Skills Tutor CD-ROM.

  ⊙ *Transferring Information from One Medium to Another,* **Social Studies Skills Tutor CD-ROM**

Answers

Map and Chart Skills

1. the Northeast
2. Texas and Florida
3. Possible answer: There may be more celebrations and traditions reflecting Hispanic and African American cultures.

Go Online PHSchool.com Students can find more information about this topic on the DK World Desk Reference Online.

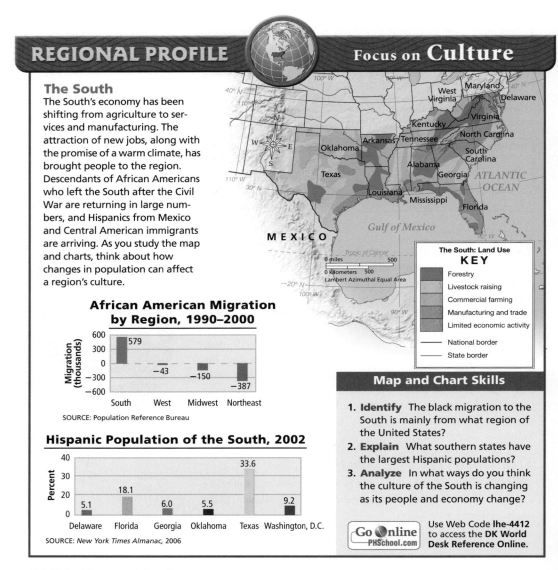

The region has a warm climate, and most parts of it receive plenty of rain. The wide coastal plains along the Atlantic Ocean and the Gulf of Mexico have rich soil. In addition, the South has a long growing season. There are between 200 and 290 frost-free days every year. Together, these features make much of the South an excellent place for growing crops such as cotton, rice, tobacco, and sugar cane and raising animals.

REGIONAL PROFILE   Focus on Culture

The South

The South's economy has been shifting from agriculture to services and manufacturing. The attraction of new jobs, along with the promise of a warm climate, has brought people to the region. Descendants of African Americans who left the South after the Civil War are returning in large numbers, and Hispanics from Mexico and Central American immigrants are arriving. As you study the map and charts, think about how changes in population can affect a region's culture.

The South: Land Use
KEY
- Forestry
- Livestock raising
- Commercial farming
- Manufacturing and trade
- Limited economic activity
- — National border
- — State border

African American Migration by Region, 1990–2000

Migration (thousands): South 579, West −43, Midwest −150, Northeast −387

SOURCE: Population Reference Bureau

Hispanic Population of the South, 2002

Percent: Delaware 5.1, Florida 18.1, Georgia 6.0, Oklahoma 5.5, Texas 33.6, Washington, D.C. 9.2

SOURCE: *New York Times Almanac,* 2006

Map and Chart Skills

1. **Identify** The black migration to the South is mainly from what region of the United States?
2. **Explain** What southern states have the largest Hispanic populations?
3. **Analyze** In what ways do you think the culture of the South is changing as its people and economy change?

Go Online PHSchool.com Use Web Code lhe-4412 to access the **DK World Desk Reference Online.**

118 United States and Canada

Vocabulary Builder

Use the information below to teach students this section's high-use words.

High-Use Word	Definition and Sample Sentence
consume, p. 119	*v.* to use up He **consumed** all of the milk and none was left for our cereal.
decade, p. 122	*n.* period of ten years She told him, "You're a **decade** old!" on his tenth birthday.

Farming One of the most important parts of the South's economy is farming. For years, the South's major crop was cotton. By the 1950s, bedspread factories in Georgia alone consumed 500,000 bales of cotton every year. Many southern farmers once depended on cotton as their only source of income. Today, cotton still brings much money to the South, especially to Alabama, Mississippi, and Texas, but King Cotton no longer rules this region. In the 1890s, the boll weevil (bohl WEE vul), a kind of beetle, began to attack cotton plants in the South. Over the next 30 years, it destroyed cotton crops across the region. Without money from cotton, many farmers went bankrupt. Today, most southern farmers raise more than one crop.

Growing Conditions Some of these crops need special growing conditions. Citrus fruits require year-round warmth and sunshine. Florida has plenty of both. More oranges, tangerines, grapefruits, and limes are grown here than in any other state. Rice needs warm, moist growing conditions. Farmers in Arkansas, Louisiana, and Mississippi take advantage of their climate by growing rice along the coast of the Gulf of Mexico and in the Mississippi River valley.

Agricultural Products Some areas of the South have become famous for their agricultural products. Georgia has taken one of its products as its nickname—the Peach State. Georgia is also known for its peanut and pecan crops. Texans raise more cattle than do farmers in any other state. All of these items are just a sample of the diversity of southern agriculture.

The Cotton Crop
Although cotton (below) is no longer the South's major crop, it is still important to the region's economy. **Identify Effects** *How did boll weevils (above) affect the South's economy and way of farming?*

The Land of the South [L2]

Guided Instruction

- **Vocabulary Builder** Clarify the high-use word **consume** before reading.

- Read The Land of the South using the Paragraph Shrinking strategy (TE, p. T34).

- Ask **How is the South's land important to its economy?** (*Farming is one of the most important parts of the South's economy. The wide coastal plains in the South have rich soil that is good for farming.*)

- Ask **How do mineral resources contribute to the South's economy?** (*Oil and natural gas are used for fuel and many products, including petrochemicals such as plastic and paint. Other useful minerals are also mined.*)

Background: Global Perspectives

Cotton Cotton is one of the most important crops in the world. China leads the world in cotton production, but the United States, India, Pakistan, Brazil, Egypt, and some of the countries that were once part of the former Soviet Union are also major producers. In addition to cloth, products from parts of the cotton plant include automobile tire cord, plastic reinforcing, packing materials, cellulose, pressed paper, and cardboard. Cottonseed oil is used to make cosmetics, cooking oil, and some detergents.

Answer

Identify Effects Over the course of 30 years, the boll weevil destroyed many farmers' cotton crops. This caused many farmers in the South to plant more than one crop. Cotton no longer rules the region.

Independent Practice

Ask students to create the Taking Notes graphic organizer on a blank piece of paper. Then have them begin to fill in the table with information from these pages. Briefly model how to identify information to include.

Monitor Progress

As students fill in the graphic organizer, move around the room and make sure individuals are choosing the correct details. Provide assistance as needed.

Offshore Drilling
The rig provides a platform for oil drilling in the Gulf of Mexico. **Draw Conclusions** *Why is drilling for oil an important industry in the South?*

Drilling and Mining In some parts of the South, what is under the soil is as important as what grows in it. In Louisiana, Oklahoma, and Texas, companies drill for oil and natural gas. These can be used as fuel and made into **petrochemicals,** which are substances, such as plastics, paint, nylon, and asphalt, that come from petroleum. In Alabama, Kentucky, West Virginia, and Tennessee, miners dig for coal. Southern states are leading producers of minerals such as salt, sulfur, and zinc. The South also produces many important building materials, including crushed stone, construction sand and gravel, and cement.

Fishing and Forestry Many people in the South make a living in fishing and forestry. The Chesapeake Bay area of Maryland and Virginia is famous for its shellfish, including clams, crabs, and scallops. Mississippi leads the nation in catfish farming. However, the South's fishing industry is strongest in Louisiana, Texas, and Florida. The timber industry is active in most of the southern states. Softwood trees like southern pine are turned into lumber or paper. People use hardwood trees to make furniture. North Carolina has the nation's largest hardwood furniture industry.

√ Reading Check **Name two kinds of crops that need special growing conditions.**

120 United States and Canada

Answers

Draw Conclusions Oil drilling companies employ many people, as do companies that process oil.

√ Reading Check Citrus fruits and rice are crops that need special growing conditions.

Background: Global Perspectives

Louisiana's Island Industry About 140 miles (84 kilometers) west of New Orleans lies tiny Avery Island, where the McIlhenny family has been producing Tabasco sauce for more than 130 years. The fiery red peppers that are the main ingredient of the sauce are native to Central America, but grow equally well on Avery Island. In fact, the name *Tabasco* comes from a Native American language and means "land where the soil is hot and humid." The sauce is almost entirely a product of the island. Not only are the peppers grown on the island, they are mixed with salt mined on the island. Once the sauce has been properly aged in oaken barrels, it is bottled and shipped to more than 105 countries.

Southern Cities and Industries

Some people still think of the South as it was in the early 1900s—a slow-moving, mostly rural region. But over the past 50 years, this region has gone through many changes. Although the South's rural areas are still important to its economy, most people in the South today live in cities. Some work in factories or in high-technology firms. Others work in tourism or in one of the other service industries in this region's growing economy. This change from an agriculture-based economy to an industry-based economy is called **industrialization.**

Textiles   One of the most important industries in the South is the textile industry. Textile mills make cloth. They were originally built in this region to use the South's cotton. Today, many mills still make cotton cloth. Others now make cloth from synthetic, or human-made, materials. The textile industry is strongest in Georgia, the Carolinas, and Virginia.

Technology   One expanding set of industries is in the field of high technology. For example, workers develop computers and other electronics and figure out better ways to use them. Some centers of high technology are Raleigh-Durham, North Carolina, and Austin, Texas.

Another high-technology industry is the aerospace business. In Cape Canaveral, Florida, Houston, Texas, and Huntsville, Alabama, people work for the National Aeronautics and Space Administration (NASA). Some people train as astronauts, while others run the space shuttle program. Atlanta, Georgia, is now a center for the cable television industry.

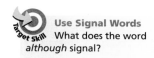
Use Signal Words
What does the word *although* signal?

Space Camp
Every year, people attend United States Space Camp in Huntsville, Alabama. As one student (left) sits in the cockpit of a space shuttle, other students (right) experiment with the feeling of being in outer space.
Analyze Images *How do these photographs reflect the high-technology industry?*

🏹 Target Reading Skill   L2

Use Signal Words As a follow up, ask students to answer the Target Reading Skill question in the Student Edition. (*The word* although *signals a contrast.*)

Southern Cities and Industries   L2

Guided Instruction

- **Vocabulary Builder** Clarify the high-use word **decade** before reading.

- Read Southern Cities and Industries with students. As students read, circulate and make sure individuals can answer the Reading Check question.

- Ask students **Where do most people in the South live—in urban or rural areas?** (*Most people live in urban areas.*)

- Discuss with students how industrialization has changed the South. (*Although farming is still important to the South's economy, many people in the South now work in industries such as aerospace and tourism. Industrialization has helped the South's economy.*)

Answer

Analyze Images They show the aerospace business, which is a high-technology industry.

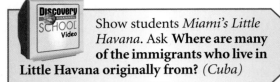

Show students *Miami's Little Havana*. Ask **Where are many of the immigrants who live in Little Havana originally from?** (*Cuba*)

Guided Instruction (continued)

■ Ask **Why does transportation play a large role in the South's economy?** (*Many southern cities are centers of transportation, moving goods in and out of the region.*)

Independent Practice

Have students complete the graphic organizer with additional information about the growth of industry and its effects on the economy.

Monitor Progress

■ Show *Section Reading Support Transparency USC 55* and ask students to check their graphic organizers individually. Go over key concepts and clarify key vocabulary as needed.

   📖 **United States and Canada Transparencies,** *Section Reading Support Transparency USC 55*

■ Tell students to fill in the last column of their *Reading Readiness Guides*. Probe for what they learned that confirms or invalidates each statement.

   All in One United States and Canada Teaching Resources, *Reading Readiness Guide*, p. 240

Answers

MAP MASTER Skills Activity **Locate** in the southern and southwestern United States **Draw Conclusions** The region's new industries and mild climate drew people to the Sun Belt.

Go Online PHSchool.com Students may practice their map skills using the interactive online version of this map.

Explore Miami's Little Havana

Transportation and Tourism A big part of the South's economy depends on moving goods and people into and out of the region. Most of the South's largest cities play important roles in this transportation industry. Miami, Florida, and New Orleans, Louisiana, are major ports. Miami is a center for goods and people going to and from Central and South America. New Orleans is a gateway between the Gulf of Mexico and the Mississippi River system. It is also an important port for oil tankers.

Some of the people the transportation industry brings to the South come to stay. Thousands come to work in the South's new industries. Thousands more choose to move to the South because of its climate. The South is part of the Sun Belt. The **Sun Belt** is the broad area of the United States that stretches from the southern Atlantic coast to the coast of California. It is known for its warm weather. The population of the Sun Belt has been rising for the past few decades. Some arrivals are older adults who want to retire to places without cold, snowy winters. Others come to take advantage of both the weather and the work that the Sun Belt offers.

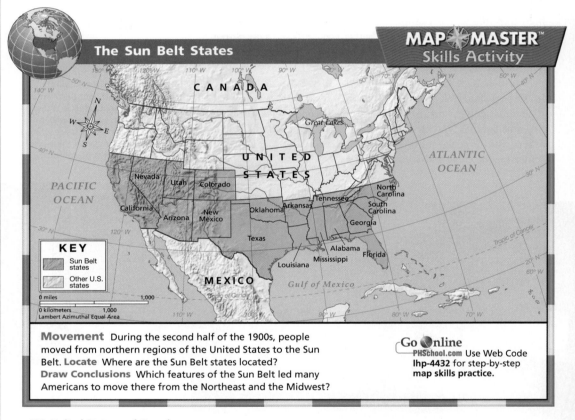

The Sun Belt States

MAP MASTER Skills Activity

KEY
Sun Belt states
Other U.S. states

Movement During the second half of the 1900s, people moved from northern regions of the United States to the Sun Belt. **Locate** Where are the Sun Belt states located? **Draw Conclusions** Which features of the Sun Belt led many Americans to move there from the Northeast and the Midwest?

Go Online PHSchool.com Use Web Code lhp-4432 for step-by-step map skills practice.

122 United States and Canada

Differentiated Instruction

For Gifted and Talented **L3**
Suggest that students choose one state in the South and create an economic activity map for it. Remind students to make a key for their map. Students can research their map in the library or on the Internet.

As a model, you might wish to have students first complete *Reading an Economic Activity Map*.

   All in One United States and Canada Teaching Resources, *Reading an Economic Activity Map*, p. 264

Warm weather also brings to the South people who only plan to visit. These people fuel the region's tourist industry. In winter, tourists flock to the sunny beaches of Florida and the Gulf Coast. In the summer, they hike in the mountains of the Appalachians and Ozarks. Southern historic cities such as Charleston, South Carolina, or New Orleans, Louisiana, draw tourists at any time of the year. In states throughout the South, there are always fun and exciting things to see and to do.

The Nation's Capital The city of Washington is not in a state. Instead, it is in the District of Columbia, which lies between the states of Maryland and Virginia. This area of land was chosen in 1790 as the site for the nation's capital. Located on the shore of the Potomac River, Washington, D.C., is a planned city. Many people consider Washington to be one of the most beautiful cities in the world. It has wide avenues, grand public buildings, and dramatic monuments, including the Supreme Court, the Library of Congress, the Washington Monument, and the Lincoln Memorial. The city's major avenues are named after the states. As the nation's capital, Washington is home to the nation's leaders and to hundreds of foreign diplomats.

Tourists on a paddleboat near the Jefferson Memorial in Washington, D.C.

√ **Reading Check** Where is the city of Washington located?

Section 2 Assessment

Key Terms
Review the key terms at the beginning of this section. Use each term in a sentence that explains its meaning.

Target Reading Skill
Review the section Fishing and Forestry on page 120. Find the word that signals contrast in relation to the fishing industry.

Comprehension and Critical Thinking
1. (a) List Name five of the southern states.
(b) Draw Conclusions How have the geography and climate of the South shaped its economy?

(c) Summarize In what ways has the South's economy changed since the 1800s?
2. (a) Recall Why has the population of the Sun Belt been increasing?
(b) Explain Why have many people in the South moved from rural to urban areas?
(c) Identify Cause and Effect How has the South's economy affected this population growth?

Writing Activity
Suppose that you work in an advertising firm in Atlanta, Georgia; Houston, Texas; or Miami, Florida. Create an advertisement persuading people to move to your city or state. It can be designed for a newspaper or a magazine. It can also be for radio, television, or the Internet.

Go Online PHSchool.com

For: An activity on oil
Visit: PHSchool.com
Web Code: lhd-4402

Writing Activity
Use the *Rubric for Assessing a Writing Assignment* to evaluate students' advertisements.

All in One **United States and Canada Teaching Resources,** *Rubric for Assessing a Writing Assignment,* p. 273

Go Online PHSchool.com Typing in the Web code when prompted will bring students directly to detailed instructions for this activity.

Assess and Reteach

Assess Progress
Have students complete the Section Assessment. Administer the *Section Quiz*.

All in One **United States and Canada Teaching Resources,** *Section Quiz,* p. 242

Reteach
If students need more instruction, have them read this section in the Reading and Vocabulary Study Guide.

Chapter 4, Section 2, **United States and Canada Reading and Vocabulary Study Guide,** pp. 45–47

Extend
Have students do library or Internet research on the economy of three southern states to make circles graphs similar to the one of the Northeast on page 112.

Answer

√ **Reading Check** in the District of Columbia

Section 2 Assessment

Key Terms
Students' sentences should reflect knowledge of each Key Term.

Target Reading Skill
The word *however* signals a contrast.

Comprehension and Critical Thinking
1. (a) Students should choose five of the following: North Carolina, South Carolina, Georgia, Florida, Arkansas, Louisiana, Mississippi, Alabama, Virginia, Texas, Maryland, Kentucky, West Virginia, Tennessee, Delaware, and Oklahoma. **(b)** The warm climate and rich soil of the coastal plains have made farming and forestry important industries. **(c)** Farmers no longer rely on one crop; some industries like textiles have grown; other industries like high technology are new; the tourism industry has drawn many people to the region.

2. (a) People are moving to the South to work in its new industries and older adults are moving there to retire. **(b)** Most industries where jobs are available are in cities. **(c)** As the southern economies become more industrialized, more people move to cities where industries are located.

Skills for Life

Objective
Learn how to read and analyze circle graphs.

Prepare to Read

Build Background Knowledge L2
Ask students to describe a circle graph and note a recent one from their studies. Then invite students to explain how a circle graph could show weather data, such as the percentage of rainy days a city has in a year. (*The circle graph could show the percentage of days with rain and the percentage without rain.*) Encourage students to sketch an example of such a graph to share with the class.

Instruct

Understanding Circle Graphs L2

Guided Instruction
- Read the opening paragraphs with students. Discuss other kinds of data a circle graph might show.

- Read the steps to analyze and interpret a circle graph as a class and write them on the board.

- Practice the skill by following the steps on page 124 as a class. Model each step by reading aloud the questions on p. 125 and answering them. Point out that the purpose of the first circle graph on the page is to show the major ethnic groups in the United States, and the whole circle represents 100 percent of the population. Identify each portion of the graph. You might conclude that although more than 50 percent of the population is white the American population is ethnically diverse.

Independent Practice
Assign *Skills for Life* and have students complete it individually.

All in One **United States and Canada Teaching Resources,** *Skills for Life,* p. 256

Understanding Circle Graphs

Chris walked across the playground with his new friend Kyung, who had just moved to Florida from Korea. Kyung looked up at the sun.

"It's really hot here. Does the entire United States get weather like this?"

"Let me think," said Chris. "In the Northwest it rains a lot, and I don't think it gets quite as hot as here. Arizona and New Mexico do, for sure. The Midwest has some really hot summers but freezing-cold winters. And then there's arctic Alaska—the summers don't get too hot there, even though the sun shines all night long. The United States gets a lot of different weather."

Boston meteorologist Mish Michaels

Meteorologists collect an amazing variety of weather information from all over the country. One way they present data on temperatures, rainfall, and other weather information is to put it into graphs.

Learn the Skill
Follow the steps below to learn how to read and interpret a circle graph.

1. **Study the elements of the circle graph.** Read the title of the graph and all the labels. Make sure that you understand the purpose of the graph.

2. **Study the information shown in the graph.** The full circle represents 100 percent, or all, of something. Identify what the circle represents.

3. **Compare the portions within the graph.** Each division of the circle represents a certain percentage, or portion, of the whole. The portions should always add up to 100 percent. Notice which piece is the biggest—that is, the highest percentage. Which piece is the smallest?

4. **Draw conclusions from the graph.** Draw conclusions about the topic of the graph. Your conclusion should attempt to explain any differences or similarities in the sizes of the pieces of the circle.

124 United States and Canada

Monitor Progress
Monitor the students doing the *Skills for Life* worksheet, checking to make sure they understand the skill steps.

Practice the Skill

Refer to the circle graph on the right and follow the steps for interpreting it.

1 After reading the title and labels of the graph, what do you think is its purpose?

2 What does the full circle represent—the circle is 100 percent of what?

3 What does each colored portion of the graph represent? Which is the largest portion? Which is the smallest portion?

4 Write a conclusion statement about the graph. Explain the meaning of the differences in the sizes of the portions.

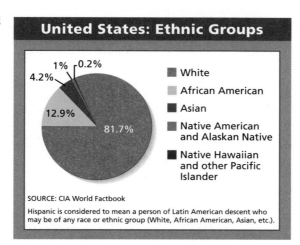

United States: Ethnic Groups

- 0.2%
- 1%
- 4.2%
- 12.9%
- 81.7%

■ White
■ African American
■ Asian
■ Native American and Alaskan Native
■ Native Hawaiian and other Pacific Islander

SOURCE: CIA World Factbook

Hispanic is considered to mean a person of Latin American descent who may be of any race or ethnic group (White, African American, Asian, etc.).

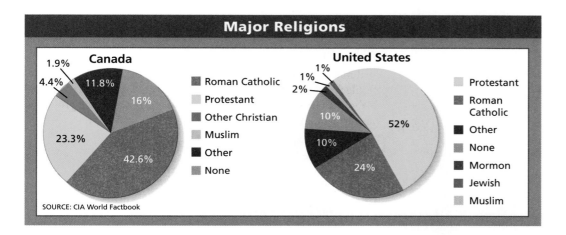

Major Religions

Canada
- 1.9%
- 4.4%
- 11.8%
- 16%
- 23.3%
- 42.6%

■ Roman Catholic
■ Protestant
■ Other Christian
■ Muslim
■ Other
■ None

United States
- 1%
- 1%
- 2%
- 10%
- 10%
- 52%
- 24%

■ Protestant
■ Roman Catholic
■ Other
■ None
■ Mormon
■ Jewish
■ Muslim

SOURCE: CIA World Factbook

Apply the Skill

Study the two circle graphs above. Following the steps in this skill, write a conclusion statement about each graph. Then compare the graphs and write a conclusion about their similarities and differences.

Assess and Reteach

Assess Progress L2
Ask students to do the Apply the Skill activity.

Reteach L1
If students are having trouble applying the skill steps, have them review the skill using the interactive Social Studies Skills Tutor CD-ROM.

 Analyzing Graphic Data, **Social Studies Skills Tutor CD-ROM**

Extend L3
To extend the lesson, have students find the circle graphs showing the major ethnic groups in the United States and Canada in the DK World Desk Reference Online. Ask them to apply the skill steps to compare the two graphs and write a conclusion about their similarities and differences.

Answer
Apply the Skill

Possible conclusion: The graphs are alike in that both show sizeable Roman Catholic and Protestant segments. In both countries a form of Christianity predominates, although Roman Catholics make up a larger portion of the population in Canada than in the United States. The graphs show larger Mormon and Jewish segments in the United States, and a slightly larger Muslim segment in Canada.

Section 3
Step-by-Step Instruction

Objectives

Social Studies
1. Read about how technology is changing life on farms.
2. Learn how changes in farming are affecting the development of cities.

Reading/Language Arts
Contrast two situations to find out how they are different.

Prepare to Read

Build Background Knowledge   L2
Tell students that the region they will study in this section has long been associated with farming. Brainstorm a list of words and phrases that come to mind when one thinks of a farm, such as crops and animals. Use an Idea Wave (TE, p. T35) to elicit ideas to write on the board. Have students note the ideas that the section supported and those it did not support as they read.

Set a Purpose for Reading   L2
■ Preview the Objectives

■ Read each statement in the *Reading Readiness Guide* aloud. Ask students to mark the statements true or false.

■ Have students discuss the statements in pairs or groups of four, then mark their worksheets again. Use the Numbered Heads participation strategy (TE, p. T36) to call on students to share their group's perspectives.

All in One United States and Canada Teaching Resources, *Reading Readiness Guide,* p. 244

Vocabulary Builder
Preview Key Terms   L2
Pronounce each Key Term, then ask students to say the word with you. Provide a simple explanation such as, "During a recession, many people cut back on buying things they don't need because they may not be making as much money as they once had."

Section 3   The Midwest
Leaving the Farm

Prepare to Read

Objectives
In this section, you will
1. Read about how technology is changing life on farms.
2. Learn how changes in farming are affecting the development of cities.

Taking Notes
As you read this section, look for details that show how changes in agriculture have caused cities to grow. Copy the chart below, and record your findings in it.

CAUSES
•
•
•
→
EVENT
Changes in agriculture
→
EFFECTS
•
•
•

Target Reading Skill

Identify Contrasts When you contrast two or more situations, you examine how they differ. In this section you will read about family farms and corporate farms. Although they both rely on technology, they differ in how they use it. As you read, list all of the differences between family farms and corporate farms.

Key Terms
• **mixed-crop farm** (mikst krahp fahrm) *n.* a farm that grows several different kinds of crops
• **recession** (rih SESH un) *n.* a decline in business activity and economic prosperity
• **corporate farm** (KAWR puh rit fahrm) *n.* a large farm that is run by a corporation, or an agricultural company

Present-day harvesting machines (below) work the land much faster than horse-driven plows once did (bottom).

Nebraska is one of several states in the middle of the country that make up the Midwest. Nebraska is a land of vast prairies and fertile farmland. Willa Cather's 1913 novel *O Pioneers!* is set on a Nebraska farm. A daughter of pioneers herself, Cather describes the farmland in great detail:

> **There are few scenes more gratifying than a spring plowing in that country, where the furrows of a single field often lie a mile in length, and the brown earth, with such a strong, clean smell, and such a power of growth . . . in it, yields itself eagerly to the plow; rolls away from the shear, not even dimming the brightness of the metal, with a soft, deep sigh of happiness. . . . The grain is so heavy that it bends toward the blade and cuts like velvet.** 》

—*Willa Cather,* O Pioneers!

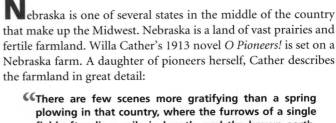

126 United States and Canada

Target Reading Skill   L2

Identify Contrasts Point out the Target Reading Skill. Explain that students can contrast two situations to identify their differences.

Model identifying contrasts by reading the *O, Pioneers* excerpt on p. 126 aloud and identifying the differences between farming in Cather's time and farming today. *(Horse-drawn farming equipment was used in Cather's* *time while tractors are used today. Also, farms today have electricity and roads leading to them unlike the farms of Cather's time.)*

Give students *Identify Contrasts.* Have them complete the activity in groups.

All in One United States and Canada Teaching Resources, *Identify Contrasts,* p. 252

Farming in the Midwest has changed since Cather's time. Tractors have replaced horse-drawn farm equipment. Electricity and roads have been brought out to rural farms. Today, technology continues to change the way people farm the land.

REGIONAL PROFILE
Focus on **Economics**

Guided Instruction ⬛2

Lead students in reading the text and reviewing the graphic material on this page. Work with the class to answer the Map and Chart Skills questions. Allow students to confer with a partner before sharing their responses.

Independent Practice

Partner students and have them each make up two questions for the other to answer. Questions should be based on the information in the Regional Profile.

REGIONAL PROFILE
Focus on **Economics**

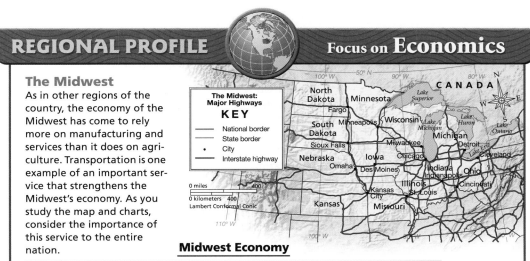

The Midwest

As in other regions of the country, the economy of the Midwest has come to rely more on manufacturing and services than it does on agriculture. Transportation is one example of an important service that strengthens the Midwest's economy. As you study the map and charts, consider the importance of this service to the entire nation.

The Midwest: Major Highways

KEY

— National border
— State border
• City
— Interstate highway

0 miles 400
0 kilometers 400
Lambert Conformal Conic

Midwest Economy

Agriculture	Fishing, forestry, and agriculture (including corn, soybeans, wheat, hay, hogs, beef cattle, and barley)
Industry	Construction, manufacturing, and mining
Services	Community, business, and personal services; finance; government and trade; transportation, communication, and utilities

SOURCE: U.S. Bureau of Economic Analysis

Pie chart: Industry 43%, Services 52%, Agriculture 5%

■ Industry
■ Services
■ Agriculture

Chicago, Major Transportation Hub

Airport	O'Hare Airport is the nation's busiest. A plane takes off every minute.
Railroads	More than seven railroads serve Chicago, the nation's rail center.
Highways	I-90 from Seattle, I-80 from New York, I-55 from the South all cross in Chicago.
Rivers and waterways	The Chicago River, Chicago Canal, and Lake Michigan carry commercial shipping traffic.

SOURCE: Chicago Department of Aviation

Map and Chart Skills

1. **Explain** Which sector of the Midwest economy is the biggest?
2. **Infer** There is a general trend for people to move from rural to urban areas. Do you think this is true in the Midwest as well? Explain why.
3. **Analyze** What feature of its geographic setting makes the Midwest an important area for transportation?

 Use Web Code **Ihe-4413** for **DK World Desk Reference Online.**

Chapter 4 Section 3 **127**

Answers

Map and Chart Skills

1. Industry
2. Yes; as more people take jobs in businesses and industry, they move to urban areas where these economic activities are located.
3. It is in the center of the nation and it is near the Great Lakes, Mississippi River, and other bodies of water that are used for transportation.

Go Online PHSchool.com Students can find more information about this topic on the DK World Desk Reference Online.

Vocabulary Builder

Use the information below to teach students this section's high-use words.

High-Use Word	Definition and Sample Sentence
technique, p. 128	*n.* method of accomplishing a desired aim The new **technique** was more effective than the old method.
prosper, p. 128	*v.* to achieve economic success The farmers **prospered** when they brought in a good crop.
efficiently, p. 129	*adj.* bringing about a result with the least waste of time She finished one project quickly and **efficiently** moved on to the next.
ethnic, p. 130	*adj.* relating to large groups of people who share a common cultural background His **ethnic** background was a mix of Swedish and Native American.

Technology Changes Farm Life

L2

Guided Reading

- **Vocabulary Builder** Clarify the high-use words **technique, prosper,** and **efficient** before reading.

- Read Technology Changes Farm Life using the ReQuest procedure (TE, p. T35).

- Have students name the technological advances that helped people build farms in the Midwest. *(steel plows, the windmill, barbed wire, and drilling equipment)*

- Discuss with students the reasons for the decline of the family farm. *(Farmers borrowed money from banks to buy more land and equipment. In the 1980s, a recession took place, decreasing the demand for farm products and increasing loan interest rates. Farmers were unable to pay loans so many sold or left their farms.)*

Answers

Graph Skills **Describe** decreasing from 1910 to 1990 and increasing slightly from 1990 to 2000 **Analyze Information** Today farming employs less than four million people, far less than it employed in the early 1900s.

Technology Changes Farm Life

The Midwest is often called the heartland because it is the agricultural center of our nation. The soil is rich, and the climate is suitable for producing corn, wheat, soybeans, and livestock. Inventions such as the steel plow, the windmill, and barbed wire helped settlers carve out farms on the plains. Drilling equipment helped to make wells deep enough to reach water. These tools also helped make farms productive. Technological advances continue to improve farming techniques today.

Family Farms Decline Until the 1980s, small family farms were common in the Midwest. Many of these farms were mixed-crop farms. On a **mixed-crop farm,** several different kinds of crops are grown. This was a sensible way for farmers to work. If one crop failed, the farm had others to fall back on.

In the 1960s and 1970s, family farms prospered. The world population was rising, and demand for American farm products was high. Farmers felt that they could increase their business if they enlarged their farms. To build bigger farms, farmers bought more land and equipment. But all of this cost money. Many farmers borrowed money from local banks.

In the early 1980s, there was a countrywide **recession** (rih SESH un), or a downturn in business activity. The demand for farm products decreased. Then, interest rates on bank loans increased. As a result, many farmers were not able to make enough money to pay their loans. Some families sold their farms. More than one million American farmers have left the land since 1980.

■ Graph Skills

In the early 1900s, about one-third of the workers in the United States worked on farms, such as the Illinois farm shown below. **Describe** What is the pattern of the number of farm workers shown in the graph? **Analyze Information** What does the information on the graph tell you about farming today?

Number of U.S. Farm Workers, 1910–2000

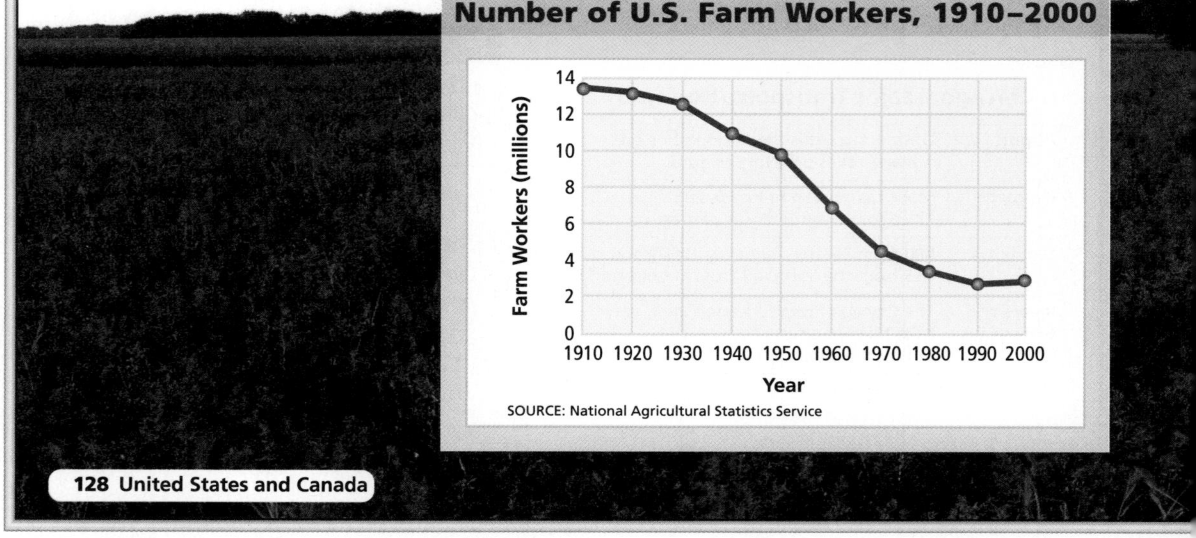

SOURCE: National Agricultural Statistics Service

128 United States and Canada

Differentiated Instruction

For English Language Learners L2
Encourage native speakers to help non-native speakers use context clues to clarify words with multiple meanings in the Regional Profile, such as *rich* and *service.*

For Special Needs Students L1
Some students may require additional help to read and understand the tables illustrated in the Regional Profile. Have students work in pairs to complete *Reading a Table,* then as a class review the tables and discuss the process of determining the answers.

All in One **United States and Canada Teaching Resources,** *Reading a Table,* p. 266

Corporate Farms Rise A small number of agricultural companies bought many of these family farms. When these agricultural companies combine several small family farms into one large farm, it is called a **corporate farm.** Large corporations can afford to buy the expensive land and equipment that modern farming requires. These large farms are run efficiently and make a profit.

Corporate farmers rely on machines and computers to do much of the work. This means that corporate farms employ fewer workers. Kansas offers a good example of corporate farming, since it has fewer workers and larger farms. In Kansas, 90 percent of the land is farmland, but fewer than 1 percent of the people are farmers. Most of the people in Kansas live and work in cities such as Wichita.

Small family farms do still exist in the Midwest. But most of them struggle to earn enough money for supporting a family. Family farmers usually need to have another job as well. Many people look to the cities for more job opportunities.

√ Reading Check **Why did so many families sell or leave their farms?**

Identify Contrasts How are corporate farms different from family farms?

Chapter 4 Section 3 **129**

ᵔᵒ Target Reading Skill   L2

Identify Contrasts As a follow up, ask students to answer the Target Reading Skill question in the Student Edition. *(Family farms are run by a small group of people, while corporate farms are run by large corporations. Family farms usually grow a smaller amount of crops than corporate farms. They also rely more on human labor while corporate farms often rely more on machines and computers to do the work.)*

Guided Instruction (continued)

■ Ask students **How might corporate farms benefit consumers?** *(Products grown and raised on corporate farms can be sold at a cheaper price because it costs less money to produce them with fewer workers to pay and more efficient farming equipment.)*

Independent Practice

Have students create the Taking Notes graphic organizer on a blank piece of paper. Use the *Cause and Effect Chart* transparency to model how to begin filling it in.

📖 **United States and Canada Transparencies,** *Transparency B7: Cause and Effect Chart*

Monitor Progress

While students work on their charts, circulate to make sure individuals are choosing the correct information to include. Provide assistance as needed.

Differentiated Instruction

For Advanced Readers   L3
Have students research a list of inventions that helped to change the nature of farming. Ask students to make a time line showing the dates of six of the most important inventions. Have students write a brief summary explaining how this technology affected farming. Use the *Time Line* transparency to model how to make a time line.

📖 **United States and Canada Transparencies,** *Transparency B20: Timeline*

For Less Proficient Readers   L1
Pair these students with more proficient readers and have them create an outline of the material as they read. Tell students to use the headings in the section as a framework.

Answer

√ Reading Check There was a recession and the demand for farm products decreased while interest rates increased. Many farmers could not make their payments on loans and so they were forced to sell or leave their farms.

Cities Develop in the Midwest L2

Guided Instruction

- **Vocabulary Builder** Clarify the high-use word **ethnic** before reading.

- Have students read Cities Develop in the Midwest. As students read, circulate to make sure individuals can answer the Reading Check question.

- Ask **What are some important cities in the Midwest?** (*Chicago, Detroit, St. Louis, Minneapolis, St. Paul*)

- Ask **How has being located near a body of water been important in the growth and development of these cities?** (*In some cases, farm products were shipped to other states via the Great Lakes. In others, people have used the lakes and rivers near these cities as points of departure. These activities have drawn people to the cities and helped them develop.*)

Links

Read the **Links Across the World** on this page. Ask students **Why do you think that the construction of buildings such as the Sears Tower did not occur until the twentieth century?** (*In order to construct such tall buildings, advances in architecture, construction, and materials were required. These technological advances did not occur until the twentieth century.*)

Cities Develop in the Midwest

Many Midwestern cities began as centers of transportation and processing. Farmers from the surrounding area would send their harvests and livestock to nearby cities to be processed and shipped east. The largest processing city was Chicago, Illinois.

Chicago Located on Lake Michigan, Chicago was surrounded by prairies and farms in the mid-1800s. Farmers sent corn, wheat, cattle, and hogs to the mills and meat-packing plants in the city. Here the raw materials were turned into foods and shipped east by way of the Great Lakes. When railroads were built, Chicago really boomed. By the late 1800s, it had become a steel-making and manufacturing center. What was one of the most important manufactured products made in Chicago? You probably guessed it: farm equipment.

Today, Chicago is the biggest city in the heartland. It is known for its ethnic diversity and lively culture. It is the hub of major transportation routes including highways, railroads, airlines, and shipping routes. Chicago is also the home of the first steel skyscraper—the Home Insurance Company Building—and many other architectural wonders. For a bird's-eye view of Chicago, go to the top of the Sears Tower, one of the tallest buildings in the world.

Links Across The World

Higher and Higher Until 1996, Chicago's Sears Tower, at 1,454 feet (443 meters), was the world's tallest building. The photo below shows the view from the Sears Tower. The twin Petronas Towers in Malaysia then held the title. In 2004, the Taipei 101 building in Taipei, Taiwan, gained the title of world's tallest building, topping out at 1,671 feet (509 meters). Today, even taller skyscrapers are being planned in cities around the world.

130 United States and Canada

Differentiated Instruction

For Gifted and Talented L3
Have students read about the Gateway Arch in the *Enrichment* worksheet. From the list provided, students should select another American memorial or monument to research. Then have them write a report on the site and present it to the class.

 All in One United States and Canada Teaching Resources, *Enrichment,* p. 255

For Less Proficient Readers L1
Remind students to read the captions that appear with photographs or other visual material. Direct students' attention to the captions in this section. Have them reread them to find one noun that names the object in the photo. When students are finished, ask them to describe each item without referring to the caption.

Major Rail Routes of the Late 1800s

MAP★MASTER™
Skills Activity

KEY
- — Major railroads
- — National border
- — State border
- • City or town

0 miles 500
0 kilometers 500
Lambert Azimuthal Equal Area

Human-Environment Interaction In the late 1800s, the midwestern cities that grew the fastest were the ones located on railroad routes. Chicago became a railroad junction—a place where a number of railroad lines meet. **List** Locate Chicago on the map and list how many railroad routes met there.
Draw Conclusions Why was Chicago's location important to its becoming a railroad junction?

Go Online
PHSchool.com Use Web Code lhp-4443 for step-by-step map skills practice.

Detroit and St. Louis Two other large cities in the Midwest are Detroit, Michigan, and St. Louis, Missouri. They have both played an important role in the country's history. Why do you think Detroit is called the Motor City? You will find the headquarters of America's automobile manufacturers here. General Motors, Ford, and Daimler Chrysler have their main offices and factories in the city.

Covered wagons, not cars, used to roll through St. Louis. Located on the Mississippi River, this city was the starting point for pioneers heading west. Its location on the banks of the Mississippi River made it an important city in the days before railroads. Today, a huge stainless steel arch beside the river marks St. Louis as the Gateway to the West. St. Louis is also a banking and commercial center.

DISCOVERY CHANNEL SCHOOL Video
Find out about the powerful Mississippi River.

Chapter 4 Section 3 **131**

Skills for Life Skills Mini Lesson

Using a Special Purpose Map

1. Explain that there are many different types of special purpose maps. Thematic maps focus on a specific topic, such as transportation routes. The key and the map title can help students identify the purpose of a map.

2. Help students practice the skill by reading the title of the map on p. 131 and identifying what the symbols in the key represent.

3. Have students apply the skill by tracing and describing two possible railroad routes from New York City to Denver.

Guided Instruction (continued)

- Ask **Why was St. Louis considered to be the "Gateway to the West?"** (*The city was the starting point for pioneers moving west.*)

- Ask students **How do you think the decline of the family farm has affected cities?** (*Some people who had to sell their farms are moving to the cities to find jobs, which is increasing the population of Midwestern cities.*)

Independent Practice
Have students complete the graphic organizer by filling in additional causes and effects.

Monitor Progress
- Show *Section Support Transparency USC 56* and ask students to check their cause and effect charts individually. Go over key concepts and clarify key vocabulary as needed.

  📖 **United States and Canada Transparencies,** *Section Reading Support Transparency USC 56*

- Tell students to fill in the last column of the *Reading Readiness Guide.* Probe for what they learned that confirms or invalidates each statement.

  All in One United States and Canada Teaching Resources, *Reading Readiness Guide,* p. 244

DISCOVERY SCHOOL Video
Show students *Taming the Mississippi* and ask **What do people who live along the river use to try to control flooding?** (*levees*)

Answers
MAP★MASTER Skills Activity **List** Four railroads met in Chicago. **Draw Conclusions** Chicago's location in the middle of the country and on Lake Michigan allowed goods to be shipped out of the city after they arrived by railroad.

Go Online PHSchool.com Students may practice their map skills using the interactive online version of this map.

Assess and Reteach

Assess Progress L2

Have students complete the Section Assessment. Administer the *Section Quiz*.

All in One **United States and Canada Teaching Resources,** *Section Quiz,* p. 246

Reteach L1

If students need more instruction, have them read this section in the Reading and Vocabulary Study Guide.

Chapter 4, Section 3, **The United States and Canada Reading and Vocabulary Study Guide,** pp. 48–50

Extend L3

If you have not already done so, show students *Taming the Mississippi* to help them learn more about this important transportation route that flows through the Midwest.

The Geography of the United States, **World Studies Video Program**

Answer

✔ **Reading Check** The world's first skyscraper was located in Chicago.

Section 3 Assessment

Key Terms
Students' sentences should reflect knowledge of each Key Term.

Target Reading Skill
There were more prosperous family farms in the 1960s and 1970s. Farming technology has advanced since the 1980s so fewer workers are needed on farms.

Comprehension and Critical Thinking
1. (a) It is the agricultural center of the United States. **(b)** There was a recession that led to decreased demand for farm products and an increase in interest rates on farm loans. **(c)** Possible answer: There will probably continue to be fewer opportunities for farmers to own their own small farms.

2. (a) They began as centers of transportation and processing. **(b)** They helped cities grow by allowing them to ship the goods they produced faster and to more places. **(c)** It is in the middle of the country and on Lake Michigan so its location makes it a good transportation hub for people and goods.

Inside the Mall of America in Minnesota

The Twin Cities Minneapolis is the largest city in Minnesota, followed by St. Paul. Together, they are known as the Twin Cities because they are next to each other on the Mississippi River. The Twin Cities were once the flour-milling center of the United States. Pillsbury and Company was founded there in 1872. Today, publishing, medical, computer, and art businesses flourish there. The city's suburbs have replaced hundreds of square miles of fertile land once used for farming.

✔ **Reading Check** **Where was the world's first skyscraper located?**

Section 3 Assessment

Key Terms
Review the key terms at the beginning of this section. Use each term in a sentence that explains its meaning.

Target Reading Skill
What are two ways that farming in the 1960s and 1970s was different from farming since the 1980s?

Comprehension and Critical Thinking
1. (a) Explain Why is the Midwest called the nation's heartland?

(b) Explore the Main Idea Why did family farmers face hard times in the 1980s?
(c) Predict What do you think the future holds for family farmers?
2. (a) Recall How did some midwestern cities get their starts?
(b) Identify Effects How did railroads affect the growth of midwestern cities?
(c) Draw Inferences How might Chicago's location affect its growth today?

Writing Activity
Suppose that you are a farmer and you have decided to sell your farm and move to a city. Write a letter to a friend explaining your decision.

For: An activity on the automobile industry
Visit: PHSchool.com
Web Code: lhd-4403

132 United States and Canada

Writing Activity

Use the *Rubric for Assessing a Writing Assignment* to evaluate students' letters.

All in One **United States and Canada Teaching Resources,** *Rubric for Assessing a Writing Assignment,* p. 273

Go Online PHSchool.com Typing in the Web code when prompted will bring students directly to detailed instructions for this activity.

Prepare to Read

Objectives
In this section you will
1. Learn about the natural resources of the West.
2. Read about the challenges facing the urban West.

Taking Notes
As you read this section, look for ways that natural resources are used and conserved in the West. Copy the table below, and record your findings in it.

Resources of the West	
Using Resources	**Conserving Resources**
•	•
•	•
•	•

Target Reading Skill

Make Comparisons Comparing two or more situations enables you to see how they are alike. As you read this section, compare how different parts of the West use and manage resources. Write the information in your Taking Notes table.

Key Terms
- **forty-niner** (FAWRT ee NY nur) *n.* the nickname for a miner who took part in the California Gold Rush of 1849
- **responsible development** (rih SPAHN suh bul dih VEL up munt) *n.* balancing the needs of the environment, community, and economy
- **mass transit** (mas TRAN sit) *n.* a system of subways, buses, and commuter trains used to transport large numbers of people

Objectives

Social Studies
1. Learn about the natural resources of the West.
2. Read about the challenges facing the urban West.

Reading/Language Arts
Make comparisons to see how two situations are the same.

Prepare to Read

Build Background Knowledge   L2
Tell students that they will learn about how the people of the West are trying to use their natural resources wisely. Call on volunteers to describe some of their own recycling or conservation efforts. Discuss how it could make a difference if everyone in the country made efforts to conserve natural resources. Use the Give One, Get One participation strategy (TE, p. T37) to elicit student responses.

Set a Purpose for Reading L2
- Preview the Objectives
- Form students into pairs or groups of four. Distribute the *Reading Readiness Guide*. Ask students to fill in the first two columns of the chart. Use the Numbered Heads participation strategy (TE, p. T36) to call on students to share one piece of information they already know and one piece of information they want to know.

All in One United States and Canada Teaching Resources, *Reading Readiness Guide,* p. 248

Vocabulary Builder
Preview Key Terms   L2
Pronounce each Key Term, then ask students to say the word with you. Provide a simple explanation such as, "Forty-niners were people who went to California to find gold in 1849."

From colonial days to the present, Americans have been drawn westward. Over time, explorers and settlers have pushed out the farthest boundaries of the western frontier. In the 1780s, the frontier was considered to be the land as far west as the Mississippi River. Twenty years later, it included all of the land to the Rocky Mountains. By the 1850s, the frontier was the region that we now think of as the West—the land from the Rocky Mountains to the Pacific Ocean. By the 1900s, it also included Alaska and Hawaii.

Although the boundaries of the West have changed dramatically over the years, one factor has remained the same: People are attracted westward by the promise of the land.

Rocky Mountains, Colorado

Target Reading Skill L2

Make Comparisons Point out the Target Reading Skill. Tell students that they can make comparisons to find the similarities between two situations.

Model the skill by reading this page aloud and identifying the similarity between the West in the 1780s and the West today. (*Its land still attracts people to move there.*)

Give students *Make Comparisons*. Have them complete the activity in groups.

All in One United States and Canada Teaching Resources, *Make Comparisons,* p. 253

Instruct

Guided Instruction L2
Ask students to study the Regional Profile map and charts and read the text on this page. Work with the class to answer the Map and Chart Skills questions. Allow students to discuss their responses with a partner before sharing answers.

Independent Practice
Display *Color Transparency USC 29: The United States: Annual Precipitation and Prevailing Winds.* Ask students to compare and contrast the amount of precipitation that falls in the West with the amount that falls in the other United States regions.

📖 **United States and Canada Transparencies,** *Color Transparency USC 29: The United States: Annual Precipitation and Prevailing Winds*

Answers

Map and Chart Skills

1. The coasts of Washington and Oregon receive the most rain.

2. Washington

3. Some issues that might be addressed are water pollution and which bodies of water can be used to produce hydroelectric power.

Go Online *PHSchool.com* Students can find more information about this topic on the DK World Desk Reference Online.

Natural Resources of the West

For well over 400 years, people have been drawn to the West by its wealth of natural resources. The Spanish had already settled in the Southwest when the Pilgrims arrived in New England in the 1620s. After Lewis and Clark's exploration of the Louisiana Territory in the early 1800s, more people moved westward.

REGIONAL PROFILE
Focus on Geography

The West
Water is an important resource of the West—more important even than gold. Farmers have always needed large quantities of water to irrigate their lands. Today, as large cities and their populations grow, people are demanding more and more water for everyday use. Study the map and charts, and think about how water availability and use are shaping this region.

California Cropland

Nonirrigated 11%

Irrigated 89%

SOURCE: National Agriculture Statistics Service

Leading Hydroelectric Power-Producing States, 2006

States	Thousands of Megawatt Hours
Washington	14,650
Oregon	7,854
California	8,088
New York*	4,173
Alabama*	1,913
Idaho	1,736
Tennessee*	1,557

SOURCE: Energy Information Administration, US Department of Energy
*not a western state

The West: Precipitation
KEY

Inches	Millimeters
More than 59	More than 1,499
40–59	1,000–1,499
20–39	500–999
10–19	250–499
Less than 10	Less than 250

— National border
— State border

Map and Chart Skills

1. **Locate** Which areas of the West receive the most rain?

2. **Identify** What state produces the most hydroelectric power?

3. **Analyze** There is a category of law devoted to water use. What issues might be addressed by lawyers who specialize in water use?

Go Online *PHSchool.com* Use Web Code lhe-4414 to access the **DK World Desk Reference Online.**

Vocabulary Builder

Use the information below to teach students this section's high-use words.

High-Use Word	Definition and Sample Sentence
pollution, p. 136	*n.* the condition of being unclean; contamination **Pollution** made the lake too dirty to swim in.
site, p. 136	*n.* location The carpenter arrived at the work **site.**
junction, p. 136	*n.* a place where two roads or rivers meet A stop sign was put in at the **junction** of the two roads.

Mineral Resources Before gold was discovered in California, Native Americans and Spanish settlers lived in the region. With the California Gold Rush, the population exploded. The sleepy port of San Francisco boomed into a prosperous city. Its population grew from 800 people in 1848 to 25,000 just two years later. The first miners and prospectors of the Gold Rush were called **forty-niners** because they arrived in 1849. They arrived, bought supplies, and headed off to the Sierra Nevada expecting to strike it rich. Few of them succeeded, but many remained in the West.

A gold strike in 1858 in Colorado led to the founding of the city of Denver. Similar events took place in Nevada, Idaho, and Montana in the 1860s. Further discoveries of valuable minerals, including silver and copper, drew more and more people to the West. A mining town formed around each new discovery.

All of these new settlers needed homes, and the timber to build them with was in large supply in the the Pacific Northwest. After the Civil War, logging camps, sawmills, and paper mills sprang up in Washington, Oregon, and northern California. At first, the resources of the West seemed unlimited. The use of these resources created wealth and many jobs. However, it also brought with it new challenges.

Learn more about the California Gold Rush.

Show students *The Gold Rush* and ask **In what state did a gold rush similar to that of California's take place?** (*Alaska*)

The Cost of Mining
Merchants and traders supplied miners with food, clothing, and tools. Supplies were hauled from the river ports to the mining camps by wagons and mules. This caused increased prices. With the population boom and the difficulty of getting supplies up to the camps, the cost of living for miners was high.
Conclude *Was trying to strike it rich worth the amount of time, effort, and money needed? Explain your answer.*

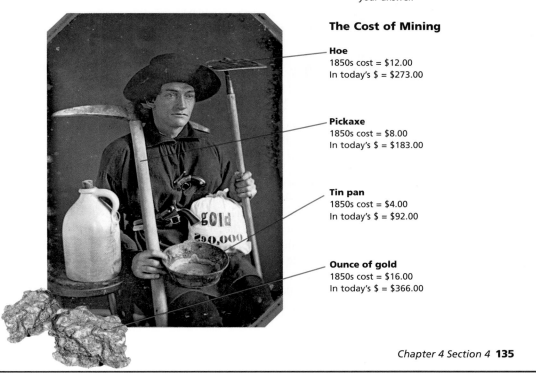

The Cost of Mining

Hoe
1850s cost = $12.00
In today's $ = $273.00

Pickaxe
1850s cost = $8.00
In today's $ = $183.00

Tin pan
1850s cost = $4.00
In today's $ = $92.00

Ounce of gold
1850s cost = $16.00
In today's $ = $366.00

Chapter 4 Section 4 **135**

Natural Resources of the West L2

Guided Instruction
- **Vocabulary Builder** Clarify the high-use word **pollution** before reading.

- Read Natural Resources of the West with students, using the Choral Reading strategy (TE, p. T34).

- Ask **What useful minerals are found in the West?** (*gold, silver, copper*) **What are some useful non-mineral resources found in the West?** (*timber and water*)

- Lead a discussion on the ways people in the West are addressing the challenge of managing resources. (*Logging companies are replacing trees by planting new ones; power plants are using advanced technology to control pollution; the number of campers is being limited in national parks such as Yosemite.*)

Independent Practice
Have students create the Taking Notes graphic organizer on a blank piece of paper. Ask them to begin filling in the ways resources are used and conserved in the West. Fill in the first detail for each column with them to model how to choose the correct details.

Monitor Progress
As students work on their graphic organizers, circulate to make sure individuals comprehend key concepts. Provide assistance as needed.

Differentiated Instruction

For Less Proficient Readers L1
To ensure that students understand the Regional Profile on the previous page, students may need further instruction on how to read a table. Distribute *Reading a Table* and have students complete the activity in pairs. It may also be helpful to explain the definition of a megawatt hour.

All in One United States and Canada Teaching Resources, *Reading a Table* p. 266

For Gifted and Talented L3
To enhance students understanding of the Regional Profile on the previous page, have students choose three states from the table and do Internet or library research to find the sources of hydroelectric power in that state. Have them present their findings in a table.

Answer
Conclude Possible answers: Yes, it was worth it if you ended up finding gold; No, it was not worth it because the chance of striking it rich was so slim.

The Urban West

Guided Instruction

- **Vocabulary Builder** Clarify the high-use words **function** and **site** before reading.

- Read the Urban West as a class. As students read, circulate and make sure individuals can answer the Reading Check question.

- Ask **How has the work people do to earn a living changed in the West?** (*Most people are no longer farmers, loggers, and miners; they now have jobs in businesses in the cities.*)

- Ask **What is the second most populated city in the United States?** (*Los Angeles, California*)

- Have students brainstorm ways in which the Western states might better meet the challenge of air pollution. Conduct an Idea Wave (TE, p. T35) to generate a list of possibilities. (*Possible answers: build more mass transit systems; limit the size of cars people can own; develop better energy-saving vehicles.*)

Old Faithful is the best-known geyser in Yellowstone National Park, Wyoming.

Managing Resources California's population continued to grow after the Gold Rush. To meet the demand for new houses, loggers leveled many forests. Engineers built dams to pipe water through the mountains to coastal cities. Next to the dams, they built hydroelectric plants. Cities like San Francisco got water and power this way, but the dams flooded whole valleys of the Sierras.

To save parts of the West as natural wilderness, Congress created several national parks and forests. Yet these parks are not trouble-free. California's Yosemite (yoh SEM uh tee) National Park now gets so many visitors that it suffers from traffic jams and air pollution in the summer. Some of the scenic views in Montana's Glacier National Park are also reduced by hazy skies.

Some westerners are working on **responsible development,** or balancing the needs of the environment, the community, and the economy. For example, Yosemite now limits the number of campers in the park. Dam building has stopped. In addition, some logging companies are working to preserve the environment by planting new trees to replace the ones that have been cut down. Advanced technology, such as power plants with better pollution-control devices, can help meet energy and environmental needs.

✓ **Reading Check** What caused California's population to grow in the 1800s?

The Urban West

Most westerners today are not miners, farmers, or loggers. Rather, they live and work in cities. Their challenge is to figure out how to use natural resources wisely.

Portland, Oregon "Your town or mine?" two land developers asked each other in 1845. They were at the same site and predicted the development of a major port city. Located near the junction of the Willamette and Columbia rivers, how could they fail? Francis W. Pettygrove of Portland, Maine, won the coin toss. He named the site after his hometown in the East.

Portland became a trade center for lumber, fur, grain, salmon, and wool. In the 1930s, new dams produced cheap electricity. Portland attracted many manufacturing industries.

136 United States and Canada

Skills Mini Lesson

Distinguishing Fact and Opinion

1. Introduce the skill by explaining that a fact can be proved true, while an opinion, which is an individual belief, cannot be proven.

2. To practice the skill, write the following statements on the board and have students determine which is a fact and which is an opinion: *San Jose is California's most beautiful city. (opinion) Many people moved to Los Angeles to work in the movie industry. (fact)*

3. To apply the skill, have each student write one fact and one opinion on a separate slip of paper, then switch with a partner and determine which is which.

Answer

✓ **Reading Check** The Gold Rush caused the population to soar.

Seattle, Washington   The port city of Seattle was founded in the early 1850s. It was named after a Native American leader who helped the area's first settlers. Seattle has grown into a bustling city of more than half a million people.

Years of unchecked growth eventually led to problems. In the 1960s, a group of local citizens started a campaign to revitalize the local economy. A bridge was built across Lake Washington to help residents commute. Sewage was cleaned up from Lake Washington, and many neighborhood parks were created. The group also kept Pike Place Market from being destroyed. It is the oldest continuously run market in the country. Farmers have sold their crops and produce there since 1907.

San Jose, California   Urban sprawl is a local challenge in San Jose. The area around San Jose was once known for its beautiful orchards and farms. Now it is called Silicon Valley because it is a part of the computer industry.

San Jose's most valuable resource is now its people. They come from all parts of the world. The greater population density has created crowded freeways and air pollution. To counter these problems, San Jose has built a light-rail mass transit system. A **mass transit** system replaces individual cars with energy-saving buses or trains.

Make Comparisons
What do Portland and Seattle have in common?

■ **Graph Skills**

The Internet boom of the 1990s saw between 7,000 and 10,000 Internet companies start up. It began to decline dramatically by the beginning of 2000.
Describe In what year did the most Internet companies shut down?
Predict If the number of company shutdowns continues, what would be the effect on urban sprawl?

Internet Company Shutdowns

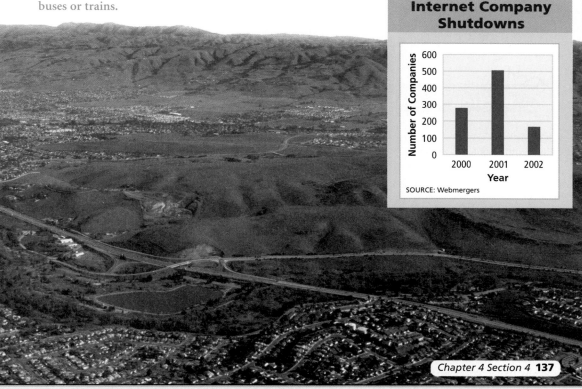

SOURCE: Webmergers

→ Target Reading Skill   **L2**

Make Comparisons As a follow up, ask students to answer the Target Reading Skill question in the Student Edition. *(Both Portland and Seattle are port cities.)*

Independent Practice
Tell students to complete their graphic organizers with more information about using and conserving resources.

Monitor Progress
■ Show *Section Reading Support Transparency USC 57* and ask students to check their graphic organizers individually. Go over key concepts and clarify key vocabulary as needed.

▱ **United States and Canada Transparencies,** *Section Reading Support Transparency USC 57*

■ Tell students to fill in the last column of their *Reading Readiness Guides.* Ask students to evaluate if what they learned was what they had expected to learn.

All in One United States and Canada Teaching Resources, *Reading Readiness Guide,* p. 248

┌ **Differentiated Instruction**

For Special Needs Students   **L1**
Have students read the section as they listen to the recorded version on the Student Edition on Audio CD. Check for comprehension by asking students to write one sentence about each city.

◉ Chapter 4, Section 4, **Student Edition on Audio CD**

For Gifted and Talented   **L3**
Assign students the *Making a Model River* activity. As they work, ask students to relate the project to the use of rivers in the West.

All in One United States and Canada Teaching Resources, *Activity Shop Lab: Making a Model River,* pp. 261–262

Answers
Graph Skills **Describe** 2001
Predict Urban sprawl might slow down.

Assess and Reteach

Assess Progress L2
Have students complete the Section Assessment. Administer the *Section Quiz*.

All in One **United States and Canada Teaching Resources,** *Section Quiz*, p. 250

Reteach L1
If students need more instruction, have them read this section in the Reading and Vocabulary Study Guide

📖 Chapter 4, Section 4, **United States and Canada Reading and Vocabulary Study Guide,** pp. 51–53

Extend L3
Have students complete the *Small Group Activity* to increase their understanding of the importance of water as a resource in the West and its various uses.

All in One **United States and Canada Teaching Resources,** *Small Group Activity: Simulation: Town Meeting on Water Use,* pp. 257–260

Answer

✓ Reading Check San Jose needed a mass transit system to help address its problems with pollution and highway crowding.

Section 4 Assessment

Key Terms
Students' sentences should reflect knowledge of each Key Term.

🎯 Target Reading Skill
In the 1780s, Los Angeles was a small Mexican village. Today it is the second most populated city in the United States, and it is a center for banking, the aircraft industry, and the entertainment industry.

Comprehension and Critical Thinking
1. (a) the Gold Rush **(b)** Many people who came to the West during the Gold Rush stayed and established cities. **(c)** More people means the use of more resources. People in the West had to find ways to conserve and protect resources.

2. (a) A developer named it after his hometown of Portland, Maine. **(b)** Trees and the Columbia and Willamette rivers made it a good location for a city. **(c)** Possible answers: Trees that are cut for lumber may be replaced by newly planted trees; limits may be placed on fishing; pollution of the rivers may be prohibited.

Los Angeles, California Los Angeles is another California city whose people are its greatest resource. It has grown from a small Mexican village in the 1780s to the second-most-populated city in the United States. The Gold Rush and the building of the transcontinental railroad helped the city grow.

By the 1920s, the movie, petroleum, and manufacturing industries all brought more people to the city. Today, Los Angeles is a center for banking and aircraft manufacturing. But, it is most noted for its entertainment industry. In addition to the Hollywood movie industry, the headquarters of many of the country's recording companies and radio and television networks are located here. Many broadcasts are in foreign languages, especially Spanish. Hispanics are the largest ethnic group in the city, followed by Asians.

The Hollywood sign hovers over Los Angeles, California, and is a reminder that the city is home to the entertainment industry. Cameramen (lower photo) shoot a movie on a local set.

✓ Reading Check Why did San Jose need a mass transit system?

✦ Section 4 Assessment

Key Terms
Review the key terms at the beginning of this section. Use each term in a sentence that explains its meaning.

🎯 Target Reading Skill
Compare Los Angeles today to what it was like in the 1780s.

Comprehension and Critical Thinking
1. (a) Recall What event took place in California in 1849?
(b) Identify Cause and Effect How did that event lead to the formation of towns and cities?

(c) Infer How did the population explosion affect the West's natural resources?
2. (a) Explain How did Portland, Oregon, get its name?
(b) Summarize What natural resources made Portland a good location for a city?
(c) Predict How might these resources be protected today?

Writing Activity
What natural resources are there in your community? In what ways do people use these natural resources? Write a paragraph describing the natural resources in your area and how they are used.

For: An activity on Denver
Visit: PHSchool.com
Web Code: lhd-4404

138 United States and Canada

Writing Activity
Use the *Rubric for Assessing a Writing Assignment* to evaluate students' paragraphs.

All in One **United States and Canada Teaching Resources,** *Rubric for Assessing a Writing Assignment*, p. 273

Go Online *PHSchool.com* Typing in the Web code when prompted will bring students directly to detailed instructions for this activity.

Review and Assessment

Review and Assessment

Review Chapter Content

■ Review and revisit the major themes of this chapter by having students relate each bulleted statement in the Chapter Summary to a Guiding Question. Use the Think-Write-Pair-Share participation strategy (TE, p. T36) to have students determine the number of the Guiding Question that relates to each statement and then have students discuss their classifications with their partners. Refer to page 1 in the Student Edition for the text of the Guiding Questions.

■ Assign *Vocabulary Development* for students to review Key Terms.

All in One United States and Canada Teaching Resources, *Vocabulary Development*, p. 271

◆ Chapter Summary

Section 1: The Northeast
- A chain of cities runs from Boston, Massachusetts, to Washington, D.C.
- The Northeast is the most densely populated region of the United States.
- Many immigrants entered the United States through one of the ports in the Northeast.

Haymarket in Boston, Massachusetts

Section 2: The South
- The South's warm climate and abundant rainfall make it suitable for growing many crops.
- Drilling, mining, fishing, and forestry are important industries in the South.
- Many people have moved from rural towns to the cities for better job opportunities.

Section 3: The Midwest
- Technology has changed the way that American farms operate.
- Many small family farms have closed because they are unprofitable.
- Many Midwestern cities got their start as places that processed and shipped farm products.

Section 4: The West
- The West has a wide array of natural resources.
- Managing these natural resources is an important task for people in the West.
- People are some of the urban West's most valuable resources.

◆ Key Terms

Use each key term below in a sentence that shows the meaning of the term.

1. commute
2. megalopolis
3. population density
4. petrochemical
5. industrialization
6. Sun Belt
7. mixed-crop farm
8. recession
9. corporate farm
10. forty-niner
11. mass transit

Chapter 4 **139**

┌ Vocabulary Builder

Revisit this chapter's high-use words:

hub	decade	ethnic
institution	technique	pollution
innumerable	prosper	site
consume	efficiently	junction

Ask students to review the definitions they recorded on their *Word Knowledge* worksheet.

All in One United States and Canada Teaching Resources, *Word Knowledge*, p. 254

Consider allowing students to earn extra credit if they use the words in their answers to the questions in the Chapter Review and Assessment. The words must be used correctly and in a natural context to win the extra points.

Answers

Key Terms
1–11. Students' sentences should reflect knowledge of each Key Term.

Review and Assessment

Comprehension and Critical Thinking

12. (a) New York, Boston, and Philadelphia **(b)** Answers will vary depending on cities selected. Possible answer: Boston and Philadelphia are both historic cities. Boston is known for its colleges and universities. It is a medical, science, and technology center while Philadelphia is an industrial center and a transportation center.

13. (a) New York City **(b)** Possible answer: It is the largest, wealthiest, and most influential city in the country.

14. (a) warm climate, plenty of rain, good soil, and wide plains along coast **(b)** cotton **(c)** Farmers might have continued to plant only cotton instead of a variety of crops.

15. (a) They make a living in mining, forestry, fishing, textiles, aerospace, technology, cable television, transportation, and tourism. **(b)** Georgia is one of the states in which the textile industry is the strongest.

16. (a) Demand for farm products decreased while interest rates for loans increased, leaving farmers unable to pay their loans and forcing them to leave or sell their farms. **(b)** Mixed-crop farms are run by small families and produce a small amount of crops, while corporate farms rely on machines and computers to do the work and produce larger amounts of crops.

17. (a) minerals, timber, and water **(b)** for mining, building homes, irrigating lands, and bringing water to cities **(c)** Today, people are trying to manage the use of resources to preserve them.

Skills Practice
Students' conclusions will vary.

Writing Activity: Science
Students' reports will vary, but should include mention of computers and large farm machines. Use *Rubric for Assessing a Newspaper Article* to evaluate students' reports. Tell students how many sources you would like them to use, if any, beyond the textbook.

All in One **United States and Canada Teaching Resources,** *Rubric for Assessing a Newspaper Article,* p. 274

Review and Assessment (continued)

◆ Comprehension and Critical Thinking

12. (a) List What are some of the large cities in the Northeast?
(b) Compare and Contrast Choose two of the Northeast's cities. How are they similar? How have they developed differently?

13. (a) Locate Which city in the Northeast was attacked by terrorists in 2001?
(b) Draw Conclusions Why might terrorists have targeted that city in particular?

14. (a) Explain What features make the South a good place for farming?
(b) Identify What was the South's most important crop until the 1900s?
(c) Predict How might farming in the South have been different without the boll weevil?

15. (a) Recall How do people in the South make a living other than by farming?
(b) Draw Conclusions How is Georgia important to the textile industry?

16. (a) Summarize How did the recession in the 1980s affect farmers?
(b) Compare and Contrast How are mixed-crop farming and corporate farming different?

17. (a) Name What are the main natural resources of the West?
(b) Summarize How have people used these natural resources?
(c) Compare and Contrast How has the way people manage natural resources in the West changed since the 1800s?

◆ Skills Practice

Understanding Circle Graphs In the Skills for Life activity in this chapter, you learned that information can be given in the form of circle graphs.

Review the steps you followed to learn this skill. Then reread the Regional Profile of the Midwest on page 127. Study the Midwest Economy circle graph on that page. Identify what percentage of the graph each part represents. Use the information in the circle graph to draw conclusions about the economy of the Midwest.

◆ Writing Activity: Science

Suppose that you are the science reporter for a newspaper covering the history of farming on the plains. Write a brief report about how advances in science and technology have contributed to successfully farming the land.

MAP MASTER™
Skills Activity

Place Location Write the letter from the map that shows its location.
1. Boston
2. New York City
3. Washington, D.C.
4. Atlanta
5. Chicago
6. St. Louis
7. Portland
8. Los Angeles

Go Online
PHSchool.com Use Web Code lhp-4444 for an interactive map.

United States

140 United States and Canada

Standardized Test Prep

Test-Taking Tips

Some questions on standardized tests ask you to analyze graphs. Study the graph below. Then follow the tips to answer the sample question.

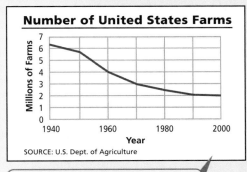

Number of United States Farms

SOURCE: U.S. Dept. of Agriculture

TIP When you study a graph, read the title to understand its subject. Then study information on the left side and bottom of the graph.

Based on this graph, it is clear that the

A size of farms has decreased since the 1940s.

B size of farms increased during the last half of the 1900s.

C number of farms steadily decreased during the last half of the 1900s.

D number of farms probably will increase during the first twenty years of the present century.

TIP Restate the question to make sure you understand what it is asking. "Based on the graph, what conclusion can you draw about United States farms?"

Think It Through Read the title of the graph. You can eliminate A and B because they are about the *size* of American farms. What does the graph show about the *number* of farms? The number line goes down after 1940, but there is no indication that the number of farms will increase in the 2000s. The correct answer is C.

Practice Questions

Use the tips above and other tips in this book to help you answer the following questions.

1. The most densely populated region of the United States is the

   A South.   **B** Midwest.

   C Northeast.   **D** West.

2. What caused San Francisco to grow into a large city?

   A the Gold Rush

   B hydroelectricity

   C the logging industry

   D Lewis and Clark's expedition

3. The Midwest's largest city is

   A Detroit, Michigan.   **B** St. Louis, Missouri.

   C Minneapolis, Minnesota.   **D** Chicago, Illinois.

Study the graph below, and then answer the question that follows.

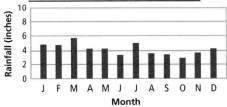

Atlanta, Georgia: Rainfall

SOURCE: *The World Almanac, 2001*

4. In which month is the average temperature highest in Atlanta? How much rain falls in that month?

   A March; 5.5 inches   **B** May; 6 inches

   C July; 6 inches   **D** September; 3 inches

Use Web Code **lha-4404** for a **Chapter 4 self-test**

Chapter 4 **141**

Standardized Test Prep

Answers

1. C

2. A

3. D

4. A

Assessment Resources

Use *Chapter Tests A and B* to assess students' mastery of chapter content.

All in One **United States and Canada Teaching Resources,** *Chapter Tests A and B,* pp. 275–280

Tests are also available on the **ExamView®** **Test Bank CD-ROM.**

⊙ *ExamView Test Bank CD-ROM*

Objectives

- Learn how the town of Parmele changed over three generations.

- Identify elements that the memoirs of the three generations have in common.

- Determine the authors' purposes and points of view.

Prepare to Read

Build Background Knowledge **L2**

Discuss the concept of family history with students. Ask them how much they know about the lives of their grandparents and their parents' childhoods. Encourage students to think about how someone could find information to write a family history. Use an Idea Wave (TE, p. T35) to help students generate ideas.

Instruct

Childtimes **L2**

Guided Instruction

- Point out that some potentially unfamiliar words are defined for students in the margin. Clarify the meanings of these words before reading.

- Chunk each memoir into sections and have students use the Structured Silent Reading strategy (TE, p. T34) to read the passages. Point out that this selection includes the memories of three women representing three generations of a family.

- Have students describe Pattie's point of view. *(Pattie is writing about events that happened when she was very young. Her frame of reference is that of a black woman living in a growing southern town in the late 1800s. She mentions that she was too young to know what was going on at the time, but was told that the town developed quickly. Students should realize that her point of view was heavily influenced by those around her. For example, she seemed excited about the prospects of new jobs for people in town.)*

Answer

√ Reading Check It was named after New Yorker Mr. Parmele who started a lumber company there.

From **Childtimes**

By Eloise Greenfield and Lessie Jones Little, with material by Pattie Ridley Jones

Prepare to Read

Background Information

How much do people know about the lives of their grandparents or their parents as children? Suppose someone wanted to write a history of his or her family. How could he or she find information?

You can learn a great deal from seeing how a single family lives through several generations. Every family history reflects the history of the place where that family lives. The following excerpts come from a memoir, or a story of personal experience, written by a mother, a daughter, and a grandmother. The book tells the story of their family, as well as the growth of their hometown, Parmele, North Carolina.

Objectives

In this section you will

1. Learn how and why the town of Parmele changed over three generations.

2. Identify elements that the memoirs of the three generations have in common.

About the Selection

Childtimes: A Three-Generation Memoir was published in 1979 by Thomas Y. Crowell.

Reading Check

How did the town of Parmele get its name?

Pattie Frances Ridley Jones—born in Bertie County, North Carolina, December 15, 1884

Parmele, North Carolina

Towns build up around work, you know. People go and live where they can find jobs. And that's how Parmele got started.

At first, it was just a junction, a place where two railroads crossed. Two Atlantic Coast Line railroads, one running between Rocky Mount and Plymouth, and one running between Kinston and Weldon. Didn't too many people live around there then, and those that did were pretty much spread out.

Well, around 1888, a Yankee named Mr. Parmele came down from New York and looked the place over, and he saw all those big trees and decided to start a lumber company. Everybody knew what that meant. There were going to be jobs! People came from everywhere to get work. I was right little at that time, too little to know what was going on, but everybody says it was something to see how fast that town grew. All those people moving in and houses going up. They named the town after the man who made the jobs, and they called it *Pomma-lee.*

The lumber company hired a whole lot of people. They hired workers to lay track for those little railroads they call tram roads that they were going to run back and forth between the town and the woods. They hired lumberjacks to chop the trees down and cut them up into logs, and load them on the tram cars. They hired

142 United States and Canada

Read Fluently

Form the class into partners. Choose a paragraph from the selection. Have students take turns reading the paragraph aloud. Ask them to underline words that give them trouble as they read. Then, have them decode the problem words with their partner. Provide assistance as needed. Have students reread the paragraph two more times to improve their reading speed. Remind them to stop at the commas and periods and to read with expression.

men to build the mill and put the machinery in, and millworkers to run the machines that would cut the logs into different sizes and dry them and make them nice and smooth. . . .

Lessie Blanche Jones Little—born in Parmele, North Carolina, October 1, 1906

Parmele

I used to hear Papa and Mama and their friends talking about the lumber mill that had been the center of life in Parmele before I was born, but there wasn't any mill when I was growing up. The only thing left of it was the sawdust from all the wood they had sawed there. The sawdust was about a foot thick on the land where the mill had been. I used to love to walk on it. It was spongy, and it made me feel like I was made of rubber. I'd take my shoes off and kind of bounce along on top of it. But that was all that was left of the mill.

My Parmele was a train town. The life of my town moved around the trains that came in and out all day long. About three hundred people lived in Parmele, most of them black. There were three black churches, a Baptist, a Methodist, and a Holiness, and one white church. Two black schools, one white. There wasn't even one doctor, and not many people would have had the money to pay one, if there had been. If somebody got down real bad sick, a member of the family would go by horse and buggy to a nearby town and bring the doctor back, or sometimes the doctor would ride on his own horse.

Most of the men and women in Parmele earned their living by farming. Some did other things like working at the tobacco factory in Robersonville, but most worked on the farms that were all around in the area, white people's farms usually. When I was a little girl, they earned fifty cents a day, a farm day, sunup to sundown, plus meals. After they got home, they had all their own work to do, cooking and cleaning, laundry, chopping wood for the woodstove, and shopping. . . .

A steam engine pulls a train through the countryside.

- Ask **What changes in Parmele did Lessie notice?** (*It no longer had the lumber mill that her parents talked about, but instead Parmele was a train town. Most people made their living as farmers or working in a nearby tobacco factory.*)

- Ask **How was the train station important to the social life of the town?** (*It was a gathering place where people went to relax after working. It was also a place where a lot was happening as trains came in all day long, bringing people and freight.*)

- Ask **What do you think the purpose of *Childtimes* is?** (*Possible answers: to recall a family's history through personal experiences; to describe a family's relationship to a town over time*)

- Have students compare the entries by Lessie and Eloise. Ask them to identify the similarities in their memoirs. *(Both discuss how people in the town and people in their families made a living; both talk about the part the train station played in their lives; both include stories that hint at the state of the economy of the town at the time.)*

Independent Practice

Have students work with partners to brainstorm a list of questions about family life in Parmele that they would like to ask the authors of these memoirs.

Monitor Progress

Circulate to make sure students are communicating effectively while brainstorming. Make sure individuals understand the assignment as it relates to the literature selection.

Pamlico Sound (PAM lih koh sownd) *n.* a long body of water off the coast of North Carolina that separates the Hatteras Islands from the mainland

✓ Reading Check

What kind of work did Eloise's father do before he went to Washington, D.C.?

Sharecroppers in the South

144 United States and Canada

Parmele had trains coming in and going out all day long. Passenger trains and freight trains. There was always so much going on at the station that I wouldn't know what to watch. People were changing trains and going in and out of the cafe and the restaurant. They came from big cities like New York and Chicago and Boston, and they were all wearing the latest styles. Things were being unloaded, like furniture and trunks and plows and cases of fruit and crates of clucking chickens, or a puppy, or the body of somebody who had died and was being brought back home. And every year around the last two weeks in May, a special train would come through. It had two white flags flying on the locomotive, and it was carrying one hundred carloads of white potatoes that had been grown down near <u>Pamlico Sound</u>, where everybody said the soil was so rich they didn't even have to fertilize it.

The train station was a gathering place, too. A lot of people went there to relax after they had finished their work for the day. They'd come downtown to pick up their mail, or buy a newspaper, and then they'd just stand around laughing and talking to their friends. And on Sundays fellas and their girls would come all the way from other towns, just to spend the afternoon at the Parmele train station. . . .

It was hard for Papa to find work. Not long after Sis Clara died, we moved to Mount Herman, a black section of Portsmouth, Virginia. Papa worked on the docks there, and even though he didn't make much money, the work was steady. But when we moved back to Parmele, it was hard for him to find any work at all. . . .

Eloise Glynn Little Greenfield—born in Parmele, North Carolina, May 17, 1929

Daddy Makes a Way

When I was three months old, Daddy left home to make a way for us. He went North, as thousands of black people had done, during slavery and since. They went North looking for safety, for justice, for freedom, for work, looking for a good life. Often one member of a family would go ahead of the others to make a way—to find a job and a place to live. And that's what my father did.

In the spring of 1926, Daddy had graduated from high school, Parmele Training School. He had been offered a scholarship by Knoxville College in Tennessee, but he hadn't taken it. He and Mama had gotten married that fall, and now they had Wilbur and me to take care of. Mama had been teaching school since her graduation from Higgs, but she had decided to stop.

Differentiated Instruction

For Advanced Readers   **L3**

Challenge students to find a book in the library that contains memoirs from someone living in the northeast in the 1800s. Have them write a short paragraph sum-marizing what they learned from the book and comparing the point of view of the writer with one of the memoir writers from *Childtimes*.

Answer

✓ Reading Check He did farm work harvesting potatoes and working in tobacco fields, packed and loaded at a tobacco warehouse, and moved houses.

Nineteen twenty-nine was a bad time for Daddy to go away, but a worse time for him not to go. The Great Depression was about to begin, had already begun for many people. All over the United States, thousands of people were already jobless and homeless.

In Parmele, there were few permanent jobs. Some seasons of the year, Daddy could get farm work, harvesting potatoes and working in the tobacco fields. Every year, from August to around Thanksgiving, he worked ten hours a day for twenty-five cents an hour at a tobacco warehouse in a nearby town, packing tobacco in huge barrels and loading them on the train for shipping. And he and his father were house movers. Whenever somebody wanted a house moved from one place to another, Daddy and Pa would jack it up and attach it to a windlass, the machine that the horse would turn to move the house. But it was only once in a while that they were called on to do that.

So, one morning in August 1929, Mama went with Daddy to the train station and tried to hold back her tears as the Atlantic Coast Line train pulled out, taking him toward Washington, D.C. Then she went home, sat in the porch swing, and cried.

In Washington, friends helped Daddy find a room for himself and his family to live in, and took him job hunting. He found a job as a dishwasher in a restaurant, and in a few weeks, he had saved enough money for our train fare.

Great Depression (grayt dee PRESH un) *n.* an economic collapse that began in 1929 and lasted throughout the 1930s, causing many people to lose their jobs

Review and Assessment

Thinking About the Selection

1. (a) Recall Why was the town located where it was? What caused the town to first begin to grow?
(b) Identify Why did building a sawmill attract more people to Parmele? How did they earn a living after the mill closed?
(c) Evaluate How did the life of a young person in Parmele compare with your own?
2. (a) Respond What do these memoirs tell you about how hard life in Parmele was at different time periods?

(b) Infer What aspect of their parents' lives most shaped the lives of these women when they were young girls?
(c) Compare and Contrast What do the three narrators have in common? How are they different?

Writing Activity

Write a Memoir Write a memoir of your own childhood. Use the point of view of yourself as an older person. Talk about the forces that have most shaped your life.

About the Author

Eloise Greenfield (b. 1929) was born in Parmele, North Carolina. She has received dozens of awards and honors for her more than thirty books of poetry, biography, and fiction. Greenfield's fiction often depicts strong, loving African American families and contains positive messages for all of her readers. She currently lives in Washington, D.C.

Literature **145**

Writing Activity
Use *Rubric for Assessing a Writing Assignment* to evaluate students' memoirs.

All in One **United States and Canada Teaching Resources,** *Rubric for Assessing a Writing Assignment,* p. 273

Assess and Reteach

Assess Progress   L2
Have students answer the assessment questions.

Reteach   L1
Have students work in pairs to make a simple chart with the name of each writer in the selection as the column headings. Under each name students should list the main ideas the writer has presented in her part of the memoir. *(Pattie Frances Ridley Jones: how the town got its name and the start of the lumber company; Lessie Blanche Jones Little: the town as a train center and the life in a small town that was mostly black; Eloise Glynn Little Greenfield: how the town was affected by the Depression, her father's struggles to find work)*

Extend   L3
Have students read *Personal Experience of Maria Antonia Pico,* a memoir from a woman who lived in another part of the United States in the 1800s. Have them answer the questions at the end of the selection. In addition, ask them to describe Pico's point of view.

All in One **United States and Canada Teaching Resources,** *Personal Experience of Maria Antonia Pico,* pp. 268–269

Review and Assessment

Thinking About the Selection
1. (a) It was located at the junction of two railroads where goods could easily be shipped to and from the town. It grew because of the lumber company that Mr. Parmele began.
(b) It created more jobs. After it closed, people made a living mostly by farming. **(c)** Answers will vary, but students should mention the similarities and differences in jobs and size of community.

2. (a) People were happy just to get any kind of job, which shows how difficult it was to make a living in Parmele. Lessie suggests that people were so poor they could not even pay for a doctor if the town had one. **(b)** The issue of finding work to earn a living seemed to shape the girls' lives. **(c)** Possible answers: They all tell about the same place and the struggles to find work. Pattie's memoir recollects more positive things about work than the other memoirs because of the lumber company. Both Lessie and Eloise recall the difficulty their fathers had finding work.

Chapter Overview

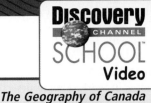

Overview

Introducing Canada
1. Learn about the provinces and territories of Canada.
2. Analyze data to compare the provinces and territories of Canada.
3. Identify characteristics that most provinces and territories share.
4. Explain key differences among the provinces and territories.

The Geography of Canada
Length: 5 minutes, 20 seconds
Provides an overview of Canada by showing its location, topography, climate, and population density.

Section 1 Ontario and Quebec: Bridging Two Cultures
1. Read about the seat of the Canadian government in Ontario.
2. Learn about the French cultural influence in Quebec.

Toronto: Canada's Financial Center
Length: 3 minutes, 48 seconds
Describes Toronto, Ontario.

Section 2 The Prairie Provinces: Canada's Breadbasket
1. Learn why many immigrants came to the Prairie Provinces in the 1800s.
2. Read about how Canadians celebrate their cultural traditions.

Canada's Prairie Provinces
Length: 4 minutes, 37 seconds
Explores the Canadian Plains region.

Section 3 British Columbia: Economic and Cultural Changes
1. Find out about the people and cultures of the Canadian West.
2. Learn what the economy and culture of British Columbia are like.

British Columbia: Canada's Gateway to the Pacific
Length: 3 minutes, 53 seconds
Describes how British Columbia became a hub for Asian culture.

Section 4 The Atlantic Provinces: Relying on the Sea
1. Learn what life is like on the Atlantic coast.
2. Discover how maritime industries affect the provinces.

Cultures of the Atlantic Provinces
Length: 3 minutes, 8 seconds
Discusses the European influence on Canada's Atlantic provinces.

Section 5 The Northern Territories: New Frontiers
1. Discover what life is like for people in Canada's far north.
2. Find out about the remote region of the Yukon Territory.
3. Understand how the new territory of Nunavut was formed.

The Northern Territories: Challenge of the Cold
Length: 4 minutes, 18 seconds
Shows cultures of northern Canada.

Technology Resources

Students use embedded Web codes to access Internet activities, chapter self-tests, and additional map practice. They may also access Dorling Kindersley's Online Desk Reference to learn more about each country they study.

Use the Interactive Textbook to make content and concepts come alive through animations, videos, and activities that accompany the complete basal text—online and on CD-ROM.

Use this complete suite of powerful teaching tools to make planning lessons and administering tests quicker and easier.

Reading and Assessment

Reading and Vocabulary Instruction

🔁 Model the Target Reading Skill

Context The context of a word is the surrounding words, phrases, and sentences that help reveal its meaning. Unless a definition is given, a reader must interpret a word's meaning by using context clues. Write the passage below, from page 152 of the Student Edition, on the board. Model using context clues to reveal the meaning of the word in quotation marks.

Canada's capital, Ottawa, is located in Ontario. But government functions spill over into the city of Hull, Quebec, located on the other end of the Macdonald-Cartier Bridge. Hull is considered Ottawa's "sister city" because a number of federal government office buildings dot its landscape.

Ask yourself aloud: What clues explain what it means for Hull to be Ottawa's *sister city? (The word* because *is a clue that a definition or explanation follows. The explanation says that Hull has government buildings, where some government functions from Ottawa are performed. So the two cities have something in common— they both have government buildings. Another thing they have in common is the bridge that connects them. They must be "sister cities" because they have enough in common to make them seem related.)* Have students choose another paragraph that contains an unfamiliar word and use context clues to decipher its meaning.

Use the following worksheets from All-in-One United States and Canada Teaching Resources (pp. 305–308) to support this chapter's Target Reading Skill.

Vocabulary Builder
High-Use Academic Words
Use these steps to teach this chapter's high-use words:

1. Have students rate how well they know each word on their Word Knowledge worksheets (All-in-One United States and Canada Teaching Resources, p. 309).
2. Pronounce each word and ask students to repeat it.
3. Give students a brief definition and sample sentence (provided on TE pp. 153, 161, 167, 174 and 181).
4. Work with students as they fill in the "Definition or Example" column of their Word Knowledge worksheets.

Assessment

Formal Assessment
Test students' understanding of core knowledge and skills.

Chapter Tests A and B, and Final Exams A and B All-in-One United States and Canada Teaching Resources, pp. 329–334, 339–344

Customize the Chapter Tests to suit your needs.
ExamView Test Bank CD-ROM

Skills Assessment
Assess geographic literacy.
MapMaster Skills, Student Edition, pp. 147, 171, 176, 186
Regional Profile Map and Chart Skills, Student Edition, pp. 154, 158, 162, 168, 175, 182

Assess reading and comprehension.
Target Reading Skills, Student Edition, pp. 157, 164, 169, 174, 181, and in Section Assessments
Chapter 510 Assessment, United States and Canada Reading and Vocabulary Study Guide, p. 70

Performance Assessment
Assess students' performance using the following rubrics from All-in-One United States and Canada Teaching Resources.
Rubric for Assessing a Student Poster, p. 325
Rubric for Assessing a Performance on a Project, p. 328

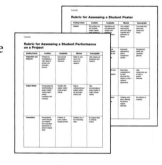

Assess students' work through performance tasks.
Small Group Activity: Writing a Newspaper Feature, All-in-One United States and Canada Teaching Resources, pp. 312–315
Portfolio Suggestions, Teacher's Edition, p. 151

Online Assessment
Have students check their own understanding.
Chapter Self-Test

Test Preparation
United States and Canada Practice Tests A, B, and C, Test Prep Workbook, pp. 85–96
United States and Canada Benchmark Test 2 and Outcome Test, AYP Monitoring Assessments, pp. 93–96, 176–181

Section 1 Ontario and Quebec: Bridging Two Cultures

 2 periods, 1 block (includes Country Databank)

Social Studies Objectives
1. Read about the seat of the Canadian government in Ontario.
2. Learn about the French cultural influence in Quebec.

Reading/Language Arts Objective
Use context clues to determine the meaning of unfamiliar words.

Prepare to Read	Instructional Resources	Differentiated Instruction
Build Background Knowledge Discuss the different cultures of Ontario and Quebec. **Set a Purpose for Reading** Have students evaluate statements on the *Reading Readiness Guide*. **Preview Key Terms** Teach the section's Key Terms. **Target Reading Skill** Introduce the section's Target Reading Skill of **using context clues**.	**All in One United States and Canada Teaching Resources** L2 Reading Readiness Guide, p. 286 L2 Use Context Clues: General Knowledge, p. 305	**Spanish Reading and Vocabulary Study Guide** L1 Chapter 5, Section 1, pp. 41–42 ELL **World Studies Video Program** L2 The Geography of Canada AR, GT, LPR, SN

Instruct	Instructional Resources	Differentiated Instruction
Ontario Discuss the governments and major cities of Ontario. **Regional Profile** Ask students to derive information from maps, charts, and graphs. **French Culture in Quebec** Discuss how Quebec's culture reflects both French and local influence. **Target Reading Skill** Review **using context clues**. **Regional Profile** Ask students to derive information from maps, charts, and graphs.	**All in One United States and Canada Teaching Resources** L2 Guided Reading and Review, p. 287 L2 Reading Readiness Guide, p. 286 L2 Reading a Population Density Map, p. 316 **United States and Canada Transparencies** L2 Section Reading Support Transparency USC 58 **World Studies Video Program** L2 Toronto: Canada's Financial Center	**All in One United States and Canada Teaching Resources** Rubric for Assessing a Student Poster, p. 325 ELL, LPR, SN L2 Outline Map 12: Canada: Political, p. 319 AR, GT, LPR, SN L3 Preparing for Presentations, p. 323 AR, GT L3 Enrichment, p. 310 AR, GT L3 Shadows on the Rock, pp. 320–322 AR, GT **Teacher's Edition** L3 For Advanced Readers, TE pp. 149, 158 L3 For English Language Learners, TE p. 154 L1 For Special Needs Students, TE p. 155 L3 For Gifted and Talented, TE p. 155 L1 For Less Proficient Readers, TE pp. 149, 158 **Student Edition on Audio CD** L1 Chapter 5, Section 1 ELL, LPR, SN

Assess and Reteach	Instructional Resources	Differentiated Instruction
Assess Progress Evaluate student comprehension with the section assessment and section quiz. **Reteach** Assign the Reading and Vocabulary Study Guide to help struggling students. **Extend** Extend the lesson by assigning a Small Group Activity.	**All in One United States and Canada Teaching Resources** L2 Section Quiz, p. 288 L3 Small Group Activity: Writing a Newspaper Feature, pp. 312–315 Rubric for Assessing a Writing Assignment, p. 326 **Reading and Vocabulary Study Guide** L1 Chapter 5, Section 1, pp. 55–57	**Spanish Support** L2 Section Quiz (Spanish), p. 43 ELL

Key

L1 Basic to Average	L3 Average to Advanced	LPR Less Proficient Readers	GT Gifted and Talented
L2 For All Students		AR Advanced Readers	ELL English Language Learners
		SN Special Needs Students	

Section 2 The Prairie Provinces: Canada's Breadbasket

 1 period, .5 block

Social Studies Objectives
1. Learn why many immigrants came to the Prairie Provinces in the 1800s.
2. Read about how Canadians celebrate their cultural traditions.

Reading/Language Arts Objective
Practice interpreting the meaning of nonliteral language.

Prepare to Read	Instructional Resources	Differentiated Instruction
Build Background Knowledge Show students the video *Canada's Prairie Provinces* and then discuss the main points. **Set a Purpose for Reading** Have students evaluate statements on the *Reading Readiness Guide*. **Preview Key Terms** Teach the section's Key Terms. **Target Reading Skill** Introduce the section's Target Reading Skill of **interpreting nonliteral meanings**.	**All in One United States and Canada Teaching Resources** L2 Reading Readiness Guide, p. 290 L2 Recognize Nonliteral Meanings, p. 306 **World Studies Video Program** L2 Canada's Prairie Provinces	**Spanish Reading and Vocabulary Study Guide** L1 Chapter 5, Section 2, pp. 43–44 ELL

Instruct	Instructional Resources	Differentiated Instruction
The Prairie Provinces Discuss people of the Canadian Plains and how settlements developed there. **Regional Profile** Ask students to derive information from maps, charts, and graphs. **Celebrating Traditions** Discuss traditional celebrations of the Prairie Provinces. **Target Reading Skill** Review **interpreting nonliteral meanings**.	**All in One United States and Canada Teaching Resources** L2 Guided Reading and Review, p. 291 L2 Reading Readiness Guide, p. 290 **United States and Canada Transparencies** L2 Section Reading Support Transparency USC 59	**Teacher's Edition** L3 For Gifted and Talented, TE pp. 162, 164 L3 For Advanced Readers, TE p. 162 L1 For English Language Learners, TE p. 163 L1 For Special Needs Students, TE p. 163 L1 For Less Proficient Readers, TE p. 164 **Student Edition on Audio CD** L1 Chapter 5, Section 2 ELL, LPR, SN **Spanish Support** L2 Guided Reading and Review (Spanish), p. 44 ELL

Assess and Reteach	Instructional Resources	Differentiated Instruction
Assess Progress Evaluate student comprehension with the section assessment and section quiz. **Reteach** Assign the Reading and Vocabulary Study Guide to help struggling students. **Extend** Extend the lesson by having students research different traditions of the Prairie Provinces.	**All in One United States and Canada Teaching Resources** L2 Section Quiz, p. 292 Rubric for Assessing a Student Poster, p. 325 **Reading and Vocabulary Study Guide** L1 Chapter 5, Section 2, pp. 58–60	**Spanish Support** L2 Section Quiz (Spanish), p. 45 ELL

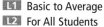

British Columbia: Economic
Section 3 and Cultural Changes

 1 period, .5 block

Social Studies Objectives
1. Find out about the people and cultures of the Canadian West.
2. Learn what the economy and culture of British Columbia are like.

Reading/Language Arts Objective
Use context clues to determine the meaning of unfamiliar words.

Section Lesson Planner

Prepare to Read	Instructional Resources	Differentiated Instruction
Build Background Knowledge Have students brainstorm ways that the east and west coasts of Canada may differ. **Set a Purpose for Reading** Have students evaluate statements on the *Reading Readiness Guide*. **Preview Key Terms** Teach the section's Key Terms. **Target Reading Skill** Introduce the section's Target Reading Skill of **using context clues**.	**All in One United States and Canada Teaching Resources** L2 Reading Readiness Guide, p. 294 L2 Use Context Clues: General Knowledge, p. 305	**Spanish Reading and Vocabulary Study Guide** L1 Chapter 5, Section 3, pp. 45–46 ELL

Instruct	Instructional Resources	Differentiated Instruction
The People of the Canadian West Discuss the impact of gold miners, fur traders, and railroads on the people of the Canadian West. **Regional Profile** Ask students to derive information from maps, charts, and graphs. **Target Reading Skill** Review **using context clues**. **Economics and Culture** Ask questions about and discuss the economy and culture of British Columbia.	**All in One United States and Canada Teaching Resources** L2 Guided Reading and Review, p. 295 L2 Reading Readiness Guide, p. 294 L2 Analyzing Statistics, p. 317 **United States and Canada Transparencies** L2 Section Reading Support Transparency USC 60 **World Studies Video Program** L2 British Columbia: Canada's Gateway to the Pacific	**Teacher's Edition** L3 For Advanced Readers, TE p. 168 L1 For Less Proficient Readers, TE p. 169 L2 For English Language Learners, TE p. 169 L1 For Special Needs Students, TE p. 171 L3 For Gifted and Talented, TE p. 171 **PHSchool.com** L3 **For:** Environmental and Global Issues: Trade in a Global Economy **Web Code:** lhd-4506 AR, GT **Spanish Support** L2 Guided Reading and Review (Spanish), p. 46 ELL

Assess and Reteach	Instructional Resources	Differentiated Instruction
Assess Progress Evaluate student comprehension with the section assessment and section quiz. **Reteach** Assign the Reading and Vocabulary Study Guide to help struggling students. **Extend** Extend the lesson by having students write a newspaper editorial about the impact of gold miners on the Canadian West.	**All in One United States and Canada Teaching Resources** L2 Section Quiz, p. 296 Rubric for Assessing a Journal Entry, p. 327 **Reading and Vocabulary Study Guide** L1 Chapter 5, Section 3, pp. 61–63	**Spanish Support** L2 Section Quiz (Spanish), p. 47 ELL

Key
L1 Basic to Average	L3 Average to Advanced	**LPR** Less Proficient Readers	**GT** Gifted and Talented
L2 For All Students		**AR** Advanced Readers	**ELL** English Language Learners
		SN Special Needs Students	

Section 4 The Atlantic Provinces: Relying on the Sea

 2 periods, 1 block (includes Skills for Life)

Social Studies Objectives
1. Learn what life is like on the Atlantic coast.
2. Discover how maritime industries affect the provinces.

Reading/Language Arts Objective
Learn how cause-and-effect clues can help you understand the meaning of an unfamiliar word.

Prepare to Read	Instructional Resources	Differentiated Instruction
Build Background Knowledge Have students study the location of the Atlantic Provinces using a transparency. **Set a Purpose for Reading** Have students begin to fill out the *Reading Readiness Guide*. **Preview Key Terms** Teach the section's Key Terms. **Target Reading Skill** Introduce the section's Target Reading Skill of **using context clues**.	**All in One United States and Canada Teaching Resources** L2 Reading Readiness Guide, p. 298 L2 Use Context Clues: Cause and Effect, p. 307 **United States and Canada Transparencies** L2 Color Transparency USC 40: Canada: Physical-Political	**Spanish Reading and Vocabulary Study Guide** L1 Chapter 5, Section 4, pp. 47–48 ELL

Instruct	Instructional Resources	Differentiated Instruction
Living on the Coast Discuss the effects of location on the lives of the people living in the Atlantic Provinces. **Target Reading Skill** Review **using context clues**. **Regional Profile** Ask students to derive information from maps, charts, and graphs. **A Maritime Economy** Discuss the fishing industry in Canada.	**All in One United States and Canada Teaching Resources** L2 Guided Reading and Review, p. 299 L2 Reading Readiness Guide, p. 298 L2 Reading a Line Graph, p. 318 **United States and Canada Transparencies** L2 Section Reading Support Transparency USC 61 **World Studies Video Program** L2 Cultures of the Atlantic Provinces	**All in One United States and Canada Teaching Resources** L2 Skills for Life, p. 311 AR, GT, LPR, SN **Teacher's Edition** L1 For Less Proficient Readers, TE p. 175 L1 For English Language Learners, TE p. 176 L1 For Special Needs Students, TE p. 176 **Spanish Support** L2 Guided Reading and Review (Spanish), p. 48 ELL

Assess and Reteach	Instructional Resources	Differentiated Instruction
Assess Progress Evaluate student comprehension with the section assessment and section quiz. **Reteach** Assign the Reading and Vocabulary Study Guide to help struggling students. **Extend** Extend the lesson by having students debate the ban on cod fishing.	**All in One United States and Canada Teaching Resources** L2 Section Quiz, p. 300 Rubric for Assessing a Writing Assignment, p. 326 **Reading and Vocabulary Study Guide** L1 Chapter 5, Section 4, pp. 64–66	**Teacher's Edition** L3 For Advanced Readers, TE p. 179 **Spanish Support** L2 Section Quiz (Spanish), p. 49 ELL

Key
L1 Basic to Average	LPR Less Proficient Readers	GT Gifted and Talented
L3 Average to Advanced	AR Advanced Readers	ELL English Language Learners
L2 For All Students	SN Special Needs Students	

Section 5 The Northern Territories: New Frontiers

 2.5 periods, 1.25 blocks (includes Chapter Review and Assessment)

Social Studies Objectives
1. Discover what life is like for people in Canada's far north.
2. Find out about the remote region of the Yukon Territory.
3. Understand how the new territory of Nunavut was formed.

Reading/Language Arts Objective
Use context clues to determine the meaning of a familiar word when used in an unfamiliar way.

Prepare to Read	**Instructional Resources**	**Differentiated Instruction**
Build Background Knowledge Have students contrast the Northern Territories with Canada's other regions. **Set a Purpose for Reading** Have students evaluate statements on the *Reading Readiness Guide*. **Preview Key Terms** Teach the section's Key Terms. **Target Reading Skill** Introduce the section's Target Reading Skill of **using context clues**.	**All in One United States and Canada Teaching Resources** L2 Reading Readiness Guide, p. 302 L2 Use Context Clues: Definition/Description, p. 308	**Spanish Reading and Vocabulary Study Guide** L1 Chapter 5, Section 5, pp. 49–50 ELL

Instruct	**Instructional Resources**	**Differentiated Instruction**
The Far North Ask how the population of the Northern Territories is affected by their geography. **Target Reading Skill** Review **using context clues**. **Regional Profile** Ask students to derive information from maps, charts, and graphs. **Forming New Territories** Ask questions about the Yukon Territory and Nunavut.	**All in One United States and Canada Teaching Resources** L2 Guided Reading and Review, p. 303 L2 Reading Readiness Guide, p. 302 **United States and Canada Transparencies** L2 Section Reading Support Transparency USC 62 **World Studies Video Program** L2 The Northern Territories: Challenge of the Cold	**Teacher's Edition** L1 For Less Proficient Readers, TE p. 182 **Spanish Support** L2 Guided Reading and Review (Spanish), p. 50 ELL

Assess and Reteach	**Instructional Resources**	**Differentiated Instruction**
Assess Progress Evaluate student comprehension with the section assessment and section quiz. **Reteach** Assign the Reading and Vocabulary Study Guide to help struggling students. **Extend** Extend the lesson by assigning a Long-Term Integrated Project.	**All in One United States and Canada Teaching Resources** L2 Section Quiz, p. 304 L2 Vocabulary Development, p. 324 Rubric for Assessing a Writing Assignment, p. 326 L2 Word Knowledge, p. 309 Rubric for Assessing Performance on a Project, p. 328 L2 Chapter Tests A and B, pp. 329–334 L2 Final Exams A and B, pp. 339–344 **Reading and Vocabulary Study Guide** L1 Chapter 5, Section 5, pp. 67–69	**Spanish Support** L2 Section Quiz (Spanish), p. 51 ELL L2 Chapter Summary (Spanish), p. 52 ELL L2 Vocabulary Development (Spanish), p. 53 ELL **PHSchool.com** L3 **For:** Long-Term Integrated Project: *Holding Community Meetings Under Different Forms of Government* **Web Code:** lhd-4507

Key
L1 Basic to Average	L3 Average to Advanced	LPR Less Proficient Readers
L2 For All Students		AR Advanced Readers
		SN Special Needs Students

GT Gifted and Talented
ELL English Language Learners

Professional Development

Reading Background

Seed Discussions

Give students the opportunity to lead their own discussions about what they are reading in the chapter. Tell students that in order to lead a discussion, they will need a strong "seed" to start with.

Model a strong seed versus a weak seed. A strong seed might be an opinion, such as: "I believe that Quebec should (or should not) be independent from the rest of Canada." A weak seed might be a restatement of fact, such as: "Francophones make up about 80 percent of the population of Montreal and its surrounding areas."

Have the class list ideas for strong seeds, such as questions or opinions about what they have learned, or things in the chapter that surprised them. Once students are comfortable with the concept, have each student write a seed on a sheet of paper. Then have students form small groups. In each group, each person should take a turn leading a discussion from the seed he or she has written. Divide time equally so every person gets an equal opportunity as leader.

Author's Craft

The way an author presents information is as important as the information presented. Explain that as students read, they should ask themselves how the material is organized. This will clarify any uncertainty about what students are reading, as well as help them remember it. As an example, present the following selection from page 183:

After gold was discovered in a branch of the Klondike River in 1896, thousands of prospectors swarmed to the area. Within two years, the population of the town of Dawson swelled to about 30,000.

Guide students toward recognizing a framework for these sentences by asking questions. Did the author use dates or present a chronological sequence? Is the author comparing one thing to another? Can you see a cause and effect relationship? Students should recognize that the author organized these sentences chronologically. A cause and effect relationship is also represented; the population grew because many prospectors came to the area.

Have students work individually or in pairs as they reread sections of the chapter. As they read, have them jot down different techniques the author used by asking the same kinds of questions themselves. When students have finished taking notes, have the class discuss what techniques they have found.

World Studies Background

Canada's Ties to Britain

When Britain passed the British North America Act in 1867, the Canadian provinces, which were still British colonies, became unified into a dominion of Canada. The British Parliament continued to hold authority over Canada, however. The Act served as the dominion's constitution until Britain's Queen Elizabeth II proclaimed the Constitution Act of 1982. At that time, Canada formally became a sovereign nation and Britain no longer ruled it.

The Pacific Rim

The Pacific Rim is the name for the islands and countries that lie in and encircle the Pacific Ocean. Canada, the United States, Mexico, Japan, China, and South Korea, among others, are Pacific Rim countries. The cities of Los Angeles, Vancouver, Hong Kong, and Tokyo are all world economic leaders that are part of the Pacific Rim. In 1989, 21 Pacific Rim countries formed the Asia-Pacific Economic Cooperation to solidify their economic ties.

Infoplease® provides a wealth of useful information for the classroom. You can use this resource to strengthen your background on the subjects covered in this chapter. Have students visit this advertising-free site as a starting point for projects requiring research.

 Use Web code **lhd-4500** for **Infoplease®**.

Professional Development

Chapter 5

Guiding Questions

Remind students about the Guiding Questions at the beginning of the book.

Section 1 relates to **Guiding Question** ④ **How do the governments of the United States and Canada differ? How are they alike?** *(Canada has a monarch and a prime minister; both elect representatives)*

Section 2 relates to **Guiding Question** ② **How have historical events affected the cultures of the United States and Canada?** *(In the late 1870s, people of European descent began moving onto the Canadian prairie.)*

Section 3 relates to **Guiding Question** ⑤ **How did the United States and Canada become two of the wealthiest nations in the world?** *(British Columbia exports resources.)*

Section 4 relates to **Guiding Question** ① **How has physical geography affected the cultures of the United States and Canada?** *(Much of the Atlantic Provinces' economy depends on fishing and shipbuilding.)*

Section 5 relates to **Guiding Question** ③ **How has the variety of people in the United States and Canada benefited and challenged the two nations?** *(The northern territories have a variety of cultures and ethic groups.)*

⊙ Target Reading Skill

In this chapter, students will learn the skill of using context. Use the following to help students practice this skill:

All in One United States and Canada Teaching Resources, *Use Context Clues: General Knowledge,* p. 305; *Recognize Nonliteral Meanings,* p. 306; *Use Context Clues: Cause and Effect,* p. 307; *Use Context Clues: Definition/Description,* p. 308

Differentiated Instruction

These Teacher's Edition strategies are suitable for students of varying abilities.

Advanced Readers, pp. 149, 158, 162, 168, 179

English Language Learners, pp. 154, 163, 169, 176

Gifted and Talented, pp. 155, 162, 164, 171

Less Proficient Readers, pp. 149, 158, 164, 169, 175, 182

Special Needs Students, pp. 155, 163, 171, 176

Chapter 5 Canada

Chapter Preview

This chapter will introduce you to the provinces and territories of Canada.

Country Databank
The Country Databank provides data of each of the provinces and territories in Canada.

Section 1
Ontario and Quebec
Bridging Two Cultures

Section 2
The Prairie Provinces
Canada's Breadbasket

Section 3
British Columbia
Economic and Cultural Changes

Section 4
The Atlantic Provinces
Relying on the Sea

Section 5
The Northern Territories
New Frontiers

 Target Reading Skill

Context In this chapter, you will focus on using context to help you understand unfamiliar words. Context includes the words, phrases, and sentences surrounding the word.

▶ **Lighthouse in Peggy's Cove, Nova Scotia, Canada**

146 United States and Canada

Bibliography

For the Teacher

Dickason, Olive Patricia. *Canada's First Nations: A History of Founding Peoples from Earliest Times.* Oxford University Press, 2001.

Molyneaux, Geoffrey. *British Columbia: An Illustrated History.* Raincoast Books, 2003.

Moogk, Peter. *La Nouvelle France: The Making of French Canada: A Cultural History.* Michigan State University Press, 2000.

For the Student

▪ Hancock, Lyn. *Nunavut.* Fitzhenry & Whiteside Ltd, 2003.

▪ Moore, Christopher. *The Big Book of Canada: Exploring the Provinces and Territories.* Tundra Books, 2002.

▪ Prophet, Elizabeth Clare. *Beginnings: Stories of Canada's Past.* Ronsdale Press, 2001.

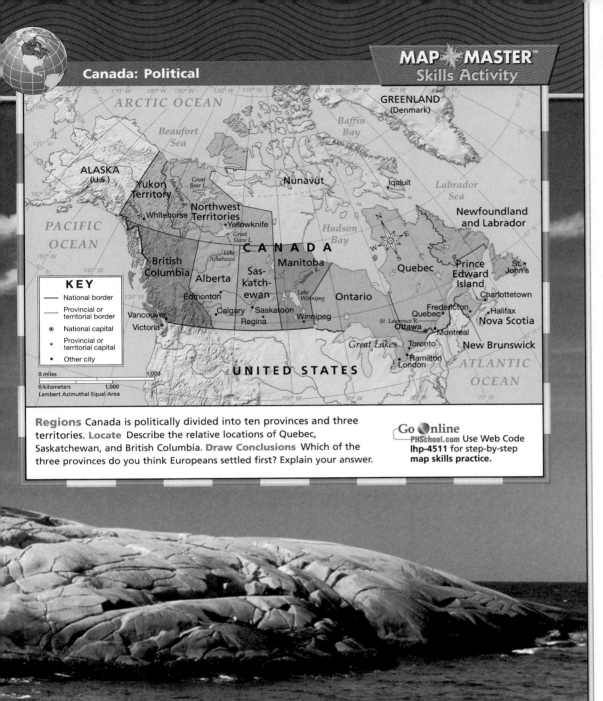

MAP MASTER™ Skills Activity

Canada: Political

KEY
- — National border
- — Provincial or territorial border
- ⊛ National capital
- ★ Provincial or territorial capital
- • Other city

0 miles 1,000
0 kilometers 1,000
Lambert Azimuthal Equal Area

Regions Canada is politically divided into ten provinces and three territories. **Locate** Describe the relative locations of Quebec, Saskatchewan, and British Columbia. **Draw Conclusions** Which of the three provinces do you think Europeans settled first? Explain your answer.

Go Online PHSchool.com Use Web Code lhp-4511 for step-by-step map skills practice.

Chapter 5 **147**

MAP MASTER™ Skills Activity

Have students study the map, paying close attention to the title and the map key. Then have them list each province and territory on a separate sheet of paper. Have students write down one piece of information from the map about each province or territory, such as the capital, any large bodies of water, or what other provinces, territories, or country it borders. Create a table on the board with a column for each province, and then have students take turns coming up and adding facts from their lists.

Go Online PHSchool.com **Students may practice their map skills using the interactive online version of this map.**

Using the Visual   L2

Reach Into Your Background Draw students' attention to the photo and its caption. Ask students **What is a lighthouse used for? Looking at Nova Scotia's location on the map, why do you think lighthouses might be important there?** Conduct an Idea Wave (TE, p. T35) to generate a list of student responses.

Answers

MAP MASTER Skills Activity **Locate** Quebec is near the eastern coast of Canada; Saskatchewan is in Canada's interior; British Columbia is on Canada's west coast. **Draw Conclusions** Possible answer: Quebec, because it is located the closest to Europe.

Chapter Resources

Teaching Resources
- L2 Vocabulary Development, p. 324
- L2 Skills for Life, p. 311
- L2 Chapter Tests A and B, pp. 329–334
- L2 Final Exams A and B, pp. 339–344

Spanish Support
- L2 Spanish Chapter Summary, p. 52
- L2 Spanish Vocabulary Development, p. 53

Media and Technology
- L1 Student Edition on Audio CD
- L1 Guided Reading Audiotapes, English and Spanish
- L2 Social Studies Skills Tutor CD-ROM
  ExamView Test Bank CD-ROM

PRENTICE HALL
Presentation EXPRESS™
Teach · Connect · Inspire

Teach this chapter's content using the PresentationExpress™ CD-ROM including:
- slide shows
- transparencies
- interactive maps and media
- *ExamView*® QuickTake Presenter

Objectives

- Learn about the provinces and territories of Canada.

- Analyze data to compare the provinces and territories of Canada.

- Identify characteristics that most provinces and territories share.

- Explain key differences among the provinces and territories.

Show students *The Geography of Canada*. Ask **Why do most Canadians live in the southern part of the country?** *(because it is warmer)* **What factors influenced where the big cities of Canada developed?** *(climate)*

Prepare to Read

Build Background Knowledge L2

Invite students to share what they know about the provinces and territories of Canada, and what they learned about the country from watching the video *The Geography of Canada*. Create a table on the board with the following columns: *Name, Province/Territory, Capital, Major Cities, Population Density—High or Low?* Conduct an Idea Wave (TE, p. T35) to generate a list of what students learned or know about each topic. Write their responses in the appropriate column on the board.

📼 *The Geography of Canada*, **World Studies Video Program**

Introducing
Canada

Guide for Reading

This section provides an introduction to the ten provinces and three territories that make up Canada.

- Look at the map on the previous page, and then read the information below to learn about each province and territory.
- Analyze the data to compare the provinces and territories.
- What are the characteristics that most of the provinces and territories share?
- What are some of the key differences among the provinces and territories?

Viewing the Video Overview

View the World Studies Video Overview to learn more about each of the provinces and territories. As you watch, answer these questions:

- Why do most Canadians live in the southern part of the country?
- What factors influenced where the big cities of Canada developed?

Explore the geography of Canada.

Alberta

Capital	Edmonton
Land Area	247,999 sq mi; 642,317 sq km
Population	3,101,561
Language(s)	English, Chinese, German, French
Agriculture	livestock, wheat, canola, dairy products, barley, poultry, potatoes, nurseries, vegetables, eggs, sugar beets, honey
Industry	manufacturing, construction, oil production and refinery

British Columbia

Capital	Victoria
Land Area	357,214 sq mi; 925,186 sq km
Population	4,118,141
Language(s)	English, Chinese, Punjabi, German, French
Agriculture	nurseries, livestock, dairy products, vegetables, poultry, fruit, potatoes, ginseng, canola, wheat
Industry	forestry, wood and paper, mining, tourism, agriculture, fishing, manufacturing

Odyssium is Edmonton, Alberta's space and science center.

Manitoba

Capital	Winnipeg
Land Area	213,728 sq mi; 553,556 sq km
Population	1,150,038
Language(s)	English, German, French
Agriculture	wheat, livestock, canola, dairy products, potatoes, barley, poultry, eggs, nurseries, vegetables, corn, honey
Industry	manufacturing, agriculture, food industry, mining, construction

New Brunswick

Capital	Fredericton
Land Area	27,587 sq mi; 71,450 sq km
Population	756,939
Language(s)	English, French
Agriculture	potatoes, dairy products, poultry, nurseries, livestock, eggs, fruit
Industry	manufacturing, fishing, mining, forestry, pulp and paper, agriculture

Newfoundland and Labrador

Capital	St. John's
Land Area	144,362 sq mi; 373,872 sq km
Population	531,820
Language(s)	English, French
Agriculture	dairy products, eggs, nurseries, vegetables, potatoes, hogs
Industry	mining, manufacturing, fishing, logging and forestry, electricity production, tourism

Northwest Territories

Capital	Yellowknife
Land Area	456,789 sq mi; 1,183,085 sq km
Population	40,071
Language(s)	English, French, Inuktitut
Agriculture	potatoes, hay, nurseries, livestock
Industry	construction, mining, utilities, services, tourism

Nova Scotia

Capital	Halifax
Land Area	20,594 sq mi; 53,338 sq km
Population	943,497
Language(s)	English, French
Agriculture	dairy products, poultry, livestock, nurseries, fruit, eggs, vegetables
Industry	manufacturing, fishing and trapping, mining, agriculture, pulp and paper

Snowy owl

Chapter 5 **149**

Instruct

Introducing Canada L2

Guided Instruction

- With students, read through each data table using the Structured Silent Reading strategy (TE, p. T34).

- Have students make a list of the provinces and territories in order of population, from highest to lowest. Ask **How do the populations of the territories differ from those of the provinces?** (*They are much smaller.*)

- Ask **Which language does all of Canada have in common?** (*English*) **What language is the second most common in Canada?** (*French*)

- Ask **Which industry do nearly all of the provinces share?** (*manufacturing*)

- Ask **Based on what you have learned about Canada's physical geography, why do you think fishing and mining are major industries in Canada?** (*Much of Canada is on the Pacific, Atlantic, and Arctic Oceans, which provide fish; many inland areas are on the Canadian Shield, which is rich in minerals.*)

Differentiated Instruction

For Advanced Readers L3
To gain a deeper understanding about the French heritage of the province of Quebec, have students read *Shadows on the Rock*, and then answer the assessment questions.

All in One **United States and Canada Teaching Resources**, *Shadows on the Rock*, pp. 320–322

For Less Proficient Readers L1
Form students into pairs to create a poster highlighting one province or territory. Posters should include the capital and major industies of the province or territory, and a picture of its flag. Use *Rubric for Assessing a Student Poster* to evaluate students' work.

All in One **United States and Canada Teaching Resources**, *Rubric for Assessing a Student Poster*, p. 325

Independent Practice

Have students show the agricultural products of each province and territory on *Outline Map 12: Canada: Political.* Tell students to use symbols to represent each product, and to include a map key explaining their symbols. Tell students to give the map an appropriate title.

 **United States and Canada Teaching Resources,** *Outline Map 12: Canada: Political,* p. 319

Monitor Progress

Circulate to be sure students are making the map key correctly and that they have chosen an appropriate map title.

Introducing Canada

Nunavut

Capital	Iqaluit
Land Area	747,533 sq mi; 1,936,113 sq km
Population	29,016
Language(s)	Inuktitut, English
Industry	mining, tourism, shrimp and scallop fishing, hunting and trapping, arts and crafts production

Ontario

Capital	Toronto
Land Area	354,340 sq mi; 917,741 sq km
Population	11,977,360
Language(s)	English, French, Chinese, Italian, German, Portuguese, Polish, Spanish, Punjabi
Agriculture	livestock, dairy products, nurseries, vegetables, poultry, soybeans, corn, tobacco, eggs, fruit, wheat, ginseng, maple products
Industry	manufacturing, construction, agriculture, forestry, mining

Prince Edward Island

Capital	Charlottetown
Land Area	2,185 sq mi; 5,660 sq km
Population	135,294
Language(s)	English, French
Agriculture	potatoes, dairy products, livestock, vegetables
Industry	agriculture, tourism, fishing, manufacturing

Cape Tryon on Prince Edward Island

Background: Daily Life

The Inuit Nunavut is the largest territory in Canada in land area, but one of the smallest in population. The majority of the population there is Inuit, an indigenous group of northern Canada that has been living in this region for more than 4,000 years. Originally the Inuit were nomads, moving from place to place, and hunting and fishing in the Arctic waters. They built houses from snow in the winter and lived in tents made from animal skins in the summer. Today, however, the lifestyle of many Inuit has changed. Most live in permanent homes in towns and cities. Hunting and fishing have remained important, but are often part of the commercial economy, rather than for subsistence.

Quebec

Capital	Quebec
Land Area	594,860 sq mi; 1,365,128 sq km
Population	7,432,005
Language(s)	French, English, Italian
Agriculture	dairy products, livestock, poultry, vegetables, corn, nurseries, maple products, fruit, potatoes, soybeans, barley, tobacco, wheat
Industry	manufacturing, electric power, mining, pulp and paper, transportation equipment

Saskatchewan

Capital	Regina
Land Area	251,866 sq mi; 591,670 sq km
Population	1,001,224
Language(s)	English, German, Cree, Ukrainian, French
Agriculture	wheat, livestock, canola, barley, lentils, dairy products, poultry, potatoes, nurseries, eggs, honey
Industry	agriculture, mining, manufacturing, electric power, construction, chemical production

Musicians in Montreal, Quebec

Yukon Territory

Capital	Whitehorse
Land Area	186,661 sq mi; 474,391 sq km
Population	29,552
Language(s)	English, German, French
Agriculture	nurseries, vegetables, poultry
Industry	mining, tourism

SOURCES: *CIA World Factbook*, 2002; *World Almanac*, 2003; *Canadian Global Almanac*, 2003, Canada Census, 2001

Assessment

Comprehension and Critical Thinking

1. Compare and Contrast Compare Nunavut and Ontario based on physical size and population size.

2. Draw Conclusions What characteristics do the three territories share?

3. Contrast How has geographic location affected the populations and industries of Canada's provinces and territories?

4. Categorize What are the major products in Canada?

5. Infer What can you infer about Nunavut if there are no agricultural products listed?

6. Make a Bar Graph Create a bar graph showing the population of the provinces and territories of Canada.

Keeping Current

Access the **DK World Desk Reference Online** at **PHSchool.com** for up-to-date information about Canada.

Go Online
PHSchool.com

Web Code: lhe-4501

Assess Progress ▐L2▌
Direct students' attention back to the columns on the board. Encourage them to suggest additional information to fill in under each heading based on what they learned from the Country Databank. Also, create new columns entitled *Land Area*, *Languages*, *Agriculture*, and *Industry*, and have students add the appropriate information. Then have students answer the Assessment questions.

Reteach ▐L2▌
Ask students to create a table on a large piece of poster board that shows the data for all of the provinces and territories in the Country Databank. Have them list the categories across the top of the table and the names of the regions along the side. Model filling in the information for one of the provinces on the board.

Extend ▐L3▌
Portfolio Activity Divide students into groups, and assign each group a data category for each province or territory that is not listed in the Country Databank, such as percentage of ethnic groups or exports and imports. Have students do research to find this information for each province or territory, and create a circle graph or bar graph that shows this information. Then have students add their work to their portfolios.

Answers

Assessment

1. Nunavut has over twice the land area as Ontario, while Ontario has over 400 times the population of Nunavut.

2. Characteristics they share include: small populations; English as at least one of their languages; mining and tourism as industries.

3. Location affects Canada's climate. Few people have settled in the colder areas where not many crops will grow. Canada's industries are affected by the natural resources of each area.

4. livestock, vegetables, eggs, and dairy products

5. that the land is not suitable to raise crops or livestock

6. Students' graphs will vary, but their bar graphs should reflect the correct populations of each province and territory.

Objectives

Social Studies

1. Read about the seat of the Canadian government in Ontario.
2. Learn about the French cultural influence in Quebec.

Reading/Language Arts

Use context clues to determine the meaning of unfamiliar words.

Prepare to Read

Build Background Knowledge L2

Ask students to suppose that while visiting Canada, they travel across the MacDonald-Cartier Bridge, which connects Ontario and Quebec. Tell them that the road signs on the Ontario side of the bridge are primarily in English, and the road signs on the Quebec side are primarily in French. Have students brainstorm the possible benefits and challenges of living in a country where neighboring regions speak different languages and have different cultures. Have students use the Give One, Get One participation strategy (TE, p. T37) to generate a list.

Set a Purpose for Reading L2

- Preview the Objectives.

- Read each statement in the *Reading Readiness Guide* aloud. Ask students to mark the statements true or false.

- Have students discuss the statements in pairs or groups of four, then mark their worksheets again. Use the Numbered Heads participation strategy (TE, p. T36) to call on students to share their group's perspectives.

All in One United States and Canada Teaching Resources, *Reading Readiness Guide*, p. 286

Vocabulary Builder
Preview Key Terms L2

Pronounce each Key Term, then ask students to say the word with you. Provide a simple explanation such as, "A Francophone is a person who learned to speak French before any other language."

Prepare to Read

Objectives
In this section you will
1. Read about the seat of the Canadian government in Ontario.
2. Learn about the French cultural influence in Quebec.

Taking Notes
As you read this section, look for ways that people in Quebec are preserving and celebrating their culture. Copy the concept web below, and record your findings in it.

Preserving French Culture

Target Reading Skill
Use Context Clues When you come across an unfamiliar word, you can often figure out its meaning from clues in the context. The context refers to the surrounding words, phrases, and sentences. Sometimes the context will define the word. In this example, the phrase in italics explains what a tariff is: Both countries charged tariffs, or *fees*, on imported goods.

Key Terms
- **federation** (fed ur AY shun) *n.* a union of states, groups, provinces, or nations
- **Francophone** (FRANG koh fohn) *n.* a person who speaks French as his or her first language
- **Quiet Revolution** (KWY ut rev uh LOO shun) *n.* a peaceful change in the government of Quebec
- **separatist** (SEP ur uh tist) *n.* a person who wants Quebec to become an independent country

The Macdonald-Cartier Bridge

152 United States and Canada

Much of the border between Ontario and Quebec is formed by the Ottawa River. The Macdonald-Cartier Bridge stretches across the river, connecting the two provinces. The bridge is named for two Canadian political leaders, one an English speaker and one a French speaker. While the bridge links the two provinces, its very name characterizes the differences between the provinces—people in Ontario speak English primarily, while people in Quebec mostly speak French.

In spite of this significant distinction, Ontario and Quebec have much in common. They are home to Canada's two largest cities—Toronto, Ontario, and Montreal, Quebec. They are the two most populous provinces in Canada. Canada's capital, Ottawa, is located in Ontario. But government functions spill over into the city of Hull, Quebec, located on the other end of the Macdonald-Cartier Bridge. Hull is considered Ottawa's "sister city" because a number of federal government office buildings dot its landscape.

Target Reading Skill L2

Use Context Clues Point out the Target Reading Skill. Tell students that terms and phrases surrounding an unknown word can provide clues to the unfamiliar word's meaning.

Model using context clues to find the meaning of *primarily* in the following sentence from p. 152: "While the bridge links the two provinces, its very name characterizes the differences between the provinces—people in Ontario speak English primarily, while people in Quebec mostly speak French." (*The surrounding information and the word* mostly *provide clues that* primarily *also means "mostly.")*

Give students *Use Context Clues: General*. Have them complete the activity in their groups.

All in One United States and Canada Teaching Resources, *Use Context Clues: General Knowledge*, p. 305

Ontario

The province of Ontario is perhaps Canada's most diverse province geographically. Located on the United States border, it reaches from Hudson Bay in the north to the Great Lakes in the south. Ontario's northern region is part of the Canadian Shield, the region of ancient rock that covers about half of Canada. The Canadian Shield has rocky terrain, rugged winters, and is sparsely populated. Ontario's southern lowlands have milder winters and warm summers. About one third of Canada's entire population lives in this southern area.

Canada's Federal Government
Canada is a federation, or union, of 10 provinces and 3 territories. In the Canadian federation, each province has its own government. Each of these governments shares power with Canada's central government, located in Ottawa.

Although Canada's formal head of state is the monarch of Britain, Canada has complete power over its own government. The head of state, represented by the governor general, performs mainly ceremonial duties, such as hosting politicians from other countries, supporting charitable causes, and honoring the achievements of Canadians. Unlike the United States, in which the president is head of state as well as head of government, Canada has a separate head of government, called the prime minister. The prime minister leads the government and is part of Canada's central legislature—the Canadian Parliament.

Ottawa Ottawa has been a capital city since the middle of the nineteenth century, when Upper and Lower Canada—present-day Ontario and Quebec—formed the Province of Canada. Ottawa was selected as the capital because it was located on the border of the two territories. In 1867, Nova Scotia and New Brunswick joined Ontario and Quebec to become the Dominion of Canada, an autonomous, or self-governing, member of the British Empire.

The Canadian Government

Diagram Skills

In the Canadian government structure, the executive, or prime minister, proposes laws; the legislature, Parliament, adopts laws; and the judiciary interprets laws. Stephen Harper, shown at left, was elected as Canadian prime minister in 2006. **Identify** Name the two houses of Parliament. **Contrast** How does Canada's head of state differ from the President of the United States?

Vocabulary Builder

Use the information below to teach students this section's high-use words.

High-Use Word	Definition and Sample Sentence
structure, p. 155	*n.* something (such as a building) that has been built "That's the largest **structure** in town," he said, pointing to a tall building.
mature, p. 155	*v.* to reach a final state Over the years, the sapling **matured** into a beautiful, tall tree.
issue, p. 157	*n.* something that is being discussed or debated, a problem to be talked over They debated the **issue** until it was time to go to bed.
margin, p. 157	*n.* the amount of the difference between two quantities It was almost a tie—John won by a very small **margin**.

Instruct

Ontario   L2

Guided Instruction

- **Vocabulary Builder** Clarify the high-use words **structure** and **mature** before reading.

- Read Ontario, using the Choral Reading technique (TE, p. T34).

- Discuss Canada's head of state and its head of government, pointing out who fills each role and how their functions differ. *(Canada's head of state is the monarch of Britain, while the country's head of government is the prime minister. The head of state is a ceremonial figure who hosts politicians from other countries and honors the achievements of Canadians. The head of government leads the government and is part of Canada's central legislature.)*

- Ask students to compare and contrast Ottawa and Toronto. *(Both cities are in Ontario, and both are capitals. Ottawa is the country's capital, while Toronto is the province's capital. Ottawa is Canada's center of government, while Toronto is Canada's largest city and its main commercial and financial center.)*

Independent Practice   L2
Assign *Guided Reading and Review.*

All in One **United States and Canada Teaching Resources,** *Guided Reading and Review,* p. 287

Monitor Progress   L2
Monitor the students as they complete the *Guided Reading and Review,* checking to make sure they understand and can answer the questions on the worksheet.

Answers
Diagram Skills **Identify** the House of Commons and the Senate **Contrast** Canada's head of state performs mainly ceremonial duties, while the President of the United States is both head of state and head of government.

Guided Instruction L2

Ask students to study the Regional Profile on this page. Remind them to read the map key to fully understand the population density map of Ontario. Also encourage them to study the table and think about the information each provides. As a class, answer the Map and Chart Skills questions. Allow students to briefly discuss their responses with a partner before sharing answers.

Independent Practice

Distribute *Reading a Population Density Map*. Discuss the differences between the map on the worksheet and the one of Ontario on page 154. Have students work in pairs to complete the worksheet.

All in One **United States and Canada Teaching Resources,** *Reading a Population Density Map*, p. 316

Ontario

Canada separated from England very gradually. It went from a dependent colony of England, to a dominion, and finally to an independent nation with ties to Great Britain through the British Commonwealth of Nations. As you study the map and charts, compare and contrast Canada's government with that of the United States.

The House of Commons

Province or Territory	Seats
Alberta	28
British Columbia	36
Manitoba, Saskatchewan	14
New Brunswick	10
Newfoundland and Labrador	7
Northwest Territories, Nunavut, Yukon Territory	1
Nova Scotia	11
Ontario	106
Prince Edward Island	4
Quebec	75

SOURCE: *Canadian Global Almanac, 2003*

Structure of Government

	Canada	United States
Head of State (ceremonial)	Queen of England Governor General (the Queen's representative)	President (elected by the voters)
Head of Government (political)	Prime Minister (PM, the leader of the majority party in the House of Commons)	President
Legislature	Parliament • House of Commons (elected by the voters) • Senate (appointed by PM)	Congress • House of Representatives (elected) • Senate (elected)
Districts	Provinces and territories	States

Ontario: Population Density
KEY

Persons per sq. mile		Persons per sq. kilometer
More than 129		More than 49
25–129		10–49
1–24		1–9
Less than 1		Less than 1

Urban Areas
- □ More than 4,999,999
- ⊙ 1,000,000–4,999,999
- • 500,000–999,999
- · Less than 500,000
- — National border
- — Provincial or territorial border

Map and Chart Skills

1. **Note** Where is most of Ontario's population located?
2. **Explain** How does population affect the number of seats a province or territory has in the House of Commons?
3. **Analyze** What is the difference in the roles of the voters in Canada and in the United States?

 Use Web Code **Ihe-4511** for **DK World Desk Reference Online.**

Answers

Map and Chart Skills

1. southern Ontario
2. Territories and provinces with larger populations have more seats; those with smaller populations have fewer.
3. Voters in the United States have a more direct role in electing government leaders.

Go Online **PHSchool.com** Students can find more information about this topic on the DK World Desk Reference Online.

Differentiated Instruction

For English Language Learners L3

Check for students' comprehension of the term *cultural mosaic,* which appears in the second paragraph on p. 155. Have students read the Spanish Support section of the United States and Canada Teaching Resources. Then ask them to write in their own words what it means that "Toronto has matured into a cultural mosaic with a very diverse population." Have pairs of students read their explanations to each other and discuss whether they both understand the term to mean the same thing. If they do not agree about the term, mediate a discussion between them about the possible meanings.

Guided Reading and Review (Spanish), **Spanish Support,** p. 42

Toronto Each of Canada's provinces has a capital. Toronto is the capital of Ontario. It is also Canada's largest city and its commercial and financial center. Founded in 1793, Toronto was first known as York. Its location on Lake Ontario made it a major trade and transportation center. Toronto has come to be identified by its Canadian National (CN) Tower, which, at 1,815 feet (553 meters), is the world's tallest freestanding structure.

Toronto has matured into a cultural mosaic with a very diverse population—nearly half of its residents are foreign-born. After World War II, a large number of Europeans immigrated to Canada, with many settling in Toronto.

The most recent wave of immigrants included a large number of Asians. About 10 percent of Toronto's residents are of Chinese ethnicity. British, Italian, First Nations, Portuguese, East Indian, Greek, German, Ukrainian, Polish, and French are among the other ethnic groups that make up Toronto's population.

✓ **Reading Check** Where is Canada's federal government located?

Toronto Cityscape
The CN Tower (right) dominates Toronto's skyline. The large aerial photo taken from the tower shows Rogers Centre (formerly the SkyDome), home of the Toronto Blue Jays baseball team. It was the first domed stadium built with a roof that opens and closes.
Draw Conclusions Why would a domed stadium be needed in Toronto?

Learn about Toronto: Canada's largest city

Chapter 5 Section 1 **155**

French Culture in Quebec L2

Guided Instruction

- **Vocabulary Builder** Clarify the high-use words **issue** and **margin** before reading.

- Ask students to read about the role French history and culture has played in Quebec in French Culture in Quebec. As students read, circulate and make sure individuals can answer the Reading Check question.

- Discuss some of the peaceful ways in which the French separatist movement in Quebec took shape. *(Early on, the government helped the French separatist movement take shape peacefully by creating better job opportunities for Francophones. Later, the government made French the official language of Quebec and required immigrants to Quebec to learn the language. Additionally, the question of whether or not Quebec should become a separate nation was decided by voting rather than by fighting.)*

Show students *Toronto: Canada's Financial Center.* Ask students to explain why Toronto is one of Canada's most important cities. *(With a large and diverse population, Toronto is the country's cultural, commercial, and financial center.)*

Differentiated Instruction

For Special Needs Students L1
Have students read the section as they listen to the recorded version on the Student Edition on Audio CD. Then have them write a summary of French Culture in Quebec as they read the section to themselves again.

⊙ Chapter 5, Section 1, **Student Edition on Audio CD**

For Gifted and Talented L3
Have students conduct research to find five aspects of French-Canadian culture that are not in the text. Have them use *Preparing for Presentations,* to help them present their findings to the class.

All in One **United States and Canada Teaching Resources,** *Preparing for Presentations,* p. 323

Answers
Draw Conclusions so baseball can be played in bad weather
✓ **Reading Check** Ottawa, Ontario

Ask students to give examples of how Quebec's culture reflects a mix of French and local influences. (*People have added local ingredients such as maple syrup to French-style cooking. Quebec's architecture is also a mix of French and Canadian styles.*)

Independent Practice
Ask students to create the Taking Notes graphic organizer on a blank piece of paper. Then ask them to fill in the ovals with the information they have just learned. Briefly model how to fill in separate pieces of information in each oval.

French Culture in Quebec

French culture first reached Quebec in the 1500s, when Jacques Cartier (zhahk kahr tee AY), a French explorer, sailed along the St. Lawrence River and landed in a village called Stadacona (stad uh KOH nuh). The Iroquois, the native people of the area, inhabited the village. Today, the site of that village is the city of Quebec, capital of the province of Quebec.

Cartier claimed the region we now know as Quebec for France and named it Canada. Great Britain, however, was also interested in the region. French and British forces fought for the land in four separate wars over a period of nearly 80 years. The last of the battles were part of the French and Indian War. In 1759, the British captured the city of Quebec. Within four years, France surrendered all of its North American land east of the Mississippi River to the British.

Despite Great Britain's victory, tens of thousands of French colonists remained in the region, and their descendants make up the majority of Quebec's population today. They are called **Francophones** (FRANG koh fohnz), or people who speak French as their first language. In Quebec's largest city, Montreal, and its surrounding areas, more than 65 percent of the population are Francophones.

French Influence in Quebec
French culture reached Quebec hundreds of years ago, and it still exists in the capital city today.
Analyze Images *How can the influence of French culture be seen in this street in Quebec City?*

156 United States and Canada

Skills Mini Lesson

Recognizing Bias L2

1. Teach the skill by explaining that a biased statement expresses a slanted opinion that is not supported by facts and often used loaded words.

2. Have students practice the skill by assessing if the following statement if biased: *French Canadian separatists wanted the beautiful, expressive French language to* be Quebec's official language and the charming French-Canadian traditions to be maintained.

3. Have students apply the skill by rewriting the sentence above to make it more fair. Students should eliminate any loaded words (*beautiful, expressive, charming*) and be sure the statement can be supported with facts from the chapter.

Answer

Analyze Images Signs are written in French.

Francophones Seek Rights In the 1960s, many Francophones began to express concern that their language and culture might die, because English was spoken in the schools and at work. They also believed that opportunities for Francophones in Quebec were not equal to those for English speakers. For the most part, Francophones got jobs with lower pay. So they set out to create change, in a movement that was similar to the civil rights movement in the United States in the 1960s. In 1960, the Liberal party, which supported Francophones, came to power in Quebec. Prime Minister Jean Lesage led the government in creating better job opportunities for Francophones and in modernizing education and health care in Quebec. This change in the government became known as the **Quiet Revolution** because great changes were brought about peacefully.

Disagreement on Separation
A Quebec resident (left) displays her opposition to separation. Other people carrying signs calling for independence and sovereignty rally to support the split from Canada (above). **Analyze Images** *What evidence is there that the woman at the left is against the Separatist Movement?*

The Separatist Movement During the Quiet Revolution, the separatist movement began to grow. **Separatists** are people who want to see Quebec break away from the rest of Canada and become an independent country. French-Canadian separatists saw important victories in the 1970s as French became the official language of Quebec and the children of immigrants to the province were required to learn French. But still, Quebec remained a province of Canada.

Not everyone in Quebec supported the idea of separation from Canada. In 1980, the provincial government held a referendum. In a referendum, voters cast ballots for or against an issue. This referendum asked voters whether Quebec should become a separate nation. A majority voted no.

In 1995, Quebec held another referendum. Again, Quebec's people voted to remain part of Canada. But this time the margin was very slim—50.6 percent voted against separation while 49.4 percent voted for it. Since then, separatists have lost power and positions in government, but they vow that they will continue to fight for Quebec's independence.

Use Context Clues If you do not know what a referendum is, look for a context clue. Here, the sentence following *referendum* is a definition of the term. What is a referendum?

Monitor Progress

- As students fill in the graphic organizer, circulate and make sure individuals are choosing logical details to place in the concept web. Provide assistance as needed.

- Show *Section Reading Support Transparency USC 58* and ask students to check their graphic organizers individually. Go over key concepts and clarify key vocabulary as needed.

  United States and Canada Transparencies, *Section Reading Support Transparency USC 58*

- Tell students to fill in the last column of the *Reading Readiness Guide*. Probe for what they learned that confirms or invalidates each statement.

  All in One United States and Canada Teaching Resources, *Reading Readiness Guide,* p. 286

Target Reading Skill

Use Context Clues As a follow up, ask students to answer the Target Reading Skill question in the Student Edition. *(In a referendum, voters cast ballots for or against an issue.)*

Skills Mini Lesson

Supporting a Position L2

1. Teach the skill by explaining that one supports a position by identifying reasons, supporting each with facts, and drawing a valid conclusion.

2. Help students practice the skill by reading the passages about Quebec and its separatist movement on pp. 156–157 and stating the position of separatists in

   Quebec. *(The separatists want Quebec to break away from the rest of Canada.)*

3. Have students apply the skill by determining the reasons why many Francophones became separatists. *(They feared their language and culture would die out, and they felt they did not have equal opportunities.)*

Answer

Analyze Images The woman is holding the Canadian flag and has the Canadian maple leaf painted on her face. She also has a sticker that reads "No" in English on her forehead.

Guided Instruction `L2`

Ask students to study the Regional Profile on this page. Encourage students to study the map, circle graph, and time lines carefully. As a class, answer the Map and Chart Skills questions. Allow students to briefly discuss their responses with a partner before sharing answers.

Independent Practice

Ask students to consider the circle graph on this page. It shows how Montreal's population is divided among different languages. Ask students to write a paragraph comparing the percentages of Montreal residents who speak English, French, both, and neither. Encourage students to include a comment on how this breakdown relates to Quebec's history.

Answers

Map and Chart Skills

1. in southern Quebec and along the St. Lawrence River

2. The names of some provinces and bodies of water reflect Canada's early history. City names in Quebec reflect French heritage.

3. Possible answer: the language law may have made some separatists more willing to have Quebec remain part of Canada.

Go Online PHSchool.com Students can find more information about this topic on the DK World Desk Reference Online.

REGIONAL PROFILE
Focus on History

Quebec

Like much of Canada, Quebec's early history was shaped by two countries—Great Britain and France. Unlike the rest of the nation, however, French influence has remained particularly strong in Quebec. The province's recent history reflects the importance of the French legacy in the region. As you study the map, chart, and timelines, think about how history and culture have interacted in Quebec throughout its history.

Languages Spoken in Montreal

- 2%
- 8%
- 40%
- 50%

- English and French
- French
- English
- Neither

SOURCE: *Canadian Global Almanac, 2003*

Quebec: Population Density

KEY

Persons per sq. mile	Persons per sq. kilometer
More than 129	More than 49
25–129	10–49
1–24	1–9
Less than 1	Less than 1

Urban Areas
- ⊙ More than 999,999
- ● 500,000–999,999
- · Less than 500,000

— National border
— Provincial or territorial border

0 miles 400
0 kilometers 400
Lambert Azimuthal Equal Area

Early Canadian History

1608 Samuel de Champlain builds a fort at Quebec for the French fur trade.

1663 King Louis XIV declares New France a royal colony.

1754 French and Indian War pits the British against the French.

1600 — 1650 — 1700 — 1750 — 1800

1610 English explorer Henry Hudson charts Hudson Bay.

1670 Hudson's Bay Company is set up in England.

1763 The Treaty of Paris ends French control of Canada.

Recent Quebec History

1968 Interest grows in a separate French-speaking province.

1976 Parti Québécois (PQ) takes power under Premier René Lévesque.

1980 In a referendum, Quebec votes to stay a part of federal Canada.

1965 — 1970 — 1975 — 1980

1977 French becomes the official language of Quebec.

Map and Chart Skills

1. **Identify** Where is most of Quebec's population located?

2. **Infer** How do the place names on the map reflect early Canadian history?

3. **Analyze** What effect do you think the language law had on those who wanted Quebec to be a separate country?

Go Online PHSchool.com Use Web Code lhe-4521 for DK World Desk Reference Online.

Differentiated Instruction

For Advanced Readers `L3`

Have students read the quotations on the *Enrichment* worksheet. Then ask students to write a summary titled "The Canadian Identity" using both the *Enrichment* sheet and the Regional Profile.

All in One **United States and Canada Teaching Resources,** *Enrichment,* p. 310

For Less Proficient Readers `L1`

Pair students with more proficient readers to read *Shadows on the Rock*. Have students take turns reading the paragraphs aloud. Then have the pairs answer the questions at the end of the reading.

All in One **United States and Canada Teaching Resources,** *Shadows on the Rock,* pp. 320–322

Celebrating Quebec's Culture One of the ways in which Quebec's people celebrate their culture is through festivals. The Quebec Winter Carnival lasts 17 days. Fantastic ice sculptures adorn Quebec City, and canoe races take place among the ice floes in the St. Lawrence River.

Another Quebec festival honors St. Jean-Baptiste (zhahn bah TEEST), or John the Baptist, the patron saint, or special guardian, of French Canadians. This festival is held June 24. All over the province, people celebrate with bonfires, firecrackers, and street dances.

French style and cooking flourish in Quebec—with Quebec variations. Sugar pie, for example, uses maple sugar from the province's forests. Quebec also has French architecture. The people of Quebec take pride in preserving their lively culture.

✓ **Reading Check** What is the official language of Quebec?

An ice slide sculpture at Quebec City's Winter Carnival

Section 1 Assessment

Key Terms
Review the key terms at the beginning of this section. Use each key term in a sentence that explains its meaning.

⟳ **Target Reading Skill**
Find the word *autonomous* on page 153. Use context to figure out its meaning. What clue helped you figure out its meaning?

Comprehension and Critical Thinking
1. (a) **Identify** Who is the head of state in Canada?

(b) **Contrast** How does the head of state differ from the head of government?
(c) **Analyze** What are the possible benefits of this kind of system?
2. (a) **Recall** How many people in and around Montreal are Francophones?
(b) **Make Generalizations** Why are French-Canadians concerned with preserving their heritage?
(c) **Summarize** What has the Canadian government done to meet the demands of French-Canadians?

Writing Activity
You have read that some people in Quebec want to remain a part of Canada while others want Quebec to become a separate country. Write a paragraph giving your opinion on the subject. Be sure to give reasons for your point of view.

For: An activity on Quebec
Visit: PHSchool.com
Web Code: lhd-4501

Writing Activity
Use the *Rubric for Assessing a Writing Assignment* to evaluate students' paragraphs.

All in One **United States and Canada Teaching Resources,** *Rubric for Assessing a Writing Assignment,* p. 326

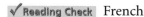 Typing in the Web code when prompted will bring students directly to detailed instructions for this activity.

Assess and Reteach

Assess Progress [L2]
Have students complete the Section Assessment. Administer the *Section Quiz.*

All in One **United States and Canada Teaching Resources,** *Section Quiz,* p. 288

Reteach [L1]
If students need more instruction, have them read this section in the Reading and Vocabulary Study Guide.

📖 Chapter 5, Section 1, **United States and Canada Reading and Vocabulary Study Guide,** pp. 55–57

Extend [L3]
Have students learn more about French Canadians and Quebec by completing the *Small Group Activity: Writing a Newspaper Feature.*

All in One **United States and Canada Teaching Resources,** *Small Group Activity: Writing a Newspaper Feature,* pp. 312–315

Answers

✓ **Reading Check** French

Section 1 Assessment

Key Terms
Students' sentences should reflect knowledge of each Key Term.

⟳ **Target Reading Skill**
Autonomous means self-governing. This definition is given in the sentence.

Comprehension and Critical Thinking
1. **(a)** the monarch of Britain **(b)** The head of state is a ceremonial figure, while the head of government—the prime minister—leads the government and is part of Canada's central legislature. **(c)** Answers will vary, but may include the possible benefit that each leader can focus solely on his or her specific duties.

2. **(a)** more than 80 percent **(b)** As a minority in Canada, French Canadians are concerned that their language and culture might be lost. **(c)** It has created better job opportunities for French Canadians, modernized education and health care in Quebec, and made French the official language of Quebec.

Section 2
Step-by-Step Instruction

Objectives

Social Studies
1. Learn why many immigrants came to the Prairie Provinces in the 1800s.
2. Read about how Canadians celebrate their cultural traditions.

Reading/Language Arts
Practice interpreting the meaning of non-literal language.

Prepare to Read

Build Background Knowledge   L2
Tell students that they will learn about the Canadian plains in this section. The Canadian plains are part of the same prairie that makes up much of the Midwest region of the United States. Have students watch the video *Canada's Prairie Provinces* and note two to three similarities between the Canadian prairie and the American prairie they learned about in the last chapter. Ask students to share their ideas using the Numbered Heads participation strategy (TE, p. T36).

📼 *Canada's Prairie Provinces,* **World Studies Video Program**

Set a Purpose for Reading   L2
- Preview the Objectives.

- Read each statement in the *Reading Readiness Guide* aloud. Ask students to mark the statements true or false.

  All in One **United States and Canada Teaching Resources,** *Reading Readiness Guide,* p. 290

- Have students discuss the statements in pairs or groups of four, then mark their worksheets again. Use the Numbered Heads participation strategy (TE, p. T36) to call on students to share their group's perspectives.

Vocabulary Builder
Preview Key Terms   L2
Pronounce each Key Term, then ask students to say the word with you. Provide a simple explanation such as, "If you have immunity to a disease, you will not catch the disease."

Section 2 The Prairie Provinces
Canada's Breadbasket

Prepare to Read

Objectives
In this section you will
1. Learn why many immigrants came to the Prairie Provinces in the 1800s.
2. Read about how Canadians celebrate their cultural traditions.

Taking Notes
As you read this section, looks for details about European immigration to the Prairie Provinces. Copy the chart below, and record your findings in it.

🎯 Target Reading Skill

Interpret Nonliteral Meanings Literal language means exactly what it says. Nonliteral language uses images to communicate an idea. Sometimes nonliteral language communicates a point more vividly than literal language. In this section, you will read about "Canada's Breadbasket." When you see these words, ask yourself: How does nonliteral language make a point about the Prairie Provinces region?

Key Terms
- **descent** (dee SENT) *n.* a person's ancestry
- **immunity** (ih MYOO nuh tee) *n.* a natural resistance to disease

Sheets of floating ice in Hudson Bay

One day in 1821, after a difficult journey, about 200 Swiss immigrants reached Hudson Bay in northern Canada. They wanted to become farmers in the region that now includes Saskatchewan (sas KACH uh wahn), Alberta, and Manitoba. Stories of good land and an excellent climate attracted the settlers to the vast plains. But no shelter, food, or supplies awaited them. The settlers survived only because the native people of the region, the Saulteaux (sawl TOH), helped them.

The winters were harsh. In summer they had to put up with drought, floods, and swarms of grasshoppers. With few trees on the plains, people built homes out of prairie sod—strips of grass with thick roots and soil attached. They cut it into blocks, which they piled up to make walls in the same way that American settlers did in the Midwest. "Soddies" were cheap, but if it rained, the roofs leaked. Few settlers had farming experience, and they did not anticipate such hardships.

🎯 Target Reading Skill   L2

Interpret Nonliteral Meanings Point out the Target Reading Skill. Tell students that nonliteral language often uses images to vividly communicate an idea.

Model how to interpret nonliteral meanings by reading the first paragraph on page 164. Point out that the information in this paragraph helps make it clear that "boomed" is a nonliteral way of saying "grew very quickly."

Give students *Recognize Nonliteral Meanings.* Have them complete the activity in their groups.

All in One **United States and Canada Teaching Resources,** *Recognize Nonliteral Meanings,* p. 306

The Prairie Provinces

Manitoba, Saskatchewan, and Alberta are located on the largest prairie in the world, stretching across the three provinces and down into the central United States. As a result, they are often called the Prairie Provinces. These provinces occupy lands where indigenous peoples have lived for thousands of years.

A Way of Life Ends The Cree and Saulteaux were among the indigenous peoples who lived on the plains in present-day Manitoba. The Cree, Blackfoot, and Assiniboine (uh SIN uh boyn) lived in present-day Alberta. The Chipewyan (chip uh WY un) and Sioux, also called Dakota, are native to Saskatchewan.

These native peoples were deeply connected to the plants and animals of their lands. Buffalo, in particular, were the foundation of their daily lives. Buffalo meat provided food, and buffalo hides were made into clothing. Regina, now the capital of Saskatchewan, was once a place the Cree called *Wascana*, which means "pile of bones." Here people made buffalo bones into tools. Despite their dependence on the buffalo, however, native peoples only used what they needed. Huge numbers of buffalo remained.

In the late 1870s, however, that changed. People of European **descent,** or ancestry, moved into the region and began killing off the buffalo herds that blanketed the region. People killed the buffalo both for sport and for their hides. In a few years, nearly all the buffalo were gone. At the same time, the government of Canada began to take over the indigenous peoples' land. Most agreed to give up their land and live on reserves. The ways of life of many indigenous peoples in the Plains region of North America had come to an end.

A Buffalo Hunt
By the 1730s, Plains Indians were able to trade for horses. **Analyze Images** *How did horses help the Plains Indians to hunt buffalo more effectively?*

Explore the Canadian Plains region

Guided Instruction

- **Vocabulary Builder** Clarify the high-use word **occupy** before reading.

- Read The Prairie Provinces, using the Structured Silent Reading technique (TE, p. T34).

- Ask students **In what ways did indigenous people on the plains rely on the buffalo?** (*The buffalo provided indigenous people with meat, hides for clothing, and bones to use to make tools.*)

- Then ask **How did the arrival of European settlers change life for indigenous people on the plains?** (*Settlers killed nearly all the buffalo and most indigenous people were moved onto reserves. Plains Indians were also affected by diseases brought by Europeans.*)

Show students *Canada's Prairie Provinces.* Ask **What factors make farming and raising livestock difficult in this region?** (*the cold climate, drought, insects, and disease.*)

Vocabulary Builder

Use the information below to teach students this section's high-use word.

High-Use Word	Definition and Sample Sentence
occupy, p. 161	*v.* to take up space, fill Someone already **occupied** the seat next to Rita.

Answer

Analyze Images Horses allowed hunters to get closer to the buffalo, and to follow buffalo herds for longer distances.

Guided Instruction
L2

Ask students to study the Regional Profile on this page. Remind them to read the map key to understand what the different symbols on the map represent. Also encourage them to study the graphs carefully. As a class, answer the Map and Chart Skills questions. Allow students to briefly discuss their responses with a partner before sharing answers.

Independent Practice

- Help students read the line graph by asking them to list approximately how many farms were in the Prairie Provinces in each of the five years shown on the graph. Then have students write a sentence stating whether the number of farms increased or decreased over time.

- Help students read the bar graph by asking them to fill in the following sentence for each product: "_____% of Canadian _____ is grown in the Prairie Provinces." Ask them to summarize the three sentences with a conclusion about whether the Prairie Provinces produce most of or only a little of Canada's wheat, barley, rye, and oats.

Answers

Map and Chart Skills

1. wheat, barley, rye, oats
2. about 200 acres larger
3. The Prairie Provinces still have the best land in Canada for raising wheat, barley, rye, and oats and new technologies have helped increase crops.

Go Online PHSchool.com Students can find more information about this topic on the DK World Desk Reference Online.

REGIONAL PROFILE
Focus on Economics

Prairie Provinces

Canada is the world's second-largest exporter of wheat, after the United States. Although the size of farms in Canada is growing larger, there are fewer of them. Farmers take advantage of science and new technology to increase their crop production. But the new methods are expensive, so corporate farms are replacing small family farms. As you study the map and charts, think about where the food you eat comes from.

Number of Farms in Prairie Provinces

SOURCE: Statistics Canada

Average Size of Farms in Prairie Provinces

SOURCE: Statistics Canada

Percent of Canadian Grains Grown in Prairie Provinces

Wheat 95% Barley and rye 90% Oats 75%

SOURCE: *Canadian Wheat Board, Canadian Global Almanac,* 2004

Prairie Provinces: Land Use
KEY
- Forestry
- Livestock raising
- Commercial agriculture
- Manufacturing and trade
- Limited economic activity
- National border
- Provincial or territorial border

Map and Chart Skills

1. **Identify** What important crops are grown in the Prairie Provinces?
2. **Note** How much larger was a Prairie Province farm in 2001 than in 1981?
3. **Draw Conclusions** How is it possible that the number of farms has decreased but the Prairie Provinces produce most of Canada's wheat, barley, rye, and oats?

Go Online PHSchool.com Use Web Code lhe-4511 for **DK World Desk Reference Online.**

162 United States and Canada

Differentiated Instruction

For Gifted and Talented
L3
Have students research crops other than wheat that Canada produces. Ask students to make a poster showing where each is grown.

For Advanced Readers
L3
Have students research to learn more about the role of wheat production in Canada's economy. Ask them to write a summary of their findings, including at least three pieces of information that they did not learn in the textbook.

Increasing Immigration The population of the indigenous peoples also began to shrink. This happened, in part, because European immigrants brought diseases to which the Plains Indians did not have **immunity,** or natural resistance. At the same time, the European population swelled. The settlers were eager to farm the prairie. The Canadian government encouraged people to settle on the Plains. Newcomers would help the economy grow. In the late 1800s and early 1900s, Canada advertised free land in European newspapers. The advertisements worked, and immigration increased. From 1900 to 1910, the population of Alberta alone increased by more than 500 percent.

Until the early 1900s, nearly all Canadians were indigenous peoples or people of French or British descent. That quickly changed. German, French, Belgian, Ukrainian, Hungarian, and Scandinavian immigrants all came to the Prairie Provinces. These immigrants farmed, mined, ranched, and participated in the fur trade.

Links to
Science

Sanctuary Visitors to Saskatchewan's Grasslands National Park see some of North America's last untouched prairies. Ancient grasses called wheat grass, spear grass, and sage blow in the wind. The park is also home to 12 endangered and threatened species. They include hawks, burrowing owls, and short-horned lizards (below).

Prairie wheat grows in Saskatchewan, Canada.

Guided Instruction (continued)

- Ask **What did the Canadian government do to encourage immigration to Canada?** *(The government advertised free land in European newspapers.)*

- Ask **What effect did these advertisements have on Canada's population and economy?** *(European immigration increased, causing the population to grow. Immigrants contributed to the economy by farming, ranching, mining, and trading furs.)*

Independent Practice

Ask students to create the Taking Notes graphic organizer on a blank piece of paper. Then ask them to fill in causes and effects from the information they have just learned. Briefly model how to distinguish between a cause and an effect.

Monitor Progress

As students fill in the graphic organizer, circulate and make sure individuals are correctly placing causes in the Causes box and effects in the Effects box. Provide assistance as needed.

Links

Read the **Links to Science** on this page. Ask students **Why do you think it is necessary to create sanctuaries such as Saskatchewan's Grasslands National Park?** *(Answers will vary, but may include the need to ensure that animals and plants are preserved from extinction.)*

Differentiated Instruction

For English Language Learners ☐L1
Pair students with native English speakers to read the Links to Science. Ask both students in each pair to read the box aloud, with the English language learner reading first. Then have the students work together to write a summary of the box in their own words.

For Special Needs Students ☐L1
Have students read the section as they listen to the recorded version on the Student Edition on Audio CD. Check for comprehension of concepts such as *ancestry* and *immunity* by pausing the CD and asking students to try to describe them aloud.

⊙ Chapter 5, Section 2, **Student Edition on Audio CD**

Celebrating Traditions L2

Guided Instruction
- Ask students to read Celebrating Traditions. As students read, circulate and make sure individuals can answer the Reading Check question.

- Ask students to name the different celebrations that take place in the Prairie Provinces, the city each occurs in, and the heritage each commemorates. (*The Calgary Stampede in Calgary, Alberta, commemorates the area's ranching heritage. Klondike Days in Edmonton, Alberta, commemorates the area's gold rush. Festival du Voyageur in Winnipeg, Manitoba, commemorates the area's fur-trading heritage. The Weyburn Wheat Festival in Weyburn, Saskatchewan, commemorates the area's wheat crop.*)

Independent Practice
Have students complete the graphic organizer by filling in the last few effects of immigrants arriving in the Prairie Provinces.

Monitor Progress
- Show *Section Reading Support Transparency USC 59* and ask students to check their graphic organizers individually. Go over key concepts and clarify key vocabulary as needed.

  United States and Canada Transparencies, *Section Reading Support Transparency USC 59*

- Tell students to fill in the last column of the *Reading Readiness Guide*. Probe for what they learned that confirms or invalidates each statement.

  All in One United States and Canada Teaching Resources, *Reading Readiness Guide*, p. 290

Target Reading Skill L2
Interpret Nonliteral Meanings As a follow up, ask students to answer the Target Reading Skill question in the Student Edition. (*the region that produces most of the country's wheat*)

Answers

✓ Reading Check because it produces so much wheat

Compare The Midwest is similar to the Prairie Provinces of Canada because the regions share similar types of farmland.

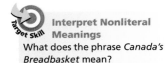

Interpret Nonliteral Meanings
What does the phrase *Canada's Breadbasket* mean?

Harvesting Wheat
This farmer harvests wheat near Saskatoon, Saskatchewan. Saskatchewan has more farmland than any other Canadian province. It is also Canada's largest producer of wheat.
Compare *What part of the United States is similar to this part of Canada? Explain why.*

Farming the Land Many of the European immigrants who arrived became wheat farmers. In 1886, the completion of the Canadian Pacific Railway allowed settlers to reach the Prairie Provinces more easily. Better transportation also meant that wheat could be carried more quickly from farms to Canadian ports and then to the rest of the world. The wheat economy of Canada boomed.

Today, more than three fourths of Canada's farmland is in the Prairie Provinces. Wheat is still the major crop. Every year since the mid-1930s, Saskatchewan has produced more than half of Canada's wheat crop. This has helped Canada to become one of the world's leading exporters of wheat. It is no wonder then, that the region is known as Canada's Breadbasket. Although corporate farming is increasing, there are still more family-run farms in Canada than there are in the United States.

✓ Reading Check **Why is this region known as Canada's Breadbasket?**

164 United States and Canada

Differentiated Instruction

For Less Proficient Readers L1
Pair less proficient readers with more advanced readers and ask each pair to make a chart titled "Prairie Province Celebrations." Students should use the following column headings for their charts: *Name of Celebration, Location, What it Commemorates,* and *Events Involved.*

For Gifted and Talented L3
Ask students to select a Prairie Province celebration that interests them, such as the Calgary Stampede or Klondike Days. Have them write a fictional account of attending the celebration. Students should use details from at least two sources other than the textbook.

Celebrating Traditions

Each year, cities of the Prairie Provinces celebrate their ethnic or cultural heritage. In Calgary, Alberta, the Calgary Stampede commemorates the area's ranching legacy. This ten-day rodeo event has been held in Calgary since 1912. It offers a large variety of events such as chuck-wagon races, cow-milking contests, and bull riding. For ten days every July, the city of Edmonton, Alberta, celebrates the gold rush with its Klondike Days. Popular events include the raft race and the sourdough pancake breakfast. (During the gold rush many prospectors ate sourdough bread and biscuits).

Festival du Voyageur is held each February in Winnipeg, the capital of Manitoba. It honors the French Canadian fur-trading heritage of the area and features traditional food, arts and crafts, and exhibits. And in Weyburn, Saskatchewan, residents pay tribute to wheat as the area's most important crop with the Weyburn Wheat Festival. A great deal of fun at this festival comes from harvesting competitions and plant shows. The smell of fresh-baked bread from outdoor ovens adds to the atmosphere.

Rodeo events take place during the Calgary Stampede in Calgary, Alberta.

√ **Reading Check** Which Canadian festival celebrates ranching?

Section 2 Assessment

Key Terms
Review the key terms at the beginning of this section. Use each key term in a sentence that explains its meaning.

Target Reading Skill
Find the phrase "buffalo herds that blanketed the region" on page 161. Explain in your own words what it means.

Comprehension and Critical Thinking
1. (a) List Which three provinces make up the Prairie Provinces?
(b) Explain What attracted thousands of European immigrants to the Canadian Prairie Provinces?

(c) Identify Effects How did the lives of indigenous people in the Canadian plains change after Europeans arrived?
2. (a) Recall Name two ways that Canadians celebrate their cultural heritage.
(b) Identify Effects How have European immigrants influenced the life and culture of the Prairie Provinces?
(c) Draw Conclusions What do you think were the advantages and disadvantages of moving to the Canadian plains in the 1800s?

Writing Activity
Suppose that it is the year 1900, and you work for Canada's government. The government will give 160 acres of land to people willing to come to the Prairie Provinces to start farms. Make a poster advertising free land. Describe conditions that would make settlers want to come.

Go Online
PHSchool.com

For: An activity on Saskatchewan
Visit: PHSchool.com
Web Code: lhd-4502

Writing Activity
Use the *Rubric for Assessing a Student Poster* to evaluate students' posters advertising free land.

All in One United States and Canada Teaching Resources, *Rubric for Assessing a Student Poster,* p. 325

Go Online
PHSchool.com Typing in the Web code when prompted will bring students directly to detailed instructions for this activity.

Assess Progress L2
Have students complete the Section Assessment. Administer the *Section Quiz.*

All in One United States and Canada Teaching Resources, *Section Quiz,* p. 292

Reteach L1
If students need more instruction, have them read this section in the Reading and Vocabulary Study Guide.

 Chapter 5, Section 2, **United States and Canada Reading and Vocabulary Study Guide,** pp. 58–60

Extend L3
Have student groups organize a fair that celebrates the different cultural groups of the Prairie Provinces. Each group should research one cultural group. Encourage students to find out about traditional crafts, dances, clothes, and art. Suggest that they obtain recordings of music or prepare food that represents the cultural group they are presenting.

Answers

√ **Reading Check** the Calgary Stampede

Section 2 Assessment

Key Terms
Students' sentences should reflect knowledge of each Key Term.

Target Reading Skill
Possible answer: the herds of buffalo were large and covered vast areas of land.

Comprehension and Critical Thinking
1. (a) Alberta, Manitoba, and Saskatchewan **(b)** The Canadian government offered free land to settlers. **(c)** The buffalo that the indigenous people relied on were killed off. Most indigenous people agreed to give up their land and live on reserves. However, many died because of diseases brought by the immigrants.

2. (a) Canadians celebrate their heritage with festivals that include contests and traditional foods and crafts. **(b)** by bringing new industries, skills, and traditions **(c)** Answers will vary. Advantages include free farm land and new opportunities. Disadvantages include lack of food and supplies, harsh winters, and few trees for building.

Section 3
Step-by-Step Instruction

Objectives

Social Studies

1. Find out about the people and cultures of the Canadian West.
2. Learn what the economy and culture of British Columbia are like.

Reading/Language Arts

Use context clues to determine the meaning of unfamiliar words.

Prepare to Read

Build Background Knowledge L2

Tell students that most people in British Columbia live closer to Asia than to the east coast of their own country. Encourage them to think about how this might affect life in British Columbia. Ask students to think back to what they learned about French Canada in Section 1, then use the Give One, Get One participation strategy (TE, p. T37) to brainstorm a list of ways that the cultures of the east and west coasts of Canada might differ.

Set a Purpose for Reading L2

■ Preview the Objectives.

■ Read each statement in the *Reading Readiness Guide* aloud. Ask students to mark the statements true or false.

　All in One United States and Canada Teaching Resources, *Reading Readiness Guide*, p. 294

■ Have students discuss the statements in pairs or groups of four, then mark their worksheets again. Use the Numbered Heads participation strategy (TE, p. T36) to call on students to share their group's perspectives.

Vocabulary Builder
Preview Key Terms L2

Pronounce each Key Term, then ask students to say the word with you. Provide a simple explanation such as, "During the gold rush, boomtowns grew quickly as places where gold miners could live and buy the things they needed."

Prepare to Read

Objectives

In this section you will

1. Find out about the people and cultures of the Canadian West.
2. Learn what the economy and culture of British Columbia are like.

Taking Notes

As you read this section, look for details about the history of British Columbia. Copy the table below, and record your findings in it.

Events in British Columbian History	
10,000 years ago	
1700s	
1800s	
Today	

 Target Reading Skill

Use Context Clues When you come across an unfamiliar word, you can sometimes figure out its meaning by using context—the surrounding words, phrases, and sentences. Sometimes the meaning of a word may not be clear until you have read an entire passage. However, you can infer the meaning of the unfamiliar word using general context clues and evaluating the information in the reading passage.

Key Terms

• **totem pole** (TOHT um pohl) *n.* a tall, carved pole containing the symbols of a particular Native American group, clan, or family
• **boomtown** (boom town) *n.* a settlement that springs up quickly to serve the needs of miners

A visitor starts her day at a tiny coffee shop. All around her, people are speaking Dutch, Japanese, Spanish, German, and English. After having breakfast, the visitor gets into her car. On the radio, she hears country music—sung in French. Driving downtown, she passes street signs in Chinese, Indian men wearing turbans, a Korean travel agency, and a Thai restaurant. Where in the world is she? It may seem like the United Nations. But it is Vancouver (van KOO vur), British Columbia—a truly international city. As the largest city in British Columbia, Vancouver is the province's major center of industry, transportation, commerce, and culture.

Dancers at Chinese New Year in Vancouver, British Columbia

166 United States and Canada

 Target Reading Skill L2

Use Context Clues Point out the Target Reading Skill. Remind students that context clues are pieces of information that help you find the meaning of an unfamiliar word.

Model the skill by reading this sentence on p. 170: "There were countless obstacles—soaring mountains, steep valleys, and glaciers." Explain that students can use clues in the sentence to find the meaning of *obstacles. (This sentence gives examples which help show that obstacles are things that can block progress.)*

Give students *Use Context Clues: General Knowledge.* Have them complete the activity in their groups.

　All in One United States and Canada Teaching Resources, *Use Context Clues: General Knowledge,* p. 305

The People of the Canadian West

The first people came to present-day British Columbia at least 10,000 years ago. They belonged to several ethnic groups and spoke many different languages. Each group had its own customs and a complex society. The people along the coast caught fish, whales, and shellfish. They also carved giant **totem poles,** or tall, carved poles containing the symbols of a particular group, clan, or family. Other groups lived and hunted game in the dense inland forests. Some people traded with one another and got along well. Others fought.

New Arrivals In the late 1700s, Spanish, British, and Russian explorers arrived in the area to trade. In 1778, James Cook, a British explorer, sailed to Vancouver Island, off the coast of British Columbia. A group of Nootka (NOOT kuh) people met the British and agreed to trade. These coastal people wanted iron tools, while the British wanted furs. When the British built a fur-trading post on the island, trade between the two groups began to flourish.

Trade changed the indigenous peoples' lives a great deal. Although fur traders did not permanently settle the area, they introduced tools, clothing, and ideas. In 1858, everything changed. Gold was discovered along the Fraser River.

Indigenous Carvings
The Haida sculptor (below) works on a small totem pole. Large totem poles (right) are sometimes used to tell the history of a family or tribe.
Analyze Images *What does this totem pole tell you about the lives of the indigenous people who carved it?*

Vocabulary Builder

Use the information below to teach students this section's high-use word.

High-Use Word	Definition and Sample Sentence
benefit, p. 172	*v.* to gain something useful; to help The extra time to study **benefited** the whole class.

The People of the Canadian West L2

Guided Instruction

■ Read The People of the Canadian West, using the Paragraph Shrinking strategy (TE, p. T34).

■ Ask students **When fur traders went to what is now British Columbia, how did they affect the lives of indigenous people? How was this different from the impact of gold miners on indigenous people?** *(The fur traders did not settle permanently; they came and went. The gold miners settled towns and pushed indigenous people onto reserves.)*

Answer

Analyze Images Possible answer: The fact that the figure in the totem pole is holding fish may mean that fishing was an important part of the lives of the people who carved it.

Guided Instruction

L2

Ask students to study the Regional Profile on this page. As a class, answer the Map and Chart Skills questions. Allow students to briefly discuss their responses with a partner before sharing answers.

Independent Practice

To give students more practice working with data, distribute *Analyzing Statistics*. Have students work in pairs to complete the worksheet. Encourage them to use the table on page 168 as a model for their tables.

All in One **United States and Canada Teaching Resources,** *Analyzing Statistics,* p. 317

REGIONAL PROFILE
Focus on Geography

British Columbia

More than 90 percent of British Columbia is owned by the government, which manages the land and its resources. The government sets certain rules about where and how forests can be cut, and then leases the land to private companies and loggers. More than 260,000 British Columbians depend on forestry for their jobs. British Columbia is the largest single exporter of softwood lumber in the world. As you study the map and charts, think about the importance of the provinces' natural resources.

British Columbia: Natural Resources

KEY
- Gold
- Silver
- Copper
- Iron
- Lead
- Zinc
- Coal
- Petroleum
- Natural gas
- Hydroelectric power
- Forested area
- Barren land
- Cropland and urban area
- National border
- Provincial or territorial border

0 miles 200
0 kilometers 200
Lambert Azimuthal Equal Area

Yukon Territory · Northwest Territories · Gulf of Alaska · ALASKA (U.S.) · British Columbia · Queen Charlotte Islands · PACIFIC OCEAN · Vancouver Island · Alberta · UNITED STATES · Fraser River · Peace River

Income From Mining in British Columbia, 2005

Mineral	Dollars (millions)
Copper	$1,130
Zinc	$528
Gold	$255
Lead	$87

SOURCE: *Price Waterhouse Coopers, Canada*

Canadian Wood and Paper Products Production

- 21% Quebec
- 31% British Columbia
- 26% Ontario
- 14% New Brunswick
- 5% Alberta
- 3% Other

SOURCE: *Canadian Global Almanac, 2004*

Map and Chart Skills

1. **Identify** Look at the map to describe the location of British Columbia's forests.
2. **Analyze Information** What is the total income British Columbia received in 2005 from mining copper, gold, zinc, and lead?
3. **Draw Conclusions** What do the charts tell you about the importance of forest products to the economy of British Columbia?

 Use Web Code **lhe-4513** for **DK World Desk Reference Online.**

Answers

Map and Chart Skills

1. Forests are located inland, and cover most of British Columbia.
2. $2 billion
3. British Columbia is among the leading producers of wood and paper products in Canada, so many people in British Columbia depend on the industry for jobs.

Go Online *PHSchool.com* Students can find more information about this topic on the DK World Desk Reference Online.

Differentiated Instruction

For Advanced Readers

L3

Have students learn more about trade by completing the online activity *Trade in a Global Economy.* As they complete the activity, have students pay attention to Canada's role as one of the world's major exporters.

Go Online *PHSchool.com*

For: Environmental and Global Issues: *Trade in a Global Economy*
Visit: PHSchool.com
Web Code: lhd-4506

The Gold Rush

The Gold Rush A few years earlier, the British had established Victoria, a trading village on Vancouver Island. It was a small town of traders and farmers. Then, one Sunday morning in April 1858, an American paddlewheeler entered Victoria's harbor. It dropped off more than 400 men. They carried packs, blankets, spades, pickaxes, knives, and pistols. These rugged-looking characters had come to mine gold in the area. In a single morning, Victoria's population more than doubled.

Within weeks, tens of thousands more miners had arrived. Victoria quickly became a "stumptown"—all of its great trees had been chopped down to build shacks and boats. The town served as a supply center for the miners who were looking for gold on the Fraser River.

Two years later, miners also struck gold in the Cariboo Mountains in eastern British Columbia. Another wave of miners came from China, Europe, and the United States. The region was far from the coast and hard to reach, so the government built a 400-mile (644-kilometer) highway to it. Almost overnight, **boomtowns,** or settlements that were built to serve the needs of the miners, sprang up along the road. When the gold rush was over, many boomtowns died out.

Changes for Indigenous Peoples The thousands of settlers who arrived were taking gold from indigenous people's land—even taking over the land itself. In 1888, the British government took steps to confine some indigenous peoples to a small reserve. The indigenous peoples protested. The reserve was located on land that they had always lived on. How, they asked, could the government now "give" it to them?

Mining for Gold
This photograph, taken in 1900, shows a group of people looking for gold at Pine Creek, British Columbia.
Analyze Information *Why would most people choose to mine gold from creeks and streams rather than by digging deep into the ground?*

Use Context Clues
If you do not know what a *paddlewheeler* is, consider these context clues. It was able to enter a harbor. It was carrying more than 400 passengers. Therefore, a paddlewheeler is _____.

Explore Vancouver, British Columbia's largest city.

Guided Instruction (continued)

Ask students **Why did immigration to British Columbia increase even more once the building of the Canadian Pacific Railway began?** (*Immigrants from all over the world went to Canada to help build the railroad.*)

Independent Practice

Ask students to create the Taking Notes graphic organizer on a blank piece of paper. Then have students fill in the events that match each date as they read.

Monitor Progress

As students fill in the graphic organizer, circulate and make sure individuals are correctly listing events beside the time periods in which they occurred. Provide assistance as needed.

An indigenous man uses a gaff, an iron hook with a long handle, to catch salmon on the Morice-town Indian Reserve in British Columbia.

Like indigenous peoples throughout Canada, they had little choice. In a few short years, native people had gone from being the great majority to being the smallest minority of the population. They were pushed onto small reserves. The government passed laws banning many of their customs, religions, and languages. Authorities took children from their parents and placed them in government-run schools.

Recently, the indigenous peoples of British Columbia have found new pride in their history and culture. Their art is thriving. They are also demanding political rights and land. As a result, tension has developed between indigenous peoples and other British Columbians. For example, in 1999 the Sechelt Indians were awarded thousands of acres of land northwest of Vancouver and more than $40 million Canadian dollars. Many people felt that these terms were too generous. In July 2002, residents of British Columbia voted to place limits on native land claims.

The Canadian Pacific Railway British Columbia officially joined Canada in 1871. One of the conditions of joining was that a transcontinental railroad would be built within 10 years. Construction began in 1875, but little progress was made until 1881. That spring, Canadians began work on the enormous project of building a railroad that would stretch from Montreal to Vancouver. The goal of the project was to unite Canada. Look at the physical map of Canada on page 4 and you can see what a huge task this was. There were countless obstacles—soaring mountains, steep valleys, and glaciers. Workers built bridges and blasted long tunnels through the mountains.

The railroad project brought more change to Canada. There were not enough workers available to complete the railway on schedule. Thousands of immigrants, particularly from Ireland and China, came to work on the railroad. Towns grew up along the railroad, and more newcomers moved in. In a few short years, British Columbia changed from a sparsely inhabited region to a settled one, complete with cities.

√ **Reading Check** Why was the Canadian Pacific Railway built?

Background: Links Across Time

The North West Mounted Police

Today, Canada's federal police force is the Royal Canadian Mounted Police. When the force was founded in 1873 in Alberta, it was called the North West Mounted Police and was the only authority to patrol the vast western stretches of Canada. The original Mounties, as they were called, took on a variety of tasks. For example, they were responsible for ensuring the fair treatment of indigenous people by fur traders, and for providing wilderness survival tips to immigrants. In 1920, the Mounties became a national police force called by the name they use today.

Answer

√ **Reading Check** The Canadian Pacific Railway was built to unite Canada.

Economics and Culture

Although the Canadian Pacific Railroad connects all of Canada, the mountains are a barrier between British Columbia and the rest of the country. Today, most British Columbians live along the coast, west of the mountains. Many of them feel that their economic future lies with other countries more than with the rest of Canada.

The Pacific Rim Many British Columbians feel a link between their province and the Pacific Rim countries—nations that border the Pacific Ocean. One link is British Columbia's diverse people. More than 15 percent have Asian ancestors.

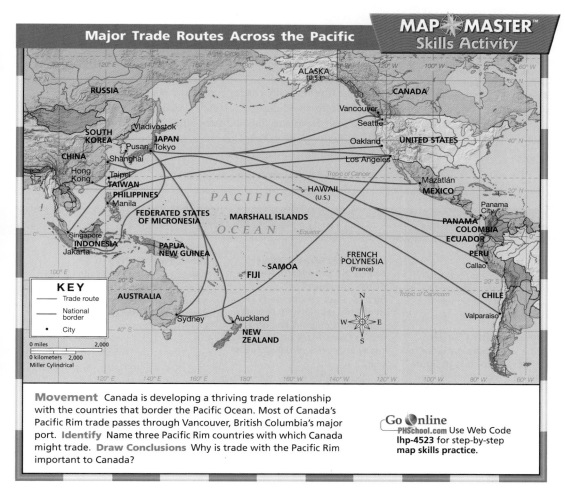

Major Trade Routes Across the Pacific

MAP MASTER™ Skills Activity

KEY
— Trade route
— National border
• City

0 miles 2,000
0 kilometers 2,000
Miller Cylindrical

Movement Canada is developing a thriving trade relationship with the countries that border the Pacific Ocean. Most of Canada's Pacific Rim trade passes through Vancouver, British Columbia's major port. **Identify** Name three Pacific Rim countries with which Canada might trade. **Draw Conclusions** Why is trade with the Pacific Rim important to Canada?

Go Online
PHSchool.com Use Web Code
lhp-4523 for step-by-step
map skills practice.

Chapter 5 Section 3 **171**

Economics and Culture L2

Guided Instruction

- **Vocabulary Builder** Clarify the high-use word **benefit** before reading.

- Read Economics and Culture. As students read, circulate and make sure individuals can answer the Reading Check question.

- Ask students **What impact does British Columbia's location on the Pacific Rim have on the province's culture?** *(British Columbia's culture is more strongly influenced by Asian countries than are other regions of Canada.)*

- Discuss the positive impact that the television and film industry has on British Columbia's economy. *(This industry brings millions of dollars to the region and provides thousands of jobs.)*

Independent Practice

Have students complete the graphic organizer by filling in the events from the given time periods that they identify in this section.

Monitor Progress

- Show *Section Reading Support Transparency USC 60.* Go over key concepts and clarify key vocabulary as needed.

  📖 **United States and Canada Transparencies,** *Section Reading Support Transparency USC 60*

- Tell students to fill in the last column of the *Reading Readiness Guide.* Probe for what they learned that confirms or invalidates each statement.

  All in One **United States and Canada Teaching Resources,** *Reading Readiness Guide,* p. 294

Differentiated Instruction

For Special Needs Students L1
After students read Economics and Culture and watch *British Columbia: Canada's Gateway to the Pacific,* ask them to write a short summary of the relationship between British Columbia and the Pacific Rim.

📼 *British Columbia: Canada's Gateway to the Pacific,* **World Studies Video Program**

For Gifted and Talented L3
After students read Economics and Culture, ask them to research an item traded between British Columbia and the Pacific Rim and write an advertisement that includes reasons why the item will sell well in this region.

Answers

MAP MASTER Skills Activity **Identify** Answers may include Japan, China, South Korea, Taiwan, Philippines, Indonesia, Australia, and New Zealand. **Draw Conclusions** Trade with Pacific Rim countries benefits Canada's economy.

Go Online
PHSchool.com Students may practice their map skills using the interactive online version of this map.

Assess and Reteach

Assess Progress   L2

Have students complete the Section Assessment. Administer the *Section Quiz.*

All in One **United States and Canada Teaching Resources,** *Section Quiz,* p. 296

Reteach   L1

If students need more instruction, have them read this section in the Reading and Vocabulary Study Guide.

Chapter 5, Section 3, **United States and Canada Reading and Vocabulary Study Guide,** pp. 61–63

Extend   L3

Have each student write a newspaper editorial from the point of view of a townsperson about the consequences of thousands of gold miners arriving in Victoria. Encourage students to consider questions such as the following before writing: In what different ways might citizens of Victoria react to the newcomers? Would they be excited, wary, angry, or welcoming? How would the population increase affect the community's businesses? Who might benefit and who might be hurt?

Answers

✓ **Reading Check** The Pacific Rim is made up of the countries that border the Pacific Ocean.

Section 3 Assessment

Key Terms
Students' sentences should reflect knowledge of each Key Term.

Target Reading Skill
Possible answer: "international" means of many different countries. The paragraph describes languages from many different countries.

Comprehension and Critical Thinking
1. (a) gold mining **(b)** The population of British Columbia more than doubled, and indigenous people were forced onto reserves and had many of their customs, religions, and languages banned. **(c)** Answers will vary. Students may say that the relationship would be better today if so many newcomers had not arrived in such a short time period and forced so much change on the indigenous people.

The water in Vancouver's harbor does not freeze. As a result, it's one of Canada's most important ports.

Trade is still another link between British Columbia and the Pacific Rim. Forty percent of the province's trade is with Asian countries. British Columbia wants good relationships with them. As a result, in British Columbian schools, students learn Asian languages. They learn Japanese, Cantonese Chinese, or Mandarin Chinese. Some even learn Punjabi (pun JAH bee), a language of India and Pakistan.

The Film Industry The television and film industry is another example of British Columbia's strong link to other countries. British Columbia is the third-largest film production center in North America—after New York and Los Angeles. More than 200 productions were filmed in the province in 2002, bringing more than $800 million Canadian dollars to the region.

The film industry creates about 50,000 jobs. The jobs are not just for actors and directors. Hotels, restaurants, and gas stations all benefit from the film industry. Only a two-hour plane ride from Hollywood, British Columbia is a good option for many American television and film projects.

✓ **Reading Check** What is the Pacific Rim?

Section 3 Assessment

Key Terms
Review the key terms at the beginning of this section. Use each key term in a sentence that explains its meaning.

Target Reading Skill
Find the word "international" on page 166. Use context to figure out its meaning. What do you think it means? What clues helped you arrive at a meaning?

Comprehension and Critical Thinking
1. (a) Recall What brought people to British Columbia in the late 1800s?

(b) Identify Effects What effects did this event have on British Columbia?
(c) Link Past and Present How might the relationship between indigenous peoples and other British Columbians be different today if this event hadn't taken place?
2. (a) List What ties exist between the people of British Columbia and the Pacific Rim?
(b) Analyze How does British Columbia's geography contribute to its economic and cultural ties with the Pacific Rim?

Writing Activity
What do you think it would be like to be a gold prospector in one of the gold rushes in Canada? Write a journal entry describing a gold prospector's typical workday.

For: An activity on totem poles
Visit: PHSchool.com
Web Code: lhd-4503

2. (a) heritage, language, and trade **(b)** British Columbia's nearness to the other Pacific Rim countries has led to cultural exchange and valuable trading relationships.

Writing Activity
Use the *Rubric for Assessing a Journal Entry* to evaluate students' journal entries.

All in One **United States and Canada Teaching Resources,** *Rubric for Assessing a Journal Entry,* p. 327

Go Online PHSchool.com Typing in the Web code when prompted will bring students directly to detailed instructions for this activity.

The Atlantic Provinces
Relying on the Sea

Prepare to Read

Objectives
In this section you will
1. Learn what life is like on the Atlantic coast.
2. Discover how maritime industries affect the provinces.

Taking Notes
As you read this section, look for the causes and effects of overfishing. Copy the chart below, and record your findings in it.

CAUSES
•
•

→ EVENT
Cod fishing ban

→ EFFECTS
•
•

Target Reading Skill
Use Context Clues Context, the words and phrases surrounding a word, can help you understand a word you may not know. One context clue to look for is cause and effect. The context clues show how the unfamiliar word is related to the cause or is the result of an action or idea. Clues to look for include *because, since, therefore,* and *so.*

Key Terms
• **exile** (EK syl) *v.* to force someone to leave his or her native land or home
• **maritime** (MA rih tym) *adj.* having to do with navigation or shipping on the sea
• **aquaculture** (AHK wuh kul chur) *n.* the cultivation of fish or water plants

Objectives
Social Studies
1. Learn what life is like on the Atlantic coast.
2. Discover how maritime industries affect the provinces.

Reading/Language Arts
Learn how cause-and-effect clues can help you understand the meaning of an unfamiliar word.

Prepare to Read

Build Background Knowledge L2
Tell students that they will learn how the people of Canada's Atlantic Provinces rely on the sea in this section. Ask students to study the location of the Atlantic Provinces on *Color Transparency USC 40.* Point out that these provinces each border a large length of ocean. Using Think-Write-Pair-Share (TE, p. T36), challenge students to make a list of industries that are likely to thrive along an ocean coastline *(fishing, shipping, tourism).*

📖 **United States and Canada Transparencies,** *Color Transparency USC 40: Canada: Physical-Political*

Set a Purpose for Reading L2
■ Preview the Objectives.

■ Read each statement in the *Reading Readiness Guide* aloud. Ask students to mark the statements true or false.

■ Have students discuss the statements in pairs or groups of four, then mark their worksheets again. Use the Numbered Heads participation strategy (TE, p. T36) to call on students to share their group's perspectives.

All in One **United States and Canada Teaching Resources,** *Reading Readiness Guide,* p. 298

Vocabulary Builder
Preview Key Terms L2
Pronounce each Key Term, then ask students to say the word with you. Provide a simple explanation such as, "Aquaculture is also known as fish farming."

Modern-day Norwegian explorer Helge Ingstad was aboard a ship in 1960 that stopped at a rocky peninsula in Newfoundland. The land formation was similar to what he had seen on ancient maps, and the scenery reminded him of the descriptions in Viking legends. After spotting what appeared to be the outlines of old building foundations, Ingstad believed he might be at the site of the first known Viking settlement in North America. Eight years of archaeological digs proved that Ingstad had unearthed a Viking settlement—possibly the very one that Leif Ericsson reached and named Vinland around the year 1000. Many artifacts were found at the site, including fireplaces, and a pit where iron may have been heated and formed into tools. The Viking settlement is now called L'Anse aux Meadows (lahns oh meh DOH). Viking buildings and artifacts have been reconstructed, and the historic site has become a popular tourist attraction.

From the time of the Vikings until today, the location of the Atlantic Provinces has had a huge influence on the region.

Some historians believe that Leif Ericsson may have landed here at L'Anse aux Meadows about 1,000 years ago.

🎯 Target Reading Skill L2

Use Context Clues Point out the Target Reading Skill. Explain that students can use cause-and-effect clues in the text to help them find the meaning of unfamiliar words.

Model the skill by asking students to use cause-and-effect clues to help find the meaning of *archaeologist* in this sentence: Archaeologists dug in Newfoundland because they wanted to find the remains of a very old Viking settlement.

Point out the context clues that can help students infer the meaning of archaeologist.

Give students *Use Context Clues: Cause and Effect.* Have them complete the activity in their groups.

All in One **United States and Canada Teaching Resources,** *Use Context Clues: Cause and Effect,* p. 307

Instruct

Living on the Coast   L2

Guided Instruction

- **Vocabulary Builder** Clarify the high-use word **neutral** before reading.

- Read Living on the Coast, using the Oral Cloze reading strategy (TE, p. T33).

- Ask students **How has location influenced life in the Atlantic Provinces?** (*Because the provinces border the Atlantic Ocean, they have developed a strong fishing industry. Also, Newfoundland and Labrador is an important transatlantic transportation and communications center.*)

- Ask **What happened to Acadians when the British controlled Acadia in 1755?** (*Acadians were exiled. Some moved to Quebec, others to Louisiana.*)

Independent Practice

Ask students to create the Taking Notes graphic organizer on a blank piece of paper. Then ask them to fill in causes and effects from the information they have just learned. Briefly model how to distinguish between a cause and an effect.

Monitor Progress

As students fill in the graphic organizer, circulate and make sure individuals are placing causes in the Causes box and effects in the Effects box. Provide assistance as needed.

⟳ Target Reading Skill   L2

Use Context Clues As a follow up, ask students to answer the Target Reading Skill question in the Student Edition. (*something that crosses the Atlantic Ocean*)

Use Context Clues
If you do not know what *transatlantic* means, look for a context clue. Use the cause and effect context clue and the surrounding sentences to figure out its meaning. What does *transatlantic* mean?

Northern gannets fly around Avalon Peninsula, Newfoundland and Labrador.

174 United States and Canada

Living on the Coast

Today, Newfoundland and Labrador, along with Prince Edward Island, New Brunswick, and Nova Scotia, make up the Atlantic Provinces. These provinces are located in eastern Canada, where they all share at least part of their border with the Atlantic Ocean. Many of the people in these provinces live on the coast. One exception is Prince Edward Island, where the population is evenly spread across the island. The people in the Atlantic Provinces are mainly of English, Irish, Scottish, and French descent.

Newfoundland and Labrador Five hundred years after the Vikings left their colony in Vinland, John Cabot rediscovered the island in 1497. He called it the *New Found Land*. About 100 years later, the island became England's first overseas colony. It was used mainly as a fishing station until settlers moved there permanently in the early 1600s. In 2001, the province's name officially changed from Newfoundland to Newfoundland and Labrador.

The province of Newfoundland and Labrador is the easternmost part of North America. Because of its location, the province is an important transatlantic transportation and communications center. It was here in 1901 that Guglielmo Marconi (goo lee EL moh mahr KOH nee) received the first wireless telegraph signals from across the Atlantic Ocean. More importantly, the province is located next to the Grand Banks, which at one time were the best fishing grounds in the world.

Vocabulary Builder

Use the information below to teach students this section's high-use words.

High-Use Word	Definition and Sample Sentence
neutral, p. 176	*adj.* not taking one side or the other in a quarrel or war My brother stayed **neutral** in the fight between my sister and me.
focus, p. 177	*n.* center of attention The teacher was the **focus** of the class when she announced the day of the next test.

The Atlantic Provinces

Long before the Atlantic Provinces were settled, European fishermen had been coming to the Grand Banks to fish. The abundance and variety of fish astonished them. Since that time, fishing, especially cod fishing, has been a vital part of the region's economy. Because of overfishing, cod fishing was banned in 2003. People in the Atlantic Provinces are beginning to concentrate on other economic activities. As you study the map and charts, think about how a natural resource can affect a region's people and economy.

Atlantic Provinces: Natural Resources
KEY

Gold	Iron	Hydroelectric power
Silver	Coal	Timber
Copper	Petroleum	Fish
—— National border	—— Provincial or territorial border	

Cod Fishing in Newfoundland

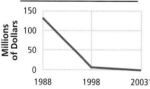

* Cod fishing banned throughout Canada
SOURCES: *The World Today Series: Canada, 2003; Boston Globe,* 2003

Aquaculture in Newfoundland and Labrador

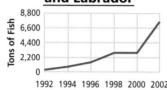

SOURCE: Government of Newfoundland

Economic Activities in the Atlantic Provinces

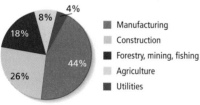

- 44% Manufacturing
- 4%
- 8%
- 18%
- 26%

Manufacturing
Construction
Forestry, mining, fishing
Agriculture
Utilities

SOURCE: *Canadian Global Almanac,* 2003

Map and Chart Skills

1. **List** What are the Atlantic Provinces' major natural resources?
2. **Analyze** How has aquaculture changed in the past decade?
3. **Predict** How do you think the cod fishing ban will affect the region? How might it help the development of other economic activities?

 Use Web Code **lhe-4514** for **DK World Desk Reference Online.**

Differentiated Instruction

For Less Proficient Readers [L1]

Remind students that it is important to read the title and labels of each line graph to understand the information it provides. Similarly, remind them to read the keys on the circle graph and the map to ensure that they comprehend all the information on these visuals. Have students practice reading graphs by copying the data from a graph into a table. For the cod fishing graph, for example, have students complete a table such as this:

Year	Millions of dollars
1988	
1998	
2003	

Guided Instruction [L2]

Ask students to study the Regional Profile on this page. Encourage them to study the map and the graphs on the page and think about the information each provides. As a class, answer the Map and Chart Skills questions. Allow students to briefly discuss their responses with a partner before sharing answers.

Independent Practice

- To help students understand the information given in the line graphs, distribute *Reading a Line Graph.* Have students work in pairs to complete the worksheet.

  All in One **United States and Canada Teaching Resources,** *Reading a Line Graph,* p. 318

- Ask students to study the line graphs on this page. Ask **Which line graph shows an increase over time?** *(the aquaculture graph)* **Which one shows a decrease over time?** *(the cod fishing graph)*

Answers

Map and Chart Skills

1. Fish, coal, and timber
2. It has increased from producing almost no fish to producing about 8,000 tons of fish per year.
3. Possible answer: The ban may cause financial hardship to people who make their living from cod fishing. The ban will force people in the region to focus on other economic activities, such as manufacturing, construction, or utilities. This should help those economic activities to grow.

Go Online PHSchool.com Students can find more information about this topic on the DK World Desk Reference Online.

A Maritime Economy ▪ L2

Guided Instruction
- **Vocabulary Builder** Clarify the high-use word **focus** before reading.

- Read about the economy of the Atlantic Provinces in A Maritime Economy. As students read, make sure individuals can answer the Reading Check question.

- Discuss the way a booming fishing industry led to the development of other industries in the Atlantic Provinces. (*Fishing required fishing vessels, so a shipbuilding industry emerged. The shipbuilding industry needed wood with which to build ships, so the forestry industry grew.*)

Independent Practice
Have students continue to fill in the boxes in their graphic organizers with causes and effects of overfishing.

Monitor Progress
- Show *Section Reading Support Transparency USC 61*. Go over key concepts and clarify key vocabulary as needed.

  📖 **United States and Canada Transparencies,** *Section Reading Support Transparency USC 61*

- Tell students to fill in the last column of the *Reading Readiness Guide*. Probe for what they learned that confirms or invalidates each statement.

  All in One United States and Canada Teaching Resources, *Reading Readiness Guide,* p. 298

Links
Read the **Links to Science** on this page. Ask students **How would the unique shape of the Bay of Fundy affect the region's economy?** (*Answers may include that it allows for a greater variety and availability of fish.*)

Answers

MAP MASTER Skills Activity

European Land Claims, 1682 and 1763

KEY
- English
- Spanish
- French

KEY
- British
- Spanish

Regions In less than 100 years, France lost its land claims in the United States and Canada. **Read a Map Key** What three countries claimed land in North America in 1682? **Draw Conclusions** By 1763, who controlled most of the areas once controlled by France?

Go Online PHSchool.com Use Web Code lhp-4524 for step-by-step map skills practice.

Links to Science

High Tide The Bay of Fundy lies between New Brunswick and Nova Scotia. Its unique funnel shape—narrow with shallow water at the north end of the bay and wide with deep water where the bay opens into the ocean—causes some of the highest tides in the world. Water in the bay can rise as much as 60 feet at high tide. These exceptional tides carry about 100 billion tons of water in and out of the bay each day.

Acadia Eastern Canada was once almost entirely populated by people of French descent. Nova Scotia, New Brunswick, and Prince Edward Island were part of Acadia. Here, in the early 1600s, the French established their first permanent North American settlement. French control of the area, however, did not last long. The English wanted this land, and the two countries fought over it many times. The area shifted from one country's control to the other's more than once. During the fighting, Acadians remained neutral.

In 1755, a time when Britain controlled the area, Britain feared that the French inhabitants of Acadia might secretly be loyal to France. As a result, Acadians were **exiled,** or forced to leave the area. Some exiled Acadians settled in Quebec or New Brunswick, while others moved to France, the West Indies, and other French colonies. Still others moved to present-day Louisiana, then a French settlement, where their descendants today are known as Cajuns. Britain gained permanent control over Acadia in 1763 at the end of the Seven Years' War. Many Acadians returned to the area only to find that the British had taken control of the fertile lands they had once farmed. So they took up fishing and lumbering instead to support themselves.

✓ **Reading Check** When did Britain gain permanent control over Acadia?

176 United States and Canada

Differentiated Instruction

For English Language Learners ▪ L1
Check for students' comprehension of the terms *maritime* and *aquaculture*. Have students read this section in the Spanish Reading and Vocabulary Study Guide to reinforce these and other concepts for them.

📖 Chapter 5, Section 4, **United States and Canada Spanish Reading and Vocabulary Study Guide,** pp. 47–48

For Special Needs Students ▪ L1
After students have read about Acadia and watched the video *Cultures of the Atlantic Provinces*, ask them to work in pairs to write a paragraph summarizing the experience of Acadians during the 1700s.

📼 *Cultures of the Atlantic Provinces,* **World Studies Video Program**

A Maritime Economy

Maritime means related to navigation or commerce on the sea. No term better sums up the focus of life in the Atlantic Provinces. The Atlantic Provinces are often called the Maritime Provinces. Much of the economy there depends on fishing.

In the 1800s, the demand for fishing vessels brought about the growth of the shipbuilding industry. The region led Canada in ship construction through most of the 1800s. The forestry industry in the area kept shipbuilders well supplied. Both industries helped the region's economy boom. Shipbuilding is still a major employer in the region, particularly in Nova Scotia.

Fishing is another major industry. However, the fishing industry has changed. In Newfoundland and Labrador, cod had been the primary catch until cod fishing was partially banned in 1992 and completely banned in 2003. The government banned cod fishing because the waters had been overfished. Tens of thousands of fishing jobs have been lost as a result of the ban.

Today, the province has turned its attention toward other types of fish to make up for loss of revenue from cod. Fish farming, or **aquaculture**, is a growing industry. Mussels are grown on Canada's eastern coast, and salmon farms are operating off the shores of New Brunswick.

Fishing village on Cape Breton Island, Nova Scotia

√ Reading Check **Which Atlantic Province is a leader in the shipbuilding industry?**

Section 4 Assessment

Key Terms
Review the key terms at the beginning of this section. Use each key term in a sentence that explains its meaning.

Target Reading Skill
Find the word *overfished* on page 177. Use context to figure out its meaning. What clue helped you?

Comprehension and Critical Thinking
1. (a) List Name the provinces that make up the Atlantic Provinces.

(b) Explain Where are the Atlantic Provinces located?
(c) Analyze How has the location of Newfoundland and Labrador made it an important communications center?
2. (a) Recall What industries did fishing help to grow in the 1800s?
(b) Summarize How has the fishing industry in the Atlantic Provinces changed in recent years?
(c) Predict What role might the fishing industry play in the Atlantic Provinces' economy in the future?

Writing Activity
Suppose that you are a French farmer living in Acadia in 1755. The British have told you that you must move to Louisiana. Write a paragraph describing how you feel about the move.

Go Online
PHSchool.com

For: An activity on Nova Scotia
Visit: PHSchool.com
Web Code: lhd-4504

Chapter 5 Section 4 **177**

Writing Activity
Use the *Rubric for Assessing a Writing Assignment* to evaluate students' paragraphs.

All in One **United States and Canada Teaching Resources,** *Rubric for Assessing a Writing Assignment,* p. 326

Go Online
PHSchool.com Typing in the Web code when prompted will bring students directly to detailed instructions for this activity.

Objective

Learn how to write a summary.

Prepare to Read

Build Background Knowledge L2

Ask students to brainstorm instances in which they chose to give a summary of something rather than all the details. Ask whether any students have recently described a movie they saw or a trip they took. Encourage students to explain why they gave a summary rather than a detailed explanation.

Instruct

Writing a Summary L2

Guided Instruction

- Read the steps to writing a summary as a class and write them on the board.

- Practice the skill by following the steps on p. 178 as a class. Model each step in the activity by choosing a sample vacation to summarize (*a visit to a national park*), stating the main ideas (*On my vacation, we had good weather, saw lots of animals, and hiked through beautiful woods and over rocky mountains.*), identifying what the main ideas have in common (*Everything about my vacation was great.*), and writing a summary paragraph (*My vacation was great because of all the interesting things we got to see and do. We had good weather, saw lots of animals, and hiked through beautiful woods and over rocky mountains.*)

Independent Practice

Assign *Skills for Life* and have students complete it individually.

All in One **United States and Canada Teaching Resources,** *Skills for Life,* p. 311

Monitor Progress

As students are completing the *Skills for Life* worksheet, circulate to make sure students understand the skill steps. Provide assistance as needed.

Skills for Life — Writing a Summary

"Hey, how was your weekend?"

If your friend asked you this question, would you tell him everything that happened over the weekend? Of course you wouldn't. You would pick a few major events and state them as a conclusion. For instance, "I went to the ball game on Saturday afternoon and the movies on Saturday night. I was really busy."

When you're asked to summarize information, you find the main ideas and weave them into a conclusion. Being able to summarize information is a school survival skill. You need it to take tests, write essays, have debates, and understand what you read.

Learn the Skill

You can summarize many types of information: a novel, a news report, a movie—even a museum exhibit. These steps show you how to sum up information.

1. **Find and state the main idea of each paragraph or section of information you want to summarize.** You can often find a main idea in the topic sentence of a paragraph. If you are summarizing a large piece of information, you might want to jot down the main ideas.

2. **Identify what the main ideas have in common.** Look for the logic in how the ideas are presented. You might find events in chronological order. You might find causes and effects or comparisons. You can also look for main ideas that describe parts of a whole topic.

3. **Write a summary paragraph beginning with a topic sentence.** The topic sentence should draw together the main ideas you are summarizing. The main ideas on your list will become the supporting details of your summary.

178 United States and Canada

Practice the Skill

Reread pages 156–157. Follow the steps on the previous page in order to summarize the text.

1 Read the heading and subheadings of this passage. List the main idea of each paragraph. For example, in the first paragraph, the first half of the topic sentence provides a strong main idea: "French culture first reached Quebec in the 1500s. ..." If no one sentence states the whole main idea, you should form a statement in your own words. Now write down the main idea for the other paragraphs in this passage.

2 The main ideas in this passage are mostly in chronological order. In what other ways are they related?

3 One possible topic sentence for your summary might be this: "The province of Quebec has struggled to preserve its French heritage in a country dominated by English culture." Use this topic sentence, or write your own, and then complete the summary paragraph by adding explanations and details. The details will come from the main ideas on your list.

A welcome-to-Quebec sign in English and French.

Apply the Skill

Reread page 167. Follow the steps to summarize the information. Keep in mind that *change* is a major part of this passage.

Differentiated Instruction

For Advanced Readers ▪ L3

Ask students to select another passage from the textbook and write a summary of it. Then have students trade summaries with a partner and challenge each student to identify the passage that the other student summarized. Allow students to revise their summaries based on their partner's responses.

Assess and Reteach

Assess Progress ▪ L2

Ask students to do the Apply the Skill activity.

Reteach ▪ L1

If students are having trouble applying the skill steps, have them review the skill by working in pairs to write a summary of The Prairie Provinces section.

Extend ▪ L3

To extend the lesson, have pairs of students select something they have both read, seen, or participated in recently and write a summary about it. Ask each student in a pair to write his or her own summary and to include at least two paragraphs. Then have partners trade their summaries and identify differences. Students may revise their summaries after seeing their partner's summary if they wish.

Answer
Apply the Skill

Answers will vary, but should show that students understand the skill steps.

Objectives

Social Studies

1. Discover what life is like for people in Canada's far north.

2. Find out about the remote region of the Yukon Territory.

3. Understand how the new territory of Nunavut was formed.

Reading/Language Arts

Use context clues to determine the meaning of a familiar word when used in an unfamiliar way.

Prepare to Read

Build Background Knowledge L2

Tell students that in this section, they will learn about the Northern Territories of Canada. Ask them to preview the section's headings and photos with this question in mind: **How are the Northern Territories different from other regions of Canada?** Have students share responses using an Idea Wave (TE, p. T35).

Set a Purpose for Reading L2

■ Preview the Objectives.

■ Read each statement in the *Reading Readiness Guide* aloud. Ask students to mark the statements true or false.

All in One **United States and Canada Teaching Resources,** *Reading Readiness Guide,* p. 302

■ Have students discuss the statements in pairs or groups of four, then mark their worksheets again. Use the Numbered Heads participation strategy (TE, p. T36) to call on students to share their group's perspectives.

Vocabulary Builder
Preview Key Terms L2

Pronounce the Key Term, then ask students to say the word with you. Provide a simple explanation such as, "The aurora borealis is a colorful, natural light show in the sky of the far north."

Prepare to Read

Objectives

In this section you will

1. Discover what life is like for people in Canada's far north.

2. Find out about the remote region of the Yukon Territory.

3. Understand how the new territory of Nunavut was formed.

Taking Notes

As you read the section, look for details about the government of the Northern Territories. Copy the concept web below, and record your findings in it.

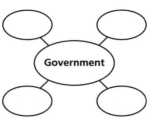

Target Reading Skill

Use Context Clues Words and phrases can take on different meanings in different situations. For example, if you are watching a play, and someone says that the *cast* is very talented, you would know that *cast* means the group of actors. But *cast* can also mean "to throw a fishing line" or "something you put on a broken arm." The information surrounding a word—whether it is a few other words, or phrases and sentences—is the context of that word.

Key Terms

• **aurora borealis** (aw RAWR uh bawr ee AL us) *n.* the colorful bands of light that can be seen in the skies of the Northern Hemisphere

• **Inuktitut** (ih NOOK tih toot) *n.* the native language of the Inuit

Named for the Latin word for dawn, the **aurora borealis** (aw RAWR uh bawr ee AL us), or northern lights, is a colorful band of light that can be seen in the Northern Hemisphere. The farther north you travel, the better is your chance of seeing these colorful bands of light. Some of Canada's indigenous peoples believed the lights were spirits. One folktale described the lights as spirits playing games. Others said that if you whistled loudly, the spirits would whisk you away.

Scientists today think that the lights, shown here, are caused by the reaction that occurs when charged particles from the sun hit gases in Earth's atmosphere. The lights still attract many sky-gazers. These dazzling displays can be seen throughout northern Canada. The northern lights are a beautiful sight in the often harsh environment of these sparsely-populated territories.

180 United States and Canada

Target Reading Skill L2

Use Context Clues Point out the Target Reading Skill. Tell students that words can have different meanings in different contexts. In this case, the context surrounding a word can provide clues to the word's meaning.

Model using context clues by finding the meaning of "pass" in this sentence from p. 183: "The end of the pass narrowed to less than three feet wide and became very steep."

(The context helps show that "pass" here means a narrow passage through mountains.)

Give students *Use Context Clues: Definition/Description.* Have them complete the activity in their groups.

All in One **United States and Canada Teaching Resources,** *Use Context Clues: Definition/Description,* p. 308

The Far North

In addition to its provinces, Canada has three territories—the Northwest Territories, Yukon Territory, and Nunavut (NOO nuh voot). The territories make up more than one third of Canada's total land area and stretch far north into the Arctic Ocean. Despite the region's size, the people there comprise less than one percent of the nation's population. The main reason for the low population is the region's rugged terrain and harsh climate. The area is made up of tundra with little vegetation, icy waters, and subarctic forests.

Modern Inuits
This modern Inuit family travels on a snowmobile on Ellesmere Island.
Draw Conclusions *How does technology influence Inuit life?*

People of the Far North Another characteristic unique to this region is the large number of indigenous people who live there. In the Northwest Territories, almost 50 percent of the population is made up of indigenous peoples such as the Dene, Métis, and Inuit. In Nunavut, about 85 percent of the population are Inuit. In contrast, only about 14 percent of the Yukon population is made up of native people. The rest of the population is of European or other ancestry.

Contact with Europeans has changed many of the ways in which indigenous peoples live. Technology has played a major role. For example, seal hunting is an important part of Inuit life. Today, Inuit hunters use snowmobiles instead of dogsleds to cross the frozen land.

A Different Form of Government Members of the House of Commons, a part of the Canadian Parliament, represent both territories and provinces in the federal government. Each territory has its own legislative, or law-making, body similar to those of the provinces.

But, the federal government exercises more authority over the territories. While territories do have control over many of the same local concerns as provinces, such as education, the federal government controls other areas, such as some natural resources. Territories also have less power to tax than the provinces do.

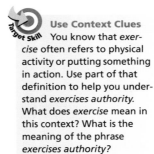

Use Context Clues You know that *exercise* often refers to physical activity or putting something in action. Use part of that definition to help you understand *exercises authority*. What does *exercise* mean in this context? What is the meaning of the phrase *exercises authority*?

✓ **Reading Check** What percentage of Nunavut's population is Inuit?

Vocabulary Builder

Use the information below to teach students this section's high-use words.

High-Use Word	Definition and Sample Sentence
environment, p. 180	*n.* natural surroundings We wore coats and hats to protect us from the cold **environment.**
despite, p. 181	*prep.* regardless of We played outside **despite** the cold weather.
portion, p. 184	*n.* part or section I ate my **portion** of the orange, while my friend ate the other part.
resident, p. 184	*n.* someone who lives in a place A **resident** of the neighborhood invited us to a barbecue in her backyard.

Instruct

The Far North L2

Guided Instruction

■ **Vocabulary Builder** Clarify the high-use words **environment** and **despite** before reading.

■ Read The Far North, using the Structured Silent Reading strategy (TE, p. T34).

■ Ask students to describe the difference between provinces and territories. *(In the territories, the federal government has more authority over such things as taxes and natural resources than in the provinces.)*

■ Ask students **What factors contribute to the low population of these territories?** *(the rugged terrain and harsh climate)*

Independent Practice

Ask students to create the Taking Notes graphic organizer on a blank piece of paper. Then ask students to fill in the ovals with the information they have just learned. Briefly model how to fill in each separate detail in a different oval.

Monitor Progress

As students fill in the graphic organizer, circulate and make sure individuals are choosing the correct details. Provide assistance as needed.

⟳ Target Reading Skill L2

Use Context Clues As a follow up, ask students to answer the Target Reading Skill question in the Student Edition. *(Exercise means putting something in action in this context. The phrase* exercises authority *means to put into action or use authority.)*

Answers

Draw Conclusions Possible answer: Technology has changed many aspects of Inuit life. In the photo, the snowmobile may make crossing the frozen land easier.

✓ **Reading Check** about 85 percent

Guided Instruction   [L2]

Ask students to study the Regional Profile on this page. Encourage them to look at the map, graphs, and on the page and think about the information each provides. As a class, answer the Map and Chart Skills questions. Allow students to briefly discuss their responses with a partner before sharing answers.

Independent Practice

- Help students read the bar graphs by asking them to fill in the following sentence for each territory: "_____ has a population of _____ people and an area of _____ square miles."

- Then ask students whether a larger land area means a larger population. Help them see that the Northwest Territories has a larger land area and population than the Yukon, but Nunavut has a larger land area and smaller population than the Yukon— so there is not a direct relationship between land area and population.

Answers

Map and Chart Skills

1. Inuit

2. Possible answer: It is easier to come to agreement when sitting in a circle because there is no clear divide between members, everyone is equal.

3. Possible answers: It would work because a vote can take place no matter how parties are seated; it would not work because representing a population as large as the whole country requires parties to be more organized.

Go Online PHSchool.com Students can find more information about this topic on the DK World Desk Reference Online.

Northern Territories

Three territories—Nunavut, the Northwest Territories, and Yukon—make up this region. As territories, they have a different status from Canada's provinces. All three territories have legislatures, but there are no political parties. Decisions are made by agreement rather than by majority vote. Most of the territories' public land is controlled by the government in Ottawa. As you study the map and graphs, think about why and how Canada's territories are different from the nation's provinces.

Northern Territories: Native North American Groups

KEY

- Champagne and Aishihik
- Gwich'in
- Inuit
- Inuvialuit
- Nacho Nyak Dun
- Sahtu Dene and Métis
- National border
- Provincial or territorial border
- ★ Provincial or territorial capital
- • Other town

0 miles — 1,000
0 kilometers — 1,000
Lambert Azimuthal Equal Area

Population and Area of Northern Canada

Population (thousands): Yukon, Northwest Territories, Nunavut
SOURCE: Statistics Canada

Area (square miles): Yukon, Northwest Territories, Nunavut
SOURCE: Encyclopaedia Britannica

Nunavut Legislature

Most provincial legislatures meet in a divided chamber. The party in power sits on one side, and the opposition sits on the other. The Nunavut legislature sits in a circle.

Map and Chart Skills

1. **Identify** What is the main ethnic group in Nunavut?

2. **Infer** How does the circular seating of the legislature serve the Nunavut decision-making process?

3. **Analyze** Would the organization of Nunavut's legislature work for the Canadian federal government in Ottawa? Explain why or why not.

 Use Web Code **lhe-4515** for **DK World Desk Reference Online.**

Differentiated Instruction

For Less Proficient Readers   [L1]

As students read the Regional Profile, have them make a two-column chart to help them keep track of the differences between provinces and territories. Have them label the first column *Territories* and the second column *Differences from Provinces*.

Explain that they should use the first column to record details given about territories, such as that they have legislatures. They should use the second column to record ways that territories are different from provinces, such as that they do not have political parties.

Forming New Territories

All of Canada's northern land used to be one giant territory—the Northwest Territories. Over time, this vast land was split up into three separate territories.

Yukon Territory The Yukon Territory was once a district of the Northwest Territories. In 1898, an act of Parliament made it a separate territory. Many people are familiar with the Yukon Territory because of the Klondike Gold Rush. After gold was discovered in a branch of the Klondike River in 1896, thousands of prospectors swarmed to the area. Within two years, the population of the town of Dawson swelled to about 30,000. Saloons, banks, theaters, and dance halls sprang up there.

It was amazing that so many people were able to get to the area, because one of the main routes was the treacherous Chilkoot Pass, known as "the meanest 32 miles in the world." The end of the pass narrowed to less than three feet wide and became very steep. But the Yukon's era of prosperity was short-lived. By the end of 1898, the rush began to slow, and the population of the settlement declined quickly. Today, fewer than 1,300 people live in Dawson.

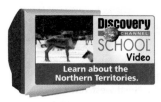

Learn about the Northern Territories.

Building a New Capital
A new building was constructed in Iqaluit to house Nunavut's legislature. **Draw Conclusions** How might the construction of a new capital have helped Nunavut's economy?

Show students *The Northern Territories: Challenge of the Cold.* Ask students to name Canada's three northern territories. (*Yukon Territory, Northwest Territories, Nunavut*)

Forming New Territories L2

Guided Instruction

■ **Vocabulary Builder** Clarify the high-use words **portion** and **resident** before reading.

■ Read Forming New Territories. As students read, circulate and make sure individuals can answer the Reading Check question.

■ Ask students **Why, during the 1890s, were many people willing to brave the Chilkoot Pass to get to the Yukon Territory?** (*to mine the gold found there*)

■ Ask students **What do you think was the most important factor that allowed for the creation of Nunavut?** (*the large percentage of Inuit people in the area; when the matter came to a vote, the Inuit population was large enough to determine the outcome*)

Independent Practice

Have students complete the graphic organizer by filling in details about the government of Nunavut.

Monitor Progress

■ Show *Section Reading Support Transparency USC 62* and ask students to check their graphic organizers individually.

   United States and Canada Transparencies, *Section Reading Support Transparency USC 62*

■ Tell students to fill in the last column of the *Reading Readiness Guide.* Probe for what they learned that confirms or invalidates each statement.

   All in One United States and Canada Teaching Resources, *Reading Readiness Guide,* p. 302

Answers

Draw Conclusions by providing work for people in the construction industry and boosting local businesses

---

Assess and Reteach

Assess Progress L2

Have students complete the Section Assessment. Administer the *Section Quiz*.

All in One United States and Canada Teaching Resources, *Section Quiz*, p. 304

Reteach L1

If students need more instruction, have them read this section in the Reading and Vocabulary Study Guide.

Chapter 5, Section 5, **United States and Canada Reading and Vocabulary Study Guide,** pp. 67–69

Extend L3

Now that students have learned how the government of Nunavut differs from the governments of Canada and its provinces, have them learn about other kinds of government by starting the *Holding Community Meetings Under Different Forms of Government* Long-Term Integrated Project. Assign students to groups to do the activity.

Go Online PHSchool.com

For: Long-Term Integrated Project: *Holding Community Meetings Under Different Forms of Government*
Visit: PHSchool.com
Web Code: lhd-4507

Answer

 Reading Check the Northwest Territories

Section 5 Assessment

Key Terms
Students' sentences should reflect knowledge of each Key Term.

Target Reading Skill
Possible answer: in this context, *bands* are thin strips.

Comprehension and Critical Thinking
1. (a) the Northwest Territories, Yukon Territory, and Nunavut **(b)** similar: they all have their own legislative bodies; different: the federal government has more control over the territories' governments than it does over the provinces'

This stop sign is in Inuktitut and English.

Nunavut In 1993, the area now known as Nunavut was carved out of the eastern portion of the Northwest Territories. A constitutional act officially made Nunavut the third Canadian territory on April 1, 1999. A decades-long dream of the Inuit people to have their own self-governing territory became reality.

The Inuit, who make up most of Nunavut's population, proposed the formation of Nunavut in the 1970s. Nunavut means "our land" in **Inuktitut** (ih NOOK tih toot), the native language of the Inuit. When the matter came to a vote in 1982, residents overwhelmingly favored the creation of their own territory.

The construction of Nunavut's new capital, Iqaluit (ee KAH loo eet), provided many jobs for people. But Nunavut still faces several challenges. Leaders in the territory must work to keep its economy strong in spite of its remote location and harsh climate. The modernization of the area, which now has an Internet provider, a television broadcaster, and cellular phone service, may be a step in the right direction.

✓ **Reading Check** **Present-day Nunavut was once a part of which territory?**

Section 5 Assessment

Key Terms
Review the key terms at the beginning of this section. Use each key term in a sentence that explains its meaning.

Target Reading Skill
Find the word *bands* on page 180. Use your own knowledge and the surrounding words and phrases to explain what *bands* means in this context.

Comprehension and Critical Thinking
1. (a) List Which three territories make up the Northern Territories?

(b) Compare and Contrast How do the governments of provinces and territories differ? How are they the same?
2. (a) Recall What event made the Yukon Territory famous?
(b) Identify Effects How did that event cause the town of Dawson to grow?
3. (a) Recall What is the newest territory in Canada?
(b) Identify Point of View Why might Inuits have wanted to create a self-governing territory?

Writing Activity
Suppose that you are Inuit, and you have always been a part of a minority in a larger territory. Describe what it might be like living for the first time in a territory where you are part of the majority.

Go Online PHSchool.com

For: An activity on Nunavut
Visit: PHSchool.com
Web Code: lhd-4505

---

2. (a) the Klondike Gold Rush **(b)** by causing thousands of prospectors to swarm to the area

3. (a) Nunavut **(b)** Answers will vary. Students may say that Inuit people might have wanted to create a self-governing territory because they have a different heritage, traditions, and beliefs than other Canadians and wanted to be able to represent and govern in accordance with their culture.

Writing Activity
Use the *Rubric for Assessing a Writing Assignment* to evaluate students' descriptions.

All in One United States and Canada Teaching Resources, *Rubric for Assessing a Writing Assignment*, p. 326

 Typing in the Web code when prompted will bring students directly to detailed instructions for this activity.

Review and Assessment

◆ **Chapter Summary**

Section 1: Ontario and Quebec

• Canada's central government is located in Ottawa, Ontario.
• Toronto is Canada's financial center and largest city.
• French Canadians are concerned about preserving their cultural heritage, and some think that Quebec should become an independent country.

Section 2: The Prairie Provinces

• Manitoba, Saskatchewan, and Alberta are called the Prairie Provinces.
• Many European immigrants settled the Canadian plains in the late 1800s.
• Disease and the destruction of the buffalo in the late 1800s led to the end of many indigenous peoples' way of life.

Section 3: British Columbia

• Following the discovery of gold in 1858, the population of British Columbia grew rapidly.
• Indigenous peoples were pushed onto small reserves and were not allowed to practice many of their customs.
• British Columbia has geographic, economic, and cultural ties to foreign countries, especially those of the Pacific Rim.

Section 4: The Atlantic Provinces

• Newfoundland and Labrador, Prince Edward Island, New Brunswick, and Nova Scotia make up the Atlantic Provinces.
• The location of the Atlantic Provinces has shaped the history, culture, and economy of the people there.
• The economy of the Atlantic Provinces is dependent on the fishing industry.

Section 5: The Northern Territories

• The Northern Territories—made up of the Northwest Territories, Yukon Territories, and Nunavut—are the least-populated regions in Canada.
• The Northern Territories have a different form of government from that of Canada's provinces.
• Nunavut is the homeland of the Inuit, and Canada's newest territory.

Totem pole

◆ **Key Terms**

Each of the statements below contains a key term from the chapter. If the statement is true, write *true*. If it is false, rewrite the statement to make it true.

1. A separatist is a person who speaks French as his or her first language.
2. A boomtown is a settlement that springs up to serve the needs of miners.
3. Colorful bands of light that can be seen in the Northern Hemisphere are the aurora borealis.
4. Descent is a natural resistance to disease.
5. Aquaculture has to do with navigation or shipping on the sea.
6. After the Quiet Revolution, Nunavut became a separate territory.
7. An exile is someone who is forced to leave his or her homeland.
8. A federation is a union of states, groups, provinces, or nations.

Vocabulary Builder

Revisit this chapter's high-use words:

structure	occupy	environment
mature	benefit	despite
issue	neutral	portion
margin	focus	resident

Ask students to review the definitions they recorded on their *World Knowledge* worksheets.

All in One **United States and Canada Teaching Resources,** *Word Knowledge,* p. 309

Consider allowing students to earn extra credit if they use the words in their answers to the questions in the Chapter Review and Assessment. The words must be used correctly and in a natural context to win the extra points.

Review and Assessment

Review Chapter Content

■ Review and revisit the major themes of this chapter by asking students to classify what Guiding Question each bulleted statement in the Chapter Summary answers. Write the Chapter Summary on the board and divide the class into groups to complete the activity. Then have a member from each group write the numbers they selected next to each statement on the board. Refer to page 1 in the Student Edition for the text of Guiding Questions.

■ Assign *Vocabulary Development* for students to review Key Terms.

All in One **United States and Canada Teaching Resources,** *Vocabulary Development,* p. 324

Answers

Key Terms

1. False. A separatist is a person who wants Quebec to break away from Canada and become an independent country.
2. True
3. True
4. False. Descent is an individual's ancestry.
5. False. Aquaculture is a method of farming fish.
6. False. The Quiet Revolution was a time during which great changes in Quebec's government were brought about peacefully.
7. True
8. True

Review and Assessment

Comprehension and Critical Thinking

9. (a) The British monarch is Canada's head of state; his or her duties are purely ceremonial. **(b)** The United States President is head of state and head of government, whereas the British monarch is Canada's head of state and the Canadian prime minister is head of government.

10. (a) The people voted for Quebec to remain part of Canada. **(b)** Many people in Quebec want to separate from Canada in order to preserve their French heritage and culture, which they worry will die out in an English-dominated country.

11. (a) Buffalo meat was used for food, hides were used for clothes, and bones were used for tools. **(b)** The traditional ways of life of the indigenous peoples of the plains came to an end.

12. (a) Spain, Britain, Russia **(b)** The indigenous people and the early explorers traded with each other. **(c)** The miners set up towns and quickly doubled the population of British Columbia, taking over the land and forcing the indigenous people onto reserves.

13. (a) Acadia **(b)** Exiled Acadians returned to find the British had taken over the land they had once farmed. Acadians then took up fishing and lumbering instead of farming.

14. (a) because of the region's rugged terrain and harsh climate **(b)** Answers will vary. Students may say that the harsh climate determines the economic activities that are available to people or that it prevents many newcomers from arriving, allowing the culture to remain mainly indigenous.

Skills Practice

Students' summaries will vary, but answers should reflect understanding of the skill and should include a topic sentence and main ideas drawn from Section 3 of this chapter.

Writing Activity: Language and Arts

Students' storyboards will vary but should include real events from British Columbia's history. Dates should be given along with clear indications of what occurred and why it is interesting.

Use *Rubric for Assessing a Performance on a Project* to evaluate students' storyboards. Tell students how many sources you would like them to use, if any, beyond the textbook.

All in One United States and Canada Teaching Resources, *Rubric for Assessing a Performance on a Project,* p. 328

Review and Assessment (continued)

◆ Comprehension and Critical Thinking

9. (a) Explain What is the role of the British monarch in Canadian government?
(b) Compare and Contrast How does the Canadian government differ from that of the United States?

10. (a) Recall What were the results of the 1980 and 1995 referendums on Quebec's independence?
(b) Analyze Why do so many people in Quebec want to separate from Canada?

11. (a) List In what ways was the buffalo important to indigenous peoples on the Plains?
(b) Identify Effects How might the destruction of the buffalo have affected the native people who lived there?

12. (a) List In the late 1700s, which countries sent explorers to present-day British Columbia?
(b) Summarize What was the relationship between the early explorers and the indigenous people of the region?
(c) Compare and Contrast How and why did the miners' relationship with native peoples differ from that of the early explorers?

13. (a) Locate Where was the first French settlement in North America?

(b) Summarize How did the lives of Acadians change after the British gained control over the region in 1763?

14. (a) Explain Why are the Northern Territories not heavily populated?
(b) Predict How does climate affect culture in the Northern Territories?

◆ Skills Practice

Writing a Summary Review the steps you followed in the Skills for Life activity in this chapter. Then reread the part of Section 3 under the heading Economics and Culture. Find and state the main idea of each paragraph. Then, identify what the main ideas have in common. Finally, write a summary paragraph that begins with a topic sentence.

◆ Writing Activity: Language Arts

Suppose that you have been asked to develop a proposal for a film to be set in British Columbia. You may choose to make a documentary or a historical film. Outline the events or the plot of the film on a storyboard—a series of sketches that show the sequence of major scenes in the film.

MAP MASTER™ Skills Activity

Place Location For each place listed below, write the letter from the map that shows its location.
1. Quebec
2. Ottawa
3. Saskatchewan
4. Winnipeg
5. Vancouver
6. Prince Edward Island
7. Iqaluit

Go Online PHSchool.com Use Web Code **lhp-4555** for an interactive map.

Canada

MAP MASTER™ Skills Activity

1. F	**2.** E
3. D	**4.** G
5. B	**6.** C
7. A	

Go Online PHSchool.com Students may practice their map skills using the interactive online version of this map.

Standardized Test Prep

Test-Taking Tips
Some questions on standardized tests ask you to analyze a reading selection. Read the passage below. Then, follow the tips to answer the sample question.

> **TIP** Read for key words that may help you answer the question. In this case, the key word is *Nunavut*.

In 1982, citizens of Canada's Northwest Territories were about to vote on whether to allow the creation of a self-governing homeland. It would be known as Nunavut and would be carved out of the territories. Someone argued, "We're asking for a share in the resources. We don't want to appear as beggars dependent on government handouts, but we are now being denied the resources that we so willingly gave up to support this nation."

Who might have made this argument?

A a descendant of a French fur trader

B a descendant of an English farmer

C a descendant of an Inuit hunter

D a descendant of a German logger

> **TIP** Try to answer the question before you look at the answer choices. Doing so may help you find the BEST answer.

Think It Through The key word *Nunavut* will help you answer the question. What does the passage have to do with Nunavut? The speaker says the government owes his people resources that had been taken away. Which group wants a separate homeland that would give them control over their own resources? You can eliminate B and D. That leaves A and C. Some French in Quebec do want their own homeland. But, their resources and land were not taken away. The answer is C.

Practice Questions

Use the tips above and other tips in this book to help you answer the following questions.

1. Who is Canada's head of state?
   A the monarch of Britain
   B the prime minister
   C the governor of Ontario
   D the president

Read the passage below, and then answer the question that follows.

In the late 1800s, life changed for a group of people who lived on Canada's plains. They could not hunt the way they always had, and their lands were taken away by new settlers. They also began to get sick in large numbers from new diseases.

2. Who does this passage describe?
   A French Canadians
   B Scandinavian immigrants
   C Native Americans
   D German immigrants

3. British Columbia has special economic and cultural ties to
   A Russia.
   B the rest of Canada.
   C the northeastern United States.
   D the Pacific Rim.

4. Who first settled Canada's Atlantic Provinces in large numbers?
   A the French
   B the British
   C the Vikings
   D Americans

Use Web Code lha-4505
for **Chapter 5 self-test.**

Standardized Test Prep
Answers
1. A
2. C
3. D
4. B

Go Online PHSchool.com Students may use the Chapter 5 self-test on PHSchool.com to prepare for the Chapter Test.

Assessment Resources

Teaching Resources
Chapter Tests A and B, pp. 329–334
Final Exams A and B, pp. 339–344

Test Prep Workbook
United States and Canada Study Sheet, pp. 124–127
United States and Canada Practice Tests A, B, and C, pp. 85–96

AYP Monitoring Assessments
United States and Canada Benchmark Test 2, pp. 93–96
United States and Canada Outcome Test, pp. 176–181

Technology
◉ *ExamView Test Bank CD-ROM*

- Students can further explore the Guiding Questions by completing hands-on projects.

- Three pages of structured guidance in All-in-One United States and Canada Teaching Resources support each of the projects described on this page.

  All in One **United States and Canada Teaching Resources,** *Book Project: Set Up a Weather Station, pp. 73–75; Book Project: Make a Timeline of Local History, pp. 79–81*

- There are also two additional projects introduced, explained, and supported in the All-in-One United States and Canada Teaching Resources.

  All in One **United States and Canada Teaching Resources,** *Book Project: Write a Children's Book, pp. 76–78; Book Project: Create a Diorama, pp. 82–84*

- Go over the four project suggestions with students.

- Ask each student to select one of the projects, or design his or her own. Work with students to create a project description and a schedule.

- Post project schedules and monitor student progress by asking for progress reports.

- Assess student projects using rubrics from the All-in-One United States and Canada Teaching Resources.

  All in One **United States and Canada Teaching Resources,** *Rubric for Assessing Student Performance on a Project, p. 85; Rubric for Assessing Performance of an Entire Group, p. 86; Rubric for Assessing Individual Performance in a Group, p. 87*

Tell students they can add their completed Book Project as the final item in their portfolios. Assess student portfolios with *Rubric for Assessing a Student Portfolio.*

  All in One **United States and Canada Teaching Resources,** *Rubric for Assessing Student Portfolio, p. 88*

Projects

Create your own projects to learn more about the United States and Canada. At the beginning of this book, you were introduced to the **Guiding Questions** for studying the chapters and special features. But you can also find answers to these questions by doing projects on your own or with a group.

1. **Geography** How has physical geography affected the cultures of the United States and Canada?

2. **History** How have historical events affected the cultures of the United States and Canada?

3. **Culture** How has the variety of people in the United States and Canada benefited and challenged the two nations?

4. **Government** How do the governments of the United States and Canada differ? How are they alike?

5. **Economics** How did the United States and Canada become two of the wealthiest nations in the world?

Project
RESEARCH YOUR LOCAL HISTORY

Make a Timeline
Read about the history of your community at the local public library. Write down dates and descriptions of between 10 and 20 important events. Then, make a timeline large enough to hang on the wall of your classroom. Draw a picture of each event and place it next to its description on the timeline. Add several major events of United States history.

Project
SET UP A WEATHER STATION

Create a Weather Log
Set up a weather station to measure and record your local weather as you read this book. Measure the temperature each day at the same time. Also record the amount of precipitation and the wind direction. Record all of your findings in a weather log.

Each day, compare your local weather with the weather in other parts of the country. You can get this information from television, radio, the newspaper, or the Internet. When you have finished your measurements and recordings, create graphs to display your local readings. Then, compare your findings with the climate map in the Activity Atlas.

188 United States and Canada

Reference

Table of Contents

The World: Political

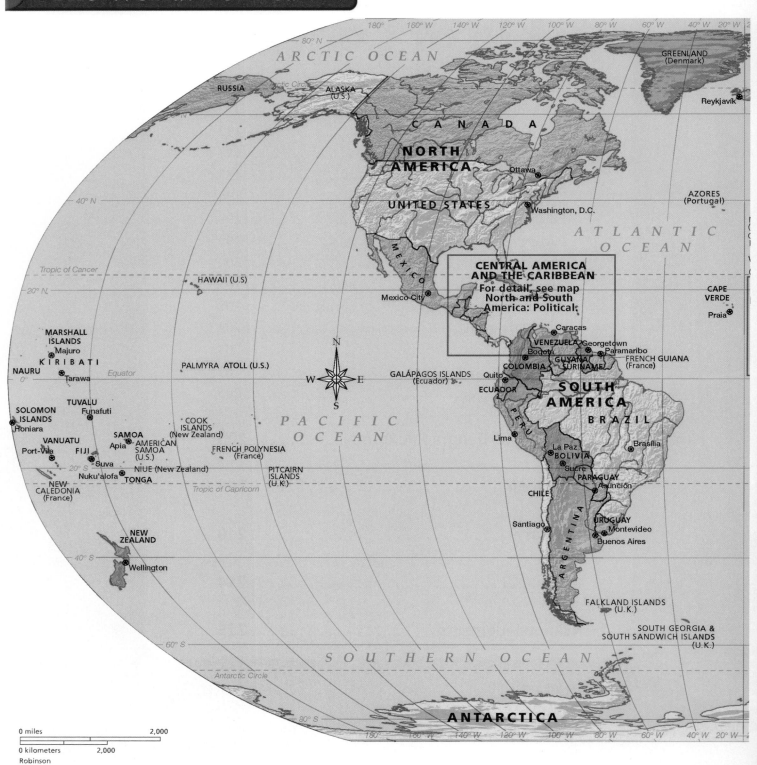

ARCTIC OCEAN

RUSSIA

ALASKA (U.S.)

GREENLAND (Denmark)

Reykjavík

CANADA

NORTH AMERICA

UNITED STATES

Ottawa

Washington, D.C.

ATLANTIC OCEAN

AZORES (Portugal)

MEXICO

Tropic of Cancer

HAWAII (U.S)

20° N

Mexico City

CAPE VERDE

Praia

CENTRAL AMERICA AND THE CARIBBEAN
For detail, see map
North and South
America: Political.

MARSHALL ISLANDS

Majuro

K I R I B A T I

NAURU

Tarawa

Equator

PALMYRA ATOLL (U.S.)

GALÁPAGOS ISLANDS (Ecuador)

Caracas

VENEZUELA Georgetown

Bogotá GUYANA Paramaribo FRENCH GUIANA (France)

COLOMBIA SURINAME

Quito

ECUADOR

SOUTH AMERICA

BRAZIL

TUVALU

SOLOMON ISLANDS

Funafuti

Honiara

VANUATU

Port-Vila FIJI

Suva

SAMOA

Apia AMERICAN SAMOA (U.S.)

NIUE (New Zealand)

Nuku'alofa TONGA

COOK ISLANDS (New Zealand)

FRENCH POLYNESIA (France)

PACIFIC OCEAN

Lima

PERU

La Paz

BOLIVIA

Sucre

Brasília

PARAGUAY

Asunción

PITCAIRN ISLANDS (U.K.)

NEW CALEDONIA (France)

20° S

Tropic of Capricorn

CHILE

ARGENTINA

URUGUAY

Santiago

Montevideo

Buenos Aires

NEW ZEALAND

40° S

Wellington

FALKLAND ISLANDS (U.K.)

SOUTH GEORGIA & SOUTH SANDWICH ISLANDS (U.K.)

60° S

SOUTHERN OCEAN

Antarctic Circle

80° S

ANTARCTICA

0 miles 2,000

0 kilometers 2,000

Robinson

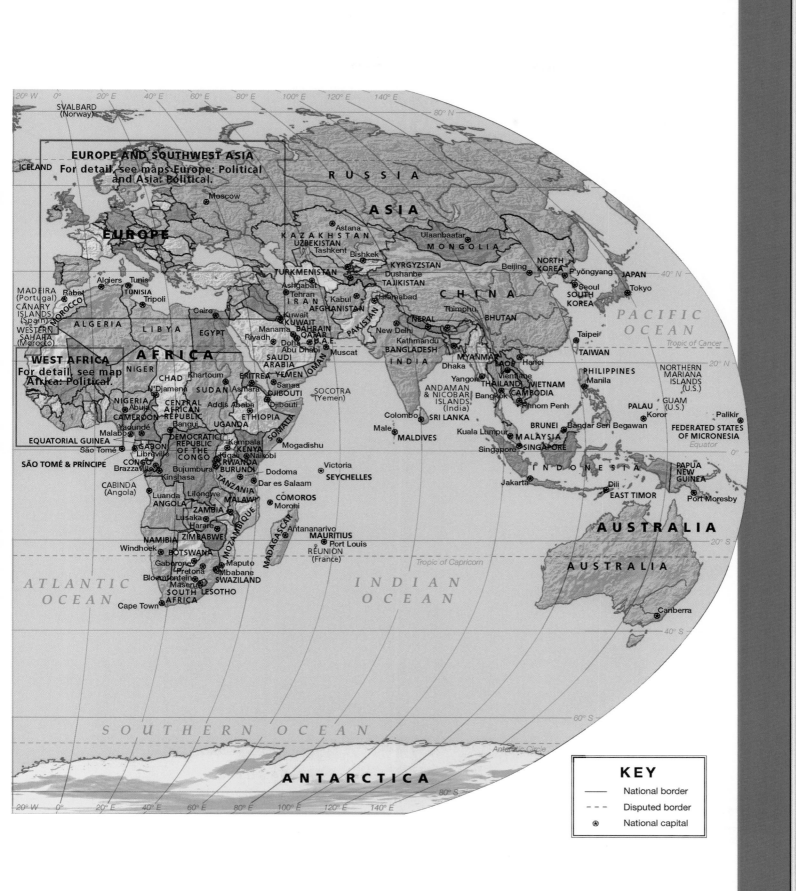

SVALBARD
(Norway)

ICELAND

EUROPE AND SOUTHWEST ASIA
For detail, see maps Europe: Political
and Asia: Political.

RUSSIA

Moscow

EUROPE

ASIA

Astana
KAZAKHSTAN
UZBEKISTAN
Tashkent

Ulaanbaatar

MONGOLIA

Bishkek
KYRGYZSTAN
TURKMENISTAN
Dushanbe
TAJIKISTAN

Beijing

NORTH
KOREA
P'yŏngyang
JAPAN

Algiers Tunis
TUNISIA
Tripoli

Ashgabat
Tehran
IRAN
AFGHANISTAN

Kabul
Islamabad

CHINA

Seoul
SOUTH
KOREA
Tokyo

MADEIRA
(Portugal)
CANARY
ISLANDS
(Spain)
WESTERN
SAHARA
(Morocco)

Rabat
MOROCCO

Cairo

Thimphu

BHUTAN

Taipei

TAIWAN

Tropic of Cancer

ALGERIA

LIBYA

EGYPT

Kuwait
KUWAIT
Manama BAHRAIN
Riyadh Doha QATAR
Abu Dhabi U.A.E.
Muscat

NEPAL
New Delhi
Kathmandu

BANGLADESH

AFRICA

Dhaka

WEST AFRICA
For detail, see map
Africa: Political.

NIGER

CHAD

Khartoum

SAUDI
ARABIA

OMAN

INDIA

MYANMAR

LAOS

Hanoi

PHILIPPINES

NORTHERN
MARIANA
ISLANDS
(U.S.)

ERITREA YEMEN
Asmara
N'Djamena SUDAN
DJIBOUTI
Sanaa

Yangon

Vientiane
THAILAND VIETNAM
Bangkok CAMBODIA

Manila

NIGERIA
Abuja
CENTRAL
AFRICAN
REPUBLIC
CAMEROON
Yaoundé
Malabo
EQUATORIAL GUINEA

Addis Ababa

Djibouti

SOCOTRA
(Yemen)

ANDAMAN
& NICOBAR
ISLANDS
(India)

Phnom Penh

PALAU

GUAM
(U.S.)
Koror

Palikir

ETHIOPIA

Bangui
UGANDA

SOMALIA

Colombo
SRI LANKA
Male
MALDIVES

BRUNEI
Bandar Seri Begawan

Kuala Lumpur
MALAYSIA

FEDERATED STATES
OF MICRONESIA

SÃO TOMÉ
SÃO TOMÉ & PRÍNCIPE

GABON
Libreville

DEMOCRATIC
REPUBLIC
OF THE
CONGO

Kampala
KENYA
Kigali
RWANDA Nairobi
BURUNDI

Mogadishu

Singapore SINGAPORE

INDONESIA

PAPUA
NEW
GUINEA

CONGO
Brazzaville
Kinshasa

Bujumbura

Dodoma

TANZANIA
Dar es Salaam

Victoria
SEYCHELLES

Jakarta

Dili
EAST TIMOR

Port Moresby

CABINDA
(Angola)

Luanda
ANGOLA

Lilongwe
MALAWI

COMOROS
Moroni

Lusaka
ZAMBIA
Harare

MOZAMBIQUE

MADAGASCAR

Antananarivo

MAURITIUS
Port Louis
RÉUNION
(France)

AUSTRALIA

NAMIBIA ZIMBABWE

Windhoek

BOTSWANA

Tropic of Capricorn

AUSTRALIA

ATLANTIC
OCEAN

Gaborone
Bloemfontein Pretoria
Maseru Mbabane
SWAZILAND
SOUTH LESOTHO
Cape Town AFRICA

Maputo

INDIAN
OCEAN

Canberra

SOUTHERN OCEAN

Antarctic Circle

ANTARCTICA

KEY	
———	National border
– – –	Disputed border
⊛	National capital

The World: Physical

ARCTIC OCEAN

Beaufort Sea

Baffin Island

Greenland

Yukon R.

Mackenzie R.

Bering Sea

Hudson Bay

Labrador Sea

NORTH AMERICA

CANADIAN SHIELD

Aleutian Islands

ROCKY MOUNTAINS

GREAT PLAINS

Great Lakes

St. Lawrence R.

Missouri R.

Platte R.

APPALACHIAN MTS.

Colorado R.

Mississippi R.

ATLANTIC OCEAN

Rio Grande

Gulf of Mexico

Tropic of Cancer

Hawaiian Islands

West Indies

Caribbean Sea

MICRONESIA

Equator

Galápagos Islands

Orinoco R.

GUIANA HIGHLANDS

N

W E

S

AMAZON BASIN

Amazon R.

SOUTH AMERICA

MELANESIA

POLYNESIA

PACIFIC OCEAN

ANDES

BRAZILIAN HIGHLANDS

Tasman Sea

North Island

Tropic of Capricorn

PAMPAS

Río de la Plata

South Island

PATAGONIA

Cape Horn

Drake Passage

SOUTHERN OCEAN

ANTARCTIC PENINSULA

Weddell Sea

Antarctic Circle

Ross Sea

ANTARCTICA

0 miles 2,000

0 kilometers 2,000

Robinson

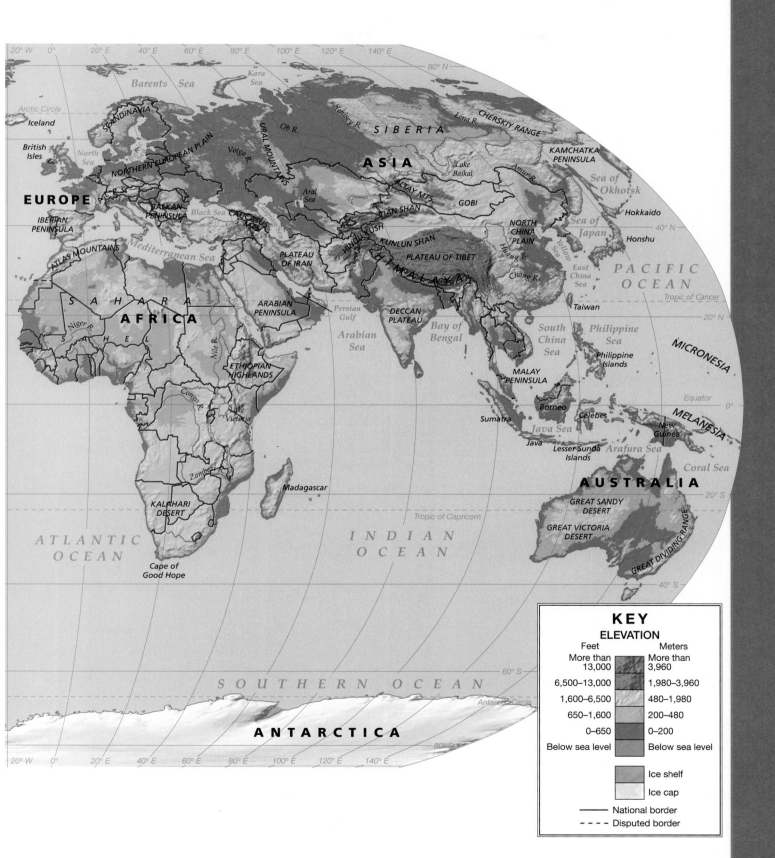

20° W | 0° | 20° E | 40° E | 60° E | 80° E | 100° E | 120° E | 140° E

80° N

Barents Sea

Kara Sea

Arctic Circle

Iceland

SCANDINAVIA

Yenisey R.

Lena R.

CHERSKIY RANGE

British Isles

North Sea

URAL MOUNTAINS

Ob R.

S I B E R I A

KAMCHATKA PENINSULA

NORTHERN EUROPEAN PLAIN

Volga R.

A S I A

Lake Baikal

Amur R.

Sea of Okhotsk

EUROPE

BALKAN PENINSULA

Black Sea

CAUCASUS MTS.

Aral Sea

ALTAY MTS.

GOBI

NORTH CHINA PLAIN

Sea of Japan

Hokkaido

40° N

Honshu

IBERIAN PENINSULA

Caspian Sea

TIAN SHAN

ATLAS MOUNTAINS

Mediterranean Sea

PLATEAU OF IRAN

HINDU KUSH

KUNLUN SHAN

PLATEAU OF TIBET

Huang R.

Yellow Sea

East China Sea

P A C I F I C   O C E A N

Chang R.

Tropic of Cancer

S A H A R A

AFRICA

ARABIAN PENINSULA

Red Sea

Persian Gulf

DECCAN PLATEAU

H I M A L A Y A

Taiwan

20° N

Niger R.

S A H E L

Nile R.

Arabian Sea

Bay of Bengal

South China Sea

Philippine Sea

MICRONESIA

ETHIOPIAN HIGHLANDS

Philippine Islands

MALAY PENINSULA

Congo R.

Lake Victoria

Borneo

Celebes

Equator | 0°

MELANESIA

Sumatra

Java Sea

New Guinea

Zambezi R.

Java

Lesser Sunda Islands

Arafura Sea

Madagascar

Coral Sea

AUSTRALIA

20° S

KALAHARI DESERT

GREAT SANDY DESERT

Tropic of Capricorn

A T L A N T I C   O C E A N

I N D I A N   O C E A N

GREAT VICTORIA DESERT

GREAT DIVIDING RANGE

Cape of Good Hope

40° S

60° S

S O U T H E R N   O C E A N

Antarctic Circle

80° S

A N T A R C T I C A

20° W | 0° | 20° E | 40° E | 60° E | 80° E | 100° E | 120° E | 140° E

KEY
ELEVATION

Feet		Meters
More than 13,000		More than 3,960
6,500–13,000		1,980–3,960
1,600–6,500		480–1,980
650–1,600		200–480
0–650		0–200
Below sea level		Below sea level

Ice shelf

Ice cap

—— National border

- - - Disputed border

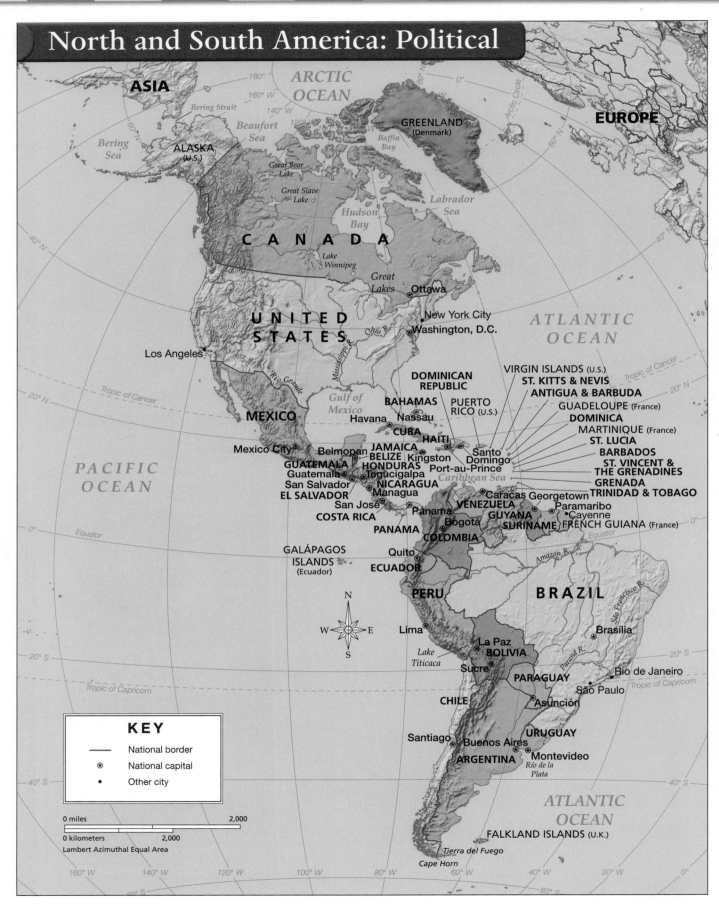

North and South America: Political

ASIA

ARCTIC OCEAN

Bering Strait

Beaufort Sea

GREENLAND (Denmark)

EUROPE

Bering Sea

ALASKA (U.S.)

Baffin Bay

Great Bear Lake

Great Slave Lake

Hudson Bay

Labrador Sea

CANADA

Lake Winnipeg

Great Lakes

Ottawa

New York City

Washington, D.C.

ATLANTIC OCEAN

UNITED STATES

Ohio R.

Los Angeles

Mississippi R.

Rio Grande

Tropic of Cancer

DOMINICAN REPUBLIC

VIRGIN ISLANDS (U.S.)

ST. KITTS & NEVIS

ANTIGUA & BARBUDA

GUADELOUPE (France)

DOMINICA

MARTINIQUE (France)

ST. LUCIA

BARBADOS

ST. VINCENT & THE GRENADINES

GRENADA

TRINIDAD & TOBAGO

Gulf of Mexico

BAHAMAS

PUERTO RICO (U.S.)

MEXICO

Havana

Nassau

CUBA

HAITI

Mexico City

JAMAICA

Belmopan

BELIZE

Kingston

Santo Domingo

Port-au-Prince

Guatemala

GUATEMALA

HONDURAS

San Salvador

Tegucigalpa

NICARAGUA

Caribbean Sea

EL SALVADOR

Managua

PACIFIC OCEAN

San José

Panama

Caracas

Georgetown

COSTA RICA

VENEZUELA

Paramaribo

PANAMA

Bogotá

GUYANA

Cayenne

SURINAME

FRENCH GUIANA (France)

COLOMBIA

Equator

GALÁPAGOS ISLANDS (Ecuador)

Quito

ECUADOR

Amazon R.

São Francisco R.

PERU

BRAZIL

N

Lima

Brasília

W E

S

La Paz

BOLIVIA

Lake Titicaca

Sucre

Rio de Janeiro

Paraná R.

PARAGUAY

São Paulo

Tropic of Capricorn

CHILE

Asunción

URUGUAY

Santiago

Buenos Aires

Montevideo

ARGENTINA

Río de la Plata

KEY

— National border

⊛ National capital

• Other city

0 miles 2,000

0 kilometers 2,000

Lambert Azimuthal Equal Area

ATLANTIC OCEAN

FALKLAND ISLANDS (U.K.)

Tierra del Fuego

Cape Horn

North and South America: Physical

ASIA

ARCTIC OCEAN

EUROPE

Bering Strait

Beaufort Sea

Greenland

Mt. McKinley
20,320 ft
(6,194 m)

Bering Sea

Aleutian Islands

Alaska Range

Gulf of Alaska

Baffin Bay

Davis Strait

Baffin Island

Labrador Sea

ROCKY MOUNTAINS

Mackenzie R.

Great Bear Lake

Great Slave Lake

Hudson Bay

CANADIAN SHIELD

Newfoundland

GREAT PLAINS

Lake Winnipeg

Missouri R.

Great Lakes

Ohio R.

Appalachian Mts.

ATLANTIC OCEAN

Colorado R.

Mississippi R.

Tropic of Cancer

Baja California

Rio Grande

Sierra Madre Occidental

Sierra Madre Oriental

Gulf of Mexico

Gulf of California

PACIFIC OCEAN

Yucatán Peninsula

Cuba

Hispaniola

Lesser Antilles

Greater Antilles

Caribbean Sea

Isthmus of Panama

Orinoco R.

Guiana Highlands

Galápagos Islands

Equator

AMAZON BASIN

Amazon R.

São Francisco R.

ANDES

Brazilian Highlands

Lake Titicaca

Tropic of Capricorn

Gran Chaco

Paraguay R.

Paraná R.

KEY

ELEVATION

Feet		Meters
More than 13,000		More than 3,960
6,500–13,000		1,980–3,960
1,600–6,500		480–1,980
650–1,600		200–480
0–650		0–200

Ice cap

National border

Aconcagua
22,834 ft
(6,960 m)

Pampas

Río de la Plata

ANDES

Patagonia

ATLANTIC OCEAN

0 miles 2,000

0 kilometers 2,000

Lambert Azimuthal Equal Area

Falkland Islands

Tierra del Fuego

Cape Horn

United States: Political

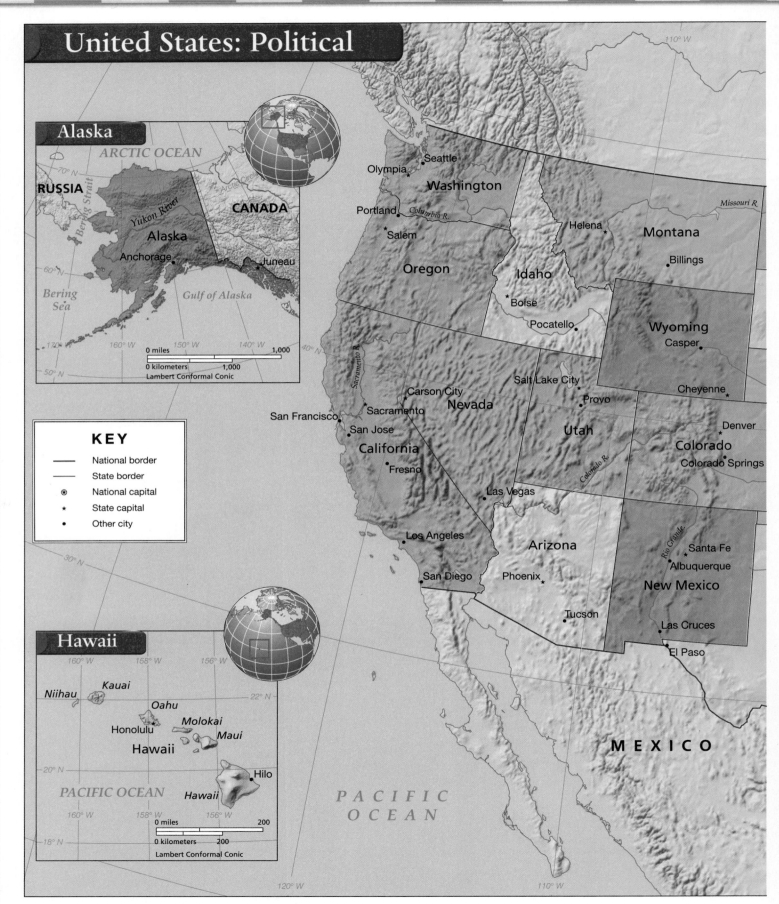

Alaska

ARCTIC OCEAN

RUSSIA

Bering Strait

Yukon River

CANADA

Alaska

Anchorage

Juneau

Bering Sea

Gulf of Alaska

70° N

60° N

50° N

170° W   160° W   150° W   140° W

0 miles   1,000
0 kilometers   1,000
Lambert Conformal Conic

KEY

—— National border

—— State border

⊛ National capital

★ State capital

• Other city

Hawaii

160° W   158° W   156° W

Niihau   Kauai

Oahu

Honolulu   Molokai

Maui

Hawaii

Hilo

PACIFIC OCEAN   Hawaii

22° N

20° N

18° N

160° W   158° W   156° W

0 miles   200
0 kilometers   200
Lambert Conformal Conic

Seattle
Olympia ★
Washington
Portland •
Columbia R.
Salem ★
Oregon
Helena ★
Montana
Missouri R.
Billings •
Idaho
Boise ★
Pocatello •
Wyoming
Casper •
Sacramento R.
Carson City ★
Nevada
Salt Lake City ★
Provo •
Cheyenne ★
San Francisco •
Sacramento ★
San Jose •
Utah
Denver ★
California
Colorado
Colorado Springs •
Fresno •
Colorado R.
Las Vegas •
Los Angeles •
Arizona
Rio Grande
Santa Fe ★
Albuquerque •
San Diego •
Phoenix ★
New Mexico
Tucson •
Las Cruces •
El Paso •

40° N

30° N

110° W

120° W

110° W

PACIFIC OCEAN

MEXICO

CANADA

North Dakota
· Bismarck
· Fargo

Minnesota

South Dakota
· Pierre

· Sioux Falls

Nebraska
· Omaha
· Lincoln

Kansas
· Topeka
Wichita ·

Oklahoma
· Oklahoma City

Texas
· Dallas
Fort Worth ·
· Austin
· San Antonio
· Houston

Iowa
Des Moines ·

Minneapolis · St. Paul
Mississippi R.

Wisconsin
Milwaukee ·
Madison ·

Chicago ·
Cedar Rapids ·

Illinois
· Springfield

Missouri
Kansas City ·
Jefferson City ·
St. Louis ·

Arkansas
Fort Smith ·
Little Rock ·

Shreveport ·

Louisiana
Baton Rouge ·
Gulfport ·
New Orleans ·

Mississippi
Jackson ·

Memphis ·

Tennessee
· Nashville

Alabama
Birmingham ·
Montgomery ·

Mobile ·

Lake Superior

Michigan
· Grand Rapids
· Lansing

Lake Michigan

Fort Wayne ·

Indiana
· Indianapolis

Lake Huron

Detroit ·

Ohio
· Columbus
Cincinnati ·
Ohio R.

Louisville ·

· Frankfort

Kentucky

Tennessee R.
· Knoxville

· Atlanta

Georgia
· Columbus

· Savannah

Tallahassee ·

Florida
· Orlando
· Tampa

· Miami

Gulf of Mexico

Lake Erie

Cleveland ·
Pittsburgh ·

West
Virginia
· Charleston

Richmond ·

Virginia

North Carolina
· Raleigh
· Charlotte

South Carolina
· Columbia
· Charleston

· Jacksonville

Lake Ontario

Pennsylvania
Harrisburg ·

Albany ·

Buffalo ·

New York

Baltimore ·
Washington, D.C.

Maryland
District of Columbia

· Norfolk

Maine
· Augusta
· Portland

Vermont
Montpelier · New Hampshire
· Concord

· Boston

Providence · Massachusetts
Hartford · Rhode Island
Connecticut

New York City ·

New Jersey
· Trenton
· Philadelphia

Delaware
· Dover
· Annapolis

ATLANTIC
OCEAN

Red R.

Arkansas R.

Missouri R.

Tennessee R.

Mississippi R.

100° W   90° W   80° W   70° W   50° N
90° W   80° W

0 miles   250
0 kilometers   250
Lambert Azimuthal Equal Area

N
W   E
S

Europe: Political

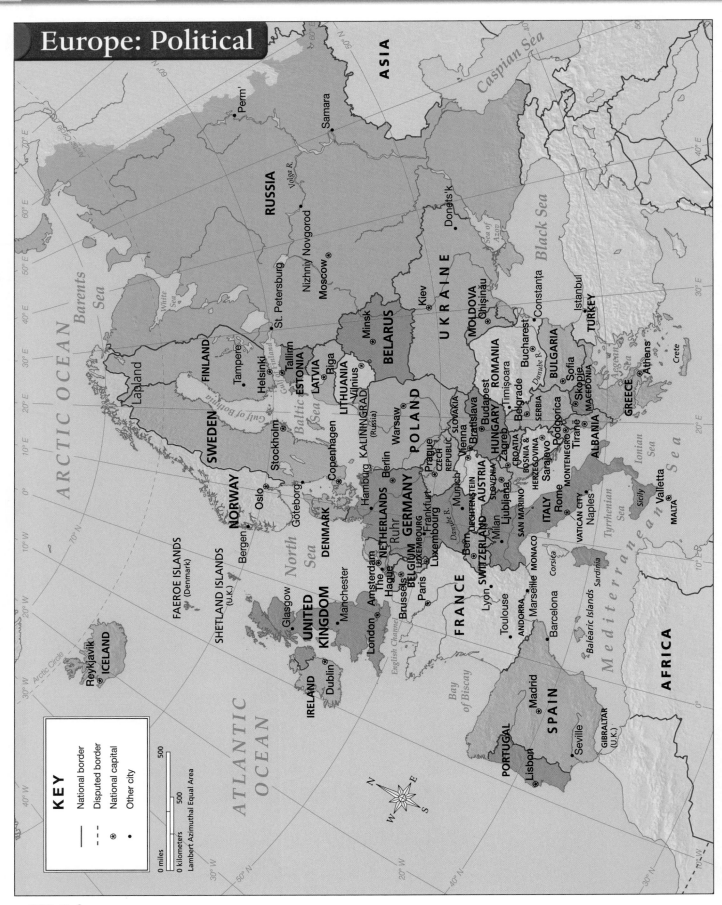

KEY

— National border

--- Disputed border

⊛ National capital

• Other city

0 miles 500

0 kilometers 500

Lambert Azimuthal Equal Area

ARCTIC OCEAN

ASIA

Caspian Sea

Barents Sea

RUSSIA

Volga R.

Perm'

Samara

Donets'k

Black Sea

Sea of Azov

White Sea

ATLANTIC OCEAN

Reykjavik
ICELAND

FAEROE ISLANDS (Denmark)

SHETLAND ISLANDS (U.K.)

NORWAY

Bergen

Oslo

SWEDEN

Göteborg

Stockholm

FINLAND

Lapland

Tampere

Helsinki

Gulf of Bothnia

Gulf of Finland

St. Petersburg

Nizhniy Novgorod

Moscow

Kiev

UKRAINE

MOLDOVA

Chişinău

Tallinn

ESTONIA

Riga

LATVIA

LITHUANIA

Vilnius

KALININGRAD (Russia)

BELARUS

Minsk

Baltic Sea

North Sea

DENMARK

Copenhagen

Hamburg

Berlin

POLAND

Warsaw

Prague

CZECH REPUBLIC

SLOVAKIA

Bratislava

Budapest

HUNGARY

ROMANIA

Timişoara

Bucharest

Danube R.

Constanţa

BULGARIA

Sofia

Skopje

MACEDONIA

GREECE

Athens

Istanbul

TURKEY

Aegean Sea

Crete

UNITED KINGDOM

Glasgow

Manchester

London

IRELAND

Dublin

NETHERLANDS

Amsterdam

The Hague

BELGIUM

Brussels

Paris

GERMANY

Ruhr

Frankfurt

Munich

LUXEMBOURG

Luxembourg

LIECHTENSTEIN

SWITZERLAND

Bern

AUSTRIA

Vienna

SLOVENIA

Ljubljana

CROATIA

Zagreb

BOSNIA & HERZEGOVINA

Sarajevo

SERBIA

Belgrade

MONTENEGRO

Podgorica

ALBANIA

Tiranë

Danube R.

FRANCE

Lyon

Toulouse

Marseille

MONACO

Milan

ITALY

SAN MARINO

Rome

VATICAN CITY

Naples

Corsica

Sardinia

Tyrrhenian Sea

Sicily

MALTA

Valletta

Ionian Sea

Mediterranean Sea

English Channel

Bay of Biscay

ANDORRA

Barcelona

SPAIN

Madrid

Seville

Balearic Islands

PORTUGAL

Lisbon

GIBRALTAR (U.K.)

AFRICA

Arctic Circle

N E S W compass rose

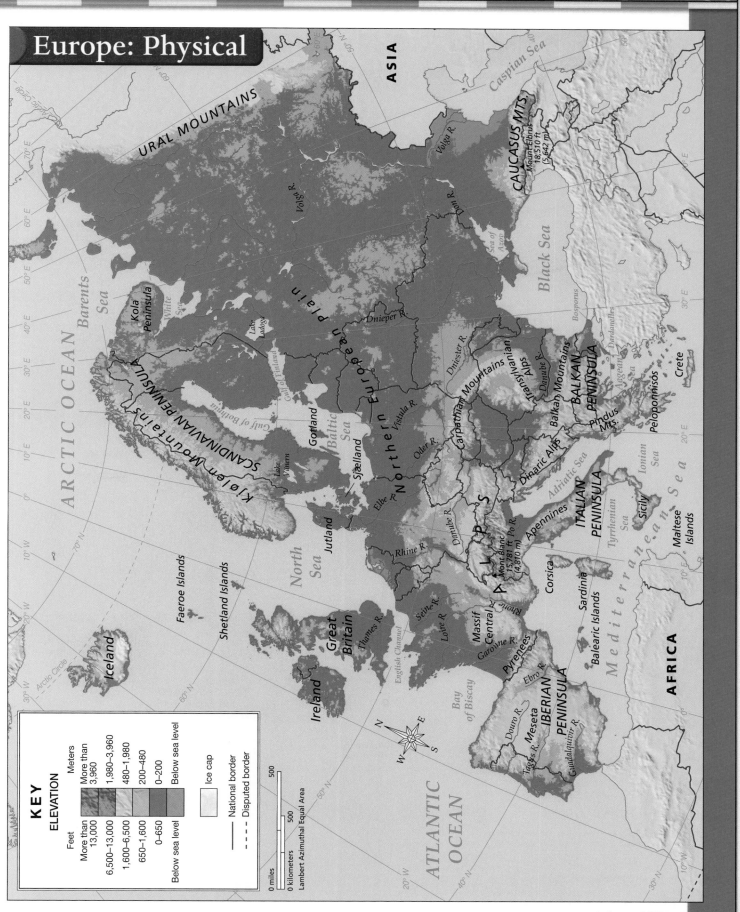

Europe: Physical

ASIA

URAL MOUNTAINS

Caspian Sea

CAUCASUS MTS.
Mount Elbrus
18,510 ft
(5,642 m)

Volga R.

Don R.

Sea of Azov

Black Sea

Dnieper R.

Dniester R.

Carpathian Mountains

Transylvanian Alps

Danube R.

Balkan Mountains

BALKAN PENINSULA

Pindus Mts.

Peloponnisos

Crete

Bosporus

Dardanelles

Aegean Sea

Ionian Sea

Dinaric Alps

Adriatic Sea

Apennines

ITALIAN PENINSULA

Sicily

Tyrrhenian Sea

Maltese Islands

Mediterranean Sea

AFRICA

Northern European Plain

Lake Ladoga

White Sea

Kola Peninsula

Barents Sea

ARCTIC OCEAN

Arctic Circle

Gulf of Bothnia

Gulf of Finland

Lake Ladoga

Vistula R.

Oder R.

Elbe R.

Gotland

Baltic Sea

Sjælland

SCANDINAVIAN PENINSULA

Kjølen Mountains

Lake Vänern

Jutland

North Sea

Faeroe Islands

Shetland Islands

Iceland

Arctic Circle

Ireland

Great Britain

Thames R.

English Channel

Seine R.

Loire R.

Bay of Biscay

Rhine R.

Danube R.

A L P S

Mont Blanc
15,781 ft
(4,810 m)

Rhône R.

Massif Central

Garonne R.

Pyrenees

Ebro R.

Corsica

Sardinia

Balearic Islands

IBERIAN PENINSULA

Douro R.

Meseta

Tagus R.

Guadalquivir R.

Bay of Biscay

ATLANTIC OCEAN

N
E
S
W

KEY

ELEVATION

Feet	Meters
More than 13,000	More than 3,960
6,500–13,000	1,980–3,960
1,600–6,500	480–1,980
650–1,600	200–480
0–650	0–200
Below sea level	Below sea level

Ice cap

—— National border

---- Disputed border

0 miles 500
0 kilometers 500
Lambert Azimuthal Equal Area

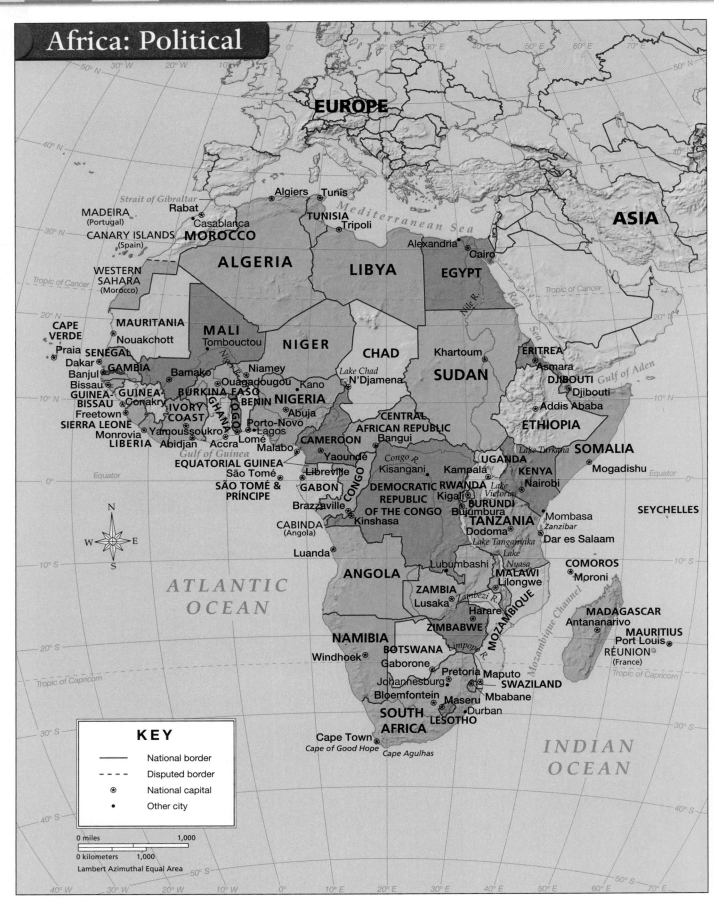

Africa: Political

EUROPE

ASIA

Strait of Gibraltar

MADEIRA (Portugal)

CANARY ISLANDS (Spain)

Algiers • Tunis
Rabat •
Casablanca
MOROCCO
TUNISIA
Tripoli •

Mediterranean Sea

Alexandria •
Cairo ⊛

WESTERN SAHARA (Morocco)

Tropic of Cancer

ALGERIA

LIBYA

EGYPT

Tropic of Cancer

Nile R.

Red Sea

CAPE VERDE

Praia ⊛

MAURITANIA

Nouakchott ⊛

MALI

Tombouctou •

NIGER

CHAD

Khartoum ⊛

SUDAN

ERITREA

Asmara ⊛

DJIBOUTI

Gulf of Aden

SENEGAL
Dakar ⊛
Banjul ⊛
GAMBIA
Bissau ⊛
GUINEA-BISSAU
Freetown ⊛
SIERRA LEONE
Monrovia ⊛
LIBERIA

Bamako ⊛

GUINEA
Conakry ⊛

Niger R.

Niamey ⊛

BURKINA FASO
Ouagadougou ⊛
Kano •

IVORY COAST

GHANA
Yamoussoukro ⊛
Abidjan •
Accra ⊛

TOGO

BENIN
Porto-Novo ⊛
Lomé ⊛

NIGERIA
Abuja ⊛
Lagos •

N'Djamena •

Lake Chad

CENTRAL AFRICAN REPUBLIC
Bangui ⊛

Addis Ababa ⊛

ETHIOPIA

SOMALIA

Djibouti •

Gulf of Guinea

CAMEROON
Yaoundé ⊛
Malabo ⊛

EQUATORIAL GUINEA
São Tomé ⊛

SÃO TOMÉ & PRÍNCIPE

Libreville ⊛

GABON

CONGO
Brazzaville ⊛

CABINDA (Angola)

Luanda ⊛

Congo R.
Kisangani •

DEMOCRATIC REPUBLIC OF THE CONGO
Kinshasa ⊛

Equator

RWANDA
Kigali ⊛
BURUNDI
Bujumbura ⊛

UGANDA
Kampala ⊛

Lake Victoria

Lake Turkana

KENYA
Nairobi ⊛

Mogadishu ⊛

Equator

TANZANIA
Dodoma ⊛

Mombasa •
Zanzibar •
Dar es Salaam •

Lake Tanganyika

SEYCHELLES

ATLANTIC OCEAN

Lubumbashi •

Lake Nyasa

ANGOLA

ZAMBIA
Lusaka ⊛

Zambezi R.

MALAWI
Lilongwe ⊛

COMOROS
Moroni ⊛

Harare ⊛

ZIMBABWE

MOZAMBIQUE

MADAGASCAR
Antananarivo ⊛

MAURITIUS
Port Louis ⊛
RÉUNION (France)

NAMIBIA

BOTSWANA

Windhoek ⊛
Gaborone ⊛

Limpopo R.

Pretoria ⊛ Maputo ⊛
Johannesburg •
Bloemfontein •
Maseru ⊛
Durban •

SWAZILAND
Mbabane ⊛

Mozambique Channel

Tropic of Capricorn

SOUTH AFRICA

LESOTHO

Tropic of Capricorn

Cape Town ⊛
Cape of Good Hope
Cape Agulhas

INDIAN OCEAN

KEY

— National border

- - - Disputed border

⊛ National capital

• Other city

0 miles 1,000

0 kilometers 1,000

Lambert Azimuthal Equal Area

Africa: Physical

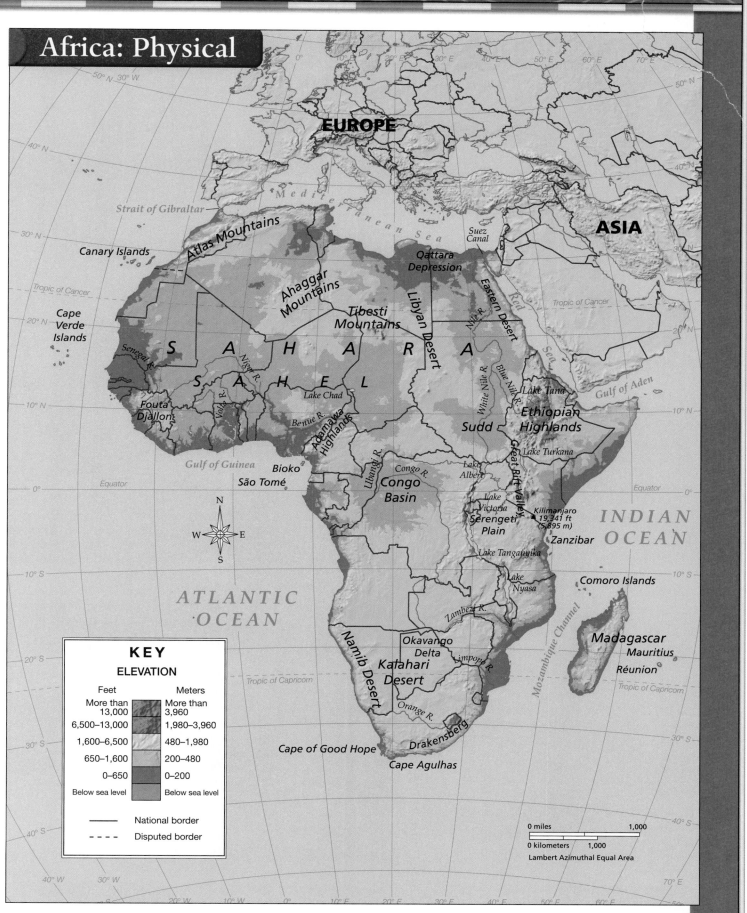

EUROPE

ASIA

Strait of Gibraltar

Canary Islands

Atlas Mountains

Qattara Depression

Suez Canal

Cape Verde Islands

Ahaggar Mountains

Tibesti Mountains

Libyan Desert

Eastern Desert

Red Sea

Tropic of Cancer

Tropic of Cancer

S A H A R A

Senegal R.

Nile R.

S A H E L

Niger R.

Lake Chad

White Nile R.

Blue Nile R.

Lake Tana

Gulf of Aden

Fouta Djallon

Volta R.

Benue R.

Adamawa Highlands

Sudd

Ethiopian Highlands

Gulf of Guinea

Bioko

Ubangi R.

Congo R.

Lake Albert

Lake Turkana

São Tomé

Congo Basin

Great Rift Valley

Equator

Equator

Lake Victoria

Kilimanjaro 19,341 ft (5,895 m)

INDIAN OCEAN

N
W   E
S

Serengeti Plain

Zanzibar

Lake Tanganyika

Comoro Islands

10° S

10° S

ATLANTIC OCEAN

Lake Nyasa

Madagascar

Mauritius

Réunion

Zambezi R.

Mozambique Channel

Namib Desert

Okavango Delta

Kalahari Desert

Limpopo R.

Tropic of Capricorn

Tropic of Capricorn

Orange R.

Drakensberg

Cape of Good Hope

Cape Agulhas

KEY

ELEVATION

Feet		Meters
More than 13,000		More than 3,960
6,500–13,000		1,980–3,960
1,600–6,500		480–1,980
650–1,600		200–480
0–650		0–200
Below sea level		Below sea level

——— National border

- - - Disputed border

0 miles   1,000

0 kilometers   1,000

Lambert Azimuthal Equal Area

Asia: Political

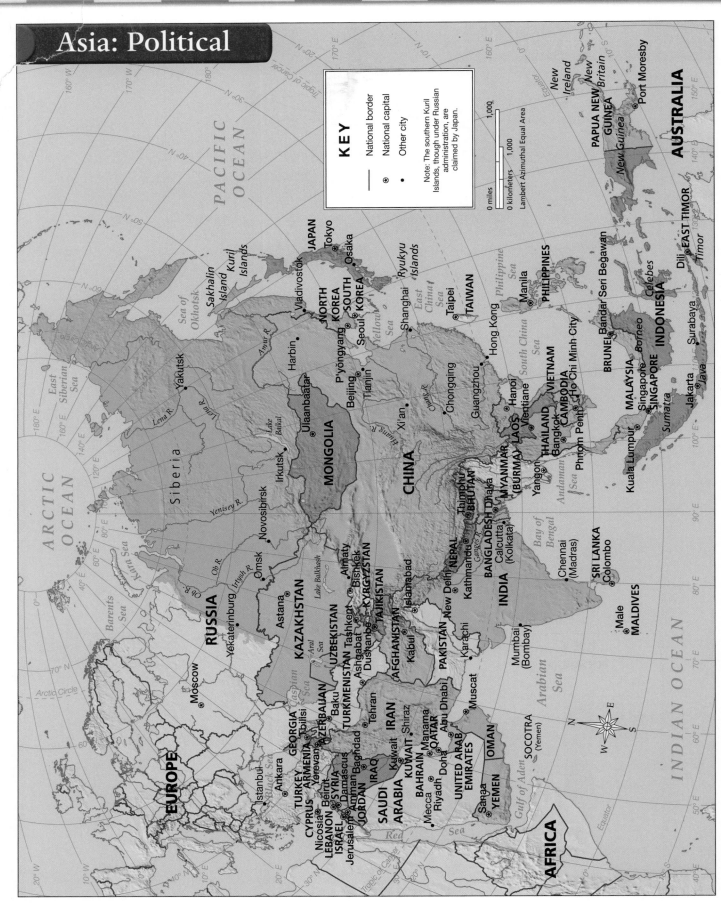

KEY

—— National border

⊛ National capital

• Other city

Note: The southern Kuril Islands, though under Russian administration, are claimed by Japan.

0 miles   1,000

0 kilometers   1,000

Lambert Azimuthal Equal Area

PACIFIC OCEAN

ARCTIC OCEAN

EUROPE

AFRICA

INDIAN OCEAN

AUSTRALIA

Arctic Circle

Tropic of Cancer

Equator

Tropic of Cancer

RUSSIA

Siberia

Moscow ⊛

Yekaterinburg

Omsk

Novosibirsk

Astana ⊛

Irkutsk

Yakutsk

Vladivostok

Sakhalin Island

Kuril Islands

Sea of Okhotsk

East Siberian Sea

Kara Sea

Barents Sea

Lena R.

Yenisey R.

Ob R.

Irtysh R.

Lake Baikal

Lake Balkhash

Aral Sea

Caspian Sea

Black Sea

KAZAKHSTAN

MONGOLIA

Ulaanbaatar ⊛

JAPAN

Tokyo ⊛

Osaka

Ryukyu Islands

NORTH KOREA

P'yŏngyang ⊛

SOUTH KOREA

Seoul ⊛

Yellow Sea

Harbin

Beijing ⊛

Tianjin

Shanghai

CHINA

Xi'an

Chongqing

Guangzhou

Hong Kong

East China Sea

Taipei ⊛

TAIWAN

Philippine Sea

Manila ⊛

PHILIPPINES

Chang R.

Huang R.

UZBEKISTAN

Tashkent ⊛

KYRGYZSTAN

Bishkek ⊛

Almaty

TAJIKISTAN

Dushanbe ⊛

TURKMENISTAN

Ashgabat ⊛

AFGHANISTAN

Kabul ⊛

PAKISTAN

Islamabad ⊛

Karachi

NEPAL

Kathmandu ⊛

New Delhi ⊛

BHUTAN

Thimphu ⊛

BANGLADESH

Dhaka ⊛

Calcutta (Kolkata)

Ganges R.

INDIA

Mumbai (Bombay)

Chennai (Madras)

SRI LANKA

Colombo ⊛

Male ⊛

MALDIVES

Bay of Bengal

Arabian Sea

MYANMAR (BURMA)

Yangon

Andaman Sea

THAILAND

Bangkok ⊛

LAOS

Vientiane ⊛

VIETNAM

Hanoi ⊛

CAMBODIA

Phnom Penh ⊛

Ho Chi Minh City

South China Sea

MALAYSIA

Kuala Lumpur ⊛

SINGAPORE ⊛

BRUNEI

Bandar Seri Begawan ⊛

Borneo

Celebes

INDONESIA

Jakarta ⊛

Sumatra

Java

Surabaya

Timor

Dili ⊛

EAST TIMOR

PAPUA NEW GUINEA

Port Moresby ⊛

New Guinea

New Ireland

New Britain

TURKEY

Ankara ⊛

Istanbul

GEORGIA

Tbilisi ⊛

ARMENIA

Yerevan ⊛

AZERBAIJAN

Baku ⊛

CYPRUS

Nicosia ⊛

LEBANON

Beirut ⊛

SYRIA

Damascus ⊛

ISRAEL

Jerusalem ⊛

JORDAN

Amman ⊛

IRAQ

Baghdad ⊛

IRAN

Tehran ⊛

Shiraz

KUWAIT

Kuwait ⊛

BAHRAIN

Manama ⊛

QATAR

Doha ⊛

SAUDI ARABIA

Riyadh ⊛

Mecca

UNITED ARAB EMIRATES

Abu Dhabi ⊛

OMAN

Muscat ⊛

YEMEN

Sanaa ⊛

SOCOTRA (Yemen)

Gulf of Aden

Red Sea

Kura R.

N E S W

Asia: Physical

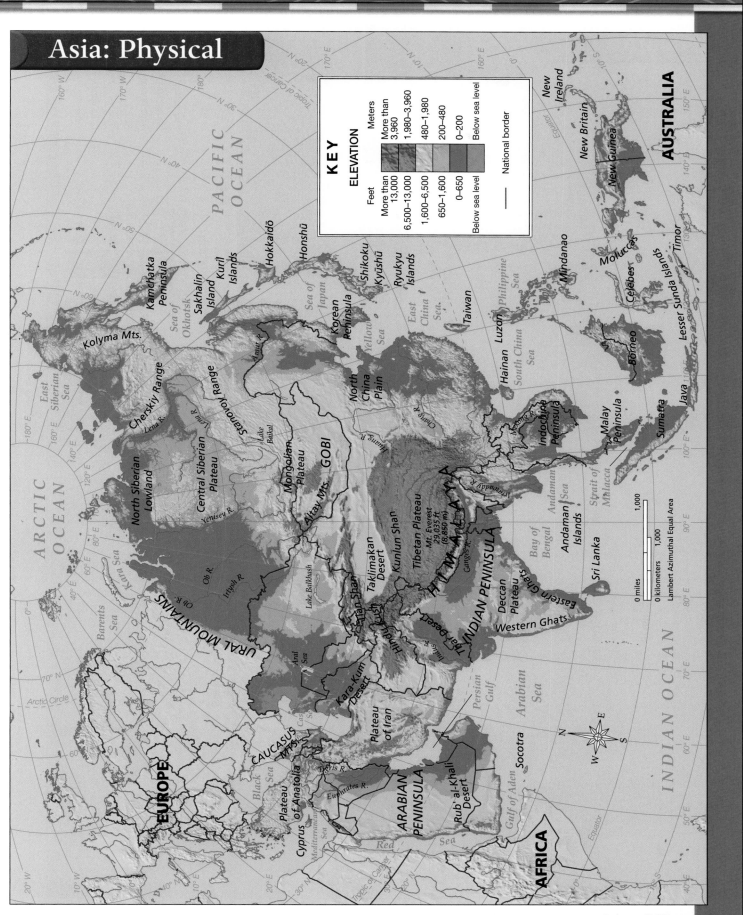

KEY

ELEVATION

Feet	Meters
More than 13,000	More than 3,960
6,500–13,000	1,980–3,960
1,600–6,500	480–1,980
650–1,600	200–480
0–650	0–200
Below sea level	Below sea level

—— National border

PACIFIC OCEAN

ARCTIC OCEAN

INDIAN OCEAN

AUSTRALIA

EUROPE

AFRICA

New Ireland
New Britain
New Guinea
Mindanao
Moluccas
Celebes
Lesser Sunda Islands
Timor
Borneo
Java
Sumatra
Malay Peninsula
Philippine Sea
Luzon
Hainan
South China Sea
Taiwan
East China Sea
Ryukyu Islands
Kyushu
Shikoku
Honshu
Hokkaidō
Kuril Islands
Sakhalin Island
Sea of Okhotsk
Kamchatka Peninsula
Kolyma Mts.
Cherskiy Range
Stanovoy Range
North Siberian Lowland
Central Siberian Plateau
Lena R.
Yenisey R.
Ob R.
Irtysh R.
URAL MOUNTAINS
Kara Sea
Barents Sea
East Siberian Sea
Korean Peninsula
Sea of Japan
Yellow Sea
North China Plain
Huang R.
Chang R.
Mongolian Plateau
GOBI
Altay Mts.
Amur R.
Lake Baikal
Lake Balkhash
Aral Sea
Kara-Kum Desert
Tian Shan
Taklimakan Desert
Kunlun Shan
Tibetan Plateau
Mt. Everest 29,035 ft (8,850 m)
HIMALAYA
Hindu Kush
Indus R.
Thar Desert
Ganges R.
INDIAN PENINSULA
Deccan Plateau
Eastern Ghats
Western Ghats
Sri Lanka
Bay of Bengal
Andaman Sea
Andaman Islands
Irrawaddy R.
Mekong R.
Indochina Peninsula
Strait of Malacca
Arabian Sea
Socotra
Gulf of Aden
ARABIAN PENINSULA
Rub' al-Khali Desert
Persian Gulf
Plateau of Iran
Caspian Sea
CAUCASUS MTS.
Black Sea
Plateau of Anatolia
Cyprus
Mediterranean Sea
Tigris R.
Euphrates R.
Red Sea
Tropic of Cancer
Arctic Circle
Equator

0 miles 1,000
0 kilometers 1,000
Lambert Azimuthal Equal Area

Oceania

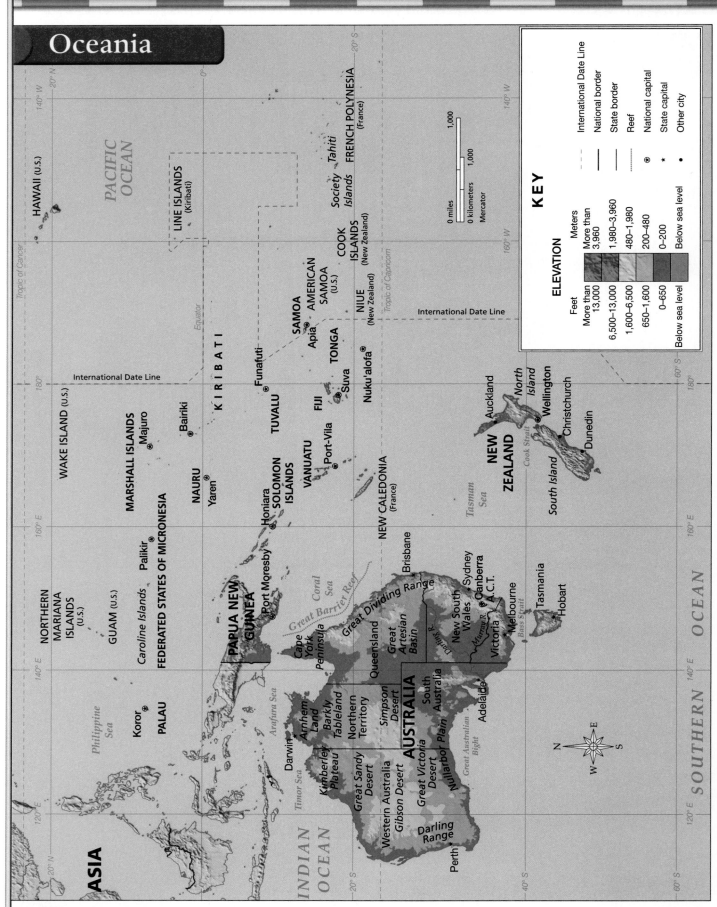

ASIA

PACIFIC OCEAN

HAWAII (U.S.)

LINE ISLANDS
(Kiribati)

FRENCH POLYNESIA
(France)

Tahiti
Society
Islands

COOK
ISLANDS
(New Zealand)

NIUE
(New Zealand)

AMERICAN
SAMOA
(U.S.)

SAMOA
Apia ⊛
TONGA
Nuku'alofa ⊛

International Date Line

Tropic of Cancer

Equator

Tropic of Capricorn

K I R I B A T I

Funafuti ⊛
TUVALU

FIJI
Suva

VANUATU
Port-Vila ⊛

Bairiki ⊛

NAURU
Yaren ⊛

SOLOMON
ISLANDS
Honiara ⊛

WAKE ISLAND (U.S.)

MARSHALL ISLANDS
Majuro ⊛

NORTHERN
MARIANA
ISLANDS
(U.S.)

GUAM (U.S.)

Caroline Islands
Palikir ⊛
FEDERATED STATES OF MICRONESIA

Koror ⊛
PALAU

Philippine
Sea

Timor Sea

Arafura Sea

PAPUA NEW
GUINEA
Port Moresby ⊛

NEW CALEDONIA
(France)

Great Barrier Reef

Coral
Sea

Cape
York
Peninsula

Great Dividing Range

Queensland

Great
Artesian
Basin

Brisbane

New South
Wales
Sydney
Canberra ★ A.C.T.

Murray R.
Darling R.

Victoria
Melbourne

Bass Strait

Tasmania
Hobart ★

Darwin ★

Arnhem
Land

Barkly
Tableland

Northern
Territory

Simpson
Desert

South
Australia

Adelaide ★

Kimberley
Plateau

Great Sandy
Desert

Western Australia

Gibson Desert

Great Victoria
Desert

Nullarbor Plain

AUSTRALIA

Great Australian Bight

Darling
Range

Perth ★

INDIAN
OCEAN

NEW
ZEALAND

Auckland
North
Island
Wellington
Christchurch
Dunedin
South Island

Cook Strait

Tasman
Sea

SOUTHERN OCEAN

KEY

ELEVATION

Feet	Meters
More than 13,000	More than 3,960
6,500–13,000	1,980–3,960
1,600–6,500	480–1,980
650–1,600	200–480
0–650	0–200
Below sea level	Below sea level

International Date Line
National border
State border
Reef
⊛ National capital
★ State capital
• Other city

0 miles 1,000
0 kilometers 1,000
Mercator

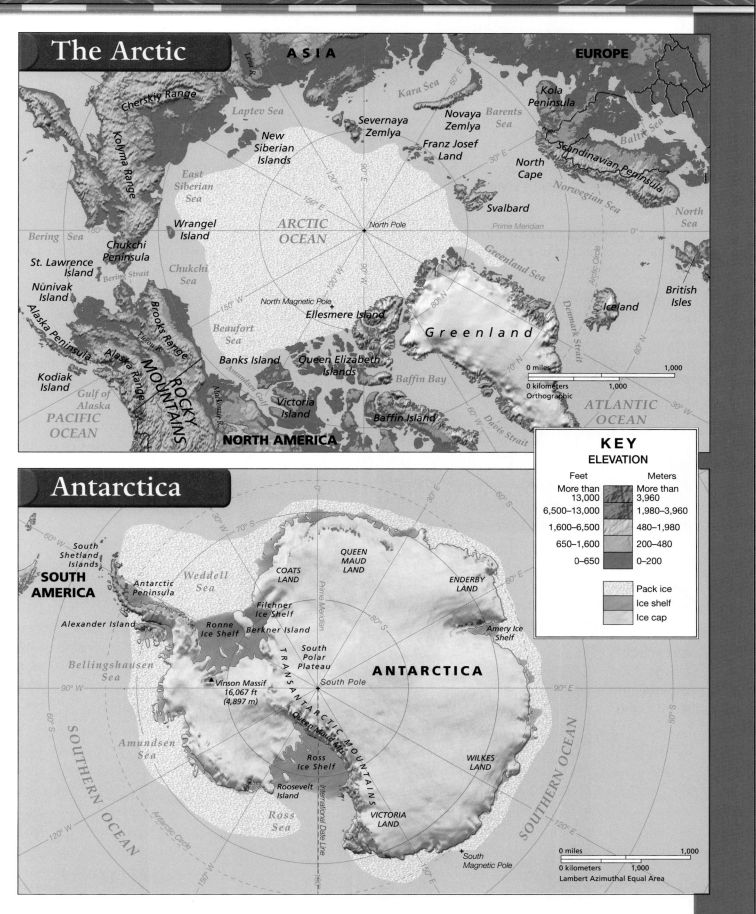

The Arctic

ASIA

EUROPE

Cherskiy Range
Lena R.
Laptev Sea
Kara Sea
Kola Peninsula
Severnaya Zemlya
Novaya Zemlya
Franz Josef Land
Barents Sea
Baltic Sea
New Siberian Islands
Kolyma Range
North Cape
Scandinavian Peninsula
East Siberian Sea
Svalbard
Norwegian Sea
North Sea
Wrangel Island
ARCTIC OCEAN
North Pole
Prime Meridian
Bering Sea
Chukchi Peninsula
Chukchi Sea
Greenland Sea
Arctic Circle
British Isles
St. Lawrence Island
Bering Strait
Iceland
Nunivak Island
North Magnetic Pole
Ellesmere Island
Greenland
Denmark Strait
Beaufort Sea
Alaska Peninsula
Brooks Range
Yukon R.
Banks Island
Queen Elizabeth Islands
Baffin Bay
Kodiak Island
Alaska Range
ROCKY MOUNTAINS
Amundsen Gulf
Mackenzie R.
Victoria Island
Baffin Island
Davis Strait
ATLANTIC OCEAN
Gulf of Alaska
PACIFIC OCEAN
NORTH AMERICA

0 miles 1,000
0 kilometers 1,000
Orthographic

KEY
ELEVATION

Feet		Meters
More than 13,000		More than 3,960
6,500–13,000		1,980–3,960
1,600–6,500		480–1,980
650–1,600		200–480
0–650		0–200

Pack ice
Ice shelf
Ice cap

Antarctica

South Shetland Islands
SOUTH AMERICA
Antarctic Peninsula
Weddell Sea
COATS LAND
QUEEN MAUD LAND
ENDERBY LAND
Alexander Island
Ronne Ice Shelf
Filchner Ice Shelf
Berkner Island
Prime Meridian
Amery Ice Shelf
Bellingshausen Sea
South Polar Plateau
TRANSANTARCTIC MOUNTAINS
ANTARCTICA
Amundsen Sea
Vinson Massif 16,067 ft (4,897 m)
South Pole
Queen Maud Mts.
Ross Ice Shelf
WILKES LAND
Roosevelt Island
VICTORIA LAND
Ross Sea
South Magnetic Pole
SOUTHERN OCEAN
International Date Line
Antarctic Circle

0 miles 1,000
0 kilometers 1,000
Lambert Azimuthal Equal Area

Glossary of Geographic Terms

basin
an area that is lower than surrounding land areas; some basins are filled with water

bay
a body of water that is partly surrounded by land and that is connected to a larger body of water

butte
a small, high, flat-topped landform with cliff-like sides

▲ **butte**

canyon
a deep, narrow valley with steep sides; often with a stream flowing through it

cataract
a large waterfall or steep rapids

delta
a plain at the mouth of a river, often triangular in shape, formed where sediment is deposited by flowing water

flood plain
a broad plain on either side of a river, formed where sediment settles during floods

glacier
a huge, slow-moving mass of snow and ice

hill
an area that rises above surrounding land and has a rounded top; lower and usually less steep than a mountain

island
an area of land completely surrounded by water

isthmus
a narrow strip of land that connects two larger areas of land

mesa
a high, flat-topped landform with cliff-like sides; larger than a butte

mountain
a landform that rises steeply at least 2,000 feet (610 meters) above surrounding land; usually wide at the bottom and rising to a narrow peak or ridge

▶ **glacier**

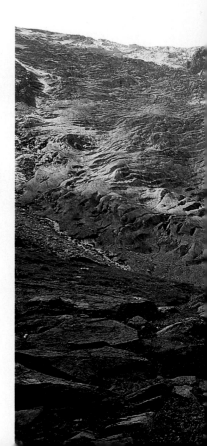

◀ **cataract**

◀ delta

mountain pass
a gap between mountains

peninsula
an area of land almost completely surrounded by water but connected to the mainland

plain
a large area of flat or gently rolling land

plateau
a large, flat area that rises above the surrounding land; at least one side has a steep slope

river mouth
the point where a river enters a lake or sea

strait
a narrow stretch of water that connects two larger bodies of water

tributary
a river or stream that flows into a larger river

valley
a low stretch of land between mountains or hills; land that is drained by a river

volcano
an opening in Earth's surface through which molten rock, ashes, and gases escape from the interior

▶ **volcano**

Gazetteer

A

Acadia (51° N, 110° W) the first permanent French settlement in North America, p. 176

Atlanta (33°44′ N, 84°23′ W) the capital of the state of Georgia, p. 121

B

Boston (42°21′ N, 71°03′ W) the capital of the state of Massachusetts, p. 113

C

Calgary (51° N, 114° W) a city in southern Alberta, Canada, p. 165

Canadian Shield a region of rocky, rugged land that covers about half of Canada, p. 13

Cariboo Mountains (59° N, 116° W) a mountain range in eastern British Columbia, Canada, p. 169

Chicago (41°51′ N, 87°39′ W) a major city in the state of Illinois, on Lake Michigan, p. 130

Coast Ranges (55° N, 129° W) a mountain range stretching along the Pacific from southern California to Alaska, p. 13

Cuyahoga River (41° N, 82° W) a river in northeastern Ohio, p. 65

D

Dawson (64°04′ N, 139°25′ W) a city located in western Yukon Territory, Canada, p. 183

Death Valley (36° N, 116° W) the hottest, driest region of North America, located in southeastern California, p. 12

Detroit (42°20′ N, 83°03′ W) a city in the state of Michigan, p. 131

F

Fraser River (49° N, 123° W) a major river of western North America, mainly in British Columbia, p. 14

G

Great Lakes a group of five large lakes in central North America: Lakes Superior, Michigan, Huron, Erie, and Ontario, p. 13

I

Iqaluit (63°44′ N, 68°28′ W) the capital of Nunavut, Canada, p. 184

J

Jamestown (37°30′ N, 75°55′ W) the first permanent English settlement in North America, located in present-day Virginia, p. 40

L

L'Anse aux Meadows (51°36′ N, 55°32′ W) the earliest known North American Viking settlement, located on Newfoundland, p. 173

Los Angeles (34°03′ N, 118°14′ W) a major city on the southwest coast of California, p. 138

M

Mackenzie River (69° N, 134° W) a large river in the Northwest Territories of Canada, p. 14

Miami (25°46′ N, 80°11′ W) a city on the southeast coast of Florida, p. 122

Minneapolis–St. Paul (44°58′ N, 93°15′ W) two cities in Minnesota; also called the Twin Cities, p. 132

Mississippi River (29° N, 89° W) a large river in the central United States, flowing south from Minnesota to the Gulf of Mexico, p. 14

Missouri River (39° N, 90° W) a large river in the west central United States, flowing southeast from Montana into the Mississippi River, p. 14

Montreal (45°31′ N, 73°34′ W) the largest city in the province of Quebec, Canada, p. 156

N

New York City (40°43' N, 73°01' W) a large city and port at the mouth of the Hudson River in the state of New York, p. 115

Niagara Falls (43°05' N, 79°04' W) a waterfall on the Niagara River between Ontario, Canada, and New York State, p. 68

Northwest Territories (65° N, 120° W) a region of Northern Canada, p. 181

Nunavut (70° N, 95° W) a Canadian territory in the northern part of Canada, p. 181

O

Ontario (50° N, 88° W) the second-largest province in Canada, p. 153

Ottawa (45°25' N, 75°42' W) the capital city of Canada, located in Ontario, p. 153

P

Pacific Northwest the region in the northwestern United States that includes Oregon, Washington, and northern California, p. 135

Pennsylvania Colony a colony in America founded in 1682 by William Penn, p. 40

Philadelphia (39°57' N, 75°09' W) a city and port in Pennsylvania, on the Delaware River, p. 113

Portland (45°31' N, 122°40' W) the largest city in the state of Oregon, p. 136

Q

Quebec (52° N, 72° W) a province in eastern Canada, p. 157

R

Rocky Mountains (48° N, 116° W) the major mountain range in western North America, extending from central New Mexico to northeastern British Columbia, p. 11

S

St. Lawrence River (49° N, 67° W) a river in eastern North America; the second-longest river in Canada, p. 15

St. Lawrence Seaway (46° N, 73° W) a navigable seaway from the Atlantic Ocean to the western end of the Great Lakes, p. 68

St. Louis (38°37' N, 90°11' W) a major city in Missouri, on the Mississippi River, p. 131

San Jose (37°20' N, 121°53' W) a city in western California, p. 137

Seattle (47°36' N, 122°19' W) a city in the state of Washington on Puget Sound, p. 137

Sierra Nevada a mountain range in California in the western United States, p. 12

T

Toronto (43°39' N, 79°23' W) the largest and most populous city in Canada; the capital of the province of Ontario, p. 155

V

Vancouver (49°16' N, 123°07' W) a city in southwestern British Columbia, Canada, p. 166

Victoria (48°25' N, 123°22' W) the capital of British Columbia, Canada, p. 169

W

Washington, D.C. (38°53' N, 77°02' W) the capital city of the United States, located between Maryland and Virginia on the Potomac River, p. 123

Y

Yukon (64° N, 135° W) a territory in northwestern Canada, p. 181

Glossary

A

abolitionist (ab uh LISH un ist) *n.* a person who believed that enslaving people was wrong and who wanted to end the practice, p. 47

acid rain (AS id rayn) *n.* a rain containing acid that is harmful to plants and trees, often formed when pollutants from cars and factories combine with moisture in the air, p. 66

agribusiness (AG ruh biz niz) *n.* a large company that runs huge farms to produce, process, and distribute agricultural products, p. 26

alliance (uh LY uns) *n.* a formal agreement to do business together, sometimes formed between governments, p. 42

alluvial soil (uh LOO vee ul soyl) *n.* soil deposited by water; fertile topsoil left by rivers after a flood, p. 26

aquaculture (AHK wuh kul chur) *n.* the cultivation of fish and water plants, p. 177

aurora borealis (aw RAWR uh bawr ee AL us) *n.* colorful bands of light that can be seen in northern skies, p. 180

B

bilingual (by LIN gwul) *adj.* speaking two languages; having two official languages, p. 59

bison (BY sun) *n.* buffalo, p. 37

boomtown (boom town) *n.* a settlement that springs up quickly, often to serve the needs of miners, p. 169

boycott (BOY kaht) *n.* a refusal to buy or use goods and services, p. 41

C

civil rights (SIV ul ryts) *n.* the basic rights due to all citizens, p. 53

Civil War (SIV ul wawr) *n.* the war between the northern and southern states in the United States, which began in 1861 and ended in 1865, p. 47

Cold War (kohld wawr) *n.* a period of great tension between the United States and the Soviet Union, which lasted for more than 40 years after World War II, p. 53

communism (KAHM yoo niz um) *n.* a political system in which the central government controls all aspects of citizens' lives, p. 53

commute (kuh MYOOT) *v.* to travel regularly to and from a place, particularly to and from a job, p. 110

Continental Divide (kahn tuh NEN tul duh VYD) *n.* the boundary that separates rivers flowing toward opposite sides of a continent, located in the Rocky Mountains of North America, p. 14

corporate farm (KAWR puh rit fahrm) *n.* a large farm run by a corporation, often consisting of many smaller farms, p. 129

cultural diversity (KUL chur ul duh VUR suh tee) *n.* a wide variety of cultures, p. 76

cultural exchange (KUL chur ul eks CHAYNJ) *n.* a process in which different cultures share ideas and ways of doing things, p. 77

D

descendant (dee SEN dunt) *n.* a child, grandchild, great-grandchild (and so on) of an ancestor, p. 156

descent (dee SENT) *n.* ancestry, p. 161

dictator (DIK tay tur) *n.* a person who rules a country completely and independently, p. 54

discrimination (dih skrim ih NAY shun) *n.* the practice of treating certain groups of people unfairly, p. 53

dominion (duh MIN yun) *n.* a self-governing area subject to Great Britain; for example, Canada prior to 1939, p. 58

E

economy (ih KAHN uh mee) *n.* a system for producing, distributing, consuming, and owning goods, services, and wealth, p. 28

enslave (en SLAYV) *v.* to force someone to become a slave, p. 39

ethnic group (ETH nik groop) *n.* a group of people who share the same ancestors, culture, language, or religion, p. 78

exile (EK syl) *v.* to force to leave an area, p. 176

export (eks PAWRT) *v.* to send goods to another country for sale, p. 69

F

federation (fed ur AY shun) *n.* a union of states, groups, provinces, or nations, p. 153

forty-niner (FAWRT ee NY nur) *n.* one of the first miners of the California Gold Rush of 1849, p. 135

fossil fuel (FAHS ul FYOO ul) *n.* a fuel formed over millions of years from animal and plant remains, including coal, petroleum, and natural gas, p. 27

Francophone (FRANG koh fohn) *n.* a person who speaks French as his or her first language, p. 156

free trade (free trayd) *n.* trade with no tariffs, or taxes, on imported goods, p. 70

fugitive (FYOO jih tiv) *n.* a runaway; someone who runs from danger, p. 46

G

glacier (GLAY shur) *n.* a huge, slow-moving mass of snow and ice, p. 12

grasslands (GRAS landz) *n.* regions of flat or rolling land covered with grasses, p. 21

Great Lakes (grayt layks) *n.* the world's largest group of freshwater lakes, located between the United States and Canada and comprising Lakes Erie, Huron, Michigan, Ontario, and Superior, p. 13

H

haze (hayz) *n.* foglike air, often caused by pollution, p. 66

Holocaust (HAHL uh kawst) *n.* the killing of millions of Jews by the Nazis in World War II, p. 52

Homestead Act (HOHM sted akt) *n.* a law passed in 1862 giving 160 acres (65 hectares) of land on the Midwestern plains to any adult willing to live on and farm it for five years, p. 50

hydroelectricity (hy droh ee lek TRIH suh tee) *n.* electric power produced by moving water, p. 27

I

immigrant (IM uh grunt) *n.* a person who moves to a new country in order to settle there, p. 45

immunity (ih MYOO nuh tee) *n.* a natural resistance to disease, p. 163

import (im PAWRT) *v.* to bring goods into one country from another, p. 69

indentured servant (in DEN churd SUR vunt) *n.* a person who, in exchange for benefits received, must work for a period of years to gain freedom, p. 40

indigenous (in DIJ uh nus) *adj.* belonging to a certain place, p. 37

industrialization (in dus tree ul ih ZAY shun) *n.* the development of large industries, p. 121

Industrial Revolution (in DUS tree ul rev uh LOO shun) *n.* the change from making goods by hand to making them by machine, p. 45

Inuktitut (ih NOOK tih toot) *n.* the native language of the Inuit, p. 184

L

labor force (LAY bur fawrs) *n.* the workers in a country or region, p. 50

land bridge (land brij) *n.* a bridge formed by a narrow strip of land connecting one landmass to another, p. 37

landmass (LAND mas) *n.* a large area of land, p. 11

latitude (LAT uh tood) *n.* the distance north or south of the Equator, p. 19

literacy (LIT ur uh see) *n.* the ability to read and write, p. 80

lock (lahk) *n.* an enclosed section of a canal used to raise or lower a ship to another level, pp. 15, 69

Louisiana Purchase (loo ee zee AN uh PUR chus) *n.* the sale of land in 1803 by France to the United States; all the land between the Mississippi River and the eastern slope of the Rocky Mountains, p. 43

lowlands (LOH landz) *n.* lands that are lower than the surrounding land, p. 13

M

Manifest Destiny (MAN uh fest DES tuh nee) *n.* a belief that the United States had a right to own all the land from the Atlantic Ocean to the Pacific Ocean, p. 45

maritime (MA rih tym) *adj.* having to do with navigation or shipping on the sea, p. 177

mass transit (mas TRAN sit) *n.* a system of subways, buses, and commuter trains used to transport large numbers of people, p. 137

megalopolis (meg uh LAHP uh lis) *n.* a number of cities and suburbs that blend into one very large urban area, p. 111

melting pot (MELT ing paht) *n.* a country in which all cultures blend together to form a single culture, p. 89

migration (my GRAY shun) *n.* the movement of people from one country or region to another in order to make a new home, p. 37

missionary (MISH un ehr ee) *n.* a person who tries to convert others to his or her religion, p. 39

mixed-crop farm (mikst krahp fahrm) *n.* a farm that grows several different kinds of crops, p. 128

N

NAFTA (NAF tuh) *n.* North American Free Trade Agreement, signed in 1994 by Canada, the United States, and Mexico to establish mutual free trade, p. 70

navigate (NAV uh gayt) *v.* to plot or direct the course of a ship or aircraft, p. 15

nomadic (noh MAD ik) *adj.* frequently moving from one place to another in search of food or pasture-land, p. 91

P

Pacific Rim (puh SIF ik rim) *n.* the group of countries bordering on the Pacific Ocean, p. 171

permafrost (PUR muh frawst) *n.* permanently frozen layer of ground below the top layer of soil, p. 21

petrochemical (pet roh KEM ih kul) *n.* a substance, such as plastic, paint, or asphalt, that is made from petroleum, p. 120

plantation (plan TAY shun) *n.* a large, one-crop farm with many workers, common in the Southern United States before the Civil War, p. 40

population density (pahp yuh LAY shun DEN suh tee) *n.* the average number of people per square mile or square kilometer, p. 111

prairie (PREHR ee) *n.* a region of flat or rolling land covered with tall grasses, p. 21

prime minister (prym MIN is tur) *n.* the chief official in a government with a parliament, pp. 60, 153

province (PRAH vins) *n.* a political division of land in Canada, similar to a state in the United States, p. 21

Q

Quiet Revolution (KWY ut rev uh LOO shun) *n.* a peaceful change in the government of Quebec, Canada, in which the Parti Québécois won control of the legislature and made French the official language, p. 157

R

rain shadow (rayn SHAD oh) *n.* an area on the side of a mountain away from the wind, which receives little rainfall, p. 19

recession (rih SESH un) *n.* a downturn in business activity and economic prosperity, not as severe as a depression, p. 128

Reconstruction (ree kun STRUK shun) *n.* the United States plan for rebuilding the nation after the Civil War, including a period when the South was governed by the United States Army, p. 48

referendum (ref uh REN dum) *n.* a ballot or vote in which voters decide for or against a particular issue, p. 157

reservation (rez ur VAY shun) *n.* land set aside for a specific purpose, as by the United States government for Native Americans, p. 85

reserve (rih ZURV) *n.* land set aside for a specific purpose, as by the Canadian government for indigenous peoples, p. 90

responsible development (rih SPAHN suh bul dih VEL up munt) *n.* balancing the needs of the environment, community, and economy, p. 136

Revolutionary War (rev uh LOO shun ehr ee wawr) *n.* the war in which the American colonies won their independence from Britain, fought from 1775 to 1781, p. 41

Rocky Mountains (RAHK ee MOWN tunz) *n.* the major mountain range in western North America, p. 11

S

segregate (SEG ruh gayt) *v.* to set apart and force to use separate schools, housing, parks, and so on because of race or religion, p. 48

separatist (SEP ur uh tist) *n.* someone who wants the province of Quebec to break away from the rest of Canada, p. 157

slum (slum) *n.* a usually crowded area of a city, often with poverty and poor housing, p. 49

sod (sahd) *n.* the top layer of soil, containing grass plants and their roots, p. 160

standard of living (STAN durd uv LIV ing) *n.* the level that a person or nation lives, as measured by the availability of food, clothing, shelter, etc., p. 81

Sun Belt (sun belt) *n.* area of the United States stretching from the southern Atlantic Coast to the coast of California; known for its warm weather, p. 122

T

tariff (TAR if) *n.* a tax charged on imported goods, p. 70

tenement (TEN uh munt) *n.* an apartment house that is poorly built and crowded, p. 49

territory (TEHR uh tawr ee) *n.* a large division of Canada, p. 181

terrorist (TEHR ur ist) *n.* a person who uses violence and fear to achieve political goals, p. 54

textile (TEKS tyl) *n.* cloth, p. 45

totem pole (TOHT um pohl) *n.* a tall, carved wooden pole containing symbols, found among Native Americans of the Pacific Northwest, p. 167

treaty (TREE tee) *n.* an agreement between two or more nations, p. 85

tributary (TRIB yoo tehr ee) *n.* a river or stream that flows into a larger river, p. 14

tundra (TUN druh) *n.* a cold, dry region covered with snow for more than half the year; a vast, treeless plain where the subsoil is always frozen, p. 21

V

vegetation (vej uh TAY shun) *n.* plant life, p. 21

Index

The *m, g,* or *p* following some page numbers refers to maps *(m)*, charts, diagrams, tables, timelines, or graphs *(g)* or pictures *(p)*.

Acknowledgments

Cover Design

Pronk&Associates

Staff Credits

The people who made up *World Studies* team—representing design services, editorial, editorial services, educational technology, marketing, market research, photo research and art development, production services, project office, publishing processes, and rights & permissions—are listed below. Bold type denotes core team members.

Greg Abrom, Ernie Albanese, Rob Aleman, Susan Andariese, **Rachel Avenia-Prol,** Leann Davis Alspaugh, Penny Baker, Barbara Bertell, **Peter Brooks,** Rui Camarinha, John Carle, **Lisa Del Gatto,** Kathy Dempsey, Anne Drowns, Deborah Dukeshire, Marlies Dwyer, **Frederick Fellows,** Paula C. Foye, Lara Fox, Julia Gecha, **Mary Hanisco,** Salena Hastings, Lance Hatch, Kerri Hoar, **Beth Hyslip,** Katharine Ingram, Nancy Jones, John Kingston, Deborah Levheim, Constance J. McCarty, **Kathleen Mercandetti,** Art Mkrtchyan, Ken Myett, **Mark O'Malley,** Jen Paley, Ray Parenteau, **Gabriela Pérez Fiato,** Linda Punskovsky, Kirsten Richert, **Lynn Robbins,** Nancy Rogier, Bruce Rolff, Robin Samper, Mildred Schulte, **Malti Sharma,** Lisa Smith-Ruvalcaba, Roberta Warshaw, Sarah Yezzi

Additional Credits

Jonathan Ambar, Tom Benfatti, Lisa D. Ferrari, Paul Foster, Florrie Gadson, Phil Gagler, Ella Hanna, Jeffrey LaFountain, Karen Mancinelli, Michael McLaughlin, Lesley Pierson, Debi Taffet

The DK Designs team who contributed to *World Studies* were as follows: Hilary Bird, Samantha Borland, Marian Broderick, Richard Czapnik, Nigel Duffield, Heather Dunleavy, Cynthia Frazer, James A. Hall, Lucy Heaver, Rose Horridge, Paul Jackson, Heather Jones, Ian Midson, Marie Ortu, Marie Osborn, Leyla Ostovar, Ralph Pitchford, Ilana Sallick, Pamela Shiels, Andrew Szudek, Amber Tokeley.

Maps

Maps and globes were created by **DK Cartography.** The team consisted of Tony Chambers, Damien Demaj, Julia Lunn, Ed Merritt, David Roberts, Ann Stephenson, Gail Townsley, Iorwerth Watkins.

Illustrations

Kenneth Batelman: 153, 182; Geosystems: 68; Jill Ort: 83, 125; Jen Paley: 10, 18, 19, 25, 29, 36, 42, 49, 52–53, 55, 64, 76, 84, 86, 89, 90, 110, 112, 117, 118, 126, 127, 128, 133, 134, 137, 141, 152, 154, 158, 160, 162, 166, 168, 173, 175, 180, 182

Photographs

Cover Photos

tl, Miles Ertman/Masterfile; **tm,** Gunter Marx Photography/Corbis/MAGMA; **tr,** David Schmidt/Masterfile; **b,** Richard Cummins/Superstock.

Title Page

Richard Cummins/Superstock.

Table of Contents

T4–T5, Andre Jenny/Visuals Unlimited; **T6,** Bonnie Kamin/PhotoEdit; **T7,** C. McIntyre/PhotoLink/Getty Images, Inc.; **T9,** Kevin Fleming/Corbis.

Professional Development

T35, Royalty-Free/Corbis; **T36,** PhotoDisc/Getty Images, Inc.; **T37,** Comstock.

Reading and Writing Handbook

RW, Michael Newman/PhotoEdit; **RW1,** Walter Hodges/Getty Images, Inc.; **RW2,** Digital Vision/Getty Images, Inc.; **RW3,** Will Hart/PhotoEdit; **RW5,** Jose Luis Pelaez, Inc./Corbis.

Map Master Skills Handbook

M, James Hall/DK Images; **M1,** Mertin Harvey/Gallo Images/Corbis; **M2–3 m,** NASA; **M2–3,** (globes) Planetary Visions; **M5 br,** Barnabas Kindersley/DK Images; **M6 tr,** Mike Dunning/DK Images; **M10 b,** Bernard and Catherine Desjeux. /Corbis; **M11,** Hutchison Library; **M12 b,** Pa Photos; **M13 r,** Panos Pictures; **M14 l,** Macduff Everton/Corbis; **M14 t,** MSCF/NASA; **M15 b,** Ariadne Van Zandbergen/Lonely Planet Images; **M16 l,** Bill Stormont/Corbis; **M16 b,** Pablo Corral/Corbis; **M17 t,** Stone Les/Sygma/Corbis; **M17 b,** W. Perry Conway/Corbis.

Guiding Questions

1t, Ohio Historical Society; **1b,** Bob Winsett/Index Stock Imagery, Inc.

Regional Overview

2, Staffan Widstrand/Corbis; **3,** R. Rainford/Robert Harding Picture Library; **4 t,** Jim Wark/Lonely Planet Images; **4 b,** Charles O'Rear/Corbis; **5,** Bohemian Nomad Picturemakers/Corbis; **6 t,** John Elk III/Lonely Planet Images; **6 bl,** DK Images; **6 br,** Inc. Luis/Castaneda/Getty Images; **7 t,** Richard T. Nowitz/Corbis; **7 m,** Yann Arthus-Bertrand; **7 b,** Peter Beck/Corbis.

Chapter One

8f l, Royalty-Free/Corbis; **8f r,** PhotoDisc/Getty Images, Inc.; **8–9,** Frank Perkins/Index Stock Imagery, Inc.; **10,** Scott Darsney/Alaska Stock; **11 t,** Andre Jenny/Visuals Unlimited; **11 b,** Discovery Channel School; **12,** Richard A. Cooke/Corbis; **13,** U.S. Geological Survey, Denver; **14–15 t,** Joseph Sohm; ChromoSohm Inc/Corbis; **14 b,** Joe McDonald/Corbis; **16,** Nancy Sheehan/PhotoEdit; **17,** J. Eastcott/Yva Momatiuk/Valan Photos; **18,** Donald Nausbaum/Getty Images, Inc.; **19,** Bob Winsett/Index Stock Imagery, Inc.; **20,** Alan R. Moller/Getty Images, Inc.; **21 t,** Gerry Ellis/Minden Pictures; **21 b,** Norbert Rising/National Geographic Society/Getty Images, Inc.; **23 t,** David A. Northcott/Corbis; **23 b,** Gordon Whitten/Corbis; **24,** Jean du Boisberranger/Getty Images, Inc.; **25,** Royalty-Free/Corbis; **27 t,** Bruce Forster/Getty Images, Inc.; **27 b,** Randy Brandon/Alaska Stock; **28,** Melvin Grubb/Grubb Photo Service, Inc.; **29,** Jeff Greenberg/Visuals Unlimited; **30,** Vince Streano/Getty Images, Inc.; **31 t,** Joe McDonald/Corbis; **31 b,** David A. Northcott/Corbis.

Chapter Two

34h l, Royalty-Free/Corbis; **34h r,** PhotoDisc/Getty Images, Inc.; **34–35,** Robert Essel NYC/Corbis; **36 l,** Ohio Historical Society; **36 r,** Ohio Historical Society; **37 t,** Discovery Channel School; **37 b,** Tom Bean/Corbis; **38 t,** Marc Muench/Corbis; **38 m,** DK Images, **38 b,** Michael Freeman/Corbis; **40 t,** Sarony & Major/Library of Congress; **40 b,** Bettmann/Corbis; **41,** Kevin Fleming/Corbis; **42,** The Granger Collection; **45,** The Granger Collection, NY; **47,** Magma Photo News/Corbis; **47 inset,** Seth Goltzer/William Gladstone/West Point Museum Collections; **48,** Bettmann/Corbis; **48 inset,** C Squared Studios/Getty Images, Inc.; **49,** Bettmann/Corbis; **50–51 t,** Corbis; **50 b,** Bettmann/Corbis; **51 m,** Library of Congress; **51 b,** Underwood & Underwood/Corbis; **52 t,** Corbis; **52 b,** Bettmann/Corbis; **53 t,** Bettmann/Corbis; **53 b,** Mirrorpix/Getty Images, Inc.; **54,** Reuters NewMedia Inc./Corbis; **55,** Christie's Images/Corbis; **56,** Library of Congress; **57,** Hulton/Getty Images Inc.; **59 l,** Getty Images, Inc.; **59 r,** Bettmann/Corbis; **60,** Paul A. Souders/Corbis; **61,** Reuters NewMedia Inc./Corbis; **62 t,** Michael Newman/PhotoEdit; **62 b,** David Young-Wolff/PhotoEdit; **64,** Illustration by ML Kirk in Longfellow, Hiawatha 1910/Mary Evans Picture Library; **65 t,** Mark Gibson/Index Stock Imagery, Inc.; **65 b,** Bettmann/Corbis; **66,** Didier Dorval/Masterfile Corporation; **67 t,** Weyerhaeuser Company; **67 b,** Joel W. Rogers/Corbis; **68–69,** Nik Wheeler/Nik Wheeler Photography; **70,** AP Photo/Martin Mejia; **71 t,** Ohio Historical Society; **71 b,** Magma Photo News/Corbis.

Chapter Three

74f l, Royalty-Free/Corbis; **74f r,** PhotoDisc/Getty Images, Inc.; **74–75,** Kwame Zikomo/SuperStock Inc.; **76,** H A Strong/Mary Evans Picture Library; **77,** Library of Congress, Washington D.C., USA/Bridgeman Art Library; **78,** Mary Evans Picture Library; **79 l,** Connie Ricca/Danita Delimont; **79 r,** Nik

DATE DUE